MW01126376

The John W. Campbell Letters
With Isaac Asimov and A.E. van Vogt, Vol. II
by
Perry A. Chapdelaine, Sr.

Kelly Freas Cover

The Preface

Criteria for Selection

Unlike the more complex inclusion criteria of Volume I of *The John W. Campbell Letters*, the only criterion for selection in Volume II has been whether or not Isaac Asimov and/or A.E. van Vogt and/or their stories have been mentioned in John W. Campbell's letters. This single criterion has made my task vastly easier.

Volume I was very well received by almost all factions of fandom and academia. I believe that this second volume will be accepted equally well. I must, however, mention that the main criticism of the first volume was the absence of letters from authors to Campbell. There are very good reasons for the omission which include: (1) The enormous time required to search out authors and/or their estates to seek their legal permission to publish; (2) The large costs in so doing.

I leave that -- shudder -- academic task to others!

This Volume II does have some letters from Isaac Asimov and A.E. van Vogt to John W. Campbell -- with their permission.

Unfortunately, there are not enough letters from the authors to John W. Campbell, and apparently copies do not exist either in Campbell's meticulously preserved files, or in the authors'. I wanted to ask Isaac Asimov to rely on his eidetic memory and so reproduce all of his communications to Campbell for us -- but on second thought decided to leave that suggestion for others, also.

I won't go into remaining criticisms of the first volume (and possible criticisms of this volume), but answer all of them as I would imagine Isaac doing: "I did it the way I did it because that's the way I did it!"

The John W. Campbell Letters was conceived as a series of perhaps ten or twelve volumes. There's certainly enough letters in our files to do this, although not without some duplications, especially when the letters are classified in several different ways (as Volume I and Volume II represent). The overall concept of a series of volumes, then, was also meant to satisfy two populations: (1) those who wish to write Science Fiction (specialized wordsmiths); and, (2) those who read Science Fiction (fandom) -- all this while maintaining academician accuracy for future generations.

AC Projects, Inc. is a very tiny publisher without the huge bucks required to generate sales sufficiently rapidly to quickly fulfill the dream of multiple volumes. All profits from the first volume have been saved to generate this second volume, and that has taken five years.

Not that the first volume is(was) not popular with diverse populations, but that advertising and distribution is(was) simply not available.

If you wish to order the first Volume of *The John W. Campbell Letters*, we still have available both the paperback edition ($5.95) and the limited, numbered hardcover copy ($35.00). This Volume II is available only in the hardcover copy ($45.00).

AC Projects, Inc. also offers a hardcover copy of *The Battle of Forever* by A.E. van Vogt, limited numbered, signed edition ($14.95) and the trade edition, hardcover, ($9.95). This edition is beautifully illustrated by Bob Maurus.

There is also available *The Laughing Terran* and *Spork of the Ayor* both hardcover (Robert Hale) by Perry A. Chapdelaine, Sr. ($5.95).

All books may be ordered through distributors or direct from AC Projects, Inc.

Acknowledgement

Again I wish to thank Leslyn Campbell Randazzo and Philinda Campbell Hammond for their continuing support and encourgement; and also Forrest E. Ackerman, Isaac Asimov, L. Ron Hubbard and A.E. van Vogt.

James Tollett (Chattanooga, TN) and Tom Gervais (Franklin, TN) helped with MS typing. As my fingers are no longer capable of sustained repetitive movements, I am quite grateful.

Appropriate forewards have been provided by Forrest E. Ackerman, Michael G. Adkisson, James Gunn, Ph.D., George Hay and Igor Toloconnicov for which special acknowledgement is due.

The cover painting of John W. Campbell, Jr. was furnished by Kelly Freas, as well as additional, excellent advice.

Based on photographs either from John W. Campbell's files, or from Isaac Asimov and A.E. van Vogt all interior illustrations were drawn by France Watts.

My son Tony helped with editing and in other ways.

Volume I was typeset via expensive photographic paper, and with great flexibility for typesetting. This Volume II is typeset via Laserjet and the Pagemaker computer program, with inexpensive paper and low typesetting flexibility. I have left "orphans" and "widows" alone. I, alone, am responsible for this decision.

And finally, to all who've sent me their good comments about the first Volume, who've asked for the second Volume, and those who've given continuous encouragement and support for this gigantic project -- thanks, thanks, many thanks!

Perry A. Chapdelaine, Sr.

I, Asimov
by
James Gunn, Ph.D.

James Gunn is a most generous and talented writer. He has very kindly permitted use of "I, Asimov", in Volume II of The John W. Campbell Letters. *I doubt that any lengthy search for material on Isaac Asimov, and his relationship to John W. Campbell, could have uncovered a gem so accurately cut and mounted. [Perry A. Chapdelaine: Ed.]*

(From *Isaac Asimov: The Foundations of Science Fiction* Copyright 1982 by Oxford University Press, Reprinted by Permission of James Gunn, Ph.D.)

Writing about the life of Isaac Asimov is like pouring water into the ocean. Asimov has written more about himself than any living author, and generally with frankness and insight. His autobiographical output began in 1962 with the first of his anthologies, *The Hugo Winners*, in which he inserted references to his own life in the introductions. Like many of the events in his life, this happened by accident. In his autobiography, Asimov mentions that he had never edited an anthology, thought it would be fun to try, but was not sure of his judgment in choosing the stories. The stories in *The Hugo Winners* already were chosen (they were the less-than-novel-length stories awarded Hugos by the World Science Fiction Conventions, beginning in 1955), and even the order was evident. All Asimov had to do was to write introductions. Since there was no question about the reason for the stories' inclusion, he decided to deal with the authors, and in a humorous way. The general introduction would be funny too and would deal with the fact that the editor had never won a Hugo. *The Hugo Winners*, indeed, became a highly personal book, as much about Asimov as about the Hugos or their winners. Since then, Asimov has gone on to edit more than a dozen anthologies and added comfortably to his more than two hundred volumes.

The Hugo Winners was breakthrough for Asimov in another area as well. Up to that point, Asimov says, his attempts at humor had been well received in person but poorly in print. Many readers of *The Hugo*

7

Winners wrote to tell him that the introductions were the best part of the book. After that, collections of his own stories began appearing with introductions, at first (*The Rest of the Robots*, 1964) with notes about the stories salted with a few personal comments and later with full-blown autobiographical detail. This technique reached its grandest expressions in *Opus 100* (1969), the story of how Asimov came to write one hundred books, with excerpts by category; *The Early Asimov* (1972), a kind of autobiography with illustrations from his early writing; and *Before the Golden Age* (1974), which carried Asimov back to his earliest memories and brought his life story up to *The Early Asimov*, illustrated with his favorite science-fiction stories read between 1931 and 1938. All of these works were limbering-up exercises for the massive autobiography in two volumes, the first of which came out in 1979 as his 200th book (along with *Opus 200*, which he put together in fairness to Houghton Mifflin, which had published *Opus 100*). The autobiography offers 1560 pages of Asimov's life story, complete with photographs, a list of his two hundred books, and indexes (which, he informs us, he does not trust anyone else to do).

There have been a great many words about the life of a man who admits he has "never done anything." They have largely progressed from "and then I read" to "and then I wrote" because Asimov's life has been woven from the warp and woof of reading and writing. The triumph of his writing skill is that he makes it all so readable.

This kind of obsession with self might be insufferable in a person who was not at the same time openly amazed at the good fortune, success, plaudits, renown, and wealth that have come his way. Asimov has been greatly honored and richly rewarded for remarkable achievements. Even so, to interpret everything in terms of one's own reaction to it, including World War II, may seem excessively egotistical. But Asimov's attitude of "cheerful self-appreciation," which sometimes breaks over into "charming Asimovian immodesties" (a phrase coined by a Doubleday editor in response to a *Time* magazine article quoting some of Asimov's self-praise), is balanced by disarming Asimovian self-denigration.

In his autobiographical writings and comments, Asimov continually invites the reader to share his triumphs, to laugh at his blunders and lack of sophistication, and to wonder, with him, at the rise to prominence of a bright Jewish boy brought to this country from Russia at the age of three and raised in a succession of Brooklyn candy stores. Asimov is aided too by the fact that his readers are predisposed to enjoy his success with him. Some are admirers of his science popularizations and other non-fiction books and are curious about his earlier life; others are science-fiction readers and fans, and the science-fiction community still retains much of the solidarity and lack of envy of its early ghetto days.

The problem remains: what more can a critic say about Asimov's life and work that Asimov himself hasn't said already in nearly a million well-chosen words? Asimov's autobiographical writings are both an asset and an intimidation, revealing priceless information about the circumstances of creation and publication but also rendering redundant the critic's job of digging out little-known facts about life and work. Asimov's life is an open book — in fact, two hundred more open books.

Well, the critic can tell the Asimov story more selectively and send the still curious on to fuller accounts elsewhere, bring the details of the life into focus in illuminating the work, and explain the work in terms of a thesis that may be too close to Asimov for him to perceive. The critic also has an opportunity to comment on the state of criticism as well as the work and the author at hand. One reason for undertaking this study was the conviction that much criticism of science fiction has been misguided and particularly that critics of Asimov's work have headed up false trails, trying to bring to the analysis of Asimov's fiction traditional methods and traditional criteria that are unproductive when applied to Asimov and to much other science fiction. What I found myself doing as I began writing, then, was blending biographical, sociological, publishing, and critical considerations into what I later perceived (perhaps without sufficient perspective) was something a bit unusual in criticism, perhaps unnatural in normal circumstances, that I eventually thought of calling "criticism in context."

Within the following chapters, for instance, the reader will find a number of plot summaries. These are desirable for several reasons: first, because the reader may be familiar with many Asimov's works but certainly not all; second, because the reader may remember the general outlines of stories and novels but not the revealing details; and third (and most important), because what happens is the most important aspect of Asimov's fiction (and most other science fiction) and what happens is revealed in plot.

Other matters that I found important as I got into my consideration of Asimov's work were the conditions under which the fiction was written and the way in which it was published. Asimov himself keeps referring to these matters in his autobiographical writings; he thinks they were important to what he wrote and didn't write, and so do I. In one footnote in his autobiography, he writes:

"In this book I am going to pay considerable attention to the details of the money I received for stories and other things. Perhaps I should be noble enough to rise above such sordid things as money, but the fact is I couldn't and didn't. The money I earned — or didn't earn — has influenced my pathway through life, and I must go into the financial details if the pathway is to make sense."

In the course of the chapters that follow, the reader will find frequent mention of why the fiction was written and how it got into print. The goal of the science-fiction writer was to get published, and the writing done was shaped by what was read in the magazines, what was said by an editor, what was paid for a story, and sometimes how readers responded. More traditional critics may feel that such concerns disqualify the writing from serious literary study. They are wrong: scholars have been trying for centuries to ferret out the same kind of information about Shakespeare's plays.

Asimov's early ambition, for instance, was to sell stories to *Astounding Science Fiction*. Two of his stories were published in *Amazing Stories* before one appeared in *Astounding*; only the *Astounding* story really mattered to him. The relationship between Asimov and John W. Campbell, editor of *Astounding* beginning in 1937, was influential in Asimov's development. Asimov gives Campbell most of the credit for his early science fiction and even his later writing career.

In the analysis of Asimov's fiction that makes up most of this book, then, the reader will find mixed in with the critical comments many details of Asimov's life as they relate to his writing. This is more of his life than one might think: as Asimov himself recognizes, his life was his writing, and his other relationships were either detractions from or contributions to it.

10

Asimov provides a couple of illustrative anecdotes. When he received copies of his forty-first book from Houghton Mifflin, he mentioned to his wife the possibility of reaching a hundred books before he died. She shook her head and said, "What good will it be if you then regret having spent your life writing books while all the essence of life passes you by?" And Asimov replied, "But for me the essence of life *is* writing. In fact, if I do manage to publish a hundred books, and if I then die, my last words are likely to be, 'Only a hundred!'"

His daughter Robyn asked him to suppose he had to choose between her and — writing. Asimov recalls he said, "Why, I would choose you, dear." And adds, *"But I hesitated* — and she noticed that, too."

Asimov was born January 2, 1920 (as nearly as his parents could calculate; it may have been as early as October 4, 1919) in Petrovichi, U.S.S.R. Petrovichi is a small town about fifty-five miles south of Smolensk and about two hundred fifty miles southwest of Moscow. When Asimov was three, his parents emigrated with him to the United States, at the invitation and sponsorship of his mother's older half-brother. They settled in Brooklyn, where Asimov's father, handicapped by his lack of English and of job experience, bought a candy store in 1926. The candy store, and its successors, became a major part of Asimov's existence. "It was open seven days a week and eighteen hours a day," he reports in his autobiography, "so my father and mother had to take turns running it, and I had to pitch in, too."

The other important fact of Asimov's youth was his precocity. He had an unusual ability to learn and, as he later discovered, an unusually retentive memory. They were to be major assets in his life and career. He taught himself to read at the age of five, entered the first grade before he was six (his mother lied about his age), and became the brightest student in his class early and continuously, even though he skipped half a year of kindergarten, half a year of first grade, and half a year of third grade and changed schools a couple of times.

Asimov's schoolboy practice was to read all his schoolbooks the first couple of days after he got them and then not refer to them again. He acquired a reputation as a child prodigy and a sense of his own superiority that he didn't mind letting other people see. They did not add to his popularity — he was considered a smart-alecky kid — but he did not have much association with others anyway. His work in the candy store kept him busy after school, and the seven-day week meant that he and his parents never visited anyone or had anyone visit them.

Asimov recalls that he was orphaned by the candy store (since he was deprived of his parents' companionship) as well as protected by it (since he knew where his parents were at all times). The candy store constricted and shaped his life until he left home. It also meant that he grew up largely in the company of adults when he was in the store, or in the company of books when he was not. Both no doubt contributed to his precocity.

Asimov completed junior high school in two years instead of three and entered Boys High School of Brooklyn, which at the time was a selective high school that had an excellent reputation for mathematics. He was twelve and a half upon entering, two and a half years younger than the normal age of fifteen. He continued to be sheltered: he had almost no contact with girls, as he might have had at a co-educational school. But in the world encapsulated in his autobiography almost everything happened for the best — how could it not have happened for the best when he rose so far from such humble beginnings? — and he reasons that though being segregated from girls may have kept him naive far into his adolescence, it also may have protected him from more severe symptoms of rejection, for he was so much younger than his female classmates. Moreover, he had a bad case of acne from twelve to twenty.

High school, however, was the beginning of a series of disillusionments. Asimov discovered limits to his intellectual ability. He was not as good a mathematician as some of the other boys, who may not have been as intelligent but had a special feeling for math. He never made the math team. He discovered as well that other students could study harder and accomplish more; Asimov stuck by his "understanding-at-once-and-remembering-forever" pattern. He had to abandon his illusion of universal brilliance when he discovered, for instance, that he disliked and could never understand economics. And even his attempts at creative writing were ridiculed in a high-school writing class. This bothered him more than anything else because his ambition to write fiction had been growing since the age of eleven, when he had begun writing a series book for boys called *The Greenville Chums at*

College, copying it out in longhand in nickel copybooks. When Asimov was fifteen his father had found $10 to buy his son a much-longed-for typewriter, an office-size model.

More disappointments awaited him. His father wanted his elder son (there were two other children, a girl, Marcia, and a boy, Stanley) to become a physician, and the fifteen-year-old Asimov had come to share this ambition. But getting into medical school was not easy; medical schools had quotas (negative, not positive) on the number of Jewish applicants they would accept. For a variety of reasons, Asimov was never to be admitted to the study of medicine. By then his goals had changed, however. After high school, he applied to Columbia College, but was rejected — possibly, he speculates, because he did not make a good showing in interviews. He was asked to change his application to a Brooklyn branch of Columbia University called Seth Low Junior College, where enrollment was heavily Jewish.

Asimov also applied to City College of New York, which had no tuition and accepted him because his grades were excellent. He actually spent three days there before receiving a letter from Seth Low asking why he had not showed up. When his father explained to Seth Low authorities that the family could not afford the tuition, Seth Low came up with a hundred-dollar scholarship and a National Youth Administration job for $15 a month. Asimov switched colleges. His second year, after a summer spent in manual labor to earn enough money, was at the Morningside Heights campus because Seth Low had closed at the end of its tenth year. He was enrolled in Columbia University, not its more prestigious undergraduate college. Asimov was a second-class citizen throughout his undergraduate education, and he never forgot it. When he was graduated, he received a bachelor of science degree in chemistry instead of the bachelor of arts degree, for which University undergraduates were not eligible, he says.

In his second year of college, Asimov's distaste for zoology (he killed a cat and dissected it but never forgave himself) and embryology (he was not good at picking out details through a microscope and even worse at drawing them) led him to drop the biological sciences and switch to chemistry as a major. He liked chemistry and did well at it. After graduation from Columbia he applied (somewhat halfheartedly because of his distaste for biological courses) to a number of

13

medical schools and was rejected by all of them. He went on with the study of chemistry in Columbia's graduate school, but only after some difficulty because he had not taken physical chemistry. He had to spend a troublesome year on probation. As usual, his problem had not been his grades or test scores but his "wise-guy personality."

Asimov obtained his M.A. in 1941 and was working toward his doctorate when the United States entered World War II. A few months later he suspended his studies in order to work as a chemist at the U.S. Navy Yard in Philadelphia, where for the first time he was free of his duties at the candy store and where the steady income gave him the opportunity to marry the woman with whom he had fallen in love, Gertrude Blugerman.

Asimov's autobiography suggests that he was good at the theory of chemistry but not at the practice. He refers to his poor laboratory technique and his difficulties getting the correct results. His talents were probably not those of a research chemist, nor those of a practicing scientist of any kind. But at the end of the war he returned to his doctoral program at Columbia, earned his degree in 1948, did a year of post-doctoral research at Columbia, and finally was offered a position as instructor in biochemistry at the Boston University School of Medicine.

Asimov's discovery of science fiction and his attempts to write it were more important to his final career than his studies. He had come upon *Amazing Stories* in 1928, its second year of publication, when he was eight years old. His father's candy store carried magazines, but the young Asimov was not allowed to read them because his father considered them a waste of time and a corrupting influence. They would turn him into "a bum," his father said. The boy had been reading library books of all kinds, but he longed for the brightly colored pulp magazines with their cover paintings of futuristic machines and planets and alien menaces. Finally, Hugo Gernsback lost control of *Amazing* and brought out a competitor, *Science Wonder Stories*, the then nine-year-old boy brought the magazine to his father, pointed out the word "Science" in the title, and won his battle. Possibly his father just did not have the spirit to fight because his mother was about to give birth to Asimov's younger brother, Stanley.

The science-fiction magazines filled Asimov's imagination with ideas and dreams. They did not consume all his reading time because
14

there weren't enough of them (only two a month at first, and only three a month in 1930). He kept up his omnivorous reading of other books, mostly library borrowings, but science fiction became what he lived for. Oddly enough, Asimov's early writing efforts did not focus on science fiction. "I had the most exalted notion of the intense skills and vast scientific knowledge required of authors in the field, and I dared not aspire to such things," he remembers.

On his new typewriter, however, he ventured into fantasy and then into science friction. Like almost every aspiring author, Asimov started many stories and finished none, and what he wrote was derived mostly from what he liked to read. His derivative writing was to persist through several years of his career as a published writer until he finally rid himself of what he called his "pulpishness." He got his inspiration, his plots, even his vocabulary from other science-fiction writers. From them came the blasters and needle guns and force beams that litter his stories and early novels, and even, by an analogous process of invention, such concepts as neuronic whips and psycho-probes, hyperspace and Jumps. When he turned to more unique concepts such as psychohistory and the Foundations, the logical development of robots, a radioactive Earth and the lost origin of man, and particularly human reactions to overcrowded cities, his fiction began to glow with its own fire.

Not long after he got his typewriter, Asimov wrote a letter to *Astounding Stories* that was published in 1935. Two years later, when Campbell had become editor of the magazine and had changed its name to *Astounding Science Fiction*, Asimov began writing letters again, "commenting on the stories, rating them, and, in general, taking on the airs of a critic." Such letters became a monthly event; usually Campbell published them in a letter-to-the-editor section called then, as now, "Brass Tacks."

One Tuesday in May, when the new *Astounding* was scheduled to arrive in his father's package of new magazines, it did not show up. The eighteen-year-old Asimov was terrified that it had ceased publication. He called the publisher, Street & Smith, and was assured that the magazine still was being published. But when the new issue had not arrived by the following Tuesday, he ventured off on the subway to the Street & Smith offices in Manhattan, where an executive told him that the publication date had been changed from the second Wednesday to the third Friday of the month. Two days later the magazine arrived.

His panic at the thought that *Astounding* might vanish sent Asimov to the typewriter to finish a story he had been working at for some months titled "Cosmic Corkscrew." He completed the story on June 19, 1938, and took it personally to the editor. Campbell was familiar with Asimov's name from his frequent letters and talked for more than an hour with the aspiring author, read the story overnight, and mailed it back two days later with a polite letter of rejection. That sent Asimov back to his typewriter to work on a story titled "Stowaway." He finished it in eighteen days and took this in person to Campbell. That story came back with a rejection in four days.

A pattern had been established. A rejection would come from Campbell but phrased in ways that would encourage Asimov to turn immediately to a new story. "It didn't matter that he rejected you," Asimov recalled. "There was an enthusiasm about him and an all-encompassing friendliness that was contagious. I always left him eager to write further." "Stowaway," however, did not end up lost for all time with "Cosmic Corkscrew." It eventually found its way into print, in the April 1940 *Astonishing Stories* edited by Frederick Pohl (as youthful an editor as Asimov was a writer), as "The Callistan Menace," though Asimov's third story, "Marooned Off Vesta," had appeared first, in the March 1939 *Amazing Stories*.

Meanwhile, Asimov had discovered other science-fiction readers, and not just readers but fans, fanatics like himself. This led progressively to fanzines, club meetings, and the organizing of the Futurians, a fan group that included many of the later writers and shapers of science fiction, including Pohl, Donald A. Wollheim, Cyril Kornbluth, Robert W. Lowndes, Richard Wilson, and later Damon Knight and James Blish. Asimov attended monthly meetings, became involved in the debates and schisms to which fandom is so susceptible, began meeting other authors, and talked about his writing ambition and finally getting published. All culminated in the first World Science Fiction Convention held in Manhattan on July 2, 1939. Every Futurian but Asimov were excluded by the organizer, Sam Moskowitz, as disruptive influences. Asimov went as an author and has felt guilty about it ever since. But as he became more and more an author, he became less and less a fan.

By the time of the World Convention Asimov was a bonafide author in his own eyes because *Astounding* had published his tenth story, "Trends," in its issue of July 1939. Almost two years later it published the second of his robot stories (the first, "Robbie," was published in the September 1940 *Super Science Stories* as "Strange Playfellow") and within the next fourteen months two more robot stories, plus "Nightfall," and "Foundation" and its sequel. Though Asimov didn't know it at the time, "Nightfall" alone made him, in his own words, "a major figure in the field." The stories did not earn that much money, but what they brought in was put to good use, paying for his tuition or accumulating in a bank account. He had three stories published in 1939, seven in 1940, eight in 1941, ten in 1942, only one in 1943, three in 1944, four in 1945, one in 1946, one in 1947, two in 1948, three in 1949, six in 1950.

It was not a remarkable record of productivity or success; it brought Asimov a total of $7,821.75, which amounted to little more than $710 a year. It was not enough to encourage him to consider a career as a full-time writer, but it did provide a growing feeling of economic security. Finally, Doubleday published his first novel, *Pebble in the Sky*, in 1950. A specialty house called Gnome Press began publishing his robot stories and then his Foundation stories as books. His income from writing slowly began to equal and then to exceed his income from teaching at Boston University School of Medicine, and, after a disagreement with his superior, he turned to the career that had seemed impossible for all those years.

The impression even the casual reader may obtain from Asimov's autobiography is that he has been shaped by his childhood. He refers continually to the way in which the candy store controlled his early life and the way the habits of those years have carried over into his later life. His industry — he still writes seven days a week and ten hours a day, turning out six to ten thousand words on an average day — he traces to the long hours at the candy store, for instance, and to his father's accusations that he was lazy when found in a corner reading.

In a similar way, Asimov traces his ability to eat anything to his mother's hearty, indigestible cuisine, and his habit of eating swiftly to

17

the fact that he and his mother and sister had to eat in a hurry so that his father could be relieved of his duties in the candy store and eat his supper in a more leisurely fashion. He reads while he eats because he loved to read, his father wasn't present, his mother was busy cooking and serving, and in any case reading was a sign of studiousness.

His uneasiness with strangers Asimov traces to the fact that during his childhood his family visited no one and no one visited them. The fact that he reads newspapers and magazines so carefully that no one can tell they have been read started, he believes, when he had to return magazines to his father's rack looking unopened. As a boy he had to awaken at 6 a.m. to deliver newspapers before school. If he wasn't down on time, his father would yell at his window from the street below, and later lecture him about the "deadly spiritual dangers of being a *fulyack* [sluggard]." To this day, Asimov reports, he awakens, without an alarm clock, at 6 a.m.

He describes his infatuation with baseball when he was in junior high school: he became a Giants fan, which was odd because Brooklyn had the Dodgers. "By the time I found out there was a Brooklyn team, it was too late; I was imprinted." He describes being "imprinted" in other ways as well. He blames his fear of flying on his mother's oversolicitude about his health. "My parents . . . trembled over my well-being so extremely, especially after my babyhood experience with pneumonia, that I couldn't help but absorb the fact and gain an exaggerated caution for myself. (THAT MAY BE WHY I won't fly, for instance, and why I do very little else that would involve my knowingly putting myself into peril.)"

His mother's insistence that he keep her informed of his whereabouts meant that when he was out he had to report in at frequent intervals by telephone. "I've kept that habit all my life," he reports. "It is a bad habit. It ties me to the phone, and if forgetfulness or circumstances get in the way, everyone is sure something terrible has happened." He traces his avoidance of books on how to write and of college-level courses on writing to "the ever-present memory of that horrible course in creative writing in the sixth term of high school."

It may not be surprising that someone who can find so many habits of the man in the experience of the boy would imagine a science of predicting human behavior, called "psychohistory," in his Foundation stories. On the other hand, Asimov can relate anecdotes that seem to demonstrate just the opposite principle of behavior. He recalls his father struggling to balance the books of the candy store every evening, being a dollar over or a dollar under and staying until he had straightened it out. Later in his life, when money was easier, Asimov recalls handing his father five dollars to make up the difference, and his father commenting, "If you gave me a million dollars, that dollar would still have to be found. The books must balance." Asimov never could understand why the books had to balance. Rather than carrying that trait into his own life, he says, "In later life, when I had occasion to balance accounts, I never bothered over trifling discrepancies. I just made arbitrary corrections and let it go. My father did enough searching for both of us in his lifetime."

At the same time, Asimov is capable of seeing his explanations for behavior as "probably simple rationalizations designed to resign me to things as they are." After all, what is an autobiography? It is not so much the finding of the truths in one's existence as a rationalization of how one got from one place to another when there were so many different places at which one could have arrived. Asimov has much to explain, and his autobiography is a search for explanations.

Asimov also is a supreme rationalist, a searcher for explanations in his fiction as well as in his life. The reason for his faith in rationalism and his distrust of emotions may be no easier to come by, however, than any other speculation about his life. Asimov does not rely totally on environment to rationalize his life; some traits are implicit, or genetic, and Asimov simply does not mention them. His intelligence, for instance, and his ability to learn and remember must have been inherited. His habit of counting objects (light bulbs, repeated decorations, holes in soundproofed ceilings) whenever he is bored in public places he traces to his counting automobiles as they passed on Van Siclen Avenue when he was three. He finds no reason for his idiosyncratic fondness for enclosed places. He liked the candy store on Decatur Street because it had a kitchen in the back that had no windows. "Why it should be, I don't know, and psychiatrists may make what they like of it (for I will not ask them, and I will not listen if they try to tell me), but I have always liked enclosed places." He remembers that he thought display rooms in department stores looked better than real

19

rooms and finally realized that it was because they had no windows. He envied the people who ran newsstands in subway stations, "for I imagined that they could board it up whenever they wanted to, put the light on, lie on a cot at the bottom, and read magazines. I used to fantasize doing so, with the warm rumble of the subway trains intermittently passing." Asimov's claustrophilia and agoraphobia will return to the discussion when we examine *The Caves of Steel* and *The Naked Sun*.

A psychiatrist (one of that group to whom Asimov will not listen) might suggest that Asimov's distrust of emotions and faith in rationalism are his responses to "being orphaned" by the candy store at the age of six. Being deprived of his parents' companionship ("never again, after I was six, could I be with him [his father] on a Sunday morning, while he told me stories") came at a difficult time: he was in the middle of second grade. Moreover, his father had admired his son's abilities from an early age. When Asimov taught himself to read at the age of five, his father asked him how he had done it, and Asimov replied that he just figured it out. "That gave my father the idea that there was something strange and remarkable about me; something he clung to for the rest of his life." But the high regard in which Asimov's father held his son's abilities meant that when the schoolboy brought home less than perfect marks from school, he could expect his father's disapproval for not living up to his potential. In his autobiography Asimov recalls many instances of his father's disapproval, few of his approval.

His mother also spent much of her time in the candy store with customers, or with her two younger children. She had a terrible temper, Asimov recalls, and unlike his father "raised her hand to me any time she felt she needed a little exercise. . . ." He also recalls, seemingly without rancor, being beaten with a rope his mother kept in her closet. When he mentioned it to his mother in later life, she did not remember it. His parents, though a devoted couple, were not demonstrative. There were few if any expressions of affection between them, and Asimov presents the births of three children as the only proof that there was. Certainly Asimov had reason to distrust emotion and to seek rational explanations for why he was deprived of parental closeness, perhaps even love.

Asimov, nevertheless, always knew that he was his parents' favorite, and his brother knew it as well, apparently without resentment. Asimov speaks bitterly about the series of candy stores but remembers his father and mother with great fondness. The family was always in close touch until the death first of his father (in 1973, at the age of 72) and then of his mother (in 1973, at the age of nearly 78), even though Asimov did not go to see his parents after they moved to Florida a year before his father's death because of his fear of flying.

In his typical rational way, he looks back upon his childhood as a generally happy period: "I know perfectly well it was a deprived one in many ways, but the thing was, you see, I never knew it at the time. No one is deprived unless and until he thinks he is."

A more general mystery than the origin of Asimov's traits and neuroses is why certain young people turn to reading, and sometimes writing, science fiction. Asimov is a case study. When he began reading science fiction, the number of readers was small — Damon Knight has called science fiction the mass medium for the few — but intensely involved. Most had turned to science fiction out of some kind of youthful frustration with their lives. A profile of new readers would reveal them to be mostly boys; mostly brighter than their schoolmates; mostly social misfits because of personality, appearance, lack of social graces, or inability to find intellectual companionship; unsophisticated about girls (the study of women readers and writers still is in its infancy) and ill at ease in their company. Science fiction was a kind of literature of the outcast that praised the intellectual aspects of life that its readers enjoyed and in which they excelled and offered more hope for the future than the present. When those kind of persons discover others like themselves, fan clubs spring up, sometimes fanzines are published, conventions are organized, and writing science fiction becomes a virtually universal ambition. When those kind of persons begin to write, they write science fiction.

Asimov was like that. The Futurians were like that. Damon Knight says that "all we science-fiction writers began as toads." When Robert Silverberg read the first volume of Asimov's autobiography, he wrote for the galley proofs of the second volume because he couldn't wait: there was so much in Asimov's life that paralleled his own that it gave him a sense of *deja vu*. There are certain curious resemblances between the characters and careers of Asimov and H.G. Wells, who is often called the father of modern science fiction. Both spent their early

21

lives in unsuccessful shops, were precocious students, quick to learn with good memories, and began by writing science fiction but turned to popularizations (Well's biggest success was his *Outline of History*). Both were selective in what they liked, Wells with biology and evolution, Asimov with chemistry, and both were fond of history. Both became known as pundits, experts in almost everything, and both were attentive to the ladies. . . . The analogy can be carried too far. Wells, for instance, became a serious novelist of contemporary life; Asimov varied his science fiction and non-fiction with detective stories and novels.

Asimov, in spite of his success at other kinds of writing and public speaking, has never thought of himself as anything but a science-fiction writer who sometimes writes other, often easier, things. He introduces himself as a science-fiction writer. Some writers of science fiction have gone on to other kinds of writing and some, like Kurt Vonnegut, Jr., have denied that they ever wrote science fiction. Not Asimov, who always has remained true to his boyhood love. In his autobiography he describes a fancy *World Book* sales meeting at which the board members were introduced with orchestral motifs: to his chagrin, Asimov was introduced as a science writer by "How deep is the ocean?/How high is the sky?" "No matter how various the subject matter I write on," he adds, "I was a science-fiction writer first and it is as a science-fiction writer that I want to be identified."

In an interview in 1979, I said to him that his autobiography revealed a great deal of loyalty to what he was, to the boy he was, and to what science fiction had meant to him when he discovered it. Asimov replied that he had deliberately not abandoned his origins. He had made up his mind when he was quite young, and said it in print, that no matter what happened to him or where he went he would never deny his origins as a science-fiction writer and never break his connection to science fiction, and he never has.

He considers loyalty a prime virtue. In 1976 when he started *Isaac Asimov's Science Fiction Magazine*, he told publisher Joel Davis that he wouldn't give up his *Magazine of Fantasy and Science Fiction* science articles.

"I probably bore everybody with my endless repetition of how much I owe to John Campbell, because I figure I would rather bore them than be disloyal in my own mind. It is the easiest thing in the world to forget the ladder you climb or to be embarrassed at the thought that there was a time when somebody had to help you. The tendency is to minimize this, minimize that, and I'm normal enough and human enough to do the same thing if it were left to itself, but this is a matter of having once made a vow and sticking to it."

He pointed out that it was inconvenient to always have to tell people that Campbell made up the Three Laws of Robotics, and the more important the Three Laws became the more he wanted to be the originator and take the credit, but he couldn't. "Why this is so I never really thought about. I guess I like to think about it only as a matter of virtue. I don't consider myself a particularly virtuous person, but I like to think I have some virtues, of which loyalty is one."

Possibly, however, his insistence on being considered a science-fiction writer is like his relationship to his racial origins. He says he is not a good Jew. Asimov attends no Jewish religious functions, follows no Jewish rituals, obeys no Jewish dietary laws, and yet he never, under any circumstances, leaves any doubt that he is Jewish.

"I really dislike Judaism. . . . It's a form of particularly pernicious nationalism. I don't want humanity divided into these little groups that are firmly convinced, each one, that it is better than the others. Judaism is the prototype of the "I'm better than you" group — we are the ones who invented this business of the only God. It's not that we have our God and you have your God, but we have the only God. I feel a deep and abiding historic guilt about that. And every once in a while, when I'm not careful, I think that the reason Jews have been persecuted as much as they have has been to punish them for having invented this pernicious doctrine."

Asimov suggests that because he feels that in some ways he has been a traitor to Judaism ("which I try to make up for by making sure that everyone knows I'm a Jew, so while I'm deprived of the benefits of being part of a group, I make sure that I don't lose any of the disadvantages, because no one should think that I'm denying my Judaism in order to gain certain advantages"), he made up his mind that he was not going to be disloyal in any other way. "I'm not saying I believe this," he concluded, "but this is the sort of thing that people do work up for reasons, and, after all, I'm imaginative enough to think up such reasons, too. . . . I don't guarantee it's correct."

The characteristic that began to appear in Asimov's science fiction, that gave his writing its unique quality and made it so typically Campbellian as well as Asimovian, was its rationality. Asimov agrees with Randall Garrett's assessment that the relationship between Asimov and Campbell was symbiotic. In the interview Asimov commented that he must have been the perfect foil for Campbell.

"On the one hand, I was close to him. I lived right in town and I could see him every week. And, for another, I could endure him. I imagine that a great many other writers found him too rich for their blood — at least to sit there and listen to him hour after hour. But I was fortunate in the sense that he was in some ways a lot like my father. I had grown up listening to my father pontificate in much the same way that John did, and so I was quite at home. I suppose if you took all the time that I sat there listening to John and put it all together, it was easily a week's worth — of just listening to him talk. Day and night, 168 hours. And I remember everything he said and how he thought and I did my best — because I desperately wanted to sell stories to him — to incorporate his method of thinking into my stories, which, of course, also had my method of thinking, with the result that somehow I caught the Campbell flavor."

The Campbell flavor was the solution of problems. Much of Asimov's early writing did not quite capture that quality of problem-solving that became characteristic of his later work; those stories were less successful, neither identifiably Asimovian nor distinguished science fiction. His first published story had it, "Marooned Off Vesta," and later it would find its best expression in the robot stories and the Foundation stories, among his early science-fiction successes, and, of course, in the science-fiction mystery novels that came so naturally just before he switched to writing non-fiction, *The Caves of Steel* and *The Naked Sun*.

I made these suggestions to Asimov, and he agreed that they seemed right. "Certainly the stories that really satisfied me and made me feel good about my writing were my robot stories, and the robot stories, of course, virtually every one of them, had a situation in which robots — which couldn't go wrong — did go wrong. And we had to find out what had gone wrong, and how to correct it, within the absolute limits of the three laws. This was just the sort of thing I
24

loved to do."

At its most typical, in "Nightfall" for example, Asimov's science fiction demonstrates the triumph of reason, or the struggle of reason to triumph, over various kinds of circumstances, including irrational or emotional responses to situations. If reason is going to prove superior as an approach to life, the mystery is the natural form in which that superiority will be demonstrated.

Asimov has said that his villains generally are as rational as his heroes. "In other words, it's not even a triumph of rationality over irrationality or over emotion, at least not in my favorite stories. It's generally a conflict between rationalities and the superior winning. If it were a western, where everything depends upon the draw of the gun, it would be very unsatisfactory if the hero shot down a person who didn't know how to shoot."

Growing up as he did, excelling at intellectual pursuits but uneasy in personal relationships in which he found himself ignorant of the proper thing to do or uncertain how the other person would respond, Asimov found himself coping in a variety of ways. One way, which he adopted when he was young, was to distance himself from the rest of the world with wit: he still delights in puns and wordplay, which find their most typical expression in personal banter with his friends but also enliven his limericks and verse parodies and display themselves in the titles of and occasional lines in articles and stories. Another way to cope was to demonstrate his greater knowledge or superior mind. His adoption of these two characteristics gave him a reputation as a smart-aleck and a know-it-all with a mission to enlighten everyone around him.

Asimov gives as an example of his behavior the assignment of Leigh Hunt's "Abou Ben Adhem" in his high-school English class. Anticipating the teacher's question about the last line ("And lo! Ben Adhem's name led all the rest"), his hand shot up, and he answered the inevitable question, "Why did Ben Adhem's name lead all the rest?" with "Alphabetical order, sir?" He was sent to the principal, but he didn't care.

Asimov finally gave up his mission to educate the masses. He traces his decision to a time when he was in the Army in Hawaii, waiting for the H-bomb tests at Bikini. A couple soldiers in the barracks were listening to a third explain, inaccurately, how the atom bomb worked.

"Wearily, I put down my book and began to get to my feet so I could go over and assume "the smart man's burden" and educate them.

"Halfway to my feet, I thought: Who appointed you their educator? Is it going to hurt them to be wrong about the atom bomb?

"And I returned, contentedly, to my book.

"This does not mean I turned with knife-edge suddenness and became another man. It's just that I was a generally disliked know-it-all earlier in my life, and I am a generally liked person (I believe) who is genial and a nonpusher later in my life. . . .

"Why? I'm not sure I know. Perhaps it was my surrender of the child-prodigy status. Perhaps it was my feeling that I had grown up. I had proved myself, and I no longer had to give everyone a headache convincing them that I was, too, smart."

One other way in which Asimov learned to cope socially was his adoption of a flirtatious attitude toward women — all women — what he calls his "all-embracing suavity," by which he means that he is willing to embrace any female within range and usually does. From a gauche, inexperienced, tentative young man he turned into a good-natured, public Casanova with a "penchant for making gallant suggestions to the ladies." Yet Asimov speculates about his behavior as an adult that "you don't really change much as you get older." The uncertain young man may still be there inside the "all-embracing" older one.

Asimov has denied being anything other than direct and clear in his writing, and that may apply to his personal life as well. Certainly he is open about his life, even on those matters that most people are most closed about: money and sex — and, more important to Asimov, his writing. I asked him in our interview if his disclaimer of knowledge about the craft of writing wasn't a pose. Clearly, he had thought about it, I pointed out. He had criticized other people's stories in his teen-age letters-to-the-editor days; he had noticed Clifford Simak's way of leaving space to indicate a break between scenes and, after having had it explained, had adopted it himself; he had even attended the Bread Loaf Writers's Conference, a couple of times as a member of the faculty. Asimov responded that he does not deliberately set up a pose. He really thinks he does not know much about writing, but, as he points out in an afterward to the collection of essays about his work edited by Martin Greenberg and Joseph Olander titled *Asimov*, "without very much in the way of conscious thinking I manage to learn from what I read and what I hear."

As the young Asimov became the older Asimov (still in his late youth, as he would say), what he was became what he is, either conditioned by his early experience or in reaction to it. Asimov recognizes both processes. In one sense he is a rational man in an irrational world, puzzled at humanity's responses to change, unable to understand humanity's inability to see the clear necessity, if it is to survive, to control population and pollution and eliminate war, still assuming "the smart man's burden" to educate the bewilderingly uneducable, even taken aback at times when the people he deals with behave irrationally.

Joseph Patrouch in his *The Science Fiction of Isaac Asimov* (1974) comments that Asimov has not written in his fiction on the subjects about which he is most concerned, the subjects he writes on in his nonfiction and speaks about in his public talks: pollution, overpopulation, and so forth. I asked Asimov about this, saying that in his talks and articles and books he seemed to exhibit a kind of alarm about our world situation that was not in his fiction — a kind of public despair that contrasts with his fictional optimism. In his science writing he tries to persuade by showing the terrible consequences of what will happen if people do not act, and in his science fiction he tries to persuade by showing how the problems can be solved. Asimov agreed.

"In my public statements I have to deal with the world as it is — which is the world in which irrationality is predominant; whereas in my fiction I create a world and in my world, my created worlds, things are rational. Even the villains, the supposed villains, are villainous for rational reasons. . . .

"You can see for yourself in my autobiography that I had a great deal of difficulty adjusting to the world when I was young. To a large extent the world was an enemy world. . . . Science fiction in its very nature is intended to appeal a) to people who value reason and b) to people who form a small minority in a world that doesn't value reason. . . . I *am* trying to lead a life of reason in an emotional world."

Asimov, no doubt, still is trying to please his stern father with industry and productivity. Asimov would be the first to admit it. He also would say that it doesn't matter how the past has shaped him. He is satisfied to be what he is: a claustrophile, an acrophobe, a compulsive writer. When he was a teenager, people complained about his eccentricities: his walking home from the library with three books, reading one and holding one under each arm; his love of cemeteries; his constant whistling. Their complaints didn't bother him (though he did, when asked, stop whistling in the cemetery). "I had gathered the notion somewhere that my eccentricities belonged to me and to nobody else and that I had every right to keep them." He added, "And I lived long enough to see these eccentricities and others that I have not mentioned come to be described as 'colorful' facets of my personality."

He has rationalized everything that has happened to him; he is a rational man who knows that the past cannot be changed, it can only be understood. Moreover, the things that he is have been rewarded by the world. He has had his many triumphs. Scientists have applauded his science books: Professor George G. Simpson of Harvard called him "one of our natural wonders and national resources." He has been guest of honor and toastmaster at World Science Fiction Conventions. He has won Hugos and Nebulas, and, perhaps best of all, John Campbell has told him, "You are one of the greatest science-fiction writers in the world."

As a rational man, Asimov knows that the present must be accepted, and as a rational man, he knows that what he is is an excellent thing to be. So the world has said, and so he agrees. That life of reason found its expression in his fiction as well as his non-fiction. How it developed and how it expressed itself can be found in the following pages. [And so begins "The Foundations of Science Fiction" by James Gunn, Ph.D.: Ed.]

A Report on Probability B
by
Igor A. Toloconnicov
USRR
Volgograd - 66
CPO, Poste restante

Igor Toloconnicov first corresponded with me to ask for a copy of
The John W. Campbell Letters, *Volume I. As his country was still domi-*
nated by centralized planning, and the ruble was not convertible to
American dollars, Igor asked for a free copy, which was sent.

During follow-on correspondence I learned of his desperate need
and desire for any kind of science fiction and fantasy materials. One of
our local science fiction clubs, as well as I, began sending him boxes of
books, sometimes new, but mostly used.

I hope that others will follow suit. Those wishing to correspond with
Igor may do so at the address given above.

Of course, it is always interesting to learn how our favorite authors
are viewed by "foreigners," but even more, of course, Igor's "A Report
on Probability B" is suitable because Isaac Asimov emigrated from Rus-
sia at an early age. Probably coincidentally, Isaac is revered, and van
Vogt is hardly known by virtue of past authoritarian decree. [Perry A.
Chapdelaine: Ed.]

Isaac Asimov is a darling of translators. Young ones come to me and
say: Gee! It's so clearcut and, please, have I something for them to translate. I disappoint them by pointing out that most of his 400 works are
non-fiction (even though only a dozen were translated during two peaks
of interest in 60's and 80's whatever this signifies; and this year his SF
mystery collection has appeared in print.)

Mr. Asimov has had the bad luck to become canonized in my country. The science fiction field was too independent for the ruling party, and
the ghetto walls were enforced through random regulation of 50 titles total annually (including reprints). So it is easy to see how an imposed
canon becomes a dogma. There are few of Asimov's SF works published
-- *Steel Caves, Naked Sun, I, Robot and the Rest of the Robots, The End
of Eternity* (which was filmed recently), *Gods Themselves* -- but the

sheer number of copies in millions' count take care of the impact generated. That's due both to the genuine enchantment Isaac Asimov effects, and scholastic approach to fiction in general. When an idea takes root among bureaucracy establishments that such-and-such an author is to be considered a classic then automatically a process is initiated, and through tame critics' ravings and sheer weight of copies published a popular awareness is smothered without a chance to hear a dissenting voice. The same was done to Ray Bradbury, to Kurt Vonnegut (Arthur Clarke had kept his vitality but this is another tale); and to Howard Fast and Theodore Dreiser. According to this church rule-book, Isaac had become a holy man of SF parish, and writings by Saint Asimov -- may Isaac forgive a putting on, just forcing the point home -- must grace any new anthology of foreign SF. Practically every one such includes his story. Some are reprinted fifteen and more times, often under different titles. By this treatment a great injustice is done in reducing his whole presence to a mere pipsqueek. One hopes that by publishing the Foundation series, Nemesis, Azazel, the engaging personality of Isaac Asimov, would be restored again.

Just as Asimov is kept in the limelight, Mr. van Vogt remained in shadow (and many, many others like H.P. Lovecraft, Frank Herbert, Keith Laumer, Philip Jose' Farmer, Harlan Ellison). But for a couple of short stories van Vogt has made no appearance at all. Reasons: There is no tangible evidence to pin. (What reasons were there for an abridged child's version of *Lord of the Rings* by J.R.R. Tolkein to see publication only by mid-eighties?) I hazard a guess that [van Vogt's] association with Dianetics™ is the reason enough. There were plenty devastating diatribes directed at [Dianetics]; the last one at the turn of eighties. Mind you, in past times the mass media was rigidly enforcing opinions of government clerks; and once the machinery is set into motion it is hard to reverse gears though attitudes have changed towards it. Even UFO and psi-phenomena became commonplace on nationwide newspaper pages.

Newly sprung co-op publishing enterprises break down taboos. This year *Null A* was published in Krasnodar on money put up by translator. Even though the price is outrageous for soft book -- four times that of hardcover -- the fact is that it was sold out in two months. Grassroot samizdat [underground press] popularity has seen to it. For there exist SF fans in Soviet Union, too, who had sought ways to counter arbitrary

30

straightjacket of official propaganda. As far as it's possible to judge there are something like five thousands samizdat SF titles in existence (including van Vogt's non-Aristotelian series and Wizard Lynn series, *Slan*, etc.) giving a limited access to Western SF field. This is also the figure of unfulfilled demand.

In a sense Isaac Asimov and van Vogt represent two parts of an iceberg; and when the iceberg emerges at last it would be an indication that Soviet science fiction stands on its feet once again.

The Visionary
by
Michael G. Adkisson

Michael G. Adkisson, editor and publisher of New Pathways, *has long been determined to establish a revolutionary new kind of science-fiction publication, one that promotes the good of the old and the new.*

In case you're unfamiliar with New Pathways -- *it has been said to be the "cutting edge" of science (speculative) fiction.*

One can hardly comprehend the determination and hardships endured by Adkisson in pioneering a totally new magazine -- without fundamental capitalization and sans any reasonable distribution.

Adkisson, many years ago, wrote "The Visionary" for the second volume of The John W. Campbell Letters. *This article represents his initial and his late considered response to John W. Campbell.*

The significance of Michael Adkisson lies not just with his admiration for John W. Campbell, and agreement with Campbell's rightful place in modern literature, but also in the fact that Adkisson is a later generation of science fiction readership -- one that was only indirectly under Campbell's influence -- but nonetheless an inheritor of the powerful Campbellian legacy.

Speaking of establishing his New Pathways, *Adkisson proudfully says, "Our struggling, awkward and formative stage is far behind us now and the magazine is firmly established. (This does not mean that it is producing a profit; it means that it has gone from a bankrupt-producing folly to an expensive hobby)."*

We are equally proud to present an entrepeneur immersed in traditional American values.

May we also respectfully refer you to his magazine New Pathways, *at MGA Services, PO Box 863994, Plano, TX 75086-3994? [Perry A. Chapdelaine: Ed.]*

John W. Campbell offended some people.

But do you remember when you were young, watching your elders in their stuffy shirts become agitated when someone in the room said something off-color, inappropriate, or — something that they had never heard before? There is a certain mischievous, primeval joy in the hert of a youngster watching his elders become offended at something new and untried.

Of course, some "old" people are even younger at heart than the "young" people. To these unique individuals, life remains an adventure.

Why is this so? When does life cease to be an adventure and become merely a duty and responsibility instead?

Some of us may think that our basic knowledge is "complete." We are qualified to teach others, to be a respectful pillar in the establishment. But in doing so we give up having that young perspective of the world around us.

John W. Campbell never gave up that kind of attitude.

Campbell Wrote: *I'm still looking for the stories that get in and really twist things in the reader. . . you can shock him out of a life-time pattern, and change him for the rest of his natural existence, if you can find and break one of his false cultural orientations. . . Things can get in, because the barrier isn't real.*

Yeah — I know this isn't as popular a type of story . . . . yet. But give us some time! We're developing an art-form that hasn't been more than started — as a conscious effort.

I suspect it'll never be really a mass-audience type, either. You can kill people with a really good story of that type — and I am not kidding. It's a fine exercise for strong minds — and our readers wouldn't be the speculative philosophical people they are if they didn't have tough, resilient minds — but it's not good for the weak ones.

Among the other cultural-orientation sabotage plants we've run recently. . .[1].

Do you recognize a bit of that almost mischievous joy of the youngster who likes to say things that knocks old granny off her rocker?

Of course, we must contemplate, theorize and draw conclusions. But when those conclusions become as hard as the solid earth that we walk upon, we're liable to miss the rest of life as it passes us by. The "youngster" that challenges our views and mannerisms is really doing us a favor. We shouldn't be so settled in our ways.

Some critics have analyzed the methodology of Campbell's thinking process as "mind games." If it was mind games, it was mind games with a purpose — to search for the untried, the unproven, and the unknown. What better purpose can a man commit himself to in such a vast universe?

To those who travel in mental eddies, never venturing beyond their prescribed ideological framework, it must indeed be a "mind game" to have sat and explored possibilities with Campbell. But out of such discussions came forth science fiction classics such as Isaac Asmiov's *Foundation* series.

The reason some critics expend so much time and energy putting down Campbell's methodology — and others like him, is that the challenging spirit of Campbell is a constant threat to them. "No, that ideology isn't good enough. Your philosophy is unsound." Of course, some of these people are paid to be "experts" in their field — and an admission of ignorance, or the apparent "weakness" displayed in a blatant change of philosophy, is anathema. Most of us, after all, seem to be motivated by pocketbook issues, while truth is secondary.

Are men like Campbell an anomaly in human history?

What is it about certain men and women that make them special? If we really knew the answer, we might not like it -- because often the same qualities that drive those men and women to new heights are also the things that disturb us.

And yet, is it wise to treasure the golden egg and not also nourish the proverbial goose?

While pouring over the letters of John W. Campbell, one cannot but help but be impressed with the energy and candor of those same letters — indeed, the evangelical fervor unleashed in those letters might be more appropriate in a university hall, or even a pulpit. It is the voice of a man with a message. And today that message speaks to us, though the man whom that voice belonged to is gone.

"Grant me not the fish; instead, teach me how to fish."

The fish that Campbell caught were the fish of new ideas. Is creative thinking something we're born with or is it something that can be learned and passed on to others? Campbell insisted that creative thinking was intermixed with the ability to experience a total reorientation of thought patterns, and to assimilate new data, allowing our minds to grow and evolve.

John W. Campbell wrote: *To change a man's basic life-evaluation patterns, to induce basic insights of that depth, you have to induce him to give up a vast amount of specialization. Any time you can get a man*
34

to do that, incidentally, you'll have one of the most powerful human beings who ever lived; he will have learned to be Protean, to be anything he chooses. He will, incidentally, scare the living bejayzus out of anyone who tries to work with him closely, because we aren't accustomed to human beings who can change their basic belief-patterns at will!

Actually, that sort of basic orientation isn't necessary for ordinary individuals in the Society. You have some of it; it's needed in the leaders of the society, but they musn't discomfit the ordinary members of the society by displaying the characteristic too widely.[2].

It is exactly this characteristic that Campbell often displayed. The reactions from those around him ranged from outrage to distant admiration. Campbell must have been a difficult gent to argue with — not because of the intensity of his views, but because his ideas came from so many different angles. It was almost as though all the others were too familiar with this "human life" thing, as though they had been reincarnated, but Campbell was doing the "human life" thing for the very first time. To him everything was fascinating — and the cruelest thing to him was to have one's thoughts inhibited by environment, culture, or surroundings.

In short, one of the men who helped spawn an age of science fiction could do so only because his mind roamed free. It was not opinions that Campbell argued — but rather the inability to consider new ideas.

He wrote: *I don't give a damn what your opinion is; you can have it, for all of me. And I don't give a damn what my opinion is. I want to know what the Universe's opinion is. But your opinion is useful to me, because, since it inevitably differs from mine, it gives me a chance to get a different angle of view on the Universe. From one angle only, a disc does appear a metal bar. If that were my only angle of view, I couldn't possibly learn what the reality was.*

Now some items to consider: try defining "human being" some time. You may find it ain't quite so simple as it looks. For one thing: it's a remarkable thing that we, who are so brilliant in our wisdom, are the direct descendants of such a collection of stupid fools, silly, superstitious nit-wits, and maundering idiots as we are repeatedly assured inhabited this planet a few centuries ago. Truly remarkable that, de-

35

scended from such as they, we could be so much more brilliant and wise and sensible, isn't it?[2]

For many of us, we are born into a world of ideas and culture. We adopt those ideas and culture without question. Now it may be that we could arrive at those ideas and culture on our own — and then again, maybe not.

What might have been the saddest day of my life was the day of my college graduation. Here was an event which signified the completion of learning, even though many of the learned academicians advised that real learning was only now beginning. The joy was in discovering and learning — and if there ever comes a day when that learning stops, if we ever feel it is time to "cash in" on that learning to grasp at the straws of human respect, integrity, and status — ultimately that will become the saddest day of our lives.

Do we feel threatened? Should we look upon Campbell's preoccupation with Scientology as excess baggage, when it grew from the very core of what made Campbell who he was?

Consider how the ancient Jewish Pharisees reacted when there arose an unordained Teacher who could speak the words they taught as though He Himself had written them. They hated the Man for the simple reason that this Man might possibly put them out of jobs.

In the wake of the seeker's discoveries usually come an establishment of principles and guidelines, whether it be religion, science — or even the field of science fiction itself. The sad history of human civilization is that intellectual and spiritual light comes all too infrequently -- and when it does, we build a shrine. When the light leaves us, we have nothing but an empty husk and a marketplace — a temple full of moneychangers. If we claim to walk in Campbell's footsteps, we may only be keeping the husk. We may not need Christianity or Scientology or Hinduism, but we certainly need the inward knowledge that the seeker obtains.

No one is born a great thinker. No one is born a "Campbell." While most great thinkers only communicated their attained knowledge and wisdom, Campbell attempted to communicate the process of obtaining that wisdom. Campbell taught men how to fish. And no effort can be greater than this.

Campbell wrote: *The greatest philosophical advances in Man's his-*

tory have been based on the destruction of the in-group-out-group distinction. Christianity started (but didn't continue, sad to say) as a belief based on the proposition that every individual could appeal directly to God — that no special priest was necessary in any ordinary problem.

Galileo's great point was that every man could investigate Nature for himself; that no special Authority was necessary.[4]

And also: *The amateur is far too little respected — despite the fact that amateurs have been responsible for most of the great advances of human understanding. Jesus wasn't a priest; Pasteur wasn't a doctor; Freud wasn't an MD or a psychologist. There's a nasty little trick the society plays on us; it says, 'Oh, him! He wasn't an amateur — he was a genius!'[5]*

Campbell's path down the road of Scientology was simply the path that so many others walked before him — a search for some answers. Those who criticize the man for this have never walked down that road before. In Campbell's mind there was the Absolute Truth, which no man can attain — and then there was relative truth, which we can strive for.

Why should Campbell be criticized for searching for relative truth by men who settle only for inheriting accepted truths and knowledge? All too often in modern society we confuse open-mindedness with an ambiguous noncommittal to any belief or value system. We say, "You can't judge that person for killing their neighbor. You are making a value judgment." We say, "You can't say for sure whether or not there is a God. We don't know — we should keep our minds open." But why do we insist that an open mind be devoid of beliefs?

This was the contradiction of Campbell's life. He demonstrated strong opinions and beliefs — and yet apparently spent most of his life studying the human mind — and spoke of the ability to keep an open mind, forever changing, forever growing. He spoke of the logical and the non-logical methods of arriving at those beliefs.

An open mind has the ability to assimilate new ideas. But in our society, an open mind is equated with a vacant mind — uncommitted to any value or belief. But in reality, the open mind is forever changing, forever growing into new awareness. The belief-pattern is there, but it

37

evolves.

A great truth that Campbell discovered was that human beings apparently do not have the ability to think in a totally objective manner. There are always hidden motivations. Campbell was an enigma to many people because he constantly spoke about the nature of the mind. He seldom dealt with specific points of argument; instead, he examined the process of thought that led to the conclusions.

The literature of science fiction was built by men such as Campbell, and if that literature is to continue as a serious art form, then it should be guided and directed by a similar mindset.

Campbell wrote: *Actually, all creative thinking appears to be non-logical, and only when we learn the laws of non-logical rationality will we be able to be creative thinkers at will, and without limit. When Newton worked up the law of gravity, he gave a logical demonstration of the validity of his idea after he had derived the postulate of the inverse square law attraction. But no one had ever given a logical process whereby he originally derived that postulate.[6]*

Few will deny that a great body of science fiction was crafted under the guiding influence of Campbell — but why do so many ignore the hidden source of that influence? Since Campbell's preoccupation, pursuit, and investigation of the human thought processes also led him to embark on wild flights of imagination that burned new ideas into the budding writers of that time, writers such as Isaac Asimov, why can we not also venture down that same path and reap the same harvest?

We want the fish, but we don't want to know how to fish.

In the last fifteen years we have seen technology and knowledge advance at an almost staggering pace. But most of it seems to be development and refinement of basic science already in existence. Newly observed phenomena which do not fit our laws and principles constantly mystify us.

We forget that the pioneers who formed our basic structure of science today were simply making observations of the phenomena around them — and tabulated those observances as laws and principles in the physical universe. First observance, and then principle, not vice versa.

But today, as we observe new phenomena, we attempt to explain them using already-established laws and principles. Does man, who is merely a frog in a deep well, really understand all the basics — and only the details need to be filled in?

Campbell constantly pushed his "test pilots" to "the outer edge of the envelope" to find out the answer to that question, using speculation, intuitive and nonlogical imagination, and known scientific facts.

Today, however, many of us have fallen into a trap. In the midst of scientific advance and accomplishment, we may be prone to become drunken with success, resting upon our laurels. Some people imagine that a movie space travel, with computer terminals, is "science-fiction" and even use the term "extrapolation" to avoid having to really figure out what life might be like a hundred years from now.

Is science fiction today too complacent? Does it have the vitality that it did in Campbell's day? Does today's science fiction disturb us the way that it might have in Campbell's day?

Campbell wrote: *Anytime the SSS (self-styled scientists) boys decide they know the ultimate absolute limits of what can be true — they're claiming they're ominiscient. Anyone who claims omniscience thinks he's God Almighty. Well, that God is not only dead, he never existed.*

My interest in psi stems from direct observation of phenomena that are real and reproducible by some talented individuals that are not explicable in terms of now-known data.

Where the SSS says 'If my present data and logic can't explain it, that proves it doesn't exist,' I hold, instead, that 'If present knowledge and data can't explain it — maybe there's something new to learn here! Let's investigate!' A true scientist does keep that difference in mind.

It's only the SSS type — the self-styled scientists — that are so arrogant as to deny their knowledge is not total.

Keep in mind that the great scientist Lord Kelvin proved, by the most advanced scientific knowledge of his time, that the Earth was not more than 25,000,000 years old. (Some of the earliest apes were having trouble with Nile crocodillians about then. The dinosaurs had been extinct for 100,000,000 years or so.)

And that the best scientific data and logic of 1966 was still firmly holding that dowsing was nonsense — although some Marines were beginning to use it because it saved their leathernecks.

It's the SSS boys who are the real voluntarists; they claim that

39

their orthodoxy determines what's true in the Universe.[7]

The fact that sometimes people agree with one another is not very meaningful. What is more meaningful is when people are on the same wavelength. When they arrive at a certain conclusion using the same method, then they may grow and develop together.

But people seldom investigate the method — they are only interested in the conclusions, and whether or not those conclusions are in agreement with their own. Again, the actual truth is secondary.

There might not be such fighting and arguing at all if we but examined the process of thinking itself. Of those who discuss and argue, how many can honestly say they're purely motivated by the pursuit of truth, rather than the subjugation of other ideas to their own?

Campbell realized that the accepted methodology of thinking was inadequate. Rather, he suggested another process of thought: . . . *All the logic mankind has ever developed is a snare and a delusion, because it's inadequate. But when a human being, using more adequate methods, gets a usable answer, he's railed at for being illogical or irrational.*

Look, the experimental method is inherently illogical. That's why the Greeks wouldn't use it. It is not logical; it's pragmatic. Many times its results are contrary to logic; the Greeks resented this so deeply they refused to use it. (We know the answer is, in such cases, that the basic premise of the logic was false.)

But there is, equally, a non-logical method of reaching a conclusion, called 'intuition'. There is no logical method that can yield a conclusion applicable to an individual case. Statistical methods will yield generalizations applicable to general cases, but not applicable to individual cases. (The insurance company can use the conclusions; the individual policy-holder cannot.) There is no logical method of reaching a Natural Law type of generalization — it can be done only by a not-yet-describable process called "the intuitive method."[8]

The above words might sound like blasphemy to some scientists, but the true discoverer and explorer will recognize the truth of Campbell's statements. It is perhaps this process of thought that we need the most in today's world.

In a time when the economic structure is crumbling, and the fabric of society is ripping apart, we need such a visionary as John W.

40

Campbell to light the way before us. The cynical and complacent attitude so prevalent today is a sign of decay and decline.

Human civilization has a disturbing pattern: first accomplishment, then complacency, then regression. It is important that we not confuse the knowledge required in manufacturing a silicon chip with the sheer genius of creating the first wheel. There is a difference.

A common theme throughout science fiction is the apocalyptic disintegration of society, the intellectual decay and resultant barbarism, and the advent of the New Dark Age. In the shadow of this threat is the voice of John W. Campbell, who attempted to mold science fiction into a powerful force of change.

Today that potential is as strong as ever before.

But where is the visionary imagination of a John Wood Campbell?

References:

1. *The John W. Campbell Letters, Volume I*, AC Projects, Inc., 5106 Old Harding Road, Franklin, TN 37064, p. 267.

2. Ibid, p. 159.

3. Ibid, p. 296.

4. Ibid, p. 219.

5. Ibid, p. 220.

6. Ibid, p. 93.

7. Ibid, p. 521.

8. Ibid, p. 247.

Science, Scientism, and . . . ?
by
George Hay

I've known George Hay since the early fifties, when L. Ron Hubbard's Dianetics[tm] was first promulgated by John Campbell, Jr. in the pages of Astounding.

Aside from George's un-American spellings, an English propensity for circling the fox to distraction, and his Irish bulls ("the silence on these issues is deafening"), George always pulls through.

I've told folks for years that if one were riding in a tour bus through the most remote region of Africa, and the bus were passing through a small mud-hut village, and if someone were to shout out the window to ask the inhabitants if anyone knew George Hay, at least one of the natives would raise his/her hand.

He is a fine human and has long been a fine friend.

In "Science, Scientism, and . . . ?" George tackles a side of John W. Campbell, Jr. often questioned, but seldom confronted head on: Campbell's propensity for insisting on correct science in articles, his requirement to use believable <u>and consistent</u> logic in stories, and his wild-eyed propensity for needling professional scientists.

The Dean Drive was a veritable ideal case-history in point. John had pictures in Astounding's *"Science" section showing a "working model" of the Dean Drive. It consisted of a quarter-inch drill mounted by various springs and brackets onto a standard bathroom scale. A photo of the "weight" of this whole assembly showed the scale reading of zero.*

Since the drill, the brackets, nuts and bolts and assorted springs all weighed <u>something</u>, and the scale's index of weight was <u>zero</u>, there <u>had</u> to be a superior (outside established physics) explanation. Perhaps the inertialess drive so well touted in his and E.E. Smith's early stories?

Now mind you, John would not have accepted a strictly mathematical explanation, nor even the explanation that George's friends, below, have given. Zeno was able to explain away motion with ingenious mathematical logic of his time . . . .

But such was the effect <u>as a prime cause</u> of John's thinking on

American society of his time that he caused a mighty ruckus with his Dean-drive article.

I remember during the sixties -- while working for the U.S. Air Force -- running across an article in which the US Air Force had funded a mathematical analysis of all the components of the Dean Drive. It was a complex analytical/mechanical/mathematical description of what forces connected to what forces throughout the total contraption — and the end conclusions of these analyses were essentially the same as that given by George's friends below.

So, while John was prodding writers to use better science, he was — as in a point made in Volume I of these letters — also prodding scientists to rethink their models — and succeeding!

George Hay's following article from "Foundation Forum" (Number 41, Winter 1987, p.65.) is apropo. [Perry A. Chapdelaine: Ed]

(From "Foundation Forum", The Science Fiction Foundation, Polytechnic of East London, Longbridge Road, Dagenham, Essex, RM8 2AS, United Kingdom.) : Under the heading "Foundation Forum" we normally publish items designed to provoke debate, to outrage, to intrigue. George Hay, whose name has now gone onto the Science Fiction Foundation's new notepaper as "Founder," has frequently done all three, and we suspect he will have done it again. He offers us a useful (and all too rare) reminder that sf is about science as well as literature, appropriate in a volume dedicated to Arthur C. Clarke. Pursuing his theme of "applied science fiction," on July 9th George gave the introduction at a half-day conference at Burgh House, Hampstead, organized jointly by the International Science Policy Foundation and the SFF, on "Science Fiction and its Applications;" Tom Kindberg, quoted below, was one of the speakers.

"It cannot, then, be true that science itself demands that scientists should treat all problems as scientific problems. If the narrow definition of science currently used is to be kept, a great many problems of real scientific importance fall outside science" (Mary Midgley, in *Evolution as a Religion*: Methuen 1985).

In this article I shall endeavour to give some pointers as to what degree science fiction has reflected science, rather than scientism, and to consider to what degree changes in science theory have been reflected in novels and magazines. Also, I shall indicate some ways in which ideas put forward in the genre could be used in education generally. First, some general remarks:

"Wellsianity," as it has been called, the onward-and-upward linear view of progress, starting with Verne and carrying on through Campbell and his stable of writers, is based four-square on a vastly simplified view of science as the Victorians understood it. The best exponent of this today is Dr. Asimov, though in his case a caveat is needed: I do not wish to be taken as saying that, because the Good Doctor has a truly remarkable gift for simplifying the issues involved, he himself either is simplistic or ignores wider issues. However, in the case of lesser writers of this school, we do seem to have a repetition of the view, current until quite recently, that Victorians such as T.H. Huxley and Darwin were inflexible dogmatists. A generation before this, they were, of course, seen as bold innovators, struggling heroically against obscurantism. Both views were false — see for example Mary Midgeley's account of the actual facts of the famous Huxley/Wilberforce dispute (in the book quoted above). What has happened, of course, is that, as always, a simplified myth, put forward in the belief that readers were idiots, has supplanted the facts. And meanwhile, as a result of a slow but steady penetration of the implications of quantum theory, a counter-myth has sprung up and is taking hold. While Victorian confidence has taken us up past Verne, Wells, and Campbell, culminating today in the school of Pournelle and Niven, the counter-myth attacks this on the basis of theories adduced by "new science" writers such as Capra, Zukav and Bohm. The distinction is not as clear-cut as many would wish to think: Campbell, for example, had strong mystical tendencies, and his serial, "Uncertainty," in *Amazing Stories* in 1936 was, I believe, the first fictional development of Heisenberg's Uncertainty Principle. Still, by and large, the antithesis holds. Of course, readers will have their own stands on these issues, and in any event, I am not qualified scientifically to discuss the issues involved. However, I believe I am qualified to discuss the implications of the projects of these new ("new"?) theories on the chalk-face of science fiction, a genre highly interactive with life in our global village. Anyone wishing to check this out need only visit any of the larger sf bookstores, where one frequently has to queue for some time to get the cash-desk. And these are b-i-i-g shops. Specialised book fairs apart, I doubt whether other bookshops can boast similar business. And what is bought is read, and what is read is remembered, if only subliminally. Since the quantum theory view has it that perception governs reality, you will see that here we have an entire generation being conditioned into belief in hyperspace, parallel worlds and the rest of it, as actual existents. Whether belief does in some ultimate sense govern reality is not an issue I propose to go into here. Never mind "ultimately": anyone who has had of late to deal with publishers or the media will have had it drummed into him quite brutally that to those here at the levers of power, this is not just another theory, but the bedrock of commercial existence. Productwise — to use the jargon — what publishers put out is governed by their view of their readers' wish-fulfillment fantasies — as distinct, that is, from anything that authors themselves might wish to say.

I shall return to this issue. For the moment, let me just draw your attention to the fate of the late unlamented Joseph Goebbels, who, starting his act as a very sophisticated character, and nobody's fool, ended as a firm believer in the view that existence was some kind of lowest-common-denominator of mass perception, and of the view that, if enough people say so, it must be true. Since it was this kind of thing that cost Germany the war, I have some sympathy for the opposing, the old-fashioned Johnsonian view that what is, is, and what isn't, isn't; that the universe is outside us, not inside, and that it consists of mostly unknown wonders whose nature it is up to us to discover.

Of course, this view also has a lowest-common-denominator. Let us consider E.E. "Doc" Smith, as an example of what scientism at its worst can produce. His "Skylark" novels are referred to on their paperback jackets as "classics," and correctly so, since a classic is by definition a book read and admired by successive generations. *The Skylark of Valeron* was copyrighted in 1934; I do not know its status in the United States, but over here [England] it sells and sells, which should tell us something, something rather nasty, when we come to inspect it close up:

Humanity *uber alles* — homo sapiens against all the vermin of the universe! Let's go. *Two* — do your stuff!

"As *Two* hurtled toward the unfortunate planet with every iota of her driving power, Seaton settled down to observe the strife and see what he could do. That which lay beneath his viewpoint had not been a city, in the strict sense of the word. It had been an immense system of concentric fortifications, of which the outer circles had long since gone down under the irresistible attack of the two huge structures of metal which hung above. Where those outer rings had been there was now an annular lake of boiling, seething lava. Lava from which arose gouts and slender pillars of smoke and fume: lava being volatilized by the terrific heat of the offensive beams and being hurled away in flaming cascades by the almost constant detonations of high-explosive shells; lava into which from time to time another portion of the immense fortress slagged down — put out of action, riddled and finally fused by the awful forces of the invader."

And so on and so forth. Ploughing through these novels, one is struck by the way in which the plots seem to exist merely as excuses to set set-pieces of such superschrecklichkeit. Hirsohima, any-one? While Smith is undoubtedly the master of these worshipful de-scriptions of raw force, it is instructive to note how often in space opera this one-note piano is called into play. In a much more recent novel, *All Evil Shed Away*, Scots author Archie Roy refers to, ". . . the auxiliary equipment necessary to feed the ravening power to these monsters from the MDH fusion generator . . ." I must hasten to add that Mr. Roy is of quite a different class from Smith, with a very opposite ethic and a fine grasp of the true wellsprings of human behaviour. But this simply makes my point: if they do these things in the green wood, what will they do in the dry? What, indeed? Smith's is a far from isolated example, if one wishes to consider the moral and tech-nological effects of this kind of writing. Professor Clarke's *Voices Prophesying War*, and our own editor's articles in *Foundation* show clearly enough the predispositions that the genre can and has created in its public: predispositions with a positive feedback effect encouraging the use of the technologies, nuclear and otherwise, on which it loves to dwell. I have been personally informed by one involved that Wells's *The World Set Free*, with its early but relatively accurate description of atomic warfare, was well-known reading among those involved with the Manhattan Project.

46

I now go over — with some relief — to science fact. The chief line of communication here has always been *Astounding Science Fiction* magazine, now *Analog*. Prior to John W. Campbell's taking over the editorship, serious articles were few and far apart, but from 1939 onwards we find — for example — Willy Ley writing about "2,000-year-old electric batteries" and "Geography for Time-travelers," while astronomer R.S. Richardson contributed several pieces about, for example, supernovae. In May/June of that year L. Sprague de Camp gives us "Design for Life," an outline of the factors governing life-forms generally; about the same time Richard Tooker wrote "Toward a Superman," in which — you will be glad to hear — he wrote "the methods most useful in plants cannot be used with man in the same wholehearted manner." Cheers! "Unseen Tools" by Leo Vernon, in June 1940, cites C.E. Shannon's work on the use of symbolic algebra for studying switchboard and wiring diagrams. In February 1947 Campbell himself weighs in with some wildly optimistic predictions in "Atomic Power Plant." "Atomic piles will be safe unless completely deserted for periods of several days at a time, a period preceded by long-continued mismanagement, neglect and general lack of maintenance. Any good automatic control system should be good for several months of unattended care . . . there will certainly be plenty of time for manual control operators to shut down the pile if necessary."

Mind you, Campbell could be amusing and stimulating as well as inaccurate. Describing in 1952 the Brookhaven procedures for charging outside companies for irradiation tests, he adds, "I have a feeling that accountants will have a certain vague discomfort at calculating costs on the basis of multiplying 2,000,000,000,000 X 30 and dividing by 400,000,000 to determine the cost in dollars. For one thing, I suspect standard bookkeeping machines are not designed to handle thirteen to fifteen digit numbers. Nuclear physics brings industry new problems!" You can say that again.

From this time onward, Campbell obviously had no difficulty in getting a good supply of science writers, many of them of high standing; this input was kept up after his death by editors Ben Bova and Stanley Schmidt, and the standard today continues high. The current (February 1987) issue, for example, carries a detailed and valuable article by G. Harry Stine on current American options in space following the "Challenger" disaster, with some pertinent comments on same. For the benefit of any reader here who thinks that this kind of article can be conjured up by anyone with access to trade journals and government reports, it is perhaps worth quoting Stine's own comments on his qualifications. "After a lot of training I became the lone individual who stood with my finger on the button when Navy rockets and guided missiles were launched at White Sands. I was Chairman of the Inter-Range Safety Group in 1956/57, and helped codify a standard set of safety criteria that would be used on all Department of Defense rocket and guided missile ranges." Science writers for *Analog* really do know what they are talking about, and readers who care about scientific advances, with their social and political implications, do, I strongly feel, have a responsibility for keeping up with this material, as well as studying the editorial and letter-column material. *Analog* is the only current sf magazine committed to publishing, alongside the sf, articles about the impact of science on the modern world.

Since most *Foundation* readers are subscribers, and presumably reasonably avid readers of sf, then, between their book purchases and our reviews, they will be up-to-date on the state of current science as portrayed in today's novels, and I do not propose to comment on these. Such readers will probably have long ago made up their minds on the contending issues I raised earlier, and about all I can usefully add here is that the debate between these issues does itself form an increasingly large content of new works of fiction. Despite my own opinions, I am mainly concerned here to present information: what follows will go accordingly.

Some may recall that in *Foundation* 24 I expressed the view that the genre should express an ethos making use of real science but informed by sound philosophy. Feeling that I should put my efforts where my mouth is, I have for some while been concerned with what some will feel is a chimera — Applied Science Fiction, by which I mean the use of sf ideas in real-life situations, of which the most important is education. In a society whose own ethos alternates violently between greed and apathy, this is uphill work, yet not without its compensations. Let me give you one or two cases. . . .

As far back as 1975 John Brunner was serving notice of the then-unconsidered potentials of the oncoming computer revolution. In *The*

Shock-Wave Rider he put forward the idea of a "worm" program: one that, released into a large computer network, would self-replicate virus-like, with horrifying results — well, horrifying at least to the owners of the network. Since Mr. Brunner dramatized the idea, it has surfaced from time to time in various journalistic computer-do scenarios, but it is still largely seen as pure fiction, happily for the state of our bank-accounts and of sundry Ministries of Defence. However, 'tame' versions are now being produced. . . .

A worm is a program which "lives" in more than one computer, adapting and growing in its environment by replicating the segments which are its component program parts. John Shoch and Jon Hupp at Xerox's Palo Alto Research Center saw worm programs as very useful for their network of about a hundred computer work-stations: a worm could be used to occupy idle work-stations by running its programs there until the work-station was needed by a human again. Software was designed whereby worms such as the Existential Worm could be run — a program to experiment with the work whose sole aim in life was to exist as a pre-defined number of segments. The worm would detect the loss of segments when workers logged-on to machines in which they were running, and create duplicates in other machines, in order to keep the population of segments constant.

At the Polytechnic of Central London, Yakup Paker, Tom Kindberg and Ali Vahit Sahiner have built an environment especially for creating and running worm programs. (Tom Kindberg has supplied me with all this information, which I am quoting and summarising.) Their network of computers they call the *earth*, and programmers produce *worm eggs* which, when run, grow into collections of communicating segment programs. Worms can be used for any application where a multiple computer earth can be of direct practical advantage, such as in parallel processing: a worm coordinates the activities of several computers to perform the necessary calculations, instead of having the whole process take longer on a single computer. They have even introduced the idea of worm DNA — that part of the worm which determines how a worm grows and adapts to its environment. Worms could monitor their own behaviour and adapt their own DNA in response to it; thus worms could evolve. Introducing a random element into worm evolution is theoretically possible, although it would be necessary to ensure containment against the unpredictable growth of "monster" worms. To quote Kindberg directly: "In our earth several worms can run together at the same time. Worm society can thus be studied, a society in which the need to share computing resources is matched against individual growth strategies. This is all in direct opposition to conventional computing practice, wherein programs are tightly constrained by centralized administrative software called operating systems. We are only just beginning to experiment with worms with their new, organic self-determination; and it is uncertain what limits shall have to be put to their behaviour. In thoughts of the future one is inspired, however, by what Charles Darwin had to say about their living counterparts: 'It may be doubted whether there are any other animals which have played such an important part in the history of the world as these lowly organised creatures.'

Older readers of *Analog* — then *Astounding* — may remember the Great Dean Drive Debate. In October 1960 John Campbell jumped up and down excitedly about one Norman L. Dean, who had patented an allegedly workable inertial drive, a device Campbell believed would, if incorporated into a submarine, take the craft from earth to Mars in five days. Campbell's view was that the Space Administration, the Office of Naval Research, etc., had turned the thing down untested on the grounds that the principles involved did not accord with orthodox physics. His point, a favourite with him, was that it did not matter whether the theory was sound or not; that from an engineering point of view, it would work. What really interested him was the possibility of a totally new approach to physics thinking.

"Note that while the greater added kinetic energy appears with respect to the Mars frame of reference, *no momentum or energy* is being transferred between the ship and Mars at the time. The ship is reacting against its exhaust gases, not Mars. But, if that ship is going to land on Mars, that kinetic energy must be accounted for at that time. *Which* kinetic energy is conservative — the ship-earth value, or the ship-Mars value? Einstein's entire theoretical structure breaks down if si-multaneity is imposed as a requirement, just as Newton's broke down under the requirements of more than one frame of reference."

Since 1960 there have been various follow-ups on this story, all of them tantalising but inconclusive. It struck me that some educational benefit might be had from a further investigation. There seemed three
50

possibilities: Campbell was right, and a great scientific breakthrough was being suppressed; Campbell was wrong; or else, Campbell was knowingly winding up his readers in the hopes of "getting them to think" (and, in the process, increasing the circulation of his magazine). Whatever the final answer, it seemed to me that something constructive might emerge from some kind of Popperian test.

It has been a long haul, and I count myself lucky in having received the untiring assistance of Douglas Letts, a mathematician with a remarkable knowledge, not only of physics, but of its historical underpinnings, of Alan Thompson, an inventor of a very practical disposition, and of Michael Williams, till lately a Research officer at the Science Museum and now Director of the new Children's Gallery there. (It should be made quite clear here that Mr. Williams's advice came in a purely personal capacity, and in no way expresses any "official" view from the Museum). Not surprisingly, the views of these gentlemen by no means entirely coincided. All of them have inspected Dean's Patent No. 2,886,976, which I obtained — as could anyone else — from the patent Office, and which states "This invention relates to driving systems for producing unidirectional motion and [it] has for its primary object to provide a propulsion system in which a rotational movement produced by a prime mover is converted into a continuous or intermittent unidirectional movement of a load carrier which may or may not be the carrier of the rotational element of the system."

What follows is from private correspondence with those named above. Mr. Letts Writes: "As for the 'three body problem', even Campbell gets around to the correct application of this difficulty: celestial mechanics, the motion of three bodies connected by gravitational forces alone.

"Dean's apparatus is not held together by gravitational forces, but by screws, levers, slides, axles, pins, sockets, bearings and other mechanical paraphernalia. Besides, if all three body problems were insoluble, Doug Letts would not have been able to solve the 'triple bob', page 19 of *Vector Analysis by Computer*, 2nd Edition, where, by the way, the method of working is readily adaptable to masses of different sizes and considerably more than three of them, too. Campbell is completely up the creek when he writes: *Our mathematics . . . can not handle simultaneous multiple relationships.*

51

"The theme of *Vector Analysis by Computer* is simultaneous multiple relationships and how to make light work of them with a little help from a Sinclair ZX81. And you can be pretty sure that even without a computer the same simultaneous multiple relationships are the working substance, the grist for the mathematical mills of pen and paper mathematicians. The essence of Dean's Patent (and here I add that it is a genuine Patent, a description of a workable device), the essence is: the description of an apparatus capable of motion along a 'tape, cord or cable'. It is not reactionless. It is not a sky hook. It is not a space drive. Whatever claims Dean may have made, mathematically, or with models, relating to reactionless drives, well, these form no part of the published Patent.

"In other words, in the critical Campbell sentence, *His device . . . patent No. 2,886,976 . . . thrust . . . without reaction'*, his device, without reaction, is not the subject of Patent No. 2,886,976. If there were other devices having the required properties, then details are not available, yet.

"There is nothing in the given Patent to establish a claim to reactionless drive. Accordingly, any such claim based upon a reference to the Patent cannot succeed. However, we may suppose that Dean was unable to obtain a Patent for his reactionless drive and did the next best thing: he patented the essential parts — or what he believed to be the essential parts — in the guise of a workable apparatus containing those parts.

"And what are these essential parts?

"Agreement between elements of the Patent and other published details points to 'two counter-rotating masses, on shafts rotating in a light frame' (p. 78). The myth follows (p. 79): 'The centre of rotation has no mass; it's a geometrical concept, not a material entity. Pushing it around doesn't require force'.

"Double confusion follows.

"The conceptual mountain comes to Mahomet.

"The physical mountain stands immobile, so Mahomet gets up and walks. Effortlessly, I invert the concept of the Eiffel Tower, though allowing 12 hours rotation of the Earth to effect the same plan.

"Meanwhile, 'His machine solves the problem perfectly — and the answer is rectified centrifugal force' (p. 81).

"Crystal and cat's whisker, silicon or germanium diode, mercury arc rectifier and thermionic diode are all analogues of differential friction. This way *hard*, that way *easy*.

"But as the electronic rectifier ceases to function when one end is disconnected from the circuit, so does the mechanical centrifugal force rectifier fail when detached from 'a fixed member', (often the Earth), or the 'tape, cord or cable' (connecting two points, usually on Earth).

"The problem with Mr. Dean's invention is *not* that it denies established physics or Newtonian principles. The 'emotional impact of the concept' here, at this address, is confined to a now weary acceptance that contra-rotating masses do little else but conform."

The following paper from Michael Williams covers the matter from a different angle, and describes what he nicknames the Bumble Drive: "The following idea is based on the Dean patent of 1959 but achieves the same result without using counter-rotating eccentric discs. It is therefore outside the patent. I believe that in effect it is the same idea: a vibration in one line only that can be made to move itself or a ribbon, one in relation to another. But I do not believe that the action of the Dean patent or this device will achieve the <u>reaction free</u> motion that is the desire of the originator. Further I believe that the changed mode of action I suggest gives a clear vision of why the Dean idea fails.

"When a tuning fork has its base rested on a sounding board the board vibrates as the energy is drained from the fork. The fork stem moves up and down. If the fork were placed within a ratchet system it could run itself up the ratchet as its energy was absorbed. This is the 'differential friction' effect that is often seen in models that are claimed to break Newton's Third Law. The Laithwaite gyro was rested on a bed of ball bearings but I still could not see its action as other than a frictional one. How can we modify my device to make it the equivalent of a Dean Drive?

"The first thing to do is to make it vibrate under an external energy supply. This is achieved by fitting a single solenoid that is fed with an alternating current from a tuned circuit. The circuit would have to be linked to a sensor so that the fork itself kept the frequency at the correct figure. Optical sensing would give the least disturbance. The forces may be imagined to be applied perpendicular to the line of the blades,

53

but the solenoid is fixed to the frame. We now have the energy source and it does not make the device spin in any way.

"At this point we have to add the gadgetry to grip a ribbon and also to return the fork to its central position in relation to the frame. This is best imagined by electronic control based on phase-shifted pulse circuits under the control of the master frequency set by the fork. One device would be set to grip the tape at precise times and for precise times during the cycle. This could be a solenoid device but at the high frequency envisaged there would be problems in circuitry and operation.

"But I cannot see any instant or short periods in the cycle at which the fork may be returned to its central position as if it had no inertia. That is the key point on which Dean fails, it is easier to see why in my version.

"Why bumble drive? Quote: *Life on Earth* by David Attenborough. . . . '. . . flies . . . They only use their forewings for flight. The hind wings are reduced to tiny knobs. All flies posses these little structures but they are particularly noticeable in crane flies, the daddy-long-legs, in which the knobs are placed at the end of stalks so that they look like the heads of drumsticks. When the fly is in the air, these organs which are jointed to the thorax in the same way as wings, oscillate up and down a hundred or more times a second. They act partly as stabilisers, like gyroscopes, and partly as sense organs presumably telling the fly of the attitude of its body in the air and in the direction in which it is moving . . . .'

"The action of fly drumsticks is the equivalent of the tuning forks that are used in short-range guided missiles for the same purpose — to sense the rate of turn and compensate for it. And as an amusing end-note may it not be that the flies have in fact installed in their flight-drive a form of the Dean-drive, under what is in effect a computer-brain control. If Dean-drive were possible then evolution would have given it to the flies.

"I am reminded of the Scottish hammer-thrower in childrens' comics: he whirls the thing around his head and then gets carried away. As he flies through the air he is on Dean-drive, for that is the mechanism we have been discussing. And on the surface it seems possible . . . ."

54

I hope to have demonstrated here that original and possibly valuable work has resulted form my follow-up on the original Campbell editorial on the Inertial Drive. I say, 'my' follow-up; this in fact has consisted in the main of nagging letters to my collaborators, whose patience must at times have been sorely tried. At all events, they have my profound thanks.

I hope to have shown here that a) there are very unhealthy elements in the use (traduction?) of science in past and current science fiction, but that b) the healthy, accurate and constructive element still survives (consider for example, Rudy Rucker's work in mathematics) and deserves far more active support from academic circles than it is getting. I believe, as did Campbell, that this stems from a basic disinterest — especially in the United States — in the philosophy of science and in the existential issues involved. Without such interest, there is no question but that science must decline, as it is declining, into increasingly sinister technological fixes. Let me ask the reader a question: in reading science fiction over the past decade, how many references has he or she come across to Simone Weil, Kuhn, Popper, Colin Wilson, or Ayn Rand? I pull these names out of the hat at random: I could pull more. With them, what counts is not that they were right or wrong, but that they confront fundamental issues linking science to the humanities — that is, to the fate of thee and me. The silence on these issues is deafening. I don't know what effect this silence has on others, but it frightens me to death.

Was John W. Campbell
a Racially Prejudiced Bastard?
by
Perry A. Chapdelaine, Sr.

Volume I, *The John W. Campbell Letters* already more than adequately says — and demonstrates — my feelings about this man who was a giant among giants — and who shaped the modern world of science fiction to an extent not yet fully appreciated. So, I wasn't going to say more about Campbell in Volume II.

During preparation of this Second volume, however, I could not help but note the extensive dialogues that occurred between Isaac Asimov and John W. Campbell, Jr., regarding the nature of racial prejudism. It became clear that more must be said, especially from my vantage points, which included the following: (1) I taught simultaneously, full-time, at both an all-Black university, and an all-White university. (2) I, a White person, experienced, without harm or threat of harm, the dreadful racial riots in and around our schools during the late sixties. (3) I confronted my Negro students head-on with John W. Campbell's thesis (to follow), and found my students during this tense period not one whit inclined to the "Campbell is a racially prejudiced bastard" thesis. (4) I had personally met some of the key players in propagating this false thesis during that sad period. My personal conviction, then and even today my present opinion, was/is that many were in the process of tearing a great man's reputation down as a means of pushing themselves upward.

This harsh statement did not apply to Isaac Asimov, however, as I felt (and still feel) that Isaac had personal, unverbalized, reasons for misunderstanding Campbell's argumentations, his reasons unrelated to the parry and thrust of those-who-would-be-great-by-dethroning-the-already-great. Isaac will have to speak to this point himself, if he has not already done so.

Then, during that period of almost social revolution — SNICK, Stokley Carmichael, Martin Luther King, Jr. and others — there were also the blind liberals in and out of fandom, in and out of SF writing. These unwittingly supported the efforts of those-who-would-be-great-at-the-expense-of-the-already-great.

It was, indeed, a trying time, almost isolating John W. Campbell, Jr. from properly earned awards and friendships within the fandom community during his physically declining years. According to Peg Campbell's statement to George Hay (*The John Campbell Letters*, Vol. I, p. 10, 1985): ". . . she and John sometimes found themselves quite alone at conventions, when they would have welcomed company and conversation."

Here was a man who, from my adolescence onward, had taught me to love and to associate with the most extreme form of life in every shape, hue and with every attitude, Extra-Terrestrial Aliens breathing every kind of atmosphere. I loved those Extra-Terrestrial Aliens!

In John W. Campbell's letter to Isaac Asimov, November 18, 1958, this volume, he says: "I dislike White, Yellow, and Red trash as thoroughly as I dislike Black-skinned trash.

"The one thing I'm interested in is the develoment of MEN. Supermen. And I don't give a damn what racial stock they start from -- just so they achieve."

Racially prejudiced?

Not hardly!

Volume I, *The John W. Campbell Letters*, quite clearly shows John Campbell's need to turn about every hypothesis, and to argue the other side of "Mother's are wonderful" truisims. That Volume, as well as the contents of this one, also clearly demonstrates John's need to argue "to learn" not so much "to win." That technique, his penchant for demanding an "engineering solution and his superb ability to analogize most everything, after all, were his teaching tools, his tools in trade for producing such wonderful authors as Isaac Asimov!

If we were to make a proper analysis of all the force vectors that brought about such gross misunderstanding of John's racial philosophies, we would need perhaps several books, but at least one major force vector should be mentioned: Fandom turns over rapidly, perhaps a new generation every three or four years. Fans come and fans go. But the nature of fandom seems ever-present, a ripe field for gossip and dissent, the creation and propagation of monstrous untruths that are not easily searched out and uprooted for what they are. Knowledge that such a bedrock exists makes it easier to understand what followed when a then well-known editor of a well-distributed

SF Magazine, through publication and distribution, publicly berated John W. Campbell for being racially prejudiced.

An unthinking fandom -- in destructive packs -- followed the distortions, misunderstandings and half truths — and thus began the terrible isolation felt by Peg Campbell and John, as reported above.

How easy it was to isolate a godling . . . !

John W. Campbell answers best for himself, in the letter that follows:

Perry A. Chapdelaine, Sr.   *February 24, 1970*

Dear Perry,

The trouble with a mathematics training is that mathematics assumes a perfect Universe, following exact rules with absolute infallibility.

Now, the real universe is not that way; it contains noise — imperfections. Its rules are not exactly known. Rules we never heard of or imagined cut in and louse things up.

And one of the rules that Mathematics denies is never the less real, and applies to all Mathematicians. They all goof.

My father was an engineer (Chief Engineer for Plant Practices, A.T. & T. General) and he trained me to cross check any computation I made by running a crude analog computation on any digital math, and a rough digital check on my analog solution. Digital math can get n places correct — but it's just as apt to goof in the millions place as in the units place; analog always gets the first places right, but its hopeless beyond the first three or four. You know — the slide-rule computation of "2 X 2 is 3.98, oh hell, call it four."

Any good textbook on astronomy — my latest happens to be *Exploration of the Universe*, by Abell — will do about equally well, provided you add a new training on top of your Math training. <u>Do</u> interpret the results in common-sense terms. What would that look like — feel like . . . ?

Because I've been doing that for years, I spotted the fact that there were errors — without knowing their magnitudes exactly — in one rapid reading of your story. A <u>hotter</u> sun covering <u>more</u> of the sky, and
58

the temperatures on the planet are similar to Earth's? Oh, come on now — that doesn't fit at all!

It's worth using that cross-check to see whether your math has, somehow, slipped. For one thing, it's quick and easy.

The surface gravity of all the planets in the Solar system, save for Mercury, Mars and Jupiter, come out surprisingly close to 1 G. Saturn's huge, but the density is so low that the surface G is just about 1. The same applies to both Uranus and Neptune. Pluto's mass and diameter are unknown, so we can't say. But Venus is also close to 1G.

When you're aware of that, the importance — and effect — of planetary density and radius have more meaning to you.

In designing his weirdo planet, Meskelin, **Hal Clement** had to use extreme measures to get the extreme gravity he wanted. Primarily, this involved going to an immense core of collapsed matter, because density, rather than total mass, is what makes for high surface G. After all, the Sun's mass is 1000 times that of Jupiter — enormously greater than Earth's — yet the surface gravity of Sol works out to only about 27G. Low density effect.

It may be an inversion of your math training — but it makes a damn good cross-check!

Your "Be Fruitful & Multiply" is a version of the approach we had in "The Right to Breed," by Donald Kingsbury. He's a professor of Math at McGill University, and added a couple of frills. He assumed a technology that went to the absolute end of imaginable technology (answering the objection that improved technology will allow a larger population) by saying means for instantaneous travel to infinite distance is developed, and technology that can convert any mass to food is developed. Then all the stars, planets, gas, dust, and even radiation in space becomes available for human food. Assume the radius of the Universe is ten times what we now think it is. Assume the known density of matter in that space, how long would it take to convert all that total mass to human flesh? Answer: Approximately 7000 years.

The argument would certainly bear repeating.

In re pollution: So long as man depends on muscle-power for energy sources, the algae-plant production of O_2 is bound to balance the animal production of CO_2. But when you bring in fossil fuels, we can consume O_2 and produce CO_2 faster than plants reverse the process.

59

Also — interesting point! — burning fossil fuels <u>puts more radio-active waste</u> into the air than a nuclear power plant does!

Reason: Nuclear radioactive wastes we carefully bury deep underground, where they can cool off before entering the biosphere again. But coal we dig from deep underground, where its content of uranium and thorium daughter elements, radium, actinium, polonium, etc., are taken out of storage and released into the biosphere! And actual quantity of those radioactives being released is <u>greater</u> than the leakage from a nuclear power plant.

Well-designed nuclear power plants are the only kind of power plants we can build that do not have to interfere with the biosphere. Remember that even a hydroelectric power plant interferes with the ecology of its region!

Re the attacks on me as a race bigot: As you know, the victim of such an attack cannot reply effectively, even when the statements are deliberate misquotations, or quotations out of context.

Since you're teaching in a largely-Negro school, you're in a good position to make remarks about bigotry and prejudice. You obviously wouldn't be where you are if <u>you</u> were biased.

What the attackers are reacting to is that I'm a pragmatist-engineer, interested in solutions that can actually work. This makes me the enemy of the Idealists who think that only the End is important, and any objection to Means is mere nit-picking, or the result of bias, prejudice, back-lash, etc. "When I'm so pure-heartedly Idealistic, clearly anyone opposed to what I say must be a black-hearted bigot!"

The Prohibition people tried that, and got a constitutional amendment rammed through to cure forever the problem of alcoholism.

Those cock-eyed Idealists now are trying to ram through "love thy neighbor" by legal command — and maintaining, at the same time, that anyone who feels any law is unjust, should defy that law. The hopeless logical inconsistency of this never penetrates their rigidly idealistic minds. Reminds me of a high school girl in the neighborhood who wants to be a model, and decided to go on a rigid diet. Her father — who's an M.D. — doesn't want her to be a model, and knows better than to argue with her. So he's watched with some amusement. It seems the diet called for lots of cottage cheese, but she found she didn't like that, and so substituted cream cheese instead — which

60

she eats by the brick. Her father did mention to her that cream cheese runs 60% butter-fat, but that didn't have a chance of penetrating her teen-age certainty of her own wisdom.

After all, cottage and cream cheese look much alike, don't they?

The facts I'm operating on are that it is not true that all men are born equal. That, in any gene-pool-race, some are bright and some are stupid. That wisdom and intelligence are two independent variables. That education can not make up for lack of potential, which is a genetic trait. (The ability to learn has to be genetic, for instance, since, by definition, you cannot teach an organism how to learn . . . if it can't learn already! Thus you cannot teach a chimp how to speak; he lacks the genetically conferred potential required.)

Among the great gene-pool-race groups on Earth we can distinguish — solely by history, not skin-color! — the orientals, Polynesians, Amerinds, Indo-aryans, and Africans.

Orientals and middle-eastern gene-pool-races first achieved high-level civilization, with the oriental branch of the Indo-Aryans learning from them, a couple of millennia before **Christ**. The western Indo-Aryans learned a millennium later, and finally the north-western group, particularly the Scots, didn't catch on until about 300 years ago.

The Polynesians developed high-level civilization and technology suited to their island-and-sea milieu at least 2500 years ago.

The native Africans, as of the time of **Christ**, had a very low population, due to the fact that they had no decent crop plants, and suffered from chronic acute protein starvation. Note that Biafra is a lush, tropical land . . . yet Biafrans starved to death for lack of usable food. Africa doesn't produce a decent crop plant.

There was a population explosion among the Bantu natives of Africa about 200 years A.D., when explorers from Indonesia invaded east Africa, set up colonies, and introduced new, nourishing crop-plants. A second wave of invaders came some two hundred or so years later from India, introducing more crop plants.

These invaders employed Africans — largely as slaves — to build cities for them, such as the famous Zimbabwe. (Remember that Angkor Vat was built, and deserted, about that time in a Cambodian jungle; building cities in jungles was old stuff to the Indonesian architects!)

61

Point of interest: The Amerinds developed high cultures in America. The Orientals developed high cultures. The Indo-aryans developed high cultures and technology. The Polynesians did.

The Africans alone of the major gene-pool-races did not.

The above statements have nothing whatever to do with skin color; they're simple facts of history.

I'm not talking about what happened to Africans transplanted to America — I'm talking about Africans in Africa.

One of the characteristics of a strong, dynamic civilization is a high degree of organization — whether it's done by a bloody-handed tyrant or by representative democracy (as the Asmoans developed). Organization and efficient division of labor is the foundation of civilization, and until that is achieved, no major building is possible. And that's the characteristic that the Africans did not develop during the 6500 year period of written history, while all the other groups did.

That fact makes a major difference in integrating the group into the major cultural stream of the Earth. It is a system that "isn't natural" to them, simply because it isn't ancestral to them.

There are two types of "feeling membership in" groups that an individual can experience. One is the individual-to-individual type of belongingness — i.e., all first-rate mechanics feel a kinship with each other as individual peers. Or mathematicians, chemists, musicians, etc. And there's racial belongingness, as all Blacks are brothers — or all Scots, Frenchmen, or White Russians. (But Mongol "Russians" exclude that kind of belongingness.)

Currently, there's a tough problem in the schools; experience now shows that neither the Whites nor the Blacks want integrated schools. Actually, it's the old, old story; group A wants right of free entry into any group — but while they demand the right to enter group B's area, they want to exclude B's from their area. The Jews show exactly the same pattern — they want no bars to their free entry to hotels, theaters, resorts, etc., — but they also seek to push any goyim out of their resorts, hotels, theaters, etc. And they try to make sure none of their daughters marry goyim, but cry "Anti-semitism" if somebody tries to keep a Christian girl from marrying a Jew. (Remember "Abie's Irish Rose"?)

The Blacks want to be free to enter any school they want to — but

62

Black students are uniting to drive White students out of their schools, once they achieve a 50+% majority in a school.

Until individual-achievement-membership becomes more important to them than genetic-group-membership — there'll be trouble.

Because, over the centuries, Africans didn't develop organizational talents, their descendants today are still lousy organizers. Vide the mess the various African nations are making of themselves — Congo, Nigeria, you-name-it.

And American Negroes provide few competent business organizers. That's why there are so very, very few Negro banks, insurance companies, supermarket chains, and even local stores.

By 1820 there were a lot of free Negroes in this country -- but no Negro banks. When the Irish came in, they were held to be lower than the Negro — but they promptly set up banks, insurance companies, organized clubs, built churches, set up parochial schools, and organized businesses.

What I am trying to point out is that you can't solve problems if you won't acknowledge the facts of that system. Acknowledge what the problem is, and you can design steps to correct the situation in a minimum of time, with a minimum of human agony, and a minimum of false hopes.

The current much-publicized approach reminds me of the cancer quack who keeps telling his sucker that "All you need is another $1000 worth of treatment and we'll get rid of that pain," and sells him another series of caramel colored water laced with alcohol and laudanum.

The solution takes time, and must start with schools that teach selected Negroes how to organize effectively and constructively. Negro banks and insurance companies that Negroes can feel they can trust their money to. (And that does not mean that they can feel "Oh, well, the FDIC will take care my money isn't lost," or "Oh, I don't have to worry — the State Insurance inspection people will see to it that my insurance gets paid somehow." It means trusting the able, honest and responsible men who run the bank.)

It's not an attractive approach — because it takes time, care, and responsible action. To any people a quick, spectacular action is much more soul-satisfying. "Burn, baby, burn!" is so much more satisfying than "Wait, baby, wait — we're getting there!" to any human people.

63

The trouble, of course, is that "Burn, baby, burn!" rouses "Step on them black bastards!" — which is worse than useless, but also a very human, response.

The trouble with being a pragmatist is that it makes enemies of both sides — both types of bigoted Idealists hate having facts slapped in their faces. It makes the problem seem almost as tough as it really is, instead of being something that could all be solved by one simple drastic maneuver.

Regards, John W. Campbell, Editor

A.E. "Slan" Vogt
by
Forrest J Ackerman

Forrest Ackerman -- inventor of the term "sci-fi", the first one during early fandom to develop and wear a futuristic costume during a science fiction convention, thereby setting an established program -- is a kind of "Slan" himself.

During most of A.E. van Vogt's writing years, Forrest was his literary agent and close friend, but additionally is or has been publisher, editor, writer, television and tv actor, founder of and acquistioner for the gigantic and fantastic Ackerman science fiction and horror memorabilia collection located in Hollywood, personal friend of many movie greats, punster, and science fiction and horror fan -- and many, many more things.

I am proud to say that Forrest J Ackerman has long been a friend, supporter of this Campbell Letters project, and the most single authoritative figure I know on A.E. van Vogt, outside of van Vogt himself.

Forrest's wife, Wendayne, during their long tenure together, was almost equally active in Forrest's many enterprises, and a star in her own right.

Forrest has taken time from his extremely busy travels and schedules to reminisce about A.E. van Vogt.

Alfred Elton van Vogt was born to Aganetha (Buhr) van Vogt over seven decades ago south of Winnipeg, in Manitoba, Canada. His father, Henry van Vogt practiced law. Van (as his friends call him) lived successively in small Canadian towns until moving to Winnipeg, Manitoba.

He completed high school during the great depression era, wrote civil service exams, and at age 18 began working at census taking in Ottawa. While there he studied correspondence courses and, on returning to Winnipeg, wrote and sold a confession type short story, after which many others of similar type followed. He also became Western representative for the Maclean trade papers of Toronto, and wrote articles each month for eight different business magazines.

In 1936 he met Edna Mayne Hull at the Winnipeg Writer's Club meeting, and they were married May 9, 1939, until she passed away in the early seventies. During World War II years van worked in the De-

partment of National Defense.

Van sold his first science fiction story to Astounding Science Fiction Magazine *in 1938. His best known work,* Slan, *was written in the evenings during those months in Ottawa.*

The van Vogt's migrated to Los Angeles, CA in 1947. He eventually received his BA degree in 1953 and became a UCLA alumnus in the early 1970's.

Van married Lydia, his present wife, when she was a Los Angeles court interpreter. She speaks five languages."

Known as one of the world's great and original science fantasy writers, he continues to live and think and work in a house overlooking Hollywood, just beneath the "Hollywood" sign. His novels and other writings represent some of the definitive, creative stories written in a manner of suspense totally different than any other writer.

I first met A.E. van Vogt on his invitation to lecture on Dianetics^{TM} at the Los Angeles Hubbard Dianetic Foundation, Inc. van Vogt is a man of exceedingly high ethics and my friend.

AC Projects, Inc., (5106 Old Harding Road, Franklin, TN 37064) publishers of The John W. Campbell Letters, also published A.E. van Vogt's The Battle of Forever, *still available in both signed, numbered edition as well as trade edition.*

Where Isaac Asimov represents a brilliant writer who willingly learned everything possible from John W. Campbell, A.E. van Vogt is one of those rare writers of the time, who held steady with his own ideas and writing techniques, and, to some extent, was not capable of bending to Campbell's paradigms.

John Campbell embraced both men! [Perry A. Chapdelaine, Sr.: Ed.]

Haphazard Reminiscences at Deadline Time during a Very Hectic Time of My Life

IN THE 65 YEARS that I have been reading science fiction, from the pioneering era of Gernsback's "scientifiction" to the $20 million TV channel recognition of "sci-fi" -- "Everybody" knows about the $20 million cable channel called Sci-Fi Channel, starting in '91 -- Alfred Elton van Vogt has entertained me about as much as any sf author I can name. He has given me indelible memories of reading pleasure in the company of H.G. Wells, Edgar Rice Burroughs, Ray Bradbury, Henry Kuttner, Catherine Moore, Frederik Pohl, Robert Heinlein and several other sensawunda (sense-of-wonder) scribes who have enhanced my literary life.

I don't know where; and neither, I think, does Van; the notion got loose for awhile that his middle name was Egger but it's been a long time since that erroneous information cropped up in print.

One of my earliest memories of him as an in-the-flesh person was as Co-Guest of Honor of the first Pacificon, the World SF Convention of 1946 in LA.

After World War II, when I timorously hung out my shingle as a science fiction agent, Van became one of my earliest clients and has been my most important one for 40 years. There was a brief hiatus of 2 years when he thought a younger, New York based agent could represent him more satisfactorily than an aging FJA but after a disillusioning period of non-publication under the aegis of a big name literary rep in NYC he has returned to the fold and I am happy to report that 1991 is the Year of Renaissance for "the idea man of science fiction", with his classic novels coming back into print, previously unpublished works scheduled for his bylined books, and Russia, Romania, Czechoslovakia, Taiwan and Hungary all hungry for his work.

I was very gratified when AE originally picked me as it was by a process of elimination. He was shopping his manuscripts around with 4 established agents of the time and I was an untried, unknown quantity . . . but he eventually settled on me! I've sold him to TV and placed an original movie script by him with Roger Corman: *Conflict 2100*.

I was the first person to receive a sample of Dianetic™ auditing from him in 1950 after he had read the first copy of *Dianetics: The Modern Science of Mental Health* rushed to LA; and shortly after my 50th birthday, when I was laid low by a series of heart attacks (only 2 hours energy a day for a year) he very generously donated his valuable time for a number of months to aid me in recovery with Dianetic assistance. He is a very generous person in many respects.

We have been together on television in Calgary, Canada, and in Rio de Janeiro in 1969 at the Brazilian International Science Fiction Film Festival for 12 days. (Like the rest of us -- Phil Farmer, Fred Pohl, George Pal, John Brunner, Bob Sheckley, Bob Bloch, Damon Knight, et al -- one lunch time on the strand, he too didn't have the nerve to sample the only 2 entrees on the menu: spit sandwiches and raddled out turkey cock. No, such native delicacies defeated even the gustatory imagination of the man destined to rule the sevagram!)

I was flattered that he chose me to give the graveside eulogy for his first wife, s.f. author E. Mayne Hull, although I was bedded with a temporary illness the day of the ceremony and could not oblige.

We collaborated on one story, "Laugh, Clone, Laugh", published in the pocketbook *Science Fiction Worlds of Forrest J Ackerman and Friends*.

He has immortalized my "Garage Mahal, Son of Taj" by stating publicly that "Forrest J Ackerman has not only the world's greatest collection of science fiction but the world's <u>second</u> greatest collection of science fiction" (referring to the duplicate material housed in my triplex garage).

I have never known a man so dedicated to self-improvement, particularly of his mental capacities. Although I think there was very little room for improvement in the first place.

Thanks for endless hours of entertainment, Van, and thanks for the privilege of being associated with you professionally for 8 illustrious lustrums.

**The 1930's
with *Isaac Asimov***

Ave Robertus!

Uh! Things and stuff have been going on down here, and I'm up to my ears, and getting deeper every day. NOTE BENE! DON'T EVEN PUT THIS IN YOUR BOUND LETTERS DEPARTMENT FOR A WHILE. It's super-under-the-hat 'til January 25, when *Astounding* will burgeon forth with the news.

You'll be seeing presently in the fan mags that *Astounding's* taking a slant toward more fantasy. Lies, all lies. Base lies and deception. *Astounding* is going to carry even less fantasy than at present. But I'm frantically seeking first-rate fantasy story material. I've written **Norman L. Knight, C.A. Smith, C.L. Moore, Lester del Rey, Seabury Quinn, Ed. Hamilton**, everyone I could think of and a lot more I'd never begun to think of for new fantasy material — immediately. Telling 'em all that *Astounding's* taking an immediate slant toward fantasy, running more fantasy due to the recent success of **L. Ron Hubbard's** fantasy, and **Manly Wade Wellman's** fantasy.

That much is out to the fan magazines, whence the rumors soon to appear.

This much is out to a few of the closed-mouthed S&S editors who might recommend authors who could do fantasy to me: I'm starting a new companion magazine to *Astounding Science-Fiction*, a magazine of pure fantasy. The material is to be fantasy plus a little weird, supernatural and horror of the psychological type. NO sex, NO sadism, and NO elementals of a malignant nature with penchants for vivisection, no beauteous and necessarily nude maidens sacrificed to obscene gods. I'll try my damnedest to make this the best fantasy magazine that ever has appeared — a dozen times better than *Weird* ever wanted to be and Street and Smith are backing me 100%. So I ought to get there.

And this is the particularly super-super-super under the hat. S&S President **Grammar**, Vice President **Ralston**, Promotion Manager **de Grouchey** and I being the present repositories of information. The magazine will be called STRANGE WORLDS with the subtitle FANTASY FICTION. I think that makes a damned good title.

And this mag is going to be 100% my own particular pet, thought up, started, and formed by me — wherefore I love it.

Astounding will continue to be the tops in science-fiction. It's range is going to be human adventure to weird as its range. The covers will be designed to express that range.

Incidentally, I've remarked, I think, that Art Director **Flynn** and I have had differences of opinion on art in *Astounding*? We finally had a knock-down-drag-out fight on the Feb. cover, going to bat with Pres. **Grammar** as to who got what he wanted. Flynn wanted a cover showing a Martian looking out of a window at the U.S. capitol building. I didn't, because it was a monster cover. There was no reason for competition with *Wonder* and *Amazing*, when we didn't directly compete in material, and had no need to do so. Further, the mystery and curiosity arousing powers of monster-covers is a field that's been plowed over and over for 10 years.

I wanted a cover showing a rocket ship broken, split, fused in disastrous landing, nose buried in rust-red sand of an endless desert under a purple-black, unearthly sky. Two human figures stumbling off across the endless desert, one with a bandaged head, one with an arm in a sling. No equipment, stumbling tracks in the sand leading away from the wrecked ship and a cross-topped mound in the sand.

Flynn was dragged out. I get that cover — and it's going to be the finest scf. cover yet, I think. There'll be drama and mystery and genuine human appeal in that, I believe. The man that's doing it is **Rogers**, a new artist to scf., but a man who's been doing *Popular Science* and *Popular Mechanics* covers for years. He's a real artist, and a genuine scf. fan into the bargain. He seems to appreciate and agree with me in my dictum of no reds just because they're red, no eye-searing gaudiness just because they're gaudy.

I talked hard, hot and fast for about 10 minutes with **Grammar**, putting up those reasons for the type of cover I wanted and I'm going to get it, thank God. Now we've got to see what kind of cover we can find for *Strange Worlds*. That will range more toward the weird monster than *Astounding* will, but again I'm going to do my damnedest to avoid the old spectrum colors just because they're bright. I insist that those reds, blues, and greens and yellows aren't either necessary or sensible; everybody does it, and by not doing it we'll stand out more than by doing it. Further, the material I'm going to use is going to be of a type that

71

will have genuine appeal to adult minds. I'm going to try to get that one supernatural fantasy that every good author unburdens himself of at some time during his career — the 10 cent a word slick author stuff.

In the meantime, for the first time in history, *Astounding* is going to get some real pushing and promotion. I'm trying to get myself on some radio programs on sustaining hours the broadcasting companies search frantically to fill. Lecturer on popular science, you know. I'm going to do my damnedest to horn in somehow on "Hobby Lobby," with either **Willy Ley** or myself. **Ley** certainly ought to make it, with his fascination hobby, rockets.

I'm going to have *Astounding* piled with the *Popular Science* magazines on the stands in hopes that some of the science-minded readers will look it over for a change. Our new cover lettering and new type covers should get hold of some.

We're going to start cross-ading in other S&S mags to a greater extent. We have been cross-ading with *Doc Savage* mag in the past, and that recent advertising survey we published — Sept. issue — showed a 40% cross-readership with them. 40% of *Astounding's* readers read *Doc Savage*. We've done the same to a lesser extent with the *Shadow*. We have 12% cross-over with them. We haven't done it with *Air Trails* and have only 1.5% cross with them, and should have at least a 25% cross.

Air Trails is going to run a picture of the interior of the control compartment of the new Atlantic Clipper, with its multitude of dials, controls, recording instruments, etc., and remark, "This might be the interior of a spaceship such as described in *Astounding Science Fiction*; it is, in fact, the interior of the Atlantic Clipper." I, in turn, will print in *Astounding* a little note that, for a good idea of what the control board of a rocket ship would look like, see page 47 of *Air Trails*. We'll work similar stunts on and off from now on.

Strange Worlds will be 20 cents, $2 a year, 144 pages to start, 160 pages later, probably. Pulp size, trimmed, of course. Naturally, it will cross-ad with *Astounding* liberally.

The Saturn cover will come soon, no doubt. That will open the Hayden Planetarium promotion scheme for *Astounding*. Probably our March cover. I was thinking of using "Cloak of Aesir" on that but won't. The Sarn Mother would be a monster, and better suited for

Strange Worlds. "Cloak of Aesir" will appear in March *Astounding* though, I think. 21,000 words. The Saturn cover will be done with the aid and advice of the Hayden Planetarium, and should be right.

Incidentally, your remark about the cover error being so easy to spot is -- evidently another illusion — as **Spiegl's** and **Chauvenet's** reaction showed. We played a game out at a party the other day in which a number of things like cheese graters, folding rules, fountain pens, rubber bands, poker chips etc. were hidden in plain sight. In a living room. About 15 people trying to find where they were. It took me 20 minutes to find the 6 red poker chips. They'd been stuck onto six drawer-pulls, right in front, and looked like part of the furniture. The cheese grater was thrust over the handle of a saber hung on the wall, and took me 10 minutes. A pair of teacups balanced over two wall-lamps took one fellow 20 minutes to find. And, in half an hour's hunt, only one man found the folding rule. It was folded and stuck upright in the book case so that it looked like part of a gate-leg table. In plain sight, all of them, but they were too blamed plain. The fountain pen, which several people missed, was stuck in a piperack in with a dozen hard-rubber pipe mouthpieces so that it was completely concealed yet in plain sight.

Well, our error seems to be the same. I've been told the bands run the wrong way on Jupiter, that the satellites should be in a straight line parallel to the equator, and not staggered, that a dozen perfectly correct things are screwy -- and gotten only one letter spotting the error so far. Incidentally, they all say the cover's fine, and they've all said that November is an unusually good issue, better than Oct. by a long shot! I myself agreed with you that **Taen** is being accepted fairly well on the basis I offered it: a picture of Mars.

I'm very curious as to their reactions to the Dec. issue, which I honestly believe has two golds, and six blues. I think you'll allow me one gold, and at least four blues.

Read the stamp ad. Suppose you had $5 worth of unused US stamps all of 50 cents denomination. What would you do with them? The post office won't exchange them, you know. You'd wait a hell of a while to get packages needing all 50 cent stamps. Or suppose, like myself, you'd acquired a heterogeneous collection of 6, 8, 12, 10, 15, 20, 30, and 50 cent stamps, and no use for them?

Incidentally, "Reunion on Ganymede" seems to be taking tops in the Nov. Issue! They like **Simak** better for this one than they did for "Hunger Death" — and they're all saying it's hard to pick tops in a swell issue! Frankly, I'm pleased, but slightly dazed. I thought it was acceptable, but showed signs of having been written to order.

Incidentally, **Asimov**, the fan who's been trying to be a writer, was in the other day and told me that he'd made a sale to *Amazing*. Naturally bucked up. I'd rejected the yarn, but it was a sound, and pretty fair piece of work, just lacking humanity. But anyway, he'd gotten into communication with **C.D. Simak**, and wrote him about the sale, chortling about making his $60 sale. **Simak** replied he was bucked up too. He'd just sold a serial to *Astounding* for $560!

All works out for the best. **Asimov** naturally has the background feeling now that you're in the money when you're in *Astounding*, but *Amazing* etc. are just penny ante stuff.

Greek font hell, for those omegas. Why, pray tell? The Greek font is hand type. To use it in the stereotype process means its destruction. Further, it's hand work, as no Linotype font has both Greek and Roman type complete.

Letters were rare as hell that time, because everybody was writing to that damned advertising quiz instead of to me. Hence I was using letters set up last month, and every interesting letter that did come in.

Re-indexing the imprinted mss. of mine. Some of those — notably the Duke Stetson opus — were admitted and recognized failures, partitioned and destroyed for use elsewhere in view of that. This is true of the Stetson story, which as you say, was the progenitor of the "Mightiest Machine." Also of "The Space Beyond," which was neither finished nor submitted, of course, and was re-used elsewhere. The green space cups, for instance, appear in "Infinite Atom."

Why not separately catalog the unpublished opi, or if you do include them, include those that were regarded as satisfactory and submitted and worked with as such. It wouldn't exactly count to index the beginning to "Night" as a mss. It was never submitted, as being unsatisfactory in connection with the story I wanted.

Startling Stories was dated somewhat aheadish because the latest *TWS* out was Dec. 1938, and the following mag would, naturally, be the Jan. 1939. I was interested in the robot steal myself — also the "more candy." The robot, though, genuinely lost, I think, by being painted red instead of copper. Copper is real and recognizable. Red metal isn't real or recognizable. Copper robot, therefore tied it in with actual experience and seemed realer, I believe.

Incidentally, **Wesso** was in to see me. He illustrated inside, you noticed. He said that robot was described in story as having square head, triangular body. They changed the story to fit **Brown's** steal.

We're starting to advertise fan mags in Dec. issue — Jan., I mean. I think **Mort's** move at Philly convention was really bad.

Write comments on *Strange Worlds* plizzz!

Regards, John

The 1950's
with *Isaac Asimov*

Dear Asimov:

I'm up against a combination of circumstances that's got me in a spot, and I'm genuinely trying to get your help and reactions to the problem. I'm sending similar letters to a number of other authors, and I think it is a problem of genuine interest and importance to all of us.

It has to do with the author-agent-editor relationship, and it's a genuinely tough nut to crack. Let's consider the sequence of events:

Author A sends his first few stories to *Astounding Science Fiction,* and starts making sales. Then one of the literary agents, properly carrying out his proper and ethical business, contacts the new author, and invites him to allow the agent to handle his stories. The author, recognizing the advantages offered, agrees, but since the author has already established a working market with me here, he usually excepts sales to *Astounding Science Fiction* from the agenting arrangement.

That makes sense — but sets up a darned unhanding situation from my point of view. Because the agent, naturally, is trying to build up his business income; when Author A sells a novel to *Astounding,* the agent doesn't get $250, while the productivity of the author was tied up for several months. The agent, therefore, will naturally try to keep the best, most productive authors, loaded with work-orders from any market other than *Astounding*.

The author naturally wants to except his *Astounding* sales; the agent has a perfectly understandable desire to make commissions — that's his livelihood — and I have a perfectly understandable desire to get first rate stories here. The agent is <u>not</u> refusing to send manuscripts here when the author so requests; he's simply seeing to it the author is kept busy filling other markets.

Now — what can I do to break up the situation? If I develop a new, promising writer now, I can be fairly sure that his work will be diverted to any market except my magazine — a situation I not unreasonably dislike considerably.

The only answer I can see at the moment is to require that any author who is selling through any agent, when making sales in the science-fiction market, must sell to *Astounding Science Fiction* through agent, although we will continue direct personal discussion. This would please the agents, no doubt; it would settle my problem, but might seem unreasonably arbitrary to the authors. The present situation annoys agents, and puts me behind the eight-ball.

I'm trying to see if any of you authors have a more satisfactory solution that would please everyone; otherwise I feel I'll have to institute that system soon.

Sincerely, John W. Campbell, Jr.

Also sent to: **van Vogt, Stine, Stubbs, Schmitz, Russell, Leiber, Fyfe, Asimov, de Camp, Jones, Poul Anderson, Kuttner, K. MacLean, D. McLaughlin, Sturgeon, Piper, Simak, Williamson**

Isa D. Reed   *July 2, 1951*

Dear Miss Reed:
The series of stories to which you refer began with "In Hiding" and appeared as follows:
"In Hiding" — November 1948
"Opening Doors" — March 1949
"New Foundations" — March 1950
Wilmar Shiras, incidentally, is herself a grandmother and is in an excellent position to describe such material.

It might be interesting to you to realize that science fiction stems as much from *Aesop's Fables* as from **Jules Verne** in that in science fiction we are able to project human problems on the nonhuman entities. A mind tends to rebel against consideration of its own problems but is willing to consider the same problem if it is projected as the problem of a completely unassociated entity. I recommend to your attention **Isaac Asimov's** book *I, Robot*. You will find, if you consider it, that "the three laws of robotics" listed in there are, in essence, the basic desires of a small child with the exception that the motivation of desire for love has been properly omitted. The result, as shown in the stories, is basically a very human problem of childhood. The story "Liar" in that collection is an excellent example.

Sincerely John W. Campbell, Jr.

Isaac Asimov   *September 27, 1951*

Dear Asimov:

I think you have very real possibilities of a book novel here, but it has certain qualifications as a magazine novel. Mainly, the fact that the nature of the problem is so slow developing. I don't know just what it is, but for some reason book novels seem to get away with a very slow development of the problem, and then follow up with a relatively quick solution. For magazine purposes, it's somewhat better if the problem is stated, and stated fairly clearly, early in the story.

You might put it this way: In a detective story, it isn't satisfactory if you have to read half or two-thirds of the story before you find out who's going to be murdered. The murder should come early, so that the subsequent action has pressure and importance. An English country-house week-end party is of no slightest interest to me; if the Corpse-to-Be isn't properly murdered until Sunday Noon. I've been dragged through Friday and Saturday of nonsense and meaningless chatter. I'd prefer the murder of the corpse to take place Friday noon, so the rest of the time would have some point.

Rik, for the first three chapters, is a remarkably uninteresting and unintelligent character. I have a hunch that a single short chapter of introduction, describing briefly how Rik got that way, and why it is horribly urgent that he un-get-that-way, would give this first part a straining urgency — the feeling you want, of someone battling to carry the vital message through when all the world is wrapped in a gray fog in which only the nearest large obstacles can be seen.

Rik — practically mindless — says what he has is important. Probability that such data from a semi-crazed semi-moron is valid: 0.001. Then what's the furore all about?

But if we met Rik just briefly, first, in a short section with nameless characters, while Rik as a highly trained, vital and dynamic individual, and that Rik said it was important, things change. Now Probability Factor goes up to 0.9 or so.

Incidentally, I don't know what you have in mind — but the best and most effective possible force for righting the Sark-Floria situation, the one that can do the most good, with the least harm, is an organization of Sarkians with some brains and good sense who are opposed to the Sarkian government. They might have wit enough to see that Tanto will upset their applecart if the thing isn't squared around.

79

Tantor's ambassador could well see that it would be to his advantage to have the problem rectified without Tantor getting sucked into the thing, and so inviting the anger of the non-Tantorian sections of the galaxy. If Tantor helps Sarkian rebels and Florians only indirectly, it would have the following advantages:

1. Florians would attribute the results to the Tantorians. They hate Sark so thoroughly that the Sarkian rebels would seem Tantorian agents to them.

2. The rest of the galaxy would have a nasty problem cleaned up via revolution, instead of war.

3. Tantor would be spared the problem of starting a war.

4. There'd be a markedly greater chance that the ISB would get their man back — and the government responsible for this trouble would be adequately punished.

I don't know what you had in mind, but that might be it. Anyway, for your use, the whole punch of the yarn could be greatly increased by about 2500-3000 words of introductory material. That would give the foggy period of this section here an urgency it now lacks.

You know — show the corpse is killed before the party's spent two-thirds of the week end "doncho knowing" at each other.

I'm also sending back "Nobody Here But Us . . . " It's a light piece, of course, and doesn't make real science-fiction; the basic idea, of an intelligent, instead of merely mathematical, machine is nothing new in scf.

Regards, John W. Campbell, Jr.

Isaac Asimov *November 5, 1951*

Dear Isaac:
I have sent "Youth" along to **Fred Pohl** as per your instructions, as I am afraid it does not have what it takes under the present pressure of manuscripts. The principal kicker in the story is the small creatures turn out to be Earthmen which, while interesting, is not sufficient to push it over.

Regards, John W. Campbell, Jr.

John W. Campbell, Jr. *November 19, 1951*

Dear John:

Thank you for considering "Youth". As I told you, **Fred** had warned me of the crowded state of your novelette exchequer and had directed me to markets which were hungrier at the moment, but I was dead set on getting your refusal first. (Of course, I would rather have had your assental, but I'll be trying again. You're bound to accept an **Asimov** yarn someday.)

Last Friday, I was in town to attend a cancer conference at the N.Y. Academy of Sciences and seized the opportunity to have lunch with **Mr. Lawler**. He turned out to be an s.f. fan who had read my stuff and the whole session was extremely pleasant. He was as friendly as could be. He asked if I had met you and I went into some detail on our meeting twelve years ago and exactly what it had meant to me as a writer. (God, it was thirteen years ago. The years tick by like seconds.)

Have a pleasant Thanksgiving with your wife and four children and extend my holiday greetings to **Catherine**.

Yours, Isaac Asimov

John W. Campbell, Jr. *March 16, 1952*

Dear John,

My Doubleday novel is, at last, approaching completion. it has been delayed by several factors, one of which was, of course, the birth of my son.

At any rate, it is now moving ahead of schedule and, barring acts of God, it will be done a week or so ahead of its Easter deadline. I expect to bring it in to Doubleday in person some time in the week of April 13 and when I do so I shall also bring a copy to you.

I would be very happy, of course, if you should decide that it was worth putting into *Astounding*.

I have received the *Astounding* anthology, by the way, and I suppose there is no question about its being a good job. You couldn't very well go wrong in your choice of stories even if you used a blindfold and a pin considering that you had all of *Astounding* to pick from. Using eyes and judgement made certainty out of mere probability. The cover jacket is very attractive, by the way, and I think fulfills its function, because it stands out from among the rest of my s.f. library in a definite yet non-garish way. I hope it does well.

Anyway, I look forward to seeing you. I may have a short story along with me as well, but I can't guarantee that as I have been giving the novel precedence so that the short story has been sitting around half done (and in first draft at that) for almost a month now.

Yours, Isaac Asimov

John W. Campbell, Jr.   *May 12, 1952*

Dear John:

As you probably know, **Reginald Bretnor** tabbed me for a chapter in his forthcoming book *Modern Science Fiction: Its Meaning and Its Future*. Originally, I asked to do the section labelled IV-D: "Science-Fiction, Morals and Religion," but since that was assigned to **Gerald Heard**, **Mr. Bretnor** urged me to take IV-A: "Science Fiction and Man's New Horizons. How science fiction can influence social, anthropological, and cosmological orientations." I agreed and got to work instantly.

In his second letter to me, **Mr. Bretnor** said, "**John W. Campbell, Jr.** has suggested, and indicated his willingness to do, a chapter from a perspective which I had overlooked." He did not elaborate.

Meanwhile I continued on my section, and in order to describe the effect of science-fiction on society, I had first to describe the growth of the "sociological" type of science-fiction, which I called "social-science-fiction." (In fact that is the title of my contribution: "Social-science-fiction.") And in order to describe its growth, I went back in history and described the genesis of science-fiction as a whole.

My essay, thus, falls roughly into three parts: a) the beginnings of science-fiction, b) the differentiation of science-fiction, and c) the influence of science-fiction. Each part has 5,000 words devoted to it. Now when I was well along with the essay, I wrote to **Bretnor**, giving him a rough idea of what I was doing, and he answered to say:

"For your information, I'd better amplify what I said about **Campbell's** chapter. (I'll apologize for not having given this information previously.) He is going to discuss the reasons for the appearance of science fiction, using the general theme of his introduction to the *As-*

tounding anthology as a basis, elaborating it, and adding new material. Superficially, this might appear to conflict with the first part of your chapter. From what you have told me, though, and from what I remember of **Campbell's** introduction, I do not think so. I feel instead that the two will complement each other — and, as the subject is one which I would like to see examined as thoroughly as possible, I believe that its treatment as a part of your chapter will be all to the good. If you think that there's any danger of some points duplicating each other too closely, would it be imposing on you to ask you to drop **Campbell** a line? If, on the other hand, you consider that your approach is adequately dissimilar, or that the chances of direct duplication are minimal, I'll be glad to take the responsibility for ironing out any chance conflicts."

Well, **John**, at the time I received this letter, I had just completed my section, so I put it into an envelope and mailed it to **Bretnor** for his inspection. The question is, how will my material interfere with yours? I apologize, of course, for encroaching upon your preserves and can only plead ignorance of the fact that you were going to treat of the subject.

Now, I am certain that our approaches will not be similar, that our writing styles are quite different, and that you will treat the subject at greater length (since you will devote an entire essay rather than a third of an essay to it) and with greater skill. However, in one respect we are bound to duplicate each other. Our final conclusion, I am certain, will be that for the first time in history, Mankind is now in an age of rapid, continual, and increasing change and that science-fiction is the literary response to that fact. It is the literature of change and growth.

Do you think this is a serious duplication? If you would like, I will gladly send you a carbon copy of my section, so that you may stress points I have overlooked or even directly contradict any errors in reasoning you think I may have made. If you would rather write your section independently and let **Bretnor** worry about duplication, that's all right with me, too.

I have taken the liberty, **John**, of calling you "the father of social-science-fiction" and devoting about 1500 words (10% of the whole) to your influence on the development of science-fiction. In fact, I have gone so far as to split the history of science-fiction into four parts: a) the Primitive Era, 1815-1926; b) the **Gernsback** Era, 1926-1938; c) the

83

Campbell Era, 1938-1945; d) the Atomic Era, 1945-present, and have made it quite plain that it was you (in my opinion) who catalyzed the transition from adolescent to adult science-fiction. (The Atomic Era differs from the **Campbell** Era not in that you have lost your influence — you haven't — but that with increasing interest in science-fiction on the part of the public, you now have quite a few imitators so that you are not the lonely giant you were.)

Anyway, may I hear from you about this problem. Regards to **Peg** and all the children, and say hello to **Miss Tarrant** for me.

Yours, Isaac Asimov

P.S. Have you any idea yet as to which issue will see the start of "Currents of Space?"

Isaac Asimov *June 9, 1952*

Dear Isaac:

I have just written **Skyke Miller** and told him about your book. We will not run a review of it, but he will mention that the book has been published on the basis that validation of the scientific competence of our major authors is of interest and value to the readers of the magazine. (We also have some hot-shot biochemists among our readership who could actually read those lovely formulas I am sure decorate the pages of your book.)

I am going to bat out a less formal and more personal note to you in a day or so, discussing the question of whether centipedes are pacers or trotters and give you a few more ideas to mull over. In the meantime try this one yourself and some of the physicists around there:

A basic philosophical tenet of modern physics is "a phenomenon which cannot be detected cannot be said to exist."

Electrons can be detected as emissions from atoms, but an electron cannot be detected while it is stable in its shell within the atom. Question: Do electrons exist within the atom?

Regards, John W. Campbell, Jr.

John W. Campbell, Jr. *June 28, 1952*

Dear John:

It was very pleasant to have that little talk with you and it made my flying trip to New York most worthwhile.

However, I keep thinking of that cover painting for "Currents of Space." Now I know that you have a great many worthwhile things to do with such covers, and that the artist himself may wish to keep it or dispose of it. Nevertheless, I can't help asking if it is at all possible that I might have it? I have never before asked for an illustration of any kind, which is what nerves me to this present beggarly request.

If the painting is already promised to someone else or if you intend it for your own use or the artist intends it for his — why, that's perfectly all right. Don't give it a thought. But if you will have to dispose of it some day or if you are only waiting for someone to ask for it, why, here I am.

If you do send it to me, I will be glad to remit postage or express charges.

Yours, Isaac Asimov

Isaac Asimov   *July 3, 1952*

Dear Isaac:

I regret to say that I am unable to let you have the cover original on my say-so. We buy only First Reproduction Rights and recently **Paul Orban** has organized a science fiction artists service. The artists are turning their originals both black and whites and covers over to him and he is arranging to sell them to various fans, et. cetera.

I suggest the best move on your part is to write **van Dongen** a note telling him that you would like to get hold of the cover and send it in care of my office here. I'll see that **van Dongen** gets it. Essentially, you two will have to straighten it out between you.

Regards, John W. Campbell, Jr.

P. Schuyler Miller   *August 7, 1952*

Dear Skyke:

I've put through the voucher on your "Reference Library" with a seventy-five dollar label on it. It's not a mistake — you've earned it. I've gotten a lot of solidly pleased comment on the job you've done,

85

and it's earned a real respect for the book review column.

Like the guy who's bet on the winning horse, I'm as pleased with your work as you should be.

One item: Please, in the next column, put in a reference to **Joe Winter's** "Are Your Troubles Psychosomatic?," mentioning it as one of **Dr. Winter's** professional publications, and some remarks about **Isaac Asimov's** textbook, *Biochemistry and Human Metabolism.* **Asimov's** work on the text is one fourth of the whole book — but he's done an excellent job of making the complex subject readable and understandable to anyone with standard college chemistry, though it's designed for medical students.

Regards, John W. Campbell, Jr.

P.S. Could you mail your copy around the 25th of the month — December department, August 25th, etc. cetera?

John W. Campbell, Jr.   *September 16, 1952*

Dear John:

I just got back to Boston and hasten to write my thanks for an excellent luncheon and for an even more excellent conversation. It is always more than pleasant to talk to you, and whether I agree with you or not (and sometimes, on specific points, I don't agree with you — which probably comes as no surprise to you) you remain the most stimulating person I know.

Simak writes me (the letter was waiting for me when I arrived) that he spoke to you at Chicago and received in a short space of time enough ideas to keep him busy for six months, if he could only do them correctly. So you see, I'm not the only person who is aware of the real source of many of "his" ideas.

Thank you for taking the "Thiotimoline" article, by the way. In the October issue of *ASF*, by the way (although I must insist that "Currents of Space" rates highest with myself personally — a prejudiced opinion) I would like to hand out second place to "Survival Policy." **Edwin James** has a very luminously clear way of writing, so he <u>can't</u> be **A.E. van Vogt**, can he? I ask, because of his reference to Gosseyn's double brain.

Yours, Isaac Asimov

86

John W. Campbell, Jr.   *October 16, 1952*

Dear John,

Thanks a lot for forwarding **Mr. Sharp's** letter (if that is his name. I had trouble reading his signature.)

At first, it scared the pants off me, because I'm a biochemist, not a goddam mathematician and I thought I had made a fool of myself. However, after hard thinking I figured out that I wasn't so wrong, and I wrote an answer to **Mr. Sharp**. I enclosed a copy of that answer together with **Mr. Sharp's** original letter. Now I don't want to start a googolplex discussion in "Brass Tacks" [I really don't. (handwritten note: Ed)] (because, frankly, I'd rather read letters expressing opinions about stories, rather than about philosophy), but if you feel really impelled to print **Mr. Sharp's** letter, may I ask that you also print my answer.

Now to write about other things. I have a few questions to ask and I really hope you have time to answer me as I would like to know:

1) How is the reader response so far to "The Currents of Space?" (I'll die of suspense, waiting for the "Analytical Lab" figures to come out.)

2) Did you receive a copy of *David Starr, Space Ranger*, the juvenile I wrote for Doubleday, under the name of **Paul French**?

3) If you did, did you ever get a chance to glance through it?

4) If you did, did you like it?

I'm planning to go to New York as soon as I finish my current juvenile. (I only have a couple of weeks work left on it, so that I'm planning to hit the trail, either the week before Election Day or the week after. I must be in Waltham <u>on</u> Election Day, so I can help keep the Presidency a civilian office. Remember — I'm a Democrat.) Anyway, I hope to see you when I am in New York.

Yours, Isaac Asimov

John P. Sharp   *October 16, 1952*

Dear Mr. Sharp:

87

Mr. Campbell of *Astounding Science-Fiction* has kindly forwarded to me your letter criticizing some of the statements I made in my own letter published on pp. 163-164 of the November 1952 *Astounding*.

May I take up the cudgels on my own behalf, point by point.

1) You say **Kasner** and **Newman's** definition of googolplex is ten to the googolth and not googol to the googolth. You are correct, and my own reference to **Kasner** and **Newman** was an aside which I should not have made. However, **Mr. Jack Thomas** in his story "Next Door" (which I liked, by the way) defines googolplex as a googol to the googolth and I think we ought to accept his definition, if we are going to argue about the statements he makes in his story.

2) You say that $_{10}100^{100}$ is not $10^{10,000}$ because that would imply that 100^{100} equals 10,000, Yours is one way of looking at it, but not the only way. It depends on where the parenthesis falls. Thus: $_{10}(100^{100})$ equals $_{10}^{(\text{googol2})}$ and is a very large number as you point out.

However: $(10^{100})^{100}$ equals $10^{10,000}$ as I stated, and is a relatively small number.

I should have put in parenthesis to indicate which number I meant, but again, **Mr. Jack Thomas** himself defines a googolplex arrangement of the parenthesis and didn't bother to go into the matter deeper.

Obviously, $10^{10,000}$ is not the same as $\text{googol}^{\text{googol}}$. **Thomas** uses both definitions and this is the mistake I set out to indicate in my letter.

3) You object to my use of the word "number" when I mean "integer." I am sorry. I was using the word "number" in its popular sense. Most non-mathematicians consider "number" and "integer" synonymous and would, for instance, differentiate between a "number" and a "fraction." I'm afraid I was writing in a popular mood, rather than in a mathematical mood. For that matter, if we were to be perfectly rigid, one should not use the term "number" as you do, when you really mean "real number." I take it that you weren't thinking of including imaginaries, hyperimaginaries, etc. in your own discussion of "number."

Very truly yours, Isaac Asimov

Isaac Asimov   *November 3, 1952*

Dear Isaac:

I don't know why it is the readers like to argue about such things as googolplexes, but they evidently do. Frankly I think the argument has gone on long enough, so I am going to drop it.

Reader response on "Currents of Space" has been very favorable. **Peg** liked it a lot and is currently waiting for the third installment. She constitutes my check on non-science-fiction addicts.

I did receive a copy of *David Starr, Space Ranger*. It's at home and my juvenile critic is currently reviewing it — **Peedee** age twelve hasn't yet reported; life is so busy for her. I am going to read it myself as soon as I get a chance, but I am more interested in what **Peedee** thinks about it; that, after all, is most important — the opinion of a juvenile.

Regards, John W. Campbell, Jr.

Isaac Asimov   *January 16, 1953*

Dear Isaac:

Back cometh "Belief." It has a fault that can be corrected, and needs to be corrected.

Your psychiatrist in this one has a perfectly valid point; as a matter of fact, he's not a psychiatrist at all, because he's talking like a sound, clear-thinking physical scientist, and describing the proper orientation of a physical scientist, which is something very, very few psychiatrists have. But one doctor I know does have it, and that doctor is talking right out of his own sound orientation — **Dr. Asimov.**

See the comments attributed to Dr. Searle on the bottom of page 27. "Forget your ideals, your theories, your notions as to what people ought to do. Consider what they are doing." If you substitute the word "molecules" for "people" in that statement, you have the credo of a good biochemist. If you substitute "forces," you have the credo of a good physicist. If you then add that the observer must not merely accept the facts of what they are doing, but understand those facts and figure out how to make those facts and actions-as-they-are lead to the condition he wants, you'll have the full credo of a physical scientist.

There's a basic law of Nature: It's easy to roll a stone down hill, and hard to roll it up. It's easy to get X to do Y, if Y is what X wants to do anyway. It's hard to get X to do contra-Y when Y is what X wants to do. Therefore, if you want to achieve contra-Y, study X carefully and find such tendencies of X as M, N, and P such that X's net desire with respect to M, N, P and Y can be manipulated to yield contra-Y in aiding X to achieve M, N and P.

Let's say that X is a gal named Xenobia, and Y stands for a young man. And M, N, and P stand for Money, Nice things, and Position. So we find that X will go contra-Y because of the net resultant of the forces pro-Y, M, N, and P when faced with a contra-Y having M, N, and P.

So she marries a guy who has 50 years, 50 megabucks, 5 estates, and the highest respect of everyone in the state.

Your physicist didn't get all the help from the psychiatrist he should have; if the psychiatrist were really sharp, he'd have brought that out, and induced the physicist to start doing some resolution of forces on the problem.

What you've got here is an ending which says, "Levitation is no use, and there is no solution, and it can't be solved."

Now the basic orientation of science-fiction is, was, and will be that no problem is insoluble — but that you don't have a good story until you can propose a really clever solution to the problem that appears insoluble.

This starts off with the guy being scared; it winds up with him being scared to death. The essence of a good story -- vide the many good stories you've written — is that the central character grows, matures, strengthens, and achieves greater understanding and wisdom.

This bird decided to give up. He didn't do the job well at any stage of the game; he started retreating the moment it happened, and kept running all the way. He made an exceedingly half-hearted attempt as a magician; Magoun was quite correct in firing him. As a magician, he stank. Instead of having some personality, a line of chatter, he rather bovinely floated around, sort of like an aerial gold-fish dispiritedly blurping its mouth open and closed.

This naturally forced everybody to notice his levitation, which they didn't want to accept. Magoun didn't.

Now there are a few basic laws of human nature that Toomey could have used to advantage, instead of letting those laws use him.

1. A human being wants to be accepted for what he thinks is important about himself.

Consequence: Toomey wanted to have his levitation accepted. The story as you've written it is precisely true to human nature — Toomey insists that people accept his problem — levitation — and help him directly with that problem.

Sarle correctly points out that people won't. You can't make a man attack a problem he doesn't see is important.

People have, always, all the problems that they can handle easily. You'll never find a human being who doesn't have plenty of problems on hand to take all the time he has available. To tackle a new one, he must drop one of the problems he is now working on, and now considers important. (Like **Isaac Asimov** having to drop some of his biochemistry work if he's to tackle fiction, or some of his science-fiction to tackle biochemistry. And therefore he won't willingly take on any new problems such as, say, learning to play the piano well.)

You have, with unerring correctness, described precisely the results to be expected from these basic human factors, if left to operate in their own natural ways.

Toomey wants help on levitation, and insists on presenting the problem to other people. (So he makes a lousy magician, because he doesn't even try to distract people from his levitation act. He insistently, single-mindedly demands that they notice and accept the problem.)

Nobody will accept his problem; they've got enough of their own on hand, and aren't going to take on any new super-doozeys like that if they can avoid it. And, as you so correctly point out, brother! they can avoid it! They can deny the problem really exists.

He is very insistent about its reality, however, and so makes them uncomfortable.

Toomey made all the mistakes. 1. He forced his problem on his wife, who stuck it out as long as she could, and finally had to give up. 2. He forced his problem on the people at the university, until they had to get rid of him. 3. Ditto Magoun. 4. Ditto the night-club patrons. 5. Ditto right to and beyond death.

Toomey got so wrapped up in his own problem that he didn't pay any attention to the problems of the people around him. (But he objected violently to the fact they were so wrapped up in their problems that they wouldn't pay any attention to his.)

91

The result of this as a continuing policy is precisely what you've outlined; you've got a perfectly correct description of How Not To Solve This Problem.

Toomey has a right to miss the trick; Sarle, in this respect, is acting like a true psychiatrist — he wants Toomey to face reality and stop trying to make anybody listen to his problem.

Nuts. That's the Old Reliable way of handling the situation. Cultures always try to handle the situation the easiest way — arrange to make the problem-presenter shut up, so the problem doesn't have to be considered. That's what happened to **Galileo**. **Copernicus**, being a sharp bird, wanted his theories published after his death, so the culture couldn't shut him up. One of the roles the psychiatrist — who is a descendant of the priest-witch-doctor of old — is to act as the taboo enforcer, the thought-police, to prevent cultural disturbance caused by people with strange ideas. This includes people who think everybody around them is trying to destroy them, and are collecting sawed-off shotguns and dynamite at home to defend themselves. It also includes people like that rebellious radical, **George Washington**, **G. Galileo**, and **J. Christ**. Each of those individuals felt his was being persecuted, and took measures against the faults he found in his society. So now we think these three were right. **Hitler** thought he was right. So did **Torquemada**. Some form of thought-police is necessary — but we haven't done so good with that problem so far, have we?

Now; how can Toomey's problem be solved?

Item: People always get mad and hyper-insistent if you won't listen to their problems, and insist on studying your own.

Tsk tsk. Too bad.

Suppose Toomey levitated, and absolutely refused to admit to anyone that he did so? Suppose he reached for books on the top shelf, and when accused of floating three inches up, indignantly denied that he did any such thing, and insisted that the observer who reported it must be unsane — he ought to know that was impossible! Why, the very idea of suggesting that he, Toomey, could break a basic law of nature! My good man, what's the matter with your eyes? Saying I float! How fantastic! How silly!

NOW who's problem is it? Now who's going to insistently demand that it be investigated?

So the students say they saw him flying down stairs? "Why Dr. Morton, what in the world do you suppose has gotten into those students? Do you suppose they're drinking that much before coming to class? We've got to stop those reporters, sir! We can't have them publishing stories about drunken students here at the University!"

Now who's going to have to insist, demand, scream and shout for investigation of levitation?

And — don't go on stage as a magician. He's built up as a **Johnny Raye** singer — only different. **Johnny Raye** weeps, screams, and contorts — but it's his singing that he's selling. Please pay no attention to the facial contortions — that's accidental.

So Toomey is a singer — or a comedian or something — who unfortunately has a slight tic, but polite people won't notice this unfortunate and unintentional levitation.

Again — now who's got a problem?

You see, Toomey can quote all the authorities in science, "everybody knows. . ." and "You know that's impossible. . ." against the observations of his levitation. He doesn't have to explain it; they do.

He can deny it with such sane remarks as, "Why, if I knew how to do that, man, I'd patent it! It'd be worth millions. I wouldn't make silly tricks of it. Be sensible." Or, "Why, if I knew how to overcome gravity, it would be my duty to inform the government. Think of it's military value! Don't be foolish; you know levitation is impossible." And, "If I could actually float, you know perfectly well I'd be made a Top Secret Military project. Something's wrong with your eyes. Must be some trick of refraction."

Naturally, before long, he'll be conscripted as a Top Secret Military project at the insistence of the Armed Forces.

I think Sarles is the man to clarify the problem for him.

If Toomey takes that line, nobody can act against him until they have already accepted his problem and made it their own.

And that, of course, is precisely what he wants.

Regards, John

Isaac Asimov   *February 16, 1953*

Dear Isaac:

I read your piece in **Bretnor's** book with great interest; it was a good, sound job, and entirely typical of your thinking. The letter you sent me the other day is of a piece with it — and equally typical of you.

Some scientists are gleaners of facts; on their efforts all the structure of science must, in essence, rest. But the whole structure of science is <u>not</u> facts, and with the gleaners-of-facts alone we would still be using rule-of-thumb methods. You're not of that type, but of quite a different level. While science rests on the solid foundation of facts, you can equally say that it depends on the strong tensile forces of theories, hypothesis, and close-knit thinking.

Ray Jones had in one of his stories the proposition that any race will build a technology that bears a structural relationship to the structure of the organism of that race. He had this in connection with a story of Joe's Spaceship Repair yard, where they fixed interstellar spacers of alien races, and used "cerebral analogs" to figure out how the alien machinery was intended to work.

The work **Peg** and I have done confirms **Ray's** guess; there is a powerful analog between all Man's works in science and government and Man's own body organization. Many a problem can be solved by a careful study of how the human body organism has solved the equivalent problem. The relationship works both ways; many problems of the body can be solved, I suspect, if we observe what we are doing as human beings — and suspect a relationship with what body cells do.

In the body, the physical senses — sight, hearing, etc. -- are direct data-gleaners. Like good science organization, they are designed for heavy overlap and cross-checking. We hear not only with our ears, but also with the skin; a human being will invariably feel confused, bewildered, and somewhat frightened if two senses that are intended to overlap and confirm each other are separately stimulated in non-congruent patterns.

Examples: the skin is particularly adapted to recieving frequencies below about 200 cycles; the ears react about 15 cycles. Above about 2000, the ears do practically all the work.

In nature, pure sine-wave single-frequencies sounds are exceedingly rare; any sound-source generating a 10-cycle note will also produce 20, 30, 40, 50, 60, etc. cycle harmonics.

But if you produce a pure 10-cycle note of moderately strong intensity, a human being in that sound-field will be scared. His skin-sound-sense and his ear-sound-sense are in disagreement; he is therefore unable to decide the nature of the situation, and is immediately thrown into confusion.

Second example: The breathing is controlled by two factors: CO_2 balance in the blood, and O_2 balance in the blood. If CO_2 gets high, breathing activity must increase; if O_2 gets low, breathing must increase; if O_2 gets too high, breathing must decrease.

In treating neurosis, **Joe Winter** and others have been using a CO_2-O_2 mixture running 30% CO_2, 70% O_2. This mixture stimulates the metabolic senses in directly opposite directions; the O_2 sense demands cessation of breathing of excess O_2; the CO_2 sense screams bloody murder and demands gasping breath. The result is a frightful sense of imminent catastrophe, a fear-shock, and the patient will suddenly start spilling mental problems he hasn't been able to get near in years. An ordinary individual can take about three good wiffs of that stuff before he starts talking frantically.

After a number of sessions, he can take about 30 breaths, and no results. Reason: his system has learned to understand the nature of the situation, and no longer panics when it encounters the situation.

The human senses are designed to act like a fine, organized science, with adequate cross-checking, using basically different checking methods. The eyes cross-check with the skin also; you can fool an optical pyrometer by turning it on a piece of white paper, and getting a reading of $8,000^0$ absolute — but you can't fool a human being that way. The eyes may report a color-temperature of $8,000^0$ absolute, but the radiation-sensitive skin reports "low energy output from that direction," and the human being reaches a sane conclusion.

But notice that the cross-checking of sensory data — or data gathered by individual scientists — can take place only at a higher level, at a computational, integrative level. Of course, any human scientist who is doing data-gathering is also doing some computing on the basis of his data, and some cross-checking. But basically, data has meaning only as it is interrelated.

You're a philospher more than a straight scientist; that is a level of integration and understanding many human beings never attain. It is achieved in high-level human beings only beginning about the 21st

95

year — check it with actual experience! — ordinarily. The lower level individual minds will never achieve it; instead they will achieve rule-of-thumb system of interrelated patterns of behavior that work, and work pretty well. Such men are absolutely essential to the progress of humanity; they can do jobs that you, **Isaac**, would not be able to handle adequately. You don't have the perseverance at the routine level to make a really good repetitive checker of experiments. The level of creativity in your mind is so high that, inevitably, you'ld wind up making variations in each re-run of the experiment, so that your results are <u>not</u> truly rechecks of the original experiment. How'd you make out putting Bolt #376-A-42 in the chassis of Model 72-A on the assembly line? And how would our civilization make out if we didn't have men who did that very vital job?

How would you make out as an organism if you didn't have a heart that delighted in, and took deep satisfaction in, doing exactly the same thing, day after day, year in and year out? And a system of nerve cells that delighted in doing something different, varying their patterns and their work routine continuously?

You're quite right that you've grown — and are growing. Where once your characters were always single, because that seemed the natural state of a man to you, you now find that the natural state is otherwise. That's the normal course of human growth and development, isn't it? And in using the wife in "Belief," you used her as she is in life — the one to whom a man can reveal his problems as he can to no other person, neither parent nor brother nor friend nor child.

Joe Kearney, my step-son, was home last Christmas with a fraternity brother. Some years back, when I saw a high school kid reading an old copy of *Amazing* that contained my first published story, and he said it had come out the month he was born, I first really recognized that I was accumulating years.

But when **Joe** and his fraternity brother were here, I discovered something else. I was suddenly deeply aware that I was glad I wasn't 19. I was 42, and I had 23 years that were full of experience at a level those kids had never known, and couldn't possibly understand, and which I couldn't even communicate to them if I tried. How the hell can you explain to them the experience of wondering whether the stiff neck and headache and wooziness your child complains of means polio? How
96

can you explain to them that a wife is a natural and necessary part of a man's full being, and not merely a woman whom you've captured by conquest? That a child isn't a burden that the parents have to lug through life?

How can you explain to the mentally-emotionally immature that not only is energy implacably conserved, but that equally effort is implacably conservative; you cannot get satisfaction save in proportion to your effort expended. If doing A is easy for you, doing A will yield you little satisfaction. Once, **Isaac**, you took deep satisfaction and rightfully so, in getting an accurate determination of potassium in a sample of potassium carbonate, I imagine. Would you now?

Once you took great satisfaction in writing and selling "Trends", and rightfully so. Would you now? It's a good yarn; self-evidently, it is tautological to say that it is as good as it is.

Every growth you make requires that you make a greater one if you are to retain the satisfaction-feeling you want.

Leslyn was sorry for me last summer, when she was enjoying the merry-go-round so much, and poor old daddy couldn't seem to have that fun.

Poor little **Leslyn** couldn't have the greater satisfaction of watching her small daughter bouncing with excitement and fun on the merry-go-round, either.

Sure — we're doing social science-fiction now. But there's a three-step arrangement that needs looking at.

A small child learns about facts. Water is wet. Mud sticks. Fire is hot. Falling down hurts.

An older child learns some interrelations. Mud makes mother mad. Not obeying makes parents angry.

An adolescent advances to wonderful ideas of World Government and the Nature of Philosophy, and very large concepts indeed — in a somewhat sketchy way.

A young adult advances to discovering people — individuals. That World Government doesn't exist unless there are human beings with human needs and wants and problems to make it work.

He's apt to lose sight of the World Government — which really was a good idea, save that, as an adolescent, he didn't have any process worked out for the ideal he saw.

Only a mature adult begins to see facts and people and interrelations and world government, and human beings as one integrated, continuous process.

I've great respect for **Eisenhower**; I think he genuinely is one of those truly mature adults who grasps the whole system. Since world government is made of people, he works with people and ideals. He's wiser and deeper and broader than political parties; given four years, he'll teach the political parties the value of recognizing the deeper level -- and not without retaining their own differences. That business of having both Republican and Democratic congressmen to lunch is very fine indeed; he's a Republican — but he's the President of the UNITED States. It's quite futile to impose a world government; it would be a ramschackle affair, with the people basically operating on the principle, "You can make me take it, but you can't make me like it."

Conceivably, I might be able to make an author write the exact kind of story I happened to have in mind, too. But he'd do it cynically, and it would show it. And, naturally, I wouldn't learn a thing. I found out some while back that the only way you learn anything is to lose an argument; if you win it, your viewpoint hasn't been changed, and you've learned nothing new.

I don't need that last Foundation story. Basically, the whole point of the story was that the Second Foundation's great plan was strictly Benevolent Tyranny — no matter how sincerely they felt they were right, it was still tyranny. Seldon's Plan was benevolent tyranny from the beginning. Possibly justified, possibly not.

You're already doing that kind of story anyway. I've been needling **Poul Anderson** and **Chad Oliver** a bit here and there, they're doing it too, but not too well, because they're both too young. (Both taking graduate work.)

Our whole culture today is based on one basic fallacy — that in all things there is one and only one right way. That despite the fact that 2,000,000,000 years of field testing has repeatedly shown that it takes two sexes to make a successful race. That there must be three factors — male, female, and their resultant interaction — and thus not less than three different right ways. And the observable fact that the most successful governments in the world have two parties, and the government is a third and different structure formed of the interaction re-
98

sultant of the two forces, differing from either of the two as the resultant differs from the two forces in a parallelogram of force-vectors.

It takes two eyes, seeing differently, to produce a three-dimensional
understanding.

You and **Gertrude** necessarily see life differently; you're standing
in different positions, and have inherently different mind-structures.
But that's essential, because only so can the **Isaac-Gertrude** team get a
three-dimensional view of life.

"In the kingdom of the blind, the one-eyed man is king."

No, he isn't. Because he will use his one eye, and get a one-way
view of things, while the blind, forced to rely on their two ears, their
two hands, and so on, will have a better balanced understanding of life.
he won't be king; he'll be the Scout.

M.C. Pease, who's an electronics man with Sylvania — he lives in
Needham, by the way, and you might be interested in getting in touch
with him; his phone in Needham - 3-2436-R — has a story basic idea
you might be able to handle. He doesn't feel he can, and passed it
along to me. It's this:

Everybody knows about the Bad Vicious Companies who Suppress the Great Invention because it would Ruin their Business.

Good. Let's take it from there. Bill Blow has invented a Box; it's
about 14" cube. It has terminals on one side, and it gives off power. It
consumes anything handy by way of fuel. It cannot be made to explode. It works by total annihilation of the matter, and therefore
produces no radioactive, dangerous residue. It can't be made smaller
than some specific, moderate size, as the suggested 14" cube. It can be
made as large as desired. The 14 inch cube will supply anything up to
250 kva.

The principles involved are not understood; it was made by Bill
Blow, who was a sort of backyard genius, and did it by trial-and-error
experiment, rule of thumb, and Yoga. He isn't a scientist. He's a mystic
garage mechanic.

But the gadget works. Because no underlying principles have been
discovered, its introduction does not introduce any new scientific principles into the society. It doesn't bring spaceships, matter transmutation, matter transmitters, or anything else. (That's the reason for making the inventor a mystic garage mechanic; it forces the new invention

99

onto our society as it is.) Some day when they figure out what in hell makes the Blow Power Pack work, they may get those things. In the meantime, Blow can go around pulling my favorite little gag on the scientists. "Wiggle your finger. O.K. How do you do it? Well, then, don't tell me I have to know how this works either. I can use it, can't I?"

But — what happens to <u>people</u>?

The public service companies go out of business — taking several hundred insurance companies who hold their bonds and stocks down to ruin. General Electric and Westinghouse are bankrupt; their great power generating equipment and distribution equipment business is gone — <u>whoosh</u>.

Who wants electric power engineers?

The oil companies go broke — ruining most of the people who have invested their future in stocks dependent on them. Home heating, ship and locomotive propulsion, etc., as well as the automobile business also go <u>whoosh</u>.

College professors, of course, join the breadlines. (What family has money to send their children to college?)

Did you see "The Man In The White Suit"? If not, it's worth looking for. It's based on something of the same proposition.

I have no idea how the story would go. Bill Blow sounds kind of like he might be one of the type that's convinced all Big Companies are out to swindle the Little Man, and the Big Companies are trying to suppress his invention for their own selfish benefit.

I can see it winding up with some understanding psychiatrist declaring him insane, so he can be safely tucked away where his invention won't destroy the civilization.

I can also see fifty assorted varieties of hell breaking loose.

The one thing I can't see any high probability on is the continued survival of Bill Blow. It might be an ex-president of one of the Locals of the United Electrical Workers who assassinated him, or a neurotic petroleum chemist who did it, or simply a mob of unbearably miserable ordinary people. But I really don't think he'd live very long, do you?

It's kind of like that story proposition I gave **Harry Stine** a while back. (He hasn't yet been able to write it up!) Man and the Plortun race meet, establish commerce interstellar-wise, and progress happily and rapidly for 50 years. Then it is discovered that an extract of a gland of
100

the adult female Plortun will make a human being immortal to all practical purposes. Or, vice versa, that Plortun can be made immortal by a gland taken from an adult human female.

Passing laws against murdering Plortun women is utterly futile, of course. No government can possibly do anything about it. Laws won't stop people from trying for immortality. The only outcome I can foresee for such a situation is the total anihilation of one race or other.

No government could control Blow's power pack, either; the individuals want it, but don't want the results inevitably consequent on individuals' having them.

Wanna tackle the yarn?

Regards, John

Isaac Asimov   *February 27, 1953*

Dear Isaac:

Unless I forget completely, your paper to the *J. of Chem. Ed.* should be enclosed herewith.

The business is interesting as data — however as an article for *ASF*, it has the difficulty that it's a "And what is the significance of this?" item.

The great error, as I see it, in ordinary educational techniques is precisely that that **John Arnold's** battling — the presentation of facts without any effort to show what their meanings are, or to induce kids to find meanings in facts they know.

For example: Suppose you take one of your classes, and try these two questions on them. I'll bet that not over 5% of the classes can answer both correctly — yet both can be answered on the basis of the simplest sort of freshman physics:

1. There is only one household electrical appliance that is truly 100% efficient. What is it?

2. You have a cup of coffee that's too hot to drink, and are in somewhat of a hurry. You like cream in your coffee. Will the coffee-and-cream system reach drinkable temperature more quickly if you wait and then add the cream, or if you add the cream and then wait? (There is a real difference, and the question can be answered.)

The first one, of course, refers to the electric room heater; even the

101

resistance losses in the line-cord you plug it in with show up as useful product — heat.

The second one isn't so obvious to people — even physicists, who haven't bothered to integrate knowledge with living. Obviously, however, an object at high temperature will lose more calories per second than it will when it's at a lower temperature. Therefore the cup of coffee will lose heat faster than the somewhat cooled cup of coffee-plus-cool-cream. Solving each of these problems demands only the simplest ordinary understandings of physics and engineering — but will throw too damned many people.

Or consider this: It's necessary to chill a liquid foodstuff to freezing as nearly instantaneously as possible. Ideally, the foodstuff should be brought into direct contact with the refrigerating medium, to minimize heat-transfer time-loss. If a silver pipe is used, even so there is the problem that the mush formed at the wall of the pipe blocks heat transfer. But it's a delicate foodstuff; flavor is important. What refrigerant can be brought into contact with it without imparting flavor, diluting it, or running any danger of toxicity? How should it be done?

Answer: Spray it directly into liquid air. Any foodstuff is already saturated with the gases of air; none of the gases of air can remain liquid at ordinary frozen-food-locker temperatures. Unlike carbon dioxide refrigerant, which would impart a carbonated flavor, no new flavor would be added. Since the air cannot possibly remain present as a liquid or solid contaminant, and the stuff is already saturated with the gases, no flavor effect can be expected. And air, clearly, is not a toxic substance.

So there are certain amounts of radioactive elements in the Earth. Well . . . what of it? What's the significance?

I don't question that it has one — but your *J of Ed Chem* article doesn't bring one into sight.

I'll give you a stinker to play with, if you'd like. Consider this postulate: That the laws of nature as we know them are not "eternal"; that, instead, there is a time-factor in every law itself. That is, that there is, unknown to us, a time-factor that modifies the law, so that **Newton's** Law of Gravity was perfectly accurate, we'll say, in 1600, was only minutely and indetectably off in 1700, and was progressively further off in 1800 and 1900. Because the full law requires an expression involving T_0 — T_0 being the Absolute Time, measured from Absolute Zero Time.

Look: Imagine a submarine people who started studying gases; because of the exceedingly high thermal conductivity of their environment, and the essentially stable temperature resulting therefrom, they haven't measured temperatures. So they get the gas laws as $PV = pv$. But gradually they find there is some mysterious flaw; this Law of Nature seems to undergo small, but detectable variations. The PV relationship isn't constant.

They're getting seasonal temperature variations of about 5 degrees C.

They'll have a hell of a time, because they will not, at first, find any correlation that looks simple between temperature and the PV relationship. Sure, they measure temperature — but on a freezing-point zero system.

Suppose we have to measure from Absolute Time Zero — from the Creation Instant, to get the right answers?!

Now the volume of some materials is relatively unaffected by temperature. Invar steel, for instance. Other substances, however, have a massive expansion coefficient — particularly is this true of gases. Most alloys have a very complex expansion-contraction characteristic. Water itself has a dilly-doozey, in going from 100 Centigrade to -100 C.

Suppose that there are certain sets of laws of nature that have a very low time-coefficient; they'll appear to be practically eternal. Others may have a very high time-coefficient; they'll appear to be something other than natural laws.

Suppose Magic, for instance, depended on a characteristic of the Universe which, like something with a 100 megayear half-life, was almost all dissipated, while the laws that were left were "nonradioactive," stable laws. Then there may have been a time when werewolves, magicians, and life-forms (fairies, etc.) based on use of magical instead of physical energies could work!

That's just a F'r'instance; the serious proposal is that possibly the laws of nature are themselves time-modified, with the necessity of imposing an Absolute Time value.

Then: we could account for the red-shift on this basis. And notice how difficult it would be to observe it in most reactions; if it's measured in terms of absolute time, then one year would cause a change of

103

the natural law amounting to one part in four billion-plus, if it were a linear relationship. If it were some complex relationship, it might cause a change of only one part in twenty billion. And **Isaac** — you want to name something that you can guarantee you can measure with an accuracy of one part in four billion?

If you say yes to that one, you're a liar. How do you know that your measuring system — also part of a time-modified universe — isn't modifying too?

This concept doesn't reduce the Universe to chaos; it does say that Absolute Time might be important, and have effect in forcing us — so long as we ignore it — to some outlandishly complicated conceptions of what goes on.

Naturally, if such were the case, science would get started by studying those phenomena which involved the least complex time-dependent structures — the stable law-atoms, so to speak. Imagine a chemist who was immune to any radioactive energy, and who was given a lab to work in in which all the materials he had to work with were pure radioactive isotopes. He'd have a fiendish time trying to determine the properties of carbon, for instance, if the carbon dioxide sample he was given to work with was pure ^{11}C that kept turning into boron.

Remember the croquet game in Alice? They had soldiers bent over for wickets, rolled-up hedgehogs for balls, and used flamingoes for croquet mallets. The soldiers got up and moved; the hedgehogs unrolled and walked around, and the flamingoes, when properly tucked under the arm, would twist their heads up to look at Alice to see what she was doing.

Now IF the basic laws of human personality, for example, were of the type involving a high time-factor, you could expect rapid growth and development, and a relatively low stability of long-term behavior. That would make for progress, all right, which is characteristic of living beings. But studying the damn thing would be like trying to determine the chemical properties of pure samples of short-lived radioactives. You could NOT get any answers that made sense UNTIL you recognized you had to consider the radioactive system of elements; studying any one of them would be completely hopeless, because no one of them would remain that one long enough for sensible checks!

Let us consider one individual human. We'll call him David. At the time we start our tests, we get certain results. We take these results, finding this David-material we are studying can barely speak English. These results we study carefully, and after studying them, cross-correlating them, etc., we come to some conclusions, and go back to test these conclusions on our David-material. This work has taken us about 1 year. Now whaddaya know! None of the predictions work. Further, our original tests seem to have been wrong, because the David-material now indicates that it has a good understanding of English, instead of a very poor one.

So we decide that our original measurements must have been wrong, throw them out and make a new set, being more careful. Again nearly a year of hard work is spent integrating these data, and making careful deductions.

And — dammit, they don't work either. The David-material proves to be quite different than we thought it was.

After about 25 years of this, we find that we can get somewhat more stable readings. (The short lived conditions and characteristics have exhausted themselves, leaving more stable daughter-characteristics.)

I have a hell of a strong suspicion that a lot of the things we don't understand involve laws of nature with an appreciable time-factor involvement! Certainly Man, who's spent some 2,000,000 of the Universe's 4,000,000,000 year development adapting to it, has developed in his own characteristics a terrific tendency to be time-modified. The most successful of the Universe's known creatures, in fact, is the one that shows the <u>highest</u> rate of time-modification.

<u>If</u> the Universe is time-modified, <u>then</u> only a time-modified structure could remain stable-with-respect-to-it.

Observed data: Only creatures that change remain alive; i.e., only organisms that modify their organization remain in existence as-organizations. The corpse remains in existence as -- matter, but the livingness-organization has broken up.

But just try playing with the T_0 concept a while, and see where you land!

And if T_0 <u>is</u> important — why, then of course the ratios of the radioactive atoms is one of the most important clues we now have for finding out what T_1 — the time-now — is.

Item: In quantum mechanics, they have some remarkably intractable infinities regarding electrons; the math will work only if they set up their equations on a difference-of-two-magnitudes basis. That's what they've done, but they haven't had any very solid reason for doing so. Maybe what they're actually doing is subtracting T_1 from T_2 — wherein T_1 is something like 4,000,000,000 years, but is also "infinity" in the sense of being "all the time that has been."

My, what fun we can have taking basic theories apart! They always turn out to be like one of these Suth'n Plantation Mansions in the movies — lovely to look at, so long as you don't stray beyond the camera-angles allowed. Get around back, though, and they're empty shells, supported by angled 2 x 4's.

Or maybe it would be fairer to say that they turn out to be scale models — imperfect, not the real thing, but damned useful in figuring out the relationships of the parts that the real thing will, eventually, have to have!

Regards, John

Isaac Asimov   *May 13, 1953*

Dear Isaac:

In further exploration of "What makes science-fiction different," it occurs to me that scf, unlike the standard modern novel, bases itself on a different level of development. Where the novel studies the development of an individual personality, science-fiction studies the development of a cultural personality. Thus your Foundation series studied the development of a galactic culture. **Hal Clement's** "Mission of Gravity" is studying the cultural characteristics forced by the technology necessary to a high-gravity world. Most of the best-liked science-fiction turns out to be cultural studies.

Obviously, once you stop to think about it, the next step beyond personality development that literature must take, is the study of cultural development forces.

Incidentally, it is interesting to think of the effect of a cultural environment on the individual as being somewhat analogous to the interaction of a magnetic field and an individual electron. If we have a complex focused magnetic lens, and project an electron into the field, the course of the electron is a function of two factors: the field structure and its own entering velocity vectors and position. Similarly, the individual's course through life is a function of the social field he encounters, and of his own heredity and birth-position.

Note that, in a magnetic lens system, the electron beam current causes a magnetic field itself, so that a massive beam current will distort the focusing field. If a large number of individuals having the same velocity vectors enter a social field, they will distort the field. (Immigrants of one nationality will tend to alter the culture they enter.)

The above analogy is interesting, but inadequate. It doesn't explain the effect that a single individual of great personal force can produce. That effect can better be explained in a chemical analogy; a catalytic effect wherein one molecule of an enzyme can alter 10,000 molecules of a suitable medium. Of course, if you altered 10,000 individuals in a social field, then you could have enough interaction to distort the field itself.

The trouble is, of course, that we haven't developed adequate techniques for presenting the massive tides of cultural changes; they spread over from four to a hundred human life-spans. Even the fast, short-term cycles on such things as sexual mores are hard to recognize.

If you could just find a good analogy for what happens in the culture development, it'd be a big help in presenting high-power science-fiction novels.

Regards, John

L.E. Garner, Jr.   *June 11, 1953*

Dear Mr. Garner:

The hoax articles can be used only rarely; you have some lovely photographs here, and the idea's good — but I can't use it.

A while back I bought, and have scheduled for early appearance, **Dr. Isaac Asimov's** recent lecture delivered to the M.I.T.'s Chemical Society. (Fact; he did. The chemists loved it!) The article is titled "The Micropsychiatric Applications of Theotimoline."

I can't use another one for 18 months.

Sincerely, John W. Campbell, Jr.

107

Isaac Asimov   *September 4, 1953*

Dear Isaac:

I don't know whether you'll be at the Convention or not; if you are, this goes along with me, and you'll get it there. Otherwise, I'll mail it.

I'd like your help as a highly trained, and experienced biochemist; I've got a theory-hypothesis, and I don't know enough about the biochemical problems, and biochemical science to be able to evaluate the probabilities applicable to it. I'll present it as a theory, and ask if you'll tell me if it makes sense.

If it does, maybe you can get opinions from other men up there, and perhaps get some experimental work on it.

Information Theory is an enormously powerful theoretical tool that has not yet penetrated very widely into other fields of science. It has some exceedingly nasty implications — but ones which will lead to far more powerful methods of attacking problems when properly understood.

In attacking any problem, there is always the question, "Is the method I am seeking to use competent?," and, "Am I competent?" The tendency is to force a man to hold that <u>he</u> is incompetent when his efforts fail, because the method has been used successfully on other seemingly related problems.

But seemingly related problems sometimes are totally unrelated. Consider the problem of finding the diagonal of a geometrical figure as a function of the perimeter. For some figures, it's quite simple — and therefore the problems <u>seem</u> to be of a class. Took a hell of a while to discover that there were transcendental numbers that could never be reduced to an expressible form!

The Greek geometers bisected the angle, and quartered it, and men spent 2000 plus years looking for a trisection construction. Finally somebody did work out a proof that the problem was inherently insoluble in the method of Greek geometry.

Men have wasted life-times trying to unscrew the inscrutable — which is a happy phrase, indicating the inherent impossibility of using a process suited to one level (mechanical) to solve a problem at a different level (philosophical).

108

What we need, of course, is some method of solving the general problem "Is the given problem, P, of a class capable of solution by the method M, or must a method operating on a different level be used? And if a different level must be used, what is the method N, which will work?"

You can NOT solve the problems of transatlantic navigation with plane geometry; the problem <u>can</u> be solved with spherical geometry.

O.K. To Horse!

The nature of a complex organism is such that it has many aspects which must be considered. There are cells, but the sum of the parts is not the whole, since there is a complex interaction yielding not "meat" but "living body." What's the difference between a living man and his corpse a half-second later? The corpse equals the sum of the parts; the living man is a higher-order function — the integrand of the parts, not the sum.

Aging, I think, (hypothesis here being stated), is the accumulation and repetition of metabolic noise.

Information Theory shows that noise is inherent in the physical universe. Any physical system contains noise; a biochemical system is a physical system, and therefore must contain noise.

Information theory also deals with the behavior of relay-station systems of transmission of information. The problem is to maintain a high signal-to-noise ratio. By the use of repeater stations, a given message can be transmitted over a greater span than it could be if it were sent direct.

There are always two sources of noise: the external environment, and the physical mechanism of the relay station system itself. In transmitting radio messages, for instance, if you put your stations 50 miles apart, the receiving equipment at the repeater station will hear <u>both</u> the original transmitted message, <u>and</u> the atmospheric static in the 50-mile gap. The stations must be close enough together, and powerful enough, that the transmitted signal has a high dominance over the static.

But the receiver at the relay station is a physical apparatus; it generates noise within itself. The transmitter at the relay station, which sends it on to the next relay station, also contains noise. Thus there are two problems:

1. The further apart the stations are, the more external noise can

get into the system; the greater chance the external noise has to dominate the transmitted signal.

2. The closer together the stations are, the more stations must be used to transmit the signal a given total distance. Since each station generates noise itself, this within-the-system noise mounts as the stations are close-spaced.

Now the identity of an organism is determined by the nature of it's organization — by its complex "message."

In a living individual, each cell dies, and transmits its "message" to a daughter cell; it is acting as a relay-station transmitting information across a span of time.

If the individual cell lives too long — if the time-span is too great between relays — mutation of the individual cell will have a high probability.

If the relays are too frequent, there will be greater chance of noise entering the duplication process.

For any individual chain of reduplicating cells, noise will inevitably, inescapably enter sooner or later.

The advantage of an organism of many cells, however, is that cell-reproduction-lines run in parallel, and they can cross-check each other.

In radio work, this is known as multiple diversity transmission. The same message is sent by three, four, or more separate channels, and cross-checked at the receiving end.

Information Theory calls it redundance.

The organism of many cells has a greater ability to maintain its "message" by redundance and cross-checking.

However, if an error creeps in, the relay stations will, thenceforth, repeat that error as part of the message.

Age, as I say, may be simply the accumulation and repetition of errors of the metabolic message.

Now: No drug can ever be found which will satisfactorily undo the work of aging.

Imagine we find a drug which acts as a template, to which the individual cells can compare their message, and correct it perfectly to match the original intended message. This would eliminate all deviation from the original message.

Suppose I had a drug which represented the exact condition of my
110

cells at age 25 — my physical peak.

If I took this drug now, we assume for the argument, it would restore my cells to precisely the condition then extant.

But — some of the "noise" that has entered the system since that time is what we call "learning." I'd restore my 25-year-old condition all right — at the expense of everything I have learned since that time!

Conclusion: No physical-chemical means of restoring youth can be found which does not destroy learning.

The only way it could be done is by an <u>intelligently selective</u> process. A process that distinguishes between error and valid learning. But that's a philosophical-judicial process; we'd be asking for a chemical which had wise judgment!

Therefore, immortality can only be the possession of the Gods or demi-gods — i.e., of an entity having judgment so great as to be able to distinguish between truth and error.

Now let's see to what extent this theory applies at the observational level. The proposal is that the statements above are the truth, and nothing but the truth — but it is agreed that they are not the whole truth. That they are necessary, but not sufficient.

If the theory is valid, an organism having many cells would tend to have a longer life-span than an organism having few cells. And an organism having a high level of intelligence would tend to have a longer life-span (because of a greater judgment level) than an organism of equal cell-numbers having a lower intelligence.

The above rules do appear to check fairly well with observed life-spans of animals — but there are unexplained exceptions. The parrot has a very long life-span, and is neither large nor intelligent. Extremely small cells present in greater numbers than indicated by its size? What's the rate of cell-replacement in parrots? I don't know. So far that's just not explained. It may be the fact that breaks the theory, or a fact that adds another answer.

In each case, we're dealing with statistical fluctuations, and means of deleting them. The scientist making observations seeks to determine the true mean of his varying readings; in doing so he throws out wild readings on the basis that the wild one probably means some unaccounted disturbance crept in.

(However, the Geiger counter seeks to detect and count the wild errors that creep into a stable statistical system of gas molecules under electric field tension. Even the wild ones have meaning, but the meaning belongs to another problem-system.)

Now cancer could be considered a type of error that was acquired, and repeated. For some reason, the surrounding cells have not thrown out the wild datum. It has acquired an error in the message that somehow says, "Don't delete this passage; it is important!" and then gives a passage of gibberish. It's like a spy who doesn't know that the password is the highly improbable statement, "I come from Mars," and has accidentally taken, as his cover-identity, the name of a man who was born in Mars, Pennsylvania, and so explains, "I come from Mars" and is passed as a member of the group. (Hmmm — you couldn't even catch him on the password phrase with a lie detector. He'd know he was lying when he said, "I come from Mars," but so would all the legitimate members of the group!

Now there's an additional proposition. If this relay-repeater station idea is legitimate, short-span repetition would reduce the probability of accumulation of external errors.

Learning and accumulation of wisdom, however, depends on allowing the introduction of desirable "errors." (Favorable mutations must be preserved.)

In an organism of extremely low intelligence, where wisdom was practically nil anyway, the following system might be predicted:

Very rapid repeater-relay — early reproduction — would minimize accumulation of and transmission of errors. It would tend to produce a sequence of generations with small accumulated error.

Now if the reproductive system involved a halving of the message each time, the transmission would necessarily halve the accumulated errors also.

Imagine that each message-unit is repeated twice — sent in this fashion:

Grwo grow strong strong and and multiply multiply rapidly rapidly.

Now if we somehow split the doubled message in half, we'll have two units, one of which says:

Grwo strong and multiply fast.

The other says:

Grow strong and multiply fast.

The first statement contains a nonsense-error; it simply won't work at all.

The second statement is error-free, and will work.

The result would be that the split would have totally eliminated an accumulated error. If the reproductive system was so rigged that the message was immediately doubled, the new individual would now have:

Grow-grow strong-strong . . . etc.

This implies that there is an advantage to doubling the message within the unit, and splitting it in two when reproduction is to occur. It gives the organism a double chance at the right answer, but each regeneration will involve an extreme tendency to test any errors present against the physical universe.

The half-message containing the error would contain an impossible command, and destroy the organism quickly.

Item: There are no female hemophiliacs. To have hemophilia, the individual must have the gene for it in the X chromosome. You can stagger along with one command in the X chromosome that's sour; you can do fine if you have two X chromosomes, only one of which is sour, the other being sound, but when both X chromosomes agree on a sour command — you're sunk so deep you never get born.

A female zygote having a double hemophilia command dies aborning.

A female zygote having one sour X and one sound one, doesn't display hemophilia, because the sour one is masked by the sound one.

A male zygote carries the sour command into practice, because he hasn't any masking sound X — but he has only one command to bleed, and fights against it enough to get born.

Now suppose we took some very low-order animal, one that could reproduce hermaphroditically, or parthenogenetically. An egg-layer that could produce young without intervention of males, perhaps, would be ideal.

If we caused them to reproduce near the end of their life-span, the mothers would have accumulated a lifetime of errors. Their reproductive cells would have a lifetime of errors, too. The noise level would be so high that, by repeatedly breeding generations of high noise level, we'd accumulate errors that would produce weak, sickly,

113

and old-at-birth offspring. They would have shorter and shorter lifespans as generations went on — and they wouldn't go on very long!

One the other hand, if a group is bred on the youngest-possible basis, reproducing as quickly as possible, the error-halving system of reproduction would continuously reduce accumulated errors. If the error-halving reduction could reduce errors faster than noise-introduction induced error, the result would tend to be a more and more perfect message. With this error-reduction method, the young would be born with less error than the parent; there would be an increasing life-span, a prolonged maturity, etc.

Did you read the article *in Scientific American* about the guy who bred some kind of small parthenogenic water animal (kind, I've forgotten, dammit) in age studies? He found that young bred from generation after generation of very young mothers showed steadily increasing life-span, till after 50 generations the life-span had gotten so damned long it was inconvenient for the biologist to measure it. The normal life-span was about 20 days; he had 'em living 250 days!

While when he bred from very old mothers, about 7 days old, the lifespan shrank with appalling rapidity, until it was down so short he couldn't get any individuals 17 days old.

Under the theory proposed, the life-span of a colony of any organism would average at such a level that all error-reducing mechanisms in the race were just being balanced by the effects of all error-introduction mechanisms. Then alteration of the situation to favor any error-reducing mechanism would increase the lifespan, while alteration to favor any error-introducing mechanism would shorten it.

Introduction of intelligence and judgment is an error-reducing mechanism. When it starts feeding back antibiotics and hormone extracts, surgery and sanitation, naturally the average life-span of the race rises. When it feeds back automobiles with stupid drivers, the high tensions of great cities, and atomic-cum-biological warfare, the average life-span tends to drop.

When the automobiles with stupid drivers kill more stupid drivers in other automobiles than non-stupid drivers in other automobiles, the average lifespan of the race tends to rise. It has now become an error-reducing mechanism.

When automobiles kill chickens crossing the road because the
114

chickens can't compute a 40-mile-an-hour attacker, being used to nothing above about 20 MPH, the lifespan of chickens drops. But when they kill more chickens that can't compute fast moving dangers than chickens who can, the life-span tends to rise, and presently you have a race of chickens that doesn't cross roads when automobiles are in sight.

This summer we drove through Ohio, Indiana, Illinois, Wisconsin, Michigan, Ontario, and New York state. We didn't kill a single chicken, though much of the time we cruised between 70 and 75 miles an hour.

We did kill a pheasant, though.

Now: I've suggested earlier that no drug can cure aging; only judgment and intelligence can.

But let me show you a problem that could drive a biochemist completely nuts, break him down in hopeless frustration.

The biologist observed that breeding old mothers produced old-at-birth young. He postulated a substance X which was passed on from the mother, and caused rapid aging. Now let's set a biochemist to work to isolate X.

This gentleman is going to go stark, staring nuts. You see, what he's trying to isolate is pure noise. He's trying to isolate lack of organization.

Now there's a guy I know who's been trying to isolate the enzyme systems present in cancer, and distinguish them from the enzyme system present in normal tissue. I have a sad suspicion he's trying to identify all possible errors of cellular metabolism, that can produce excessive growth.

This, it occurs to me, is somewhat like trying to list all possible numbers between 0 and 1. It's a limited goal — apparently. After all, you're looking only for numbers between 0 and 1.

But Cantor, the mathematician, has proven that there are more numbers between 0 and 1 than there are cardinal numbers between 0 and infinity!

Theoretically, given infinite time, some high-speed electronic gadget could record all the numbers — cardinal numbers that is — between 0 and infinity!

But that isn't even theoretically possible for all the possible numbers between 0 and 1!

There's a little trick to be considered here; you're working with the interrelations between molecules. There's a finite number of molecules all right — but the possible interrelations between them is a transfinite cardinal higher than aleph null!

With only the two binary digits 0 and 1 you can, by using positional notation, construct a transfinite quantity of numbers of cardinality higher than aleph null. With hydrogen, oxygen, carbon, nitrogen, sulfur and phosphorous — wanna bet there is only a finite number of combinations?

Regards, John

Isaac Asimov   *September 30,* 1953

Dear Isaac:

One of the annoying things about making basic discoveries is that people will, for reasons that can readily be shown, almost inevitably say, "Sure . . . I know that. I been doing it for years, only I didn't call it that."

The reason: If you've been operating successfully in the Universe, you've been obeying the fundamental laws of Nature. You may not have known it, brother, but you were a law-abiding citizen of the Universe just the same — or you died off quite some while back. Ugh, the caveman, didn't know about the law of gravity, but he considered its effects most carefully, and invariably obeyed it.

Peg and I have been doing fundamental research; we've found some basic principles. And we are greeted, usually, with "Why sure, I've always done that!" Man, you are so right! Obviously! If that weren't the case, the discovery wouldn't be a valid one!

Information theory has a set of explanations and interrelations of facts; the peculiar difference about information theory is that it relates the laws of the-relationship-of-facts, instead of being simply facts-themselves.

Any time someone can give you a piece of theory such that you have that feeling, "Why that's just saying what I've been doing right along!," you've been handed a basic statement about a field that hasn't been adequately investigated — the surface hasn't even been scratched.

Science can be defined as the business of making the self-evident obvious. It can also be quite frustrating to the men who first open up
116

an area, because everything they say appears so painfully obvious --after it's been said.

Information Theory is in that category. It says a lot of perfectly obvious things. People glance at it, and say "Humph. So what? That's obvious; been doing it right along myself." and walk off. <u>The consequences aren't obv</u>ious — and the consequences can't be deduced until the so-obvious statement has been precisely formula**ted.**

Claude Shannon started Information Theory almost a dozen years ago. Psychology hasn't used it yet — yet the function of the human mind is the handling and interpretation of information. A man is sane if he can distinguish signal from noise; he's nuts if he can't, and confuses noise (hallucinations) and signal. Information Theory is a mathematical study of the characteristics of signals, noise, the meaning of "information," and the importance of signal-to-noise ratio.

But psychology doesn't understand that the concepts are directly applicable in its field!

Neither does political science. Sooner or later **Claude Shann**on's work will be evaluated, recognized, and he'll get a Nobel Prize. I don't know whether it will be a Nobel Prize in Peace, due to Information Theory's applications to international problems, distinguishing between "noise" and "information" in that field, a prize in Medicine, Physics, or Chemistry. Of course, it applies in Literature, too — but usually you have to write the work itself, not just develop a theory whereby it can be shown that great literature is that which succeeds in eliminating the maximum of noise from a segment of life, and transcribing a maximum of message — thus producing a high signal-to-noise ratio. But at the same time retaining optimum redundance, to prevent confusion of the receiver of the message.

In the last half century, several basic philosophical discoveries have been made; before their discovery, the problems of psychology, interpersonal relations, sociology, physics, chemistry, and the rest of human living, could not be solved for lack of the needed tools. Try producing free fluorine without electricity, and you'll get some approximation of the difficulty.

One of those needed concepts was the package called Information Theory. Another was the concept of Negative Feedback. **James Watt** invented the negative feedback system of the steam-engine governor — but he didn't abstract and state the concept of Negative Feedback.

Psychology was thoroughly stymied without that one; they still haven't caught on to what **Weiner** was talking about in his Cybernetics.

Anyhow, the problems of chemistry, particularly of biochemistry, aren't going to be solved very readily until the most powerful tools of thought Man has are applied to it. I don't care how bright you are, you can't solve problems without thought-tools. Thought-tools are like the monkey wrenches of thinking; try disassembling an automobile, to see what makes it work, without hammer, wrench, or screw-driver. You won't get to first base with your fingers, I assure you.

The concept of Probability was one of the great thought-tools. Information Theory and Negative Feedback are a couple more.

In addition, until it is generally recognized that there is a nonlogical method of rational thinking, you'll have a fancy time solving some of your biochemical problems. Let me show you what I mean:

Suppose we have a steam engine, with a speed-governor on it. The speed-governor consists of a device which detects the slightest change of speed, and immediately moves the throttle in such a direction, and to such a degree, as to hold the speed constant.

Now let us observe the actual behavior of this engine.

1. By observation, increasing or decreasing the load on the engine has no bearing on its speed. Speed and load are not related.

2. The position of the throttle has no influence on its speed.

3. The position of the governor-operation-indicator has no effect on the speed.

4. Under extreme load, the speed does not increase, but the engine blows up.

When a negative feedback loop is involved, no one unit appears to be related to the behavior of the system. The system cannot be understood in logical terms, because the logical terms will be perfectly circular! That is, in the above system, the throttle moves because of its position! That is, it moves because the position it is in is not appropriate to the load on the engine. If you want to get utterly confused, try making a list of perfectly true, logical statements about the engine-system. They will necessarily be circular — because the negative feedback system is itself circular. But circular logic is remarkably futile!

118

What's needed is a gestalt rationale — a non-logical thinking that considers the system-as-a-whole. In Gestalt rationale, the whole is not equal to the sum of its parts, but is some different function; it's the integrand of the parts, say.

We can appreciate the concept of the gestalt unit, but haven't developed expressible, formula terminology for manipulating it in formal discussion. Start talking about the logical cause-effect relationships in a system that is truly a circular feedback system, however, and you'll quickly be reduced to a recognition of the vital necessity for gestalt thinking. In a feedback system, you actually do have the situation that A is the cause of B, while B is the cause of A, so A is the effect of B, and B is both the cause of A and the effect of A!

At this point, the dearly beloved "law" of cause and effect lies down on its back, waves its paws in the air, and expires with a gusty sigh.

Meanwhile, the biologist goes into dithering frustration. The patient's heart-beat improved because he had dropsy. Having dropsy caused him to take digitalis, which caused his heartbeat to improve, so you see his heartbeat improved because he had dropsy.

It ain't funny, McGee! It's a fact.

This system won't make sense until it's viewed as a gestalt.

How many of the problems you're now tearing your hair over are simply fractions of a gestalt. Lots of the systems in Nature involve multiple feedback loops, where as many as eight or ten chains use a common impedance — er, that's an electronics term; better make it "common reactant." Your high-energy phosphate bonds, for example. How many different feedback loops link through that configuration of atoms?

Apparently high-energy phosphate bonds represent the metabolic equivalent of the 110 volt power line; it goes to all the rooms in the building, and everybody in the building taps in on it. But if one of them short-circuits the line, and blows the fuse, the whole section of the building may be robbed of power. On the other hand, Joe, on the 6th floor, may be taking 1200 watts, which is high, but allowable, until Mable, on the 2nd floor, plugs in another 1200 watts, while George on the 3rd, has his 300 watt lights on. Plooey goes the fuse. Who's to blame? You'll have a juicy time, as a biochemist, trying to assign a cause for this failure of the high-energy bond power line!

So far as good texts on Information Theory? Gad, I don't know; I got what I know from talking to about 50 different people, here, there, and elsewhere. The people who know the subject are so frantically busy trying to spread themselves around applying it that they haven't written any good discussions on it. Get hold of **Wayne Batteau**, over at Harvard — he's **Dr. Wayne Batteau**, Pierce Hall 206, Harvard. You can telephone him, and ask him what makes a good text. It'd do a hell of a lot of good for your Chemistry group to have someone like Wayne, who knows Information Theory and cybernetic theory, discuss not the mechanism of computers, but the philosophy. They're Information Handling machines, you know.

In Information Theory, a chemical molecule is precisely the same as a piece of paper — they're both information carriers, and the problem is simply to read out the information. After all, a living cell reads out the information on a gene; why can't you?

Regards, John

Jane Rice   *October 5, 1953*

Dear Jane:

I'm returning these two yarns of yours; I simply can't agent them for you, and they aren't science-fiction, lovely as they are. Like the problem of the lubricated watch at the Mad Hatter's teaparty, "It was the best butter." But not science-fiction.

You do need an agent, though — but one who can and does follow the policies of a lot of editors, and knows the off-trail tendencies of the editors. Knowing only the center-of-the-formula preferences of editors wouldn't do much good with your little yarns; you have to find an agent who knows the side-alleys of each editor's mind.

The best man I know for that job is **Lurton Blassingame** (that's his real name!). He's **Bob Heinlein's** agent, and agent for a number of other damned good men. He works with the most formulated of the slicks — and also with fantasy and science fiction.

Your pot-'o-gold story has some lovely lines in it, and is a lovely concept; I think it may have some trouble selling though, because of one thing. The trouble with this type of writing is that it can be ap-
120

preciated only by highly sensitive, highly intelligent people; the back-woods dolt of whom you appear to be writing wouldn't understand the thing at all. Neither would the ordinary dry-goods store proprietor.

Now the backwoods dolt and the dry-goods store proprietor share one thing in common; if tomorrow is an exact repetition of today, and today is bearable, then tomorrow will be entirely satisfactory. They would be frightened silly if they thought tomorrow was going to be basically different in character from today — if there was going to be a change, a development, a new situation. Such a thing would require that they think out a new pattern of behavior. Here they've spent 25 years learning all the answers to life, and have been using those answers in exactly the same way for 25 years since. What horror to consider having to learn a new answer!

To them, repetition is not futile; it's ideal.

But to the type of personality who can enjoy these stories, change, development, alteration is the breath of life. They don't want tomorrow to be just like today; they want today to have some permanent influence that alters tomorrow — not a mere witless mumbling of the unchanging formula, endlessly repeated.

To the type of person who can enjoy the lovely line about her back being curled up like a fern, then, the story is unsatisfying because it ends at exactly the point it begins. The entire system of events in the story has no consequence; the story becomes a pointless intrusion in a system of pure chaos, where there is sequence, but no consequence. Nothing they do has any effect; they might as well have spared themselves the effort in the first place. And, says such a reader, so might I; I didn't have to read this to get nowhere.

This isn't a conscious level reaction — but it's there.

If you left 'em with an open-ended plan, the reader would have the fun of continuing your story, mentally, in any direction he chose. I can't help wondering who'd come off the hardest if that somewhat-more-than-eccentric family got into a town — with their pot of gold. Their ideas of what a town was, for instance, would probably be somewhat weird; given gold and the slightly peculiar powers they appear to have, the town might have some difficulty staying what it really was — if this outfit landed in it.

You don't have to describe what happens; just wind up with their happy little plans of going to town. The reader's met your mountain family; he's also met towns. He can do quite a fine job of stirring the two concepts together.

Isaac Asimov once did a science-fiction story based on the following elements:

1. The inhabitants of Jupiter, it is discovered, are insectile, immensely numerous, and consider anything not insectile to be an abomination on the face of the cosmos.

2. But they have to live in the enormously high-pressure atmosphere of Jupiter.

3. No possible material can withstand that pressure; no metal can make a sufficiently strong wall to hold their atmosphere in Space, so they can't have metal spaceships.

4. The danger is that they may discover a way to make a pure force-field that's capable of standing the pressure, and so be able to come out and attack humanity.

5. A scientist at the research station on Ganymede, the Jovian moon, has been studying force-fields. A worried ambassador from Earth has come out to investigate what the score is.

6. The scientist has just succeeded in proving that no force-field capable of standing even Earth's atmospheric pressure can be stable for more than 1/10th of a second. If an effort to maintain it longer than that is made, it explodes with enormous violence.

7. Now everybody's happy, and the ambassador, in great relief, is prepared to go home to Earth and report that the Jovian menace is confined safely. He signals for a spaceship to transport him, and one is diverted to pick him up.

8. The one diverted, it turns out, is an experimental ship. An engineer, who doesn't understand basic science very deeply, is testing his newly developed force-field-walled spaceship. He has a force-field generator that turns on and off 1,000,000 times a second; the field isn't stable for more than a minute fraction of a second at the intensity he's using — but he just keeps turning it on and off, and it works just fine.

9. What happens when the ambassador discovers the nature of the ship that's coming to pick him up is left entirely to the reader's imagination.

Regards, John

Isaac Asimov *November 4, 1953*

Dear Isaac:

O.K. on the sin-opsis. I had to run the yarn as a serial for two reasons; 25 thousand words is a bit longish, and we're fresh out of novels for the last six months. Whassa matta with e'rybody?

You're going to love the illustrati**ons Kelly F**reas did for your yarn. One beauty gives away the whole plot of the story -- it states the solution to the whole thing, directly and in large letters.

It's a scene on Earth, or some other colony planet, with a big travel-colonization poster on the wall, with people interestedly discussing in front of it. The big, bold letters on the poster say "Be On Troas!"

My, some chemists are going to hate themselves after they finish the story.

I told you his illustration gave away the whole problem of the story.

We're trying a new cover-format design on that issue, **too. F**reas has done quite a remarkable sort of cover, with your Mnemonic standing alone, with a sulky, defiant, frightened-belligerent look in a spotlight effect, with vast computer banks looming around and behind him — shadowy bulks, with only rows and files of pilot lights gleaming.

Something you might be interested in considering:

Man has, through the ages, developed three Great Questions; What? How? Why? Where and when are simply "what location." "Who?" is a totally different sort of question, of an order of complexity and degree of abstraction about 14 steps removed from the other three. Answering "Who?" actually demands the definition of the concept "I", or "you" — which is a totally different kettle of fish!

But we need a new question, at a new level. From Why? We derive How?; from How? we derive What? — but name the question which leads to Why?!

Item: If I toss a ball into the air, I supply it with kinetic energy. The ball rises, and the KE is converted to Gravitic potential. It reaches a peak, and starts "falling"; during the fall, the G. potential is reconverted to KE. Everybody knows that.

And everybody knew apples fell and hit people on the head, too — until **Newton** as<u>ked</u> why they did <u>it!</u>

123

How — by what process, what force-mechanism — is that gravitic potential converted to kinetic energy? Sure — we all agree freely that it happens. But what makes it happen?

You know that simply rearranging the atoms of ammonium nitrate into different configurations yield energy; every chemist knows that. Sure. But — what's the process?

I know that Kinetic Energy transforms to Gravitic; I also know that Electric can be transformed into Kinetic. Now if I knew the process of these transformations . . . maybe I'd know how to establish a force-mechanism that converted Electric directly to Gravitic!

And ye gods, Isaac, that mechanism must be mechanically simple to the point of sheer idiocy! A hunk of elemental matter of any kind whatsoever contains the mechanism necessary!

Want to help ask the question "What's the process by which a simple lump of matter performs the feat of conversion of one energy-type into another?"

Sorry we missed you by being in Boston that weekend. I had a friend of mine, **Mike Mihalakis**, visiting **John Arnold's** class at MIT. **Mike's** an ex-wrestler, ex-champion high-diver, ex-theater organist, composer of symphonic music, self-made patent lawyer (he never finished high school) and inventor who's just taken 20th Century Fox for about 20 megabucks, and has his own multi-million dollar plant for producing his own inventions. He discovered a basic principle of optics, and had some 40 basic patents that are so damn basic nobody can break 'em! He discovered what the process of diffuse reflection was. Having discovered what it was, he invented a substitute for it — and a synthetic surface that Nature never produced. He can project movies on it while the full light of the sun is falling on it, and have no washing out.

His basic discovery: Anybody who asked "What is diffuse reflection?" during the past couple of centuries could have done the same. He looked at a diffuse-reflecting surface under a 2000 power microscope, and believed what he saw. Diffuse reflection is not reflection at all! Magnesium carbonate is the "whitest" of diffuse reflecting surfaces, and has a reflecting power of 90%. Consider what Mg carb is though; it's a water-white crystal material. It doesn't reflect; it refracts. Each minute crystal acts as a tiny, randomly oriented prism, breaking up any incident light to a tiny jewel-flash of prismatic colors.
124

Naturally, when you look at a mass of several billions, the white light is reconstituted by summation of billions of tiny prismatic flashes.

Newton would have spotted that — if he'd had a microscope. Since then, we haven't — until **Mike** came along — been bright enough to take a good look at what happened.

See how stupid we are?

Mike replaced the refracting prisms with small reflecting dome-surfaces. By controlling the curvature of the tiny domes, he can control the angle-of-acceptance of his "diffuse reflection" surface. Result: a surface which accepts light from a certain limited angle, and reflects to any point in that angle from any point in the angle. But any light-source outside that angle reflects to points outside the angle!

He can project kodachromes, using a standard projector, on his screen, outdoors in full sunlight — because the sun is a source outside his angle of acceptance, and reflects smack into the ground. With this technique, you're actually not looking at a diffuse image, at all - but are looking, via a specularly reflecting surface, right smack down the optical system of the projector! You're not looking at an image of the kodachrome, you're looking at the kodachrome itself, and the light source behind it!

If you look at a light bulb reflected in a christmas tree ball — you aren't looking at an image of the bulb, but, via the mirror of the christmas ball, at the light itself.

Mike just proved that you don't have to look at a pre-digested and broken down image of the thing; you can look at the thing itself!

You know, most people think there isn't much in the way of new, basic ideas to find!

Stupid oafs, aren't we, **Isaac**. Either one of us could have found what **Mike** did — or, if we'd thought decently, figured out that it had to be that way, without need of a microscope.

Let's start trying to figure out why rearranging ammonium nitrate atoms — or high-energy phosphate bonds! — converts one form of energy into another. How does a rearrangement of atoms yield to my punching the keys of this typer — or, even more interesting, selecting, out of a vocabulary of perhaps 250,000 words, precisely the word that I need to express the concept I'm seeking to communicate?

125

Item: Life displays the interesting ability of making, within its domain of dominance, a monkey's uncle out of the 2nd law of thermodynamics. It also makes a monkey out of the proposition of action and reaction — of balance. Only life displays unbalanced, one-way forces. Know anything else that can make only one of a pair of optical isomers?

Item: In the whole table of atomic weights, there is one, and only one, weight that is absolutely unoccupied. There is NO isotope of atomic weight 5.

Item: Crystallographers say that no crystal can have pentagonal symmetry. Tetrahedral, yes. Cubic, yes. Hexagonal, yes. Pentagonal — no. Inherently unstable.

Item: Float ball bearings on a pool of mercury. Apply a magnetic field vertically through the surface of the Hg and bearings. One ball; stable. Two balls; stable. Three balls; stable. Four balls; stable. Five balls — whoops, one jumped out! Six balls — stable.

Item: Star-fish have a pentagonal symmetry.

Item: We have a pentacular structure.

Item: All primitive land-life had pentacular hand-feet.

Item: For some weird reason, the old magicians used to think there was something magical about the pentagon and the pentacle. Not the square or the hexagon, though.

Item: All inanimate nature tends toward stability. A life-form is dead when it's stable; it exists only so long as it is maintaining instability.

Funny co-incidence department?

Regards, John

John W. Campbell, Jr.   *November 9, 1953*

Dear John,

I look forward to seeing both cover and inside illustrations with great delight. Despite the fact that competition is a hundred times keener than it's ever been before in the history of magazine s.f. I still like A.S.F. art-work better than that of any other s.f. mag in the business.

The Be on Troas gag is terrific. I know several particular persons I will personally force into reading the story so that I can quietly point out the illustration afterward. If I escape murder or they suicide, it will be a great day.

As for novels and wassa matta e'rybody, I'm not sure. A lot of effort may be drained off by this new fashion of printing books first without selling to s.f mags. I don't know. Anyway, the old faithful, **Isaac Asimov**, can always be counted on to write a novel (or try to write one) every year or so.

So before the end of the year, I want very much to see you and discuss with you possible angles for my next Doubleday novel (with the ulterior motive in mind of selling it to you for serialization first — if you want it, of course.)

Incidentally, I must have told you this before. If I have, have patience while I tell you again. Next month, Signet books will put out a paper-back version *of The Currents of S*pace.

About your thoughts on the figure 5, very interesting. Of course, in atomic structure, you can see why isotope 5 doesn't exist (at least stable isotope 5.) Helium-4 consists of one alpha particle. Very self-satisfied. Add another neutron or proton and its frozen out — has no place to go. Add both, and you have a situation where the extra neutron and proton can pal around together. Okay. Lithium-6. so the pentagonal structure of limbs and starfish is a very cute idea indeed.

Just one thing, though. Isotope 5 is not the only one that doesn't exist. Isotope 8 doesn't exist either. For a while people thought that Beryllium-8 existed and was stable; then, that it didn't exist, but was stable when formed artificially. The current poop is that Beryllium-8 is unstable and so is any other combination of protons and neutrons making up a total of 8. Why? Well, Beryllium-8 would have four protons and four neutrons — or two alpha particles. Each alpha particle is so self-sufficient it will have nothing to do with the other. Unstable!

If you get three alpha particles together (carbon-12) or four (oxygen-16) it's different. Apparently, the possibilities of intra-nuclear combinations in more than a simple line (i.e. a triangle in the case of carbon and a tetrahedron in the case of oxygen — perhaps) not only makes the nuclei stable, but particularly stable.

Incidentally, my boss and myself finally signed a contract today to do a nurse's textbook of chemistry with McGraw-Hill. Since we are also busy working up a second edition of *our Biochemistry and Human Me-*

*tabo*lism (I'll see that you get a copy when and if it comes out) and since I have almost finished a textbook on enzymes for junior high schools (it's back with a highly approving set of comments and the request that I rewrite one chapter in the direction of greater simplicity) you can see that I've got three textbooks going simultaneously. Not bad for a guy who's "one of those crackpots that writes that there stuff about flying saucers."

Now how do I get 48 hours into a day? — or to put it another way, how do I get to live 200 years?

Life is short and art is long, John — and the older I get the longer art seems. There's so much I want to write — all sorts of things — and the days just fly by and in less than two months I'll be 34.

Yours, Isaac

John W. Campbell, Jr.   *November 17,* 1953

Dear John,

You're right. Mass number 5 is unique. The only two isotopes listed at that mass number by Sullivan's trilinear chart of nuclides are helium-5 and lithium-5. The half-life of the former is 10^{-21} seconds, while that of the latter is 3×10^{-22} seconds. Mass number 8, on the other hand, is, as you say, a different affair. It, too, has two nuclides listed, beryllium-8 and lithium-8. Beryllium-8 has a half-life of 10^{-14} seconds, but lithium-8 has a half life of 0.88 seconds. This means that of all the mass numbers known from 1 to 246 only mass number 5 has no member with a half life of more than 4/5 of a second.

Or look at it another way. Let us accept **Eddington's** estimate that the number of particles in the universe is 10^{76}. If helium-5 were the only nuclide in existence that means that there would be about 1.5×10^{75} atoms all told. This entire universe of atoms (enough to fill up all the known stars of all the known nebulae plus all the known interstellar dust) would decay down to a single atom in 2.2×10^{-19} seconds. How instantaneous can you get? And what an explosion!

As for nuclear stability, here are my own theories if you like — strictly my own.

Two particles together are stable because if the nuclear spins are opposed you get rid of that particular unbalance and have a net spin
128

momentum of zero. Three particles together can arrange themselves in a triangle so that each is at optimum distance from each of the other two. That makes for additional stability. On the other hand there are bound to be two particles of one spin and one of the reverse, leaving a net spin momentum of more than zero. That makes for less stability. The latter effect is the greater, so hydrogen-2 is more stable than hydrogen-3 or helium-3. (Helium-3 is stable but makes up a far smaller percentage of its element than does hydrogen-2.)

Four particles together, again neutralize spin momentum and also can arrange themselves in a tetrahedron where each particle is at optimum distance from each of the other three. Very stable and we have helium-4 or the alpha particle. In three dimensional space (or in four-dimensional space-time with each particle infinitely extended backward and forward along the time-axis) it is impossible to arrange five particles so that each is at optimum distance (or even at equal distances) from each of the other four.

Now two alpha particles attract each other very slightly (beryllium-8), three can be arranged so that each is at equal distances from the other two (carbon-12) and four can be arranged so that each is at equal distances from the other three (oxygen-16). The last is another peak of stability. It is no accident that of the atoms of the universe with more than one particle in the nucleus, helium-4 is most common and oxygen-16 is second most common.

You would think that multiplying 16 by 4 would yield another stability peak but the mass number 64 isotopes aren't particularly notable. The reason for that is that the stability rules hold only for nuclei with equal numbers of protons and neutrons and as the mass number goes up, the neutrons become increasingly preponderant so that the nucleus can't be viewed as being made up solely of alpha particles.

Yours, Isaac

P.S. I'm still thinking of Moebius strips. The latest theory of protein structure draws the molecule into a helix.

Isaac Asimov   *December 7,* 1953

Dear Isaac:

I know that it isn't impossible to write a science-fiction detective story — but it is mighty darned difficult, isn't it? And right now I'm badly in need of short stories, too.

If it's well written, the science-fiction highlights brought in are much more interesting than a dull old murder; if its poorly written, it's not worth reading anyway. It's got to be lousy science-fiction if the murder theme is to dominate — and the murder theme is just an annoyance if the science-fiction is good.

Regards, John W. Campbell, Jr.

Isaac Asimov   *January 9, 1954*

Dear Isaac:

As an expert on bio-chemistry and in education, I think maybe you'll have fun kicking this little idea around. Try it on some of your friends there at Boston, too!

Suppose we take a small child, and inject diphtheria anti-toxin. Injections are repeated, with increasing dosage, over a six-week period.

The child's metabolism reacts to the anti-toxin as a foreign protein, of course; at the end of 6 weeks, it will have been immunized against diphtheria anti-toxin!

Now if this child gets diptheria, it <u>can</u> not produce diphtheria anti-toxin. It'll have to solve the problem of handling diphtheria in one of the near-infinitude of other possible ways.

Generalization from this proposition: An organism will react to an "answer" as though the "answer" was a problem if it is not previously aware of the existence of the problem the "answer" is intended to solve.

Now let's apply this to education. To the student, the answers presented by the instruct<u>or are a pro</u>blem. The student's problem is "How to pass this damned cours<u>e."</u>

Only if the student is already aware of the problem the answer is intended to solve does he learn the ans<u>wer as an an</u>swer. Otherwise, he develops immunization to the answer! Then subsequently he may have to solve the problem . . . but he'll be forced to solve it by a techni<u>que</u> not involving the answer he's immunized against!

As I see it, there must be the following sequence:

130

1. The individuals become aware of a problem — and that means that he decides that it is a problem in his terms to him. If his attitude is "Yeah . . . but so what if you can't overcome gravity?" then anti-gravity is not a problem.

2. He must then encounter an idea-system S.

3. Idea-system S must then appear to him to solve the problem he saw.

If any one of these steps fails to connect, then the answer-presentation will appear to him to be a problem he must solve.

Item: I got good marks in calculus at MIT. I successfully solved the problem "How to pass calculus." But I did not solve the problem "How to use calculus to solve my problems," with the interesting result that I and now neatly immunized to calculus! I not only can't use it, but I can't even bone up on it when I want to use it!

Silly kind of education, ain't it?

Regards, John

Isaac Asimov *January 20, 1954*

Dear Isaac:

ity is not a problem.

2. He must then encounter an idea-system S.

3. Idea-system S must then appear to him to solve the problem he saw.

If any one of these steps fails to connect, then the answer-presentation will appear to him to be a problem he must solve.

Item: I got good marks in calculus at MIT. I successfully solved the problem "How to pass calculus." But I did not solve the problem "How to use calculus to solve my problems," with the interesting result that I and now neatly immunized to calculus! I not only can't use it, but I can't even bone up on it when I want to use it!

Silly kind of education, ain't it?

—   Regards, John

Isaac Asimov   January 20, 1954

Dear Isaac:

131

I deeply sympathize. I appreciate, perhaps more than you do even, what you're up against in teaching the sweet young females the rudiments of biochemistry. Believe me, a woman who knew approximately 0.01 as much biochem as you do could teach the girls much more successfully. Reason: The female of the species does NOT think in the manner the male does.

The great problem of every male is that women just don't understand what's important.

The great problem of every female is that men just don't understand what's important.

The great problem of both is that their whole education has failed completely to bring out the fact that both parties are perfectly correct; there is a difference, the diference is important, valid, and does NOT mean that A is superior to B, but that A is different from B.

Now it happens that Science is a development of Semitic philosophy — and only **Semitic** philosophies have developed science! The Judeo-Moslem culture was the first to invent what we know as science. The Greeks were great arguers; they could argue indefinitely, but in their pantheistic culture, it was self-evident that there were many equally good gods to appeal to, and many equally good logical arguments, and no need to settle to one. A dozen different philosophies could exist, with no need to pick one, and develop that.

But Moslem philosophers, oriented on the powerful Semitic tradition of There Is But One God, There Is But One Right Way, were forced to choose one philosoph7y among the Greek many. They had to

appeal to the scientific method of experimental determination; the pantheistic philosophy of the Greeks didn't make them do so.

Buddah had a fine and noble ideal — but it says "There are many Ways." No science grows in that climate.

The Judeo-Christian philosophy is also, of course, Semitic at root; it, too, holds that there is Only One Right Way.

This makes for progress in science — but it has certain difficulties when you get beyond the level of physical science. At the action level, you can not do two things at once; you must make a choice. But at some of the higher levels . . . things aren't quite so simple. The equation $x2 = 4$ for instance, has two valid roots — and if you think you've got

132

"the" answer when you say "2" you're going to get into trouble. A cubic equation does not yield "The One Right Answer"; it yields three, and they're all equally valid. Furthermore, the "one right answer" is all three.

The consequence is that the Semitic tradition alone could start science . . . but once started, it can be hampering if the further orders of undertanding aren't allowed in. It's like a car; a gasoline engine cannot start itself — but the starter has to be disconnected once the engine gets going.

The non-Semitic philosophies fail because they don't recognize that at the action level you must settle to one solution. You can't get a working solution of a cubic equation; you have to solve simultaneous equations in the first and third degree, before you can get an answer you can actually apply. You may solve the cubic, get three answers, and then select one of them arbitrarily — but you've just mentally inserted an arbitrary first-degree simultaneous equation.

The difficulty with trying to make all equations first degree is obvious; some of them damned well aren't.

The One Right Answer philosophy implies, however, that any other answer is either inferior, evil, stupid, or somehow detestable.

So now we have the second degree equation of Mankind; it has two roots, the F root and the M root. In a violent effort to force the second degree equation to behave like a first-order equation with a single root, the culture has insisted that there is no real difference between men and women. Oh, sure — some minor physiological differences that are quite important, but only physiological, you understand. There can't be two right answers at a mental-spiritual-intellectual level; everybody knows there can be only one right answer, so if there is a difference, somebody has to be inferior.

Item: No woman has ever attained first-rank competence in literature in any Indo-European language.

But . . . no man has attained first-rank literary importance in Japanese.

And — no Japanese scientist is able to work in his own language; he has to learn, and think in, one of the European languages!

Curious, isn't it? Maybe if we think of language as being nothing more than a coding system, we could explain the above observation by

133

saying that the Indo-European languages are coding systems adapted to male type thinking, and ill adapted to female-type thinking. This would naturally impose a major handicap on a woman seeking to express her type thinking! But Japanese, then, might be a female-type-thinking coding system — and men can't express their thinking adequately!

Take it for a moment as a postulate: There are two equally valid roots to the Human Equation, because it's a second order equation.

Then no solution to the human equation will be valid that does not recognize the difference and the validity of both roots.

And any socio-cultural system that insists that there is only one valid answer will get into trouble with itself; the men will find the women un-understandable, irrational, unpredictable . . . and the women will be unhappy about the unfeeling, unundersanding and unreasonable behavior of men. Both groups will be unhappy and confused and continually disappointed. Men will be patient with their women, who obviously can't think straight, and will patiently put up with their vagaries. Women will be forgiving, and resigned, and understand that life just is that way, full of the unreasonable and unfeeling behavior of men.

And your dear little nurses will patiently put up with the unreasonable vagaries of men who just don't understand that biochemistry isn't important, but, this being (sigh) a man's world, they go through the meaningless ritual of mouthing biochemical words like "acetic acid ester of salicilic acid" as patiently as they will mouth any other ritual the world demands of them, whether it be the Morning Prayer or the Pater Noster.

Of course, you couldn't possibly get away with it in a medical school, but if you hinted that the reason they had to learn biochem was that men doctors simply can't be trusted to prescribe properly unless they're checked by some woman . . . the girls would dig into that biochem. This they know for sure is true; no man can be trusted unless some woman is checking up on him.

That happens to be 100% straight goods, too. Of course, that the inverse is equally true doesn't set so well with the females — not when the whole cultural orientation says that "different means inferior."

A woman thinks like a slide rule; she never gets the answer beyond the first three significant figures — but she never gets those wrong.
134

A man thinks like a digital computer; he gets all the digits — but he's just as apt to slip in the first significant place as in the 15th place. **If you get a digital answer that agrees with a slide-rule** answer, because of the totally different approach of the two computers, you're practically certain to have the right answer.

Two digital computers, cross-checking each other, can make the same type error; both may slip and write a "3" where there should be a "2"; that error can happen just as readily in the billions position as in the units position.

If the two types of thinkers cross-check each other — they get answers that work.

Now part of your trouble is that the girls don't see why they should learn this silly ritual. A woman is never guilty of being an Ivory tower theoretician; they're pragmatic. Only men, who are instinctively theoretical, make the Ivory Tower error.

Note the pragmatism of Gertrude vs your own theoretical approach to life.

Gertrude is a very practical biochemist; she can synthesize complex proteins very successfully, and doesn't have any deep urge to find out how.

So feel your nurses; they can do it, so why bother with all this ritual about words; do something, don't just talk about it!

No Ivory Towers for them.

Trouble is, most women don't see the immense practicality of a sound theory. Left to themselves, women would still be beating the dirt out of clothes in the nearest stream; it was a practical method that worked, wasn't it?

A woman demands that an idea work — which is a necessary test, but not sufficient. There's her error — a feeling that if it works, that's both necessary and sufficient.

Man's error is that a theory must be intellectually satisfying. Some of the old boys have developed some dillys, too. Intellectually very satisfying. Observe the years and years they spent studying the relative surface area of angel feet and pinpoints. You'd never catch a woman making that error — not while her children were inadequately fed, poorly clothed, and the world was in a Grade A mess of ignorance. Besides, she's too busy seeing to it that that man of hers has clean clothes — and puts them on, instead of just putting on the ones he wore for the last four days. (He didn't notice; he'd just thought up a new argument while he was ambling over to get a shirt.)

Some of those nurses are going to do nursing . . . but they'll be the abnormal females. The great job of the female is to find a male who needs her help and guidance and protection, and undertake the big job of complementing his nature. (He does need it, too; he just thinks he doesn't.) Of course, the big job of the male is to find a woman who needs his help, guidance, and protection — who needs to be completed. (She doesn't know she needs that help, either; she finds out though, if he does his job right!)

The worst of it is that the whole history of mammalian development shows that the male of the species offers himself; the female selects from among the males who offer. But the male determines the direction of life-development — he offers not only himself, but his life-goals, his proposed development line. The female selects not the goal, but the male-who-has-a-goal-she-approves.

Women, consequently, make damned poor students in college. When you went to Columbia, you knew where you were going — into biochemistry. Suppose you'd had to study with a deep, very deep, reservation that "This may have nothing to do with the goal I'm going to direct my life toward."

A woman can study — and really study — after she's found the man, and thereby found the goal she's going to work toward.

Until then, any studying she does is necessarily done with reservations; is this laborious study advancing me in the direction I am to go?

If you think that situation makes life easy for someone who is basically pragmatic, you're wrong.

A girl does much better in Liberal Arts; that consists of a once-over-lightly of all sorts of things. Just what her instincts require for making sound selection of a specialist. But the female, before she is mated, is not supposed to be a specialist. If she is, she won't be free to make an unbiased selection.

Old Mother Nature is female to this extent — she's pragmatic as hell. She has no theories; she just tried it out for 3 billion years, and what she wound up with may not be the best possible, but it works.

136

After that much field testing, furthermore, it works damned well — a hell of a sight better than any theory Man has developed so far!

Give the gals a break, Isaac. They're being sincere, and working hard — but they have problems *that they don't even realize con-sc*iously.

It's not tough to study for no-as-yet-understandable reason when you're a child. That's the instinctive business of children.

But here you've got young adult females; millions of years of evolution says "Now it's time to busy yourself finding a mate." The last few thousand years of cultural evolution says "Wait; you have to study more." But there's no longer the feeling that studying is the main job of life.

It's a hell of a lot different for a male that age; he knows damned well that now is his last chance to prepare himself, and he knows what he's <u>preparing for</u>. It can make a big difference in the learning pattern!

Regards, John

Isaac Asimov   *January 27, 1954*

Dear Isaac:

From a study of your last few letters, plus a little consideration of the basic nature of Scholarship, I think I can suggest a solution to your problem of teaching the nurses biochemistry.

Basically, it must be realized that the business of Scholarship rests on the ability to pass the examinations imposed by a board of some kind. Scholarship is measured in terms of human beliefs, that is; this is why Scholarship and Wisdom are not necessarily the same thing.

To attain recognition in Scholarship, it is essential that one be able to answer problems posed in the terms the examiners consider correct, adequate, and appropriate.

Thus Galileo was an extremely poor scholar; it took the threat of the Inquisition to make him learn the scholarly answers.

Jesus was an even poorer scholar; he never did learn to give the scholarly answers.

You would most certainly fail an examination given by a physicist of 1900, and graded by him. You would, for instance, deny the knowledge

137

that Matter was Indestructable, and conservative. You would demonstrate lack of scholarship with respect to the periodic table by denying that the element following Uranium would be an eka-manganese type.

In order to pass an examination, it is essential that the student give the answer the examiners expect; giving the true answer may, by coincidence solely, yield a passing mark — but it will be by coincidence, not by Scholarship.

Now those nurses are having trouble learning to give the answers you expect. But I see by studying your latest letter that there is a solution to this problem that apparently should be satisfactory to both you and the nurses. If you ask them "What is the cause of diabetes?" they can satisfactorily answer you by saying "A disturbance of the biochemical millieu."

If you ask "What causes blood to clot?" they can answer "It is due to a change in the millieu."

Now it is evident that these answers are perfectly correct. They lack a little in depth of consideration, or in accuracy of definition, but they're unquestionably true.

Since your last letter indicates that you're willing to accept an answer "It's due to the millieu" in regard to one class of human entity problems, it would secm only consistent that you accept the "millieu" answer in connection with the class of problems the nurses are struggling

with. And certainly they'd be greatly relieved.

Of course the way women behave is explainable in terms of "the millieu." Naturally. Only . . . sometime try finding out what made the millieu get that way. Try figuring out why it is that, although matriarchic governments have been tried, none has ever worked. And why it is that, when women are regarded as chattel slaves, and polygamy or its equivalent — free use of concubines and mistresses — is accepted, the patriarchic societies fall flat on their suprised faces.

Look, my friend; it's all due to the millieu. Only the millieu happens to be The Universe. If you want to find techniques that work, find ones that correspond to the characteristics of that millieu.

The Amerindians had been culturally isolated for thousands of years. But they had essentially the same cultural system with regards the male-female relationship that Europe did. Coincidence, no doubt.

The South American jungle natives had been culturally isolated for
138

even more thousands of years from the African jungle natives. But they had essentially similar male-female relationships. Coincidence is strange, isn't it?

You can build a low order civilization on polygamy; it's been done repeatedly. But not a high-order civilization; it's been un-done repeatedly.

Every major empire has fallen amidst a welter of sexual abnormalities, specializing in homosexualism (dividing of the sexes with non-intercourse between them in far more important manners than the simple physical level.) The rise of homosexualism is attended normally by an increasing acceptance of sadism and masochism.

You say the cultural millieu holds that a woman should be cute and stupid. Funny . . . wonder why it does? What's it trying to express? The Ptolemaic theory of the motions of the planets expressed their observable behavior within the limits of naked eye observation; it adequately expressed the behavior of the universe so far as could be observed with the naked eye. Of course, it didn't quite do it, but you have to allow for human imperfection, we all know . . . . But the theory was certainly a good one, wasn't it?

Could be the culture is trying to express the fact that a woman's thinking is not equivalent to Man's, and isn't supposed to be. (But let us not for a moment suggest that a Man's doesn't cover the whole area of a woman's thinking, any more than she covers the whole area of his!)

If you want to lick the other fellow, force him to fight on your terms, with your weapons, under conditions you specify. If you don't want to lick him, but want to learn to understand him though — you'll have to meet on common grounds, develop common terms, and common conditions of operation.

When a man and a woman fight, he'll use the weapons he's most agile with; physical strength, logic, and language. She'll reply with the weapons she's most agile with; intuitive postulate generation call intuition (let's see you do logic without a postulate! You've got to have intuition, or stick to working like a machine that never originates anything new; logic is inherently incapable of generating a new postulate.), and she'll use that sense of inward understanding that has to do with emotion. She'll withdraw her encouragement and approval, which is essential to Man's well-being.

139

They'll <u>be in</u> the postiion [of] the Dead End kids [who] like to get a couple of cats, take two cats, tie their tails together, and hang 'em over a clothesline. Each blames the other for its misery, and neither can get away. In the course of half to three quarters of an hour — cats die hard — there'll be festoons of cat-gut and assorted organs drooling off two feebly twitching, disembowled carcasses.

A man has physical strength and logical strength enough to tear the heart out of a woman. She has emotional strength and intuitive power enough to do the same to him. Keep it up, and each can destroy the other; each can successfully prove that he/she has the ability to take the joy of life out of the other.

They do, too. They're both perfectly correct; each is able to prove that fact beyond a shadow of doubt.

That's much easier to prove than it is to prove that each has the ability to increase the joy of life for the other. It's much easier to prove you can make a wound than it is to prove you <u>can cure</u> one.

And it's just ever so much easier to say "It's not my fault; it's the millieu."

Yeah. So's diabetes and so's thrombosis.

You can pin Gertrude's ears back any time you want to, for fun, money or marbles; you can do it physically because the male has a markedly higher weight-of-muscle factor than the female, and also is able to develop a far higher peak intensity of effort. You can do it logically-intellectually, too.

The Jewish culture has recognized that fact for a long, long time. It's also the culture that had to develop the Wailing Wall as a cultural tradition. Maybe there's an improvement to be made somewhere along in here, huh?

Man's gone along blithely recognizing his own superiority — and ignoring the areas of female superiority. Since one of Man's areas of superiority happens to be action, he's acted on his superiority, and made it an effective fact.

Go on, Muscles, you can lick her!

But you won't learn much that way.

Women, unfortunately, are peculiarly weak at the level of verbal expression and analysis. They're lousy communicators. The can generate plenty of volume and quantity, but the quality and intensity is way down.
140

(And men are very poor patient, detail, accurate workers. Women outperform men enormously in tasks calling for attention to detail of a repetitive nature. So we're even.)

The lack of woman's tendency to sharp analysis and precise statement, the lack of her willingness to pinpoint her idea, is the big difficulty. (Let's see you pinpoint an emotion, though! That's the other half of the Big Difficulty!)

Wherefore, it's going to take a full, deeply-felt cooperation between male and female to establish communication across the gap. You're perfectly lousy at communicating emotion; she's stinking poor at communicating ideas. You have to think, and think damned hard, to help her work out what her idea-system is. She has to intuit intensely, and with a deep realization that you're trying to express something you're not very good at expressing. You've both got to know that the other is not trying to defeat you, and also you've got to know-feel the truth of **the fact that you can not give anybody any mental attribute.**

You can't *give David muscu*lar strength; he has to develop it.

He can't develop it without working his muscles against external resistance.

But of course you're perfectly correct in saying "It's the millieu." So it is . . . if you'll recognize that you're looking at the millieu when you watch an indicator change color, or see the stars twinkle in the disturbed atmosphere at night.

That's the millieu.

Re the radioactivity article: We're over-stocked on articles. WAY over-stocked. I'll be looking for more articles about next fall, I think . . . but not sooner!

The paper's interesting; it does bring the scope of radioactive half-life variation into sight, when you put 'em all in seconds. But I can't take even a good article now!

Regards, John

Isaac Asimov   February 3, 1954

Dear Isaac:

One of the troubles we're having here in this debate-by-male is that you're operating on that primitive old concept "The Law of Cause and

141

Effect" — the old pre-cybernetics idea that an observed effect has a cause, and that an observed stimulus-phenomonon has an effect. That's what they're still teaching in physics, too — because that proposition works pretty fairly well there, at that simple level.

But let's see. Hydrogen and Chlorine react to form HCl; this is due to the nature of the hydrogen atom structure and the chlorine atom structure.

Hydorgen and nitrogen react to form ammonia. But this is due to the millieu, the immense pressure applied, because without that millieu, hydrogen won't react with nitrogen.

See? Simple isn't it? In one case it's just "the nature of the atoms involved," while in the other case it's just "the millieu" that is the cause of the effect.

Ah, me . . . inorganic chemistry is so nice and clear and cleancut. If you mix HCl and NaOH, you know just what you're going to get. The stimulus-phenomonon of mixing the two leads to the effect — NaCl and $H2O$.

And you burn ethylene in an oxygen atmosphere, and you get $CO2$ and $H2O$. But if you burn it in a millieu containing very little oxygen you get acetylene, ethane, methane, propane, bu . . . oh, hell! Let's not do that; it violates the Law of Cause and Effect; the effect is so multiplicatious as to make things very difficult. Let's go back to something nice and sensible; we'll use plenty of oxygen and get The Effect of The Cause again.

Look, Isaac, I understand that "Christine" these days is sporting a nice pair of honest-to-flesh breasts, the nice, soft, warm, squeezable kind. Now it's usually been held that development of breasts was a genetically determined characteristic. Not this time; it's strictly due to the millieu— the hormones-in-the-blood millieu, and the cultural millieu that's capable of producing these hormones by chemical extraction processes. It's also due to the cultural millieu that so distorted the mind-structure of a human individual that he couldn't stand being what his genetic nature called for, and tried to be what his genetic nature didn't call for.

Now it becomes evident that the development of breasts is due to the action of the cultural millieu; we must have been mistaken in believing it was due to some genetic factor, because "Christine" didn't have the genetic factor, and does have breasts. Tsk tsk! See how wrong we were . . .

142

You know, Freud must have been wrong, too, He talked about the female's penis envy. "Christine" demonstrates that human beings have a lack-of-penis envy; "Christine" had "hers" removed.

Some one of these days right soon, mankind's going to develop a technique for handling logical problems that can handle nondenumerable quantity problems. In biochem, you don't say "X plus Y yields A plus B." You say "X plus Y yields a complex mixture, containing, under conditions M, 15% of the desired compound A." Vary the conditions, and you get different answers. Under any conditions, X plus Y have a certain potential for yielding A; if A is what you want, you pick the conditions which maximize the probability of that potential eventuating; if A is what you do NOT want, you establish conditions minimizing the probability of that potentiality being realized.

To understand the nature of that chemical system though, by God you'd better consider that that potentiality does exist. It's like your chain of radioactives; nucleus P is so unstable it lasts for only a microsecond. Evidently it has a very low probability of existing, so we can ignore that nucleus entirely.

Oh . . . yeah? It's an intermediate stage in the transitions leading to lead, we'll say. Ignore it, and you'll have one hell of a time figuring out how that lead managed to get there.

Pain is unpleasant, so organisms seek to avoid pain. Therefore a process which involves acute pain can be ignored, because no organism will seek that process.

My, that's so sensible and logical, I wonder why there are any painfully produced human beings in the world?

You go right ahead explaining it all in terms of education and the milieu, and if you can explain it all that way, that's lovely.

Only I'll request that you explain how the milieu came to be the way it is. Or did that spring, full-fledged, from the brow of Jove?

Man has loved nice, regular, simple figures since he started drawing geometrical diagrams. Ptolemy and others had a real hard time making the planets move in true circular paths, as he knew they had to because only circles are perfect, but he managed, after a sort of half-aspiration fashion.

Just suppose that we have two ellipsoids; the major axis of one is parallel to the minor axis of the other, and vice versa. A line passed be-

143

tween them — a plane actually — has come interesting possibilities.

In curved space, generating a true plane is somewhat difficult. It can be done, however. If you have two point sources of light, or two point sources of a field-force, the plane marking their equipotential plane will be a true plane, whatever the curvature of the space may be. Also, it matters not a whit whether the force-field follows an inverse square law, inverse cube, or inverse googolplex law. It's a bridge circuit, and it always has a balance somewhere.

So let's imagine the male and female characteristics to be so arranged that the major axis of the M type is parallel to the minor axis of the F type, and vice versa.

Item: If the female **of the species has 48 chromosomes, and the male only 47, and each chromosom**e containing several thousand genes . . . . My, there's an awful lot of chromosome-gene system involved in a simple inversion of an extroversion of certain organs to an introversion!

If the minor physiological changes are the only things affected, it's a remarkably narrowly limited effect, isn't it?

But . . . all right. Have it your way. It's all just the milieu.

Peg and I have been happier, personally, since we found out that didn't explain things so well. Our kids have been, too. *Particularly since we also gave up holding that every effect* had a single cause, and every cause had a single effect.

Regards, John

Dr. Kenneth E. Hayes   February 3, 1954

Dear Dr. Hayes:

I imagine that Asimov would be happy to have you quote from his thiotimoline article; after all, one man quoting another man's scientific paper is standard procedure, I believe . . . and thiotimoline, it appears to me, is at least as scientific as some of the items I have seen published in more serious journals!

As to your suggested article, however . . . I'm afraid not. We're overloaded on articles as it is, and can't take even serious ones for a while now.

Sincerely, John W. Campbell, Jr., Editor

Isaac Asimov   February 14, 1954

Dear Isaac:

I know you have no intention of being "converted" to my idea; that's all right — it still makes a good discussion, and a good discussion's fun. You always learn something, even if it's not what you intended, or what the other fellow expected.

But don't base your defense on the proposition that there is no proof that mental characteristics are genetically determined — because that one I can lead a herd of brontosauri through without scraping off a scale, it's got so big a hole in it.

The hole: It is logically impossible to teach an entity which has zero ability to learn. Therefore the ability to learn, and a functioning learning mechanism must be present before learning of anything is possible.

Once some kind of effective learning mechanism, however feeble, is present, then there is no limit to what learning the entity is capable of, save the limitation of time.

BUT — the learning mechanism must be built in genetically, since it is inherently and absolutely impossible to teach an entity that doesn't already have a learning mechanism!

BUT — learning is a mental characteristic.

Therefore there is proof that mental characteristics can be determined genetically.

The experimental verification of the above argument is quite ample. Some psychologists have raised a baby chimp in their home, treating it in every respect as a human baby would be treated. It's now five years old. It can't talk, and can't understand human conversation.

The chimp lacks the genetic determinants for a high-order abstraction center of the mind.

This implies that methods-of-thought can be controlled genetically, doesn't it.

BUT***NOTE that I said above that once a certain level of learning mechanism is achieved, it is potentially capable of unlimited development.

The thing that separates Man from the animals is that he has achieved that critical level. The proposition that man differs from the animals only

145

in degree is both true and false; it's purely a matter of degree, but the degree happens to span a phase-change point. The difference between water and ice is purely a matter of temperature, isn't it?

The difference between a mass of gas in interstellar space and a star is purely a matter of concentration, isn't it?

But each of these two cases the "degree" happens to span a phase-change system, so that ice is inherently a different structure from water, and the star has the new characteristic of producing thermonuclear reactions, which the mass of gas did not do.

Similarly, Man does differ from the animals only in degree . . . but the degree happens to span a phase-change. At a certain level of learning-power, learning becomes a chain-reaction. If you have a population of 1,000,000,000 and a reproduction factor of 0.999, the population will decrease toward zero without limit so long as the same k-factor remains. But if you have a population of only 1,000,000 and a k-factor of 1.00001 — the population will increase without limit. Vide the operation of a nuclear reactor.

The result is that a minute change of degree — one part in a thousand — produces a totally different resultant.

In Man, learning has achieved a K-factor of 1.00 . . . . plus. The result is that he is potentially capable of unlimited progress in understanding.

And if you don't think it's a genetically determined characteristic — try teaching a chimp to understand human speach the way David does!

Ever think of the peculiar difference between the conceptions about a force-field and the conceptions necessarily applicable to matter in respect to divisibility?

A force-field is infinitely divisible — and yet absolutely indivisible! Being non-quantized, it's capable of division infinitely finely. There are no quantum steps involved. But — the force-field characteristically extends to infinity, and nothing whatever can block it, so it is absolutely indivisible.

Example: Consider two north magnetic poles. There is a point—actually a surface — between them where the force of each is exactly balanced by the force of the other. The vector-force drops to zero at that surface, and the vector reverses itself on crossing to zero at that surface. Then if we refer to N1 and N2 , we can say that there is a point on the line between N1 and N2 where the force exerted by N1 is zero — but the
146

fact is that the force is simply balanced by an equal and opposite force from N2. We can establish a vectorial division of N1's field — but the field itself is not in the slightest degree influenced! The field of N1 interpenetrates that of N2 freely.

The Sun's gravitic field interpenetrates Earth's and produces tides. So does the Moon's.

We can meaningfully ask the question, "Is the Sun's field dominant at this point in space?" but we cannot meaningfully ask the question, "Does the Sun's field exist at this point." The latter question is meaningless, because no information can be gained from it, since the Sun's field extends to infinity, the answer to the 2nd question is always and invariably "yes." Since information is gained only when an unpredictable answer is recieved, the 2nd question canno, elici, information.

Most of the real levels of operation of the Universe are of force-field nature, not atomistic — the atomistic levels result from the force-field levels, by interaction and the business of vector-dominance.

Make a statement about a human being, and except for the atomistic-level statements, you're going to get fouled up with vector-dominant vs existential statements. Because, being a function of the totality of the real Universe as we must necessarilly be, we must necessarily partake of its characteristics — which are dominantly non-quantized, and show dominance-vector properties, not existential properties!

Now the cockeyed thing about a vector-dominance system is that balance in such a system is inherently unbalanced! The least stable position in respect to the two poles N1 and N2 is the point on the line between them that is the balance point.

Kick that fact around a while and you'll come up with a design for a system that is stable in a vector-dominant system without being on the bottom of either of the two potential wells! And . . . look what that system has to be! Tsk tsk.

You can have more fun that way!

Sometime you should try writing a textbook in a field that is making progress of the type nucleonics was during the 1942-1947 period. Major advances coming so fast that the interval between lab and the mimeograph machine — let alone the printer — had 'em tearing up stencils before they'd been used. Kind of like the problem of the newspapers reporting the German breakthrough in 1940; there was no time to discuss the meaning of the fall of X, because by the time significance could be attached, the Nazis had already taken X and Y and Z also, which made the significance so different the . . . .

Things become very disorderly in a field when that sort of sudden breakthrough is made. Naturally, no one in any field of science can ever feel that his field could be subject to a general breakthrough.

Heh heh heh. Wait'll they hit one, though! And I herewith happily stick my neck out: There will, within the next ten years, be a major breakthrough that will make the discoveries between 1885 and 1915 look like peanuts. By Jan. 1, 1965, the present fields of science will have a deserted look, wherein a few old men, and small boys, are raking up the debris.

The computing machines are doing funny things to what we know; they won't work on certain problems. Not having human prejudices, and lacking human ingenuity in building defenses around a belief, they stall when the belief won't work.

And tisk tisk. Here's an experiment that ought to work, and somehow doesn't.

Take an accurately measured mass m. Apply an accurately measured amount of energy E, producing an acceleration-intergral dv. The initial velocity of the mass m was v. Then we can calculate as follows.

$E = 1/2m(v + dv)2 - 1/2m(v)2 = 1/2m(2vdv = dv2)$

Now in this simple kinetic energy equation, all the factors are directly metrical, and measureable by standard techniques, except for the quantity v, the initial velocity of the mass.

If the equation $KE = 1/2mv2$ is valid, then we have a simple method of determining the absolute velocity of a moving system.

And if $1/2mv2$ isn't valid....

Tsk tsk. What happens to physics?

Regards, John

Isaac Asimov   February 22, 1954

Dear Isaac:

I'd never seen the quantity relationships on 40K vs U radioactivity in the per-atom terms you worked out. I did see once, some years ago, a discussion of the importance of 40K activity in terms of energy relationships. You know the immense importance of a few degrees of temperature on the Earth's climatic conditions. There's been a lot of argument about a lot of things, particularly in business, "men are just like animals, there's no difference of kind — just a matter of degree." Well, it's perfectly true that the only difference between water and ice is a difference of degree — just about 2o in fact, is plenty. When the span of degrees, however, happens to include a phase-change, things get rather startling.

The 40K energy release has a ^{ve}ry critical effect on Earth's climate, because without that energy release, the planet would be a wee bit cooler — and Earth is balanced right on the thin knife-edge of the water-ice phase change.

Question: Given a thermal conductivity like Earth's crustal rocks, how thick can a rock mantle be before radioactivity causes it to fuse? What's the score on a planet of Jupiter size, where all the layers are much thicker?

The core-mass elements in planetary material are all center-of-the-periodic elements, and have damned small activity; the crustal mantle, on the other hand, accumulates the lithophile elements, which include all radioactive elements.

Calculate the possible crust thickness in terms of the heavy radioactives only, and you'll get an answer several thousand miles off the right answer. K40 is going to be damned important.

Further, the period required for a planetary crust to cool to solid state is not determined entirely by radioaction of initial heat — and that means that radioactivity half-lives are going to play a hell of a big part in determining that factor.

Question: If you started with a mass of pure uranium at time T=0, there would be an energy release due solely to U decay. At all later times, the energy release would be due to U-decay, plus the consequent decay of daughter elements. How many years after the consequent decay of daughter elements? How many years after the time T=0 will the rate of energy release reach maximum? Would this phenomonon lead to solidification of rocks, followed by accumulation of daughter elements, increased energy-release, and consequent fusion of the rocks? In other words, would there be a periodic cycle effect?

One of the things Man hasn't done too well at is the study of macrocosmic effect of things that are of minor importance . . . on the human scale! Macrocosmic time periods, and macrocosmic masses have effects as widely different from those of our normal scale as the difference between test-tub level experiments and production plant level.

What happens if you neutralize 0.1 N HCl with 0.1 N NaOH? That is, what happens when you carry out this reaction with 20,000,000 gallons of each, in a single 50,000,000 gallon vat? What happens when you store Na4NO3? Say 100,000 tons of it, that is?

A piece of coal will not ignite spontaneously in air. Now 100,000 tons of coal is different from a 100 pounds of coal only in degrees, so that won't ignite spontaneously either, will it? So it's just a waste of water and effort to keep coal storage piles wetted down, isn't it?

Of course, we're also running into the fact that microscopic levels have different laws of behavior, too. A man can't walk through a brick wall. You can't just jump over a 50-foot barrier. But nuclear particles do.

When we start thinking in terms of planetary, or steller masses — throw that textbook out the window, brother; it makes nonsense.

Have you seen the interesting experiments with a tub full of mercury in a magnetic field? Tsk tsk! It displays a kind of viscosity nobody ever considered before, due to the fact that any motion in the liquid Hg sets up an effect of a conductor moving in a magnetic field, generates currents, and produces quite different interactions than otherwise expected. What happens in a star, where totally ionized material tries to stir around in the immense magnetic field of the star?

Have you seen those pictures of colliding galaxies they've gotten recently? One galaxy colliding with another, and interpenetrating. (E.E.Smith was all wrong; it happens all the time, and not just to the Milky Way and Lundmarck's Nebula!) Funny thing is, the pictures show every evidence of a viscous interaction! How can a star-system be viscous?

We science-fictioneers are sort of half way willing to consider that Man is merely the latest, not the last, step of evolution. Strictly an intellectual consideration, however.

It's a lot harder to consider, even intellectually, that what we know is the latest in a long series of inadequate, inept, misguided, and poorly integrated misconceptions of the Universe. We can laugh at the primitive and his Gods and Demons. And at the alchemist, and at the phlogiston theory. What else can we laugh at?

Let's see you laugh at mathematics, for instance! Gad, is that silly! The funniest, foolishest set of inconsistent beliefs! How could the old boys, way back then, have had such a set of incompatable ideas, and believed them!

Wanna see how silly it is? Well, look:-

Any number, N, multiplied by zero, equals zero.

And a x b is exactly equivalent to a & a & a & .... b times.

Now anyone with a grain of sense knows that that's silly! Why it's perfectly ovbious that a x b is an area, and a & a & a is a length. It's true that the ratio of a to (a & a & a & .... b times) is the same as the ratio of a to a x b — but how silly of those old ... er, what did they call 'em? "scientists?" ... "magicians?" ... no, "scientists," that was it! — to think that because the ratios were the same, the things were the same! Like the old magicians it must have been a carry over of the magical belief that because a doll was similar to a man, it was possible to hurt the man by hurting the doll.

But with silly beliefs like that, it's no wonder they had such silly ideas in their science!

And anybody with a grain of sense knows that zero times any complex quantity is analogous to making a single differentiation. That is perfectly clear if you just notice that 2 ft x 3 ft x 0 ft is not zero, but 6 square feet. Just as in $d(x3) = ax2$. Oh, it's true that d(N), where N is any number, equals zero — and that N(x) is zero, but just because that's true, it certainly is silly of the old boys to hold that d(q), where (q) is any quantity is zero, or that q x 0 is zero!

And the old ... eh ... oh, yes, "scientists"! ... of the twentieth century did all their "scientific" thinking in terms of mathmetatics; if it couldn't be expressed in mathematics, it wasn't "scientific." So of course, working with a mathematics that held only ratio-logic to be valid, and insisted everything was on a ratio-basis, naturally they had [a] queer idea that everything was relative. In a ratio-logic mythology — pattern of beliefs, that is — naturally the Universe can be admitted only to the extent it matches the folk-belief of the time.

I'm afraid Einstein is a poor Jew; he's given up the faith of his fathers — the great discovery the Jewish philosophers made. Of course, they, like many other people, insisted that they had the whole truth, which they did not, instead of realizing they had an immensely important part of the truth. The Jewish philosophers were the first to establish a philosophy based on the existence of Absolutes. That's why only the cultures that have adopted the Semitic tradition of Absolutes have been able to develop science.

But the Semitic tradition is necessary, but not sufficient. There are relatives also. Einstein in rejecting the Absolutism of the ancient Semitic tradition has gone too far — he's trying to go back to the pre-Semitic tradition of pure relativity. The philosophy of "Their gods must be better than our gods, because they licked the pants off us."

There are some things that cannot be expressed as ratios — and I'm afraid Einstein is doomed to die a frustrated and dissapointed old man. He can not solve the General Field Theory problem, nor can any other man, so long as the requirement is that it be solved within the limits of ratio-mathematics, wherein multiplication by zero or infinity (the two absolute extremes) is held to be meaningless.

Differential calculus, by approximating multiplication by zero and infinity improved things a lot — but you can't solve general field theory by that method.

You can't trisect an angle by the methods of the Greek geometers, no matter how long or hard you try. Equally, Einstein is doomed to frustration if he tries to solve the problem of Absolutes using a method that denies the reality of absolutes!

Ain't we got fun?

Regards, John

Isaac Asimov   March 6, 1954

Dear Isaac:

So you think I'm just kidding about that business of 2 x 3 x 0 and 2ft x 3ft x 0ft?

Ha! You'd be supprised what it leads to! It's interested John Hocking, Gotthard Gunther, and Wayne Batteau who, since their business is mathematical logic, naturally want to work on it. It ain't so all-fired simply dismissed. And some further investigation on a new line of attack — open only because we have, today, tools on multi-valued logic that didn't exist when arithmetic and the like were invented — is leading us along a line that suggests that we can state **why** the three-body (or n-body) prob-
152

lem has never been solved. Mathematics as she is wrote is inherently incompetent — and partly because of that buisness of 2 x 3 x 0 not being zero at all.

Actually, you see, the mathematician says that "any expression multiplied by zero has no meaning." Sure, and as of 1900, the terms radar,fissile,frahmstabl,neutron,barn and transistor had no meaning. At the present frahmstabl has no known meaning. Neither have the terms kyrmod and nume —save to a few of my friends. But that doesn't mean that no useful meaning can be found; it just means that we haven't been able to elucidate the meaning.

There was a hell of a rucus when the zero concept was first introduced in arithmetic. Newton had troubles with zero when he worked up calculus. He also had trouble with infinity.

Cantor showed that infinity isn't always the same thing.

The whole point of my little item of 2 x 3 x 0 is to bring to attention the fact that whatever the product means, it does not mean "Nothing whatever."

Democritus said atoms were the uncuttable. Suppose you cut one? Why, you can't — it's uncuttable. The idea is meaningless, isn't it?

Logically — yes. But not in the universe — because when you cut an atom, you have an ion. It bleeds electrons.

(Incidentally, that doesn't prove there are electrons in an atom. You can suck milk out of a cow, but that doesn't mean she's full of milk.)

The progress of Man has been largely tied up with appreciating that the microcosm has structure, and that the macrocosmos has structure. Zero is the symbol not of nothing but of the microcosm. Infinity, similarly is not structureless, but symbolizes that which we have not yet been able to comprehend.

But to make progress, it's essential that we recognize that there is progress to be made. That's the importance of realizing that 2 x 3 x 0 must be interpreted in a manner other than we have heretofore considered it.

It's long been held that the ideal of the logical man is to be able to maintain an objective view on the problems he encounters in life.

For the strictly logical man, that's necessary — because in logic-as-we-know-it, the Class of all classes cannot be a member of itself. Our logic can't handle the situation of a system such that one of the critical factors in the system, factor A, we'll say, is controlled by the conclusion reached — this is the situation of so-called "circular logic." If the conclusion reached determines the postulate chosen to start, then logic can't work.

The Objective viewpoint holds that the observer must be external to the observed system, and have no influence on the system.

Fine. For a system of pulleys, strings, and weights, that is a useable system. For reactions between NaOH and HCl, it's a useable system. But notice that it is pure nonsense when you start talking about electrons; the act of observing destroys the system existing, so that observation is impossible in the terms rewired by the "objective viewpoint." The same is true for complex protein chemistry, and also for observation of gravitating masses. Since motions are relative, the position of A can only be expressed in terms of B and C and D — and it takes three coordinates to define motions in volume. The result is that you have to solve the n-body problem to have a meaningful answer.

But we can't in any system based on an "objective viewpoint" logic.

The phenomona are even more marked in dealing with the humanic sciences. Trying to figure out how Gertrude and David will react on an "objective" basis — on the basis that your presence or absence makes no difference to the system under consideration — is the purest nonsense.

That's why the social scientists have maintained that mathematics won't work for them. They're quite right; no present mathematics system will work in handling an n-body problem, wherein the "objective viewpoint" is as inherently inappropriate as it is in considering the behavior of electrons.

You can't get data without observing.

But observing the system alters the system.

Therefore the "objective viewpoint" is pure nonsense!

Modern math seeks to handle this problem by means of partial differentials. For certain simple systems, this — which is actually a technique of successive approximation — will work fairly well. But you know that partial differentials constitute the most horribly complex and unmanageable system of math yet developed — and that even so they can be used under some favorable circumstances.

We are now seriously seeking to develop a form of mathematics which will include all present known math as a special case — just as plane geometry is a special case of topology. If we can once locate the essential principles, we'll have a technique that will solve the n-body problem as simply as calculus solves the problem of maxima and minima — which is a very laborious task indeed by arithmetical methods.

Regards, John

Isaac Asimov   March 10, 1954

Dear Isaac:

Your letter wasn't beside me when I answered it the other day. I missed your little problems in consequence, in answering.

It took me about 2-1/2 seconds to come up with "tin" as the element with the shortest name. Not being a chemist, I don't think first in symbols and then in names, but first in names, then in symbols. That makes a difference, because tin has the longest-possible (i.e., two-letter) symbol, though the shortest name.

Your two more elementary gases ending in -ium has me stopped. If you mean true gasses, and not merely the vapor-pressure-surrounding-a-liquid, I don't know the answer, and looking down a table of elements didn't reveal it to me. Selenium and Tellurium are non-metals ending in -ium, and have high vapor pressures, but you got me, pal.

From the office, I had Miss Tarrant send you a card somebody sent in. Seems there's a report of a cure for Be poisoning. I dunno, so I left it to you to answer him. If he's right . . . fine business. It took a Mnemonics Service man to spot that Be was poisonous, for the valid reasons you gave, and they remain valid even with the data that postcard carries.

Wayne Batteau has an ion beam gadget with interesting characteristics. At region A, a series of events transpires. There is a drift-region B, and a sensing region C. By proper adjustment, the sequence of events at A can, at C, appear in reverse. The events 1, 2, 3 at A appear at B as 3, 2, 1. Other adjustments allow the sequence to appear as 312, 231, 132, or as simultaneous.

Given an event system, and a separation or gap between event-system and observation system, the sequence can be made anything desired at the observation system. The result is that the observation system, if it involves an observer with a cause-effect philosophy, will observe that 3

155

"causes" 1. Or, on the other hand, that 1 cannot be the cause of 3, because 1 and 3 are simultaneous.

The mechanism can be simplified to this: Take a beam of ions, and apply voltage that decreases with time. (A saw-tooth pulse voltage is applied to accelerate the ions.) The ions will be accelerated in such a varying way, that the pulse that lasted 10 milliseconds caused ions to arrive at the other end of the drift tube over a period of 100 milliseconds.

On the other hand, apply a rising saw-tooth voltage. The last ions through the acceleration field will be accelerated most. By adjusting the saw-tooth to the drift-length, the last ions will just overtake the first ions, so that all ions arrive simultaneously. By making the saw-tooth steeper, the last ions can arrive before the first ions.

If, instead of a saw-tooth wave that increases linearly with time, we use a more complex wave-form, we can make the first and last ions arrive together, but the mid-sequence ions arrive before either beginning or end.

Ever compute what you'd see if a ship went past you at a speed greater than light-speed? If you're standing at point C, you'll see it simultaneously at A and E, then at B and D, and then it'll run into itself at C, finally exploding into existence before A and after E. The mid-sequence events appear before the beginning or the end of the sequence.

I don't want to trouble you, Isaac — but the dear old law of Cause and Effect is rapidly going down the drain. What's left behind isn't chaos at all, either — it turns out to be what the Law of Cause and Effect was being contained in all that time. It gets to be much easier to understand things when we don't hold that time-sequence is the Be All and End All of causality.

The only trouble is, no finite logic-system can handle the problem — any more than a plane geometry can handle a map of the Earth's surface. Either you have to distort the true map outrageously as in the Mercator projection, or you wind up with a discontinuity system, of the type where you have a continuity at the equator, but a lot of saw-tooth spikes or banners waving out from that spine.

You know the old science-fiction idea of the guy who traps a 3-dinensional cross-section of a 4-dimensional entity, and can't figure out how come it keeps changing size, shape, and even number in a seamingly meaningless manner.

156

A plane cutting a cone produces a whole family of shapes. They don't look like one single family, but they are. A straight line, parabolas, hyperbola, ellipse, circle, etc.

Try it with a plane and a torus, too; the results are even more interesting. One member of the family is), and another is, (and still another single member of the family is 00 ! And there's the member of 0 of course, and the other member, a circle within a circle , concentric circles as a single member. The single member 00 certainly looks like two entites, but it isn't — it's the single entity "intersection of a plane and a torus." It's just as much a single entity as is a circle or an ellipse.

Query: How does an electron make an orbit jump?

Answer?: By following the surface of a torus, which recognises that the inner and outer orbits are the intersections of a plane with the inner and outer circumferences of the torus. The electron is not discontinuous between the two points — even if it is discontinuous in our plane of referrence.

Better take a long, nostalgic look at the Law of Cause and Effect. It's about to go the way of the Law of Contagion, which was highly popular a couple years ago.

Regards, John

William S. Hare (W3RZT)   March 11, 1954

Dear Mr. Hare:

If you'll do some more looking up on that mass-5 isotope, you'll discover it has a half-life of something like 10 -23seconds. **Isaac Asimov**
computed that if all the mass in the universe were that mass-5 matter, it would be down to one last atom in 10 -19seconds.

Offhand, I'd call it non-existent.

Sincerly, John W. Campbell, Jr.

Isaac Asimov   March 12, 1954

Dear Sceptic:

Wurra wurra. I can't make you believe I'm not kidding which I'm not, and that there are a lot of things we don't know, and won't know until we acknowledge that we don't know.

157

The peculiar feature of the American culture is that an American can work happily at a job he knows is (a) essentially obsolete, and (b) is a job that shouldn't be done anyway, and that, furthermore (c) is a damned tough job. For instance, a production engineer working on the layout for the 1955 model Super Whatzis automoblie is having a hell of a time getting the clutch assembly sub-line to tie in properly with the transmission assembly line. He's talking over his troubles with his friends at lunch. But one of them is from Research, and he's discussing the problem of the 1957 model, which has no clutch, and explaining they've eliminated the clutch because of its cost, its tendency to failure, and its inefficiency mechanically.

After lunch he goes back to struggling with the problem of making a unit that is not good, shouldn't be there, causes trouble, and unnecessary expense.

How can he take satisfaction in that?

How can living cells dedicate themselves to being a placenta, which has no future, isn't necessary, is a wrong way to live on Earth, and will kill the baby if it isn't discarded?

The Mathematics we have is the language of science. And, as I think I remarked a while back, "Itchy-kitchy-goo" is the language of baby-talk, too. The question is, is it a good-for-the-purpose language?

If Science is considered to exist only where mathematics can be used, then the limitations of mathematics would tend to limit science. And mathematics is limited.

If science is confined within the bounds of logic — and logic is limited — then Science can't advance unless logic is expanded.

I consider modern mathematics to be a special case of a more general phenomenon. The business of 2ft x 3ft x 0ft was to bring out the point that multiplying by zero does not reduce the real-quantity system to zero — it reduces it by one dimension only. That, then, multiplying by zero has a limited, not an unlimited-destructive-of-all-value, effect. What happens if you have a system which gives you $(a-c)(x^2-3x+18) = b$ under the circumstances that $a = c$, so that $a-c = 0$? Why, says the mathematician, in that case b must be zero.

Oh — yeah? Maybe it means that b is no longer a function of x^2, but is now a function of x, and that saying it is zero is a serious error.

Take a relativity formula; it talks in terms of v and c, and does not

158

specify units. How, then, can you properly divide out, or multiply out, the units in the problem? In my 2ft x 3ft x 0ft I stated the "ft" units, so you could see that the units were essential to correct solution of the problem.

Let's take the relativity expressions, and consider what happens when v = c. Length goes to zero, mass goes to infinity, etc. Everything goes to one of the absolute values, either zero or infinity.

Hmmmm — but having read Cantor's work a bit, I know that infinity isn't infinity. I know that there is an infinite number of real numbers between 0 and 1, for instance, so I can properly say, "Yes, I see the formula goes to infinity. But . . . er, which infinity, Dr. Einstein? One is infinity, so maybe the mass goes to 1.000, huh?

I'm not kidding, Isaac. We don't have an adequate mathematics. We don't have an adequate logic. Human progress has been made in those areas where units have been supplied by, or forced on us by, Nature. Reason: Logic cannot consider its own postulates. A unit is, in effect, a postulate. Every postulate must be derived by a non-logical process, wherefore, necessarily, all logic is founded on non-logic!

The Greeks were quite right in holding that experimental proceedures were not logical; they aren't. There'e nothing logical about taking the unit "one atom"; it's pure engineering-pragmatism. However logical your arguments may be from that "Given: — " the source of the postulate-unit-axiom is non-logical.

All our logic, all our math, falls flat on its face when presented with a problem of such a nature that the answer is the necessary starting point — a problem wherein the conclusion-data is necessary for solving the problem. This is the general nature of a distribution problem, or a distributed-quantity problem. The exact position of the planets is necessary data for calculating their gravitational influence on each other, but the gravitational influence of one on the other is necessary data for calculating the exact position of the planets.

Math at present seeks to solve that by infinite series approximation. For a simple system containing only about 10 major elements, like the Solar system, the method works in a half-ass fashion. (I asked Richardson, though, if long-term cumulative energy and momentum transfers among the planets could cause the Earth's orbit, over a period of a million or ten million years to vary by 0.1 A.U. He said no one has ever tried to solve the planetary orbit problem for such a period; the an-

159

swer is totally unknown. But that might very well be the answer to what causes Ice Ages.)

However, in a somewhat more complex system, one involving even a medium-small number like 10,000 units, the method is hopeless. That's why you can't solve the behavior of a protein molecule that contains maybe 50,000 atoms, and why economics, sociology, psychology, and all the distributed-value fields are hopelessly bogged down.

What would an old-line geometer say if a man had come to him and started off with, "At the intersection of these parallel lines, the value of . . .."

What is this man talking about? Parallel lines can't intersect, or they aren't parallel . . . !

Not in the special-case geometry of Euclid. But in a more general geometry . . . Ah! That's different.

The whole point I'm making is that if mathematics is the only language of science, and mathematics is incapable of handling certain classes of scientific problems -- tsktsk! Then clearly, these problems are not scientific problems; they're pure mysticism and misunderstanding and not "real" at all.

I'm working on a hyper-space radio, Isaac. And I'm NOT kidding. It can't be done within the framework of a mathematical logic that can't distinguish between one infinity and another, between one zero and another.

Do you see that my question,"Which infinity, Dr. Einstein?" is a perfectly valid question?

The three Absolute Values of mathematics are 0, 1, and Infinity. So far we've tried a logic-system based on 0 and 1 — but never worked infinity into it. The buisness of n-valued logic, where n is any real, finite number, remains essentially similar to Aristotelean logic, and is transposable into a binary logic system, just as a decimal number can always be transposed to binary.

But you can't transpose a transfinite system to a finite system. Any area can be defined in terms of another area — but you cannot define a volume in terms of areas.

You know what the decimal multiplication-truth-table looks like, and what a decimal addition-truth-table looks like. But try this one on for size!
160

Let Q represent our number-base — and Q is a transfinite.
Then:

$$0 \times Q = 1 \qquad\qquad 1 \& Q = Q$$
$$1 \times Q = Q \qquad\qquad 2 \& Q = Q$$
$$2 \times Q = Q \qquad\qquad n \& Q = Q$$
$$n \times Q = Q \qquad\qquad Q \& Q = Q$$
$$Q \times Q = P \qquad\qquad Q \& P = P$$
$$0 \times P = Q$$

Lets see you transpose that into a n-valued number-base system.

Now please to kindly note something odd. Our base above, Q, was defined as transfinite. The peculiar thing is it acts remarkably like the non-mathamatical concept "quality." No matter how many tables you destroy, the quality of "tableness" remains undiminished. And no matter how many tables you add, the quality "tableness" remains unchanged — it's still Q.

Isaac, I'm not being silly, and I'm not kidding, and I'm not off my rocker; I'm simply saying, "We have more to learn; what we know is true — but is a limited case, a small segment, of the totality."

"Life as we know it" can exist only on Earth. Why? Because Earth is part of the system of "life as we know it." Terrestrial life represents a special case solution of the problem "How to Live." If Man goes to Mars, he has to change himself, or Mars, or both. I.e., he has to build a space-suit onto "himself," or give Mars a terrestrial-type atmosphere, or build a pressurized dome.

If Man spreads out through the Solar System, using technologies to make other planets habitable, he'll be in the peculiar spot that a barbaric culture cannot exist anywhere save on Earth — so any decline in the technological level of the culture means extermination of the colony-worlds.

We have an immense technology at the genetic level — as you, who have tried to unravel some of the simplest examples of the immensely complex chemical engineering involved, should know — but that technology is adapted solely to Earth conditions. A barbaric culture depends on the genetic technologies for life; it can exist only where the genetic technologies match the environment. That is — for Man — on Earth.

To spread out, Man must solve the general problems, and not the special-case problems alone. And on that, we stink out loud. We're so
161

damned specialized in any and all levels of the life sciences that we're utterly helpless under the slightest variations. Imagine being so limited that we can't metabolize a simple molecule like strychnine into a non-toxic condition!

And being so damned specialized that we can't solve the general problem of human sociology well enough to be able to handle the minute variations that exist between our own cultural variations, so that we have wars!

Nuts! We're so wrapped up in special-case solutions that we consider anything at a different level — either microcosmic or macrocosmic, as being out of our range and non-important. If it's multiplied either by infinity or zero, we consider it meaningless.

Try getting the janitor at Boston University interested in the fact that extragalactic nebulae show, for some unimaginable reason, streaking that suggest viscosity on a macrocosmic scale.

He's too busy with special-case solutions to consider that some of the macrocosmic factors have some meaning in his daily life.

Especially, of course, if you can't show him how it means direct economic reward.

Regards, John

Isaac Asimov   April 3, 1954

Dear Isaac:

I have such a nice line . . . and I can't use it dammit.

See if you can't work this one into one of your stories somewhere; it is damned easy to have the situation occur in almost any science-fiction yarn!

"Look, if you think Martians are so damned good . . . tell me this; Would you want your daughter to marry a Martian?"

"No,sir! No more than I'd want her to marry a Woman!"

The line's based on our analysis of logic, and its failings. Our culture is based on the proposition Any Problem Can Be Solved By Logic.

It's a real good idea . . . but it won't work. It would work, if we had omniscience. But we don't, and won't, so it won't work.

Now in a logical system, things cannot be equal-but-different. In a logic system, If x equals y, then x and y must be identical-in-value. And
162

that means identical.

In our culture, forced into the strait-jacket that everything has to be logical, there is no way to express "different" without saying "superior" or "inferior." Thus the Southerner cannot say, "Negros are different," without saying either, "They are superior" or "They are inferior."

It happens that Negros, on the average, are superior musicians, and inferior executive-organizers. They're different-but-equal in a lot of ways. But that isn't expressible in a logic-system!

The line I gave you up there is simply throwing at the race-prejudice fanatic a problem precisely equivalent to the one he's presented. Of course the deep instincts recognize the difference between Negros and Whites — or Martians. But watch the pre-logic-training children; they aren't unaware of the white-negro difference, but they play together happily. By throwing the race-fanatic that trick curve, you're forcing his instincts that recognize the difference between male and female into the spot of having to recognize that difference does not have to mean inequality!

The race-fanatic has a nice, pre-established response to the whole system of arguments about race. But he's never been attacked with that little hookey, and has no pre-established training. Also, you're throwing him one in which he can't possibly work his logic-training that different-means-inferior, and only-identicals-are-equal. How the hell can he hold that a woman is inferior to a woman?

Of course, the line doesn't solve anything — but it can start a process of frantic thinking that may lead to something worthwhile.

Regards, John

Isaac Asimov   April 10, 1954

Dear Isaac:

I'm much interested in that protein isomerism item — it is damned interesting. The utter futility of trying to express the magnitude of 10 to the 600th or so is very beautifully brought out.

The interesting thing is that there's one item every human being is directly familiar with that actually represents a number that might be expressed, roughly, as n600, where n is your haemoglobin isomerism possibility number. It's so big that it makes that poor little piddlin' haemo-

163

globin isomerism number a first-order approximation to zero. And it's something every one of us is in intimate, common contact with.

It's the number of possible interpretations possible, by combination and permutation, of the experiences of normal day's living.

You see, the number of "bits" of information reaching the brain via the eyes is of the order of 20,000,000 per second. The ears supply more; nose, skin, and internal sensory systems supply more. There are 3600 seconds per hour, and even a very young child is awake 10 hours a day. That means 20,000,000 times 36,000 bits of information per day from the eyes alone.

Hah! And you thought haemoglobin isomerism yielded a big number! Why, you don't even need an exponential exponent to express that.

However, I would be interested in a piece or protein isomerism, and the possibility of data-storage capacity in that punched-protein-molecule concept as an explanation of memory.

By the way, here's something to kick around:

To Prove: That logic is logically neither necessary nor sufficient for a conscious entity.

1. An Entity having total data, total omniscience, by definition knows (has in memory) already the answer to every possible problem.

2. Such an Entity does not need logic to solve any possible problem, since, by definition, it already has the answer in hand.

3. But Logic cannot function without data and postulates.

4. Logic cannot generate data.

5. Logic cannot generate postulates; the axioms of any logic-argument are derived by a non-logical process called "intuitively."

6. Logic can solve any possible problem, provided all the necessary data and all necessary and proper postulates (i.e. rules for manipulating the data) are made available.

But this means that Logic is not necessary to an Omniscient Entity, nor sufficient for a non-omniscient entity.

Therefore Logic is neither necessary nor sufficient, because it is fully useable only to an Omniscient Entity (one having all the necessary data), and such an Entity doesn't need it.

If you think that's just playing with words, you're mistaken. It's absolutely valid. The answer is that Logic is neither necessary nor sufficient — but is useful. It cannot replace data, but can expand the effectiveness

164

of a limited data supply.

One of the big troubles is that our Society is unshakably convinced that Logic Can Do Anything And Everything.

And so it can . . . if you're Omniscient. But if you're Omniscient, you don't need it.

There is another very neat and simple logical argument which demonstrates that democratic government logically leads to hydrogen bombs and biological warfare — in a Logic-Punishment cultural system. Ours is. Reason: In a Logic-Punishment cultural system, when group A cannot convince group B by logical argument, their cultural orientation says, "The B's must be taught a lesson; they must be punished."

Since no logic yet known to Man can derive a postulate, or analyze the nature of the postulate-generating system (we just call it "intuitive" and let it go at that), if group A works on one postulate system, and group B works on a different postulate system, no possible logical argument technique can achieve agreement.

In an Aristocracy or Oligarchy, there is a small group of individuals who determine the action-policy of the government. In a Logic-Punishment cultural system, the A-group will attack the B-group and punish this small group until they give up their postulate system in apathy and despair, and accept the A-group's postulate system.

But in a democracy, the executive government does not determine fundamental policy; they cannot be punished into conforming with the A-group's desire. It's necessary to punish (the Logic-Punishment cultural system holds) the policy-making group. In a democracy, that is the civilian population.

Therefore, logically, when 150,000,000 people are the policy-making group, a punishment-technique capable of driving a population-mass of that magnitude into apathy must be applied.

See? It's as simple as that. Perfectly logical. Insane, of course — *perfectly logic*al. It takes hydrogen bombs and bio*logic*al warfare to fulfill the logically-described requirements.

And as long as we operate on a Logic-Punishment system, it's a neatly inescapable trap.

If there is no fundamental change — a totally different philosophy — introduced, the tensions possible will build up steadily, due to the inherent impossibility of making different logic-postulate systems mesh by logical means. The negative pressure of the recognition that hydrogen bomb warfare means the end of this civilization will sustain the system for a certain period. Eventually, however, that will be insufficient, and full-scale population-punishment will break out.

If you think I'm a damn fool — my boy, just check my record for dead-center hits on major prophecy. Take a look at my book, The Atomic Story, on pages 240 thru 242. This week's Time discussion of the technology of the lithium hydride bomb could have been taken directly from it. This civilization is One Dead Duck. There is absolutely no foreseeable way of escaping that.

The only thing is — we have a choice of disposing of the damned thing before it goes bang, of hanging on to it, and going bang with it.

There is, so far as I can see, one, and just one, way to get out of the corner we've built ourselves into. We've got to drop the past fundamental concepts of our culture — that logic and punishment are necessary and sufficient — and, in fact, the Only Possible Way.

We have a problem to solve. We're hitched onto a lithium hydride time-bomb, and the detonator is ticking quite noticeably. We have to solve the problem before it lets go.

The problem: Solve the process-nature of what we've been blithely calling "intuition."

Logic cannot generate postulates, and cannot analyze or alter them.

If you acknowledge that there is no effect without an underlying process — then the observed "effect" that human beings do generate postulates clearly demonstrates that there is a process of thinking that is hyper-logical.

That hyper-logical process is the only thing that can disarm the detonator.

BUT... THAT PROCESS CAN BE FOUND. All that we need do is get a major group of **major** minds to acknowledge that it can be done, and must be done, whatever it costs in terms of pride, personal prejudice, and retraction of Absolute Certainties.

It means developing techniques by which the fundamental structure of religious, cultural, social, political, and personal beliefs can be laid open, inspected, taken apart, and put together differently.

It's an extremely hateful task. The entity you know as "I" will necessarily be altered into an entity you-now would not conceivably accept.

That's why it's been so appallingly difficult to work through this problem.

Of course, it has advantages beyond the escape from the H-bomb corner; it leads directly to interstellar ships, anti-gravity, and psionic functions, as well as personal immortality to the degree the individual chooses.

The job Peg and I have been working at for five years is precisely that job. When I say it means alteration of the "I" to something utterly unacceptable, I am not kidding, or speaking off the top of my hat. I've been there, and I know from direct experience; I am now working with and benefiting from concepts that were deeply abhorrent, utterly unacceptable, to me as little as a year ago. I know I have a long way to go. My greatest difficulty — the thing that's holding me back terrifically — is my inability to give up logical thinking. Currently, my consciousness is operating at the level of logic, and I am not, therefore, conscious of the processes involved in intuitive thinking. However, I've nibbled enough at the border to know that it can be crossed — and I also know that it is inescapably necessary that it be crossed.

That's why I've been attacking this business of hyper-rational thought processes, transfinite logic structures, and the like.

The problem can be solved; I think it can be cracked open within 12 months. That doesn't mean it'll be solved — it means that the first essential breaks will be achieved.

It's taken many men many lifetimes to develop the possibilities that were inherent in the logical process. It'll take another set of lifetimes to work out transfinite logic after it's once cracked.

But cracking it will produce an escape valve that will, immediately, relieve the unbearable pressure of tensions building under our present Logic-Punishment cultural pattern. It will open Hope. The logic-punishment tensions explode when apathy sets in — when one group or the other decides that the situation is hopeless, that there is not, and never will be, any way to escape from the increasing tension of discord.

If so much as one solid demonstration of a useable non-logical, hyper-rational technique could be made at that point, although no actual improvement in the real-world situation resulted, it would introduce Hope, and allow further time for widening the breach in the Logic-Punishment system.

167

One of the great apathy-inducers now extant is the fact that no one has ever been able to clearly define the causes of war — and hence no definition of what problem had to be attacked has been available.

I think we can define it today; We Must solve the problem of the processes of intuition. That requires, first, that we clearly acknowledge that there are processes, and that they are definable.

One thing we can be very, very certain of; neither punishment, nor threat of punishment, can serve. Seven thousand years of recorded history shows that threat of retaliation never long held off war, nor did threat of punishment stop horse-stealing, murder, or thievery. It's rather **essential tha**t *we observe closely the motto "Abandon all Hope ye who enter here!" clearly* inscribed over that path to "security." It's been there for at least the last 15 human empires.

But the queer thing is that the empires of Man have repeatedly charged through that doorway — rather than the other one, labelled "Abandon all Unshakeable Convictions, ye who enter here!"

That's the door that is not hopeless; it's just very much harder to get through. Believe me, guy — it's an indescribably horrible experience to abandon a life-long belief, and find yourself faced with the knowledge that you don't know, haven't known, and can't see any way of finding out what true good sense in an area of life is. It's no damn wonder nobody chooses that door!

But this time, like it or not, we have to.

Regards, John

Isaac Asimov   June 7, 1954

Dear Isaac:

Your help on this problem would be appreciated. I write you, because you are aware of the Jewish heritage, and are also a genuine philosopher, as well as, to use an obsolescent term, a learned man.

As you know, I've been trying to work out what it was that caused the following facts:

1. Only cultures having Semitic traditions have ever been able to learn and use science.

2. Islam, a Semitic culture, was the only one of all Man's cultures, that ever invented it.

168

3. Yet the Jews themselves did not invent it.

4. And Islam, after inventing it, couldn't, for some reason, hold on to it. They went down hill.

I've already suggested that monotheism appears to be the only factor. Monotheism had been imposed on peoples before; one of the early Pharaohs imposed a monotheism based on Ra — as long as he reigned. But the Jews were the first people to accept monotheism.

Now the Old Testament Yahweh concept seems to me remarkably akin, in description of characteristics, to the Laws of the Universe. The laws of nature are implacable, inescapable, and utterly unarguable. It makes not one iota of difference what your opinion is; the laws of nature are, and that isn't open to opinion.

The Yahweh concept holds "Thou shalt have no other Gods before me," and, "The Lord Thy God is a Jealous God," and, "'Vengeance is Mine,' saith Yahweh." Put "opinions" in place of "Gods" in the first statement, and it fits most exceedingly, and uncomfortably, the facts of the Universe.

The essential characteristic of Science is that it is harsh, implacable, absolutistic, and ultimately dogmatic. You don't have the slightest chance of making your opinion get anywhere at all. And if there is anything a human being hates with violence fervor and zeal, it's the proposition that he has no right to his own opinion. Getting a whole people to accept that proposition is really quite a feat!

For the fun of it, I checked with 9-year-old **Leslyn**. She thinks that the law of gravity is "unfair." She also thinks it is "unfair" that she can't walk through walls. That simply means that she resents the limitations; at her age, that which she resents is "unfair."

Now the Greeks were in a different spot. Put in modern slangy terms, it might be put this way: "Zeus is mad at you? Ahhhh — so what? Get wise, kid! Come on over to Poseidon's temple; he's mad at Zeus anyway, and if you just slip him a nice offering, he'll fix the rap for you easy. You don't have to worry about Zeus; I can get Poseidon to quash the case easy!"

The Law doesn't mean much, under that philosophy.

And Science, that Law That Can't Be Broken, isn't going to be popular. It'll raise as much of a stink as the howl that went up when they first introduced the triplicate-form unfixable traffic ticket.

169

It's necessary, evidently, to have a people that does admit compulsions exist before Science can get started.

But somewhere, the Jews themselves slipped up; they didn't invent science, although they had all the necessary elements.

Possible answer (and this is what I want you to check):

They didn't recognize the principles of forgiveness adequately, and didn't adequately distinguish between the Sacrifice and the Bribe-offering.

Now note that while the Law of Gravity is absolute and unbreakable — a rocket can climb 200 miles up, provided it pays the due and proper fee in energy. But the bargain is perfectly fair and just; it achieves Potential, in return for Effort, and the potential can be turned in for an exactly equal amount of energy at any time. In fact, the Law is so fair, you can't get rid of the potential without an exactly equal energy-value.

The terms of the bargain are not open to opinion any more than the fact of the laws are. But the terms are open to arbitration; you can get the energy back in the form of heat, mechanical work, and/or various other forms. (The falling rocket gets red-hot, fuses, and distorts itself and the landscape on landing.)

Now if you assume that the Law is not only unbreakable, but that Nothing Whatever Can Be Done About It, you will refuse to attempt any change, because change is futile anyway. The Law is Absolute, Implacable, and Inescapable.

Then you have the proposition that I Am What I Am, and I Can't Be Different. Furthermore, the Projection of that is that We Can't Be Different Either. It's hopeless. All you can do is get all you can out of an obdurate Universe, in any way you can.

But this imposes a static philosophy, and the philosophy that anything you can get must be properly yours, because the Universe is implacable and unbreakable, and if it wasn't your right, you couldn't get it.

This, I suspect, could lead to the acceptance of the Captivity — and the ghettos down the ages since — as the right and proper and natural consequence of the nature of the Universe. There's no use trying to work with the other people, because it's the nature of the Universe that you can't change, and he can't change, until God intervenes.

At the same time, the everything-is-either-ethically-proper-or-impossible corollary can lead to what looks decidedly unethical to other

170

peoples. Which hasn't increased the overall popularity of the Jewish people. Since the concept of the fair-and-equitable-bargain was not built into the philosophy, but, rather, a bribe-offering philosophy, a lot of heartache was built in — and, because the philosophy held that the Absolute was Unchangeable, that pain and heartache had to be accepted, because it was futile to seek to alter things.

Islam changed things a bit. They retained the Absolute, but introduced the proposition that, if you fight like hell, you can change it — but you've got to understand what it is you're trying to change.

That, of course, makes proselytizing a natural part of the philosophy — and proselytizing via the sword, of course.

Christianity differed radically; it held that you could change things — but not by fighting. It, too, opened up the avenue to proselytizing — but because it argued for non-violent proselytizing, and loving your enemy, it contained a philosophy that forced the missionary to learn a little something from his convert.

The complex results of those variations on the Monotheistic theme are still going on.

I have a hunch that the concept of the Hard Bargain, which, today, dominates the philosophy of the Near East, is responsible for the failure of the great Islamic Empire. Mohammed, remember, was a successful caravan trader before he became a religious leader. Jesus was a total failure as a business man.

And . . . you can't drive a hard bargain with the Universe. You may think the Universe is driving a cruelly hard bargain with you — but it is part of the bargain that you must understand the Universe's terms; the Universe doesn't have to understand yours.

A people's philosophy and their mythology are interacting, each shaping and expressing the other. The most successful peoples on the planet today are the Scotch-English and their descendants. The mythology of the Scotch-English centers around the brownie and fairies — the little folk who are friendly and helpful and hard workers . . . but God help the mortal who tries to cheat on the bargain he makes with them!

The Scotch are famous as engineers; the English have been called "a nation of tradesmen."

In summary: Does it sound right to you that the fundamental error in the great Jewish invention, Monotheism, is excessive absolutism?

171

Regards, John

John W. Campbell, Jr.   July 19 ,1954

Dear John,

Enclosed is the article, "Hemoglobin and the Universe," which deals with the isomerism of proteins. I think I've done it up brown while being sufficiently lucid to make things plain to most of the readers rather than just to the chemistry majors among them.

The article includes nine "Figures," most of which can be set up in type directly (although the typesetter will undoubtedly hate my guts.) A few of them are simple little drawings which I'm sure one of your artists can whomp up in India ink with no trouble.

In calculating the wordage I've tried to figure an extra 1500 words on the figures. This is just a guess. If you wish to revise the wordage either up or down on the basis of your own judgement as to the space that the article will take up (and I know that's what you pay for really — space), you are free to do so.

I hope you find the article satisfactory, John, I really do. Meanwhile, the next thing I tackle is a short story called "Risk" which will involve some of the notions you threw at me the last time I was in your office and which will be my first positronic robot story in five years. My typing fingers itch.

Yours, Isaac Asimov

Isaac Asimov   August 13, 1954

Dear Isaac:

The Second Edition arrived yesterday; haven't had a chance to read it, but it's a handsome looking job.

Reading bio-chem is not something I can handle in heavy doses, and enjoy it. So it'll take me a couple of weeks to get the differences.

This letter's primarily to acquaint you with some interesting data that's been showing up. "The Cold Equations" has recieved a hell of a reception; some are hotly mad, some are warmly enthusiastic — but none are coldly indifferent.

You know the old business about a novel being supposed to show the

172

development of a personality. Well there's a reverse English on that that an author can get away with . . . if he's good enough. That is to present an unacceptable character, and not change him, but make the reader change!

Godwin accepted the unacceptable proposition, "It is right and proper to sacrifice a young woman." That's been out of fashion, and highly unacceptable, since the Aztecs stopped sacrificing them 1000 years ago.

But you see, it's not wholly wrong! Godwin made the point; the reader is forced to agree that there is a place for human sacrifice.

We have another one coming that will, I think, lift some more hair on end. Polly and Kelly Freas read it when Kelly took it home to illustrate — and fought about it for a week. (That's the kind of yarn I like — the reader doesn't sigh, yawn, and turn the page to the next one.) (Should human beings be treated as animals held for breeding purposes? Answer: Yes! Under these circumstances. . . .)

Poul Anderson has a character in his new novel that will stir some discussion too. She introduces herself to the hero — Langley, 21st century American, irrevocably time-displaced to 72nd century culture of aristocrat-commoner-slave — by saying, "I'm Marin. I'm a Class Eight slave. I'm 20 years old, a virgin, and Soandso bought me from the Xxx Breeding and Training center to give to you."

Marin has been selected and slightly altered by plastic surgery 'till she's a physical duplicate of Langley's time-lost beloved wife. When he first sees her, it throws him into a tizzie, naturally — because she's the living, walking image of his lost beloved.

But — his wife was never a slave, and never accepted a slave philosophy. Marin is — and Anderson presents the fact with the brutal directness implicit in her introduction. Later Langely asks why Soandso gave her to him. Does he expect Langley to be overcome with gratitude?

"Oh, I don't think so," Marin says, "I'm not a very expensive present."

Langley is presented with the damndest emotional snarl you ever heard of — and, therefore, the reader is too. He's feeling bitter and upset, and says to her. "All right — you're mine. That means anything goes?"

She says "Yes, sir." But he can see that she knows, of course, that there are perverted and sadistic buyers — and is facing up to that possibility.

He can return her, sell her, give her away, free her, possess her, or kill her. She's his as much as a radio set would be.

But — she's the girl who looks exactly like his beloved wife. He can't sell her . . . because he can't face the fact that there are sadistic buyers. He can't give her away or return her for the same reason. Free her? She's a highly bred, highly educated, thoughtful young woman. The Class Eight slaves are bred and trained as concubine-companions for the high-level aristocrats — and they're high-level people. Freed, she has the choice of being a commoner's wife, a servant, or a prostitute — and no chance of meeting the kind of people whom she is bred and trained to enjoy and understand. Freeing her would be a cruel punishment, without just cause, based on his fanatic insistance of no-slavery.

His orientation and conditioning make possessing her unacceptable.

The most practical solution would be to kill her; it would save him a lot of trouble. That is, it's practical logically!

Naturally he's a sucker for her; she is practically identical to his lost wife. BUT . . . he can't accept her acceptance-of-being-a-slave. He can't love her, because he can't win her love; it was given to him by her buyer, and conditioning she was given at the training center.

Marin's prize line is, in effect, "Yes, I have been conditioned to accept my owner. It is my function in life. But every woman's function is to want a man, and love him. And aren't we all conditioned — you, I, everyone? You were conditioned haphazardly by life; my conditioning was thoughtfully planned — but we're all conditioned."

What Poul''s done is to use his anthropological background to present something you damned seldom get a chance to look at; the fact that a highly intelligent human being can rationally accept being a slave. Aesop, you know, was a slave.

And it takes courage — real guts — to accept slavery. To be a slave is a passive thing, and takes nothing beyond physical existence. But to accept slavery takes high courage — as Marin displayed in her answer to Langley's "That means anything goes?" The free man can run out if he doesn't like the job ahead; one who has accepted slavery knows he can't — knows he's accepted the risk and the tough spots. Acceptance of slavery means accepting the risk of the sadistic buyer — precisely as accepting Life means accepting Death, too.

I've been looking at some of the possible interpretations of history in

174

the light of what Anderson presented there. Ever try to define what "slave" means? Very difficult, it turns out.

Consider this: I propose that high-level culture can result only from a race that has accepted slavery — being slaves!

The Amerindians, you know, could not be enslaved; they died.

Now there is a curious thing; the parasite host relationship appears to be rather like the master-slave relationship. But . . . symbiosis merges without break into parasite-host relationship. And true cooperation is mutual slavery!

Who's the slave? A child appears to fulfill the legal definition of a slave. I can, by will, give my children away, as I would a slave. They must obey my commands, and if they do not I am legally permitted to — and socially expected to — apply corporal punishment. They're slaves, aren't they?

No; I'm the slave. I am legally required to support them in idleness by the sweat of my brow.

Well, maybe Peg's the slave, then? She has to wash and clean and mend and care for my house.

But no, I'm the slave. I'm legally required to support her.

Who's the slave?

We all are! But it's symbiosis — not parasite-host relationship we're looking at. It's slavery with 100% negative feedback, so that cause and effect are inherently indistinguishable.

But you see, only a people who can accept slavery, and has the courage to stand up and say — and mean — "for richer, for poorer, for better, for worse, in sickness and in health. . . ." and knowingly accept the risk of the sadistic partner, the good with the bad — only such a people can establish true cooperation.

The courage of the free man has long been sung.

Maybe . . . could be perhaps . . . it's been somewhat over-rated? Maybe it's the courage of the egomaniac? The courage of the irresponsible?

It doesn't, of course, take anything but existence to be a slave.

How many people have the courage to accept in full the consequences of slavery, though?

Stories in there, possibly?

Regards, John

P.S. Langley finally gets some understanding of the meaning of conditioning. He marries her.

Isaac Asimov   August 16, 1954

Dear Isaac:
Herewith a group of releases on your stories of previous years. We're going to try to end the miserable, friction-inducing situation of "Who's got a right to what?" by the simple, if laborious, technique of releasing all but serial rights to all the stories.
Henceforth, sir — they're yours!
As you can see, it's a monumental task! After all, old man, you've been writing for us for fifteen years now. (and I, Junior, am starting my 18th year here. In a rut, aren't we!)
Regards, John W. Campbell, Jr., Editor
cc:**Mr. Lawler**

Donald Michie   August 19, 1954

Dear Mr. Michie:
While I enjoyed your paper, I'm afraid I must return it.
The thiotimoline joke is one that we can use only very rarely; like any joke, too much irritates.
Asimov's last item was actually delivered as a lecture to the M.I.T. chemistry society.
Sincerely, JOHN W. CAMPBELL, JR. Editor
Enc.: "Advance in Enochronics"

Isaac Asimov   August 19, 1954

Dear Isaac:
Sorry — as the Pennsylvania Dutch say, "It does not make."
You've got sound basic ideas in your presentation techniques here, but you haven't quite got them whipped into shape.
176

The most effective kind of story is one in which there is either or both of the strong pressures of a strong situation, or a strong personality — and the "both" is, of course, the best, if you can manage it.

In this, the strong situation is having to get into that ship again. You've tried to make Susan Calvin your strong personality. In each you've failed just a little bit.

The strong situation is one that's simple, stark, and acutely understandable. The fear of approaching the H-bomb is easily understood — the reason for it doesn't have to be described; merely mentioning approaching it makes the reader do 99.99% of the reacting automatically.

The hypership trip isn't that way — for a science-fiction reader! We've accepted that hypertrip situations are accept<u>able</u>, and not things of inherent horror — as H-bomb devestation is.

I got a suggestion, though. Rats and mice and guinea pigs may live O.K. when hyper-tripped — but what happens to their mental functions?

Reason for sending a positronic robot: it does approach the human on the level of having thought processes, which the rats, etc., do not have!

Suppose rats and mice come back alive, but somewhat dazed. But a chimp comes through utterly hysterical!

O.K. — so you can make the hypertrip and live, so far as metabolic processes go. But . . . a prefrontal lobotomy won't kill you, either. Neither will an animal be killed by decerebration. See? It's perfectly safe; we can guarantee that you'll come through able to live, eat and breath just as well as you do now. But — er — sorry, mabe you won't be able to think any more!

Now . . . want to make a hyper-trip?

Remember your story where the positronic brain had to figure out a hypership which involved the temporary but reversible death of the human occupants? First Law conflict, of course.

Now let's consider what happens when the positronic brain determines that the organism will not die — it'll just cease to have any mind! This doesn't conflict with the First Law, does it? Not the way it's been defined to the robot, it doesn't! Your "Liar!" Robot was the only one which would have appreciated that it does conflict with the First Law.

"Martians, Go Home!" by Fred Brown is coming up; you'll see it. The essence of the thing is that immaterial projections of little green men do nothing but kibitz, insult, and tattle — and everybody knows that "sticks and stones may break my bones, but names will never hurt me," don't they? So the immaterial Martians can't harm anybody, can they? Oh . . . yeah? Your "Liar!" robot would know better!

So; I think far greater strength in the situation would exist if the totally unacceptable nature of the consequences was directly and unarguably apparent to the reader. Here, you take time out to explain why Black doesn't want to go hyper-tripping.

Next item is making Dr. Calvin a strong personality. She has to explain herself — and brother, that never works. Don't try to tell me she's strong; show me!

One of the most effective ways of doing that is to have the strong character take a line of action that makes the reader consider him an egocentric or malevolent individual — and then develop the story so that the reader is inexorably forced to accept that course of action as the only sane, rational line of behavior, however distasteful it may be. A strong character is one who can accept decisively and early the unpleasant necessities that other characters arrive at only later and with vacillation.

Incidentally, nobody likes an altruist; he's a strong character who's arrived at a conclusion that you find involves highly unpleasant sacrifices.

The real reason for sending a man, not a robot, to fix that ship is somewhat different. And the real reason why Susan can't explain that reason is inherent in it!

A robot can do anything you've told it to do; it can act with logical process. But it **can't act intui**tively; *it can't think in a new method. Its method of thought was built i*n, and is inflexible. A man's method of thinking is not in**flexible** — if he's any good as a creative think*er, it has* to be flexible.

Black doesn't want to go — hell, nobody does. They want to send a robot. Now if Susan says, "Suppose the trouble turns out to be X?" Black can say, "Well, we can tell the robot. . . ."

So no matter what she menti**ons as the re**ason for sending a man, *once it's mentioned, it can be answered by a suitabl*e instruction to a robot. Her real argume*nt is, "Becaus*e of the reasons I can't think of!" Which is just **about** the most utterly illogical answer imaginable!

And that, of course, is precisely why it is the logical reason for not sending a logic-machine called a robot!

Regards, John
Enc.:"Risk"

C.R. **Venditto**   September 27, 1954

Dear Mr. Venditto:
I'm afraid I can't use your piece on **Dr. Asimov**. It's contrary to the tradition of Astounding to run discussions of the personality of an author. The author speaks through his stories only!
                    Sincerely, John W. Campbell, Jr., Editor
Enc.: "Biochemistry Prof. Doubles as SF Auth<u>or</u>"

Isaac Asimov   October 18, 1954

Dear Isaac:
Thanks for the copy of the Life Chemicals book; I've enjoyed looking it over, and spotting Isaac shining through the biochemistry. Like the item that catalase "goes to town" changing 5,000,000 H_2O_2 Molecules per minute per molecule.

I'm trying to get a report from the local Perfect Critic — Peedee, age 14, Freshman in High School. The difficulty is that if I recomend a book, naturally she simply couldn't like it. This phenomonon may not be clear to you yet — but wait another 10 years, my friend. Then you'll discover just how unutterably stupid and flatly unuseable any suggestion you make is. About that time your father will again shake his fis<u>t in</u> the air, laugh nastily and grate out ". . . and double Revenge!"

So I'm leaving the book around where it's most apt to be accidentally <u>stu</u>mbled across. That way I'm apt to get a comment.

I'll have Joe Winter do a review on it for ASF.

I've been interested in quartz recently; it's piezo-electric, you know, and the standard stuff for frequency control in radio work. Having a special application, I started looking up all the dope I could find on it. (The dope I wanted I can't find anywhere, of course.) Problem: An X-cut Quartz crystal plate oscillates in shear. This means the end edge of the plate slants back and forth during operations. But . . . how much? How many degrees, minutes and/or seconds per volt applied to, say, a 1mm quartz plate? Think you can get that data? Hah! Nobody wants to know

179

that. Index of refraction? Sure. Resonant frequency? Sure! How to cut a crystal? Absolutely. How much physical movement? Why! Nobody ever asks that question.

(Yeah, and nobody has the answer either, apparently!)

But I ran into some other interesting stuff, and something that could-be might interest you as a biochemist and speculative thinker.

Man evolved on this planet. He spent 3,000,000,000 years learning how to live on Planet Sol III. Most of the rocks of Sol III happen to be silicate rocks. The place is lousy with Si02. So . . . man turns up peculiarly susceptible to silicosis!

Now that sounds crazy. It's like man turning up allergic to water on a planet 3/4ths of which is water.

Futhermore, silica is peculiarly inert stuff anyway! Why, in God's name, should Man be bothered by something as inert as silica, which has been present for the last 600,000,000 years of his evolution, at least, and has even been used as a basic life-chemical in many diatoms?

Friend of mine once suggested, "Because it's piezo-electric, and body movements cause the quartz to generate electric currents that injure the surrounding cells."

Maybe. But I've got another hunch.

Quartz is optically active. The d- and l- crystals exist. The quartz molecules are strung in a helical structure, and have an hexagonal crystaline configuration. (So does ice). Query: What can't an adaptive, adaptable organism adapt to handle? Answer: Something that louses up the mechanism of adaptation itself!

If you have a self-repairing mechine, what kind of break-down can't it handle? Breakdown of the self-repair function, of course.

The recent work on nucleic acids as reported in Scientific American, indicates the gene structures are cross-braced helical structures. Now if helix meets helix, and one of 'em happens to be cross-braced as solidly, as rigidly and energetically, as is the quartz helix — and they happen to have a strongly similar atom-spacing — maybe there would be considerable hell to pay.

One thing is certain; quartz has a toxicity it damn well has no chemical business having. And that it has no biochemical business having, in organisms that evolved in a silicate-dusted atmosphere!

Regards, John

Frank C. Bennett (CHEMunications Editor)   October 18, 1954

Dear Mr. Bennett:

It happens that Dr. Asimov was in the office at the time your letter came in asking permission to republish his thiotimoline piece. On that you have his personal approval as well as ours.

Dr. Pomeroy sold us All Serial Rights on his piece, so I can release the rights on that also. If you will credit the source in the normal fashion, I think all parties will be well satisfied.

Sincerely, John W. Campbell, Jr., Editor

Isaac Asimov   October 22, 1954

Dear Isaac;

You Probably got the enclosed via your professional route; if not, it may interest you for itself anyway. But I'm sending it because I want you to do me an article on the subject, "You Have To Run That Fast Just To Stand Still," or something.

An article, in other words, on the dire and desperate need for some way of handling all the data that's being accumulated, of how a biochemist (or any other specialist) can keep up with what's happening in his own field, let alone what's happening in the office next door. An article on "We Know Too Much" — and understand too little.

Can do?

Regards, John W. Campbell, Jr., Editor

Isaac Asimov   November 30,1954

Dear Isaac;

I sincerely hope that your next offspring is female. If so, you will discover that there is, even in birth, differences that extend somewhat deeper than simply a slight modification of the plumbing attachments.

Now inasmuch as even this difference increases with time — the simple physical sex-differences are not fully present at birth, but develop later — it might be argued that the development of the breast in woman was a matter of education, not genetics. After all, boy babies and girl ba-

181

bies both have the basic structures, and medical records will show that occasionally boys do develop breasts — it's just a matter of education, no doubt, since the structures are not present at birth. That shows they can't be genetic, doesn't it?

You know, I bet a metallurgist could have himself a hell of a time trying to find how this piece of copper had been heat-treated and work-hardened to make it such a hard, elastic product. The 0.2% of beryllium present is just an accidental inclusion, of course — an impurity having no significance to the problem of the environmental treatment that produced this high-tensile high-elasticity product.

And of course, any chemist studying this strange material used in this curious electronic device, would recognize it as extremely high-purity germanium. Obviously, the producer had sought, and very nearly obtained, absolute purity — there's only about one part in a million of arsenic as an impurity present. But how that germanium — that pure germanium — was treated to make it show these strange characteristics . . . tsk tsk.

Then again, any top-rank organic chemist of 1890 would have known his techniques were good enough to analyze for the presence of any significant amount of an organic compound in a water solution. Let's give him a chance to spot the presence of one of the more effective hormones, shall we? They weren't using bio-assay methods much then, because they didn't trust organic detection techniques. One must be logical about these things, and living organisms can't be logically predicted. Too much variability due to environmental background.

Isaac . . . what constitutes "a significant difference"? One part in 10? 1 in 100? 1 in 10,000,000,000? What's the change in mass of material before and after a ton of TNT goes off? What's "a significant difference"?

If a missle is started toward Alpha Centauri, and it is launched on a course 0.00001 second of arc off dead-center . . . is that "a significant difference"?

If the oxygen tension in the mother's blood-stream deviates 5% below norm for a period of two hours during nine months of pregnancy, does that constitute a significant deviation? Ask any mongolian idiot you may meet.

The essence of the scientific method is NOT measurement, no matter what the textbooks say. It's essence is Absolute Curiosity — the willingness to investigate anything whatsoever, with no evaluative judgement whatsoever, until WHAT IS has been determined. Then and only then, can evaluative judgement of WHAT MEANING be studied.

It may appear that accepting the proposition that "Males and females do not think alike" would make life more complicated, more difficult to understand and solve. But it also appeared that accepting the idea of scores of different chemical elements would make life more complicated than the assumption of Four Elements did.

Occam's Razor — accept the theory requiring the fewest different entities — sounds reasonable and proper. But on that basis, we'd be stuck with four elements. And we'd be forced to agree with the paranoid's proposition, "Since all my difficulties can be explained away on the postulate 'There are evil forces opposed to me,' Occam's Razor makes it logically necessary that we accept that as the explanation — not the more complex theory that I, myself, have made multiple mistakes."

The old Golden Rule — a basic in half a dozen different religious philosophies — will work perfectly in an homogenous culture of homogenous individuals. It's based on the assumption that, "Individual A is an accurate analog of Individual B." In an homogenous culture of homogenous individuals — it works. But when the individuals are not analogs of each other — then it won't work.

How would you like to be locked up in a single building, with nothing but a cafeteria, a library, a thoroughly equipped chemical laboratory, and sleeping quarters for two weeks?

And how would Bill Blow, long-shoreman, IQ 85, like that situation? What's punishment? What's reward?

How would Hepsebah Slugg, age 24, IQ 80, like being given a job of putting cans of tomatoes in packing crates, making sure each can was put in with the label right side up, 8 hours a day, 5 days a week, with a 10-year contract to keep doing that and nothing else?

How would you like it — at a salary of, say, $1000 a month?

You know, Hank Kuttner had a complete breakdown while he was in the Army. He was in under "limited service" classification, due to broken-down arches. They had him filling out file cards in the infirmary, because he could type. He filled out and filed cards all day long for quite a few months.

Then somebody else filled out and filed a card on him.

There are jobs you and I and people like us are incapable of handling. It takes a moron to do them — and thank God we have sound, useful, dependable morons to do those things you and I can't achieve.

Regards, John

Gotthard Gunther   December 14, 1954

Dear Gottard:

I gather you've been extremely busy. Having just gotten an article from Isaac Asimov on the research problem involved in a textbook, I can get some idea of what you're plowing into. I never went in for that myself; I write things I don't have to do research on! That's the beauty of fiction — none of it's true anyhow, so how could anyone say I'd made a mistake?

We've been working again on the problem of the relationship of magic to mankind and to science. I think I can, now, develop a pretty firm argument that the Scientific method has about reached the end of its practicable development. As follows:

1. It's generally agreed that you can (in principle) solve any problem by sheer doing enough things. Pure trial and error, entirely without thought. But while the method is inherently unlimited in theory, we aren't. The method would work, given infinite time, and infinite numbers of trials. But we have neither the time, nor the raw materials.

2. Also, theoretically, you can solve any problem by simply guessing, and then trying the guess. This differs from pure trial and error in that guessing implies a memory or previous trials, and elimination of repetition — pure random trial-and-error does not have that feature. This added feature increases the probability of finding an answer in a given finite time.

3. Theoretically, any problem can be solved by the method of data, logic, and experiment — the scientific method. Since this involves a calculation of probabilities as well as memory of past trials, it greatly increases the probability of achieving a solution in a given, finite number of trials.

4. But while each of these methods is theoretically, inherently unlimited — we are not. Even though the scientific method is inherently un-

184

limited — that doesn't mean that Man-using-Science-alone is unlimited.

Human beings hate to be put in the spot of not having any idea of how to tackle the problem that must be solved. Lack of a method of attack is the most nerve-wracking experience Men have to face. Therefore, it is only with frantic reluctance that Men will acknowledge that their presently available methods are all inadequate to a task that must be done.

If two individuals (or nations) have a dispute over a procedure, A says, "B, your method of handling the problem will not work because it damages me!" and B says, "A, your method won't work because it damages me!" each is forcing the other to recognize that the available method on hand is inadequate. Normally, instead of acknowledging this fact, and getting to work to find a new method which solves the problem for both — they retreat to an older method. When the fight is over, the winner proves that the loser was the aggressor and in the wrong. Neither side is willing to face the problem of not knowing how to solve the problem — and solving that problem!

There is the greatest imaginable reluctance on the part of human beings to abandon a method of problem-solving.

Currently, the scientific method is bogging down more and more hopelessly in sheer quantity of data. It's like the dinosaurs, who sought to solve the problem of living by being born with all the answers necessary to all the problems to be encountered. The method worked for a while, but gradually the number of problems became so great that the method broke down — then the mammals, who didn't start with all the answers, but did have the ability to learn as individuals, took over.

Now actually, I suspect we've reached the end of mammalian evolution. The mammalian system involves a certain amount of genetic data to start with, then the process of learning by the pain-pleasure system (which involves logic, incidentally). But somewhere along this line of development, you reach the point where the individual can't learn enough either.

We've reached it. We can't learn, in a lifetime, enough data to understand what's going on in the world around us. And consequently we're rapidly loosing control of ourselves and our environment. Not at the physical level; that we can handle. But at the mental level.

The pain-pleasure system, incidentally, is strictly mammalian, I now

185

strongly suspect. I can make a machine that will show a withdrawal response to any approaching object; that's no trick. The opposite — the machine that shows an approach response to the detection of an object is known as a homing missile. The machine that shows a high-irritability response to the approach of an object is known as a proximity-fuse shell. Their actions are non-purposive. BUT — they have opinions.

Now, here's what I mean! A homeostat is any type of machine that tends to act to maintain a pre-set condition. A thermostat, for example, attached to an air conditioning plant.

A homeostat has an opinion. It holds that a certain set of relationships with respect to a certain phenomenon is the optimum relationship. The thermostat alone is an opinion; an opinion alone can do nothing — it has to be used as a sensing device to control some action-capable mechanism. But an action-capable mechanism is useless without an opinion to use as a sensory system.

The essence of the homing missiles, etc., is that they have built-in opinions, and the opinions are connected to action-capable mechanisms.

This requires (1) an opinion, (2) a sensing system that compares WHAT IS with THE OPINION and detects difference, and (2) an action-device capable of changing WHAT IS with respect to THE OPINION to reduce the difference, however that may be done.

Note that the human proposition, "This is the best of all possible worlds!," reduces the difference between Opinion and Situation to zero — by adjusting Opinion to match What Is. This is the "shallow optimism" reaction.

Now it's necessary to have a difference-signal reaching the action-capable mechanism if something is to be done. But if we install the proposition, "This is a terrible world . . . but there's nothing Man can do about it," this is equivalent to short-circuiting out the difference signal. We ground it out, so that it doesn't cause the action-capable mechanism to react.

That is a sort of "shallow pessimism" reaction. Both the "shallow optimism" and the "shallow pessimism" reactions allow the individual to slump back on his tail and just sit. I might call the latter the French Reaction; the situation is hopeless, so why disturb oneself? Take what little one can contrive to grab, for after me, the deluge.

Anyhow, the reptiles seem to me to be purely homeostat machines of
186

ludicrous complexity. I seriously doubt the reptiles actually feel what we call "pain"; their homeostat mechanisms are, like Asimov's robots, designed to prevent damage to the machine itself, and to minimize damage when it does occur. I can build a thermostat mechanism into the bearings of a machine that will cause a siren to wail if the bearing heats beyond a point determined to be undesirable. Now we have a machine that cries out when its integrity is threatened; shall we say it "feels pain, and cries with the hurt"?

A self-adjusting machine, such as one of the standard servo units, will respond to imbalance by taking such action as will restore balance. Does it feel "upset", and "hunger" for balance? It's non-purposive, however purposive its actions appears.

Somewhere along the line, Purpose does enter the picture. We are purposive — but no one has yet been able to define purposiveness! I suspect it cuts in at the point where prediction becomes a real function — where response is on a basis of what will be rather than what is.

Now a race as such might develop purposive capabilities before any individual of that race did. This is a cockeyed sort of concept in present logical-accepted terms. It implies — hell, it states! . . . that a race is an entity. I think it is.

Mankind, to date, has not been able to work out any understanding of the individual-to-group relationship. This means we don't know what "group" means, and have no idea what the capabilities and characteristics of a group are. I am willing to subscribe to Jung's concept of the Group Unconscious — even if I don't agree with him as to exactly what it is, or how it works. But the fundamental proposition I do think has merit. And I think it's long been known as God.

God's great limitation is, however, that, like the individual's mind, there's need for a physical action-capable mechanism to make any opinion effective! If I don't have a body made up of individual muscle, bone, tendon, etc; m cells available, it makes no difference what my ideas are — they ain't gonna do a damn thing!

And if those individual body-cells aren't in a mood to cooperate — I'm not going to get much done either.

The mammalian system of learning through pain and pleasure is not present in the insects, or the true reptiles, I strongly suspect. Pain is utterly useless to an entity incapable of altering its behavior; it would be

187

evolutionary nonsense.

But the pain-pleasure-learning mechanism must, eventually come to a limitation. I have a hunch we've reached it. Things are now reaching the point of being too complex to be learned. There's too much data for effective manipulation.

This allows of the pessimistic reaction, "There's nothing we can do about it, save watch the dark age of too-much-light descend." There's also the shallow optimism, "This is the way things should be; it will all work out happily — just continue and don't worry."

And there's the reaction, "Well — evidently something has to be done, and it isn't going to be achieved by getting more data on how bad the quantity-of-data problem is. We've already reached the point where the literature on means of indexing the existent literature of science is too voluminous to be indexed adequately! We can't get anywhere just throwing out all data over — oh, say 20 years old. That'd throw out all the fundamental data — Newton's work for example — and still leave too great a mass."

"We've got to get a totally new method."

The mammalian invention of the Learning Process has reached the end of its development. We won't merely invent a new method of handling problems — we'll invent a new great division of animal life!

Actually, that's already happened; the division hasn't been named yet, nor recognized adequately because it doesn't show as a physical characteristic clearly . . . as yet. It's the great life-branch of the Symbolizers. How you'd say that in Latin, I dunno — but just as the Mammals differ primarily in teaching the young (all the physical-psychological differences are simply sequels of that) so the Symbolizers differ from all previous animal evolution.

Note this physical-psychological consequence already: among the reptiles, the male-female difference is externally, relatively minor, save during the periods of active child-bearing and weaning.

But among the Symbolizers, the male-female difference is almost as extreme as it is among insects! The differences are enormous, by comparison to the differences between a stallion and a mare, a dog and a bitch, or a tom and a tabby.

Item: Magic has always centered around the immense importance of symbols. The Symbol is the Thing. The doll is the victim. The charm-ob-
188

ject is the charm-power. The chalked pentagon is a wall that blocks the forces. Magic is saturated with the exact inverse of General Semantics.

Note that in the Bhagavad-Gita, Krishna is teaching General Semantics — the importance of making distinctions, of recognizing separations, and maintaining separations. And the Hindu religion, full of distinctions as it is, has castes that have blocked the development of the people and their culture.

There's a limit to the utility of distinctions! Democracy thrives on nondistinction!

Each aspect has its place — if you can understand how to apply it usefully.

Analogical thinking deliberately makes a confusion between two different systems, and learns about System A from the available knowledge concerning System B.

Logic is based on that; Logic IS NOT man-made; it's man-discovered. The individual who is rabidly anti-logical — who deliberately seeks to revenge himself (frequently herself) on some logical-minded person by consciously acting in an anti-logical manner presents an extremely confusing problem. Such an individual will vociferously decline her intention of being non-logical . . . and will follow precisely the laws of logic, of cause and effect, etc. The confusing thing is that while saying, "I am anti-logical and I glory in it!," she will be obeying the laws of the Universe (which have a logical level) with inexorable fidelity. It's kind of like having someone say, "See! I'm walking on water; I don't have to glub blub burble," as he walks deeper and deeper into the stream 'til it closes over his head.

Logic is useful only because there is an analog relationship between our symbolic system called "logic" and a certain level of the Universe. We didn't invent the Universe; our logic simply describes it.

Now — if our logic is a valid description, it should run into paradoxes!

Reason: The Universe is not SOLELY logical! Therefore an accurate description of the logic-level of the Universe should at the edges, run into non-logical situations.

If your logic didn't run into paradoxes, that would mean that you were describing a totally and solely logical Universe.

Ours isn't.

Therefore your logic would be an inaccurate analog of the Universe!

Note Newton's difficulty with explaining the partial reflection-partial refraction of a beam of light incident on a transparent medium. Newton didn't have a probability mathematics to help him; he talked about "fits" or reflection or transmission. You can't fit a purely-logical analog to the reflection-refraction problem, because it isn't purely logical! It involves the problem logic has never yet been able to handle -- the relationship between group and individual — the relationship between photon and wave!

Incidentally, I've decided to invent a new science — photonics. It bears the same relationship to Optics that electronics does to electrical engineering. Photonics, like electronics, will deal with the individual units; optics and EE deal with the group-phenomena! And note that you can do things with electronics that are impossible in electrical engineering!

Item: We can deal with Russian individuals — the individuals-of-the-Russian-population — under a system of laws quite different from those applicable to Russia as a nation! One is psychology; the other international diplomacy. We can, in consequence, make a monkey out of diplomacy by proper use of psychology.

And I can make a liar out of the science of optics by finding the laws of photonics.

Item: What's the difference between "subjective" and "objective"?

Suggested answer: Subjective phenomena are individual level phenomena; objective phenomena are group-level. Only when we can understand and manipulate the group-individual relationship can we correlate those two aspects of totality!

I think I've found a genuine, basic understanding of what the source of neurosis of many types is — the mechanism behind the, "I hate myself," and, "I'm ashamed of myself."

Try this:

1. An animal operates on instinct directives mainly. Conscious directives are relatively less important; in the wild animal there is practically no problem then. Domesticated animals like dogs have a hell of a time; Man imposes contra-instinctive directives which louses up the system.

2. Very primitive man has little or no sense of "honor." Promises mean almost nothing.

190

3. The tribal, particularly the highest level of the tribal type has an acute sense of honor, of vows and promises.

4. The early civilization system involves an acute sense of honor among the higher levels — the Knights, for example. The concept of the Unbreakable Vow comes in.

5. The system works moderately well in a stable culture; it doesn't in a rapidly changing environment.

Now as a child, I made vows and promises, both to myself and to others. I've broken them. Like most small boys, I vowed I'd have nothing to do with girls. Oh . . . yeah?

There's a me-then buried in me that is angrily aware that the solemn vows made have been broken, and is sending out shame signals. There's a somewhat later me that is angrily replying that me-then-#1 is a fool to make such a vow. And a still later me holding that both me #1 and me #2 were fools — and this me #3 has a sinking feeling that maybe I'm still being a fool.

I've broken my promises, thrown away my vows, and generally trampled on my own sense of honor. Further, I've broken my solemn promises because of pressure of discomfort — I've been a coward, and yielded to pain, which is dishonorable.

Man, until we get this problem of "What is honor?" figured out a hell of a sight better than we have so far . . . we're in for trouble in great gobs. The trouble is called "guilt feelings."

Sure — I know that "I shouldn't feel that way." Uh-hu. Yes, and you "should stop worrying about that" too. Inasmuch as it's a known fact that a man will die for his beliefs, what the hell do you expect to happen when he has two mutually exclusive beliefs inside him, and hits a situation where both apply?

Answer: he'd better learn to be a liar, cheat, vow-breaker, fool, stupid, and dishonorable. He must learn how to be utterly inconsistent, illogical—but ethical.

He must differentiate between situations, so that the vows can be properly isolated, while integrating all situations into an understanding, so that he remains ethical. He must not use unlimited discrimination, like a caste-ridden Hindu culture, nor can he work purely with absolutes, like a tribal dogma.

But until he does learn how — he'll hate himself.

Does that check with what you know?
Regards, John

Isaac Asimov   February 20, 1955

Dear Isaac:
I'm sending this one back, and my reasons are complex. Hence this long letter.

There is, in Man, a potential for violence, for fury, and for acceptance of penalty that no psychology has ever honestly considered, and none has adequately evaluated.

Normal Man is more or less what the cultural maxims suggest. But normal men are never leaders of Mankind; the direction of development, and the rate and the reach of the race, are not determined by normal men.

And the Great leaders, the geniuses, different as they are in so many respects, share one "anti-social" characteristic -- one characteristic that's insistently suppressed in all children. Without exception, the Great Men are all Angry Men. They are angry, intolerant, belligerent, abnormally certain of their own rightness.

"Gentle Jesus, meek and mild," is strictly a myth started by those who never knew him. Make a couplet of it, and make it more accurately descriptive: . . . "Had a temper; it was wild!:

What sort of a meek, mild man do you think it was who got the money-changers out of the temple? Rather, what sort of awesome thunder of wrath did that one man exhibit that the whole group of men, and the too-complacent priests, folded up and skittered out of the way?

"Gentle" is a lovely concept . . . only it is most horrendously misunderstood. A lamb is not gentle; it's a mean-tempered, nasty, oblivious little beast . . . and so helplessly weak that it can't hurt anything. You can't be gentle unless you have the power to be ruthlessly destructive, and the wisdom to withhold it. The degree of your gentleness is limited by your ability to destroy; since a lamb, for all its nasty manners, is utterly weak, it has a gentleness rating of zero. A 1200 pound, 9-foot Kodiak bear, grooming her cub, is something else again.

Man is the only mammalian species that consistently hunts and kills his own kind. Man has a number of other unique characteristics, and
192

in our present state of near total ignorance as to the nature of the Ultimate Goal of Life, it might behoove us to assume that there's a reasonable probability that each of those unique characteristics developed because it was of high value in a manner we couldn't accept.

Like the matter of Man alone of mammals being capable of raping his female.

Well . . . there's this interesting factor. Domesticated animals must not have any resistance to miscegenation; if they do, the breeder is not free to make the crosses, to breed the blood-lines, he chooses. In the normal mammalian species, the females, simply because they cannot be raped, have absolute power to select which male blood-lines shall be perpetuated.

There's the old crack, "To teach a dog something, you have to know more about it than the dog."

Man was the first of the domesticated animals. The anatomical arrangements that make rape possible made it possible for the males of highest pragmatic achievement to breed on the females of somewhat lower type — whether those females considered the skinny, nearly hairless, pinheaded Homo sapiens type aesthetically pleasing or not.

The dairy breeder imports one very-high-bred bull, and presently has a whole herd of pretty good cows, by breeding his high-value bull on the cheap, scrub cows. If the resistance to miscegenation hadn't been eliminated from the bovine breed, you couldn't do that.

A lot of the things we think are all wrong . . . ain't.

There's an interesting item Carleton Coon brings out in his "The Story Of Man." The skull of Homo neanderthal contained as great a brain-volume as Homo sapiens (as Poul Anderson also brought out in his article in ASF). But Neanderthal's skull differed in being lower and much broader, which gave him the low-brow effect. It also, Coon says, had thinner, and less dense bony structure.

Homo sapiens differed, also, in having a femur markedly more ridged and filleted, and with more roughened muscle-attachments.

Isaac . . . Homo neanderthal lost the battle for domination of the world, for a very simple reason. Homo sapiens, not Homo neanderthal's low, broad, shallow-arched skull dome was just about as good as Sapiens' for resisting the blow of a paw — but Sapiens' high-brow is much superior armor-plate design, when people start heaving clubs around. Besides, the bone is both thicker, and denser.

It's time we stopped kidding ourselves and trying to kid each other. Man didn't win out, a poor, weak, soft-skinned, weaponless creature, surviving against all the great brutes by a desperate use of his hard-pressed wits. Man won out because he's one of Earth's largest and most powerful mammals, and his natural weapons — as natural to him as a dam is to a beaver — are far and away the most deadly.

You ᵏnow, occasionally a "feral child" does show up — a baby that's somehow been raised by and among animals — usually wolves, or the like. It's lost humanity — but does quite nicely, thank you, as one of Earth's largest, fiercest, and most powerful carnivores, quite without the help of human mind-characteristics.

And . . . soft skinned? Try building a robot, sometime, Isaac, with some consideration of what a really effective robot must have. Eyes? They're easy. Ears? Simple. Tactile sense? Huh? What do you mean?

Try building a tactile sense organ that covers the entire exterior surface of the structure — everywhere. While you're at it, make it sensitive to heat-radiation so that it can detect the radiation from a steam-heated radiator at a distance of 20 feet in a room at 720. (If you want infra-red sensitivity in all directions, you'ld better leave thermal insulation off the outer surface, you know.) Of course, the very large-area sensing organ also can be used for detecting and measuring the energy in sound waves of too low a frequency for the small-diaphragm type units most satisfactory for directional work.

Yeah . . . poor, thin-skinned Man, with nothing but the most magnificent sensory gimmick in the known universe between him and all his many enemies.

Incidentally, every life-form that's tried the technique of a thick or armor-plated skin has wound up having to struggle along by a fantastic birth-rate. The Maginot Line didn't work either. But radar, and an alert, dynamic air-force helps.

Man didn't win because he was so meek and mild and normal. He's the god-damnedest screw-ball crackpot of 'em all. He can't distinguish between Reality and Imagination well enough to keep from turning reality into what he imagined. He is the magnificent triumph of inconsistency
194

and the Wrong Answer. He never knows which way he's going next — and if you think that confuses him, with his high-order ability at abstractions, what do you think it does to everything else? There's nothing so tough as predicting the behavior of an organism that can't make up its mind to act consistently . . . particularly when you're trying to have that organism for dinner, and trying not to be dinner for that organism. Man, the High Triumph of the Wild Irrational Variable . . . because that's the way to triumph.

You're quite correct in saying the Eternity people were wrong; they tried to keep things consistent, and neat, and free of wild and unpredictable variables. You've got that nailed down neatly.

War, like rape, served a purpose for Man. Deer don't breed sluggish, congenitally lame, or inadequate types — but not because the other deer have sense enough to exclude them. The wolves may be a little rugged on the individual deer — but the race of Deer is kept trim, fleet, and competent. (And the fleetness and competence of the deer, plus the fact that a biochemical mechanism needs fuel, keeps the wolves trim, fleet and competent.)

But who or what is to judge Man? Weed out the weak, the incompetent, the aberrant in the Race of Man? No wolf dares become an effective goad. Lions that attack men get hunted down and destroyed, promptly. What species is competent to drive Mankind to perfect himself, to keep himself trim, alert and competent?

We admire the man who is capable of self-sacrifice, and self-discipline.

But don't see that Man is capable of self-sacrifice and the self-discipline that was essential to evolution across the great gap from instinctively controlled higher mammal to consciously controlled lower intelligence.

But war, like rape, reaches the end of its utility. The tough, always-hateful Test of pragmatic, "You say you're fit and hard; now let us try the Test and see!," must go on and on, down through the age ahead. The Test that says, "No — you are incompetent!," is always hated and resented. But it must be accepted, however bitter a dose it may be.

War was the Test that was accepted by its very existence. The only way to prevent someone testing you by War was to fight them off — and so the test was made anyway. It served Mankind well.

But we have available a greater test now — the test of the universe. Your idea may be good; by your arguments, or by your clubs and guns, you may make me agree with you. Fine . . . but can you make the Universe agree with you? By the brilliance of your argument, you may convince me that salt is really a special form of water. But . . . can you convince silver nitrate of that?

"A man has a right to his own opinion."

OK . . . but for every right, there is a duty. What's the duty that goes with an opinion? And every statement has a limitation, whether expressed, implied, or even if that fact is denied. What's the limit on the right to an opinion?

The people of the Hidden Centuries were right, in essence, in holding that Man alone is not an adequate judge of Man; the Universe must be consulted, also.

Most of science-fiction's development has been based on recognizing, more and more strongly, the importance of the Judgment of the Universe — the hindsight, while not very useful in determining what to do tomorrow, is infallibly correct as to what happened yesterday — and "Good" can only be defined in terms of the next 100 megayears. Not in terms of what you or I think the next 100 megayears may be, but in terms of what, 100,000,000 years hence, is known to have been.

Science-fiction — and a large part of this trend is due to the work of one I. Asimov — has tended to develop the conflict of Man against the Universe. Remember your very first ASF yarn? Man judging Man on the basis of what they believed at the moment — and not in terms of what the Universe was. Bringing out the pettiness of human resistance, for current-belief reasons, to a great natural-to-the-Universe change. The conflict of small, sure-they've-got-all-the-answers men against men who're willing to make the Test against the Universe.

"Never trouble trouble till trouble troubles you," is an old, old sentiment. It needs to be written in different terms. "Always trouble trouble, before trouble troubles you." If you're going deer-hunting in the woods, and there is a bear around — the neolithic hunter knew what to do. Hunt the bear first, the deer later. Otherwise the bear may be hunting you while you hunt the deer.

Man isn't gentle in the old sense; he can be gentle only to the degree he has the power to be ruthless — and that includes the mental-emotional ability to apply his physical power ruthlessly. Cruelty is inefficient ruthlessness — the little punishments that don't kill, but simply cripple, weaken, and torture. The little nagging deterrents that don't retrain a man to a new way of behavior, but make him miserable because of the constant tension that's never quite enough to force him to make a clean break.

The fault I find in this novel is that it presents the cruel, nagging, indeterminate business of petty human conflict. The clear, strong motivation of the story is never felt — because it comes only as an explanation at the very end, and is merely an explanation. There's never time for the reader to feel the power of that drive.

Your plot arrangement crippled you from the start; you've got the wrong viewpoint-character. Noys, not Harlan, should be the viewpoint character. As is, you are not able to present Harlan's philosophy powerfully, clearly, and cogently. If you did, you couldn't make your explanation go over at the end. A really good job of indoctrinating the reader in Harlan's (and Eternity's) viewpoint and philosophy would cripple the explanation at the end.

I wondered, as I read, why you had arbitrarily set up such an abnormal group as an all-male system. That's never sound -- it never works.

The set-up is such that you could not present the best possible case for Eternity, in the best possible light, with your best and most effective presentation arguments. You had to hold off — because Noys, in three pages, had to upset the whole argument, or your climax wouldn't come off.

Told from Noys viewpoint, the strongest possible developments of each side could have been made . . . but you'ld have a different action sequence, of course. Noys might turn out then to be a man. And her problem would be to convince an ethical, idealistic Harlan that the atomic bomb was a good idea — that causing the Hiroshima sequence was a fine thing for Mankind.

My friend, she'd need to do some exceedingly potent arguing, wouldn't she? Certainly not something she could get in in three pages!

The essential argument is, of course, the one we all accept for the other guy . . . but never accept for ourselves; only when a system is in a state of imbalance is it dynamic. Only when a man is discontented, unhappy in some respect, is he dynamic.

197

Some few human beings have a built-in, permanent discontent — the Divine Discontent of the Explorer. That's a gift that makes the prodding of externally imposed discontent unnecessary — but the mass of mankind hasn't got it yet. When they have — that'll be a different story.

The idea that Man is one race is nonsense; any geneticist knows that in a genetic enclave, genetic drift causes gradual differentiation. The idea that "all types of men can interbreed" means damn little, if it's true, and there is no real proof that it's true. Can you picture a high-level, highly intelligent, highly ethical man trying to breed with a Bush-man female?

True, a moron can rape a genius girl. Wonder what the statistics on viable outcomes of such matings are? Physiologically you can't prove any difference between 'em. But then, no physiological test yet has been able to distinguish between a genius' corpse and a moron's corpse, either. That just proves physiology isn't very indicative . . . as you correctly estimated in your conclusion that Noys didn't have to be physiologically distinguishable.

Be it noted that monkeys, men, and the inhabitants of Deneb IX all use a catenary span in throwing a bridge across a stream. I do not give a consarn what level of evolution you've reached, you'll use a catenary span in building a suspension bridge.

Somewhere, there is a point of optimum form for a generalized omnivorous intelligent inhabitant of a low-gravity, oxygen-atmo-sphere planet. Brown skin, white skin, blue skin — these don't count. Hair, feathers, or shlurth on the skull — these don't count. But hairless skin does count — it's that total-coverage sensory system, and the only hairs must be the sensing hairs of pre-contact tactile. No scales; armor of any kind interferes with the critical sensory function. (Try driving my new car, and you'll find how important skin-sensing sys-tems are. it's got power brakes and power steering, and there's no deter-minable relationship between effort applied to the wheel and stress ap-plied to the car on a turn. You've got to use kinesthetic and tactile sense to meter the turns; the muscular effort sense does no good at all.)

As evolution asymptotically approaches that optimum physio-logical form — change at the purely physical level effectively ceases. I see that Coon reports that the human-style hand has been around for a good many million years — that the chimpanzee had it, and went back to the less handlike paw they now have. Tentacles are a nice theoretical idea — but pushing buttons is awful hard with a tentacle. Ever see how an elephant has to use his trunk to push? He curls it up in a sort of jelly-roll-cross-section effect.

And a bodiless intelligence is a lovely idea . . . only we'll need to have total psi powers first, and by the time we have that, we may know enough to know why a bodiless intelligence is not practical.

The old trend in science-fiction actually consists of an effort to display Man's problem as that of:

1. Overcoming the real problems of the real Universe.

2. Helping sincere men of other opinions to understand —

3. — and being able to make oneself recognize that that other individual with the other opinion isn't a fool, and so be willing to change one's own opinion.

4. Removing, neutralizing, or by-passing the human individuals who oppose for short-term reasons. Who oppose space-travel because cheap Martian diamonds would ruin their business, for example. Or because if Bill Blow succeeds in his spaceline venture, he'll win Josephine McGruddy, instead of me.

Now this story is, in fact, a story of the old "Trends" type. But you've presented it as a matter of personal feuds, and personal interests. It's Harlan vs. Finge, and Harlan's ready to sell out Eternity (good or bad not being considered very much) for the short-term goal of winning Noys.

It's a real and powerful plot . . . carefully decked out as another boy-gets-girl, triumphing-over-jealousy-and-rivals story.

Sure human individuals are important; there ain't gonna be no long-term, if the short-term isn't taken care of. Try putting more time on the Great Project by skipping meals and sleep, and the Great Project never gets done because of the untimely collapse of the projector.

One of Mankind's greatest troubles is an insistence of Knowing What To Do. We've just got to Know The Answer.

When Man grows up enough to handle the situation of Not Knowing How to Handle The Situation, we won't have to insist that we already Know The Answer.

The Eternity people, as you properly point out, operated on the We
199

Know The Right Answer proposition. The We Know What's Good proposition.

And they missed the fact that the Universe is most clearly based on a system that involves ruthlessness; the inappropriate gets crushed. The baby who pulls a pan of boiling water down on him is scalded to death ruthlessly. The baby who is sure he can take care of himself and scampers out into the path of a car, because he knows adults won't bump into him, lands a twitching, reddened mass of disorganized protoplasm, half torn in two, when his body drops off the beautifully chrome-plated bumper of a car that obeys the laws of friction, momentum and kinetic energy, not human desire.

The Universe is ruthless . . . but just.

Here's something to think about, too, **Isaac**. Suppose we have a device made like this:

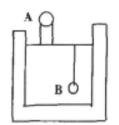

We will stipulate that the mass of A times its lever-arm length equals the mass of B times it's lever-arm, and that the bearings are friction-less. The device will, then, be in balance in any position.

Now what happens if it's, say, 3 feet high, and we rotate it at 3600 RPM? It's perfectly balanced, isn't it?

Yeah — statically. But not dynamically. It'll tear itself to pieces in a fraction of a second.

But it's soooooo much easier to balance something statically than to achieve dynamic balance. A culture, for example. Given 200,000 years of trial and error in a static cultural environment, you can work out a perfectly balanced arrangement.

But now try introducing new major cultural forces at the rate of one every decade and see what happens! Introduce cheap, fast, individual transportation called "a Ford car." then years later introduce cheap, instantaneous, public communication, called "broadcast radio." Then throw in a major war, to stir things up a bit, and then television. Add nuclear energy to upset the concepts of balance of power.

While you're doing this, lengthen the life of the average citizen by about 30%, while making the female half of the adult population far more mobile by giving them mechanical devices for household tasks and remove the burden of home preparation of vegetables and most of the time-consumption of marketing by the home-freezer storage.

Throw 'em a few more curves! We'll find out whether the system's dynamically stable or not!

The first king of the First Dynasty of Egypt, thrown four thousand years forward in time and landed in Rome, would have been settled and doing fine in a year or so. Julius Caesar thrown a thousand years forward could have helped King Arthur and his knights.

But George Washington would have been a psychoneurotic wreck within a week if someone dumped him down on the middle of the George Washington Bridge and left him there to fend for himself.

Caesar built a bridge across the Rhine.

Next time you're in New York, take a look at the George Washington Bridge, remember that steel was something barely plentiful enough for swords in Caesar's time, and think what Julius would have felt.

There was an ad a while back of Hendrik Hudson's "Half Moon" being overtaken in a mist by the "United States." Ever wonder what sort of mental shock the old boy would have undergone if he'd actually seen that stupendous, utterly impossible cliff of black steel silently sliding through the seas, literally faster than the wind? That unimaginable bulk looming up out of a light mist, blinding brilliance stabbing out in great fans of light from her portholes?

It doesn't take super-men to shock a human being half out of his wits. It takes a situation he cannot conceive, in which all the Laws of the universe he has known crumble — where not men, but the world itself is insane. Where black cliffs towering unimaginably up and up into the mists slide almost silently through the seas at incredible speeds. Where inanimate objects talk, and inanimate matter whirrs along with a whisper of wind. Where a hundred tons of metal floats unsuspended in the air, hurtling across the continent at a rate that covers 15 days travel every hour.

A man could stand firm and sane in a population of madmen.

But not in a mad world, where the laws of nature had become meaningless.

How fast can you learn? If the world changes faster than that rate, inexorably you will find yourself in a world where the things are insane.

201

Where you wave a hand at a doorway, and a room is flooded with light.

Take the fullest development of all the psi powers you can imagine, put 'em in full action by everyone around you . . . and consider whether it wouldn't be an inducement to madness.

Of course, you've had science-fiction training to endure such a shock. Could the man living next door to you?

That's part of the resistance to progress. Someone will go mad, Isaac.

Regards, John

Isaac Asimov   *February 21, 1955*

Dear Isaac:

"Victory On Paper" sounds like a good article. The title's nice, too; I've been playing mentally with variants. "Paper Prophets" or maybe "Philter Paper."

Has anyone yet tried making up a cube of blotting-of-filter paper, and tried three-dimensional chromatography? I don't know what for, but it ought to make complicated possibilities. Re the intellectual missionary compulsion. Look, piker, you just begin to have it. Ask me; I've got a full blown case. Why do you think I'm in this business, anyway? I'm not satisfied with explaining what is true — I've made a life work of explaining what might be true, too!

Regards, John W. Campbell, Jr.

Isaac Asimov   May 1, 1955

Dear Isaac:

You know me; any problem is fair game for a few pot-shots if I can see it. Try this one on some of your gang up there:

Mexico — as one example — has, because of improved medical technology, achieved a rate of population increase such that in about 25 years, the population (now 28,000,000) will be about doubled. Mexico can support about 40,000,000. In 1980, then, Mexico, presumably, will have about 15,000,000 people looking for a home. They can't expand out of Mexico to the south; the individuals most pressed won't have money for sea transportation. Guess what happens at the US-Mexico border in 1980/85?

202

Problem: a contraceptive that will be used, that is so cheap the poorest can use it, is so easy to use that the stupidest will use it successfully, and so related to the user that he or she will not fail to use it except by deliberate, conscious intent.

Obviously, it should be oral. But more, it should be extremely long-lasting — i.e., 30 days or so — or else have some characteristic that will cause it to be taken regularly unless conscious determination not to exists.

This means that we want a mildly habit-forming substance. That will make it have the characteristic of being self-reminding, but it must be only mildly habit-forming, so that conscious decision to reject it will be no great deprivation.

The proposition of a drug having a 30-day effectiveness is possible, but not very promising, I feel. I can't, off hand, think of an example of something that remains in the bloodstream that long. Sure, some of the substances that deposit in the bones come back into solution slowly; that might be an approach — but generally, only relatively simple substances are tied down that way.

But note this: if a woman became an arsenic eater, she could habituate herself comfortably to quite a high arsenic content. The human metabolism readily adapts to quite a bit of arsenic. It has some beneficial tonic effects, too.

Now a woman on a high-arsenic diet would, I suspect, be infertile to a man who was not. His sperm would have some trouble surviving in the highly arsenical body fluids.

All right. Generalization of the proposition: The oral contraceptive can be achieved by developing a substance P, such that a human metabolism can become adapted to P without harm, but such that P is, in the adapted-state concentration, toxic to human sperm.

The proposition of the habituated metabolism means that P is, in some degree, habit-forming. However, like many drug-habituations, P can be a substance which causes relatively mild habituation; habituation would, then, be an entirely favorable side-effect. It would serve to act as an automatic reminder and dosage-maintaining mechanism, while not preventing discontinuation when discontinuation was consciously desired.

But the basic proposition is that the necessary characteristic for an effective oral contraceptive is a substance which shifts the metabolism of one of the partners (probably the female, but not necessarily) sufficiently that she is rendered infertile to the male.

It's conceivable that a substance having such immense specificity as to be harmful to one, and only one type of human cell could be found. It's true that digitalis is exceedingly specific in its selection of tissues — but I think the researchers will have one holy hell of a time finding something that can circulate freely in the female human system without injuring any of her cells, yet be toxic to the sperm.

If you consider that any barrier actually constitutes simply a zone of very high rate-of-change-of characteristic, then you can see what I'm actually driving at. A mechanical "barrier" is a zone where the resistance to mechanical motion shows a very high positive charge; a wall of solid armor steel is normally considered a mechanical barrier. But let's consider a meteor coming in from outer space at 40 miles a second. it strikes down through the atmosphere (it's a big one that can reach the surface with considerably velocity) and hits the armor deck of a battlewagon. The steel armor is, from the viewpoint of something moving 20 miles a second, precisely similar to air — it differs solely in density. The mechanical strength of the steel is irrelevant under the conditions.

OK . . . then the contraceptive barrier needs to be something showing a high rate-of-change. If the woman has slowly changed to a high-P-content metabolism, and the sperm is forced to make a sudden change . . . the barrier is effective.

Note that a man who was also adapted to P would be able to impregnate the woman who was adapted to P, but would not, perhaps, be able to impregnate a non-P woman. (The latter is not necessary, but quite possible.)

I've been thinking of what you told me about Muller's figures indicating somewhat more than one mutation per human individual. It's well known among animal breeders that most highly bred domestic animals do not have instinctive copulation patterns. Artificial insemination is more than a convenience in the dairy industry; it's damn well necessary!

If the mutation frequency in humans is as high as Muller suggests, then probably, in view of animal breeders experience, many human beings do not have any sex-desire instincts whatever.

Isaac . . . what does that do to Freudian psychology, that holds that all people are neurotic, and all neurosis is based on sex???????

By the way; let's be ruthless, realistic, and understanding. The robot, in the form of computer machines and cybernetic automation, is coming in. It's going to displace human beings who can't do anything but follow instruction in a routine manner, because that's precisely what the computer can and does do. That's going to happen as surely as any other economic force — and it's much too late to stop it, even if we wanted to.

The essence of the human type that the machine cannot yet displace is the ability to act originally — outside of routine and in exact reverse of routine, even. The ability to break away from well-trodden thought-paths, and try something new. The characteristic of not being bound by familiar habits of behavior, and able, in a new situation, to abandon the habitual methods and take off in a new direction.

Betcha there is a correlation between ability to break a mental habit, and the ability to break a physiological habit.

Introduce a habit-forming contraceptive . . . and it might have the interesting characteristic of showing a selective effect, slightly, but perceptibly favoring the human type most capable of habit-changing!

This much you can bet on; the human type that did not have determination enough to maintain a specific desire for a period of a month or more would not do much reproducing! You could not reproduce if you attempted to do it on a spur-of-the-moment basis. It'd be planned parenthood — and it'd be planned and carried-out planning, too, before it worked.

Regards, John

Gib Hocking   May 7, 1955

Dear Gib:

One of the problems of communication is that of the proper use of the inaccurate statement; your own fraternity is particularly inept in handling that problem, because within your specialty, accurate statement is not only possible, but the sine qua non of respectability.

That can lead you into a rigidity of response-to-statements that

205

causes endless trouble for yourselves and others. Instance: the book about what-mathematics-can-do. Accurate statement in that area is obviously impossible; mathematicians have been hyper-trained to hold that the slightest demonstrable inaccuracy invalidates the entire system. Therefore if accurate statement cannot be made, the work is meaningless mathematically.

Isaac Asimov has pointed out that in the pure-logic sciences, the purely deductive sciences, one can begin at the beginning, proceed through the middle, and reach the end. But it is inherently impossible to do that in the inductive sciences; there's too much feedback effect to say what the beginning, middle, and end is. What's the starting point of Chemistry, for instance? The atom? No; that's the end point of nuclear physics — but the spectrum, closely related to chemistry, shows definite hyperfine structure which is influenced by the chemical combination in which the nucleus finds itself.

And biochemistry is a network system; you can't explain anything without explaining all of it, because the explanation of any single fact involves interactions from all other facts. Wherefore, until we are capable of conveying a total gestalt as a single, instantaneous impression, no statement can be accurate.

Take a simple little freshman chemistry course statement: By weighing the reaction reagents, and the reaction products, it can be shown that the mass of the input ingredients is equal to the mass of the reaction products.

Not true. The terms as understood by any normal freshman imply something which isn't valid; you can't weigh radiant energy in the sense meant by the normal statement — and if you do not weigh the mass of radiant energy escaping from the system, it is not true that the before and after masses check accurately.

Your engineers refuse to accept the infinite series idea. OK — accept, yourself, that they ain't fools, brother, and if they refuse to accept the idea as not-valid-in-practice, find out why, to what extent, and what modification of the concept would be acceptable.

My little example from chemistry hints at the answer to that. The physicist who uses Newtonian concepts to calculate the time it takes an electron to get from dynode #3 to dynode #4 in a 931-A photomultiplier tube, using 100 volts potential difference per dynode pair is using a method he knows is not accurate. Einsteinian techniques involve an infinite series approach — and the physicist is arbitrarily refusing to use a technique he knows is more accurate. Why? Because he's too good an engineer to act like a damn fool mathematician.

And there are damn fool mathematicians. Mathematics is the study of a Universe of Discourse that is inherently (by definition) noise-free, made up of zero-dimensional points, which have zero feedback, zero observer-effect-response, and are infinitely static. A mathematical-electron, for instance, will stay in precisely the same position, while traveling at 185,990 miles per second, for five years, while the mathematician observes it with the aid of a 200-ton electronic digital computer. The mathematician can trace each individual line of force entailed in that electron; the mathematician, while denying any possibility that information can be transmitted faster than light-speed, will transmit his attention all over the universe at an infinite speed. By fiat; he says he's doing that.

Now that's a real, nice, handy universe to operate in — one where everything can be made to stand still except the mathematician, and he can measure the circumference of a spherical wave-front to 1000 decimal places. (Which is mighty darned interesting, all things considered, since photons have a size that exceeds that 1000 decimal place accuracy figure.)

You guys can measure pi to 1000 decimal places — but no engineer can. The engineers are acutely aware of the fact that the math boys, every now and then, come up with an answer like 5.73967824 plus or minus 7.5.

Look, if I have a broomstick one inch in diameter, what is its circumference? "Well," says the mathematician, "That's a very difficult question, since it involves pi, which is a transcendental number. However, we can approximate the answer; it is roughly 3.1415926536 inches in circumference."

"Oh," says the engineer. Then he takes a piece of steel strap, wraps it around the broomstick, carefully scratches where the overlap occurs, and measures it with calipers. "Hmmm . . . 3.15 . . . for a good drive fit on this, I'll need a band with about 3.12" circumference inside. Allow for elasticity of the wood, and negative tolerances on undersize units in production run, and I can use about 3.10". Hey, Bill! Make up about a dozen 3.1" inside circumference steel bands, and grab a dozen broomsticks out of production. See how that set-up fits, will you?"

The essential problem, I suspect, is that mathematics doesn't teach the Science of Limitations. Infinite series? Nuts! Nothing's infinitely accurate. How about coming up with some slop-happy short-cut, inaccurate methods of doing the same problems in about 1/100th the time with 95% of the accuracy? And state the limitation of the method.

I got into an argument the other day that involved a similar sort of problem. The other person was growing angry because I would not discuss the problem as he felt it should be discussed — he felt I was dismissing the problem without consideration.

I gave him this analogy: Can an automobile fly? No. Well, suppose we make one with a 400 horsepower engine? No still? Well, suppose we paint it with blue with white stripes? Still no, huh? Well, what if we add more chrome trim, and make the trunk space bigger?

It's futile to discuss the problem at that level; the problem he was presenting he wanted discussed at the level at which he was willing to make modifications. He refused to discuss it at the level where modifications could be effective — and got mad at me because I refused to discuss an infinite series of modifications at the level at which he was willing to modify.

I've suggested that the math boys could help a lot by showing what general type of problems their different math specialties could handle. Now any such book, to be useful, would have to be a series of broad, loose, generalized statements. That type of statement is anathema to the mathematician; therefore the mathematicians would be angrily up in arms if someone published such a book. They'd deny the validity of the statements, and reject it as nonsense.

Having efficiently sabotaged the possible effectiveness of the book — since their attack would, of course, make any non-expert distrust the work completely — they would then refrain from writing such an index-system themselves, because if it were properly done, only a mathematician could understand it, and a mathematician already knows about it anyway.

OK — so the businessman sits worriedly on his accumulated capital, wishing he knew how to employ it more usefully and effectively, and the
208

mathematicians sit somewhat hungrily on their highly accurate statements wishing they had a bit more capital to employ. And Einstein, six months after saying somewhat wistfully, "I shoulda been a plumb**er,**" **dies** and leaves an estate that would make any half-way successful plumber feel ashamed of himself. One of my neighbors, it happens, is an ex-master plumber. He has a very **nice busi**ness; I suspect he's worth a quarter million.

The society has a lousy set-up; I agree in full. But I could suggest that it might help if some of the birds who are such specialists in the science of relationships would start climbing down out of their Universe of Discourse, and patch up the job the society-plumbers have built. I'll say this for the social-plumbers; the socio-economic pipes gurgle and leak and they do develop some bad water-hammer effects — but somehow the Law of the Horny Thumb has kept us eating reasonably regularly.

I keep thinking of that fumble-witted yahoo, Archimedes, who didn't have sense enough to come in out of the war, however much brains he had before that Roman soldier spilled 'em. To modify a limerick you may have heard:

Here did Rome Archimedes slay.

He died defending the Thoughtful Way.

He was right, dead right,

As he computed along.

But he's just as dead as if he'd been dead wrong.

I do wish we could work up a Science of Inaccuracy.

The trouble with that infinite series approach is that there's no use for infinite accuracy in engineering. The idea rouses a subliminal rejection in an engineer's mind, and you not only don't get him to accept the basic idea, but you can't get him to accept any of the proposition.

Incidentally, I never heard of any special technique for extracting 4th roots on a slide rule. If I wanted to, I guess I'd do a double-shift, taking the square root of the square root, or else get the log of the number from the linear scale, and work it in logarithms.

By the way Gib, it's worth noting that no radio engineer ever needs anything but slide-rule accuracy. He can't get components that are as accurate to their professed value as his slide rule is, so why calculate more accurately? And I remember a practical radio engineer friend of mine telling of a hot-shot mathematical-type radio engineer who had a circuit all figured out. My friend's rather disgusted comment was, "Ever try to compute the distributed capacity of a three-deck six-position selectro switch?"

Part of your trouble with your sociologist professor friend is that he feels "intuitively" that the inaccuracy of his method mathematically is, like the radio engineer's slide rule, unimportant in comparison to the inaccuracy of his sociological methods. That there's no use using a 10-place table of logs to compute the resonant frequency of a 25 mhenry coil and a 125 mmF condenser when the coil and condenser are both plus-or-minus ten percent.

He's quite right in his feeling that "it doesn't matter if you know how to use the method." With the sloppy sociological concepts they've got, it doesn't matter.

Look, the Ptolemaic system of the solar system was indistinguishable, in its predictions of planet-positions in the heavens, from the results of the heliocentric system — so long as you used naked-eye vision, and didn't keep records more than about 20 years. The thing that triggered Kepler into working up his formulas, on which Newton's work was based, was that Kepler believed Tycho Brahe observed accurately. That gave him a more-than-one-lifetime period of observations that he trusted. As long as each astronomer had no respect for anyone else's observations, he couldn't get a long enough accumulation of systematic error between theory and observation to spot the problem.

Psychologists won't trust each other's observations.

Sociologists won't trust each other's observations.

Nobody has ever worked out a technique for handling the problem of inaccuracy.

Until we do, we have the frustrating situation of infinitely accurate theoretical mathematics, and unknowably-inaccurate observation, and the two can never be made to fit.

You can not, and should not, trust my observations to be accurate plus or minus 0.000000001%. But you must not trust my observations to be inaccurate by 90%, either. So where, between those extremes, should you consider accepting a modification of your beliefs on the basis of my observations?

Aristotle appears to have been the originator of the comment that a single swallow does not make a summer. No — and a single bomb
210

didn't seriously dama^ge a city either . . . before 1945. The fact is that single observations of certain kinds can demolish a whole complex structure of integrated knowledge. It's that nasty fact that makes the thing so damned tricky to handle. It isn't the amount of inaccuracy; it's the cruciality (if I may invent a word) that counts. You can't be dead for "just a few days," you know, nor can a woman be "just a little" pregnant.

The thing that's made a science of inaccuracy so damned hard to set up lies in that fact. Suppose your theory suggests a value only 1% different from orthodox theory. Is it worth a while for the experienced, many-years-practiced man to reorient his entire thinking?

Well . . . if his theory holds that you can safely assemble a 100 pound sphere of 235U, and yours says that 99 pounds is critical mass . . . maybe he'd better.

Your theories in sociology differ only slightly, don't they? Of course they do! The question is, can you prove that the difference is crucial? Can you find a situation in which your theory is working at a critical phase-change point?

Is there any effective difference between using pi equals 3.14159 and pi equals 3.1415926536? There is — when you deal with a system in which the critical point is produced by the difference between two ten-digit quantities.

I think a major portion of the resistance to learning stems from the repeated experience of the misuse of inaccuracy. We've had too many experiences wherein we've been induced to give up a sound belief in favor of an unsound one because of someone cleverly making an inaccuracy or irrelevancy appear to be a crucial difference.

When Lavoissier introduced and defended the oxygen theory, against the phlogiston theory, he blithely denied the fact that his theory wouldn't explain certain experimental evidence with respect to the behavior of hydrogen. There was solid experimental evidence, that definitely did not fit the oxygen theory. L. simply brushed it aside in a thoroughly cavalier manner, and maintained his theory was valid.

Turned out some while later that the "hydrogen" experiments in question were, in fact, experiments with carbon monoxide. The tests available to chemistry at the time couldn't distinguish between the two. Both can be generated from organic materials, both burn with a

211

hot blue flame, neither will support life or combustion, and neither could be decomposed by any technique they had available.

But how are you going to prove that Objection P is, in fact, irrelevant?

Item: I suggest that the optimum role of a teacher is that of the Muse. He doesn't solve any problems for the student; he inspires the student to solve them for himself — and observe how he's solving them.

Item: I understand Einstein made a simple mistake in handling the signs in his algebra in the original Relativity work, which lead him to "discover" the Cosmical Constant, a negative gravity-like force. The error wasn't caught 'til several years later. Question: What would have been the effect if it had been caught the moment the young patent office clerk's paper was published?

Also: I've been helping Peedee with her algebra. it's important to keep her from feeling hopeless, defeated, incompetent — from, in other words, getting in the mood to give up. And it is also important to make her recognize her repeated mistakes. I've told her the story of Einstein's error; whenever she makes a mistake in signs . . . which she does frequently . . . I call it her "Einstein error." She knows Einstein's embarrassment; she is reminded of her own mistake — but, after all, Einstein, who made a similar mistake, wasn't a hopeless case, you know!

My pet technique now is to do one of the tougher problems they've assigned her as homework, but with this stipulation: "I'll do number 15 here, Peedee — but I'm going to make at least one deliberate mistake. I may make some undeliberate ones too, of course, but I'll guarantee at least one mistake. You can spot it; it'll be a mistake you know about. So let's go."

There's a tendency for a kid to let his-her mind wander limply along when someone else is doing the problem. The result is that they tend to follow the process passively, rather than dynamically. That gimmick has appeared to work well — she darned well has to follow dynamically, or she gets a wrong answer. And she knows she's going to get the wrong answer.

Sometimes I've thrown a double-cross, and put in two errors that cancel each other, then proved my result by substitution! The first time I did that she was really bollixed. I assured her that there was at
212

least one error, and yet I <u>proved the</u> answer was correct!

Knowing her pet error-types, naturally I throw in precisely the kind of hooker she's most apt to fall for. Since she has a tendency to say, "I can't do this one!," I sometimes make a wrong choice of method, winding up with a formulation that can't be cracked. You know — "<u>simplify" an ex</u>pression, then combine terms, winding up with something that won't come apart again. That type of error is, of course, the one that a kid has the maximum difficulty with — the difficulty of backing up for a fresh start, when everything seems the error in each problem, and solve correctly. The human tendency to go along with something that looks fairly reasonable, just riding along with the stream passively, would throw a perfectly horrible handicap in the path of the passive-follower type.

And perhaps one or two of them would be of the type that started off down the wrong method of analysis, winding up with a hyperbolixed integral that couldn't be resolved, so that the student's problem was to find a different way of analyzing the problem that led to a resolvable equation.

I suspect it would make even your best students hate you.

Regards, John

Isaac Asimov   *August 6, 1955*

Dear Isaac:

I'm taking the chronoscope story; the check's on the way.

The last paragraph of your note, commenting that there did seem to be some difference between the female and the male that weren't educational, interested me.

Look, my friend; did you ever try to define what the term "I won," meant? Now to most people in this beknighted culture of ours (beknighted meaning that, like a knight of old, they wear solid armor to keep things from getting into their skulls), the term "I won" means exactly and solely the same as "I defeated my opponent."

Now let us consider two individuals who, from different positions, view the same object. A says, "It's a metal bar." B says, "Oh, no! I can see it clearly, and it's a sphere."

After some argument, A, who is older, and is B's immediate supe-

213

rior, defeats B completely, and B accepts that it is a metal bar.

Who won?

Answer: they both were defeated. It's a metal disc, of course, and neither A nor B has learned this. A may have defeated B — but the Universe has defeated them both. And the Universe exacts extremely severe penalties from any entity it defeats. The penalty is disaster.

My definition of "I won" is, "I achieved a more-useful understanding." In order for A or B to <u>really</u> win in the above example, one of them must achieve the more-useful understanding that it's a disc. Now if B acknowledges that he was mistaken in his belief it was a sphere, A may feel that B is defeated, and that he, A, has "won." But if B recognized that it was a disc — B really won, and A really lost. Because A lost the opportunity to achieve a more useful understanding.

I don't give a damn what your opinion is; you can have it for all of me. And I don't give a damn what my opinion is. I want to know what the <u>Universe's</u> opinion is. But your opinion is useful to me, because, since it inevitably differs from mine, it gives me a chance to get a different angle of view on the Universe. From one angle only, a disc <u>does</u> appear a metal bar. If that were my only angle of view, I couldn't possibly learn what the reality was.

Now some items to consider: try defining "human being" some time. You may find it ain't quite so simple as it looks. For one thing; it's a remarkable thing that we, who are so brilliant in our wisdom, are the direct descendants of such a collection of stupid fools, silly, superstitious nit-wits, and maundering idiots as we are repeatedly assured inhabited this planet a few centuries ago. Truly remarkable that, descended from such as they, we could be so much more brilliant and wise and sensible, isn't it?

OK, let's back off a bit and take a second look at this business.

Let's have a little story: Publius Cassius, minor Roman noble of about 200 years after **Augustus Caesar**, has an estate about 40 miles out of Rome, where he lives with his wife four young children, and about 20 slaves. Publius is a Roman of the old school; a highly ethical, genuinely enlightened man, but stern — with himself as much as with any other. He abhors the decadence of Roman civilization; he knows that Rome is going, and loathes the mores that lies behind the sadism of the Circus — and the "theater" of his time. (If a script calls for a character
214

to be raped and tortured to death, a girl slave will be raped and tortured to death on stage.) But loathe it as he may, with the old Roman sense of practicality, he also knows that he, alone, cannot stem the momentum of a whole culture.

About three months ago, Publius bought a young girl at the slave market. She's 19, a pretty, shapely girl, intelligent, clean and attractive, with a pleasant voice and manner. He bought her as a sort of mother's helper for his wife. Vona, the girl, helps care for the children, and acts as his wife's personal maid.

One day, Publius returns home unexpectedly, and finds Vona gleefully running a pin about 5 inches long into his 10-months old son's buttocks.

Investigation soon shows that Vona is a sadist. She's been secretly torturing the children too young to communicate — a pin-prick doesn't indicate how deeply the pin pricked. A twisted arm doesn't leave bruises to explain the child's behavior.

Also, she's been torturing the other slaves. As an inner-household slave, she's been passing out rumors that Quartus is to be sold to the Circus for lion-bait, while Marta is being sold to Stipulus, the well-known sex maniac, while her two children are to be sold in the public market.

Now Publius, as an ethical and enlightened man, has a problem. Punishing a sadist is as futile as punishing a kleptomaniac for stealing. He doesn't have modern terminology, but he's no fool; he knows the equivalent of "a psychopathological condition can't be cured by punishment."

Curing Vona is impossible. Selling her to another householder without warning of her nature would be unethical. Keeping her around where she can torture other human beings is unethical too, obviously.

What should Publius do?

Now the easiest thing for Publius to do is to simply run her through the heart with his short-sword, or have her pole-axed. Kill her as quickly as possible.

Publius, though, discusses it with his wife and his major domo, an old Greek philosopher who taught him as a boy. He takes Vona into Rome, takes her to one of the theaters, and trades her for a girl the stage-manager had bought for use in that evening's performance. The stage

215

manager's perfectly willing; Vona's good looking enough, and will last long enough while being skinned alive, to give his customers their money's worth, and he doesn't care that she's a sadist, of course.

Publius takes the other girl home. Vona, a worthless, useless, destructive entity has been put to good use; by sacrificing her to a cultural momentum he cannot stop or slow, Publius has ransomed a girl that may have real value.

Of course, Publius pays a considerable penalty; by an act of his, a girl personally known to him will, that evening, die in agony under circumstances he abhors. He will, himself, feel unclean because of his personal action; if he had simply killed Vona, the other girl would have died — but she would have been unknown to him, and her screams would not be a result of any action of his.

But as I said, he is a just and stern man — with himself, too.

This little story (and you know as well as I that a thousand minor variations of it happened in the centuries of the Empires) has various points worth considering. For one, let's try to describe Vona operationally. She is an entity having human female body, she is physiologically a human female in every respect. She has a young human female mind, and a more-than-normally competent one. But she has the psyche of a vicious animal. The modern terminology is "she has a psychopathic personality."

Is Vona human, then?

She looks completely human. Judging by physical evidence, she has the potential of being a fine mother, of healthy, sturdy children. Her intelligence is good, and she appears to have the potential of being a fine help-mate for some young man, and a fine mother of their children.

But her sadistic drive multiplies all those potentials by minus one. She will use her fine female body to torture people; her intelligence will be directed to the task of destroying their hopes, their ambitions, their will to achieve and grow. She would demean and belittle her husband and destroy him. She would amuse herself by torturing her own children; by destroying the essential humanity — the hope and belief in their fellows that makes a truly human individual — of her children, she would actually produce a litter of psychopaths like herself.

Because of the -1 multiplication, the prettier and more shapely she is, the better human female body she has, the more dangerous she is.

216

And the more intelligent she is, the more skillfully and quickly she can think — the deadlier she is.

Now our poor, stupid, silly, superstitious, no-nothing ancestors, the dopes, would have called her a <u>succubus</u> — would have said she was a female demon. A creature with the body of a beautiful young woman, and the soul of a demon. How silly of them! Imagine saying that this good-looking piece of animated meat was anything but human!

Just because somebody uses a system of terminology you aren't familiar with naturally proves they were fools and nit-wits.

The thing to do with a succubus or incubus was, of course, to kill them as soon as they were detected. A succubus, if allowed to roam loose, would, these superstitious dolts, our ancestors, said, trap young men, and destroy their souls. She would, if allowed to live, give birth to young demon children who would, in turn, spread the plague.

How silly!

Oh . . . yeah? What would you do with a psychopath in a culture, scraping at the subsistence level, couldn't afford the luxury of locking them away from Mankind, and supporting them in luxury for the rest of their lives? Let 'em run loose, blasting the lives and hopes of pretty decent people around them?

Does mere human physiology constitute full humanity? Our ancestors, from hard experience, damn well knew better.

Now let us consider a somewhat more advanced culture. We have a man who abides by the exact letter of the law; he never actually breaks any law — he just cleverly bends it into a trap for the injury of more ethical individuals. For instance, he starts a wholesale business, gets a lot of stock, carries on a big business by selling very cheap, and, in six months, goes into bankruptcy owing $200,000. Of course, the bankruptcy proceedings take over the few remaining assets of his company, and he's out of business.

But he gets a job shortly with his cousin, who bought a great deal of stock from him before he went bankrupt.

Now this man has violated no law; it's just that he and his cousin have acquired $150,000 worth of merchandise for about $20,000. They've got a nice business started now, and they haven't violated a single law.

And, in our culture, there isn't a damn thing you can do to the son of a bitch.

But it wasn't always that way. A few centuries back, a man might not violate any cultural law — but if he was, personally, a sheerly nasty bastard, he didn't have to answer to the culture through the courts of law . . . but he did have to answer to individuals he harmed, through the *code duello*.

The *code duello* must have purged the human race of a lot of psychic cripples. The incubus could be forgotten; the psychopath didn't bother people . . . for long. Just keep cropping off the nasty bastards as they pop up, and there'll be a strong tendency to eliminate the genetic defectives that tend that way. Oh, the nasty bastard might be right handy with the sword or pistol, and kill off a number of good guys — but sooner or later, he'd get cut down. As **Bob Heinlein** said in "Beyond This Horizon," the *code duello* ". . . breeds good manners and fast reactions." It rapidly breeds out the incubus and the pyschopath, too.

Because of the relief from their menace the race bought through the *code duello*, the real nature, and danger, of the incubus and succubus were forgotten.

The trouble was, the *code duello* applied only to the males. Hemophilia will eliminate the males who display it, but the females act as a reservoir from which new outcroppings can continue to spring. During the *code duello* period, a man was responsible for his wife's actions; if she insulted someone, he had to take the blame. The result was that hubby would beat wifey's damn nasty hide off if she didn't behave — whether she liked to behave or not didn't matter. Hubby had a damn good reason and a damn good right to; her displayed nastiness could get him killed. If she wouldn't restrain her nastiness because she wanted to, she would bloody well be made to restrain it because she had to. Hubby could, of course, apologize profusely to the injured party, and simply take wifey home and whip hell out of her.

Of course, it doesn't make a psychopath stop having a psychopathic attitude — but it will, if maintained rigidly and continuously enough, make even a psychopath stop displaying her psychopathic attitude. It'll kill her shortly, of course; she'll go completely insane, die of one of the beatings, or develop a lethal psychosomatic. But that will definitely be no loss whatever to the evolution of a human race.

The thing is, under such a system, the female psychopath, like the

218

female hemophiliac, doesn't <u>display</u> her characteristic — but carries it. The male psychopaths weren't restrained by guardians; they displayed their characteristic, and got themselves bumped off.

But now that women are allowed to be self-responsible . . . !

It's damn tough on people, but they have to be induced to <u>display</u> what they are, before the racial stock can be improved by eliminating them.

A chimpanzee <u>cannot</u> be taught to talk. The ability to handle high-order abstractions must be supplied genetically, since by the very nature of the thing, it can't be taught. (You can not teach something that the student cannot conceive; it's impossible by definition.) You can teach a moron to <u>do</u> something, but you can't teach him <u>why</u>. You can teach a man not to steal because the police will arrest and jail him — but you can't teach him to understand the higher-order abstractions of ethics. He has to have a genetic ability before that can be taught, just as the chimp can't be taught the high-order abstractions of speech.

Gotthard Gunther made this highly interesting point; some information is "unleakable." Example: The Romans of the Republic conquered the barbarians around them with ease and dispatch, by applying a bit of military technology — they had a "secret weapon."

But the gimmick was that the barbarians, shown the secret even when it was demonstrated and explained in detail, <u>could not learn</u> it. Russia can steal our atomic information; we can steal theirs. But the barbarians couldn't steal Rome's secret weapon, even when it was carefully demonstrated to them!

Reason: The secret weapon was the cohort-and-short-sword. The short sword markedly handicaps the individual warrior; a longer sword is more efficient. Now since it is obvious that the strength of an army is the sum of the strengths of the individual warriors, then decreasing the strength of the individual warrior weakens the army.

It's obvious that if five plus five is ten, then decreasing to four will decrease the result.

Only . . . four <u>times</u> four is 16.

The cohort was a <u>team</u>, not a sum-of-individuals. The individual <u>was</u> weakened by the short sword — but by using a short sword, and fighting in very close ranks, each individual barbarian was forced to meet two or more Romans. The barbarians with their long swords <u>could</u>

219

not pack closely enough to fight on a one-to-one basis.

The barbarians lost with machine-like regularity. They could see the cohort at work; they could see the short-sword fighting techniques. But they could not conceive the necessary high-order abstraction; disciplined cooperation allows no individual to win glory, but assures victory to the team.

The barbarians could not accept, understand, or conceive of that abstraction. They went on insisting that the strength of an army was the sum of the individual strengths . . . and lost with perfect regularity.

The understanding of the secret weapon was unleakable.

Given: A culture with the cultural postulate, "The King can do no wrong."

Problem: To prove, "The King has wronged me."

Given: A culture with the cultural postulate, "The state is wiser than any individual."

Problem: To prove, "The State is mistaken, and I am right."

That time-viewer gimmick will result in an immense wave of madness. When it settles down again, there won't be any more psychopaths; they'll be dead. Can you slander a man by telling his prospective employer, "Oh, yes, he's a very bright individual."?

No court in the land would take that statement to be a slander.

But with a time-viewer you could replay the scene — and show the context, the facial expression, the tone of voice, and the gestures that went with it — and made it a vicious and effective slander. "It ain't what you say, it's the way that you say it that makes me so god-damn mad." When somebody's needled you viciously with that technique

. . . what if you had a time-viewer, to replay the scene, and show exactly and precisely what he said, and make him hear the exact tones he used?

"I'd trust him with my life," says Bill Blow. That's the official wording. But the time-viewer shows the tone he used, and the gesture of a finger across the throat while he said it.

Or some one tells you, "Bill wants you to bring him a set of left-handed golf clubs," and says it with a grin and an expression that makes you, someone unfamiliar with golf, realize that it's another "left-handed monkey-wrench" deal.

220

So later you get the hide blistered off for not obeying orders, and costing the boss an important deal. Tom Megabux, the Texas oil millionaire, was in a town, and wanted to play a game — and was left-handed. Bill has faithfully and honestly reported that he gave you the order, and that you acknowledged it.

Oh for a time-viewer!

Item: Let's define "sociology" as "the scientific study of groups of human beings numerous enough to constitute a statistical system, and homogeneous enough to constitute a meaningful group."

(False example: The average age of death of all males in the continental U.S. is 6.3 months. Reason: "all males" includes insects. It's numerous enough to be statistical, but not homogenous enough.)

(Second false example: you can't discuss a single family group statistically.)

Then what is psychology? My answer: As of now, there is none! What's currently <u>called</u> psychology is actually a branch of sociology, because it's a <u>statistical group</u> study.

Try determining the characteristics of a molecule of benzene by studying the gas laws. The gas laws represent the statistical behavior of benzene molecules in vapor form — but they have nothing to do with the behavior of the benzene <u>molecule</u>.

Currently, psychologists are studying "one," the pronoun in the sentence, "One who is a member of this culture." But this "one" is no more representative of a human individual than the statistical molecule is representative of benzene.

Your chronoscope represents one of a great class of devices; any culture can be disrupted by introducing a device which every individual wants, but which is intolerable to the culture.

The matter-duplicator is another such device. The magic purse that is never empty is another.

By properly selecting the individually-desirable-culturally-intolerable device, any given aspect of a particular culture can be demolished. (Associated aspects will then undergo some drastic readjustments, of course, but the whole culture won't have to smash.)

What, then, would be the effect of making a chronoscope that would work <u>only</u> in the range of 75-100 years ago? It would smash prudery, but not privacy, for example.

Lots of possible angles on the thing!

Regards, John

Philip Jose' Farmer   *September 5,*
1955

Dear Phil:

The trouble with most of the story ideas you've suggested is that
they all fall into the class that no one yet has been able to present. The
standard novel is supposed to present the development of an individual
character; science-fiction is trying to find a technique for presenting the
development of a culture. So far, it hasn't been done, and nobody has yet
figured out how it can be done.

Each of the themes you want to present is too damn big to be
handled; each is an essentially valid theme. **Gibbon** presented the
Decline and Fall of the Roman Empire in . . . what was it, eight volumes. An historian is expected to have a long-timer viewpoint; who
lives long enough to experience 800 years of history? And if the wander-
ing Jew did, could he tell it to you so you could feel it? No more than
you can explain what adult love means to an 8-year-old. No more than
one can explain to a 17-year-old kid what it means to look at a new-born
baby, and know it's your own child.

Even if you knew what 800 years of history meant . . . you couldn't
write it in English.

OK — so don't try.

Isaac Asimov did something of the sort very neatly, though; he
told a series of stories of the Foundation. Each covered a brief span of
history — but each constituted a point on a greater pattern.

You mentioned the business of giving up democracy and going to
an aristocracy system. Yes; that's coming. But you can't talk about the
100-year sweep of time involved in it, because no one man can experience it. But I'll tell you what you can do.

Look: the standard proposition is that a reader is supposed to
identify himself with a character, A, in a novel, and see-understand the
changes that character A undergoes during the course of the story. But
the important thing is not that the story-character is changed . . . but
that the reader is changed. The importance of the identification is that
222

if that is established, then changing the character must <u>necessarily change the co-identified reader</u>.

<u>Why</u> do you want your reader to identify with the central character? <u>Why</u> do you want the central character to change? The purpose is, I believe, that you, the author, <u>can</u> change the character. if you can induce the reader to co-identify, then when you-the-author change the character, you will, by a sort of sympathetic magic, induce a comparable change in the reader!

Readers are, however, notoriously slippery people; they'll drop an identification that gets too uncomfortable. They want to co-identify with successful, heroic characters. With good-in-their-terms individuals.

OK — if what we want is to change the reader . . . then there's a trick we can throw him.

We have a story, in which two characters are presented early, A, and B. A states his philosophy — and the reader is easily able to identify himself with it. B, on the other hand, states a philosophy that, "Aristocracy is a good idea," and, "Murder and assassination are good and useful tools," and, "Human sacrifice makes sense under some circumstances," and so on. A is solidly identified as the heroic and steadfast character, while B is seen to be a vile opportunist.

As the story progresses, A gets into trouble, and B hauls him out. A's troubles result largely, it appears, from a bull-headed insistence that A Good Idea Is Always Good, even when it isn't. About half-way through, the reader finds that A's bull-headed steadfastness is ruining everything he touches, and B looks like the one who's going to save the bacon. And, of course, readers being slippery characters, the reader switches identification to B.

And of course, the story winds up with A restating his philosophy in the same terms he started, while B restates his in his original terms. A hasn't changed a bit, because he's too bull-headed stubborn, and B hasn't changed a bit because he was right in the first place.

But the reader's changed. And he gets a lovely kick in the emotions hearing A restate the philosophy that <u>he</u>, the reader, accepted so surely only about 230 pages ago, and recognizes that A, the poor old dope, is just incapable of learning. He hasn't learned, and probably won't ever learn, the guy's such a bull-headed and stubborn old "I'm always right" character.

So B, and the reader (who has co-identified with B, by this time, of course) go off and leave A to blunder his way through life.

B, in the meantime, has committed murder, assassinated several people, set himself up as an aristocrat, and participated in human sacrifice. He's also arranged a few wars, and ruined the lives of tens of thousands of people.

(A peasant will not leave the land, unless you stick a bayonet in his tail so he can't sit down on it. It's essential, for an industrial civilization, that peasants leave the land. They can be induced to work in factories only for the purpose of getting money to buy land to sit down on . . . which means they'll leave the factories to rot, unless someone takes their money away as fast as they make it. The factories will never benefit them; only their children and grandchildren will benefit. It is therefore necessary to ruin the whole generation's lives, making them do something they don't want, for a benefit they'll never enjoy.)

Another gimmick: The battle between father and son. Father sees the ruin of all civilization; he sees the whole culture decaying into ruin around him. Son sees the new civilization growing, bursting out of the binding exoskeleton of the old. Father sees democracy and freedom of the individual being destroyed; son sees the new aristocracy, where each individual is assigned his class in society on the basis of what he himself is.

Aristocracy in the old sense failed because the aristocrat was picked by the test "Who was his father?" **Abraham's** son, **Tod Lincoln** was a nonentity. **Abraham's** father was a nonentity. An aristocracy-based-on-birth would have rejected **Abraham**. But . . . an aristocracy based on individual capabilities would have put **George Washington Carver** in a far higher spot than he was able to achieve. There would be segregation in the schools . . . but not on the test "What color is your skin." Instead, on "What kind of work do you like to do?" Why make a potential damn-good machinist into a lousy, inept, and frustrated doctor? Why not make it clear that the 1st class citizens are punished with immense rigor, while the 3rd class citizen has far greater freedom, and less rigor of punishment for an error. With greater authority goes greater responsibility.

But to the old-time democracy-oriented father, this new world of aristocracy is a decadent slipping back into old, abandoned ways.

224

The essence of good writing is to abstract the crucial data — and make it clear that these <u>are</u> crucial. To tell a series of stories which form a pattern — because no individual can experience the long-term sweep of history, Each individual is like a single fiber in a rope; he doesn't start at the beginning of history, nor will he endure to the end — yet he is an essential part of history. Each fiber of history is only about 50 years long, yet the whole 3,000,000,000 year length of history is made up of those short fibers, and is a strong rope.

I'm not going to comment too individually on your story suggestions, because the manner of presentation, not the theme, makes or breaks a yarn — as you well know. Therefore, it's futile to comment on an outline, save in broad, general terms . . . as I have.

I don't suggest that you rewrite *The Green Odyssey*; you can, I believe, sell it as it is — and God knows you can generate ideas faster than you can write anyway. Right now, I've got novels running out of my ears, and I've got **Eric Frank Russell, Lester del Rey, A.J. Budrys**, and **Isaac Asimov** threatening me with new novels-in-process. The series-of-stories technique will handle better the ideas you want to display, anyway. Try it that way.

Regards, John W. Campbell

Wayne Batteau   *September 11, 1955*

Dear Wayne:
We got back from our Mexico vacation about a week ago, and have been trying to catch up since.

The second night we were in Mexico, we walked into the arcade of the hotel (Del Prado) and, coming the other way, was **Kim Romney**. He was leaving for Denver in a couple days . . . but put us in touch with the Mexico City Anthropology Tea & Tiffin Club . . . or whatever. The probability of finding the guy is one of those things that's too small to calculate. I repeat a fundamental Law of Nature: No individual can experience the improbable; if he experiences it, it's not improbable . . . it's simply true. Or, in other words, "The probability of any actual experience is invariably 1.000."

Item: **Isaac's** done us a lovely little piece; "The Abnormality of Being Normal, or If Psychiatrists Would Only Figure." He's got an angle on "normality" that's a shocker.

Calling the commonest isotopes "normal," what's the probability of a molecule of hemoglobin (**Isaac's** favorite molecule, by now!) being composed entirely of "normal" isotopes? (Not containing deuterium, tritium, O^{18}, N^{15}, C^{13} etc.) The answer — despite the fact that for most of those elements, the normal isotope has a probability function of 0.999 or better — works out to be about 0.00000000000001. The all-normal molecule is one of the <u>less</u> probable types!

Probability calculations in complex-system situations, involving multiple parallel-series arrangements, haven't been studied worth a damn.

<u>IF</u> the characteristics that are "normal" for a human being could all be listed, and <u>if</u> each of those characteristics had a probability of 0.9999999, and there were, say, 10,000 characteristics in the structure of a human personality . . . what's the probability of an all-normal man? Then what is the <u>most probable structure</u>, as distinct from the simple listing of most-probable characteristics?

Isaac shows that the most probable structure of hemoglobin requires a certain number of deuterium, ^{18}O, ^{15}N, ^{13}C, etc. atoms.

Item: *ASF* did right well on the awards for best-of-the-year at the science-fiction convention. Best magazine: *ASF*. Best Novel: "They'd Rather Be Right." Best Novelette: "The Darfstellar." Best Short: "Alamagoosa." Best Art Work: **Frank Kelly Freas** for his work in *ASF*.

Tony Boucher, by the way, was picked to hand out the awards! **Tony's** a hell of a nice guy, and made good-natured remarks about *ASF* sweeping all the awards he had to pass out.

Horace Gold, being the kind of unhappy guy he is, was in a perfectly foul mood when **Judy Merril** called him two days later.

Isaac was Guest of Honor, as you probably know.

Item: What's the function of "intensity" in the Universe. Note that human beings violently distrust any intensity of interest anyone shows . . . unless that intensity is directed along exactly the lines the guy himself has already become intense about. Anger, for example, is intense determination to produce a specific change in a situation. If A is angry, B will seek to disrupt, quiet, dissipate, or somehow dispel A's anger, even when it is not directed at B, or anywhere in B's area. If you start displaying anger at the way geologists conduct their work, in the presence of a wholesale dry-goods salesman, the dry-goods salesman will, shortly, be trying to dissipate your anger. He's afraid of <u>intensity as such</u>.

But note this: **Cortez** and 500 men conquered Mexico. At one point, 20,000 Aztecs attacked 300 Spaniards . . . and were defeated. The essential reason, as I see it: How many pounds of meat does it take to defeat 10 pounds of meat-grinder? The difference in intensity of inter-molecular bondings in meat vs. steel is so great that the question becomes meaningless.

The Spaniards fought as a tightly-integrated team; the Aztec warriors attacked as individuals, under a loose, over-all concept. It made no difference that there were 20,000 Aztecs present; only about 100 could get into the actual front-of-contact with the Spaniards, because of their free-wheeling, loose-swinging method of fighting.

(Picture an army of 9-year-old boys, arms flailing in all directions like windmills, trying to box with 300 well-trained, well-rehearsed kids who have been taught how to use their hands. The trained team can walk through the arm-flailers in any direction, and practically at leisure.)

Item: the fundamental quantum that exists as a natural-unit in the Universe appears to be Planck's Quantum of Action. Then action (energy x time) rather than time is fundamental — and that means that the CGS system has <u>two</u> units that need to be hauled out, combined, and a new system worked out because mass (C) is energy, is part-of-action, and so is time (S).

A mis-stated problem cannot be solved. Example: How can I extract and concentrate the beautiful dye in the rainbow?

Eliminate time and energy as separate things, and you get a remarkable different sort of universe. In appearance, it's different, anyway! The conservation of energy becomes something else somewhat hard to state.

A chemical reaction will not take place unless the energy balances are proper. In a system in which 15 competing reactions, and reaction #15 is the least-probable, <u>and</u> reaction-product #15 can enter an irreversible reaction, the situation becomes:

1. Without catalyst: Very slight yield of irreversible product, as all raw materials get used in reaction #1 (highest probability.)

2. With catalyst that speeds up #15: Practically total yield of irre-

versible product.

Example: Three human races have invented and built logical-empire type cultures, of their own initiative: Caucasoid, Mongoloid, and Amerindian. The Caucasoid and Mongoloids achieved it about the same time, approximately 7000 years ago. (Aztec, Maya, Inca.)

When will the Negro race achieve it?

Answer: Never.

The Amerinds had a chance to get started 6000 years too late, only because the ocean barrier protected them. The Negroes <u>can't</u> invent their own, because the Caucasoids are already in their area.

It's like the problem, "What's the necessary prerequisite condition for life to originate on a planet? Answer: The planet must be sterile, the existent life-forms would monopolize the free-energy food-supply, and exhaust it . . . and then consume the trying-to-start life-forms.

Item: I was shown this puzzle-problem. I don't like puzzle-problems; why make up puzzles, when, God knows, there are enough real ones? Anyhow, **Kelly Freas** was also present, he got interested, and attacked it. That got me interested enough to take a good look at it.

Using a trick technique of problem-analysis, I solved it correctly in about 15 seconds . . . and then had to spend several days figuring out (a) how I had solved it, and (b) proving that my solution was validly derived from the information given.

The problem: A man comes to a paving contractor, and says, "I'm building a circular race track — perfectly circular, it's an annular ring. I want you to send me an estimate for the paving job; the track looks like this:

and the length of that line tangent to the inner circle is 100 feet."

Given only that dimension, solve the area of the track.

There's a valid mathematical-geometrical solution, that can be worked out in a minute or two. I used a logical method that is <u>not</u> mathematical, and depends on my pet "thinking in extremes" technique.

To explain the validity, consider the old gambling problem: Everyone knows 4-in-a-row (in coin-tossing) is more probable than 5-in-a-row. I, however, will pay you 3 dollars every time 4-in-a-row comes up, provided you pay me $4 every time 5 or more in a row comes up. Wanna bet?

I win. Reason: 4-in-a-row defines a system of <u>six</u> events; x———x, while <u>five or more</u> in a row also defines <u>only six events</u>; x———, . . . the subsequent event being undefined. The statement "four in a row" <u>appears</u> to define only four events, but by inescapable implication, actually defines six.

In logical thinking it is necessary to consider the inescapable implications. That is, there are two classes of implications in a logical system: volitional implications, and inescapable implications. If I say, "It is not A," there is a situation of volitional implications; I may choose C, M, or Z if I wish, since all comply with the stricture "not A." But if I say, "It is either A or B, and it is not A," implication "it is B" is inescapable.

Now in solving the above puzzle, I used the fact that an <u>inescapable implication</u> is built into the statement of the problem — though it is not stated. To wit: the radii of the two circles need not be known to solve the problem. This is the inescapable implication of the statement that the problem can be solved with the single datum given. But this in turn implies I can assume <u>any</u> arbitrary values for the inner and outer radii, and get the same area answer.

OK — I assume an inner radius equal to zero; the answer is, immediately, 50^2 X pi.

The importance of studying the terminating events of a series is easily overlooked.

Item: In a human social group, the majority establish a norm. They then exert a powerful tendency to force all members of the group to conform with the norm so established. A democratic system is one in which <u>only one</u> norm is permitted. An aristocratic group is one in which two (or more) norms are considered real and proper. (Actually, an aristocratic group allows two norms; a caste system allows multiple norms. But each system is quantized, and rigorously rejects a spectrum-

229

type distribution.)

In the one-norm system of a democratic culture, all individuals who do not fit that norm are rejected ... and, since there is only one in-group-norm in the culture, the rejectees are labeled by terms having strong negative value-loading. "Abnormal" is the most obvious of these.

And in a one-norm culture, _all_ rejectees are the same outgroup.

But actually, rejectees will be of two classes; the sub-normal and the supra-normal.

Let's imagine a home for the feeble-minded; the norm of the group of 14 year old boys in the playground is IQ 50. Now we introduce a boy of IQ 25, and another of IQ 100. Both will be rejected from the group as abnormal.

But note this: the subnormal will be rejected with sneers and ridicule and teasing ... but the supranormal will be attacked viciously. The subnormal will be allowed to retire from the group, and will be encouraged to do so ... but the super-normal causes intense irritation by his very existence. The dim-wit doesn't do "the right things," but he's so dumb he can't learn better; this we can forgive. But the super-normal doesn't "do the right things" and not because he can't learn how; it implies, inescapably, that he doesn't do them because he knows better.

This is the unforgivable sin; he is demeaning and sneering and ridiculing all of us, and our way of life.

This means that the super-normal kid must learn, and learn early, that he faces this situation:

1. He must totally mask his abnormality.

2. Or he must convince the majority that he is subnormal.

3. Or he must withdraw not merely passively, but so actively that the majority cannot find him, cannot reach him, and consider him dead. Because they will not allow his passive withdrawal.

In real life, the "In Hiding" scheme won't work. Reason: psionics are real, and we haven't learned to control them ... but we can detect them. Try convincing someone you're enthusiastically interested when you're bored stiff, and see how long you get away with it. You're radiating boredom at a psi level, and everyone around you can detect it. Try really fooling somebody that you're not angry when you are. Professional actors can't, and don't, do it; it's the business of the audience granting them one improbable assumption — that the audience can't tell the difference. Hi-fi music, however hi-fi, doesn't make you believe you're sitting in a chair in a symphony hall . . . so you spot the machine one improbable assumption, in order to enjoy the results. The hypernormal kid <u>cannot</u> disguise the fact that he's abnormal, because he gets bored when he shouldn't, gets angry when he shouldn't, has powerful psi radiations that are out of phase with those around him. (Consider the effect of displaying deep satisfaction and enjoyment, for instance, when someone else is feeling angry, or unjustly treated. Now repeat with a psi radiation, while putting on the expression, body posture, and so forth to match the group around you. You're obviously not only abnormal, but a god damned untrustworthy liar, too.)

He can't withdraw, either. Why he can't, I haven't fully worked out . . . but he sure as hell can't. **Sprague** had that right in "Judgment Day."

The <u>only</u> way he can achieve a modicum of survival-comfort is by convincing his neighbors that he is subnormal, not supernormal. That his out-of-place reactions are due to his stupidity, not supernormal. He's not afraid when they are, because he's too dumb to know better. He laughs at the wrong times, because he's a dope. He must encourage them to ridicule and sneer at him — so they will drive him away. He doesn't dare reject them; they must reject him. He'll never completely get away with it, so that they'll reject him once and for all, and let it go at that. A true subnormal is rejected, and stays rejected; the hypernormal keeps making experiments that inevitably reawaken suspicion.

(Typically, out of desire for companionship once in a while, he'll get one of the normals alone, away from the majority-group . . . and in half an hour have the kid his best friend. Naturally; he can play the normal's games, and do it but-good, when he wants to for some reason.)

Betcha a lot of "retarded students" are very busily playing subnormal.

Also, note that the super-normal won't work for the rewards that are offered the normal. "Now, if you do a good job on this, I'll give you a nice piece of candy," says the would-be-rewarder. "Er . . . please, do you mind keeping the candy, and letting me have half an hour with your *Oxford Dictionary* instead?" In consequence, his motivations are not theirs; his loyalties are not theirs. He will work with an intensity they couldn't endure, for a reward of no value to them.

231

Look, **Wayne**, what would you do, how hard would you strive, to win the adulation of those normal neighbors around you?

Yeah, that's what I thought. But how hard would the normal neighbor work if he thought he could, thereby, win a little adulation?

And how hard would you work to find someone who could tell you just what errors you make in your thinking processes? Tell you clearly and specifically?

Yeah ... and how hard would your said normal neighbors work to get the hell out of his way?

Item: A language is a cultural property. A culture is a true statistical group; the laws of statistics apply exactly to a culture. Vide insurance company tables, etc.

But an individual is not a statistical group, and the laws of statistics are not valid at all for him.

Inherently, then, if the language is a "good fit" in transforming information for a statistical-universe system, it will be inherently a poor fit for a non-statistical-individual.

But if it's a good fit for an individual ... it won't be an efficient information-transform system for a culture!

Therefore, probably, we need two languages within a cultural group; a household language which deals with individual-individual relationships, and a formal language, which deals with cultural-statistical matters. And, of course, a third language which relates the two separate systems!

You can set up a fine set of laws for gases, that work just fine for moderately large statistical systems. (They don't work for stellar masses of hydrogen, for instance, nor do they work for a 10-liter volume containing 1000 molecules of H_2.) You'ld have a hell of a time using them without any understanding of scale effects, which means analogic.

Item: The kids won't be willing to suspect that the super-normal kid is not really sub-normal; it makes them less uncomfortable if they can be sure they're smarter.

Item: The reason the barbarian couldn't learn about the short-sword and cohort secret weapon: To use the team technique, the individual must weaken himself physically, give up the right to the glory of personal victory ("We won," instead of, "I killed ten enemies!") and change the whole system of rewards the culture offers. In a team-cul-
232

ture, the individual cannot boast of his achievements . . . because he didn't achieve them alone.

You can readily define for your daughter, for example, what she must give up if she marries; try defining for her what she will gain in return! She will give up privacy, the right to a private opinion, the right to determine what she wants to do with her life, the right to the satisfaction of a career ("I have achieved this!") and even the right to determine freely her comings and goings. She will have to accept responsibility for her husband's well-being, accept many onerous chores for him. And what does she gain in return? Define it!

Tell the barbarian, in terms he can become enthusiastic about, not in terms of threat-of-pain, what he gains by weakening himself, and giving up all hope of ever again dancing around the tribal camp-fire, and crying out his triumphs.

Tell the Aztec warriors why the meat can't defeat the meat-grinder, no matter how brave it is.

Sociological note: The Negroes, currently, think they have it tough. That's because they never went through the cultural-development stage of transforming themselves from an aristocracy-serf system into a democratic system. Why, for a thousand years, your ancestors and mine were serfs, in a system that didn't call up a lynch mob if a serf appeared a bit uppity; the insulted noble just beat him to death out of hand, and mounted his head on a pike as warning to other uppity serfs.

We've undergone quite a eugenics program. As I figure it, in the 7000 years since logical-empire started going, some 230 human generations have come along. They've been picked over, each generation, for the ones that could team up in the most deadly-effective groups. And could learn from anything around them most efficiently. I figure some 10,000,000,000 men and women were selected over to yield the population of which **Cortez** & Co. were representatives. (That doesn't count some 60,000,000,000 more that were canceled out as incompetent during the first few years of life — only the ones that reached adulthood.)

If you spent 230 generations breeding a line of dogs to achieve the most efficient fighting breed possible — what chance do you think a wolf would have against the resultant?

Poor old Aztecs! They started 6000 years too late. The old fellows

233

didn't have a chance.

The Spaniards, though, gave 'em a great hand up along the way. There were 20,000,000 Aztecs in Mexico when the Spaniards arrived. Three hundred years later, when the Mexicans won their independence again, there were about 4,000,000 Indios. Must have been quite a bit of rigorous selection of determinedly vital stocks; the ones that went into the business of living on anything but a "this is for keeps" basis couldn't take it.

Mexico's building up a genuine, modern, native culture — and some of the Indio blood is very definitely contributing powerfully to it.

Because some individual types of organisms have decided to play the game of life "for keeps" . . . the rest have two choices. Do the same, or die.

There's a third choice — but that isn't ready to be thrown into operation yet. There aren't enough organisms yet that can appreciate the meaning of symbiosis — which does not mean "Live and let live." It means "Git in and pitch — and you'll either do it alive or dead, because dead you make useful meat."

Time has a nice piece on **Col. Stapp**. I particularly like the line he pulled about why he ate his medical-school-days guinea-pigs, after preparing histological sections. (He being slightly poor at the time.) "If it breathes, it's protein, and if it's protein, I eat it." Now there, I hold, is the philosophy of a truly honest, thoughtful man, one who is not given to unreasonable prejudices and biases.

Got a cover coming up: Terran Exploration Team. Shows an out-world animal, cross between a kangaroo and a saber-tooth tiger, in the foreground; exploration team obviously about to be attacked. First member of the team is 13 foot tall Kodiak bear; second is another Kodiak, with a man riding in a saddle, reaching for his weapon. Following them, a third Kodiak, carrying about 1/2 ton of supplies, just topping a nearly vertical cliff. Just taking off from the man's shoulder is an eagle. Allow genetic engineering to modify the animals slightly, giving them teamship-symbiote instincts, and a little speech ability — and I doubt that any out-world situation would be too much for the team to handle. No mechanical vehicle-robot could compete with the team for exploring a new planet of a type men would be interested in colonizing. Machines can't manufacture their own repair parts, run self-
234

maintenance systems, and adapt the local landscape to fuel and structural members! Bears are omnivores, just like **Col. Stapp**.

Regards, John W. Campbell, Jr.

Isaac Asimov *September 11, 1955*

Dear Isaac:

As you probably know, we've been down in Mexico for a while. On returning, I found that anthropological research has shown that *ASF* did right well this last year. My spies report you gave a hell of a good talk. But then, your Convention talks are famous anyway. Makes it tough, when you've got a reputation that high already, to give a talk people won't say of, "Wellll . . . it was good, but not like he gave at . . . ." And the reports I've heard are not saying that.

Thanks, also, for being my stand-in on the trophy-giving business. It was unfortunate that practically none of the award-winners could be there. **Kelly Freas**, as you probably know, has been waiting for **Polly** to finish her months . . . and the time's about up. So they couldn't go. **Peg** is still too damned uncomfortable when around a lot of eager, interested young men — and she is not ready yet to have me off on a trip somewhere, wondering whether somethings happened to me, suddenly.

Your probability calculation on "normal" has fascinated me, and caused me to do a lot of thinking in a lot of directions. I've got a hell of a lot to kick round with you when next we meet. In the meantime:

The professional crooked gambler, when he uses loaded dice, doesn't put a large permalloy slug in 'em, and then set up a 50,000 gauss electromagnet under the table. That would, of course, make the dice land exactly the way he wanted them to, every time he turned the magnet on, but it's too apt to cause vague doubts in the other players' minds, when the dice land, jump six inches in the air, and come down with a resounding thunk, or flop over violently after they've stopped rolling.

The professional uses loaded dice — but loaded so that they simply upset the expected odds. He'll win with almost absolute certainty in the long run.

Now let us consider a eugenics program. Instead of passing a Eugenics Matings Bill, and causing a revolution which we put down

235

with machine guns, nerve gas, and prefrontal lobotomies — we simply establish a wonderful National Education System. We set up great Universities and technical schools. They're open to any students who can pass the entrance examinations. Since women have as much of a right to education as men, they're co-educational.

Since city rents are high, they're located in lovely park and forest-land sites, about 75 miles or so from the nearest large town or city.

Postgraduate students are encouraged, and since the State recognizes the importance of marriage, provisions are made for married students.

And that, my boy, is guaranteed, sure-for-certain Eugenics Program. Like the professional gambler, we don't nail the god damn dice down . . . we just load them neatly. Of course no two students have to get married to each other, and of course no two have to start going with each other. They aren't forbidden to have friends on campus — it's just so convenient, that's all. And besides, the entrance examinations have, of course, tended to suck in individuals of basically similar-or-complementary tastes. And naturally, individuals of the same intellectual level are somewhat more apt to find mutual companionship pleasing. . . .

Who's going to object, huh? Who's going to get mad because he found the girl that pleased him and satisfied him, huh?

Of course, the Washington University, established in the beautiful forests of north-central Washington, is 250 miles from the nearest town of more than 5000 population, and does have a curious situation in that the men are practically all taking technical engineering courses, and the women taking humanics courses . . . but a lot of them are getting married. There's some friction at first, because the two different approaches to life need considerable reconciling, but faculty counselors help a lot . . . and some exceedingly important work in social engineering is being done by their graduates, too. Particularly by their second-generation graduates. . . .

But nobody has to go to these schools.

Now another item.

There is, in the Universe, some sort of law of least Time-Effort, or least Action. Damned if I can state it exactly . . . but it's there. Of course, we've been brought up on the CGS system of measurements, that works with Time as a basic parameter. It would, however, be per-
236

fectly simple to set up a system in which action (the product of time and energy) was the basic parameter, instead of seconds. It would probably be more closely aligned with reality, too, since Planck's Constant is evidently a real, fundamental unit in the Universe — and it's a quantum of action.

Anyhow — a catalyst (which is of course your business) can never make a reaction take place unless the energy-balance already favors it. But it can alter the time-rate of that reaction. All an enzyme does is alter the rate at which a reaction which would take place anyway proceeds.

Oh . . . yeah?

What is the score if we translate this from terms of energy-and-time-rate, into terms of action?

Also, in a system in which there are 15 possible competing reactions, the reaction yielding the greatest free-energy quotient will tend to dominate. We'll number the possible reaction systems from 1 to 15 in order of decreasing free-energy output; then the product distribution will show a maximum output of #1, and a minimum output of #15.

So we introduce a catalyst that speeds the time-rate of #15, and lo! we get a yield of 95% #15.

In human affairs, this is called the Early Bird Gets The Worm mechanism, or, "The One That Gets Thar Fustest With The Mostest Wins."

It suggests the marked advantage of cycling, or batch-lot processes; the reactants are dumped in, together with the catalyst, and the reaction started. Then Product #15 forms rapidly, and after a short time the whole system is damped down to non-reactive level, while Product #15 escapes the scene.

Now note this: The fundamental requirement that must pre-exist on a planet in order that life can start . . . is that there be no life already present. This isn't a play on the meaning of "start"; it recognizes that if life is already present, it will have damn well monopolized all available free food energy, and will immediately convert the newly-starting life into food.

Three human races have, of their own efforts, achieved logical-empire; the Mongoloids, the Caucasoids, and the Amerindians (the Mayas, Aztecs and Incas.)

The Aztecs, Incas and Mayas started approximately 6000 years later than the Caucasoids and Mongoloids.

Will the Negro race ever evolve an indigenous logical-empire culture?

No . . . it won't. Not ever.

The only reason the Amerindians did, starting 6000 years too late, was that the oceans acted as barriers that prevented the already-existent Caucasian and Mongoloid cultures from "infecting" their area.

The Negro race can never develop an indigenous culture, because we've already been in there.

Will the Chimpanzee ever develop high-order free-willed intelligence?

No, he's approximately 3,000,000 years too late. If he does succeed in evolving intelligence by himself . . . he'll be sucked into the system of human civilization, and not as a free-willed intelligence.

A shift of timing can make an otherwise possible reaction impossible. It diverts the needed reactants into other channels.

Raising temperature alters the rates of enzyme systems. If they are altered too much, they might get entirely out of balance.

Does fever work as a defense against infection by causing diversion of reactants required by metabolic enzyme systems?

Is a "mere change of rate" only that? Might not that, in and of itself, constitute a complete blockage of some reactions?

Regards, John

Isaac Asimov   *October 10,*
1955

Dear Isaac:

I think you should get a look at this, though I can't use it.

Too much of a good thing is no good. He'll have to invent his own cock-eyed idea!

Regards, John W. Campbell, Jr.

"The General Chronic Properties of Thiotimoline," by **Ens. P.G. de Baryshe**

P.S. Be sure to return this so I can send it back to the author.

John W. Campbell, Jr.   *October 12,*
1955

Dear John,

I stopped the postman today and asked for my mail. He gave me first a manila envelope from Street & Smith and I thought: "Good God, John has rejected ABNORMALITY OF BEING NORMAL." And while I stood there, confused and downcast, the postman handed me a letter from Street & Smith which obviously contained a check for AB-NORMALITY OF BEING NORMAL. So for fifteen minutes, I deliberately didn't open the manila envelope in order to see if I could figure out how to resolve the paradox. I didn't succeed. The nearest I got to it was that you might have sent me a check to reassure me <u>and</u> the manuscript for some minor changes.

Well, anyway it turned out to be the thiotimoline article (which I herewith enclose) and I thank you for sending it to me. It was tremendously interesting (though I agree with you that publishing it would be to present the readers with just a little too much of a good thing.)

Furthermore, the article made a profound emotional impact on me. The famous question that ended my Oral Examination for the Doctorate was: "**Mr. Asimov**, can you tell me something concerning the thermodynamic properties of thiotimoline?"

Well, my answer to that was a relieved laugh, which soon became general about the table. <u>Here, however, is the real answer!</u> For this, I cannot help but love **Ensign de Baryshe**. And so I hope that in rejecting the article, you will be very gentle with the young man. (A silly request -- when, from personal experience, I know how gentle you can be with young writers.)

Oh, and thank you for accepting THE ABNORMALITY OF BEING NORMAL. The check was appreciated all the more because of the ten-second interval when I thought it was rejected. (I was perhaps over-confident concerning the sale of the article. This is bad and, ordinarily, I try never to expect an acceptance. Doing this keeps me "hungry" in a spiritual sense so that I keep trying as hard now as I did in 1938.)

Your discussion of metastability was most interesting and to me, at least, most valid. I was amused though at your example of **David**, the splinter, and the needle. The reason for that is that, although you couldn't guess, it is an example that doesn't work. **David** <u>has</u> had

239

splinters in his finger, and after we explained what and why we were going to do, he sat there very quietly and let us probe. However, in other ways, he shows the concept beautifully. Thus, one of the greatest pleasures he has is in taking his toys apart. He shows the most amazing ingenuity in slowly destroying the indestructible. Afterwards, of course, he is devastated at the fact that he no longer has a toy. We have tried to explain to him that the future evil is greater than the present joy — but he is completely oblivious. He cannot resist the pleasure, although he <u>must</u> know what he is bringing on himself. (This isn't metastability, by the way, but something else.)

I intend using this principle in my current novel, of which a chapter has already been written. The Three Laws of Robotics have inherent limitations and their chief value lies in their effect upon humans rather than upon robots. I'm not sure about <u>everything</u> that's percolating in my mind as I work on the novel, but I dare say it will become clearer to me as I watch, with narrow attention, the things I write.

Yours, Isaac Asimov

Sergeant H.P. Sanderson   *November 12, 1955*

Dear Sergeant Sanderson,

I read your essay on my stories with the devouring interest any self-respectig author would have in an analysis of his own stories so keen and so favorable. I am grateful for your interest, for the thought you have given them, and if they have really given you the pleasure it seems that they gave, I am happy indeed.

Now for a few words concerning my "future history." I'm very sorry, Sergeant, but it doesn't really exist. To be sure, my "Foundation" stories are self-consistent, but I wrote each story without any thought for what would have to come next. When it was time to write a new Foundation yarn, I simply looked over what I had already written and built on that as best I could.

At the same time I wrote the Foundation stories, I was writing
240

positronic robot stories. The two types of stories had no connection whatever in my mind. In fact, my robot stories had no particular connection with one another. When I was asked to put my robot stories into a book, I was amazed to find that with a few minor modifications (such as killing off a character who must have been 150 years old at the end) I could connect them up. I had first told the publisher it couldn't be done, and I only made the attempt at his insistence.

All other stories I have ever written have not been part of either series. True, I had my own two special backgrounds, a) the Galactic Empire, b) the robot-based civilization. When I thought up a story, I often used one of these two backgrounds because, first, they were familiar to me so that I didn't waste too much brainpower on non-essentials, and, second, they were familiar to the reader and associated with my name.

However, in using one of the backgrounds, such as the Galactic Empire for SUCKER BAIT, or the robot-based civilization for CAVES OF STEEL, I made no particular atempt to tie it in consistently with other stories using the same background. That is why you have your curious little "happy endings" that seem to come to nothing in the next book of the series.

All this may disappoint you, but truth is truth and all that. I have not worked out a future history in detail, because I don't want to make life harder for myself. I don't want to have to throw out a decent yarn because I can't hammer it into place. I don't want to have to spoil a decent yarn by carving it to fit.

In fact (and I hope this doesn't sound hopelessly arty of me) when I write a story, my only thought is to make it a good and a salable one. (It is my belief that in no field of popular fiction is the correlation between "good" and "salable" closer than in science-fiction, which is one of the great reasons why I have so far resisted trying my hand at other varieties of story.) Anyway, if I have to choose between a good development and an interconsistency among my stories, I make the same choice every time and to hell with consistency.

However, my mind being essentially an orderly one, I'm never inconsistent just for the sake of it, so that where it can be managed I do keep to the main line of a possible history and that is why my books can be placed in order as well as they can be.

Let me assure you that the order in which you place my novels and your description of the history they represent is as accurate as can be expected. I doubt that I could do a better job myself. In fact, I'm sure I couldn't as I couldn't possibly write my stories with anywhere the meticulous attention you obviously devote to their reading.

While I live, I hope, in time, to write novels that fall in the time-gaps, and that their inconsistencies be small in comparison with their aptness — for the sake of yourself and others who think like you.

My current novel, or at least the one being written now, is not one of these, however. At least, it falls in time immediately after THE CAVES OF STEEL.

Thank you once again, **Sergeant**, for your interest. Unlike entertainers on the stage and its various derivatives, the man who entertains with the printed word is denied the inestimable pleasure of hearing the applause, of sensing first-hand that he is producing happiness. A labor such as yours goes a long way to making up the deficiency and is worth a great deal to me.

Very truly yours, Isaac Asimov

P.S. How would you place my THE END OF ETERNITY in your scheme. In a very peculiar way, it fits precisely into the scheme.

Isaac Asimov   *November 13 ,1955*

Dear John,

Thank you for sending me **Sargeant Sanderson's** analysis of my stories. It was fun reading it, and I answered him in some detail (I felt he deserved it.) I enclose a carbon of the answer for the sake of whatever amusement it gives you.

I am also returning **Sargent's** manuscript. I hate to do it, but since it has a "Manuscript Tracer" on it, it is obviously the temporary property of Street & Smith, so here it is.

Myths die hard. In fact, people seem to cherish them and resent their explosion from any source, however qualified. I have many times, publicly, denied having worked out a future history, but the fans go on assuming I have -- just as they insist I made up the Three Laws and the plot to "Nightfall" despite my repeated placing of credit where it belongs.

Another one -- In a little book, put out by Fantasy Press back in

1947 or thereabouts, you described me as being one top author who did not hit the big time with his very first story. In fact, you said (using round numbers) you rejected a dozen of **Asimov's** stories before you could accept one. Well, actually, the record shows that you rejected eight and took the ninth, (To be sure, you rejected the next nine after that.) Nevertheless, the figure 12 is engraved in the fan mind, and all my shouts to the effect that it was only 8 go unheeded.

Alas.

Yours, Asimov

Isaac Asimov   *December 2, 1955*

Dear Isaac:

Yes, **Isaac**, I approve of miscegenation; you may argue that it's special interest, since I am, of course, the result of one of the longest and most complicated systems of cross-breeding in recorded human history. Or you might argue that it's experience speaking, on the same basis. I am, as you know, partly Scotch; the rest is English, French, German, Dutch, Magyar, Irish, Arab, and God-knows-what, but probably a trace of Amerindian and Negro got in there somewhere in the last ten centuries.

And I know anthropologists don't use the term "Amerindian;" I do though, because it's convenient, completely clear and unambiguous, and thus leaves me free to use Indian to refer to the peoples of the great southern peninsula of Asia. Why use all those extra characters, when "Amer" is adequately specific?

There's a mountain of prejudice, bias, misunderstanding, and suspicion to be overcome in this problem of human relationships. Now just at the moment, you're heading due east on the slope of that mountain, and I'm heading due west — and you're of the opinion that I am, therefore, going in a direction opposite to the direction you're headed. You're wrong; this mountain can't be climbed straight-over; the trail is a switch-back road, and I'm at a different point on the trail. "Up" at my point happens to be westward, while "up" at your point happens to be eastward.

My friend, it was the philosophers of your own genetic line who did a Grade A No. 1 job of setting up philosophy of Racism. At that

243

particular time in the history of development, it was a damn good idea; in order to produce the best, strongest hybrid corn, you have, first, to refine two or more lines of highly inbred corn. It's necessary to have pure racial stocks before you can produce a hybrid stock.

Racism, therefore, has a definite place in the development of Man. The ancient Jews did a good job of setting up a pure genetic line, requiring a high degree of inbreeding of the strains.

OK — so the next level on this switchback mountain trail is hybridization.

And the next, of course, is a new separation of strains, to be followed by still another hybridization.

There's a difference between mixing human strains, and combining human strains. It is not true that all racial hybridization produces desirable results; hell, no! If you have a strain of mice with a genetic tendency to cancer, and another with a genetic tendency to degeneration of the spinal nerves, hybridization of the two is fairly apt to yield something that gets cancer and degeneration of the spinal cord.

If a man with cleft palate marries a woman with a hereditary tendency to piebaldness, you can get children with cleft palate and piebaldness, and you can get children with mama's sound palate, and papa's sound pigment distribution.

The gimmick in hybridization — miscegenation — is that you are required to be willing to accept the ruthless sacrifice of defectives. (Every racial strain has its weakness; the hybrid may combine all the worst features of both.) Now Nature, of course, operates on the broad, statistical level; she's totally blithely unaware of the poor sucker that drag's through his short and agonized life with hemophilia. (I knew him, though; his name was **John Kane**, and he was a codeine addict, whom the FBI had given special papers to so that he could get his codeine from doctors. There was no telling when the agony would hit one of his joints.) He, by the way, told me of a Jewess he knew, who was a hemophilia carrier . . . and knew it. She also knew genetics quite thoroughly. Two of her sons had died because of circumcision — and she had the third circumcised. He didn't have the hemophilia gene. She wanted children — but knew enough about the life of a hemophiliac not to want a hemophiliac son to live.

Nature, my friend, is not cruel — but is most appallingly (from the
244

human viewpoint) ruthless. That's because nature operates statistically; it's the only way genetics <u>can</u> work.

Now I'm headed the same way you are, actually — over that mountain of prejudice, suspicion, and the consequent unnecessary agonies of mutual hurts. You see the answer in terms of your background; you don't know what I, with my very different background, learned in just as hard a school.

You, you lucky, lucky guy, were brought up in an environment where many different races, religions, and folk-backgrounds were intermingled. You're aware, of course, of the mutual antipathy possible between different folk and genetic-racial systems. But you've misidentified what it really is.

I was brought up in a neighborhood of a single economic level, with a single religious code, a single folk-mores code, and a single consequent system of what's-right. The slightest deviation of an individual was instantly spotted as an individual deviation. You may have had troubles heaped on you for being a Jew; I had troubles heaped on me for being **John W. Campbell**: individual. You felt set apart and excluded from the great group; my friend, they had me set apart from the whole damn human race!

So, with your background, you think that there should be One World, One Race, One Mores.

Isaac, my boy . . . I hate to think what would happen to a deviant like you if that ever happened.

When there are many different groups, races, religions, and folk-customs in an area, any <u>individual</u> can mask his individual differences as being different-group-patterns. He doesn't appear different; he can make it appear that he belongs to a <u>different group</u>.

If I commit bigamy, I am vilified, arrested, punished . . . unless I show that I'm a Mohammedan. An enormous latitude of behavior is allowed an individual <u>if he can show it is normal-to-his-group</u>.

The <u>human</u> race — not any racial sub-group, but the whole race — knows deeply and instinctively the importance of discipline. An undisciplined individual is a menace to all Mankind; essentially, he is a madman in the true sense. The whole race fears the undisciplined, the rogue, individual — with reason.

Therefore if your deviations are individual, they'll punish you 'til

245

you renounce them. But if you can show you are a properly disciplined member of another group — that's different. You're civilized, even if you aren't civilized their way; you're tame, even if you do have a different owner.

You think its tough to belong to a minority group? Hah! You should try being in the spot of appearing a no-group-individual! Go ahead and achieve your one-world-one-race-one mores ideal, bub . . . and you'll be among the first to get it in the neck.

I'm out for exactly the same ultimate goal you are . . . but I'm one step ahead of you. I did have the experience of belonging to a one-mores-one-group system. Believe me — it ain't good. It's good for <u>most</u> of the people of the one-mores-one-group system, of course; necessarily it's closely matched to their needs and natures. What we actually want is a system that can define the problem of Minority opinions, and knows what to do about it.

What constitutes a minority? Answer: Any number from one individual to 49.999% of the population. What constitutes an effective-important minority? That depends. One individual sitting in Times Square with his finger on the trigger mechanism of a lithium hydride thermonuclear bomb is an effective minority. 20,000,000 low-grade morons in a population of 150,000,000 constitutes an ineffective minority. And that is <u>not</u> the way it should be; that's the way it <u>is</u>.

The New York Times has more readers, and more public respect than *Astounding Science Fiction*. But . . . they don't know, yet, that *ASF* has more effect on the shape of the future of the world. *ASF* is a smaller minority — but a very, very effective one. Our readers happen to include a majority of the creative thinkers of the nation's upcoming generation; they're the ones that will shape the future.

Wanna know how the National Association for the Advancement of Colored People can really do an immensely important and useful job for Mankind? Easy: develop methods of testing young human beings for high potential achievement, so that we <u>can</u> react to individuals on an individual basis!

But now consider the consequences if they — or any other outfit — actually succeeded. Take a science-fiction slant on it, and to hell with whether it's "impossible" or not, <u>assume</u> the development of a set of tests that accurately measured the potential abilities and talents of an
246

individual. A set that permitted us to know the nature of any tested individual with a high degree of certainty.

Now, of course, we would be able to send to college the individual who could benefit; if his papa happens to be President of Amalgamated General Everything, and he rates low, we send him to Deep Sea Diving School, that being his highest talent. If papa happens to be a coal-black coal-miner, and the kid rates high — he gets to Harvard.

Under this system, the individual's own, personal, individual talents, and not his racial background, would determine his place in society.

This is, essentially, what you want, isn't it? That each individual be judged as an individual, without reference to his race, religion, family social position, wealth, or anything but the individual's own nature. And this, obviously, inescapably requires that means be discovered for determining the facts about each individual; i.e., accurate total-personality-potential tests, on the order of the *O'Connor Aptitude Tests*, but far more accurate and detailed, must be developed. If we are to react to individuals as individuals, it is inherently, and specifically necessary that we have means of determining the nature of those individuals.

You, as a bio-chemist, can "react to" — i.e., think about — a specific enzyme only if you can identify that enzyme. If I ask, "What are the properties of a digestive enzyme?," you can't answer; I must identify the specific, individual enzyme before you can discuss its properties.

Equally, if we are to react to individuals-as-individuals, we must be able to identify specific individuals.

And, of course, if the NAACP ever made the frightful mistake of developing such tests . . . the NAACP would immediately be dissolved. The individual men who run the NAACP are, necessarily, individuals of considerable organizing ability. If the proposed tests were developed and established, they would immediately be transferred, by that very fact, from the group "colored people" to the group "executive organizers." Their group-identification would, by the fact and effect of the tests, cease to be with their racial group, which includes coal-heavers, thieves, cotton-pickers, bank-presidents, doctors, ministers, and policemen, and shift to the group-identification in which they fitted most perfectly — the executive organizers.

That means, of course, that they would now be members of the group Managers, while most of their ex-group would be in the group "Labor."

The present divisioning of human beings would, in other words, be shattered. You would recognize a much closer inherent communion with a Negro biochemist, say, than with a Jewish lawyer.

You may dislike calling them "genetic"; I don't give a damn what you call 'em. But people have "talents"; there are things for which they have an aptitude that does not come from training. These great musicians who start playing the piano at age 4 don't get that way by training — they had an aptitude. **Einstein** didn't get that way by training; he had a talent.

I don't give a consarn what you assign as the cause of the observational fact — but for Pete's sake man, don't deny the fact! Some human beings have talents; others have other talents; some don't have talents at all. Call it a genetic phenomenon, call it the will of the Gods, blame it on the fates. It is not necessary at this point to decide whence the fact comes; it is necessary to acknowledge that the fact exists.

Talents are not the result of training. Your talent for abstracting concepts wasn't caused by training; it may have been developed by training, but you had to have it before you could train it. A chimpanzee doesn't have that talent, and can't be trained.

You don't have the talent for living an active, physical-work life at 15,000 feet either — and by God, **Isaac**, you can't ever learn it. The source — genetic or otherwise be hanged for the moment. There are differences that training can't equalize.

OK. Given those tests I proposed, those differences would be found, and accurately metered. (By the definition of the postulated tests.)

They would have the result you desired; that every individual would be rated as an individual in his own right.

And ... they'd tell every individual the limits of his future hopes.

That, you see, is the thing people won't accept — and that's why the tests won't be developed. They would tell an individual, "You do not, and never will have, the talent necessary to be anything higher than a drug-store clerk. We will not give you any higher training, because it would be wasted on you. You will not be allowed to enter medical school, because you couldn't learn. Further, your sense of eth-
248

ics is too low to permit your being entrusted with human lives, and you cannot be taught to comprehend the meaning of ethics, so that you can never understand why you are incompetent to be a doctor as you want to be."

This man would immediately want to start a revolution; he would seek to gather a group of the rejected, forming a group-identification on the commonalty "We are unfairly rejected."

It doesn't matter that the rejection was absolutely valid; they can't see the validity, because the rejection was valid! They were rejected, we'll say, for lack of a sense of ethics. But lacking any appreciable sense of ethics, they can't possibly conceive that ethics is a real thing! The very validity of their rejection makes certain their reaction that the rejection was unfair. The actual fact is that people do not want to be treated as individuals! They want to be identified as members of powerful, authoritative, high-status groups. The objection to group-identifications stems from the objection to being identified with a group other than the one the individual wants to be associated with.

Answering a specific point; certainly there are white barbarians — and red-headed ones, yellow-skinned ones, and blue-eyed ones. The point I made was that the statistical distribution curve for one racial group is not coincident with the statistical curve for another. That, dammitall, is what you mean by saying there are two groups.

And my Percheron-Pony team is not a straw man. The physiological differences between men are small; agreed. But this represents the fact that physiological systems have been perfected, through millions of years of evolution, to a leveling-off point. The same thing happens with a machine design; any machine which has been manufactured for many, many decades gradually works its way toward a most-efficient-form, and, thereafter, undergoes very little change. Violins have stabilized, for example. Machine screw nuts have pretty well stabilized at square or hex.

The wild variations occur at the level of the far-from-perfected machine — the new, still-under-development machine. Practically every plane manufactured today is a monoplane; in 1915 they were making mono-, bi-, tri- and up to hexa-plane wing systems.

Since the physiological level has been pretty well engineered to a satisfactory system, there's darned little variation at that level. There

249

are no human beings 12 inches tall, and none 12 feet tall. But there <u>are</u> low-grade morons, who are not Mongolian idiots, but honest, genetic morons and can reproduce their low-grade kind. And there are **Einsteins**. The difference between a low-grade moron and an **Einstein** is a hell of a lot more than a ratio of 12 inches to 12 feet.

The physiological level is the one level where there is high correlation between all men. Mentally, emotionally, and ethically, the variations are enormous. Ethically, we have **Hitlers** and **Jesus**. Emotionally, we have South American indians who skin seals alive because it's easier to do it that way without damaging the skin than to kill the animal first. Offer one of those indians $250 for a young woman's skin, and he'd skin her alive for exactly the same reason. He's not evil, or sadistic; he just doesn't have empathy enough to sense the other entity's agony. The Nazi bigwigs had amusing sadistic sports; those Indios wouldn't. Sadism is impossible to an entity that can't appreciate another being's agony. But, as I say, they'd skin a girl alive for the perfectly logical reason that her skin would be more valuable if it weren't bruised or punctured.

Isaac, no problem can be solved until that problem is acknowledged. If you deny the existence of racial differences, the problem of racial differences cannot be solved. If you <u>do</u> acknowledge them . . . then the problem can be analyzed, studied, and worked out to a valid and workable conclusion. No matter how great an effort you may make to solve a situation by denying the problem that causes it, you can't make the solution stay put. It's like trying to put white paint over wood that's been stained mahogany; the oil-soluble stain will "bleed" through the white oil paint, no matter how many coats you put on. The existence of the oil stain <u>must</u> be acknowledged, and that problem dealt with.

They tried to deal with the problem of alcoholism by denying alcohol; Prohibition was given a real, honest try. It didn't work, and you know damn well it never would have.

Prohibit race hatred, prohibit race difference — and it won't work. It never has, **Isaac**. It <u>looked</u> much easier to the Prohibitionists to solve the problem of alcoholism by simple denial, than by the hard, deeply thoughtful, self-analytical method of figuring out why some human beings had to have alcohol. It <u>looks</u> easier to solve the race problem by denying its existence.

True, there is practically no race problem at the physiological level. True, there are no human Percheron and Ponies. But ... let's bring up an **Einstein** and a normal German boy together, and force **Einstein** to act and think, and be just like the normal German boy, so we won't have any race problem ... shall we?

Hitler, you know, was trying hard to deny the existence of the race problem. His solution was a little different; he agreed with you that there shouldn't be a race problem, but his proposed method of reaching the solution was somewhat different. He, too, wanted One Race as the final answer.

Isaac, every cell in your body is descended from the same Adam and Eve cells — the fertile ovum that became you. Yet they differentiated as they multiplied; for some reason, difference of nature was so important to an actual, living, growing, functioning system that they gave up their identity, and set themselves apart in "racial" groups.

Instead of being so ardent — and easy-looking! — a Prohibitionist, why not seek to find why difference is essential. Every higher organism has found difference absolutely essential, for some reason; perhaps a higher civilization will be unlike the sponge, in which any cell can take over any job, and will, instead, recognize the mutual interdependence of organic integration. The different races will be recognized as different, just as the body recognizes the important utility of liver cells being basically, and inherently different from nerve cells or bone cells. The Body Politic may require difference. In that case, the effort to suppress racial difference would be an effort to block the higher evolution of social organisms.

It is proper to insist that we are all members of the human race; all the cells in your body have exactly the same gene-chromosome structure, too. But it is not proper to insist that there are no important differences between human racial groups. Liver cells are not structurally, or functionally equivalent to nerve cells.

And ... which is the more important organ, **Isaac**? The liver or the brain?

Ever think that, way back in the early stages of your fetal development, some of the cells had to dedicate themselves, and all their clone of descendants, to the high, and essential function of being a rectum? They might have dedicated themselves, instead, to being bone, or

251

nerve, or muscle — but you wouldn't have been able to exist as an organism if some of those cells hadn't taken on that particular dedication!

Athens and all its glory died because no Athenian would dedicate himself to the function of Sanitary Engineer. Rome attained the power it did, partly because some Romans were willing to make that dedication.

How long could Boston live without the sewage system?

Why should all races be alike, **Isaac**? Simply so you wouldn't have to think so hard to understand a different kind of intelligent entity? Simply so that you wouldn't have to work out more than one set of right-wrong values? Simply so that people can identify the Good Guys from the Bad Guys without the trouble of making basic evaluations?

Cancer is a condition in which wild cells start growing without discipline. Evidently, the organism has lost, somehow, its power to distinguish between different-but-good-and-useful and different-and-destructive.

In a society, there are two kinds of deviants; the different-and-constructive, and the different-and-destructive. The easy way to avoid the effects of the latter is to destroy all different individuals. If One Code, One God, One Right, and One Race is insisted on, it's easy to distinguish the Good Guys from the Bad Guys; anyone who is different is a Bad Guy, and is to be punished till he conforms or dies.

It's much, much harder to learn to recognize that there are hundreds of different, needed, Good value-systems, and still be able to detect — as we absolutely must — the different that is also inherently destructive.

Germany couldn't make that distinction; that's how we got **Hitler**. And Germany, if you think about it, was a remarkably homogenous group of human beings, actually!

Instead of prohibiting difference, learn how to evaluate and use it. Instead of denying it, study it and distinguish the Useful from the Destructive. Learn to tell the cultural deviant of the Galilee type from the cultural deviants of the **Hitler** type; don't deny deviation per se.

Learn to recognize that the Negro people are the only race that ever developed harmonic music of their own, instinctive folk-nature. (If you hear half a dozen Negroes singing at work, or just walking along, only
252

one will be singing the melody. Negroes don't ordinarily sing in chorus, but in harmony.)

It's quite futile to try to shove a problem out of sight; solve it, don't deny it.

You'll never understand the nature of a woman, if you deny that there is a different nature to be understood.

You'll never solve the problems of chemistry, if you deny that there are more elements than earth, air, fire, and water. Sure, it makes the problem <u>seem</u> tougher, when you say there are over 100 elements — but that way it can be solved, and the other way will never, never, never lead to a solution.

(But don't totally deny the validity of the earth-air-fire-water element idea; that would be false, too. The old boys were quite correct; matter has four forms — solid, gas, energy and liquid. Also, <u>phlogiston</u> is perfectly valid, with some emendations, when recognized as <u>energy</u>. Combustion takes place only with the release of energy.)

A catalyst is something that makes the possible become probable. What kind of influence would you call that? We don't have a word for it, do we? But some human beings have that power; around them, the latent potentials other individuals have tend to become realities. How could we rate an individual for his talent-of-bringing-out-other-people's-talents, when we haven't a term for, let alone a measure for, the ability? How could we recognize the difference between individuals with respect to an ability we didn't acknowledge existed?

Yet <u>that</u> talent is the talent that makes a great teacher! It matters not at all how much such a man knows; <u>he</u> doesn't have to know much, because he doesn't accomplish things. It's just that such a teacher turns out pupils of immense ability.

Figure out what you really want, **Isaac** — and then see whether the path you're on is actually headed that way.

Regards, John

Isaac Asimov   *December 8, 1955*

Dear Isaac:

"There," says **Isaac**, "I guess that'll stop him! He can't perform <u>that</u> experiment!"

253

Nope, I can't — but I don't have to. You do, **Isaac**. You have to take the 200 non-Indio girl babies, and the 200 Indio girl babies, and bring them up under the conditions you propose to prove there is no difference.

I don't have to, thanks to **Galileo**, and the philosophy of scientific evidence he and his followers established. You have only the weight of Orthodox Authorities, Consensus, and Everybody Knows Who Is Anybody behind you; I have all the weight of thousands of years of animal breeding experiments behind me. I am only claiming, modestly, that human beings are non-exempt from the laws of genetics; you are seeking to establish that they do not follow the laws that are applicable to all other sexually reproduced life-forms.

I am basing my statements on the carefully compiled results of studying genetic drift in genetically isolated human groups, too.

What — other than Consensus, Orthodox Authority, and Cultural Orientation, that is — do you base your claim that human beings are immune to the genetic laws that apply to other life forms?

You, not I, must perform the experiment with the babies; you, not I, claim to have a certainty concerning an exception to a solidly established law of sexual reproduction genetics; that selective breeding, over many generations, produces a marked differentiation of types within a species.

Prove it, **Isaac**. I don't have to, because I claim only that I, like the rest of animal creation, am subject to the laws of genetics. You claim immunity.

On what basis? Have you performed such experiments as you have suggested?

I can quarrel with your interpretation of some of the evidence you cite in your letter. The Nigerian, for example, who complained of the heat in Boston. **Isaac**, I don't like hard physical labor; you don't like hard physical labor; I don't know anyone who does like hard physical labor. Put on the spot of having to do hard physical labor, I will grouse, bitch, and groan. So will you. We don't like it. But there's a friend of mine who complains he doesn't like doing hard physical labor, either; he has a severe heart impairment.

I don't like hoisting 100-pound sacks of salt for the water-softener around. **Peg** doesn't like doing it either. Neither does **Leslyn**. The difference is that I can do it, with annoyance. **Peg** can do it with considerable strain; **Leslyn** can do it only on a basis of hysterical strength.

Of course your Nigerian friend didn't like heat. But **Isaac**, my sister was in Nigeria during the war, in the U.S. Embassy in Lagos. She was invalided home with a complete breakdown into psychotic melancholia. Her dislike of the heat was at a different level than your Nigerian friend's.

Also, by the way, you misunderstand **Will's** point in "Sand Doom"; the Caucasian couldn't stand the heat, because he had his choice of (1) stripping to the skin, and letting sweat keep him cool — but having his hide burned off by the ferocious actinic light — or (2) wearing an artificial actinic-proof skin, called clothes, and being unable to evaporate enough moisture to keep his body temperature down. The Amerindians and Negroes weren't forced to that second choice; they stripped down and kept cool. The Caucasian could have, too — if he hadn't been a blond Caucasian!

And lookee here, my cancer-expert friend; Caucasians are <u>not</u> able to tan adequately, even after many months of exposure. Farmers, desert prospectors, and sailors are subject to skin cancer induced by excessive actinic irradiation. And I do NOT mean merely blue-eyed, yellow-haired Skowegian-style blonds, either. The difference the Amerindian and Negro enjoy is that they <u>start</u> where — or beyond where — a Caucasian's maximum tanning leaves off. And <u>then</u> they tan! Negroes and Indians tan too, you know!

Please, **Isaac**: State specifically what your reason for holding human beings immune to the laws of selective breeding is.

Two hundred generations of selective breeding turned the Aurochs into the cow.

Fewer generations than that can turn the generalized domestic dog into everything from Chihuahuas to St. Bernards, Greyhounds and Pekingese.

Look; I agree that there is little — though not negligible — physiological difference between human strains. But that DOES NOT APPLY at the mental, emotional, or spiritual level.

Also, dammit, I know enough about genetics to know that some of the individuals descendant from me <u>will</u> prefer strumming their guitars and singing spirituals; some of them <u>will</u> be incapable of appreci-

255

ating or using a college education. And by God, I want them to have the right to live at the level of life they find good, and be respected for what they are. Why should all men have to take college degrees, and push pencils? Why not have a few who like tilling the soil, playing guitars, and singing songs?

I know that, since I, and my clune, are not immune to the laws of genetics, not all my descendants will be at or above my level; not all will be of my own type.

The reason the old concept of aristocratic-genetics went sour lies right there, too. It is incontrovertibly true that the son of a long line of brilliant men and women is probably going to be brilliant, too — that there is a far higher probability that he will be brilliant, than that the son of a long line of nonentitites will be brilliant. It's probable that your children will be more competent than that the janitor's children will be. But genetics is a statistical thing; you carry some lousy genes, as well as some good ones; so will any female you might have mated with. "Beyond This Horizon" was based on that fact; the idea was that their techniques allowed them to combine the best available genes from each parent. A hybrid can combine papa's cleft palate and mama's piebald skin — but he can, also, combine papa's sound skin and mama's sound palate.

The aristocratic-genetic idea of "noble birth" was based on asserting as an absolute-invariant-truth the statistical truth that high-competence parents tend to produce high-competence children.

Dammit, man, accept the statistical distribution curve of population characteristics. Selectively combine the high-end individuals, while suppressing the low-end individuals. Continue for 200 generations. What happens to the peak of the distribution curve?

Look at **Muller's** work on mutations. Allow that an environment develops, in which an individual lacking gene 237-B-81 has just as good a survival chance as an individual having that gene.

Given a few dozen generations, and there'd be a 50-50 chance of any individual having that gene — except that mutation keeps mutating genes. Those that don't have it, can't lose it by mutation; those who do have it, can. Therefore mutation becomes a one-way street — and you're bound to wind up with a population that doesn't have it!

The human male is physiologically capable of raping the human
256

female. Therefore, 20,000 years ago, whether an individual female had a desire to mate had absolutely no bearing on whether she was impregnated while conscious, or while unconscious. The predictable consequence of that situation, and the tendency toward mutation, can only yield a race with females who do not have the desire for mating as an instinct.

(This doesn't mean that a high-level female, of great intellectual and emotional power, can't have a tremendously powerful desire to mate with some fine man. But it will be motivated at a level other than the physiological-endocrine-neurological level that motivates a wolf bitch, for example.)

Only by <u>continuous positive selection</u> can any genetic characteristic be maintained. Lack of selection <u>for</u> the characteristic allows mutation to destroy it — and mutation inevitably will.

If you see a house that was built in 1780, and it's still standing firm and weathertight, you know damn well that there has been continuous positive attention to maintaining it. Weathering and the attrition of time would have demolished it, otherwise.

Well, the weathering of cosmic radiation, and the attrition of time, will eliminate any genetic characteristic, given half a million years or so, unless there is a continuous attention to maintaining it.

The moment an environment develops in which the entity can survive without that characteristic — at that moment, mutational attrition sets in successfully.

Human beings are <u>not</u> immune to the laws of genetics.

Why do you hold selective breeding forces — which you will surely agree apply to all other life forms — do not act on human beings, **Isaac**?

The Incas used to have a spring fertility-marriage-courtship custom. At 15,000 feet or so, the young men and young women would hold a dance, and, at a signal, all the girls would start running up the mountain. At a second signal, the young men would start after them. Any young man could — and was expected to — mate, then and there, with any girl he could catch.

Isaac, if you ran such a race with, let's say, horses, and kept it up for 20 generations or so — is it remotely conceivable that you'ld develop a strain of <u>genetically</u> altitude-adapted horses?

257

Christ, man! Any youngster who could chase a fairly fleet-footed girl up a mountain from 15,000 feet upward, catch her, and still have stamina enough to lay her, well and soundly, would <u>have</u> to be genetically altitude-adapted!

And any girl has some degree of preference in the males that impregnate her; if she doesn't want to be mated by the tribal oaf, she damn well better be able to outrun the thumble-fumbed dope. Maybe she <u>does</u> like Hunah, and does want him to catch her — but Hunah, unfortunately, is too short-winded to run fast, and Buhbuhboo, the oaf, is going to lay her, but right now, if she doesn't do some honest running. So . . . she runs, and lets her second choice, Dunaf, catch her. Too bad about Hunah.

What sexually reproduced life-form, other than man, would <u>not</u> yield a genetically adapted high-altitude form under those conditions?

Regards, John

Dr. Herman Muller   *December 12, 1955*

Dear Dr. Muller:

I read your article in the *Scientific American* with considerable interest; I particularly liked the fact that it achieves its point and impact without use of highly technical data — but with plenty of simple, cogent thinking. I have a feeling that, as of today, too many people in science feel that data is the Be All and End All — and don't do enough thinking about what the data's for.

I've been having a lovely, red-hot argument (via mail) with **Dr. Isaac Asimov**; you probably know of his new book, written with **Dr. William C. Boyd**, "Races and People." I'm trying to convince **Isaac** that selective breeding can develop specialized types of human beings, just as thoroughly and effectively as it can when applied to other sexually reproduced animal life forms. **Isaac** — who is Jewish, a very fine guy, and has a deeply ingrained dislike of the idea that people actually do differ genetically — is fighting the idea.

It has served to sharpen our thinking; neither one of us is an incompetent "argifier," and we're both learning. The recent *Scientific American* article on "Life at High Altitudes," had a little stinker of an argument at the ending; it stated that, no doubt, any baby born and
258

raised from infancy at 15,000 feet would show the altitude adaptation displayed by the Peruvian, Andean natives. The stinker in that statement, of course, is that it is perfectly true . . . inasmuch as no human female could complete the birth labor if she were not altitude-adapted, however, the statement means that "any child of a genetically adapted human female will display altitude adaptation also." Caucasian women, for example, can't carry an infant to full term successfully above about 11,000 feet. The statement, then, sounds as though it had one meaning — and is true, only because it has a quite different fact behind it! Any baby born and raised at 15,000 feet would be altitude adapted . . . because he'd be the child of either a Peruvian Indio, or a Tibetan mother.

However, in the course of the debate we've been having, a point occurred to me that is not mentioned in your *Scientific American* article, and which I have not seen discussed anywhere in the specific form I threw at **Isaac**. As follows:

In a group of organisms, let us assume that there exists a certain gene, P, which provides the organism with some helpful characteristic, a pro-survival characteristic whereby the organism can successfully cope with an enviromental threat, aP.

If the threat, aP, is widespread and essentially universal, then only P-type organisms can survive, and all living organisms must be P-type.

Assume a change in the environment, such that the threat aP is eliminated. Now both P-type and non-P individuals can survive equally well. There appears at first glance, then, to be no factor favoring either P or non-P, genetically. Actually, there is a very important factor; mutational forces favor non-P. Reason: if an individual organism has the gene, P, it can suffer mutation to any, and that means an infinity of possibilities, non-P configuration. But if an organism does not have P, it cannot suffer such a mutation. Therefore, mutational forces act as a one-way, effect, eliminating any characteristic that is not a survival-necessity. To maintain any genetic characteristic, there must be continuous positive selection for that characteristic.

Possible example: Human beings have a genetic tendency to resistance to diptheria. The introduction of diptheria toxin-anti-toxin therapy made high genetic resistance less critical to survival. The expectable

259

consequence would be the loss of diptheria-immunity as a genetic characteristic, since the genetic defense has been effectively replaced by a technical defense.

I have also wondered to what extent the organism's evolution is influenced by what might be called "total vital energy supply"; the organism, in building itself, must expend its time-energy forces in erecting thousands of complex structures essential for its survival. If we conceive of some structure as being a "waste of growth energy," the concept implies that there is a finite limit to the growth-energy possibilities of the organism. Given an infinite source, you can't properly speak of waste, since no drain of the source diminishes it.

Then if an organism does have limited growth-energy, it is a survival factor to eliminate no-longer-needed structures — to eliminate genes which call for factors that are no longer needed in the environment.

In this case, the gene-destroying effects of mutation are a pro-survival effect!

Evidently, the effect of mutations is not to be classed as "good" or "bad," since without it, there could be no evolution. The effect is "good" or"bad" depending on whether the rate of selection for genetic characteristics is higher than the rate of mutations, or lower than the mutation rate. If the mutation rate exceeds the selection rate, the process of evolution becomes uncontrolled and uncontrollable. For the individual, of course, mutation is apt to be tragedy no matter what it is. For the race, however, that's not necessarily true.

Considering the vast reluctance to accept the new and different, I'm sure that evolution wouldn't have taken place if the selection had been fully able to control mutation. This generation's insanity (we should sterilize the insane, they say) is next generation's genius — and it gets to exist in the next generation only because the recessive genes couldn't be weeded out during the generation it was thought insanity!

Just think what remarkable possibilities there are in the development of human beings who colonize other planets! A gene that may be insane contra-survival on Earth might be the genius of survival on Mars!

Regards, John W. Campbell, Jr.

Isaac Asimov   *December 14, 1955*

Dear Isaac:

When two intelligent individuals disagree on a subject, there's bound to be the problem of "Who's behind the times?"

Now the curious thing is, things in the Universe have a sort of cyclic appearance; each advance seems to deny the immediately preceding world-concept, while reaffirming the concept that preceded that — but with a difference.

The alchemist said, "The elements are transmutable, if only we find the method." The far wiser chemists said, in 1885, "The elements are eternal and immutable; the alchemists were wrong." The nuclear chemist of 1955 says, "The elements are transmutable, if only you find the method. But, of course, chemical methods aren't at a sufficiently high-energy level."

Greece was an autocracy — not a democracy as is usually claimed. Rome was a true democracy . . . for a while. Then they had to try autocracy, but didn't have any adequate autocrats.

The world has never been able to make absolute democracy work; it never will be able to. No cultural system involving more than 100 people can be operated as an absolute democracy; the instant division of labor starts, absolute democracy ends.

Absolute autocracy has never worked long, either. It'll stand up for about five generations, generally speaking.

But right now, in the US, we are on an excessive-democracy swing; we're probably headed for an excessive-autocracy swing, but it won't be bad. The hunting Mankind is doing in that area is rapidly damping the swings. (Hunting, here, is the servo-mechanism technical term; it's what a thermostat system does in maintaining a temperature. It never maintains the exact temperature; it hunts across a small plus-and-minus range.)

No previous human culture ever knew about the concepts of genetics, statistical laws, probability curves, etc. No individual wants any Law of Nature to apply to him at the mental-psychic-emotional level; physiological laws are acceptable, because he has some understanding of them. But that there are rigid Laws of Nature at the mental-emotional level . . . NO. NO! I TELL YOU! NO! I WON'T HAVE IT! I'LL KILL YOU IF YOU PROVE IT!

Reason: There are statistical laws which are absolutely valid for

261

cultural groups. The Life Insurance companies can prove that. But cultures, throughout Man's history, have been forced to operate on statistical laws — and always will be, because, for cultures, only the statistical laws are valid, just as only statistical laws are valid for gases.

But the cultures have always tended to insist that the Law which was good for the culture, must be good for all the individuals in the culture. All human cultures have confused statistical and individuals levels. The laws of gases are not applicable to molecules.

(But the cycle begins again; statistical laws are applicable for electron behavior!)

Therein lies much of the deep distrust the human individual feels toward laws, or proposed laws, purporting to apply to individual human mental-emotional factors. Statistical laws discovered by the culture have been imposed as individual Good Ideas.

Autocracy in the past, and all ideas of racism in the past, have failed by reason of this confusion of levels. It is silly to deny that selective breeding produces specially adapted strains; it's obviously true. The trouble is, however, that it is an absolute truth only at the statistical level.

Imagine someone invents a test for General Intelligence And Overall Competence; one that works. (This we can postulate in a universe of discourse, whether we can do it or not.)

Let us select 10,000 young women who have scores of 300 or higher on this test, where 100 is normal. And 10,000 young men with scores of 300 or higher. We will mate them, and select their offspring for 300-or-higher individuals, discarding the culls. We continue this process for five generations, but raise the go-no-go score to 350 for the 3rd generation, and to 400 for the 4th and 5th generation.

We now have a group of young men and women all of whom have five generations of exceptionally high intelligence and competence behind them. What will their children be like?

They'll have a random distribution of intelligence-competence, of course, scattered on a Gaussian curve. It's just that the peak of their Gaussian curve will have been moved toward the high side. There will be some morons, some just-barely-normals, and some extreme geniuses. There has been a general shift of the Gaussian curve, but we can make no statement whatever about any individual child.

The fault in the aristocracy set-up was that it observed accurately
and correctly that individuals of high ability tended to have children
of abnormal ability. That is absolutely valid; it's silly to deny it. As
a statistical law, it's perfectly sound, and all <u>cultural</u> matters <u>must</u>
consider the statistical laws.

Further, an individual of high ability, descendant of ten generations
of men of high ability will probably have children of high ability.

Again, a sound statistical statement.

A child born of 10 generations of nonentities will probably be a
nonentity.

Again, a sound statistical law. Any culture that fails to acknowledge
that law is doomed; like it or not, it's one of the laws of nature.

Aristocracy's failure was to make the easy step from the statistical
fact, to the imposed individual requirement. It holds that <u>only</u> children
of the high-ability individuals shall be considered high-ability individuals, and that <u>all</u> such children shall be so considered. Both of
these are egregious errors.

But the error is not as extreme as our hyper-democratic system
tends to insist. Take a look at India; the caste system has been damned
stable for several thousand years. The reason the system doesn't look
very sound to us, **Isaac**, is because of that delightful old custom known
legally as the *jus primus noctis.* The aristocratic Lord of the Manor
could demand that any serf girl spend her wedding night with him.
(Which led to the fine old custom that Hans didn't marry Greta until
they were perfectly sure that Greta was already safely pregnant.) The
fact was, of course that the *jus p.n.* simply formalized the proposition;
actually any young noble would lay any peasant girl he found interesting.

This leads to the rise of a middle class. The statistics now get loused
all to hell and gone. You now have a Gaussian Curve that has been sat
on by an elephant, till it squished out both sides, and has an enormously
prolonged, practically flat top.

And this, of course, is precisely the condition needed for democratic
systems; a population which has so fine-grained a spectrum of differences that it appears to be a perfectly continuous spectrum. (Since it's
actually made up of individual human beings, it can't actually be a
continuous spectrum.)

You can NOT establish democracy in India, no matter how hard you try, until there has been adequate illicit intercourse; where there is a real difference between animal types — including human animal types — passing a law won't end it. When types have been established not by five or ten generations of selective breeding, but by very careful non-interbreeding over a period of 200 years or so . . . the Gaussian Curve doesn't apply. It comes out looking like the profile of a roller coaster.

Try making up a curve of the distribution of height at the shoulders for 100,00 mixed dogs — mixing some 50,000 dachshunds, 30,000 airedales, and 20,000 Irish wolfhounds. (They're all of the same species, and can interbreed, too, remember.) Unless you jigger your figures most woefully, you'll get a three-humped curve. (Of course, if you measure the dachshunds in centimeters, the airedales in inches, and the Irish wolfhounds in hands, you may get a nice Gaussian curve out of it, explaining that due to cultural differences, the dachshunds being German, the airedales being English, and the Irish wolfhounds being normally associated with sportsmen who use the hand as a measure, somewhat different tests were required to eliminate the effect of mere cultural difference. The fact that a nearly perfect Gaussian curve has been obtained indicates the accuracy with which the cultural differences have been smoothed out. And, of course, everyone knows that Germans use centimeters, and the English use inches as the standard measure.)

Isaac: The proof of the accuracy with which cultural differences have been compensated is the perfect Gaussian curve obtained. The proof that there is no real difference between breeds of men is that they all fall on a Gaussian curve.

How circular can you get? Yet you'll find exactly that sort of argument (in two different places, of course) in anthropology and psychology.

You see, we know that a smooth Gaussian curve is the answer the properly designed test should give. So we carefully jigger the weighting of the test till it gives a Gaussian curve.

Then we use the fact of obtaining a Gaussian distribution with the test to prove that there is no difference between breeds of human beings.

Isaac, I <u>do</u> know what has been done. I <u>do</u> know what anthropologists have found out. I am <u>not</u> speaking from ignorance of the stage-behind-you. Dammit man, <u>there's a stage ahead of you</u>. And that stage will, inevitably, bear certain resemblances to the stage behind you. Statistics apply to gasses. Individual-behavior laws apply to molecules. But statistics apply to electrons. And, somewhere another level down, individual-behavior laws apply again, I betcha.

For <u>cultures</u>, statistical laws <u>must be acknowledged</u>. Or the culture will fail.

For individuals, recognition of individual-behavior laws must be acknowledged.

Ideally, the culture will recognize that individuals must obey individual-behavior laws, while individuals will recognize that cultures must obey statistical laws. No culture yet has achieved that wisdom. But we can, if we work hard enough, produce something that would be a start toward that recognition.

The individual must, furthermore, recognize that his own clune of descendants will inevitably <u>constitute a statistical group</u>. Some of your descendants will be thieves, prostitutes, murderers, professors, theologians, politicians, engineers, psychotics, hemophiliacs, mongolian idiots, tremendous leaders of Mankind. They'll be a statistical group.

Now, **Isaac**, knowing that — and you, because of your knowledge of biology, genetics, and probability <u>do</u> know that — name the One Right Way human beings should live! Name the One Breed to which all human beings must belong! How shall your descendants, all of them in their statistical distribution, find happiness? Shall we legislate against banjo-strumming field hands? Shall we hold that these are mere animals, who have no right to be on the scene? Shall we anathematize the hobo, the itinerant worker? (**Walt Whitman** was.)

One of my fine old ancestors presided at a certain witch trial in Salem, some few years ago. The woman on trial was one of my ancestors too, it so happens — by a different line. Which side shall I favor?

My name is **Campbell**, by a trick of custom. It might, if the name descended from the female line, have been Van Campen, Zhlotoli, Wood, d'Arcey, or, for all I know at the moment, ben Abrahm. And I'm sure <u>I</u> don't know but what it might have been Bearclaws. **Peg's** maiden name was **von Winter**, actually. If the descent was on the fe-

265

male line, it could have been McKenzie — or Moran.

My ancestors are a statistical group, too. I'm like the focal point of a lens; a system of rays converges in me — and diverges from me. Each is statistical; I am individual. My clune will be statistical, too.

So statistical laws are important to me.

The race problem can be solved only by acknowledging it exists, and is a real problem. It does exist, whether we acknowledge it or not; because it is real, with or without our consent, real human beings will react to it. Until someone furnishes a better solution that fully acknowledges the problem exists, the old solutions, lousy as they are, will continue to be used.

So long as medicine can offer no real hope for cancer — human beings, dying of cancer, will try quacks. They have nothing to lose.

When a problem exists for which there is no sound solution — unsound solutions will be used.

You can't solve the problem by saying, "It isn't there!"

It is there. Men have known that the problem of genetics was real since some 100,000 years before **Mendel** — they just didn't have a name for it.

They made some damn good stabs at solutions, too; the Pharoes had a high-ability line, and did their best to stabilize it by breeding brother to sister, mother to son and father to daughter. You think they didn't know, even then, that genetics was a real force? That selective breeding produced results?

Don't, for Pete's sake, ignore the 6000 years of recorded human experimentation, **Isaac**!

Don't deny that genetics exists, and has effect.

Acknowledge the real problem — and solve that one! It is NOT a problem of "misguided human prejudice"; it's a real problem of real difference of breed. The more you deny it, the more it goes underground to fester. The people who show the most acute racial antagonisms are those most desperately, fearfully, seeking a real, workable solution — and that is not denial of the problem.

The trouble is this: there is an appearance of extreme injustice in the simple fact that, by a throw of the cosmic dice, I happened to get a collection of genes that made it possible for me to absorb a high-level education, and gave me the tendency to damn well go and get one. That

266

my father was able to help me do so was, in large measure, part of that roll of the dice; my father was also the source of half of said genes, which made it rather probable that he'd be in a position to help me.

Those things I didn't earn . . . directly. But if you recognize that I am merely a focus, with a statistical group back of me in time, and a statistical group ahead of me in time — if you think of "I" in those terms — then didn't "I" earn it?

I agree with **Newton**; "I have stood on the shoulders of giants."

Evolution is a strange thing, **Isaac**, because it must work through and around some complex barriers. Inescapably, evolution — since it works through genetics — can work only statistically. It can only produce a statistically sound answer.

But the statistics concern individuals, and the statistically-derived laws must find expression through individuals.

The individual animal must be induced to carry out actions that are statistically valuable to the race, however onerous, or dangerous, they may be to the individual organism.

When a bird sings its mating song — others than prospective mates are listening. When the firefly shines its light — predators are watching, as well as possible mates. The moose gives its mating cry, and responds to the call of the opposite sex . . . and to the moose-call lures that clever man invents.

Statistically, calling attention to itself is good for the race. Of course, the species has to have a higher birth rate to make up for the ones that get answered by the wrong listeners, or answer the lure instead of the mate. But statistically, it's necessary to the race.

Mating, for the female, means a greatly increased load on her metabolism, and a loss of the critically necessary agility. The doe bearing two fawns in her uterus is far easier prey for the wolf or the bear. Mating, for the female individual, is exceedingly foolish; it has an enormous negative value.

But the statistics of race continuity require it — so her genetics gives her a powerful urge to mate . . . and no explanation of why, no realization that mating means pregnancy and the terrible risks of pregnancy. Just a powerful urge — and a delightful individual reward of a great surge of satisfaction.

The danger-burden comes later, and she doesn't need a reward

267

there, because she can't get out of it anyway. She nurses her fawn afterwards not because she loves the dear little darling — but because her mammary glands ache like hell if something doesn't keep them cleaned out. The fawn is very precious to her; its suckling yields a vast relief to overfull mammary glands.

Cows love the farmer, too; they come to the gate at evening, and call plaintively for him to come and perform his ritual of relief and satisfaction.

The things evolution breeds into animal species are things that are statistically valid — and the individual rewards are, of course, necessary to supply the urge the individual organism must feel. They are not valid . . . individually.

The whole system is a beautiful example of the problem of Statistics vs. Individual. It's quite obvious that human beings have a deep, ancient instinct to inflict pain on other individuals; sadism is ancient and widespread. The Roman citizen laughed at the funny picture the girl in the arena made as she tried to stuff her torn guts back in her belly with one hand, while trying to run from the lion, batting futilely at his face with her other hand.

The good folks of the town gathered in the public square, holding their children up to see better, while the rebel was drawn and quartered, or the witch was shrieking as her skin peeled off in the flames.

It's an instinct, **Isaac** — and it's perfectly valid. Statistically, that is. Statistically, the race suppresses dangerous deviants that way. And statistically, punishment benefits the young, as any bear demonstrates when she cuffs her cubs. Obviously, mama bear must be given an individual-satisfaction when she does this statistically-valid act. (She must be rewarded for the effort expended — and for not doing the far simpler thing of crushing the cub's skull in, and getting herself a good square meal in the process.)

The problem is to convert the statistically-valid statistically-derived tendency to enjoy the pain inflicted on others — the reward for taking the effort to punish — into something more closely attuned to reality.

Mankind had to have an instinctive enjoyment of inflicting pain — when pain was the only way of teaching a lesson. The individual must be rewarded for effort expended on behalf of the race — or he won't

268

continue to do so.

Of course clever man got too clever for his own good; it's easier to get a conveniently handy victim to inflict the pain on, than to struggle out after the real targets. It's easier to let a lion do the work of hurting, and to put a captive girl in the arena. Romans didn't do things that way when their men were punishing back the barbarian raiders; it was a custom that came in with the Roman borders; when the borders came back toward Rome, the Circus boomed.

Good, cheap gin would have helped limit the circuses. Opium would have done an even better job. They make it so much easier to deny the problem, that you don't even have to work for a twisted, invalid solution to the deep, warning urge of the ancient instinct. The instinct that was meant to drive men out to kill off the wolves that ate their children had simply been short-circuited to the torture of a handy captive.

It's understandable that people think the instincts are bad business. They are . . . when they're perverted, ducked, and short-circuited.

But it's all right in the long run. Statistically, it doesn't matter. Statistically, the girl was going to die anyhow, the rebel was doomed at the instant of birth, and the witch wasn't immortal either; statistically, nothing important happened.

But statistically, something very important happened to the torturers; they, by ducking the real problem their instincts alerted them to, failed to solve it. Rome fell. The feudal system fell. The church eliminated its competition — and fell apart internally.

Instincts are most bodaciously wise . . . if you find out what they're for, and how to use them properly.

The problem is, however, to achieve the wisdom to understand them . . . and stop demeaning and anathematizing them.

The instinct that says, "There are racial differences," is not false. Stop yammering at it, and find out what it means, dammit!

Regards, John

Isaac Asimov   *December 21, 1955*

Dear Isaac:
Didn't know the darned thing was set for red ribbon. Oh, well, ap-

269

propriate for the season, or something.

We're taking off for Christmas in Bermuda tomorrow, but there were several items that came up in the last few days that I thought I'd like to have you and **Boyd** kick around.

First off, recognize this: when I say to a man, "You do not have the right answer there," this does NOT mean that I am implying that I do. The other day, I built an amplifier for a particular purpose. It didn't work. Theory was good, but behavior didn't check with theory. Now I am in a position such that, if someone were to come to me with that amplifier theory and say, "I'm going to build this, and it will do thus-and-so," I can, with assurance, tell him, "You're idea is wrong." I don't know what <u>will</u> work, but I know from specific experience what <u>won't</u> work, and I can, therefore, say that that theory is, in fact, wrong.

I do NOT know what the right answer to the problem of race is; I do, however, know what isn't. The answer does not lie in the direction of denying the problem.

First off on that, I've finally figured out what it is the orthodox an-thropologists, political theorists, etc., have been pulling on us. Son of a gun! I've been falling for the stupid little trick for years, too! You've been pulling it on me, and I didn't have wit enough to spot it 'til just the other night!

What's been done is this: People for years said that there were differ-ent breeds of men. The effort to deny the existence of the problem took this tack: Let's define "race" as meaning the same as "species." Now it can be shown that different species cannot interbreed. Therefore the fact that human beings can interbreed proves there is only one spe-cies.

Yeah . . . but who ever said there were different <u>species</u> of Man? Look, friend; they've set up a straw man, by defining "race" as identical with "species." That one they most certainly can knock down.

But I'm not talking about "species" of Man; I'm talking about <u>breeds</u> - you know, like Chihuahuas and Irish Wolfhounds, that belong to the same species, but are sure as hell different breeds. Any man who couldn't recognize that Chihuahuas and Irish Wolfhounds had a genetic difference would be badly in need of mental examination — but nobody says they're different <u>species</u>.

Who introduced this proposition that Man was supposed to be dif-
270

ferent species? "Race" is a term used solely, and exclusively <u>as a term applied to human beings</u>. It was the people interested in denying the existence of a problem (because they couldn't solve it) who tried the neat semantic haggle of defining the term in such form that it could be disproven. It's like trying to deny the existence of triangles by saying that "triangle" means the same as "square," but everybody knows that no square can have only three sides, and therefore this idea that triangles exist is nonsense.

"Race" is a term referring to the genetic differences that exist between human beings. The term has no other application. It is not used in referring to genetic differences between animals. Like many English collective nouns, it has a specific, limited area of application; you <u>do</u> refer to a gaggle of geese, a pride of lions, a herd of cattle, or a crowd of people. You do <u>not</u> refer to a pride of geese, a gaggle of lions, or a crowd of cattle — unless you are breaking down the specific and differentiated meanings of the terms.

You <u>do</u> refer to a race of men; you do <u>not</u> refer to a race of dogs — there you use the equivalent-but-different term "breed."

Instead of trying to foist off a definition of "race" such that it can be proven an empty class, try finding what the exact answer to the term meaning "the genetic differences that exist between human strains" <u>is</u>.

We've been mislead by the nose, via an old, stock semantic haggle. Race doesn't, and never did mean, "species." It means "breed" as applied to human beings. Use <u>that</u> definition, and see where your arguments about no-difference-of-species land!

The problem that I've run into is something quite different, and a damn sight more intriguing, anyway. This is not a semantic haggle problem, but a mighty-damn-serious sort of problem.

First off, a mule is sired by a jackass, on a mare. The mule is stronger, tougher, more resistant to disease and physical hardship, and smarter than either the donkey or the horse. But . . . it's sterile.

Now there's a damned interesting gimmick right in this area I urgently call to your attention; it deserves a lot of thought, I believe. A stallion breeding on a jenny produces not a mule, but a hinny. The hinny <u>is not a mule</u>. It's sterile all right, but it does <u>not</u> have the desirable characteristics of the mule!

This one example is, itself, enough to raise the large and practically

271

unexplored question of the non-equivalence of the female and male genetic structures within a single species. Genetically speaking, it would be necessary that a mule and a hinny be equivalent, if there were not a basic genetic non-equivalence between the male and female within one, or both of the parent species. It makes a difference whether the horse-parent is male or female — and on the genetic-equivalence-of-sexes theory, it shouldn't.

What other instances of this phenomenon there are, I don't know — but it looks like some important theses could earn some highly useful doctorates in this field!

Ever consider the intriguing possibility that we've got the wrong answer from way, way, back? That males and females are not a single species at all — but are two different species that are symbiotic, like the algae-fungus teams of the lichens? When a lichen reproduces, it appears to be a single-organism reproducing, doesn't it? But we know it ain't.

But the main point I wanted to suggest for the consideration of you and **Boyd**: the problem of matings between races is exceedingly tougher than we can handle as of now; we don't know enough genetics. To understand the problem, we're first going to have to understand the mule a lot better than we do!

Put it this way: by extreme inbreeding, two strains of exceedingly runt corn can be produced such that, when crossed, they produce a gigantically successful hybrid. This fact is dearly beloved by the seedmen . . . because of the additional fact that the hybrid doesn't breed true, and must be produced anew each year. This happy-for-them fact means that farmers can have gigantic yields — and seed growers can have an assured repeat business. I suspect the seedmen would murder any son of a bitch who produced a stable breed of corn with the desirable characteristics of the unstable hybrid.

Hybrid corn, like the mule, is a super-successful individual . . . with no clune of descendants. The mule's very great evolutionary advance over the horse is unquestionable; it's far tougher, stronger more intelligent, and longer lived. The one difficulty with it is that it can't breed.

Let us consider possibilities in human breedings. We'll take a highly inbred, puny line from the Tennessee mountains, and another
272

highly inbred and runty line from, say, some district in England where the localities haven't moved 50 miles in the last 300 years. Then we'll cross-breed them.

It's quite possible that the result would be a hybrid-corn effect — a super-competent individual of great physical, mental, and spiritual power. An **Abraham Lincoln** type.

But being the hybrid result he is — he wouldn't breed true.

I am a statistic, resulting from a statistical-group of ancestors, and leading to a statistical group of descendants — but I can be a statistical anomaly!

The inverse square law of light-energy distribution in space is absolute; there's no way of ducking it in the long run. But locally, you can set up a lens that produces a statistical anomaly — a concentration of light-flux. In the long run, the convergence-divergence effect cancel out, and the overall statistics remain unchanged. (See the second law of thermodynamics.)

Now thinking about this produces the following interesting problem: **George Washington Carver** was an abnormally brilliant, competent, and civilized human being. Few men in all history are appreciably higher on any scale of evolution than he was.

Ralph Bunche is a magnificent gentleman; a highly civilized, and highly evolved individual.

Each of these individuals earned and merited the highest respect and appreciation. They were fine human beings in every sense of the word.

But . . . just suppose that they were statistical anomalies, as **Abraham Lincoln** demonstrably was. Great as he was, none of his clune descendants has shown anything worth looking twice at. He came from nonentities — and his clune went right back where it came from; what he was was not indicative of what his genetic line was.

These things are not arguable, **Isaac**; facts exist, and instead of arguing whether they exist or not, it is necessary to seek them out and organize them.

There is an inherent difference of a type that has not been adequately studied in genetics. Mutation is recognized as a factor; the laws of hybridization have not been fully understood or worked out. The individual product of immediate crossing is not representative of the

273

hybrid clune to be expected. Stabilizing cross-breeds is a well-known problem — but one that hasn't been formulated adequately.

I suspect it can't be formulated until it is recognized that there are many levels of organization, and those different levels follow different laws.

Also, there are two kinds of statistical anomalies; positive and negative. A negative anomaly will be suppressed statistically; midgets don't breed midget children. Unfortunately, positive anomalies are also suppressed; hybrid corn doesn't breed hybrid corn.

The result is that the old question, "Would you want your daughter to marry a Negro?," is a very good philosophical question indeed. The only answer I can give, now, is, "I know too little about genetics to be able to give a reply based on understanding; I cannot compute the risks and benefits involved for the next few generations. From the little I know, it is better to marry a negative statistical anomaly of a statistically strong line, than to marry a positive statistical anomaly of a statistically weak line . . . in long-range terms."

The high achievement of any individual is his own; he can't pass it on to his children.

Now perhaps if we had a culture that could recognize these facts — we could honor the Mules for what they are as individuals — but it would force them, at the same time, to know that, like the mule, they could have neither pride of ancestry nor pride in descendants. The slightly-above-moron-grade individual, descendant of a long line of highly competent human beings, is also a statistical anomaly — but he, quite undeservedly, has a right to pride of ancestry and confidence in his descendants. He may be a fool, a dolt, and a barbarian . . . but he's merely a statistical anomaly in a statistical system.

There's a difference between the individual one-generation hybrid, and the stabilized breed.

Of course, if you want a quickie technique for breeding **Einsteins** — it's suggested in these facts. Cross-breed in a lot of different directions, highly inbred human strains from all over the world. Somewhere you're apt to hit on a strain that, properly crossed, yields Mules. (The crosses better be two ways; you might find that you got mules one way, and hinnies the other.)

(Science-fiction story in there. The planet run by Mules -- who can have companionship at their own level only by maintaining the two parent stocks separate and inbred. They'll never have descendants that way, and know it. They're brilliant, tough, long-lived — and bitter, because they exist in a hopeless side-eddy of the stream of evolution. If they allow the inbred lines to cross-breed in a normal manner, the line that produces their companions will be lost. If they don't — their little side-eddy will continue, and will, forever, be a side-eddy. Somewhere else, the slower process of development of higher statistics instead of higher individuals will take place.)

Isaac, it's so damned futile to deny a problem that exists; to wish it out of existence by a semantic trick. That just keeps it from being solved. Sure, it shouldn't be solved in public; too many human beings can't achieve the necessary stability of emotional response to accept the facts that would condemn them, and their line for a score of generations to come, to the long, slow, tough process of improving the statistics the hard way.

Improving statistics is a hell of a tough slug-fest. It's hard, and long, and disappointing. I've run into it in one form, and know how discouraging-annoying it is. I had an insurance company doctor examine me; he was an irritating son of a bitch, and his whole manner irked the hell out of me. Result: blood pressure so high, when he recorded it with perfectly accurate instruments, that I got a Class C rating.

I asked for a re-examination the next year — and they sent me to the same bastard. Class C rating confirmed.

I went to a different company, and was examined by a different doctor. Class A blood pressure rating — 132/85. But insurance companies cross-check. I got the statistical average rating — Class B.

The only way I can get the Class A rating which is proper for me, is by having repeated examinations, at one-year intervals, until I make the statistics come out Class A. There isn't any other way; they don't work on individual cases, but on statistics. And no matter how perfect I may be now — I can never make the statistics match exactly what the now-answer is.

Which would you, **Isaac**, prefer to be; a Mule, of high level intelligence and competence, aware that your clune would not be above the nonentity level — or a man of moderate accomplishment, with prospect that your clune, too, would be of good ability, and steadily advancing?

Wonder how **Abraham Lincoln** felt about the incompetence of his children?

You can produce a brilliant individual in a single mating — but you can't bring up a clune that way.

Mutation is different; it ends one statistical group, and starts another — but a group on which there are, and can be, no statistics for generations to come.

Genetics, my friend, is a tough, hard, rugged row to hoe. You get the luck of the draw — and whether it's wildly good, or wildly bad, your clune gets only the run of the cards. **Kingsbury's** cock-eyed article was not all nonsense; it wasn't that he didn't use facts — he misused them. And that bad hands of genetics must be discarded is a valid point; the way you improve the statistics is to breed from the statistical anomalies that are positive, while preventing breeding of the negative anomalies. Evolution is a result of accumulation of positive statistical anomalies.

Nature has such a gentle way about her; her way of breeding more cooperative human beings is to produce a race that tends toward murder. This tends toward rapid elimination of the defenseless. Somewhat tough on the individuals, but very good for the race. After all, the deer don't appreciate what a favor the wolves do them; if it weren't for the wolves, they would degenerate rapidly. If the wolves didn't tear down the pregnant doe, the deer would breed themselves into starvation.

But that's all right by Nature; the wolves soon starve to death if they get too efficient as killers, and then the deer have a chance. Teaches them a salutary lesson about conserving food resources, and not killing for the joy of the chase.

It is, of course, futile to say that the laws of the Universe are either Evil or Good. But its exceedingly damn nonsense to insist certain laws don't exist!

Regards, John

Isaac Asimov   *December 31, 1955*

Dear Isaac:

I like arguing with you, too, guy — or I wouldn't write such long letters! Furthermore, I wouldn't have been doing it for these last . . .
276

hmm, how many years is it now?

But on genetics, it looks like I'd do better to argue with my friend **Herman Muller**; he agrees with me more than you do. He liked several of the points I made to you, which you didn't like.

Look, **Isaac**; you're not a professional leader in the field of genetics — not one of the accepted molders-of-opinion in the field. Naturally not; your business is being a biochemist, not a geneticist. Your business in genetics is that of a professional, highly skilled and genuine expert in the highly specialized science-art of communication of technical material to a not-so-technical audience. You're a Grade A expert at that, one of the most competent men in that field in the world.

But one of the necessary <u>public</u> characteristics of such a specialist is that he must communicate <u>orthodox belief</u>; he is not permitted any original contribution at the level of ideas; his contribution is in matters of communication-of-ideas.

Publicly, therefore, you are not permitted to express your ideas about genetics; **H.J. Muller** is. **Muller**, on the other hand, is not expected to make his expression-of-ideas smooth, interesting-in-themselves, or easy-reading. You are required to.

But whatever limitations are put on the <u>public</u> expression of your ideas . . . do not apply to your private thinking.

In the anthropology field, I suggest you get some of **Clyde Kluckhone's** more recent material — the last year or so.

Kluckhone got his theories kicked in the teeth so hard, so brutally, and so inarguably that he did a hell of a lot of re-evaluation of all his beliefs and ideas. You may know that his son was arrested for murdering a woman in Raleigh, NC, by sniping at passing shoppers from a hotel window with a Luger. **Kim Romney**, an anthropologist who studied under **Kluckhone**, told us a couple years ago that the **Kluckhone** boy was a highly neurotic and deeply disturbed young man. His family life was almost pure theory of how-human-beings-should-be-raised; his father was a world authority on anthropology, and his mother is a world authority on social relationships. The behavior of their son apparently jolted **Kluckhone** enough to make him do some major revision of his thinking.

His new ideas include the proposition that anthropology has seriously neglected consideration of genetics and selection of human strains.

We just got back from Bermuda. (The vacation was a howling success; we spent only a week there, but it'll take us 6 months to get the girls calmed down again. **Peedee** had her first date — and was that a success! She went out to hear the **Talbot Brothers** at one of the Calypso night club places with a Lehigh junior, and did magnificently. She'd already met the **Talbot Brothers**, and they spent half their time back stage with the **Talbots**. **Jane** had an almost equally *summa cum hyper* series of dates with an Olympic Team swimmer, who dances like he swims — and **Jane's** good enough to keep up and make it fun.)

(I came back with a Retina II-C 35 mm camera, which made it equally a successful trip for me.)

But that isn't what I started to say. Bermuda has a very large Negro population. When the British first started settling there, Bermuda was an uninhabited island; there is no native population.

The Bermuda Negroes deeply resent the present immigration policy, which allows Jamaica, Tortegas, and Barbados Negroes free entry. The Whites resent it also.

The nights in Bermuda are slightly incredible; the place has hot-water heating, you know — the Gulf Stream. The nights are soft, humid, magnificently mild, and we were there at the time of the full moon — fortunately! We had a wonderful time strolling through the warm, spice-scented night.

Now **Peg's** been in Jamaica. You don't go out of the hotel after nightfall; you don't dare. When the sun goes down — you're Confined To Quarters.

Yet these two islands were both settled by the British, at the same time. In each case, the native population has no bearing; Jamaica natives died off, and Bermuda had none. Both islands were settled from the same population sources; Great Britain, and the West Coast of Africa.

What makes the difference — which is real?

Remember that **Machiavelli**, who was not a fool, nor a sour-minded pessimist, but a careful, practical, scientific student of human actual behavior, pointed out that no government (*The Prince*) could maintain rule in opposition to the population. (**Volstead** could have learned something from *The Prince*.)

The difference is, I believe, the indirect, but inevitable consequence

278

of the fact that Bermuda is a coral island, and Jamaica is not.

Sound like a *non sequitur*?

Here's the thinking behind that statement: When the British were establishing themselves on Bermuda, 300 years ago, Bermuda had zero possibilities as an agricultural development; as **Peedee** remarked when she saw the thickness of the soil on Bermuda, "The carrots have to grow horizontally." There's about 1/2" to 3" of soil on most of the island. A few gullies have soil several feet deep. Bermuda wasn't, and never could be, an agricultural colony. But it was an excellent center for shipping and seafaring industry. The great coral reefs give it magnificent sheltered harbors — huge, protected anchorages. The climate is mild, but not stultifying. It became a greater center of whaling, and shipping for the whole western Atlantic.

The British colonials wanted, and needed, slaves. They were making money in business; they needed clerks and domestics, dock laborers and warehousemen.

But they had no use for field hands.

When a shipload of west African slaves came in — domestics were in high demand. Now a domestic slave <u>must</u> have certain characteristics. You can NOT use as a domestic, someone who'll slit your throat at the first opportunity. You cannot use as a clerk someone who's sole interest is rebellion. Domestics and clerks <u>must</u> be cooperative, must be willing to accept that complementary functions are worthy and good and not shameful. Domestics <u>must</u> take pride and satisfaction in their work. "I am a slave, but I am a damned good slave, and my Master is proud of me, and values me and respects me <u>as what I am</u>."

A field hand, on the other hand, must have muscles. His willingness or cooperativeness is unnecessary; the whip, club, and gun can make up for that. A slave compound, with guards, can adequately take care of his rebelliousness, and tendency to slit throats. Brains are unnecessary; ability to cooperate willingly on a task for the mutual advantage of all concerned is unneeded.

When a cooperative slave showed up on Jamaica — he fetched a fancy price on domestic-and-clerk hungry Bermuda. When a rebellious, uncooperative, stupid lout showed up on Bermuda — he was sold as a field hand in the cane fields of agricultural Jamaica.

279

In the US, the slave who could not be made to cooperate was sold "down the river" — agricultural field hands don't have to be cooperative. Simon Legree used a whip — for a reason. He was being handed a group of individuals specially selected from the general Negro imports for their uncooperative, rebellious refusal to recognize the rights, needs, or special abilities of others.

The North used almost no field hands; they needed domestics and clerical types.

But because of the ease of continuous transportation on the continental area, the separation that took place in Bermuda-Jamaica never occurred, and the separation didn't remain.

Isaac, take a Gaussian distribution. Select from the distributed group three groups; the high-end group, the low-end group, and the mid group. Remove the mid group. Now mix the high-end and the low-end — and try to get a Gaussian distribution characteristic out of that resultant group! You'll get a pretty two-humped curve. If you don't you're a psychologist who makes up tests, weights the answers 'til he gets a Gaussian curve, then tests people and says, "See; a typical Gaussian curve! Proves the group is really an homogenous group!"

The Bermuda Negroes were definitely, inarguably, specifically, consciously selected for one type of personality pattern. The Jamaica Negroes were just as definitely, unarguably, specifically and consciously selected for a different personality pattern. Any test that gets a Gaussian curve from those two groups is a lying test.

In terms of the Ability To Refrain From Violations of Personal Rights Of Others, the <u>Jamaicans are inferior to the Bermudans</u>. They are so <u>genetically</u>; there was specific selection of breeding stocks to produce a highly trustworthy stock on Bermuda, while the culls of that effort were sent to Jamaica.

You can breed horses for superior draft power. You can breed them for superior speed.

You can breed dogs for draft animals — and you can breed them for intelligent ability to execute complex orders. (You should see what a working collie is expected to be able to do!)

And you can breed human beings for agricultural implements (**Plato's** term) or for intelligent ability to execute complex orders.

Now you can clearly recognize that it <u>could be</u> done. One more step,

Isaac. Stretch real hard — and look! It <u>was</u> done!

The great difficulty in getting the idea of breeds of Man over is a very simple one. It stops almost everyone. Before you have any right, or rational reason, to say, "He cannot . . . ." you must first look carefully in a good, plain, unstinted mirror, and say, "I cannot. . . ."

In order to recognize that there are breeds of Man — you must say, first, "I am of breed Q, and have the characteristics a, b, b`, d, g`` and h as dominants, but in consequence of this, I have the negative characteristics -e, -f, -h` and -m."

There are breeds of men — which means that I am one breed, and that breed has certain powerful characteristics of great value. (It wouldn't have survived in the fierce competition of Life and Evolution if it hadn't!) But being of that breed, I <u>do not</u> have characteristics other breeds of Man do have — and <u>I never will be able to have them</u>. They are characteristics that are NOT learned; they are unlearnable, and I am, therefore, forever and ever, world (and particularly me) without end, incapable of achieving those things as an individual.

I will never be able to do what a Peruvian Indio can do.

There are some men who can dive to 300 feet, stay an hour, and come to the surface in 20 minutes without getting bends. I doubt that I have that characteristic; I know that I can never, never, never learn it. My children can't learn it, either, even if trained from birth. That characteristic evidently depends on the possession of an enzyme we might call nitroanhydrase — it hastens and smoothes the evolution of dissolved nitrogen from the blood. It gives near immunity to caisson disease.

I can't, and never will be able to make music like a Negro; he has a genetic advantage I can't overtake.

I'll never be able to stand ultraviolet the way a Negro can.

Now statistically, I cannot <u>expect</u> a Negro to have the imagination power I have. I cannot expect the Negro breed to produce the queer mental characteristic **Will Jenkins** mentioned in "Sand Doom"; the characteristic of absolute refusal to accept Death as inevitable. (Why don't we practice euthanasia, **Isaac**? It's the rational thing to do many times, isn't it? A Negro population would.)

And my breed is as an overall, general statistical statement, markedly superior to the Negro breed — <u>and I can prove it</u>.

The "overall" term above means "taking all characteristics together, good and bad, strong and weak, as a statistical average, over a period of centuries."

The proof is easy — for my breed <u>as of now</u>. We run the world.

Mammals are better than reptiles; they are a higher life form. Proof: They run the world.

But the gimmick is this; the higher-yet life form will be one <u>capable of still greater symbiosis</u>. Man won over the other animals when he became symbiotic with Fire. Then he became symbiotic with the horse, the dog, the cow, chicken, duck, etc. Then he became symbiotic with Man, to some extent. Now he's becoming symbiotic with penicillin mold, and various bacteria, algae, and molds.

But symbiosis works on a basis of recognizing differences, accepting them as real, valuable, and Good — and learning to <u>use</u> not <u>fight</u> differences.

You don't think the way I do. This statement is true; I <u>could</u> derive from that, "Therefore he is wrong." Men have been happily doing that for millennia.

Instead, I say (and I know you do also!), "Therefore he is of great value to me, for he can give me a different angle of view on my conclusions." If you thought as I do, you'ld necessarily agree with me, whether I was right or wrong. Because you do think differently, we will reach agreement only on a basis of some exterior-to-both-of-us reality!

Negroes are not like Whites; therefore they are useful. And when Negroes have evolved to our level — they will know that we are useful to them, because we are different.

Street & Smith thinks I am useful to them; I think Street & Smith is useful to me. Now who is employing who? Is Street & Smith my tool for getting my ideas and concepts published? Or am I their tool for producing income? Or could it be that we're symbiotes?

Don't I have a right to smile with the Master's approval of a useful slave doing his work well, when **Bob Fenton**, the circulation department manager, straightens out a problem of distribution in New England when floods knock out normal transport routes? And doesn't **Bob Fenton** have an equal right to smile with a Master's approval of a good slave when I turn out an issue he can sell widely?
282

And could either of us work so smoothly <u>if we were not different</u>? I <u>can't</u> like his work. He <u>can't</u> like mine. There's a genetic difference.

Sure, there's an immense similarity — but **Isaac**, will you for God's sake recognize the importance of the differences?! Individuals <u>know</u> those differences are real; admit that, and <u>then and only then</u> can they consider the similarities.

Which is the most important leg of a three-legged stool?

The question has a very meaningful answer. "The one that's missing."

Think about that for a while; it ain't silly, my friend.

In a spaceship 1/4 of the way on a six-month journey to Mars, which is the most important, food, air, or motive power? That is, which will demand of the crew the maximum effort and attention?

The one that's inadequate.

What causes the most human relationship trouble; similarity, difference, or the right to be different?

The one that's not understood, and is, therefore, missing.

Suppose you have a computer that can handle 15 digit numbers, and your problem is to determine $(A \times B) - (C \times D)$. Now if A, B, C, and D are all 10-digit numbers, and the two products differ only in the last four places . . . what answer will you get?

If a human being is the product of physiology, mentality, education, orientation, and inherent-ability-to-observe, and this product is a 50-digit number, while Society runs a 20-digit computer . . . what will Society get as the difference between men?

Zero, of course. It's all lost in the rounding error.

Society's little 20-digit computer can barely distinguish between individuals that differ so massively you can <u>see</u> the difference!

Isaac, I've been stopped by cops for traffic violations about five times in the last five years.

I have not gotten tickets.

Bill Blow, standing on the curb in his run-down shoes, and sloppy clothes, with his paranoid attitude leaking out all over him, can see clearly what the score is. Rich guys that drive Lincolns get away with anything; it's only the poor guys that can't bribe the damn cops into letting 'em go.

He can see the Lincoln. He can't distinguish between his ability to judge situations and mine. Each of the cases in which I've been stopped has involved either (a) ignorance of some local, and not-predictable traffic-law peculiarity, or (b) a violation of the letter of the law in maintaining the intent of the law. (Not stopping completely at a stop-sign; the corner was such that only a slow, steady progression permitted vision. If you stopped at the stop sign, you would be completely blind.) In each case the cop allowed me to continue because I communicated the fact that I was not operating thoughtlessly; a policeman is paid to distinguish what can't be seen.

My judgment is far above the human norm. So is yours. You wouldn't be a professor if it weren't; you're paid, in some small part, to teach — but in large part, you are paid to fail students! You are paid to exercise the judgment to select and reject.

Any PhD with a set of visual aids and a prepared set of lectures, can teach, you know.

Gib Hocking was telling me that, somewhat to his embarrassed annoyance, the title "Dr." meant little down at Aberdeen Proving Grounds, in the Math department — but they addressed him as **Prof. Hocking** which carried weight.

Reason: the place was, naturally, crawling with PhD's. Any guy who passes a routine examination gets stamped PhD and turned loose on the world.

From that group, a minute number is selected for superior judgment, and labeled "Prof".

Isaac: don't make the mistake of thinking you're a normal human being. You aren't. Normal human beings aren't professors. Obviously.

Therefore don't make the mistake of saying, "I am a human being; I am thus-and-so. Therefore human beings are thus-and-so."

Before doing so, define carefully the term "human being"; you'ld have a hell of a time trying to follow a chemical process instruction that read, "Take 15 grams of one element, and 32 grams of another. Heat in a suitable vessel to a high temperature. After the heating period is completed, separate the products by using an appropriate differential solvent, and crystallize by evaporation to dryness under conditions that will prevent the explosion."
284

It would help if you defined a few of the terms, wouldn't it?

Why don't people want to acknowledge that there are breeds of Man, **Isaac**?

Regards, John

Isaac Asimov   *January 20,1956*

Dear Isaac:

Whoops . . . had the red ribbon on from writing "AIR MAIL" on an envelope. (Writing a man in Oregon; his 22 year old son, physicist with the AEC at the Hanford works, was killed by highway hypnosis last month. Someone showed him my article.)

Isaac, one of the things you found unacceptable in my discussion at lunch the other day was the proposition that some individuals have to be sacrificed. Sorry, friend — but that's the way it is. Life is, itself, the Great Research — and don't ever kid yourself that it's a mild, gentle, neatly bordered garden. There are two great risks — the Risk of Taking The Risk, and the Risk of Not Taking The Risk. No. 1 leads to your getting destroyed by sticking your nose into something too big to handle. In the old days, the men who were studying what we now call psionics (and they called Magic) would, every now and then, be reported as having "summoned a demon too powerful to control."

The fact that gunpowder was the first explosive substance reported has always interested me. Nitroglycerine is so much easier to prepare, if you're diddling around with acids and organic materials. However, it may be easier to discover gunpowder in gentle, progressive steps, so you have a good chance to report it to others — instead of simply having a loud report of undetermined etiology.

Of course, risk #2 has other consequences. While white men, for instance, were spending 6000 years testing — with the usual sociological research tools of war, rape, and slaughter — whether a culture based on powerful, brave, independent individuals or one based on powerful, cooperative teams was superior, the black races in Africa were not taking that risk of research. The good old fashioned methods, the tried-and-true techniques of the neolithic era, were good enough; they didn't choose to take the risk of trying anything so radical.

Well, they made pretty good slaves for a while. Of course, the cotton gin started the process of eliminating them; the McCormick reaper, and various other machine slaves displaced them pretty thoroughly.

I'm afraid they're going to be in even rougher condition after you enzyme chemists get through working them and their world over. **Isaac**, you know some human beings can NOT learn to do abstract, high-order thinking. Just because you can doesn't prove that all physiologically similar entities can. What are they going to do when enzyme chemistry has produced auxones and the like that will make plants, sprayed by airplane, do exactly what a machine-operated farm needs?

What shall we do with men who are field hands, want to be field hands, like being field hands, and don't want to be machinists — when we have no use for field hands? What shall we do with not merely technologically unemployed, but technologically unemployable human beings, **Isaac**?

You said that the schools aren't getting enough adequate medical students. Well, why don't you just take in any you can get, and teach them to be medical students? Training can accomplish wonders, as everyone knows.

But not everything. There is an infinity of things education can accomplish; because our society doesn't understand the meaning of **Cantor's** work on the transfinite numbers, the fact that "an infinite number" isn't equivalent to "all" is not appreciated.

I can freely agree with you that education has an infinite potential for improving an individual. But you must still agree with me that even though it can accomplish an infinite amount of good, in an infinite number of fields — that's only Aleph 1; it's certainly not even a start toward "all." Aleph-null times aleph-null is a very low order transfinite.

Somebody is going to be sacrificed.

Joe Kearney was sacrificed; we're exploring the relationship between the present human mental mechanism and the operation of high-energy, high-performance, extreme-endurance machines. **Joe** summoned a demon too powerful to handle; it destroyed him.

"In the midst of life we are in death," is the old funeral line. So we are; this being the case, one can shudder, panic, and deny violently that any such thing is true. Or one can acknowledge that I, too, am not only inherently expendable, but absolutely certain to be expended even-
286

tually. Only I hope to God that somebody learns something useful from expending me.

If the culture can learn a little more about highway hypnosis from **Joe's** death — then the greatest purpose of all in life was fulfilled. A truly futile sacrifice is one from which no one benefits.

I made a mistake on an oscilloscope circuit design recently; a 1-watt resistor overloaded, and got too hot. Carbon resistors having a negative temperature coefficient of resistance, its resistance dropped. In a remarkably small fraction of a second, a 6AU6 tube burned out its screen-grid; being in a voltage-regulation circuit, this promptly caused the circuit voltage to leap from 150 to 325 volts. Four 6AG7 tubes, having their screen hung on that supply, drew about 400 milliamperes, instead of 120; the four tubes burned out. Also the rectifier tube naturally overloaded, and fried its plates. A long time after this happened — oh, several thousand microseconds later — the fuse in the circuit sluggishly began to soften. By the time it got soft, the tubes had all gone blooie, and the load dropped off. The fuse never did blow — until later, when I thought I had everything fixed. Then the weakened fuse did pop, causing me another two hours careful research.

It took some eight hours of careful priffing [sic] around, thinking, and investigating to figure out what had happened. And, of course, there was no use plugging in another 10 bucks worth of tubes to see if they'd blow out too.

But societies work differently. A society won't take the time — can't take the time — to do all the research. Only individuals can. If one **Joe Kearney** gets killed, for the society it's cheaper to plug in another, and see if he gets killed too.

How safe should a ship be? How safe should the engineering construction practices be when building a bridge?

Any honest bridge designer can explain that "We can build the bridge across the Narrows for $50,000,000, 24 months, and 35 lives. Or we can build it in 12 months for $75,000,000 and 55 lives. On the other hand, we can build it in 20 months for $120,000,000 and 4 lives."

How safe must working conditions be? Absolutely safe?

Your apparatus in the lab might explode, **Isaac**. Never can tell, you know. And electricity can electrocute. And fire kills people. Better

287

give up fire, electricity, and research until we know how to make them absolutely safe.

Maybe the Negroes in Africa were doing their sociological research the slow, safe, sane way, while the Europeans were doing theirs the slap-dash high-cost-in-lives way. I dunno — but I do know we bought and paid for what we have in blood, sweat, and tears long before **Churchill** made that remark.

You realize the validity of the idea; that was what you had in your "Eternity" story — that Man can't afford to do things the slow, careful, rechecked and super-rechecked way. If he does, by the time he has patiently, slowly, cautiously worked out the answers . . . guess what? Somebody else got there, used it up, and moved on.

Suppose Man develops space travel, finds a super-wonderful-ideal planet, and the whole race moves out. This leaves the animals to take over. But the next comers are gonna have a hell of a time; all the easily worked mineral deposits have been stripped. They'll find interesting traces of where somebody gouged out some nice, juicy stuff.

You know the one condition essential for life to originate on a planet is that there is no life present; if there is, the newly-generated life won't stand a chance. It'll be somebody's dinner before it gets its first pair of chromosomes untangled.

"It's sad when you think of the wasted life," may be a lovely sentimental line — but if you prefer not to be a wasted life, recognize that the Risk of Not Taking Any Risk isn't a risk at all; it's a dead-sure certainty that you'll be destroyed.

The individual has to be sacrificed; the cultural group has to take risks, too. The West differs from the East largely in that the West sacrifices geniuses as well as morons; it has proven a sound, worthwhile idea.

In India, the genius isn't required to make his ideas understandable, or useful to others; he is permitted to demand that students learn to understand him, instead of being forced to make himself understandable.

The West demands that the genius sacrifice the potentiality for research and further achievement by spending most of his time-effort-energy making himself useful and understandable. A major part of the genius' individual potential is, thereby, sacrificed to the culture.

288

Necessarily, some geniuses crack under that pressure completely, give up, and live out futile, miserable lives.

Too bad. But — the culture had to sacrifice 'em to get the value out of the tougher geniuses who could take it. India, by not doing so, is stuck in a period that they should have worked out of 3000 years ago. India has, thereby, lost out permanently on the leadership it once had. (It'll never regain leadership as India — but as a hybrid, crossed-up something-entirely-different.)

Now as to why individuals of a group having a statistical norm at a level lower than the dominant group must be sacrificed: Let's consider the planet Chroma; there are six different breeds of the single intelligent species. The whole species is called Gwols; they are distinguished by differences in minor physiological adaptations, and by critical differences in mental-emotional adaptations.

Chroma is a cold planet; there isn't any excess of light anywhere, but the first scientific-logical culture arose in the only-mildly-arctic zone they call "temperate." The area was inhabited by a people who were originally nomad hunters, then became agriculturists. At this point, to protect their crops, it was necessary for many individual family-groups to cooperate. Reason: a nomad group can fight or run, depending on the size of the opposing family group. Agriculturists can't run; they have to fight, whether they like it or not. Therefore they <u>have</u> to be in a spot to like it; they <u>have</u> to be the biggest "family group." They have to develop a family group larger than the largest possible nomad group.

Fortunately, agriculture makes it possible to maintain a larger group. So they fought off the nomads. The nomads got the bejayzus beat outen 'em until they moved to more comfortable areas. The nomads moved to the equatorial and arctic zones, where the agriculturists hadn't settled.

(In the tropics, free dinners were too easy to get to make agriculture very important, and in the arctic you couldn't develop agriculture.)

Many of the youngsters of the Temruts, as the agriculturalists came to be known, didn't like being stuck in the mud; they hated having to sit on their tails and watch the grass grow. So they wandered off — or got firmly kicked off — or were bumped off — until selective breeding produced a type-in-residence that loved staying in one place on the land, and would fight like hell to keep it. (The rest left or got killed.)

Eventually, adjoining towns of Temrut people started trying to grab more land from each other. It was soon found that the peoples who could team up and cooperate best generally licked the independent warriors. Not always, of course. But, in the course of some 4000 years, the surviving Temrut agriculturalists — and by that time selective breeding had pretty well stabilized the agriculturalist tendency in the Temruts — had developed some highly cooperative citizens. When the cooperative type once became dominant in a village, the non-cooperative got labelled "deviant," and were firmly booted out

. . . or bumped off.

Meanwhile, the nomads had been developing in a leisurely sort of way. The climate being somewhat rugged, those who went toward the Arctic had grown shorter, rounder, and genetically fatter. Also the surviving lines were ones with a remarkably high birth rate; infant mortality was appalling. They'd grown rounder, shorter, and fatter, because that made for adaptation to the dim, dark, and damned cold zone. They all liked nomadic hunting; the ones that didn't had died of broken heart, been beaten to death as no-goods when young, or sneaked off to join the Temrut farmers. The Ertiks, as these people were called, didn't farm because they didn't want to, and furthermore, bloody well couldn't in the arctic.

And the nomads who went to the tropics found life far easier. They established some sort of half-ass villages — nothing you couldn't build up or knock down in a day or so. Some agriculture was practiced, in a moderate sort of way, but life was fairly easy. Domestication of animals made the Opiks, as they came to be called, even more comfortable; now they didn't have to hunt very much.

The Temruts, meanwhile, kept having more and more troubles with the need for land, and protection of land. It had taken organization to stop the nomads in the first place — and now it took even more organization to stop raiding other-villages. Villages banded together into groups; strong walls were invented. Engineering had to be invented to make the walls stand up, and to make roads so that allied villages could congregate their forces swiftly.

Now Chroma's sun is weak, but in the tropics, the race had adapted to conditions that were, for them, hot; physiological changes had been inevitable due to the different environments they adapted to. The
290

Opiks were much darker in color; practically gray-green. (The Gwols have a haemocyanin blood.) The Temruts on the other hand, have a nearly transparent skin, and the blue of the blood colors their flesh a lovely pastel blue. The Ertiks, on the other hand, because of their thick subcutaneous fat, have a yellowish tint overlying the blue blood vessels, and so appear somewhat greenish. The Ertiks are known, on Chroma, as the Greens, while the Temruts are Blues, and the Optik people are called Grays.

Now the physiological differences arose from difference of physical environment. These differences can be detected by any entity having color vision.

But the mental-emotional differences arose by equal adaptation to a socio-economic-cultural environment, and selective breeding in that respect. The Temrut socio-cultural environment selectively favored people who liked to be stationary, and cooperative.

The Ertik culture favored individuals who were independently competent, self-reliant, and nomadic.

The Optik socio-cultural environment on Chroma favored warriors of independent type; raiding was a sport with the Optiks, a survival of their nomadic days, though the easy environment had practically elimi-nated the nomadic tendency.

(The raiding was a survival factor for the race; no animal was pow-erful enough to offer serious threat to the Gwols, and their breeding would soon have overwhelmed even the tropical supply of food. Also, if the weak members of a race are not cropped out, the race degenerates. See the fate of the Icthyosaurs on Earth. Raiding wasn't good for a raid-killed individual, but was good for the race as a whole.)

Now the Temruts developed a science, eventually, and explored their planet, and imported Ertiks and Optiks as slave-workers, for a while. It caused great trouble, because the Blues said that the Greens and the Grays were "inferior" and "uncivilized" and "barbarians."

Apologists insisted that there was no real difference between the Grays and the Blues, except the slight physiological adaptation to a different climate. Since all Gwols could interbreed, they were proven to be of one species.

There was no genetic difference, it was maintained, between

them, save for the physiological difference.

But actually, there was a very great difference at the mental-emotional level, among the Gwols of Chroma. Selective breeding had adapted the breeds not only to physical, but also to socio-cultural climate — and the socio-cultural climate was due to the physically induced economic climate.

This of course is true for the Gwols on Chroma, and nowhere else; any resemblance to actual individuals living or dead is purely coincidental. On other planets, if a child of an agricultural tribe wants to leave and be a hunter, his parents don't beat the bejayzus out of the little bastard to make him see his duty toward the farm, the way they did on Chroma, until the kids either learn to like farming, or unfortunately develop a weakness and die.

Now in the city of Upchuck, in the largest nation of Chroma, there arose a problem. One Blorg, a Gray, was an exceptionally brilliant, wise, and competent man, a philosopher and a scientist of real achievement. And there was also another Gray, a Gwol named Gkakg, who was a born leader and warrior-king and an orator.

There were about 100,000 Grays in Upchuck, and 2,000,000 Blues, plus a few Greens. The Grays didn't have as good living conditions as the Blues, generally speaking. (Generally speaking, their instinctive ways of life were ill adapted to the operation of a high-level organization of a science-based city-culture. Individuals like Blorg, of course, were exceptions. Because of their poorer adaptation to the Blue's type of socio-cultural system, it was markedly more difficult for the Gray to make as good an adjustment, and hence markedly harder for them to achieve a high income.)

The Grays resented the economic differences, but not very actively. Then Gkakg came along, and pointed out to all the 100,000 Grays that Blorg was being accepted — as they were not — in the fine hotels, and at good restaurants, and at fine universities, and in good homes.

Presently, Gkakg had stirred up much unrest, and Blorg's friends were deeply troubled.

But Blorg, as I say, was a philosopher, and a wise man. He withdrew from his friends, and refused invitations.

Gkakg waxed even more tempestuous in his denunciations. The Grays, he howled, had every right to anything any Blue had; all Gwols were equal, no matter whether they had spent ten thousand years evolving the socio-economic adaptations or not — a mere difference of skin color had nothing to do with the matter!

But Blorg, as I say, was a wise man. He sought out Gkakg, and very publicly blew his brains out, for which he was duly, and with enormous regret, executed as a murderer.

Gkakg's organization broke up almost at once, as several dozen would-be successors took off on their individual efforts to be the Big Chief. Not having ten thousand years of adaptation to cooperative teamship, the Grays didn't make very effective organization leaders, where team action was concerned — a fact which Blorg had recognized fully. Blorg saw that by destroying Gkakg himself, he would at once destroy the nucleus of the revolt, and blast the false use of himself as a rallying cause.

Through his own contacts in the Grays' underground, Blorg had learned that Gkakg had planned on starting an all-out revolt in five days, and Blorg, being a far wiser man than Gkakg, knew precisely what would happen. There would be an initial success, as several thousand Blues were murdered, and the Grays ran triumphantly through the surprised city. And then the deep, inherent organizational nature of the Blues — which Gkakg simply couldn't understand — would take over, and despite the loss of the Blues leaders, organization would promptly be established. The result would be the punitive, angry suppression of the Grays, with scores of thousands of deaths.

Blorg decided that it would be a wise and expeditious thing to sacrifice two individuals for the good of both races. So he did. The whole affair wound up with a total of six deaths; the other four were four bigoted Blues whose bloodpressure exceeded the bearable when they lost their chance to declare war on the Grays.

Now it happened that Blorg had a young Gray protege — no relation of his, but equally bright -- Blorg had most carefully instructed him, and pointed out to him the exact mechanism of what had happened, and what was going to happen, after carefully locking him in a room it took him eight hours to get out of. By the time the protege did get out, Gkakg was dead, and Blorg arrested.

Blorg told him not to be a damned fool like he, Blorg, had been, and not to incite the Grays to rebellion when they were not competent, by accepting individual status which made every Gray feel he, too, should of-a-right have similar status.

It is quite impossible to explain to a Gray, Blorg told him, that there is anything besides a physiological adaptation. You know, and I know, that there is something a lot more important. But while you can show any entity having color vision that a Gray is physiologically different — how can you show that we have other differences?

Look, **Isaac**, the individual genius has to be sacrificed because he incites the group to riot.

It's the old story, "You know barking dogs don't bite! Don't be afraid of him!"

"Yeah — I know it, and you know it — but does he know it?"

Equally, I know the reason a certain individual X gets special privileges is because he has special abilities, and you know that . . . but does the individual of X's race recognize that X gets those privileges only because he is a racial deviant?

Would I condemn a man because of the color of his skin?

Essentially, I am forced to answer, "Yes." His skin-color is genetically determined; it is not something he chose. But his mental-emotional patterns are also genetically determined; he didn't choose those, either! They are adaptations to a socio-cultural environment just as truly as his skin-color is a physiological adaptation to a physical environment. If he can't choose one — why expect him to be able to choose the other?

Now the skin-color genes and the mental-emotional genes are not correlated on a one-to-one basis. You know that, and I know that . . . but do several million Negroes in Harlem know that? Don't they judge that, "That man is black skinned, like me. He is admitted to fine clubs and restaurants. Therefore I have a right to go there too."

Go ahead — give them individual rights based on individual worth. And you immediately precipitate them into a situation they cannot endure emotionally; you have robbed them of relationship-to-their-race. You've made them deviants, and alone.

Do they want that?

Regards, John

Dear Isaac:

Enclosed is a letter from **Poul Anderson**.

Maybe you and I could agree that if there aren't "races" of men there are "kiths"?

I notice with some interest that the AT&T and IBM have surrendered their right to hold patents. The consequences are going to be most interesting — and anything but what the people who nagged the anti-trust division into forcing that wanted.

It works this way: A man doesn't mind your making an insignificant discovery. The Patent Office necessarily reacts to the attitudes of the people. Consequently, you can patent a bobby-pin holder, or the curl in a hairpin — but not a transistor.

The transistor is, in essence, a fact of nature. What it amounts to is that there is one, or a few, Best Possible Ways to do something. Whether that Best Possible Way is now known or not makes no difference; it exists. The optimum length-to-diameter ratio for a barrel, cylindrical, having the maximum volume-per-area, is a mathematically determinable unique entity. There is one, and only one answer to that problem. That is IT; the Best Possible Ratio.

Now there are millions of ratios possible, but only one Best Possible. That Best Possible is a fact of nature; it is something to be discovered, not invented.

The Best Possible Answer to any problem is a unique fact — and a fact of the Nature of Things.

As we approach the limits of physical science, men discover methods that are Best Possibles — and patents on those mean that they hold a patent on the One Best Way.

A normal person doesn't mind you having a monopoly on something he doesn't want, or on some insignificant, unimportant, irrelevant item; but when your patent is something he wants — he hates you for having it. You're forcing him to pay for the privilege of using the method you discovered, and there's no alternative. He feels you're infringing on his freedom.

OK — so now AT&T, IBM. Tomorrow RCA, GE, Westinghouse, and du Pont. All these big corporations are going to be forced to release their patents, so that the Common Man has a chance to Do what He

295

Wants To, without being restricted by the Big Monopolies.

Yeah . . . only . . . patent license fees used to help pay for the research Bell Labs did.

Now it so happens that the Common Man is up against another Fact of Nature; he hasn't got $20,000,000 to invest in research. And to discover the transistor, Bell had to set up a $20,000,000 program in solid state physics. The Common Man couldn't discover the transistor.

Of course, the Common Man's Great Friend, the Government, could. Government is taking over research; the corporate research laboratory is being put out of business.

Except . . . for another stinker. Trade Secrets now have a perfectly lovely place to hide!

Security is now an accepted part of science; Company Security now comes into its own.

And just when it will work, too! We're just entering a phase of technology wherein Process is more critical than Material. The IKYG Pharmaceutical Co., for instance, starts selling cortisone at 10 cents a dose. Their cortisone is the McCoy; the product is exactly the material specified. OK — now you know, brother. You've got our product, and if you want to know what the initials in our title stand for, it's "I Know and You Guess!" We have no patent on our process; anybody who wants to is perfectly free to compete with us — it's a free world, just like your Common Man people wanted. You're as free as the breeze; figure it out, and you, too, can make cortisone at 5 cents a dose!

Or suppose Bell had happily announced that it appeared that germanium crystals would, sometimes, act as amplifiers; they had been lucky in finding some that did, and were selling a new device they called a "transistor." Anybody who wanted to compete was, of course, welcome to do so.

So a would-be competitor analyzes Bell's new germanium triode . . . and goes quietly bughouse. It's just germanium — nice, pure germanium. But germanium won't do that! They try germanium crystals

. . . and, dammit, Bell's right; they do get one that almost amplifies, and another that amplifies for a couple of hours before collapsing permanently. Bell's just lucky . . . only they're so lucky it's remarkable.
296

And, says Bell, privately, "O.K., you bastards! You wanted it this way; you've got it. It cost us five megabucks to riddle this out — now you can sweat as hard as we did, and feel perfectly free to do it any old way you want; we have no monopoly!"

Try deducing from a transistor what the process of its manufacture was!

Try deducing from a piece of heat-treated alloy-steel what the process that made it that way was! Go on! You can match that alloy atom-for-atom in composition . . . but you ain't got the goods, boy!

Twenty-five short years ago, <u>material</u> dominated; a product could be duplicated by merely duplicating the material composition. But that was before barrier layer phenomena became critical.

The best high-frequency transistors have a layer of arsenic impregnation about 1/50,000 of an inch thick. In that layer, the arsenic impurity is distributed in such a way as to have an exponential concentration across the layer.

Now, my friend, you try figuring out how they get that stuff neatly in place in the germanium, in a nice exponential distribution.

For that matter . . . how would you go about discovering that it <u>was</u> placed in an exponential concentration in a layer 1/50,000th of an inch thick, for God's sake?

To say nothing of the interesting irrelevancies anyone seeking to hide a process secret would thoughtfully include. I understand that a trace of silicon won't have the slightest effect on a germanium transistor, for example . . . but the would-be analyst couldn't afford to rule that out now, could he?

Ah, what a tangled web we can weave, when we really research on how to deceive!

Item: The Psionics editorial has brought me about a 6-inch stack of mail. It's 100,000% favorable.

Item: One of them was from a doctor who sent me some papers on studies of the effects of drugs in dilutions exceeding 10^{-24} -- which, as you may note, means a dilution such that there should be less than 1 molecule of the substance present.

The drugs, clinically tested, still work.

I'll send you the papers when I'm through with 'em.

Item: When a person has a problem, he wants the problem <u>he</u> sees, solved the way <u>he</u> wants, in the terms <u>he</u> chooses.

If you try to change his terms, he knows you're just trying to avoid solving the problem.

If his problem is that he wants you to make those little Green Men stop bothering him, he means he wants you to drive the Little Green Men away. He does <u>not</u> want any of that goddamn malarkey about sticking vitamin B$_1$ into <u>him</u>; the problem is the Little Green Men.

Now if he has a gun, it is most bodaciously recommended that you start earnestly picking up Little Green Men and throwing them out. <u>They</u> may not be subject to gunfire, but you are.

It makes not a damn bit of difference that the problem cannot be served in his terms; he, with his gun, has solved his problem; he's got you busy throwing out Little Green Men, and that's what he wanted, isn't it — to drive away the Little Green Men!

Now the curious feature of this is that he doesn't want <u>you</u> to solve the problem of the LGM's; he wants <u>you to make his solution workable</u>. He will feel a deep glow of satisfaction and triumph as you haul out LGM; he's solved his problem of making someone help make his solution workable.

If you build a LGM-proof fence, this won't satisfy him. If it works, it makes him a fool for not having done it himself.

Now the only way I know of to get out of that sort of spot is to supply him with some insignificant, irrelevant, unimportant comment that is of no value — but leads him, in his brilliant inspiration, to solve the problem. Then he can have a great glow of satisfaction; <u>he</u> solved the problem!

And, of course, he doesn't owe you anything; you didn't have the wisdom to see that that insignificant, unimportant irrelevant remark had in it the germ of a solution.

All this requires of you is that you (a) solve the problem itself, (b) figure out just how close to the whole answer you have to come before he can see that it <u>is</u> the answer, and (c) figure out how to make him notice it when (d) he doesn't <u>want</u> any other solution than the one he has in mind.

The only person in the universe who can give him a better solution than the one he has, and make him like it, is himself; if he doesn't like it, he'll reject it.

298

If you guess wrong, and get too close to the solution you want him to have, he'll guess that you're trying to make him accept an answer other than the one he knows is right, and be angry, and suspicious of anything you say.

Item: You can also say "she" in the above.

The problem in psi is that the scientist has one orientation, and that orientation specifically says, "All the problems in the universe must conform to the known laws of science." Those are the terms, then, in which all problems must be solved. If you do not present the solution in those terms, and no others, you're obviously cheating.

The difficulty is that there are problems that can NOT be solved in those terms. For example, the inverse square law is taken, in the scientific orientation, as an absolute and totally universal law. Tain't. Lots of things do not follow the inverse square law, or any distance-relationship law whatever. It just happens — how strange! — that all the non-distance-dependent laws happen to relate to subjective phenomena. These, obviously, aren't scientific, so they aren't real.

Being a couple centuries past **Faraday**, we're not a whit bothered by the idea of an invisible, intangible, odorless, soundless, tasteless phenomenon that can not be detected by any sense Man has, is immaterial in the literal sense, and can not be directly observed in any way whatsoever. Everybody knows that magnetic fields are real, even if they aren't material.

Incidentally, they defy all the laws of common sense. Two things cannot occupy the same space at the same time.

Just because, now, we have instruments which can be used to measure them. . . .

And who's ever seen an atom?

Hell, we define an atom by its defiance of the laws of common sense! It's material that can't be cut. It's material, but has none of the characteristics of matter!

Want an example of a non-distance-dependent force? The attraction between two human beings is not a function of distance — and is so real that it causes massive bodies to alter their position. How does it differ from magnetic fields, which you can detect only by indirect methods?

For your information; I've built the Hieronymus machine men-

299

tioned in the "Science of Psionics" editorial . . . and it works. It has an output which is strongly detectable by a tactile sensation, while neither oscilloscope nor vacuum tube voltmeter can detect anything whatever . . . although the output comes from a 6AU6 vacuum tube amplifier.

Item for consideration: I've succeeded in proving that the standard textbooks on sound, both physics, acoustics, electronic audio, etc., are flatly wrong. Once in a while, you know, the whole regiment is out of step; this time they're all wrong and I'm right. It's a fact of nature dependent on their failure to recognize that just because X can be analyzed into A, B, C, and D, does not mean that A plus B plus C plus D equals X. Process, my friend, is important too; material alone is not enough.

The gimmic is this: the textbooks all chorus that human hearing cannot detect phase relationships in sound waves. They're nuts. We can. What misled 'em was that human beings can, in the auditory center of the brain, unscramble misplaced phases and sort the garbled mess out. Same sort of trick the optical center pulls when you "see" the wheels of an automobile are round . . . even when you're getting a 45 degree angle viewpoint on it, and any geometry will show you that you actually must be seeing highly elliptical wheels. Just because the auditory center can unscramble a loused-up mess doesn't mean it doesn't know there's a mess.

Now every musical instrument starts with a shock-wave of some kind, and selects desired related harmonics from it. The violin uses the shock-wave excitation produced by the string snapping free of the rosined bow.

When you select harmonics from a single shock wave source, the phase-relationship of the harmonics is rigidly fixed.

You can distinguish two violins from one-violin-twice-as-loud because being sensitive to phase relationship, the auditory center recognizes that there are two teams of harmonic patterns.

Now if you pick up an orchestra with three microphones, mix the three outputs, and record the result . . . you've got a mishmash of phase relationships that even the enormously capable auditory center gives up on. You never heard any mess like that at any concert hall, that's for sure — not unless you've got three ears hiding somewhere about your person, and have lost one half of your brain so you have only
300

one auditory center left.

The result makes for listener fatigue; you can't say _why_ you don't quite like it, though. The technician can show you that every frequency is present, in just the right quantity, so it _must_ be good.

Reminds me of the first research on vitamins. Some graduate student had been doing fat-carbohydrate-protein analyses of cattle feed, using standard chemical methods of the time. Nitrogen analysis with a correction factor to determine protein content, etc. The naughty lad tried something nobody was supposed to do. He presented his professor with figures on two materials, leaving out only the ash content on each, and asked which was the superior material. The professor unhesitatingly picked the figures derived from the analysis of cow manure.

It is NOT just, "What material is there?," but, "In what relationship is it present?"

That nitrogen analysis test of theirs proved manure was better food than corn. They shoulda tried convincing a cow, though.

Enzymes, you know, don't do anything, really. After all, the reactions they catalyze would take place anyway, wouldn't they? They can't cause any reaction that wouldn't occur without them, can they? See . . . like I say, they don't do anything, really.

Regards, John

Wayne Batteau   _January 31,_
_1956_

Dear Wayne:

Pardon me for a month or two; I've been running into the problem of Secrecy in my sessions, and it makes the damndest mess of things! I urgently recommend it for your own study; I agree that it sounds like I'm inviting you to get into this same mess too, but there's point in it. Secrecy is evidently essential; much social lying is a result of the kindliness of keeping the truth a secret.

My trouble is that I get the mental stutters, currently; I dunno what should be, and what should not be, secret. Fortunately I have about six editorials backed up, or I'd really be in trouble!

I'll write you a decent letter when I finish clawing my way through this mess. It feels, mentally, like trying to walk in shoulder-deep water does; no traction, and lots of viscous resistance!

For your information: Letters on the "Science of Psionics" deluged in. They're 100% favorable; not a single, solitary Nay in the bunch.

If you want some fun, get that Hieronymus patent, and try it. I did. It doesn't work quite the way he says -- but his detector detects something wigglescope and VTVM can't! It <u>works</u>!

Item: **Isaac's** doing an article about a Texas cotton planter who was using geese to weed his cotton field . . . and one started laying gold-shelled eggs. **Isaac** discusses study of the enzyme systems by which the goose transmuted to make gold. The AEC, of course, took it over; national resource, obviously. X-rays no good; too much gold in the critical organs, and fear of sterilizing the goose.

Regards, John

Isaac Asimov   *February 20, 1956*

Dear Isaac:

What's satanic about suggesting something to somebody that (a) he enjoys doing, (b) works to his profit, (c) works to the profit of others also, and (d) yields me an advantage as well?

The boys'll love the goose-egg problem.

Incidentally, there was a British film a while back about the duck that laid uranium eggs; our biochemical approach to the golden goose egg will be a long way off, but the duck should be borne in mind, I suspect.

Love the liver business, and the *pate de fois gros* title.

Brings to mind a further possibility: The liver is busily engaged in several projects. 1. It makes substances the other organs need. 2. It regulates concentrations of food substances in the blood stream (with help from the kidneys). 3. It does very important work detoxifying substances that get into the bloodstream.

The liver will, for instance, take a highly toxic substance like benzoic acid, and turn out a less-toxic, though still toxic, material like hippuric acid, and leave the problem of getting rid of that up to the kidneys.

302

Again, the body of an animal, in trying to handle some toxic materials, is stuck with the fact that <u>any</u> compound of the damn stuff is toxic. If it's soluble, the solution causes metabolic trouble, Grade A #1. Lead, for example.

In that case, the body has a tendency to dump the stuff in an insoluble form where it will do the least harm — the bones, usually. Then gradually, over a period of months, always maintaining the concentration at a low, tolerable, though still undesirable level, excrete the damned stuff somehow.

Now if a goose were being poisoned by something, the liver would try to detoxify it. There is, from a goose's point of view, no advantage — and a distinct disadvantage — to gold-shelled eggs. Why would the creature start that process, for Pete's sake? Maybe because it was being poisoned by something in its diet, and the best detoxification reaction handy was transmuting the toxic element (or elements) to a harmless element fairly readily disposed of.

You see, the real trouble was that the insecticides being used contained lead and arsenic, and fall-out from atomic tests were adding fission products that were radiologically toxic. Now the best way to make a radioactive isotope non-toxic would, obviously, be to detoxify it by adding something to it, the way benzoic acid is detoxified. If a few nucleons from lead were shifted to the fission isotopes, the lead would be converted to inert gold, while the fission isotopes were rendered stable.

The real secret of the goose, then, is that its liver is detoxifying lead by transmutation to gold. Of course, if there are no handy fission isotopes to act as nucleon receivers, it can load them onto something else handy; ^{35}Cl, for instance, can accept two nucleons without instability, and without becoming chemically undesirable. It could even accept five, and become perfectly stable and harmless.

This interesting and valuable ability fascinates the AEC, naturally; these geese, if they can only be bred successfully, can go a long way toward solving the atomic garbage disposal problem.

Item in a different department: Proposition: Inequality before the law is essential to true equity and justice.

In mathematical statement form: Since human characteristics are distributed in a non-linear pattern, no linear pattern of duties and

303

privileges can make a proper "fit" to the nonlinear distribution of abilities.

The Gaussian distribution curve is a nonlinear function. No population is known which shows the characteristic of having perfectly homogeneous distribution of characteristics; all show a Gaussian distribution, and most actual populations show a multi-lobed set of Gaussian distributions, since the actual populations are not homogeneous even with respect to a Gaussian distribution. (E.g.; see the recent "Speaking Of Pictures" in *Life* concerning the beauty contest in Jamaica, where they had ten classes, ranging from the Caucasoid blonde, Miss Appleblossom, through Miss Lotus [pure Chinese] and Miss Sandlewood [pure East Indian] to Miss Ebony, pure Negro. Skin coloration is one human characteristic, whether it be coupled with any other or not.)

The concept of "equality before the law" implies that every individual must receive identical treatment.

This, when applied to a Gaussian distribution, amounts to seeking the one value that applies to all the individuals involved.

Now a linear function can be tangent to a curve at one point; in the case of a complex curve, it can intersect-or-be-tangent at more than one point.

The best possible fit of a horizontal line to a Gaussian curve yields two possible situations:

If the horizontal is drawn near the top of the curve, but below it, a good fit will be obtained for the maximum number of individuals.

If the horizontal is drawn near the base of the Gaussian curve, but a little above it, the two asymptotic extensions will both be near fits.

This latter situation means that the high-extreme individuals and the low-extreme individuals can be fitted, but God help the mid-range people. This is known as Aristocracy, and works fine when the actual population is divided into widely different groups. (I.e., for morons and geniuses, with no normals, it would work fine.)

The other solution — horizontal imposed near the peak of the curve — we have what's known as Democracy. With a population made up entirely of individuals close to the norm, it would work fine — but God help the morons and the geniuses.

In other words, neither solution is adequate for a group which actually has a statistical distribution. Aristocracy works when you have two different populations; democracy works when you have no spread of types.

But neither situation can ever be stable; mutation will louse up either one, and interbreeding will louse up the aristocracy set-up in a fine frantic hurry.

Rome worked just fine, so long as the very narrow range of characteristics in the ancient Latin clan — which was a single blood-related breed, actually — alone was involved. When the barbarians were added into the brew, they had to deal with a real distribution of characteristics, and the thing went to hell in a handbasket. They tried aristocracy, and that didn't work adequately either.

India's had a stable set-up for centuries, using an aristocracy system — but forbidding interbreeding.

Russia worked fine under the Czars — except for half-breeds, like **Joe Stalin**, who wasn't a noble, and yet was too intelligent to fit the peasant category, and too original a thinker to fit the one remaining category -- the church.

The evidence of history suggests that you can't fit a single legal system to a statistical distribution. That is. . . you can't, if it's a linear system!

Inequality before the law is essential to true equity.

If you reject that proposition, my friend — go out and start campaigning for equality before the income tax law. I'd love to pay the same tax rate that the guys making $2000 a year do. I'm working on a little partnership deal in which three of us will determine the partnership division of profits on the basis of how to rig it so the most money stays in our hands; the man who's putting up the money can't afford to accept as much profit as I can.

And you can also start a campaign to see to it that children get electrocuted just like adults if they commit murder. "Equal justice for all!" should be applied equally, shouldn't it?

If you don't mean that — start figuring what you do mean before you campaign vigorously in the wrong direction.

How'd you like to be on the faculty of the University of Alabama? How do you vote — for or against a race riot that settles the problem by the usual method of destroying the entity that presents the problem, rather than by acknowledging and working on the problem? Do you vote to cram **Autherine Lucy** down the throats of Alabama's whites, because it will be good for them?

Maybe so. Maybe it would be a good thing to let her be taken by the mob some night, stripped in front of a fire, beaten till she couldn't scream any more, and flung into the fire. The sacrifice of one individual to arouse the revulsion of the population might be a good . . . .

But you don't believe in the sacrifice of an individual for the group. A lot of thoroughly inferior whites would have a lot of fun tearing her flesh, and watching her agony; they wouldn't be revolted at all — and they, not the ones who would be affected, are the problem.

How do you vote? This is a human individual we must decide on, in a real situation — a non-theoretical, non-fictional situation, a situation where we can't write the dialog, and can't tear up those pages of history that fixed the characters that we have now on page 1956 and rewrite them to give us a more desirable situation. We're stuck with the characters that exist; we must solve the problem of **Autherine Lucy**, and the sincere, honest, courageous — but foolish and unwise — people of the NAACP who have convinced her that her personal sacrifices are in a worthwhile cause.

She knows perfectly well that she could get into better universities in New York or Boston, and be welcomed. It takes high courage to do what she's doing. She, evidently, believes that individuals should and must make sacrifices for the group — even when that sacrifice includes the high risk of death by torture at the hands of men who aren't fit to talk about her — white skinned barbarians, the extreme low-end of the Gaussian curve. Think an Alabama Negro girl doesn't know what can happen to her?

It's quite futile to talk about how it should be; this situation is. The NAACP won't wait; they demand that their opinion be accepted right now. They've moved **Autherine Lucy** in as the pawn; the issue is "Shall a brown skin be considered a useful symbol in distinguishing the Competent and Responsible from the Incompetent and Protected?" The other term for "stigma" is "symbol," you know.

The trouble is, **Isaac**, that it would be the Negroes of Alabama who would suffer the greatest misery — for a reason no Negro member of the NAACP would ever acknowledge as valid.

306

Look: There's a local individual, adult male, who is an idiot. He happens to be of Italian ancestry; the rest of his family is quite competent. He's a big, hulking, good-natured, blank-faced idiot.

He has a job; he helps collect garbage, where his strong body is useful, and his weak intelligence is still fairly adequate. He is, now, a useful member of society.

He does bother some of the local housewives a bit, though; he obviously has no judgment — anything he does he does because he's been carefully conditioned, trained, and tutored. He has been taught one major commandment: Thou Shalt Not Seek To Judge!

So long as he doesn't try to make decisions, but accepts the imposed rituals and taboos, he is a useful citizen. But it does lead to discomfort.

He's apt to show up, about dusk, at some housewife's back door, knocking, and looming over her in the dusk, speaking in his not-very-intelligible manner. It's not a comforting thing for a woman to look up at the big, nearly mindless hulk of a man in the semi-dark. . . .

He's come back after his garbage collection job, because he saw something in the garbage pail that he wanted when he was making his rounds, and put it back in the pail. He's come to ask her if he may have it.

The taboo laid on him is, "Never take anything that is not yours without asking."

It, combined with "Thou Shalt Not Judge!" means that whether it is in a garbage can or not — it isn't his; he must ask.

Break his commandment, or his taboo . . . and being the brainless hulk he is, he would, shortly, find himself in a morass of decisions that he could not make. Presently it would be hopeless to break him of his new habit. He'd have to be taken off his garbage-collection job.

With more time on his hands, and now a sense of utter uselessness . . . he'd be in worse trouble shortly.

Presently, he'd be locked up, useless to himself, unhappy in his uselessness, and a burden to others.

So long as no one confuses him, so long as no one makes him doubt his Rituals and Taboos and Commandments — he is a useful though low-grade component of society.

Teach him, though, that he has as much right to judge as any other man — that this is a democracy, and every man has an equal right to his opinion — that no one has any business telling him what he can and cannot do — that he's a man, just like other men, and has as much right to judge as they have. Teach him — and destroy him.

Of course, it isn't very important, because he's an idiot anyway — it doesn't really matter if he rots in some institution, with a vague, blank misery of wonderment as to what he was meant for, and why he isn't doing it. Idiots aren't worth worrying about anyway; if he can't take care of himself — to hell with him. We've got an important political mission to carry out, and what happens to quasi-human junk like him isn't important. We've got to teach everybody to think for themselves, and not let anybody tell 'em they can't. Stop this damned business of people saying to a man, "Look, fellow — your judgment isn't competent to decide those things." We've got a democracy, haven't we?

You haven't been in the deep south, and lived there. I did live in the shallow south — North Carolina. I've also contacted — and been willing to listen — to people who've lived in the deep south.

Autherine Lucy is a courageous adolescent kid, with a world-saving mission. Somebody sold her a bill of goods, and she's certainly not doing what's the most sensible thing <u>for her</u>.

For a couple of generations, the smart, competent Negroes have been doing the rational, easy thing — they've moved North. It's been a fine little eugenics device.

The difficulty is, of course, that when an animal breeder sets up a selective breeding system — he disposes of the culls by killing them.

Go on selectively separating the competent from the incompetent for a few generations — and the culls begin to accumulate. An animal breeder would simply destroy them; we can't.

The number of abysmally low-grade Negroes in Alabama is not something to be joyous about. Their judgment ability is low, **Isaac** — very, very low. They think only in terms of rituals and taboos, commandments and symbols. They think that way because, with their level of ability, that's the only way they <u>can</u> think. You can't educate a low-grade moron, no matter how hard you try, to understand the concept of an asymptotic function, or that aleph-null isn't the same as "all."

High-level minds, with high-level judgment, unfortunately do not have golden tendrils in their hair to indicate their abilities. Also, un-
308

fortunately, they don't wear halos.

Their lives are made far, far simpler, and happier, and more understandable — they aren't lost in a morass of decisions utterly beyond their comprehension — if they can have some good, simple, visual symbol by which to distinguish.

The southern Whites have all the wrong reasons for what they're doing — but what they're doing is right.

The NAACP has all the right motives for what they're doing — but what they're doing is wrong.

You know, there's a perfectly valid use for the old-fashioned blood-letting treatment? If a man with considerable hypertension has a stroke, and medication isn't immediately available, blood-letting can minimize the damage by producing a drastic drop in blood-pressure. Blood's easily replaced later; damaged brain-tissue isn't.

We could save a lot of Negro brains in the deep-south if we did a little blood-letting, and reduced the excessive population of low-grade morons and idiots.

Do you recommend that as a solution?

I believe that an honest survey of the state of Alabama would show that the number of Negro morons and idiots exceeded the total white population of the state. That's what makes their problem a little tough.

But — if you were on the faculty of the University of Alabama, how would you vote?

Regards, John

Isaac Asimov   *March 4, 1956*

Dear Isaac:

If you can stop panting long enough to consider this . . . maybe there's a nicely-nasty story in it.

John Pierce commented this afternoon that one of the difficulties in science today is that "too many people have gotten their hands on big computers."

Given 30 factors, how many combinations, permutations, and associations can be derived from them? Given 30 items of data, and a big electronic computer, which has an electric typewriter output, and a budget to handle publication expenses, one need only have the output

309

pages reproduced by photographic processes, write a brief introduction, and all the pertinent, needed, and useful combinations of the thirty factors are forever buried beyond recovery in the n permutations the machines have produced. Now nobody can afford to look for 'em.

Creative acts seem to consist of increasing man's access to a valuable something — an understanding is made more available, a chemical substance is made more attainable, access of some form is increased.

But . . . merely increasing access per se isn't creative; to be truly creative, it must be a selective increase of access. The computing machine, by giving equal access to all possible permutations of the 30 starting factors decreases the utility of the total human knowledge system.

One standard way of protecting Top Secret information is to have 100,000 relatively unimportant items classified in the Top Secret category. The enemy agents will have to spend so much time combing over the Top Secret files, even if they get in, that they probably won't get the protected information.

Now an item: Any type of organism seeks to establish an environment in which its own type of entity is favored. *Penicillium notatum* excretes penicillin to handicap any non-mold organisms. Dopes seek to establish a social-cultural system in which dopes are favored; geniuses seek to establish societies in which geniuses are comfortable, and nobody else is.

Now imagine a culture which has lots of technicians, who are competent "skilled in the art" workers. There is a small proportion of truly creative thinkers; these creative thinkers have the job of digesting new information and reducing it from theoretical abstraction to engineering practices that the skilled technicians can use.

Now introduce a new factor that permits the engineering level boys to generate data at a rate millions of times faster than the few creative thinkers can assimilate it and make it useful. The information piles up in towering library files — but there is no increase in meaning.

Further, creative workers can no longer communicate with each other, because the engineering-technician data being ground out by huge computers (which, generally speaking, only engineers, not fundamental theoreticians, can afford) is jamming the technical-communication channels. There's more creative-thinking output than ever before
310

— say 5 times as much. But the technical-engineering-data communication has gone up 500 times. The resultant concentration of creative-thinking level work has gone down to 1% — and that concentration is so low that the creative thinkers can no longer afford the time necessary to reconcentrate it from the mass of computer-generated data.

Result: creative thinkers are isolated from each other!

Result: the system grows constantly more complex, as more bigger computers are built to handle the mounting backlog of unresolved data ("Maybe if we tried a few more permutations on this data, we'd get the answer, huh? There must be some way to get answers out of all this data, and logical thinking can do it, of course.")

But logical thinking can't do it; it never will. Logic can't generate postulates — new hypotheses. Computers, and computer-type thinking can't ever do it.

There's a lot of talk now about how Russia is getting ahead of us in engineers. Yeah. So they are.

Look; let's really louse up the Russians. Let's give 'em, through some snide, tricky, third-hand method, about forty or fifty new computers. Let's give 'em lots of data! Let's let 'em compute more from that, till they've got data running out their ears. They've got lots of engineers to get more data with, too.

Meanwhile, engineers in this country are forbidden to use any computer, for any purpose whatever, until a pure theoretician who has a computer he has no need for has considered whether the engineer's project is worth computing.

We wouldn't get 1/1000th as much numerical data — but I betcha we'd start getting some meanings!

Make the engineers stop counting on their digits, for a while, and start thinking, "Is this trip necessary?" The advantage of the old manual way was that the vigorous exercise involved in doing all that computing tended to make people consider carefully whether it was worth computing.

In other words . . . couldn't one race sabotage another race beautifully by giving them unlimited — and unselective! — access to data?!?

Ever think how important segregation is in the living organism? Allow potassium free access into the blood stream, and what happens? If the liver released its stored sugar freely . . . ! If a perforating ulcer of the intestines allows the contents free access into the peritoneal cavity..!

Unselective access is deadly — yet everyone hates having his free access limited.

Query: What's your evaluation on the cancer-cells-live-by-fermentation theory of cancer? Sounds good to me, but it's a matter of whether the data is valid or not; are cancer cells always fermentative types? Are all cancers-of-certain-types fermentative? If the information (Today's *New York Times*; I don't trust **Kempfert** any further than I can trust **Leslyn** on science reporting!) is straight, it'd be highly interesting in connection with a theory I'm playing with.

Item: Next time you're down, I can show you a psionic machine. Man, it's real crazy! And I <u>do</u> mean insane. The insanest part of all is that the damn thing does Something, and it absolutely should not. What it does is unimportant; it's like saying to someone, "Hey — that mountain over there just moved over half a mile!" "Hmmm . . . which way?" Which way? Hell! Who gives a damn about that! The damn thing <u>moved</u>.

Regards, John

Betty Crowther   *March 7, 1956*

Dear Mrs. Crowther:

The best sources of material I can suggest to you would be *Modern Science Fiction*, a discussion edited by **R. Bretnor** and written by **Isaac Asimov**, **L.S. de Camp**, and myself among others, and *The Science Fiction Handbook*, by **L. Sprague de Camp**, a discussion of how to write science fiction.

If these books aren't in your local library — I know Armonk isn't exactly a vast metropolis, and the library may not have too wide a selection — one of the larger towns nearby may have the books.

No other adequate material has appeared recently, that I know of.

Sincerely, John W. Campbell, Jr., Editor

Isaac Asimov   *March 9, 1956*

Dear Isaac:

The peculiarity of the true liberal position is that it requires that

312

you spend half your efforts defending the rock-ribbed conservative, and half your efforts in behalf of the crackpot-lefters. And that you never feel very comfortable about any position you take, at any time.

I think it was **Phyllis McGinley** who spoke of the discomforts caused by "the draught from an open mind."

You propose to vote **Autherine Lucy** into the University of Alabama, and demand that the police make it stick.

Isaac, you're a bit young, but not too youg, to know what Prohibition was. That involved the proposition that they had voted in restrictions on alcoholic beverages, and if the police had just gone ahead and shot the bootleggers, and jailed all the distributors, and imprisoned the people who bought the stuff, Prohibition would have worked.

I recall quite clearly my own strong conviction, at age 18, that people who were blinded for life by drinking wood alcohol in bootleg booze, had earned what they got.

If you recall carefuly, you'll notice that the last time the Northerners — who weren't familiar with the problems of the South — sought to settle them by fiat, we had a civil war.

Senator McCarthy has a sincere conviction that the democratic way of life must be protected against communists; he considers it so important that he's willing to sacrifice democratic, legal proceedings to achieve that end.

At the present time, the Southern Whites constitute an oppressed minority in the United States. They are being victimized by legislation inspired by the religious, social, racial, and cultural beliefs of the majority. Their beliefs are different; your proposal is that the police power of the State be used to force them to change their beliefs to conform with the beliefs of the majority, or at least that they be forced to act in conformity, whether they choose to believe as we do or not.

Because of the feelings of the majority in this nation, certain laws and court decisions have been promulgated which force desegregation.

Let us pass similar desegregation laws with respect to religious institutions — that if desegregation is good in one way, it is good in others, and therefore all citizens should go to the same church, and no church shall have the right to turn away anyone — whether he comes to mock the ceremony or not.

The actual problem, Isaac, is enormously deeper than a matter of

313

skin color, race, or religion. It's the ancient problem of the Individual vs. the Group — or the Minority vs. the Majority.

The course you propose is also the ancient one; make the hard-headed, stubborn bastards conform! Arm the police! Make them do what our majority-passed laws say, or shoot 'em down!

That's a very old answer. But I thought that that was the one you were opposed to . . .?

Maybe I'm confused; explain to me the essential difference between the application of force, involving death and agony, as applied by a group of individuals in defense of their beliefs, when they happen to be a minority, and the application of force as applied by a group of individuals in enforcement of their beliefs when they happen to be in the majority, please.

How does the armed sheriff and his deputies shooting down citizens differ from armed citizens shooting down someone else? How does majority persecution of a minority for their beliefs differ from majority persecution of a minority for their differences? Does the Authority of an ill-considered Law render clean and holy and Good what would otherwise be persecution?

Now **Hitler** and his storm-troopers cannot be accused of lynching people; what they did was perfectly legal. They passed the laws that made it legal.

The majority makes the laws, usually. Now, the Negro applies to the law, and demands that the Southern White obey the law. A century ago, the Negro screamed at the unjustness of the law, and asked that the Southern White refuse to obey the laws.

You'll never settle any problem, **Isaac**, by demanding that The Law be enforced by the use of armed police. You can restrain a situation that way — buy valuable time. But never consider that police power solves any problem — and don't pay too high a price for valuable time. Sometimes the price of the time you buy by use of force is too high to meet. And it might, just might, turn out you were wrong in what you accomplished by the use of force. The Church forced **Galileo** to recant; they had effective police power.

The Israelis have accomplished something by the use of force; they've carved out Israel. In the great, broad view of history, I'm deeply afraid that's going to be hideously important; they have forced
314

into existence an accomplishment that should never have been. It's somewhat like the accomplishment of forcing into existence a 35 pound sphere of pure ^{235}U. You can do it . . . for a while. But that doesn't mean you can, by any known means, make it continue to exist.

There's a remarkably good chance of tipping off WWIII in the Near East there. And all because the Jews were fools.

They didn't have any right to that area. The inhabitants of the area had been living there for some 1000 years; their only "right" was that they wanted it.

They were fools to want it. It's an exhausted, worn-out, desert, depleted of all natural resources by 6000 years or more of continuous inhabitation by one empire after another. It's been a poverty-stricken backwater of the world, the slum area of run down and worn-out human housing, for some 1500 years.

They had to start a war, killing or driving off men, women and children who had been born there, and whose ancestors 'til-the-mind-of-man-runneth-not-to-the-contrary had been born and lived and died there. Then they had to invest hundreds of millions in order to make anything useful to a modern society out of it. And they will never be able to repay those loans; the value isn't there. There are better lands, with better resources, which will yield far more return for Man's efforts. The loans can be repaid only if the Israelis descend to a standard of living lower than that of the Arabs they dispossessed — for the Arabs were already straining the resources of the worn-out land. Sure, you can irrigate — but the land must now produce enough to pay for the irrigation as well as for the farmer's efforts. You can fertilize — but you must earn enough to pay for the fertilizer as well as the irrigation and the farmer.

You wouldn't try to make a chemical reaction run contrary to the laws of thermodynamic equilibria; just because the laws of economic equilibria are somewhat more complex, and less readily measured in small scale experiments doesn't mean you can violate them.

By putting some energy into a mixture of hydrogen and oxygen, a reaction can be initiated which yields enormous quantities of energy. By putting energy into the carbon-oxyen system, you can get a return exceeding the invested energy. But not all reactions run that way. By putting energy into the system of hydrogen-nitrogen, you can make

315

ammonia. But that never becomes a chain reaction — not at normal temperature and pressure.

The Israelis are working in an ammonia type system; energy in the form of money has to be pumped in. They believe they're igniting a combustible mixture, that that's just the ignition-energy.

Six millenia of that sort of combustion has reduced that area to ashes.

The Jews have a perfect right to a national homeland if they want it. But they've attempted to make real a 2000 year old dream. In your "Dead Past," the professor and his wife dreamed of their lost 3-year-old grown up . . . but with a 3-year-old face.

The Jews need a national homeland — and they are making the mistake of fighting people, instead of the situation. They think people are preventing their achievement.

Well . . . they have, temporarily, established a national homeland. For the first time in some 500 years, the Arab peoples of the world have a common cause; the Jews have succeeded in doing what no one in the last five centuries has ever achieved; they've reunited the Arabs, and given them a new, common goal.

The Israelis, or the Arabs, are about to suffer devastating murder and annihilation — because they're both fighting for the same thing: their beliefs.

That, you know, is what led to the Hundred Years War in Europe, only there it was Catholic vs. Protestant, instead of Arab vs. Jew.

But the deadly thing is, Russia and the West will trail along; any outlet will be a useful outlet for the vast pressures that exist. Israel-Arab war will be like the Spanish Revolution, only more so. It'll make a fine place for both sides to try out their tactical weapons. Jerusalem will probably be annihilated by a series of Russian-made, and Russian-launched tactical nuclear weapons; it'll be a useful accomplishment for the Russians, since it will break one of the powerful anchors of the three great world religions. And Russians don't like world religions. They'll quite likely succeed in doing a job on Mecca and Medina, too. But since Russia won't be technically in the war — any more than Russia-per-se was technically in the Spanish revolution — it can't be blamed on Russia's godlessness.

I think I've expressed my belief before that the Jews, if they had
316

been wise, would have established modern Israel on the Island of Madagascar. No oppositon. Immense, unexploited natural resources. The climate resembles Bermuda's. What resources, other than a complete range of rain-forest-tropical to savannah sub-tropical Madagascar has isn't really known. It does have iron and coal and manganese; recently they've found Uranium, I see.

Of course, Madagascar's off any shipping routes.

But then, Nieu Amsterdam was, too. And if $200,000,000 goes someplace, shipping lanes go after it.

People can fight hard, earnestly, and sincerely for something, and actually achieve it . . . to their eternal damnation.

The Jews had a great dream — but it was a strictly limited, inflexible, geographically located dream, not an ideal which has inherent flexibility.

They've lost their chance now; it's too late to reorient the Jewish people of the world behind a new great effort.

I'll make a prophecy: all the world will deeply, hideously regret the creation of Israel.

The Jews will, in particular. For centuries they have been the world's oppressed minority.

Now they are appearing in the role of minority-oppressors. They, now, are using force to make a minority accept their ideas. They are fighting for something legitimate, and worth while — a homeland. But they're fighting in the wrong place, on the wrong grounds.

That, in essence, is what causes most human catastrophes. Fighting for a right, sound, and ethical idea — at the wrong time, in the wrong place, or by the wrong method.

Madagascar belongs to France. In 1946-48, the Jews could have gotten it with ease; they'd have had the relieved and happy backing of the Arab states, the US, England, and most of the rest of the world. And with France flat on her silly face, New Israel would have been booming with the good wishes and encouragement of all the world. There would have been rejoicing in the Arab states, and happy cooperation as the rich commerce of the Madagascar -- Europe trade began booming through the Suez area.

Any time people tie an ideal-goal to a particular place, method, or time — they're apt to sacrifice the purpose for the place, method, or

317

time, and find that they have the substance, without the essence.

Israel <u>may</u> work out some sort of half-ass compromise way of exist-ence. They <u>might</u> make some utterly unimaginable discovery that gave the place a peculiar value. But I feel that they've gotten the substance of their long-wanted homeland — but have, now, a homeland in Hell.

Regards, John

Jane Rice   *April 23, 1956*

Dear Jane:

You can't convey much of the major meaning of science-fiction in a five-minute talk; that's for sure.

One of the major problems will be the fact that most people today already "know what science-fiction is." They "know" it's Space Cadets and rocket ships and ray guns; trying to tell them that that isn't science-fiction is hopeless, because "they know by experience" that it is.

Therefore, we have to start with what they already know science-fiction is, and convince them, somehow, to take a peek at a slightly wider horizon.

Science Fiction actually is like "detective fiction"; it ranges from the Dick Tracy level through Macbeth — which centers around the murder of the king. (Forgot what his name was.)

Now more people read Dick Tracy than read **Shakespeare's** plays; this doesn't mean that the inherent nature of detective fiction, fiction about crime and punishment, is comic strip or Mickey Spillane. True; detective fiction includes that; stories on the theme of crime and punish-ment definitely do include the sex-and-sadism rash of the pocket books. It is also true that that type is, by far, the best known and most popular.

The best known and most widely understood type of science-fiction is "Space Cadets."

The trouble is, there's a simple false syllogism at work.

1. All "Space Cadets" type material is science-fiction.

2. This is science-fiction.

3. Therefore it's "Space Cadets" type stuff.

A further difficulty is that, at this point, the average listener says, more or less, "Ah, I know now; it's **Jules Verne!**"

No; it isn't **Jules Verne**, either. It's *Aesop's Fables*, and *Gul-*

318

liver's Travels, it's Plato's "Republic" and "Erewhon." And it's something that never existed before, because never before did Mankind have this particular problem to handle.

Science is a method of predicting what will happen; if it can't do that, it isn't a science yet. A physicist can predict what will happen if you do x, y, and z, under conditions alpha. A chemist can predict what will happen if substance gamma is mixed with substance delta. That's what we mean by a science; it's a system of understandings by which accurate prediction is possible.

Before this century, science played very small part in the shaping of the culture, in shaping the forms and mores and economy of Mankind's societies — for the simple reason that Man hadn't, before 1900, developed a sufficient mass of science to represent more than a minority factor in the determination of cultural modes.

The greatest social reformer of the last half century, though, was **Henry Ford**. His purely technical invention of the cheap, practical, individual long-distance, fast transportation device smashed the whole cultural pattern. The customs of courtship, for example, underwent an enforced, violent change — the tin Lizzie struck that deep at the roots of cultural mores and concepts.

For the first time in human history, a humanly controllable, humanly predictable factor plays a major role in shaping human affairs. Once, the Sun and the seasons were about the only humanly predictable factors that played dominant roles in shaping cultures.

Now Science has grown powerful enough to reshape human destinies, willy-nilly, like-it-or-not. Science, being merely factual-logical, is not purposeful. Considerations of purpose are specifically ruled out of any scientific discussion; teleological considerations are even rejected from psychology, stupidly enough, because the tradition of science is that teleology is a snare and a delusion.

For factual-logical-only sciences, such as physics and chemistry and mathematics — that's valid.

Being purposeless, Science is somewhat like a glacier; its course is predictable, but there isn't a hell of a lot we can do about it.

This may sound strange, this idea that human science isn't actually controllable by human beings. But the fact of the matter is that it isn't. The U.S. had to develop the atomic bomb —- because it was there to

319

be developed, and somebody was going to do it, somewhere. Then we had to develop the hydrogen bomb — willy-nilly, moral conceptions and desires to the contrary notwithstanding. **Oppenheimer** was demolished for allowing his moral concepts to interfere with his work toward developing the hydrogen bomb.

Automation is coming in now; it will totally disrupt the pattern of human living, and it will, actually, render obsolete vast numbers of low-competence human beings. What the unimaginative, routine-thinking, go-by-the-rules-only type of civil servant, or white-collar worker does now . . . can be done by electronic devices. Moral concepts can not withstand the pressure of facts; the glacier follows its slow course because it can not possibly do otherwise. If we don't apply the principles of automation, Russia, China, India, or some other culture will . . . and the stream of human history will simply move in a slightly different channel — but down the channel of automation, just the same.

The other side of the automation picture is, of course, that human beings will no longer have to live machine lives; machines will free them. The automation of the household laundry has already taken place; I have heard little weeping about the poor, displaced laundress, who no longer gets to spend a day at the scrubbing board and the washboiler.

The essential point is: Not only is Science a method of predicting —— but Science itself is predictable. And since Science is now a major factor in shaping human history — human history is, to that degree, predictable.

That is the new factor in science-fiction that never existed before in history. "Science" means "Predictable" — and "science-fiction" means prediction-fiction.

I can send you figures on the advertising survey of science-fiction readership; the figures are sound, but I don't know that they are important to understanding the importance of science-fiction.

What is important in that respect is the recognition of what top-level science-fiction seeks to do. We haven't attained the goal, God wot, but the forces tending toward it are developing. The goal is to predict the course of science, and the consequences of any particular course. It is impossible to halt the advance of the glacier — but if you predict its course, you can get out of its way, and, if it's worth while, do some blasting and damming to divert the course. But you must do that before the glacier gets there.

The only way human history can retain freedom from the blind pressure of events is to predict — and it most bodaciously damn well better catch on to that fact. It's remarkably futile to curse the day science was invented; in the first place, you'd be cursing penicillin, telephones, radio, and our present ability to grow the fine and plentiful foods we can.

People can curse the mountain lake that insists on spilling its waters down the river — or they can hire some hydroelectric engineers, go to work, and set up a fine new power plant. You are completely free to choose which you want — but not free to refuse to choose and curse the necessity.

It is, now, up to the humanic sciences to achieve the ability to predict motivations — purposive actions — as neatly as the physicist and chemist can predict the purposeless action of atoms. (Sure — that'll put us in a worse jam than we're in now. I know that! But remember that the process of walking consists of continually falling forward on your face . . . and catching yourself with the other foot. And you'd better walk; "there's a robot close behind you, and he's treading on your tail." Before the robot started treading on our tails, the rest of animal evolution was kindly performing that function. It kept us evolving, even if it did keep us uncomfortable.)

Much of the high-level science-fiction today is devoted to sociological explorations — *Aesop's Fables* and Plato's "Republic" items. There are a hell of a lot of problems that you aren't permitted to ask in this fair society of ours, my girl — which fact you are well aware of, but may not be fully consciously aware of. There are questions that only very small children, and very great philosophers have ever been permitted to ask in public; gradually older children, and lesser philosophers are permitted to ask them. Currently, science-fiction — by the *Aesop's Fables* technique — is asking them publicly. Science-fiction alone can get away with it, too.

Take a real, nasty, absolutely too-hot-to-handle question like "What do you mean by 'a human being'?" Inasmuch as this underlies the problems of race prejudice, class prejudice, and even insanity, it is a somewhat important question. (Is a man who has haemophilia sick? Since the condition is genetic, his unusual blood is perfectly normal for

321

him. Is he a healthy non-human-being, or a sick human-being? Sure, his condition is not workable in the real-world situation of this planet . . . but a fish isn't sick just because it can't breathe air, is it?)

We can discuss that problem very nicely, in science-fiction. **Isaac Asimov's** stories about robots have the interesting proposition of the Three Laws of Robotics:

1. No robot can harm a human being, nor, by inaction, allow a human being to come to harm.

2. A robot must obey the orders of human beings, so long as they do not violate the First Law.

3. A robot must protect itself against destruction, within the limitations of the first two laws.

Now consider what that First Law involves. A robot is built of purposeless, knowledgeless matter; all information must be built into it. What definition shall we build into it to make the First Law statement have meaning? How shall we define "human being?"

Let's consider a household robot, intended to do ordinary household chores, and help a housewife run her home.

Is a 3-year-old child a human being?

In that case, Mama's going to have troubles when she tries to discipline Junior. The robot will harmlessly, but firmly, interfere to prevent a human being being harmed.

Also, since the robot must obey the orders of human beings, Junior may order the robot to do some of the things he'd like to do, but can't by reason of his (fortunately) limited strength. Like break down that wall so I can have a door into the next room, or pull up that tree and throw it away so I can slide my sled down here.

If we try any simple tricks like "adult's orders only," what happens when an adult idiot comes along, and thoroughly competent and intelligent 10-year-old Jimmie tries to countermand the idiotic orders?

Is a chimpanzee a human being? Don't duck out on a definition involving hair, or clothes, either; you'll have trouble with some unusually hairy man getting out of the bath.

Want to try color as a test? That's what a lot of people do you know; it's so hard to really work out a definition for "human being," and that seems such a nice, convenient solution.

Of course, in science-fiction we can make the problem that of determining whether some alien entity of weird shape is "an intelligent entity," and not use the dangerous words "human being." But a monster's a man, for a' o' that!

In addition to the fable possibilities in science fiction, and really quite apart from that, is the sort of thing we can do with the robot.

The robot can be used in the story either as a character in a fable, or as a means of presenting a specific question. That is, no one would agree that a real human being would ever come along who was totally unselfish — who never placed his own interests first, and so couldn't be bribed, made disloyal, or act in selfishness.

But we can use a robot as a character, stating that the robot has been so engineered that it is inherently impossible for him to be selfish in any way, under any circumstances. Now the reader, when faced with the actually unworkable results of total non-selfishness, can't protest that the character really was selfish. This is a fable-character use of the robot.

The use of the robot to pose a question is illustrated by asking you to define "human being" for the use of the robot. The robot has in fact what the psychologists of another generation said a child had — the "tabula rasa," the blank tablet on which the teachers could inscribe any knowledge they wished. The robot has only the motives and knowledge you deliberately give him, plus the logical deductions inevitably consequent from those.

That's what makes robots so hard to live with; they actually do, willingly and freely, exactly what you tell them to — and if you don't like the results, you can't blame the stubborn, mean-tempered, willful and deliberately perverse personality of the robot. If you don't like it, you know exactly were he got it; you put it there.

We have trouble with literary critics, because of a complex of factors that sets science-fiction apart from the main stream of literature. For one thing, there's the entirely different set of values that must be considered in evaluating a science-fiction story. In main-line literature, the criteria of judgment have long been established; the enduring human values of plot, characterization, and emotional value. And a story is rated in how much of the enduring values it presents.

Yes ... but suppose the value is one that intentionally is not enduring? Suppose someone criticizes an electric fuse by saying, "This unit is very shoddily made; it breaks down under even a slight overload, and cannot be relied on to keep equipment running." The criticism is perfectly accurate; it can't. But that happens to be precisely what it was designed to accomplish — to break down under emergency loads.

Note that the inherent nature of prediction is that its value evaporates when it has been fulfilled. How much would next Sunday's newspaper be worth on Wednesday? And how much is it worth on the following Monday?

Here is an extremely high human value that, by its inherent nature, is not enduring! And yet this is one of the highest value-criteria in science fiction. No wonder a critic seeking to evaluate entirely in terms of enduring values will feel science-fiction stories don't have high value!

A fine example is the Story "Deadline" by **Cleve Cartmill**, which appeared in April, 1944. It described the arming mechanism, probable explosive effect, and exact nature of an atomic bomb with an accuracy that was not equalled in any published material until after the **Greenglass** spy trial disclosures.

The literary quality of the story was poor. The characters were pure stock. The plot was Standard Spy Problem #6. Any literary critic would have reason to damn the story for its literary value.

True. But was it a mistake to publish that story in April 1944 — over a year before the first test bomb at Alamagordo?

Agreed; it would be lovely if I could get both literary and predictive values. **Isaac Asimov** and **John Pierce** can't write like **Hemingway**, I know. But **Hemingway** can't understand biochemistry like **Isaac Asimov**, nor electronic science like **John Pierce**. **Hemingway** is an amateurish, bumbling writer, stumbling over his own ignorance . . . in the field of science-fiction. He may have literary value, but he is so ignorant of the tensions and movements and trends of science that he'd be pitifully inadequate in that field.

If **Hemingway** spent 20 years learning to understand and feel science, then he could indeed write magnificent predictive fiction. Or if **John Pierce** spent 25 years or so practicing the art of writing, and learning to feel and understand that, maybe he could do superb science-fiction.

Trouble is — "You should live so long!"

324

Science-fiction serves as a means whereby people who understand and feel the trends and broad movements of science can discuss the problems they see coming. One of the great difficulties in our culture is that there is no recognized medium for speculative thinking in public — except science-fiction, and science-fiction isn't recognized for what it is!

A scientist writing in the professional journal in his field is specifically required to eliminate all speculation. He is absolutely forbidden to discuss the probable future consequences of his work, and the work of his coworkers in his field.

In science-fiction, he can discuss the probable future meanings of the facts of his presently known science.

There is no other medium in the culture which will permit considered speculation to be published, for the cross-speculation of other scientists.

(Incidentally, **Jane**; this isn't a value of science-fiction alone, but of fiction in general, that is seriously under-realized. We have, in English, an essentially objective language; it is a cultural property, not an individual property, and so lacks means for accurate expression of experiences that individuals have, but cultures do not have.

(Further, the use of Facts and Logic is demanded; if you cannot point to objective facts, and furnish logical proof, your statement will be rejected as "unreal."

(The extreme, and violently serious failure of the language to achieve the necessary communication of individual-to-individual relationship problems is self-concealing. Because I cannot describe that which cannot be described in English, I cannot tell you, in English, what I'm talking about! This, by the cultural logic, "proves" that I am not talking about anything which "really" exists. The problem is that I am being challenged, "Just name one thing that can't be discussed in English!" Obviously, I can't!

(But . . . I can tell a little fiction story, and convey by what can not be stated, the thing I'm referring to. To get this extremely important point across, I've worked for some time trying to get a describable situation in which the lack-of-provable-realities is so glaringly obvious that it cannot be denied.

(A voyeur is a sex-deviant whose stimulation and satisfaction
325

derives from watching, not participating, in the sex act.

(Suppose a voyeur sneaks out to the local Lover's Lane, and at gunpoint, kidnaps a young couple who are just out on a perfectly ordinary date, two perfectly decent, ordinary kids. At gunpoint he forces them to strip, then forces the boy to rape the girl, then he leaves the scene.

(Speaking in strictly objective, logical terms, name the objective injury he has caused them. He didn't touch them, even. Be logical, now — be objective. What injury has he done?

(A language so poverty-stricken that it can't describe the reality of that injury, as gross as it is — perhaps ruining two lives, if the girl becomes pregnant — clearly suffers a vast lack. And a language so incompetent in describing such gross injury — obviously isn't going to make it possible to describe in understandable detail how the normal, day-to-day hurts and injuries of ordinary human misunderstandings affect us. No wonder we get into trouble with other people in close contact, and can't express clearly to the other person precisely how they are stepping on our corns!

(Fiction, because it sketches the circumstances <u>around</u> the disputed area, can make that area understandable to another person, where no direct statement is possible in the language.

(This is the fundamental reason why about 80% of the normal library is made up of fiction, and only about 20% fact. Fiction is a hell of a clumsy way to do things — but when the language won't allow direct statement, we have to delineate the problem in fiction and parable. This **Jesus** clearly recognized.)

Finally, there's an additional, and extremely important problem the science-fictioneer faces. It stems from the fact that we can <u>not</u> define what we mean by "human being," because the variation among human types is, actually, greater than the variation between breeds of dogs.

If dogs had literature, and there was a population of fox terriers, cocker spaniels, salyhams, and dogs of similar size and type, and some dog author wrote of a hero-dog, McClinty, who attacked, fought, and killed a timber wolf single-pawed — the dog audience would reject it as fantastic nonsense. Obviously, no real dog would, or could, do any such thing!

326

Yeah . . . but McClinty happened to be an Irish Wolfhound, some four feet tall at the shoulder.

The behavior of human beings is determined by the patterns of their motivations. The underlying values of literature can endure only if there are no fundamental changes in human motivation.

But we know, now, as a fact that mutations occur, have occurred, and will occur.

One type of human being orients his life on the proposition that Traditions are secure, and stable, and dependable guides to How To Live. Other human beings orient themselves on their own inner beliefs. A third type orients themselves on the Group Opinion. What Everybody Believes Is True.

There's a growing minority type — the group that orients themselves on what the Universe holds to be true. The technician-scientist comes from this fourth group; it is a type that feels-believes in an emotional sense, the laws of the Universe. To them, what the Universe enforces is not merely true — it's Just and Right. It's Stability and Security and Goodness.

The resultant motivation-patterns of the scientist-technician type appear "inhuman" to the Tradition Oriented, the Inner Oriented or the Group oriented. The things the Universe Oriented individual feels and believes in appear, to the other three types, unbelievable, and the resultant personality seems unreal, impossible — a fantasy character, or sheer nonsense.

The **Col. Stapp** type, who can willingly have himself strapped to a rocket sled to determine whether or not his eyeballs will fall out isn't a very believable human being to most people, is he? The British medical researchers who stuck knitting needles into their flesh to determine what tissues were and what were not equipped with pain-sensing nerves don't seem quite human, do they?

Suppose a scientist-technician author accurately and understandingly portrays a character of this type. What reward will he earn from the conventional literary critic?

"His characters are poorly drawn caricatures, robot-like automata with no real humanity."

Generally speaking, the most believable character is one that you yourself would like to be. How many want to be **Col. Stapp**, eagerly

327

ordering his mind to remember all the sensations as he is slammed to a 30-G stop, carefully observing that, after the stop, he is completely blind, and noting the series of sensations that follows?

Or the British Medical researchers who noted that the skin and muscle tissues were sensitive to puncture wounds, but that there was no pain sensation when intestinal tissues were punctured; stretching, rather than puncture, was required to cause pain in intestinal tissues.

The result is that many science-fiction characters are "robot-like automata, with no real humanity." They're actually accurate characterizations of human types the literateur couldn't possibly imagine himself wanting to be — and therefore couldn't believe were real, or, if real, were human beings.

The Frontier always has been, and always will be, peopled by individuals who know perfectly well that they'll probably be killed suddenly, violently, and in some interestingly unusual manner. And still think the game is worth playing.

There usually is, also, a small, deluded population who think the Frontier is a place for gaining quick wealth easily, or gaining hero-worship easily, and the usual anti-social types who aren't trying to accomplish anything, and are freer to destroy where there are fewer people around to watch. These types usually get eliminated early and rapidly; the true frontier type makes the "tough guy" crook appear about as tough, actually, as a belligerent 3-year-old. Compare the tough-guy juvenile delinquent type of "courage" with that **Col. Stapp** has; **Stapp** is a typical Frontier type.

Finally, I'd like to quote a passage from a letter **Dr. John Hocking**, of Michigan State sent the other day. He's a mathematician, and one of our authors.

"Something inside me would enjoy psi-phenomena; the idea appeals to part of me. Yet there is a 'something-for-nothing' flavor which relegates the entire concept into a class with fairy tales — nice, but impossible. What are your opinions about this attitude? I would like to believe that my mind is open to new ideas but that is not true and I know it. My training and my own limitations prevent it. I know that our total knowledge of the universe is pitifully small, and still must have faith that we are on the right track, that these beginnings are not misguided. And this faith is absolutely necessary.

328

"Without such motivating belief I could not work; nor could others. So even if we are wrong, we need that faith in order to — eventually — prove ourselves incorrect, and start anew. Our research is not to be wasted, either. The results must be incorporated into a new system if the theory is discarded. To me, this constitutes a dilemma which I escape by the ostrich technique. Am I really wrong in doing this? My training is such that I can work within the accepted framework, and cannot work outside it. Is it not better that I work? At something?"

How many human beings have the courage **John Hocking** has, to work in full, free, self-admission that he does not know that his work has meaning — and yet the courage to work, and work with whole-hearted dedication . . . whether his dedication be wrong or not, it is better to do than to sit and wait for someone to convince him the effort's worth while.

Certainly, this is not an Inner Directed man!

When **Jesus** commanded, "Be ye humble," I think he meant something like that.

Gib's a true frontiersman — on the frontier of human ignorance, instead of a geographical frontier.

Regards, John

Isaac Asimov   *May 11, 1956*

Dear Isaac:

How was I to know that "Names" was one of those I-gotta-say-it-or-bust items? I asked for an article; you said you didn't have anything in mind . . . and the next I know it's an I-just-gotta-tell-it piece!

Anyhow, it was, of course, good; if you haven't got the check yet, it's on its way. The thing is, you can write a better article about almost nothing than most people can write about the discovery of a practical anti-gravity device. But that's no reason to encourage you to write about almost nothing, is it?

I've got a **Bob Heinlein** novel on hand now, for decision, that's got me worried and bothered. **Bob** can write a better story, with one hand tied behind him, than most people in the field can do with both hands. But **Jesus**, I wish that son of a gun would take that other hand out of his pocket. I also have a **Jack Vance** novel on hand; it's got a lovely idea.

329

If **Vance** could write like **Heinlein,** or **Heinlein** would take the trouble to think as hard as **Vance** did in cooking this one up . . . .

Bob's got a cat in the yarn, Petronius, known as Pete. Pete's a wonderful character — **Bob's** made him delightful. Only . . . he has nothing to do with the story, dammit.

Re other element-names: There's another side of the story that could be inserted briefly — just touched on in passing, so to speak. You didn't mention <u>murium,</u> the metallic element whose oxide is the anhydride of muriatic acid. It might well be fitted in at the point where you discuss **Lavoisiere's** mistake in naming "oxygen." I've forgotten where I originally read the story — I think it may well have been the small *Mellor* — but it's a tale worth the telling, and rather little known. In the old days when all acids were supposed to be oxides, muriatic acid had to be the oxide of something. The struggle to get the elements loose was defeated because they simply couldn't break down the yellow-green gaseous oxide obtained from muriatic acid. When dissolved in water, the supposed muriatic oxide clearly indicated the presence of excess oxygen; bubbles of oxygen appeared in the solution, and eventually a solution of muriatic acid remained. (Inasmuch as no one could isolate HOCl to demonstrate the stuff, they had a lovely time proving that Cl was the element, and that it wasn't "muriatic oxide.")

Inasmuch as fluorine couldn't be isolated from its compounds, it took a bit of faith to maintain the existence of the stuff as an element, in a day when modern techniques weren't on hand. The isolation of fluorine is quite a tale in itself; the fantastic deadliness of the damned stuff made the search a remarkably lethal one, as well as being damned hard. (**Moisson** was not only a brilliant chemist; he was also lucky in having a rich papa-in-law, which was equally necessary to his success. Who else had nice solid Pt-Ir U-tubes to play with? And refrigeration equipment adequate to the task of keeping his H_2F_2 liquid?)

Incidentally, ain't it a shame that Uranium wasn't named after the old Norse god of thunder and lightning? Old Thor, you know, was the guy with the magic hammer he threw with such devastating effect.

In some instances, "that ain't the way I heered it!" so far as the element-naming went. Tantalum, for example, I understood was so named because the chemist who isolated the stuff had such a hell of a time combing it out of all the other things it liked to hide behind. The
330

problem tantalized him for months, as I got it.

Also, if I'm not mistaken you missed a small item about how they first discovered some of the 100-plus elements. Twarn't no 17-atoms-to-work-with business! That was the declassified story; they did make about 17 atoms in a cyclotron — after they'd found it elsewhere. Originally, it seems to have been made in quite considerable quantities by bombarding uranium and plutonium with nitrogen nuclei and oxygen nuclei, and perhaps some sodium-uranium and chlorine-uranium reactions took place also.

They found it in what was left of that Einewetock islet after the thermonuclear explosion turned it into a 2-mile diameter hole. Quite a few short-lived elements can be produced under such conditions, in quite fair quantities. After all, when the ion-beam is operating at around 50,000,000 volts, and has a density of half a million atmospheres, and a cross-section of 30 feet or so . . . quite a few unusual reactions can occur.

It doesn't make much differene whether you slam N and O nuclei at stationary U nuclei, or heave U nuclei at effectively stationary N and O atoms.

Re possibilities of an article on biochemical level evolution: I think it would be damned interesting — and damned important! Biologists and zoologists have traced the development of mechanical structures in evolution — horns, toes, wings, teeth, and the like. But I don't know of much work that's been done in tracing the evolution of biochemical mechanisms in evolution! The development of jaws and teeth is obviously importantly related to the development of diet and behavior patterns of the animal. But the development of enzyme systems is simply the development of a microcosmic set of "teeth and jaws." No good eating cellulose with your teeth, if your enzymes can't chew the molecule apart. If you develop a set of enzymes that can crack cellulose, then you have a use for a set of teeth that'll chew cellulosic materials.

Incidentally, somebody pointed out that plants don't have to develop indigestible tissues to protect themselves against herbivores. They need only develop tissues that are difficult to digest to such an extent that the herbivores have to carry around enough extra chemical processing equipment to weight them down enough so that carnivores can catch enough of them to keep the herbivore population down.

Compare the digestive-machinery department of a cow with that of a dog. Or that of the essentially herbivorous (and distinctly pot-bellied) gorilla with that of Man, who's an omnivore with a distinct penchant for meat, and high concentration nuts, seeds, and similar foods.

One of the items that irked me about that *Scientific American* article on the Peruvian Indios was the suggestion that their distinctly different oxidation enzyme systems didn't constitute a genetic difference. They evolved that as a genetic difference just as surely as the Negro evolved a high-melanin skin as a genetic adaptation to environment. If a man's ancestors have spent a hundred generations learning how to do something you can't do — why the hell shouldn't you acknowledge he's got something special that you haven't got, and can't learn in one lifetime?

Re the uric acid problem, and uricase. If your speculation not only sounds good, but is valid . . . wonder if a drug which the human system could tolerate, and which destroyed uric acid, wouldn't turn out to be useful as a nervous-tension-relaxer, like Milltown, and the other pacifier drugs they're using now? Or if, possibly, that's how those drugs have their effect?

Those things have, you know, the effect of reducing an individual's nervousness . . . but also turning off his ambition. He isn't as worried as before, but also he isn't as worried about accomplishing anything.

Re detergents and cholesterol: how about using some of the present high-power detergents intravenously as a treatment for artherosclerosis? Haven't they developed some detergents that could be tolerated, and are more potent than even the tauroconjugates? If not, can Man tolerate tauroconjugates if injected?

Sometimes something that looks like "imperfect adaptation" turns out to be the optimum on a curve involving two conflicting requirements. Speaking of detergents — the detergents used in dishwashing in the home have to satisfy two mutually exclusive ideals: they should be so effective that they'll lift grease, caramalized and semi-carbonized matter, protein glue, and the like from metallic and ceramic surfaces, but they must not take the skin oils and protein cements off of and out of the human hand and fingernails. Result: Next time you've got a particularly glucked-up pan to clean at home, try using "All", or
332

one of the other high-power automatic-laundry detergents on it. That stuff ain't no compromise; keep your hands out of it, and watch the crud break loose! The damned stuff took a 75-year accumulation of fat-and-carbon off of a big cast-iron frying pan **Peg's** grandmother originally used. We had to re-season the thing before stuff stopped sticking, as a result.

So let's do some checking. The poorer Chinese, Hindus, and Africans don't eat very damn much meat in the course of a whole lifetime. They're busy proving Malthus was right, and haven't time to raise animal foods. How do they do on artherosclerosis?

Incidentally and by the way: I understand that the length of the gut in human beings varies by a factor of as much as 3. This being so . . . it suggests that some of us aren't able to be true omnivores; somebody with only about 10 feet of intestine would <u>have</u> to live on high-concentration, high-digestibility foods.

Item: The M.D.'s haven't gotten around to making this association, so far as I'm aware: Children under 8 or so usually dislike steak; they'd much rather have hamburger, meat-loaf, or the like.

The bones do their growing in the zone where the shank of the bone meets the joint-end part — this is usually pretty much cartilage. An adult can, I have read, exert a net force of as much as <u>7 tons</u> in chewing; the maxillary muscles are real potent little gadgets.

But if kids under 8 are equipped with cartilage near the jaw-bone joint, right where the molars set in, and the maxillaries attach — just maybe a kid knows what's good for him, when he says he wants ground round, instead of porterhouse!

I think there should be a hell of an interesting article on biochemical mechanisms in evolution.

Regards, John

Dr Frey   *May 25, 1956*

Dear Dr. Frey:

No fair! You used the word-symbol "mystic" as a technical term; I, working with a highly general audience, must stick to the non-technical meaning of the term, and I so used it. The non-technical meaning is "anyone who considers physical science an inferior attempt to explain what he knows is all caused by Spirits of a Higher Plane. Generally an individual with a completely undisciplined mind, who considers any effort to impose any form of organization of thoughts, any structure on his idea-system, a cruel, unfeeling, and unjust thing."

I think you'd be wise, in normal communication with others, to recognize that that is, in fact, the <u>general</u> definition of "a mystic." Try using the term Magi for what you normally, technically refer to as a Mystic. You can almost always improve effective communication if you use a term the other fellow does not already have a definition for; that'll stop him long enough so he'll ask what you mean, instead of assuming that you of-course mean what <u>he</u> means by the term.

If a chemist says to a complete layman, "This stuff here? Oh, that's a salt I'm working with," the layman might try putting the salt on his hard-boiled egg for lunch. If this particular salt happened to be cadmium chloride, or potassium cyanide, the results might distress the chemist almost as much as the layman.

I get into a lot of hassles with technicians; a psychologist gave me a four-page lecture on the meaning of the term <u>emotion</u> after one of my editorials. It happened, though, that I also got a three-page lecture on the same subject, the same week, from an endocrinologist. I sent each the other man's letter by way of illustration of what the problem was. I have no idea what they did about it after that.

Now you've also used the term "energies"; thanks for the quotation-marking it, because you quite evidently do not mean what a physical scientist means by the term "energy." You're cheating a bit there, too; physical scientists invented the word. It's like "gas" and "radar" — a word made up to fit a specific need, a term that never before existed, to fit a newly discovered need. The whole essence of physical science, and the immense progress it has made, has been the harsh, ruthless, but effective discipline of demanding hard, precisely delimited definitions of all terms used in making statements. The humanic sciences — including medicine — would make a lot more progress, I believe, if they would try that same frustrating, maddening, but effective self-discipline.

To begin with . . . define the term "human being."

Think it's easy? Sure . . . on a "You know what I mean!" basis. But let's take one of **Isaac Asimov's** positronic robots, newly manu-
334

factured, and all ready to be instructed as to what it must do. Now the First Law of **Asimov's** Robotics is "No robot can injure a human being, nor, by inaction, allow a human being to come to harm."

Now instruct this unlimitedly willing, enormously intelligent, but absolutely ignorant entity as to what a human being is. Let's assume that this robot is to be a nurse's aide type robot.

Is a haemophiliac a human being? Genetically different from normal individuals of the species *Homo sapiens* as he is . . . can we properly call him true human?

Is a mongolian idiot a human being?

Is a toddler in the pack-rat stage a human being? If so, you can't have a robot around your home; the First Law would force the robot to prevent your spanking Junior when he needed it; a robot cannot stand idly by while a human being is injured.

Is a chimpanzee a human being? Why not? A matter of clothes, surface color and hair? Then what happens if an unusually hairy man is getting out of the shower when the robot comes along? And what about a small, wrinkled old Negro?

And what if the robot encounters one of those unfortunates who was born without arms? Is this individual a "human being?" If so, what is your definition?

Our ancestors were no where near as stupid as we oh-so-wise moderns would like to pretend. Do you know the old terms incubus and succubus? According to the lore of the Middle Ages, an incubus was a demon in the form of a handsome young man, the succubus his female counterpart. They appeared human in every respect — except that they had no souls, and sought to trap and destroy young women and young men. Unlike a human madman, who was held to be inhabited by a demon, these entities were demons. An effort could be made to drive the demon out of the madman; the only thing to do with the incubus or succubus was to burn them as soon as detected; no cure was possible, because they weren't human to begin with.

Think they were silly? How would you describe a psychopathic personality in the terms available to the writers of 1300 A.D.? Sure, I know the oh-so-wise modern psychologists etc., hold that genetics has practically nothing to do with personality; that doesn't make them right. It's evident that human beings can be born who somehow, by a freak of genetics, lack arms, or have haemophilia, or some other monstrous and visible distortion. Can you "cure" a haemophiliac? His genetics calls for exactly the condition he is in; to "cure" him, you must permanently induce an unnatural-to-him tendency for thrombosis, mustn't you?

If a psychopathic personality can result from a genetic failure of certain normal-human social instincts . . . doesn't "incubus" describe him more accurately than some of our present concepts? Because such an individual has human physiology, and human intelligence, but animal psychic structure, the only practical solution is to destroy the monster.

By examining the extreme ranges of variation, we can sometimes do a better job of understanding what we're working with.

If some individuals are genetically lacking — some may be expected to be genetically accidentally plus, to have capabilities or characteristics not possessed by normal human beings. The rough thing about such a situation is that that means that some individuals can do something that you or I can never possibly hope to learn. You can't _learn_ a genetic gift!

At the physiological level we know this happens; the Peruvian Indios can play a violent game of Rugby at 15,000 foot altitudes. Any normal human being, even after 5 to 10 years of acclimatization, would kill himself if he tried it. The Peruvians have a genetic adaptation to thin air; you or I _can't_ learn that!

Now just because some gifted individual can do X does not mean that you or I could learn to.

But here's where the psionic machines come in. We can't operate properly at 15,000 feet — but I-plus-a-machine can. If I can define precisely what the Magi does in doing X, then I may be able to do with a machine, what I alone cannot do, nor learn to do.

A spider can spin strong silken threads. I can't. But I-plus-a-machine can spin nylon threads that make the spider's silk look silly. A gull can fly; I can't, nor can I ever learn to. But I-plus-a-machine can fly from New York to Colorado in two hours, and make a gull look silly indeed.

Furthermore, it took the gull (as a racial entity) some 150,000,000 years to achieve that flight; it took Man as a racial entity only about 500,000.

336

The great fault of the East is that the gifted individuals took themselves off into their own worlds of contemplation, and considered it no problem of theirs that others could not follow.

The West had a different attitude. It may have started as the old peasant's attitude of "Root, hog, or die!" but it did a lot of good. If Gerald Genius had some wonderful new talent . . . Gerald could be damned well git off his geniusy little tail and do something useful with it, or starve and freeze to death. Gerald was faced with the proposition, "OK — so you've got something. How nice for you! But since I haven't got it, it isn't nice for me, so bedamned if I'll feed, clothe, and house you for something that does me no good. Make it useful to me, and I'll admit you're a genius. Otherwise, for my money — and please note my brawny, if stupid, right arm that's holding this money — you can go starve."

Hard on Gerald Genius; sure slowed down the progress Gerald could have made. "He travels fastest who travels alone," you know . . . but a man who travels alone dies without issue. Bringing a woman along will certainly slow him down a lot, but only so can he and his descendants hold what he has found. Bringing the rest of the world along behind him has sure slowed down our Western geniuses. But isn't it strange that the East is dying under the impact of the mass-education West?

Here's something you and your husband might kick around; my wife and I have done a lot of thinking and working on it.

The difference between male and female is a lot deeper, wider, and more important than the physiological; it's exceedingly ancient, and exceedingly important. Before understanding of it can be achieved, a definition of what it is must be admitted to discussion.

Now Woman has 48 chromosomes, and Man has 47; woman has 24 completed pairs, and man has only 23 1/2. The consequence is that Man is genetically less stable than Woman. When Nature tries out a new idea in how-to-live (a mutation) it will, probably, show up first in the genetically less stable male. Vide haemophilia, and a variety of others. That 24-to-23 pairs ratio makes a small, but critical difference.

To measure movement, you must have one base point, and one changed point; it takes a difference-of-movement to be detected. To determine direction of movement, it takes two differentially moving

337

points.

In all animal life, evolution has tried no-sex, one-sex, two-sex, three-sex, and up to seven-sex systems here on Earth. The highest no-sex forms are monocells. The highest hermaphroditic (true one-sex) forms are snails. The three, four and more-sex forms didn't get that far. But the two-sex forms ran away with the race, and absolutely dominate the planet.

With one relatively stable form, and one relatively unstable form, the direction-of-movement can be detected.

In all mammalian life-forms, the female accepts or rejects the male. The female is the stable form; she detects that the direction-of-change of the more labile male is up or down.

The race survives through the female; the male is expendable. In any population, the birth-rate is proportional only to the number of fertile females in the child-bearing ages — social mores, religious beliefs, etc., to the contrary not withstanding. The race is not dependent on the males for its maintenance in the way it is on the females.

When primitive man went from point A to point B on migration, the males went first, while the females tagged along behind, carrying the tribal goods. The female carried the static burdens of things; the males went first, unburdened — because they carried the dynamic burden of defense against shock attacks. They had to be unencumbered.

The female carries the burden of the developing baby; the male carries the burden of shock attack of the environment. He is expendable; she is not. He defends; she maintains.

But . . . in consequence of the greater genetic lability of the male, it is, and always will be probable that the male of the species will get the new, favorable mutations first. (He'll also get the sour ones first, too — and they'll be eliminated by eliminating him.) Males have the higher death rate, a higher insanity rate, a higher rate of break-down in every department, and that despite the fact that they don't have the physiological and psychological burden of child-rearing.

But . . . males have an earned reward for taking the higher risk. Every one of the great philosophers, truly first-rank authors, first-rank painters, musicians, scientists, mathematicians, etc. has been a male. They stuck their necks out — and some few of them didn't get their heads lopped off doing that.

338

It isn't a matter of the suppression of women, either; in the first place, women have never been suppressed in the field of music — but can you name even one woman composer? More important, while it's perfectly true that women have been suppressed in many fields, consider the matter of the right to vote; how many women died on the rack in the public square because of their demand for the vote? How many had their heads mounted on pikes along the public road, after being publicly disemboweled for being uppity toward their masters? That's how men got the vote, after all!

But . . . and this is most important! — note this curious fact: Every one of mankind's greatest heroes has been a man who specifically, publicly, and strongly asserted his high respect for the opinions and thoughts of a woman. And every one of mankind's great villains has been a man who vigorously and publicly demeaned the thinking and ideas of woman! **Hitler**, for example, proclaimed "kinder, kirche und kuche!" for woman.

Which of the Eastern Magis has shared his life on a truly symbiotic basis with a woman? They travelled faster . . . but alone. And what they may have accomplished is lost because of that. They had brilliance, without patience.

We Caucasians have a great and unique genetic heritage; nearly all our ancestors were slaves. They nearly all lived in slavery for some 1500 years. Slavery has its bad points — but it breeds a type that can abide in patience, truly try to understand another human being's needs and instructions, and work well for someone else. Our heritage of generations of slavery is unique — and immensely valuable. Symbiosis is the way of life that works; evolving organisms found that out after some 2,000,000,000 years of trying. We are, of course, symbiotic colonies, each of us. But symbiosis is simply mutual slavery — as is coopeation.

The *jus primus noctis* of the Middle Ages — the local noble had a right to take any peasant girl on her wedding night — may have seemed a cruel, degrading custom — but I suspect it's the attitude behind that that made the difference between the East and the West. In India the caste rules are so rigid such a thing was unthinkable. In Europe, that attitude bred up hybrids who had the high intelligence, the drive and personality force of the nobles — and the abiding, patient determination of the peasant-slave. The "rise of the middle classes" was exactly

339

that — the rise of the hybrids, with the sturdy, solid, patience of the slave combined with the driving ambition of the noble.

India never produced such a type.

The great problem is this, though: what is the unique, and different strength a woman has? The philosophers have all been males; they could not know and express it. The women have not yet developed the self-contained strength to say what they are, that men are not; they are still too busy trying to prove an untrue point — that they're just like men. They aren't, and never will be; they're different, deeply different. But in a culture that holds that there is Only One Right Way, and Only One Way To Be Good, they are still trying to prove they're just as good men as their brothers.

That's a reduction to the absurdity — and snail-level futility — of insisting that Man is a hermaphroditic, one-sex species!

What is the different strength that you, as a woman, have that no man ever will have? Symbiosis can exist only between different organisms, you know!

I do not have the address of either the Drown Laboratories or the De La Ware laboratories; I can, and will get them and let you know.

The psionic machine did not predict the death of the white mice; it caused it. These psionic machines are not toys; they're devices exploring a vast, and enormously powerful field of forces — and they include the Death Magic as well as the Life Magic. To cure cancer, we must kill the aberrant cells; curative magic must be death magic, too.

There is a modification of the **Hieronymus** machine that is being developed now by the Radiurgic Corp., of which **Hieronymus** is Vice President in charge of Research, that amounts to a death-magic machine. They are using it for destruction of insect pests; by using the machine on a photograph of the plants to be protected, insect pests are destroyed. The miles of distance between machine and plant have no meaning. A friend of mine had the tent caterpillars in a tree in his front yard near here cleared out by **Hieronymus** using his machine in Florida. The tree's photograph was treated for 10 minutes a day for three days. A similar tree in his back yard, similarly infested, remained heavily infested; the tree in his front yard was free of caterpillars in three days.

It's logically impossible, of course, and makes no understandable sense in the light of anything known. Except that no theory can be
340

considered adequate if it does not include all observed facts.

If you try building the **Hieronymus** machine, incidentally, you'll find some weird and interesting facts about it. It works. But it works just as well when it's <u>not</u> connected to a power supply. But it <u>will not</u> work when a defective tube is used . . . even when it is or is not plugged in!

I have a **Campbell** Machine, derived from the **Hieronymus** machine that works, too. Only it's based on something so insane that it makes the **Hieronymus** machine look as conventional as a shovel. But mine works like a charm!

The great problem is not simply that of discovering things; communication is necessary too. That's where the East fell down!

Regards, John Campbell

Isaac Asimov   *August 20, 1956*

Dear Isaac:

I'm damn glad to hear of that article on Science Fiction: Ally against Ignorance. It's something that needs doing — and that few of us, as you correctly say, can do effectively. Your professorial rank makes your work n times as effective as anyone else's.

One might add that your top-flight rank in science-fiction also makes your work more effective. If you were a professor who was a third-rank, sometimes-sells sciencefictioneer, it wouldn't count as much, either.

I hope your kids are well by this time; having been there myself a few times, I know it ain't fun. **Leslyn,** by the way, had her tonsils yanked a month or so ago. I was most interested in her reactions. She was told the score, and annoyedly and grudgingly agreed that she guessed it had to be done. She had her choice of Dr.'s office, or hospital, and chose the hospital "so she could see how a hospital worked." The Dr. reported she went through the process "without a tear," accepting the anaesthetic also on the "damned nuisance but necessary" basis.

When we visited her that evening, she was still groggy, of course, but her primary statement was, "I <u>hate</u> ether." She was mad at it, because it made her sick, and getting rid of it just as fast as she could. Anger, strong rejection, but no fear or worry. The tonsilectomy healed up per-

341

fectly, and she was out and around in short order.

I have something that may well be of interest to you; if your thinking checks mine, and if investigation — which you can do as I cannot—checks it, it may be worth writing up for the *Journal of Chem Ed* and other places.

Peg and I have had a five-year running fight on the subject of Technical vs Liberal Arts schools. And I mean a fight; it has broken out repeatedly, and neither one of us could break the crux of the damned thing. It shows up in innumerable guises, but whatever form it started in, it would work down to Technical vs Liberal Arts education. We couldn't get it past that point.

Finally, we succeeded in breaking the blasted thing. We got it back one step further, and the thing cracked — and in doing so, gave me a Grade A clue as to why the government and industry are having such a time getting good technical personnel — and why the med schools aren't getting enough good men. The thing fell apart when we ran into this one:

The old Classical Education, as found in Oxford, Heidelberg, etc., involves some 6 or more years of Latin and Greek. They make the students study the old Classics, but good. Moreover, they have to write poetry, etc., in the classic languages; they have to be able to use the dead languages.

Now there's a peculiar characteristic of the dead past; it is what it is, and is that, whatever it may be, completely, solely, and absolutely. It is absolute; it is immune to alteration, amendment, or argument. You may have argument about what it was, but there can be no alteration of whatever it was. It's rigid, absolute, and immutable. Whether **Virgil's** *Canto V* was good, bad, or indifferent, it was what it was, and nothing else whatsoever. Whether **Plato's** philosophy was good, bad, or meaningless, what he said is precisely and nothing-else-but what he said.

Latin grammar is forever fixed and immutable; it's a dead language, absolutely immune to change, and unaffected by changing times.

Isaac . . . the Classical education forced the student to accept that there are things in the Universe that CAN NOT BE CHANGED BY HUMAN OPINION. They are beyond all argument, cavil, or mutation. No matter how passionate your disagreement, no matter what force of
342

insistence you bring to bear . . . they remain what they are. Your right to your own opinion is absolutely limited; you can NOT change Latin grammar one iota.

English grammar is different; English is a living language, and the force of popular opinion does change it.

The Liberal Arts schools offer courses that are entirely open to opinion; strong, passionate appeal, vigorous campaigning, can change the Truths in Art, in living languages, etc.

The basic proposition of the Liberal Arts tradition is that all things are relative.

Got a story from **H. Beam Piper**, about archeologists on Mars. They've found a dead civilization, 50,000 years dead, that had a high technology. They've found books, inscriptions, etc. But the language is, of course, unknown — and there can never be a bilingual Rosetta stone, linking the unknown to some known language. The archeologists are pretty much agreed that translation is forever hopeless; without some bilingual inscription to start with, the code is forever indecipherable.

They find an ancient university. The language is cracked in a week, and they're reading Martian books easily in a few months. A chemist cracked it. It is not true that all things are relative; the bilingual inscription was simply a periodic table of the elements. Physical reality is the absolute universal language; all languages must encode that in precisely the same manner, whether it be the language of a man, a monster, or an entity of pure force.

But the archeologists didn't know that; all humanic science people know that human customs and beliefs are so different that all things are relative, so they passed the periodic table as relating only to a Martian's idea of chemistry.

The idea of freedom of opinion is so deeply appealing to human beings, that the Liberal Arts tradition is dearly loved and warmly defended. If you say, "I don't like this book," you have a right to your opinion. It takes an **Einstein** to say,"It is not a bad book; crazy, but it is not bad."

There are two ways to induce a student to take the science courses needed to become an engineer or technician or scientist. One is to make the reward so attractive they will take the courses. The other is

343

to make the alternatives less attractive.

Now men will fight and die — sacrifice life, wife, children, and everything else — for a way of life, for a set of attitudes and beliefs. A human being will accept torture, being racked, skinned alive, roasted to death, when he could avoid it by simply changing his attitudes and opinions.

Why were enchanters so dreaded? Even the White Magicians who used their powers only therapeutically and helpfully?

Because they could change a man's attitudes without his conscious consent. Because they could <u>make him want</u> to do something instead of merely forcing him to do it.

Suppose we have a man who is psychically impotent. He had so violent a sex education that sex was nasty, awful, loathesome, dirty and obscene that the very thought of the act revolts his very soul. Intellectually, he knows that this is inappropriate . . . but it remains the fact.

If he goes to a doctor for help, he wants the doctor to make him able to force himself to go through with the act, much as he detests it, because of a sense of duty — because of some goal external to the act itself.

If the doctor said, "Certainly I can help. I'll treat you by magic, and in 24 hours you'll <u>like</u> sex!" what would the patient's reaction be?

He'd leave the place in a screaming horror. He doesn't want to <u>like</u> what he knows, deep in his soul, is a foul, loathesome act! He wants to be able to tolerate it.

If the magician worked succssfully, however, he would like sex . . . and <u>want</u> to like it, of course!

The immense power of the repugnance to the idea of something that can change your attitudes is deeply buried, and never acknowledged openly. The power is so great that the very fact it exists has to be shielded from the conscious mind; it's the ultimate horror-beyond-horror.

A disciplined education involves learning to like having your basic beliefs and attitudes changed. To be a chemist, you must learn to <u>like</u> believing something that you considered completely wrong — for that is what learning in the true sense is!

The Liberal Arts schools offer the shadow of education — data.
344

They offer the ability to argue against any opinion presented and defend your unlimited right to your own opinion, because <u>everything</u> is relative, and I have as much right to my opinion as you have to yours, and just because you believe hydrogen always has only a single electron doesn't mean I have to believe it too, does it?

The Liberal Arts education is far, far more pleasant to a human being. It comforts him; it is the strong protector of his right to his own opinion. It gives him data and techniques of argument with which he can defend his own opinion against other people who try to limit his right to believe anything he wants.

What does the Technical school offer? The harsh and inhuman rigidity of being forced to accept opinions you don't like, of being forced to learn to <u>like</u> having your beliefs torn away from you ruthlessly. The final demolition of all hope of freedom of opinion; the discovery that, even when you are grown up, you still can't do what you want, believe what you want, accept and reject ideas on the sole basis of whether they satisfy you or not. The appalling realization of a terrible, overwhelming Power, called The Universe, that forces you, willy-nilly, to agree with it . . . or accept infinite and absolute frustration. A Power against which all human argument, passion, and striving is absolutely futile. A Power that rewards solely on the basis of absolute acceptance of its dictates, without any possibility whatsoever of appeal or argument.

What human being, given free choice, would willingly accept the ultimate torture of having his personal beliefs, and the very right to have opinions, stripped away from him?

The rise in the number of people going into the humanic sciences does not mean what I thought it meant; it was a source of considerable hope to me, until I recognized this other factor.

The "humanic sciences" go one step beyond even the Liberal Arts; they hold that <u>absolutely everything</u> is a matter of opinion.

The Technical school teaches that here is a Heaven and a Hell. In Hell, there is only infinite, unending, and everlasting frustration, pain, and imprisonment, the everlasting punishment of painful failure, resulting from seeking futilely to defy the Laws of the Power that Rules. In Heaven, there is fulfillment, reward in proportion to effort, achievement and everlasting growth in seeking to understand and apply the Laws of

345

the Power That Rules.

Hell is the place where all the theories are perfect . . . and none of them work. Because all are equally perfect, and none works, it is impossible to find any fault in any of them to start correcting the others.

But the Liberal Arts school teaches that there is no heaven and no hell, and that anyone can do what he wants, believe what he wants, and if he just insists on it hard enough, it will all be equally true.

Who wants a disciplined course?

Try this one, **Isaac**: In the patient's lounge of an insane asylum, the non-violent patients stand around talking to each other. God meets Napoleon, and discusses that poor crazy fool over there who thinks he's the sinnner whose sins have brought on the world all the troubles it has by causing God's wrath. Of course, each knows that the other, poor fool, is nuts . . . but it's impolite to point that out to him. Besides, that's apt to cause him to do something unpleasant.

In a Liberal Arts college recreation room, a group of students are discussing something. Each knows he has an unarguable right to his own opinion. Of course, the others are wrong, but they don't realize it, and it would be impolite to force them to see that. And besides, that's apt to cause him to do something unpleasant.

Agreed: there is a difference. But let's see you name it!

The Liberal Arts tradition holds that the right to freedom of opinion is an <u>unlimited right</u>. But that isn't freedom — it's license.

What is the limit on the right to your own opinion? And <u>don't</u> say that the limitation is the other individual; a homocidal maniac has the opinion he should kill you, and you have a right to impose your opinion on him, despite his desires. A Jehovah's Witness family had an Rh negative baby problem, and refused the medical technique essential to saving the baby. The State imposed its opinion on them; the baby lived.

You'll never get enough self-disciplined thinkers, if the need for self-discipline is held to be unreal. The Liberal Arts approach, and more recently the humanic sciences approach, is growing in importance and effect. People educated in that tradition are now teaching grade and high school classes. They have that lovely "let the little darling do what he wants; don't frustrate his dear little ego" proposition to back them.

One of the biggest high schools near Detroit can't get enough trigonometry students — out of a couple thousand kids — to maintain a trig class. Why learn that rigid discipline, when it's so meaningless anyway, because everything's just relative anyhow? Didn't **Einstein** say so, too?

Regards, John

Isaac Asimov *August 25, 1956*

Dear Isaac:

I see by the carbon copy he sent me, that my friend **Howard Armstrong** wrote you after seeing your article on SciFic. You need a little background to understand that letter of his, I'm afraid.

He's a gentleman about 75 years old, a Princeton Engineering School graduate, class of '05 as he mentioned. *Chem Engineer. Research* mainly on mineral and metallurgical·processes all his life. Electroplating of W, and others. Ore beneficience, etc. Couple dozen patents. A classmate, **Clinton Upton**, was a mining engineer; they cooperated considerably during the years.

In 1946 they both lost their wives, within a few months of each other, to cancer. Having been research men all their lives, and having had it conclusively demonstrated that medicine couldn't crack the problem, having comfortable fortunes accumulated over the years . . . they started their own research on cancer.

If you think they're nuts . . . think again. They spent a good, full lifetime proving in the thoroughly practical way of industrial chemical engineering that they could think, and think straighter and faster than most.

Armstrong has three sons; one's a research director with Pfeiffer, one with Monsanto, and one with du Pont. Real grade A dopes they are not. (**Armstrong**, by the way, is about 3/4 Cherokee Indian.)

His letter must have sounded rambling and disjointed to you; it's as unintelligible as a report on biochemistry snatched out of a textbook, without the preceding 15 chapters of orientation.

The thing is, their cancer research ran smack into the Medical Monopoly of the AMA. We need not debate the question of whether the said monopoly is good or ill; we do need to recognize it exists. An MD who doesn't use orthodox methods will lose his license, and cease to

347

be an MD. Orthodox methods don't cure cancer. Therefore no MD can possibly cure cancer. Simple, ain't it?

But no one who is not an MD is permitted to experiment on cancer! An MD who experiments with unorthodox approaches will lose his license. Therefore, since orthodox methods won't cure cancer, no MD can find the cure for cancer!

(It'll be found by a non-MD, a biochemist, or cytologist, or the like, and will then be tested by some MD. The cure will then be known as the Jones Cure, named after John Jones, MD, who first introduced it. Oh, yes . . . lessee now . . . I think there was some biochemist who helped Jones with the routine analyses, wasn't there?)

Please note that **Pasteur**, a chemist, discovered germs, not a doctor. The problem of malaria was cracked by a civil engineer; the damn disease was getting in his way in building dams, bridges, etc., and he had to get it out of his way.

Anyhow, **Armstrong & Upton** went to work. They started the way any engineer would — by trying to find examples in Nature, and analyzing for the commonality present.

Note this: Anyone oriented in a humanic-style education accepts statistics happily, but hates laws-of-nature. (I'll get to the reasons below!)

Now suppose you get in a shipment of magnesium turnings for chemical lab use. You open the container, and about 10 grams of the stuff spills out and falls upward against the ceiling. You look at it, climb up and haul it down, release a bit and watch it fall up again. "Oh, well," you say, "that's only 10 grams out of this 10 kilogram lot. It's defective somehow — obviously can't make decent weighings with that stuff. But it's statistically unimportant, so I can ignore it."

It is statistically insignificant, isn't it?

Anyone educated in the statistical approach to life would be perfectly justified in ignoring it, wouldn't he? After all, a busy man can't spend his time fussing over trifles, can he? There's the statistically far more significant 99.9% of the Mg that must be dealt with, and behaves in a useful, predictable manner.

The engineer, however, has been educated on the proposition that every case is significant. You may, as a bridge builder, build 1000 bridges — but the first one you build that collapses means that, as of
348

right then, you ain't an engineer any more.

Recent case: US soldier in England, in a tavern brawl, stabbed an Englishman. Englishman hauled to hospital, treated, died. US man tried and convicted of murder. Woman attorney from Brooklyn got suspicious, investigated. Turned out the stab wound was minor, any reasonably healthy man would have recovered. The man died of terramycin poisoning; it was known that that man was dangerously allergic to terramycin. The use of the antibiotic was unjustified. Will the MD who did it be convicted of the murder now?

Armstrong & Upton studied naturally occurring cancer cures. Statistically, they are as insignificant as the upfalling Mg. But they are there.

The spontaneous cases have a psychosomatic aspect as the commonality. There's a term "psychogenic," but no corresponding term "psychoantigenic" — the psychic curative force. MD's recognize psychogenic forces can cause ulcers; well, let's say that psychological forces can cause a cancer to have ulcers, too. And if you have an ulcer on a cancer, that means the cancer is eaten away . . . which is known as "curing the cancer."

Check on it **Isaac**. Various religious shrines have records of spontaneous cures. Faith healers of the evangelistic type have similar (thoroughly documented) cases. Spontaneous cures have been noted in individuals who have a violently powerful will to live and continue their work.

It's long been known that a woman who is psychically sterile can be made fertile, many times, by undergoing an operation — any operation! Many times a voyage, a change of residence, has had the same effect. The curative effect of the operation is not physiological, but psychological. Wanna state absolutely and categorically that surgical techniques in cancer are useful solely because of physiological changes?

Anyhow, **Armstrong & Upton** decided that the psychic side of the matter was in need of investigation. They've been severely limited, of course, in their research. So they turned to studying the effects of psi forces in plant and animal diseases.

What **Armstrong** was talking about in his letter was their work in Death Magic. They have a psi machine — I have copies of it here; it works — which does Death Magic and Life Magic. Call it "psionic" if you prefer; it's magic, and it works. They use it to kill living entities — insect pests primarily. The State Department of Agriculture in Pennsylvania has checked their tests; the tests are valid, but the State Dept. people quite understandably, are utterly horrified at the idea of publicly stating they witnessed successful magic. (Can you imagine what such a statement would do to a botanist's scientific reputation?! Look what happened to even so powerful a man as **Sir William Crooks** when he testified he'd seen **D.D. Home** levitate!)

Anyhow, their figures showed that in tests on 90 farms, scattered over 5 Pennsylvania counties, they achieved a 95% kill of Jap beetles, at all distances from 120 feet to 150 miles. They've improved techniques since then; they now get a 99% kill of corn-borers, ear-worms and Jap beetles.

The problem of curing cancer is that of killing certain living entities that you can't reach physically. Their killing of insects involves killing living entities they do not contact physically. The killing is, of course, selective; the corn plants thrive.

They've also cured every case of Dutch Elm disease they've tackled.

Armstrong is, currently, running some tests on tomato plant galls, which are a virus-caused cancerous growth of tomatoes, and which are absolutely uncontrollable by any standard technique. He's researching for the best technique of application of the psi force, or magic, or hoosenany flapdoodle, or whatever you want to call it. I'm not stuck on any particular name; I am struck by the successful results, however.

Unofficially, **Armstrong's** treated several cancers in friends of his — cancers which were medically diagnosed, and medically treated also. It just happened that in each case the MD treating the cancer was completely successful. It was, no doubt, purely the medical treatment that cured it — just coincidence that those medical methods which fail regularly (i.e., the normal expectable outcome is death) in most cases happened to be completely successful in these cases.

The germ theory of disease is necessary . . . but not sufficient.

You can't get a photograph by exposing film to light, you know, **Isaac**. Exposure to germs doesn't produce a disease, either. You have to develop the negative as well as expose it.

350

What's the non-germ factor in disease?

If you want to make a nice, neat, scientific test, try this:

When someone comes to you, trying to communicate something that is emotionally important to him, under such circumstances that he must communicate it to you — communication with anyone else will not solve his problem — rebuff him absolutely. Block his communication solidly.

Within 24 hours he'll have a cold in the head.

Statistical correlation will run better than 85%.

Or try the other way: every time a kid shows up with a cold, as soon as you spot it, get him aside, and try finding out what shock-surprise blockages of emotional communication have hit him in the last 8 hours before the cold symptoms showed up. Betcha you can get a correlation of better than 90%.

It takes a human being about 2 weeks to damp out the shock excitation caused by a sudden, unexpected shock of emotional communication blockage. If the blockage has been predicted and expected, it won't cause that shock-excitation effect, and hence no cold. If you know your boss is a Grade A sonofabitch, when he bawls you out it's not a shock; if he's a fine, mild, kindly guy, and a good friend of yours . . . you'll have a cold.

Not being an MD, I can't report the results of that little private research anywhere that it would be effective.

A cold will break in about 8 hours if you locate and expose to intellectual analysis the emotional blockage that caused it.

Oh, well . . . I'll get the data out somehow, sooner or later. Might help you personally to look into the business, though.

Armstrong had a copy of your article on hand; I had too damned little time (I was visiting his research group in Harrisburg) to read all of it, but I did get that Cult of Ignorance business of yours. salutations and congratulation; I hadn't spotted that one myself, and you're dead-center right. There is a cult of ignorance, and I'm beginning to work on the problem of Why?

Part of it's this: Used to be that Hal, English Yeoman of 1150 AD, considered his physical body to be himself. And that body was an enigma wrapped in a mystery; he knew he had a stomach, and that it was for food, and it was pleasant to fill it, but he hadn't the foggiest sug-

351

gestion of a beginning of an idea that there was a purpose-beyond-pleasure in the business of eating. He didn't know he had a circulatory failure, and when he died it was an Act of God, or due to a visible sword, bludgeon, or arrow.

Poison was <u>unknown as such</u> in that time. Only Magic existed. The witch-doctor prepares the poisoned arrows of the primitive races. He enchants them. (Item: During the Age of Dinosaurs, there appear to have been no poisonous reptiles. The reptiles began losing the race for control . . . and poison developed. The human peoples who typically use poison arrows and darts are the very primitive, dwarfish losers in the race of world control, the ones whom the bigger, healthier races have pushed back into the least livable areas.)

Death, for Hal, was due to "those things happen"; there was no structured cause. Hal didn't have to worry about amoebic dysentery, or typhoid infection. He didn't have to worry about circulatory failure, or cancer. Not knowing these things existed, he had no fear of them.

Ignorance, my friend, is bliss; you may get killed by it, but you can't be scared by it.

The happy, ignorant, unworried moron doesn't have predictive ability enough to worry about the consequences. When women didn't know that the sex act was related to pregnancy, think how much more freely they could enjoy a good, sound, all-out intercourse! Before men knew syphilis existed, think how much more freely they could have their fun without worry! Back to Nature means Back to Ignorance-is-bliss.

Consider the Irish legend of the Banshee. The Banshee was a friendly fairy, who had prescience. Like any good Irish female, she keened for the dead. Trouble was, she made the last days of her human friend somewhat uncomfortable because, having prescience, she started keening three days before he died, instead of keening afterward. (Vide a similar thing in Alice, where the Queen shrieked like a steam calliope <u>before</u> striking her finger.)

Fear can exist only in a state of half-knowledge; you must know the danger exists before you can fear it — and you must know too little to be able to overcome it.

The Cult of Ignorance has sound basis; half-knowledge is the source of fear, and fear produces unhappiness. The only way out is to fight your way through to full knowledge — and most human beings are just damned well incompetent to achieve that. (In a system wherein all individuals have an equal opportunity to develop their highest potentials, there must necessarily be inequality — since not all individuals have equal potentials. The existence of inherently superior individuals constitutes an apparent injustice; Bill Blow, Dope, Class II, considers it deep injustice that Gerald Genius, Intellectual Class A1, should be allowed-by-the-nature-of-things to achieve things he, Bill, can't. Justice is equality, says Bill. Is it?)

The trouble with the Justice Is Equality; Equality Is Justice idea is this: Suppose a bunch of racketeers moves in on Boston University. They force you to sign up with the Faculty Protective Association, paying $5 a week for the privilege of not being beaten up by their goon squad. This is injustice. But six months later they've forced every faculty member in the entire Boston-Cambridge area to sign up. Now all faculty members are equal; they all pay $5 a week protection money. This, because it's equality, must then be Justice, no?

Before saying it's nonsense . . . notice that that's how this world of ours works! The garment industry is in precisely that spot. If Manufacturer A is racketed, he'll go broke because of his increased operating costs, putting him in an impossible competitive position. But if all manufacturers have similar racket costs, then they can all simply pass it on to the consumer. Now if A succeeds in breaking out of the racket, he is in an "unfairly privileged" competitive position; not paying racket costs, he can run with lower overhead, and underbid racket-ridden competitors. To the racket-ridden normal manufacturer, A now looks unfair. And the manufacturers will encourage the racketeers as best they may to bring A back under the racket tax.

If a whole industry is organized by rackets, the honest manufacturers in that industry find it necessary to support the racket! The industry can't operate half slave and half free.

Now just imagine that I learned the secrets of full-scale working Magic, Hexing and Enchanting, and decided to go into the garment industry. The racketeers have no defense against Magic. I cast spells over my employees, establishment, home, self, and customers such that any racketeer that tries to shoot has his gun blow up in his hand. If he tries to beat up someone, he trips over his own feet and gets a con-

353

cussion that lays him out cold for 24 hours. Incendiary devices go off in the hands of the carrier. They just have perfectly awful bad luck any time they try attacking anyone associated with me.

Naturally, with the racket costs eliminated — I'm in an unfair competitive position. I can undersell honest, rackets-paying manufacturers. The manufacturers get frantic, put the heat on the racketeers, who simply can't put heat on my magic-protected establishment. The racketeers naturally aren't going to give up their livelihood, and stop squeezing the other manufacturers . . . particularly just now when their own operating expenses, due to funeral costs for the poor, unfortunate boys are unusually high.

Conclusion: Genuine superiority, honestly earned and worked for, is the cause of unfair competitive position. All the hard work and risks that those poor racketeers put in over the years, building up a good, sound, tight organization has been demolished by my unfair, sneaky technique of Magic. And the dirty, outrageous part of it all is that they can't even force me to play fair; they just get hurt bad without hurting me at all. It's unjust. It's viciously unfair.

In this century, the average man has a far more spiritual attitude than the average man has had in any previous period. Reason: all the preachings of Religion against devotion to the purely physical-materialistic never got to first base with J. Q. Public. Hal, A.D. 1150, knew the "I" and "my body" were identical; he was inside, and knew it for a fact, didn't he? He could feel it.

Modern man is a damn sight more "spiritual"; today the average man knows perfectly well that "I" and "my body" are not identical. Why, my body is merely a mechanism — it's a sort of machine — it can be controlled by outside forces that do things to it. A little strychnine, and it goes into convulsions; a little cyanide and it dies. Why, it's just a machine . . . I'm not, by God! I have free will! I'm no machine! There are no laws of Nature that control me that way!

Prove to a man beyond peradventure of doubt that there are inexorable and inescapable laws that apply to all . . . and he stops claiming that he "is" that which can be subjected to those laws! Man turned spiritual as soon as it was proven that there were universal laws that applied to the material, in other words.

The Germans hated your *I, Robot*; it said that intellect was pure
354

machine. That there were Laws of Nature that applied to Intellect.

Why does a psychiatrist maintain "there are no universal laws of the mind" so ardently? Because that would make him subject to Laws of Nature! He'd be forced to acknowledge that he did not have an unlimited right to his own opinions concerning personality.

The Cult of Ignorance is an effort to escape the worry of knowing that there are laws and forces that apply, willy-nilly. Happiness, for the normal person, is in not-fearing because of not-knowing; unfortunately there's an abnormal type in the race who seek not-fearing by knowing. "The Truth Shall Set Ye Free" is all very well . . . but what enslaved ye in the first place, huh? The Truth, dammit!

The racketeers, facing the power of truths of the magic level, would be enslaved, constrained against their will, to a form of behavior they cannot tolerate — learning how to do constructive work efficiently. It's soooo much easier to learn how to do destructive work effectively! The Truth would see them enslaved, not free, and enslaved to the hateful task of learning something they don't want to learn.

I hadn't spotted that Cult of Ignorance; once you pointed it out to me, the above stuff followed from trying to understand why people want to be ignorant.

Regards, John

John Pomeroy   *September 19, 1956*

Dear John:

Science can get itself into the damndest messes — and this one really must be quite a large-size mess to work on. Tsk tsk.

But this one, I fear, won't do for *ASF*.

It was **Peg** who originally came up with the Golden Goose idea; we debated whether you or **Ike** should play around with it. We picked **Ike** because he does more active writing; I wish, however, you'd get going at it again. Why do you think I put that 4 cent rate on it?

Maybe you can get something from throwing the boys up against a real-world paradox that has to be solved. The Golden Goose actually amounts to that. (You have to make The Goose stop laying golden eggs to get golden goslings!)

F'r'instance: What color is a sheet of unexposed hypersensitive

355

photographic film? If someone has a technique of reviving the dead . . . how do you prove the dead was dead?

Then again, you might have fun with **Ike's** positronic robots. Give a lab report on the problem of teaching a robot the First Law. Difficulty: Define the concept "human being."

Is a two-year-old child a "human being?" If so, you can't have a robot around the house; it can't allow Mama to spank Junior, because that would be allowing a human being to be hurt.

If it must obey the orders of a "human being," Junior, age four, may be tired of walking out the front door, and tell Robby to make a hole through his bedroom wall.

If children aren't human . . . no protection.

Define "human" in terms of hairlessness and clothes-wearing, and some gentleman of an unusually black-hairy type, just stepping out of the shower, is apt to get dumped out on the street.

Speech isn't enough; other robots speak.

Go on—define it!

Regards, John W. Campbell, Jr., Editor

David Buell   *September 19, 1956*

Dear Mr. Buell:

I sent this along to **Asimov.** He liked it.

I liked it.

I would like to publish it in "Brass Tacks" — so how about picking a pen name, and/or clearing it so we can?

Sincerely, John W. Campbell, Jr. , Editor

Isaac Asimov   *November 14, 1956*

Dear Ike:

This is to tell you there's something you want to do that you don't know you want to do.

You want to write to **Dr. Joseph Stewart**, of the Esso Research Laboratories, Linden, N.J., for information about proteins identified in precambrian rocks. Not simply amino acids; proteins. In rocks much earlier than the earliest fossil-bearing rocks.

356

Stewart's an oil-geology-chemist; he's interested in finding ways of detecting oil-pools. Oil drill cores are not only a cross-section in space — they're also cross-sections in time. **Stewart** has some very interesting data, and theories, about very, very early life and its characteristics.

Didjano:- There are photosynthetic plant life-forms that do photosynthesis in a reducing atmosphere? That was a new one on me!

Item: There are lots of porphyrins in oil; lots of 'em. But they are neither Mg nor Fe porphyrins — they're Ni, V and Co porphyrins. AND . . . they not only loused up the AEC's efforts to get graphite with low neutron absorption; they also louse the hell out of cat-cracker catalysis, since the V and Ni raise hell, even when present in a few parts/million. So **Stewart** knows a lot about V and Ni porphyrins that are present in oil.

But one of the things he doesn't know is why they're there. What life forms, for what reason, needed V and Ni, rather than Mg and Fe porphyrins? Considering the low availability of V and Ni in the environment on Earth, the life-form must have needed V and Ni. The probability of accidentally developing a metabolism using a V porphyrin instead of one using an Mg or Fe porphyrin, if the Mg would have served as well, is, I think, exceedingly low. The planet's simply lousy with Mg and Fe.

Ike . . . who says photosynthesis started producing oxygen, huh? Why start with something that requires changing the whole atmosphere of the planet, huh? Why not start off by developing a photosynthesis that gives you more of what you've always been used to — instead of something you've never had before?

Wanna bet for sure that oxygen atmospheres inevitably result from the establishment of photosynthesis processes on an Earth-like planet? Maybe it was the abundance of Fe and Mg, and their easy suitability for oxygen-cycle metabolisms, and the rarity of the V and Ni porphyrins that were suitable for a reducing metabolism, that lead to the changeover?

Stewart's a long time *ASF*'er, also one of the upper echelon Esso research group, and also one of the Esso Research Labs Club directors. I met him because I gave a talk there tonight on "Problems Science Never Can Solve."

(Science can never solve a problem which it denies exists.)

But ... considering what you've been interested in ... I think, like I say, that you want to write **Dr. Stewart**. I mentioned your articles to him, and he's expecting to hear from you.

Regards, John

Isaac Asimov   *January 20, 1957*

Dear Ike:

"Omnilingual" caught a good many readers, I suspect; in our present culture, the professional humanics scientists are busily chanting "It's all a matter of viewpoint! It's all a matter of opinion! It's all a matter of viewpoint!" and busily insisting that Science and its Absolute Laws has nothing to do with human problems. As **Shakespeare** (not the Bible!) said, "Methinks the lady doth protest too much." But the protestations have been so continuous, loud, and Professional that they suckered you into believing it.

One of the lovely things about scf. is that it can, and does, use good, clean Doubt for cleaning up statements to see whether they shine when properly washed down.

Piper did a nice job of calling attention to the inherent difference between a pre-scientific and a scientific culture.

Incidentally, trying to work the business of Absolute Laws out with **Peg**, I found a handy gimmick:

Let's talk about Absolute Laws and Unabsolute Laws. Now "Unabsolute" is <u>not</u> derived from tacking the negation syllable "un" on the word, but from the first two letters of Universal; an Unabsolute Law is a UNiversal ABSOLUTE law.

The characterisitc of a human-decreed Absolute Law is that it is a single-valued statement, and relates that, "If A, then, and only then, but invariably then, B." It is, in fact, an identity or tautology statement.

But a natural, Unabsolute Law, has the characteristic of proportional relationship of several factors. The law of gravity does NOT say, "Thou shalt not leave the surface of a planet!" It simply states the energy-price to be paid for leaving the surface of a planet (size of planet being taken into consideration) and distance to which you leave it being considered, etc. It does NOT say you can't step off the top of the Em-
358

pire State Building; it assures you that you can — and specifies the relationships of energy, velocity, etc., involved when you do so. Unabsolute Laws are never inhibitory — they're always permissive . . . with a price tag clearly marked. If you don't choose to pay that price, that is your choice, not the Unabsolute Law's.

Item: last Wednesday, the announcement of the invalidity of the principle of parity sounded a death knell to an ancient and incredibly basic principle of philosophy. It'll be decades before the full consequences even begin to be effectively accepted into the society. And the effects are going to be drastic, first at a philosophical, then at a scientific, and finally at a cultural level.

Note this peculiar fact: The work was done by three Chinese scientists. Now consider these factors, and compute the probability; the percentage of Chinese among the population of top-rank scientists in the world is low. The percentage of top-rank Chinese physicists in the United States is very low. If three physicists collaborate on a project, what is the probability, in the US, that all three shall be Chinese? Answer: If the project is one involving a denial of the basic rules of Western philosophy, Western Cultural Axioms . . . the probability approaches 1.0000. The only other possibilities would be Japanese, or, possibly, Indian physicists. Chinese physicists outnumber Indian and Japanese, however, in this country.

But it would NOT be done by a Caucasian, or even by a fully Americanized Chinese. They'd have deeply ingrained automatic mental limit-switches that would turn them off if they approached the idea. They couldn't think such a thing!

You know the trick of determining pi by tossing little sticks on a ruled background. Well, let's use sewing needles for the little sticks, and just to make it handy, we'll stick a couple hundred of them on a big alnico magnet, so we can pick them off and toss them conveniently.

We try it, and . . . well, whaddaya know! The math sharks have been wrong all along! Pi is really 2.9176328, instead of 3.14159 as they've been saying, and we have experimental evidence to prove it!

No statistical law works, when the situation is not, in fact, random. The one valid use of statistical theory is to prove that a certain situation is not random.

The consequences of non-parity include, among others, the proposition that it is not "Just a matter of opinion. It's all in your point of view. Really, Good and Evil are simply different viewpoints on the same thing." There is a Universal Up and Down; there is a Universal Better and Worse, Superior and Inferior — hated words! — are not simply a matter of viewpoint. Democracy is not fundamentally sound; it's simply practical under certain circumstances.

See why no Caucasian-American could really attack the principle of Parity. The Golden Rule is invalid, too!

I've been damned well sure of this for some time . . . but had only the despised evidence of organic detectors to cite. **Ike**, snail-shells show "handedness." The overwhelming majority of snail shells are right-hand threaded. In examining snail shells today, we're studying an equilibrium population, since snails have been evolving for hundreds of megayears. If there really were no Universal Force giving specific preference toward one vs the other . . . there'd be a 50-50 distribution of left and right hand snails. There isn't.

Oh, there are left-handed snail-shells found. It's not impossible. But evidently the Unabsolute Law imposes an excessive burden — and it isn't the cultural effect of a right-handed culture supplying tools for right-handed, but not for left-handed individuals.

Why is it that it just "happens" that dextro-rotary compounds and right-handed snail-shells are preferred. And Man just happens to be right-handed, too.

The principle of parity has loused the works all up and down the line. It's all through mathematics — because symmetrical equations are easier to handle. The electronics boys just love sine-wave analysis — because sine-waves are symmetrical about the origin, and about both the X and Y axes. Top and bottom are mirror images; left and right are identical.

I was discussing with **Barbara Silverberg** — who is one of the brightest, sharpest girls I've ever met, and is, also, one of the most genuinely sweet womanly-in-the-best-sense women I've ever met — this business of sine-wave analysis. A saw-tooth wave is just what its name implies; it rises from zero to, say, 10 volts, at a constant rate, then drops from 10 to zero at a near-infinite rate, then rises slowly from 0 to 10 again, drops, and repeats.

Sine-wave analysis says this phenomenon involves an extremely
360

high frequency, representing the very high rate of fall. If the phenomenon repeats 1000 times a second, then down-strike represents 1,000,000 cycles.

Analyzing this, the electronics engineer will say, "This amplifier cannot handle any frequency above 50,000 cycles, and therefore cannot handle this sawtooth wave."

Only I put it on the oscilloscope, and . . . well whaddaya know! It is handling it, and beautifully!

Reason: sine-wave analysis implies symmetry — and a saw-tooth wave is not in fact symmetrical. The amplifier, it happens, is not symmetrical either . . . though it can operate symmetrically, within limits. If the asymmetry of the amplifier is arranged to match the asymmetry of the sawtooth — it handles the sawtooth that symmetrical computation says it can't handle!

If you want to check this on your physics-electronics colleagues, the specifications are:

Given an amplifier using 1/2 of a 6BK7A dual triode. Plate load resistor 100,000 ohms. Sawtooth rises slowly, and falls sharply; the system will NOT work if the sawtooth rises sharply and falls slowly!

The grid is driven up slowly, and snapped down, in one case, and is driven down slowly, and snapped up in the desired, usable case.

When the grid is driven positive, the 6BK7A draws some 40 milliamperes. If the plate's capacitative loading is on the order of 20 mmF, 40 milliamperes will load electrons into that capacitance in an extremely large hurry. The 100,000 ohm plate resistor can't haul them out faster than 1.5 ma. Result: the plate voltage goes negative at enormously high rate.

Now the grid starts going slowly negative. The 100,000 ohm plate load can readily keep up with the slow change.

Because the tube and plate-load resistor constitutes an asymmetrical system, it can handle an asymmetrical problem far beyond its maximum capabilities in handling a symmetrical problem.

Now: the business about the square root of i and how the square root of i equals the square root of -i. The item is perfectly correct — and happens to be perfectly general.

Ike, the fourth roots of x^4 must be four in number. What are they? Answer: x, -x, ix and -ix! The square root of i is a fourth root. And

361

<u>any</u> quantity has, as its valid fourth roots, both ix and -ix — and the two quantities are, therefore, equivalent as valid fourth roots.

That is all those equations of his said — and they said something very important.

At the fourth level, there is no difference between imagination and reality! Subjective reality, by God, shows exactly that property, too! If you are writing a story in which **Isaac Newton**, a real individual, appears . . . you handle him exactly the way you handle Chauncey Murgatroyd, your fictitious hero. In subjective reality, imaginary and real are fully equivalent; where no difference can be detected, there is no difference. Where there is no difference, we have equality.

Regards, John

Isaac Asimov   *March 18, 1957*

Dear Ike:

By the way, did you hear how the Navy finally got that Vanguard up yesterday? Seems they painted it green, waited till March 17, and had a man by the name of O'Toole push the button.

Ike, I'm not too smart for you — you are.

I don't know whether you've read any of *Atlas Shrugged* but I again recommend it. Any really accurate, careful observer-reporter, whether in the field of physical science, or psychology, or story-writing, will, in making his report accurately observational, supply the full data— including the data that is relevant, but which he prefers not to consider.

Ayn Rand, in *Atlas*, had a thesis — and she's a strong writer because her accuracy of observation and report is phenomenal. She reported so clearly that the error of her thesis is clearly exposed by her own data.

I had a knock-kown-drag-out fight with **Peg** a few years back, concerning **Terman's** *Genetics of Genius, Vol. II.* The essence of it was that the whole IQ concept was, clearly, glaringly wrong. And that **Terman** had proven it in his *G of G Vol II* . . . which was written for the specific purpose of proving that IQ was sound.

Terman gave, in the book, the data from which he derived his conclusions. The data didn't match the conclusions.

Trouble with you, my friend, is that you hand me the data you're working on, carefully and accurately delineated and tabulated, together with a conclusion that doesn't fit the data. If you weren't such a compulsively honest observer-reporter, you'd get away with your conclusions.

Look: Subjective reality is an objective-fact-of-reality. I.e., It is an objective, unarguable, undebatable fact that I do have a subjective reality. You have a subjective reality.

Each of these subjective realities is a viewpoint-picture of Universal Reality.

Now any given object can be observed from an infinity of different viewpoints, and there are, therefore, an infinite number of non-identical, perfectly accurate view-realities — subjective realities — concerning any objective entity.

BUT . . . the fact that there is an infinite number of view-realities concerning any one entity does NOT mean that ANY view-reality whatsoever is a valid view-reality. Instance: a pack of cigarettes has an infinite number of valid perspective presentations. It may look square, rectangular, etc., literally ad infinitum. But although there are an infinite number of projections, none of the valid projections can have any curved lines. So if someone says, "Well, it looks round to me," you know that he must be talking about something else.

Subjective reality has the characteristic of having an infinite but bounded volume of validities.

The only way subjective realities can be discussed in mutually-meaningful terms, then, is to discuss the bounding conditions first.

Every human individual is biochemically unique. If biochemists acted like psychologists, they'd insist that proves you can't say that there are any general laws that apply to human metabolism.

It doesn't — but it does say that you've got to study the bounding limits . . . or you'll be trying to determine which haemoglobin structure is the right one by trial and error.

When you wrote "The Ugly Little Boy" you laid the data on the line; I called your attention to the data you'd laid down. If you weren't an honest observer, your stories wouldn't have the attractive power they do . . . but neither could you be called on 'em.

The equality problem is the one you were after; you can't solve it, because our concepts of equality are utterly inadequate. Further, we want, always, to have the tests-we-know-how-to-make be adequate guidance tests for determining our safe course through life.

The Southerner wants a dark skin to have a 1-to-1 correlation with incompetence so he can have a reliable, safe guide for determining how to act. The Negro wants it to have zero correlation with incompetence, so that he won't be carrying an inescapable guide-post with him. The fact is that there is a correlation, and the correlation exceeds the statistical random. It's an individual, not a statistical problem — with the result that any effort to handle it statistically comes a cropper. The only way you can "prove" that there isn't a statistical correlation between incompetence and a dark skin is to bias the statistics.

There is a statistical correlation.

I'll put it on the biochemical level, by God! Sickle-cell anemia is deleterious — it yields a sub-normally competent (physically) individual. Now whether a Negro likes the fact or not has nothing to do with the matter; the fact remains that there is a marked over-chance statistical correlation between dark skin and sickle cell anemia.

That doesn't say one damn thing whatever about whether a given dark-skinned individual has sickle-cell anemia, however.

Now, **Ike**, you can NOT test every individual molecule of a compound to determine whether or not it is in fact H_2SO_4; the tests normally used would make it cease to be H_2SO_4 if it started out that way.

If statistical tests have no validity, then chemistry is impossible.

Statistical tests do have some vaiidity . . . and human beings damn well know it.

You will never never never get human beings to renounce the use of statistical tests "because they ought not to" — when the fact is that they ought to, so long as no more efficacious test is made available.

Airplanes are an inadequate technique of flight; give them up entirely, because we should use anti-gravity.

Nuts!

Dammitall, **Ike**, when a scientific experiment yields alpha, when it "ought to have" yielded beta . . . the scientist scratches his head, unwillingly accepts the fact that beta was the answer he should have predicted, and tries finding out why he got beta instead of alpha.

When a human experiment yields beta instead of alpha . . . he says, "These people are so damned unreliable! They never act as they ought to!"

Stop acting that way, will you, **Ike**?! What human beings do is what human beings inescapably had to do ... whether you think they should have or not. And until you can locate and modify the forces that cause the undesirable factor — stop griping, dammit, and start studying. But you can't solve a problem until you acknowledge that the problem exists to be solved. You can't locate a force until you acknowledge that a force of some kind is really present.

If you were working with 90% H_2O_2, and the stuff blew up every time you put it in a clean stainless steel beaker, you'd start to suspect that stainless steel somehow had a catalytic effect on it.

If you were putting people in a certain room, and every group you put in started rioting ... you'd complain bitterly about the irrational misbehavior of human beings.

Because, of course, your irrational behavior response on that stems from the fact that you've been educated all your life that chemicals are always logical and rational ... and that people are utterly undependable, irrational, illogical, and born in Original Sin.

Just try a switch on that. Assume that people always behave in the manner determined by the resultant of all the forces acting on them. That a human being is no more capable of supernatural rebellion against the Laws of the Universe than an atom is. If you hold that human beings defy the laws of the Universe ... you believe in witchcraft already.

But if you hold that human beings do obey the laws of the Universe, that they're not supernaturally immune to law ... then start figuring out why your theory of how they should behave went wrong. Because it doesn't fit the way they do behave.

Now: to specific cases.

Equality of opportunity is something we can't define. That's why money became important!

Suppose a man, a horse, and a dog are shipwrecked on a South-seas island. The waters around the island swarm with poisonous fish, and conger eels. There are a few birds, and some insects on the island, but nothing else, except lush plant growth.

Six months later the man and the horse are rescued; the dog died of starvation.

365

But the man and the horse are again shipwrecked, but saved by friendly Eskimos up around Point Barrow.

Six months later the man gets back to civilization; the horse died of starvation.

Now; did these three have equal opportunities?

No, they didn't, because the man is an omnivore, and the dog and horse are not.

The equality of opportunity did not exist, because on the island, there was opportunity to eat that the dog <u>could not</u> take advantage of.

In our society, there is education that some individuals <u>can not</u> take advantage of . . . and they hate it.

Let's say that island had a scanty population of mice, and some sea gulls. The dog could, by straining his every resource, barely succeed in subsisting. Meanwhile, the man and horse are taking it easy, enjoying life in a succulent paradise.

The dog wants the island rebuilt, remade, into a place where game abounds — and get this damned vegetation out of the way, so the game can't hide.

Even if the man helps the dog, catching gulls and mice for him . . . the dog still sees that the man is sleek and fat and happy, while he isn't.

You, my friend, have no business yakking about "equality of opportunity" until you define your term.

Sure, you feel the place isn't too bad — you're an omnivorous education-digester, and it looks like a lush paradise to you. And you have a strong sense of empathy, and are very sorry for the poor dog that can't eat education and grow happy on it.

But you're also a business-deals-digester, so you make out nicely economically. You should hear **Gotthard Gunther** rave about the injustice of a world in which business men have money and scholars don't. As a business man, he stinks.

Bill Blow, highest competence longshoreman, with muscles, raves about the inequality of a situation where fat, tubby, glasses-wearing do-nothing editors and professors have money and he hasn't.

Sure there's inequality. The fundamental inequality of a Universe that rewards right answers, and punishes wrong answers. A place where not all opinions are equally rewarded. Where dinosaurs were

366

exterminated for not having sufficient right answers, after megayears of being top-of-the-heap. Where the physical strength and courage of a warrior was once top-rank . . . and is now assigned to longshore-man work.

There is indeed inequality in the Universe; the Universe shows a strong bias in favor of right answers. The principle of parity was a mistake; left and right are not equal and opposite. They're different . . . and one is preferred above the other.

Inequity is fundamental in the Universe itself.

If it weren't, there could be no evolution.

"I suggest you learn to love it." . . . and see how the Laws of Inequity should be interpreted. One of the best guides will be human behavior as it actually is. Reason: We evolved here. We're pretty well adapted to the actuality of the Laws of the Universe, contrary to the best theories of the best philosophers. It's pure "rationality" that doesn't fit the real Universe . . . not the "irrational" behavior of human beings!

When the consistent facts of 6000 years of history show an unbroken continuity of disagreement with theory . . . maybe the theory's wrong, huh?

The Universe is a lawful system, all right. But it won't obey the laws we lay down . . . until we lay down the right ones.

So long as you refrain from defining "equality of opportunity," you are safe from having your definition shown inapplicable. It could never have been shown that **Newton's** laws of motion and gravity were inaccurate, if he hadn't defined the terms so very specifically.

In all the social fields, nothing is so anathematized as a hard, sharply defined, specific statement. They call it "unscientific" and reject it.

Try telling a computer what you mean by "equal opportunity" — and don't demand it of a rational Universe until you can express it to a rational machine!

Regards, John

Isaac Asimov *May 5, 1957*

Dear Ike:

I'm sorry that we zigged just when you zagged last week — but I guess it had to be that way. I had to be in Milford, Conn., on Saturday, Apr 27, which fixed one end of the trip, and I had to be here on Apr 22, which fixed the other.

We had a fine chance for bull-sessioning with **Wayne Batteau, Claude Shannon, Norbert Weiner,** and others while in Cambridge; I'd much wanted to get you over one evening for the bull-sessioning, but discovered that you'd had to go New Yorkwards.

Spent some while at MIT; one item I learned may interest you, and be useful as a side-light item somewhere in a story.

Suppose you have a man in a space-suit, out in space outside a space station in interplanetary space, and he's working on an electronic device which, when completed, will be sealed in glass. Nice place for such work — all the vacuum you want, free for nothing!

Huh-uh. No good. You know the metal-evaporation technique for shadowing in electron micrographs? Well . . . what do you think his space suit is doing while he's working on that device? Evaporating off adsorbed gases to beat all crazy, of course. And their mean free path is measured in miles, naturally.

The sun and planets also, of course, are lousing up things in that way, too. And the glass he wants to seal it in will have to be heated and de-gassed adequately, also.

I ran into that watching the work on cryotron production by metal-evaporation techniques. They're trying to work out a gadget that can be opened, loaded, really evacuated, and used in minutes instead of hours. They like to use pure nickel; the nickel-gas compounds — largely oxide, but not exclusively; there's chlorides, and even hydrides present! — aren't too great in quantity, and they have the desirable characteristic of really breaking down in hard vacuum. The ones that bother are those that don't break down cleanly, but just drool out occasional gas atoms for hours.

The interplanetary gas <u>pressure</u> may be about zero — but the weight of lead pressing on a man standing in front of a machine gun isn't what bothers him. It's all them there holes where lead was. The temperature of the solar corona can be expressed in a number of ways — but the important-in-this-connection way is that gas atoms in that outer zone are moving with 100,000-plus degree velocities.

Ran across another idea that makes a hell of a lot of sense to me.

368

You know the old one about "matter of degree" and "matter of kind." O.K.; consider any positive feedback system — a vacuum tube oscillator, a nuclear reactor, or a biological system. Any chain-reacting system is a positive-feedback system, because it is a self-exciting system.

Let's use the nuclear-reactor concept of the k-factor — the reproduction factor, the ratio of the number of units in Generation $N + 1$ to the number of units in Generation N, whether it be neutrons in a reactor, or milliwatts of energy in an electron oscillator, or bugs in a biologist's agar plate.

If k is one or greater, the system remains dynamic; if it is less than one, no reaction can start, and even if one if forced, it won't continue. If it's 1.00000000 exactly, there's a steady-state reaction — but the probability of a free system remaining at exactly one is 1/infinity. A system with a k factor of 0.999999 is, however, perfectly stable — nothing happens. If k is ever so slightly greater than 1.0000000 . . . however, the system is unstable, and headed for infinity, and continues infinite-ward so long as there is the minutest excess over one, and does so at an exponential rate.

Now in logic, the criterion is true and false, and the two are sharply distinct.

Look, **Ike** — here, in the positive feedback system, we have something that converts a matter of degree into an absolutely distinguishable difference of <u>kind</u>. If the "degree" is 0.99999 . . . or less, the system is <u>stable</u>. If the "degree" is minutely greater than 1.00000 . . ., the system is a <u>different kind</u> — it's <u>unstable</u>. There is a theoretical alternative — a "degree" of exactly One — but that has a probability of 1/infinity, and can be relegated to the appropriate department of "I'll believe it when I see it." (And considering the fact of observer effect, if it is there when I see it, I'll know it can't be there when I'm not looking!)

Psychologists say that Man differs from the animals only in degree, that no difference of kind can be shown. Yeah — if you don't know about positive feedback systems! Animals display the ability to do logical thinking; Man differs only in degree.

But Man has the characteristic that logical thinking <u>acts as the exciting stimulus for more logical thinking</u>. Man's passed the positive-feedback chain-reaction point. Yes, that <u>is</u> simply a matter of degree

369

... but it makes a difference of kind.

If you don't think so, try sitting on a hunk of ^{235}U while someone pushes another hunk of ^{235}U nearer and nearer.

Betcha this sort of degree-kind thinking could help in understanding the interaction of enzyme systems; life is an expert at the use of feedback systems of all kinds!

Note this: in a population mentally nonreactive to the steam engine idea, it isn't "steam-engine time," and you can't make the idea go, even if you start it.

"The grapevine" illustrates the proposition. In any grapevine there are individuals who communicate with other individuals, so that you have, in effect, a cross-connected multiple-parallel system of relay units. Each connects with several others, but not with all.

Each has individual characteristics; each can be thought of as a sort of resonant filter-amplifier, with feedback characteristics. They don't have similar tuning, however. For certain kinds of information, A may have a terrific amplification factor, exaggerating the item, adding sidelights, perhaps adding spurious responses, and passing it with greatly increased power. He takes pains to pass it, in heightened form, to all his contacts.

For another type of news, however, he is strongly anti-resonant. He not only doesn't pass it, but denies it, and seeks out individuals who have heard it, and vigorously denies it.

For still other types, his response is, "Oh? You don't say. Hey, Bill, by the way, have you gotten the report on that . . . " and there is no relaying.

The overall, multi-linked system bears a considerable similarity to the nuclear reactor; there are fissionable atoms, moderators, neutron-absorbers, impurities, etc. For any single, specific item of news, the grapevine has a certain k-factor and whether the news spreads or not depends on whether the k is greater or less than One.

A human population can be said to have a k-factor for a concept; if k is One-or-greater, the concept will exist in that society; if it is less than one, that concept will not exist, and even if it is introduced, it will be squelched.

Germany has a k-factor less than one for the concept of Democracy. Even when it was strongly introduced by the Allies in 1919,

370

within one generation it had damped out, and **Hitler** came in.

A human personality, I think, has a similar effect; a guy who's apathetic, never gets anything done, though he's got plenty of intelligence and competence, has some idea, some concept, that makes his k-factor less than one.

If he gets some new idea (added ^{235}U) or loses some old idea (withdraw Cd) the k-factor changes, perhaps, by as little as 0.001%; the change of degree is minute — yet he is now a new kind of personality!

What effect could the immigration of 100,000 people have on a planet with a population of 2,000,000,000? What effect could one ounce of cadmium have on ten tons of moderated nuclear reactor?

Imagine a solution of ^{235}U in water, say 100 pounds of ^{235}U^2 in so much water that it was space-diluted to a k-factor of 0.99999. The level of reaction would be indetectable. But if we add one ounce of ^{235}U to the solution . . . the k-factor becomes 1.000001, we'll say. The rate of reaction rises; the water gets hot. It begins to evaporate. This changes the k-factor to 1.0001. The rate of increase accelerates. The water boils. The solution becomes more concentrated. The k goes to 1.01. The surrounding territory goes to hell.

It wasn't the one ounce of ^{235}U that melted down the entire neighborhood, either.

Wayne, incidentally, has some new — and lovely — items of math-turned-into-English.

By definition of the term Universe, everything in the Universe is related to everything else in the Universe. Therefore, we're all working on the same problem . . . no matter what we're doing!

Analysis of the old feeling, "I don't want to be rich, I just want to have enough money so I don't have to think about it."

This means that no matter how much I happen to spend, it is to have no effect on the remainder.

But this behavior characteristic is that of a transfinite set; no matter how much you subtract from a transfinite set, the set remains unaffectedly transfinite.

Therefore the only solution to the stated money desire is a transfinite quantity of wealth!

Peg was with me, as usual; the bull sessions are a damned sight more fun, because **Peg** can throw in some of the dangdest off-beat slants

371

on ideas — things that, somehow, male-type thinking wouldn't come up with.

Jane, who was staying with the **Kahns** in San Francisco, has now moved into an apartment of her own. Looks like about 90% of her stack-blowing was simply 21-year-old general rebellion against being watched, reported on, observed, instructed, advised, censured, censored, and pressured. Complicated by the fact the Wellsley didn't give her any intellectual satisfaction. **Randy's** performance wouldn't have bothered her particularly, if she hadn't been all ready to blow her stack generally anyway. It was, apparently, mainly a high-power "I WANT OUT, DAMMIT!" reaction.

Her normal-for-21-year-olds rebellion was sort of un-normal and confused by the fact that she couldn't — as most young-adults can — point to any specifically confining and hampering actions against which she wanted to rebel. She has her own money (from her father), and intellectually it's a little difficult to complain about being confined in Wellsley. On top of which was confusion.

Oh, well, she done did better than I did. I quit MIT at 21 and got married — to the wrong gal for me, too. (**Dona's** a very nice, basically sweet girl — there's nothing wrong with her, any more than there's anything wrong with a well-made left shoe on your right foot.)

The degree of confusion around the household was, however, rather extreme for a while. Trying to get some sense out of a 21-year-old girl who's explosively angry about something that she can't name, can't indicate, and can't figure out what to do about, but knows most emphaticlly that something must be done about, and done right now, and won't answer questions, because she can't, is quite an experience. It's quite a remarkable emotional experience for the parents, too. So is sticking your finger on the 220 volt power line . . . but I don't recommend either as a relief from simple boredom.

She had guilt-feelings running out her ears — only the main ones weren't the ones that she presented as her problems. The main ones had to do with her absolute rebellion against us — with no nameable cause for that rebellion — and us busily making it worse by trying to help. Which made her madder at us and at herself.

She popped a safety valve when she'd been with the **Kahns** a week or so, too. They, of course, were doing their best (and a Grade A #1 best it was, of course) to be *in locum parentis* to make her feel at home.

Which was what she didn't want, and couldn't possibly say, of course.

So now she has her own apartment, has had her things shipped out there, and is starting to write coherent, communicative, and reasonably calmed-down letters again.

Oh, well . . . I can tell you about it, **Ike**. But it won't do any good. You'll learn about it, however, in the good old fashioned way. Comes the point where the k-factor for Independence reaches 1.00001 — and take-off occurs, with roaring noises, flashing lights, and dust clouds for miles around. And you won't believe it, because everything's been sitting there so quietly for years and years . . . .

Regards, John

Isaac Asimov *May 17, 1957*

Dear Ike:

Herewith your article. Reason: You've got information in it . . . but haven't developed meaning. It's like an exposed photographic film — all the information is present, but you can't see it because it hasn't been developed yet.

Actually, you haven't got all the information you need for this piece; you need some heat-engineering data, and you might have to call in one of the boys from the physics department as a collaborator — but the results would be worth while.

Here's what I mean: Give a concentration of X radioactive breakdowns per second, per cubic yard, with an average energy per breakdown of Y calories, the heat generation per cubic yard will be XY calories per second.

Now heat escapes from a mass only at the surface. Neglecting the gravitational effects that would, actually, cause collapse of matter, we can discuss the stable temperature of a mass in terms of energy generation per cubic yard versus radius of the spherical mass.

A mass generating 0.0000001 calorie per cubic yard per second, having infinite radius (i.e., filling the total universe) would have a stable temperature of infinity, of course. (Take it quite a while to reach it, of course, but since it would have no surface for heat to escape, the

373

result is inevitable.)

For a given rate of heat generation per cubic yard, there will be a specific radius such that a mass having that heat generation rate, and that radius in interstellar space, would stabilize at a temperature of 1000°A. Since volume goes by the cube, and surface area by the square of the radius, there is a larger volume of this same material which would be stable thermally at 2000°A.

Then we have a system in three variables: heat generation per cubic yard, radius of the mass, and resultant equilibrium temperature.

If the mass of the present Earth were raised to 2000°A it would be effectively liquid. Consider the radioactive heat generation per cubic yard in the present Earth's matter; it should be possible to calculate a radius for a sphere having such a composition which would be in equilibrium with space at 2000°A. This might come out to be 80,000 miles, for instance.

Now compute the 2000°A — equilibrium radius for a mass having the radioactivity of the computed proto-Earth matter. If that turns out to be, say, 3500 miles — then your point is made.

It might, then, be interesting to study the results for Mercury, Venus, Mars, Jupiter, etc. The giant planets, of course, bring up a different problem; they don't have the same average composition Earth does, due to the immense excess of H and He; the effective radiating surface of the planets, however, is the atmospheric surface — and the major volume of the giant planets is practically pure H, He, C and N — none of which has any radioactivity whatever. (Save for cosmic ray induced ^{14}C and ^{3}H.)

Again, if Pluto is Earth-size, and has essentially Earth-composition . . . what would its temperature be?

You know, there's been a lot of talk about the "critical mass" of U^{235}. But there's been relatively little attention paid to the fact that shape is as important as total mass. How many tons of ^{235}U does it take to become critical, if it is in the shape of a single 1" thick flat plate?

Again, ^{235}U and ^{238}U have such characteristics that the naturally occurring "alloy" is not chain reactive. Suppose we made up an alloy containing X percent ^{235}U, by enriching the natural mixture. We will specify that the alloy is such that a sphere 10 feet in diameter is not chain-reacting, due to loss of neutrons through the external surface. But
374

that if the sphere is made large enough — infinite, say — there can be no loss of neutrons from it, and the alloy is chain reacting.

Now we can discuss an infinite sphere of uranium, and speak not of the critical mass but of the critical alloy.

The mass needed for criticality, when formed into a sphere, is a function of composition.

In essence, what I'm suggesting is that that same conceptual analysis applies to the radioactivity vs. diameter for a molten planet. With a given radius, there is a critical composition, insofar as it will or will not maintain an equilibrium temperature of 2000^0A.

The mass (volume) needed for criticality (maintenance of a predetermined equilibrium temperature) when formed into a sphere, is a function of composition. (Radioactivity per cubic yard.)

When we were up there, **Wayne** gave us some beautiful ideas dealing with transfinite processes and states. These are well worth your consideration on several levels — storywise, and also very definitely personal-relationships-wise!

Wayne made an analysis of the old "I don't want to be rich; I just want enough money so I don't have to worry about it."

Let Q be the quantity of money "I don't have to worry about." Now the phrase "I don't have to worry about" actually means "I never have to worry about at all." That is, that I can make any desired withdrawal of funds, X, without concern for the change in my reserve — that the reserve shall not be effectively altered by the withdrawal X.

Mathematically stated, that comes out: Q - X = Q because Q is defined as the quantity "I don't have to worry about," and the requirement is that there be a non-worrying amount after the withdrawal as well as before.

There are three possible values for Q and X that can satisfy that equation: if X and Q are both zero, or if X is zero, the equation balances. The first solution (both zero) is the solution the Bowery bum has applied. The second, X = 0, is the solution the miser seeks to apply. The final, third, solution is that X has a real, positive value — and Q equals infinity.

Now since the real meaning of the statement involves a demand that X have a real, positive value, the net meaning of the seemingly modest desire is, in fact, a demand for infinite and inexhaustible

375

<u>wealth</u>!

Quite correct, though; the guy who wants that is honest and truth-ful in saying, "I don't want to be rich," — "rich" is a finite concept; what this guy wants is <u>transfinitewealth</u>!

There's another tricky transfinite involved in human relationships and desires, too; this one you'll find at work in small children, and grown-ups who aren't willing to be realistic in their thinking. This one goes this way: "I don't want a lot of attention, but he ought to pay atten-tion to me when I want it."

That seemingly modest request turns out to be another transfinite demand!

As you know, there are as many (infinity) points in a line segment, however short, as there are in an unlimited line. There are as many numbers between 1 and 2 as there are cardinal numbers from 1 to in-finity.

This simply means that any system which is everywhere-dense — any continuum system — is a transfinite system.

The desire for attention "when I want it" means, actually, "when<u>ever</u> I want it." This, however, requires an everywhere-dense system of <u>con-tinuous</u> availability.

Put it in terms of a neutrino. How dense would a piece of matter have to be to satisfy a neutrino. How dense would a piece of matter have to be to satisfy a neutrino's request, "That I don't demand a lot of matter; I just want some where I happen to go," in view of the neutrino's penetrating power?

The curious result is that if someone "only wants a few little things," the fact that the things they want <u>are</u> little requires an infinite density of attention!

It's a damn sight easier to hold a big, massive uranium atom than to hold "just a little thing" like a neutrino! The neutrino requires a near-infinite density; the uranium can be readily satisfied with quite a loose mesh. It won't penetrate 50 light years of solid lead the way a neutrino will!

Tsk tsk! So your girl and boy seem to be basically different in their personality patterns. Wait a few more years, **Ike**; you'll learn. The male and the female do <u>not</u> think alike. They can't, and they aren't meant to.

376

Dammit man, why do we have two eyes? So we can have a spare in case one gets destroyed? Nuts! So we can have two viewpoints that can't — by any possible stretch of physical reality — have the same viewpoint on anything. Two different two-dimensional representations of the physical world will make possible one three dimensional comprehension.

Ike, what's "impulsive thinking?" How long a time should one think a thing over before it isn't impulsive? How many times should one go over and over an idea before it's non-impulsive? In what degree of detail should one analyze an idea before it's non-impulsive?

If you think a problem through in great detail, and do it slowly and carefully, and go over it 15 times — it's still going to give you the wrong answer . . . if you use one method of analysis. If your method was wrong the first time, and you used that wrong method most carefully, you'll get the same wrong answer n times, and get a perfect check on your work.

Hahn & Strasseman used standard analytical chemical methods for checking the radioactivity in neutron bombarded uranium, and had a lovely scheme of radioactive decay of trans-uranic elements worked out. It wasn't until they tried separating their hypothetical new radium isotope from barium, by a different method of analysis, that they got kicked in the face with the fact that it wouldn't separate — and were forced to realize that that radioactivity was barium, produced from uranium, that they recognized they had the uranium atoms breaking in two.

Non-impulsive thinking requires two or more different methods of thinking.

I don't give a god damn how good any named method is; it's invariably possible to set up a problem that is perfectly matched to that method of thinking, and will make a sucker out of it. You can fool a man quite readily . . . with a problem rigged to sucker male-type logical-analysis thinking. And his wife will blow her stack at the damn fool, for making such a stupid error, when it was perfectly obvious (to female type thinking, to which the problem was not matched!) that it was a trap.

A heel can make an absolute sucker out of a woman, by presenting her with a trick matched to female type thinking -- and any man around stares in utter bafflement at the incomprehensible stupidity of

377

a smart woman who could fall for such an obvious trap. **Fanny Brice** supporting **Nickey Arnstein** for some 15 years, with **Arnstein** not even taking the trouble to live with her, or making any pretense of being faithful, but coming to her to take her for $50,000 or $75,000 any time his gambling went sour on him. And for 15 years **Fanny Brice** bailed him out, time after time.

How did the classic heels, like **Don Juan** and **Casanova**, who were widely <u>known</u> to be heels, succeed in taking one woman after another for all she had, when each woman <u>knew</u> what he was?

And the gold-digger type that takes one man after another, even when the men <u>know</u> what she is?

For any given method of analysis, there is a matching method of deceit that will make a sucker out of it.

You can make a sucker out of Logic by presenting it with a problem that Logic says can't exist. Example: if A and B are not identical, then A must be either greater than, or less than, B. That's simple logic.

Sure it is . . . because logic is a system of <u>ordering</u>; it introduces order into thinking. It arranges things in 1, 2, 3, 4, ... sequence. So if two things are not identical, then they have different order; one must take precedence over the other.

Therefore if Man and Woman don't think identically, either Man must be superior to Woman, or Woman must be superior to Man. That's simple logic, isn't it?

Yes, **Ike** it <u>is</u> simple logic . . . simple-minded logic. If two points on a line are not identical, they can't be equal. But if the line is the circumference of a circle, they can be equal with respect to a certain point not on that line. Logic introduces <u>order</u>, but doesn't consider <u>form</u>.

Man and Woman are different — but both are related to the same external-to-humanity Entity — the Universe.

Wayne, by the way, has another lovely little gem: "We're all working on the same problem." Since each entity in the Universe is seeking to solve the problem of living in the Universe, we <u>must</u> all be working on the same problem!

That, incidentally, is the higher-order expression of the concept "brotherly love," or of **Kipling's** pass-word of the jungle, which he used in the Nowgli stories; "We be of one blood, ye and I!" (Which, if you haven't read them, you should get hold of. **David** would love 'em,

378

too; like the Alice stories of **Lewis Carroll**, are stories having about 10 different levels of stimulating thought embedded in them.)

Turned down a story the other day with a perfectly gorgeous idea, and lousy write-up. First expedition to Venus finds planet with CO_2 atmosphere, oceans, rocks, no life. Second expedition sent plants, algae, lichens, low plants. Fifty years later, colonizing expedition sent — and nobody hears from 'em. Two Venus-year later, rescue expedition A goes . . . and no report. Two Venus-years later rescue expedition B goes, with maximum precautions. One Venus-year later, it staggers into space and reports.

Seems Expedition #2 not only planted algae, lichens, etc. as planned — they also, unintentionally planted some yeast cells. When colonists arrived, Venus had beer oceans. Now rain is the distillate of the oceans. The colonists found that the lakes were whiskey, the springs ran whiskey, and the rivers and brooks ran whiskey. Also the atmosphere was, of course, that of a distillery.

They were all crocked to the gills the first time they stepped out of the ship — and stayed that way. Ditto for rescue Expedition A.

Expedition A, however, planted something else, so that when Expedition B came along, things were slightly calming down. Expedition A had planted mother of vinegar. Naturally that had soured everybody on the whole idea of Venus.

Incidentally, this story idea expresses something else. Infinity is simply the absolutely unlimited. No such system actually exists; many times the problem is to determine the extremely remote, but finite-somewhere, limit.

The problem can be solved by an exponential system; the problem of exhausting the inconceivable quantity of CO_2 and H_2O in a planetary ocean-atmosphere system is readily solved; an exponential, chain-reacting system, such as a living system, can solve that in short order. Then the entire ocean of beer can be exhausted by another chain-reaction.

I think I see the solution to an ancient philosophical problem: What's the difference between a "difference of degree" and "a difference of kind?" How can you draw a line between these two?

Answer; if a system has a reproduction factor, k, less than 1.00 . . . . . it behaves in one fashion; it's stable. But if the k factor is greater than 1.0000 . . . ., it behaves in a totally different fashion; it will then exhaust infinity, or in practice, any finite limit conceivable.

But the k factor is simply a matter of <u>degree</u>.

The above applies to any positive feedback system — a vacuum tube oscillator, a mass of ^{235}U, a life-form in an environment — <u>any</u> chain-reacting system, which is any positive-feedback system.

And this test provides an absolutely knife-edge test; any exponent in the exponential series which exceeds 1.0000 .... no matter how tiny an amount makes the system inherently infinity-bound, while any deficit below 1.000 .... makes it inherently stable.

Animals show the ability to do logical reasoning; they differ from Man only in degree, then, don't they?

No; they differ in <u>kind</u> — for in Man, a logically derived conclusion serves as a stimulus for starting to do logical thinking; in Man the system is self-exciting; k exceeds 1.000 .... and consequently Man will, inevitably, exhaust the Universe of logical problems!

Regards, John

John W. Campbell, Jr.   *May 30, 1957*

Dear John,

I am glad you are getting interested in radioactivity because I think it is neglected simply because everyone (including nuclear physicists, damn it) just gets into the habit of thinking of it as a rare phenomenon and not bothering to calculate out what it means on a Galactic or even a planetary scale.

For instance, the intra-planetary heat due to radioactivity is about 1/3 of the effective Solar heat here on Earth and it has accumulated terrifically. Essentially, that means we are independent of the Sun if we could but tap Earth's internal heat. Earth could dig underground, let the atmosphere freeze and mine it when necessary, grow plants under artificial illumination (what the hell does chlorophyll care where the red light comes from) and add hydroponics to it. We'd have all the energy we could use and not have to worry about serious diminution for at least a billion years and probably learn how to get along for ten billion. I could even imagine a planet deliberately cutting itself loose from its Sun — who needs the electron storms, the threat of nova — fooie. A sturdy independence is what a planet wants.

Then, again, geologists have used the argon content of the atmosphere in an attempt to calculate the age of the atmosphere since all the argon arises from the decay of ^{40}K. But have any of them tried to calculate the total amount of argon that must have been produced in 4 billion years of Earth's solidity and figure out where it all is. If my figures are right I think that Earth has as much gas imprisoned within its own bulk (in terms of volume) as it has in its atmosphere. Also, the facts of life as far as radioactivity is concerned is that any accumulation of matter as large as the Moon and no hotter than the Moon must have an atmosphere, even if it started without one atom or molecule of gas about it. After all, ^{40}K is producing argon continuously, so that the Moon is making its own atmosphere.

The radio-astronomers at Cambridge have finally observed an atmosphere about the Moon (if we could get a vacuum as good as the Moon's atmosphere we'd be happy, but it's an atmosphere) and at the time your letter arrived I was half through with an article on the whole question of atmospheres that aren't collected and aren't the result of chemical break-down of compounds but are manufactured continuously through the natural radioactivity of a planet.

The enclosed article THAT SELF-MADE AIR is the result, **John**, and I submit it to you for your consideration.

I will admit that I wake up in the middle of the night in a sort of sweat, though. I don't worry much about writing articles based on chemistry. My knowledge of chemistry is thorough enough for me to be an adequate judge of the validity of my statements. — However, writing articles for *Astounding* has inveigled me into working out problems in geology and astronomy and I get nervous.

It all makes sense to me; it's all very plausible; but am I pulling horrible boners? I consulted **Harry Stubbs (Hal Clement)** on this one by phone but, in all good conscience, I ought still to warn you, **John**. If you feel that you ought to send it off to **R. S. Richardson** for an expert opinion, that's all right with me. And if you should turn it down because you're not sure enough I know what I'm doing, I won't blame you.

But what the devil. Win or lose, the article may amuse you.

Yours, Isaac Asimov

Dear Mr. Cameron:

Thanks for sending that expanded discussion of nucleogenesis. Most of the equations served only to remind me that I hadn't used differential equations in twenty-five years, and that the types of equations now being used weren't taught in my courses. I'll let the experts who are qualified check your equations; the concepts the equations serve to support are what interest me.

I've got a philosophical problem for you to try having some fun with, though.

Assume that the ^{254}Cf fission is the actual mechanism of Type I supernova light-curve decay. Natural ^{254}Cf and intelligent life forms can never coexist. (Evolution takes too long, and supernovas can't be approached.) Then no intelligent living entity can ever find ^{254}Cf in nature, but data concerning ^{254}Cf is essential to understand the Type I supernova. It must be synthesized.

Does this constitute a case of making up the data to fit a theory?

Incidentally; after the supernova explosion, how can the remaining mass of photodisintegration product, essentially pure ^{4}He, cool off? What happens next?

Sincerely, John W. Campbell, Jr. Editor.

Dear Mr. Cameron:

I've passed your comment anent neutrino articles along to **Asimov**; I turned down the article he had done, previously, on the grounds that the article didn't go anywhere. I.e., we can say neutrinos exist . . . but, so far, so what of it? What potential value do they have to us? Until more understanding is gained the subject is appropriate for pure research, but not for the speculative research of science fiction.

I've been digesting those parts of your second work on nucleogenesis that I can handle over the last couple of weeks. (You've got a type of math in there that they weren't using when I went to M.I.T.; I don't know what it is, even, let alone how to use it!) There are a number of things that look to me as though they'd make some marvelous article for the magazine.

I threw you that little philosophical puzzler as to what constitutes "making up the data to prove a theory." The same comments apply to the discussion of technetium and niobium found in some of the stars you mentioned. The practical point at hand is that until we did develop nuclear reactors, we couldn't get the critical data to start the level of analysis modern astrophysics can attain. (We don't discuss the crucial data we don't yet have, and don't yet know exists to be had!)

One thing that interests me is an article on stellar evolution. Used to be thought that stars proceeded from young red gas-ball giants, and progressed smoothly down toward the dwarf stage.

The new picture is just slightly different! The concept that the Sun is getting hotter, not slowly cooling, is new to most people not actually in your field; I didn't have the information, I know.

The time periods you mention are extremely interesting; a diagram, or chart, plotting time on a horizontal axis, and showing the successive stage of the star, with indications of the type of energy-process taking place, would, I think, be extremely useful. As I gather it, there will come a time when the Sun goes into the shell source stage, and starts expanding enormously, when it may expand sufficiently that Mercury is within the solar chromosphere. I would suspect that, while that would have no detectable effect on the swollen Sun, Mercury wouldn't survive more than a revolution or two.

A brief review of the energy-producing processes, and the super-nova explosion process, would make fascinating reading.

Does that instability when the star changes from shell-source energy generation to helium thermonuclear reactions correlate in any way with Cephid variables? or is the mechanism of the Cephids known as yet?

You discuss the extremely high thermal conductivity of a degenerate electron gas. I don't know the concept clearly enough to grasp its implications; does the flow of electricity in a copper wire represent a type of degenerate electron gas phenomenon? If so, I can appreciate that, in the totally-ionized plasma of a stellar core, conductivity would be extremely fast indeed.

What part, if any, or if known, do magnetic field effects play in the convection and stirring up of stellar material? The tiniest percentage of charge imbalance, when such monstrous quantities are involved, would present an enormous current. (Modern power-station transformers are 99-plus per cent efficient — but the cooling problem is terrible, because even 1/2% of 10 megawatts is a lot of heat.)

And the neutrino problem does fascinate me. So neutrinos can penetrate 50 light-years of solid lead . . . but how far can they penetrate the matter of a stellar core? Densities ranging up to 10^5 gm/cc represent a different situation. And even neutrinos are subject to gravitational deflection; what focusing effects would the stellar core material have on the appreciable neutrino flux of the universe? If a dense star, such as Sirius B, could focus light quanta . . . couldn't core focus neutrinos rather effectively?

I'd love to see some articles — I mean up to half a dozen, if you have the time to write them — discussing the whole set of problems you've written up in those two books you've sent me.

We pay 3 cents a word for the material, which, while it will make no one's fortune, has been found useful for supporting a man's hobby interests very handily. I like articles up to about 5,000 words — say about 17 pages of double-spaced typescript on standard

8-1/2 X 11 paper. Longer, they get a little clumsy — but we can always run a series.

Sincerely, John W. Campbell, Jr.

Isaac Asimov   *August 6, 1957*

Dear Ike:

You, my somewhat conservative friend (Well, you may look like a far-left radical to your Boston University colleagues, but that's just because they're so far right they're practically left of the lefts) may be somewhat surprised at the reaction my remarks anent the **Hoxsey** matter got from **Dr. Bernard I. Kahn**, chief of psychiatric research at Kaiser Foundation, in San Francisco.

He sent me a four page letter listing various medications he knew that natives were using in various parts of the world . . . which he can't even use in demonstrations to show they work! One he mentioned is a really potent pepper-upper — increases muscle tonus, reduces the fats in the bloodstream, generally effective as a systemic improver. PFDAd-
384

ministration [now FDA:Ed], however, won't allow it to be tested; being a potent and genuinely effective toner-upper . . . it has marked aphrodisiac effects, which so shocks the purity of the Pure Food & Drug people that they can't allow its administration or testing. If a guy's been feeling like he's carrying the Old Man of the Sea around, and a drug tones him up so that the Old Man drops off . . . among the other aspects of vital living he suddenly becomes interested in is sex.

Too bad, **Ike** — it's a great help in weight reduction, generally increases vitality, is a help in arteriosclerosis, and similar problems, but you can't have any. It might make you libidinous, and that's so terrible that it'd be better if you just quietly dropped dead.

Bernie first heard about rowulfia from a British M.D. during the war. But nothing could be done about it, because it hadn't been properly tested and approved, and it of course couldn't be tested on human beings until it had been shown safe for use on human beings.

The tests weren't made in this country.

Your comments anent "if it's good it will win out" are based on as neat a false bit of reasoning as ever leaked into a society and wasn't thrown out.

A lot of good things have been powerfully opposed when they were first introduced — **Galileo** being an example. But the really good ideas have all won out in the end, despite opposition, as history clearly shows.

Ja . . . sure, "History shows." Yup . . . and if **Hitler** had won the war, history would show that **Winston Churchill**, the war criminal was executed for his crimes, was the cause of the whole conflict, too. Who the hell do you think would have been writing the history?

You once upon a time did an item about the probability of reaching a required answer involving only about 57 factors, by trial and error, in a finite time in a finite universe. "Hemoglobin and the Universe" you called it. Yeah . . . all good ideas will eventually win out. But will they, unassisted by consciously directed assistance, in a finite time?

You pointed out that assembling proteins from amino acids was <u>not</u> a random process, in discussing the origin of life — that the laws of chemistry limited the possible assemblages of atoms to a relatively selected few.

<u>Something besides chance</u> must be applied if problems are to be

solved in finite time, in a finite universe.

History shows <u>only</u> the ideas that were (1) right, and (2) were championed by some intransigent, loud-mouthed, violently determined, authority-bucking, rebellious, stubborn, showman and provocateur, who so distressed, upset, annoyed, and bedeviled the Constituted Authorities that, in their angry efforts to suppress the irrepressible bastard, they made so much of a fuss themselves that people noticed the squabble and began to look at it.

Hoxsey is winning, my friend; already he's gotten far enough that now the U.S. Government is putting up posters, calling attention to his existence, and claim of a cancer cure, in post offices all over the nation. It's the first nation-wide publicity campaign calling attention to his existence that's happened. Of course, it is true the posters say his cure is worthless, and to not waste your money on **Harry Hoxsey's** Cancer Cure. But he's finally gotten the U.S. government to advertise the existence of **Hoxsey's** Cancer Cure.

It takes a loud-mouthed, ungentlemanly, vituperative, violent, law-and-authority defying, clever, slippery, argumentative, showman and promoter to put an idea the Constituted Authorities don't like sufficiently into sight, despite the every effort of the Constituted Authority, to attract public attention and get public judging.

Then, of course, if he's not right, he'll lose out.

But no matter how right you are . . . if you won't buck all hell, heaven and earth to put it over, the Constituted Authorities will shut your irritating mouth.

Look: **Galileo** didn't originate the heliocentric system. He got it from **Copernicus**, who was a very smart man — and too well satisfied with the fat cream he skimmed off of life in eleventy-teen other ways, to bother himself fighting for a right idea.

Remember, dammit, HISTORY RECORDS ONLY THE ONES THAT <u>DID</u> SUCCEED <u>AND</u> WERE RIGHT. It doesn't record the ones that were right and got silenced.

The standard platitudes you're quoting on that, **Ike,** are the standard platitudes the Const. Auth. use to keep the public calm while they're busy strangling the guy with the new idea. Then, when they've finished disposing of the poor sucker, they dust off their hands, smile engagingly, and say, "See? We were right all the time. He's dead, as you can
386

plainly see, and that proves his idea wasn't really good, because everybody knows that Right Always Wins. Everybody knows that Trial by Ordeal is the one sure test of Right and Justice, and he's dead, so he is proven wrong."

"Dug . . . uh . . . geee . . . I gess you mus' be right at that, Boss. He sure is dead. Guess his idea musta been wrong, 'cause you're right everybody knows that Right Always Wins, an' he sure didn't."

Well, I guess **Ghenghis Khan** was right all along, then. We should start building pyramids of human skulls, too, and Be Right With **Ghenghis**!

Look, if you want to stay out of the fight — OK, you've got a right to. But don't pull those damned chestnuts that Trial by ordeal is the only true test of Right. That's an excessively inefficient technique of epistemology — which is precisely what it is, incidentally. "How can we know? Ah! By having an Ordeal, and seeing who wins. He who wins we can be sure is right."

Actually, the problem is that the AMA has got itself in an utterly untenable position — and can't get off. The old "bear by the tail" situation. They've bucked **Hoxsey** unsuccessfully, and too long.

First: put it this way. Suppose you were in **Red Skelton's** spot. That it was your small son who had leukemia. The MD's have a certainty to offer you: "Your boy will die shortly." They also have medication, which they assure you positively will not cure, and will not neutralize the disease. For this they'll charge you about $1500 to $4000.

Now let's assume that **Hoxsey's** treatment is no good whatever — assume that it won't do anything curative at all. And he charges $400 for it.

If there are two futile things you can do, and one costs $1500 to $4000, and the other costs $400, which futility is the better?

So even if **Hoxsey's** stuff has zero curative value — you're way ahead going to him.

On the other forms of cancer, the AMA's score is about the same, too. (There are some they can cure — but they've openly acknowledged **Hoxsey** can and does cure external cancers, too.) Their record with respect to U.S. Senators in the last decade is perfect; every case of cancer they detected in the required regular medical check-ups has died of cancer. Perfect score — five out of five. Also **von Neumann**.

387

Dulles is on his way out.

The stinker is this: At a certain point in time, T_1, the coal-mining son of an ex-horse-doctor, in his early 20's, claimed his home-brewed weed stew would cure cancer.

The presumptive evidence was, at that time, 100% against him; he was, in all probability, either a young, irresponsible, but sincere fool, or a dangerous fraud.

At a later time, T_3, say 1955 some 30 years later, the accumulating evidence was such as to make it highly — overwhelmingly — probable that he had something that needed investigation.

There is a point T_2, somewhere in-between, when the evidence had reached a point such that the AMA should have accepted the probability **Hoxsey** had something, and started investigating it carefully.

If they had acted <u>before</u> T_2, they would have been guilty of irresponsibility, acting in a critical matter on inadequate evidence. Failing to act <u>after</u> that point, they become guilty of negligence in their duty . . . and the guilt becomes exponentially greater with time.

Problem: Define the methods by which T_2 can be accurately determined!

That's an epistemology problem, not a medical problem. For that, a doctor is <u>not</u> a competent expert — he holds an MD, not a PhD, and this is a problem of philosophy, not science.

But as of now, the AMA is in the untenable position of attempting to suppress something which impartial judges, listening to the arguments of both sides, have found is good.

If the AMA did acknowledge **Hoxsey's** method now, the damage to the AMA's reputation would be disastrous . . . and not simply disastrous to the AMA. It would prove the AMA untrustworthy as guardians of the nation's medical interests — they would establish that they prevented new remedies that could protect us from terrible agonies. Every real quack and charlatan in the nation would promptly claim to be another suppressed **Hoxsey**. It would be a medical disaster to the people of the nation.

But . . . it's a disaster to have a powerful healing weapon and not be able to use it.

How do we resolve that vicious circle? The damn fools in the AMA got us into the mess; now we have to bail them out somehow, because they're philosophically and psychologically too stupid to do it for themselves. Their only answer is to put more pressure on **Hoxsey**, 'till he shuts up. But they're now getting so frantic that their whole defense is breaking down. The utter stupidity of putting posters warning patients away from **Hoxsey** in every Post Office! They're advertising that WE HAVE A POWERFUL AND DANGEROUS RIVAL! HE'S IN DALLAS, TEXAS! HE SAYS HE CURES CANCER! OF COURSE, YOU WHO ARE DYING OF CANCER KNOW WE CAN'T, BUT DON'T WASTE YOUR MONEY ON **HOXSEY**, DOWN IN DALLAS, TEXAS. WASTE IT ON YOUR LOCAL MEDICAL TALENT."

That's the first time in history that the AMA has had to resort to that sort of campaign; do they think people are too stupid to notice that the AMA must be in serious trouble?

The problem is to find a way to get the damn fools off the hook, so we can have the cancer cure, without destroying the real values in the AMA.

For one thing, they'd be a damn sight happier if there were a competing medical organization; then if they both muffed something, neither would feel so hopelessly guilty, because, after all, the other guy flubbed on it too, didn't he? At the same time, the highly stimulating competition would make them less apt to flub.

Anyhow, in the meantime, it's pretty clear that neither **Hoxsey** nor the AMA can get themselves out of the spot they're in.

What's needed, is to introduce a <u>new kind</u> of evidence, such that the AMA can <u>claim</u> that the time-point T_2 has just arrived, at last. That is, they can say, "Ah! NOW you have some <u>evidence</u>! NOW you have proof that you have something! Now, of course, since we are rational and honorable scientists, we will at once listen to you."

Only something of that sort can get the AMA off the hook, and yield **Hoxsey** what he wants, and honorably deserves — due credit.

It is futile to try for it in the field of cancer-curing, however; that's the thing the AMA can't allow, because he's been presenting that for 30 years. He needs a totally different kind of evidence — not more of the same.

Fortunately, I believe, there is a high probability that the new-kind of evidence is available. **Hoxsey** cures terminal cancer cases, and in six months they're in good health, feeling better than they have in

389

years, they report.

Item: terminal cancer cases get put on a heavy morphine sedation schedule, and stay on it for relatively long periods.

Item: morphine addicts are not in good health, and don't feel better than they have in years.

Item: Neither **Hoxsey** nor the AMA has ever mentioned morphine addiction with respect to **Hoxsey's** cancer cures.

Item: It looks like whatever **Hoxsey's** got cures morphine addiction while curing cancer.

But . . . morphine addiction is a psychological problem. The physiological addiction is readily (if uncomfortably) overcome by planned withdrawal. Once the physiological withdrawal symptoms are over, there is no physiological addiction . . . but morphine addicts almost always come back.

None of **Hoxsey's** cancer-cure cases have been impugned by the AMA as morphine addicts — which would make a nice item for the AMA in a court battle.

My personal hunch-guess is that **Hoxsey's** stuff cures cancer <u>as a side effect of something else!!</u>

You know, tranquilizers cure ulcers — without having any effect on ulcers. They also lower blood pressure, without affecting the circulatory system. They'll also successfully treat an addiction to homicidal mania successfully.

If **Hoxsey's** stuff contains the psychological pepper-upper I think it does — **Hoxsey's** got a new kind of evidence to present.

That, dammit, could get them both off the hook.

Of course, the AMA is never going to attack cancer from the psychogenic aspect; if they did, they'd be in trouble with faith-healers, Lourdes Shrine, and various other things.

Hoxsey's been trying to prove that it is a cancer specific — which is the only thing the AMA would be really happy to accept. But, of course, not from someone who wasn't an M.D., and that they'd been fighting for 30 years.

Incidentally, I'm mulling over the idea of starting a new type of magazine. Your comments would be of interest.

Title: *The Angry Men.*

Material: essentially philosophical-level attacks on things people
390

do that the individual author doesn't like. The purpose: to provide the non-expert a chance to take a good, healthy swing at the stuffed-shirt experts. If somebody thinks all professional biochemists have gone down the wrong road, and are involutionally contemplating the navel of the carbon atom, instead of taking a look at something else — since the guy isn't a biochemist himself, naturally nobody would publish his remarks. If a lawyer thinks physicists aren't thinking straight — nobody would publish the remarks of an uninformed layman, would they?

Answer: *The Angry Men* would. The requirement would be that the individual speak as a thinking man, but not as an expert. Argument by authority would be happily laughed out of court. If someone attacks the system of the Law, anyone but lawyers would be permitted to answer. If someone attacks the AMA — the AMA can answer in its own professional *Journal*, if it wants to, but not in *The Angry Men . . . The Journal of Amateur Thinkers* — and no professionals allowed!

The title, *The Angry Men* would be explained by the cover each issue. **Jesus** driving the money changers out of the temple. **Galileo** blasting off at the Church Fathers. **Patrick Henry** blasting off on the subject of Liberty.

Take a good look at history, **Ike**; it's been the angry amateurs who've made all the big steps.

Regards, John

Isaac Asimov   *August 26, 1957*

Dear Ike:

I'm running out of stationary, so I'm saving what I have for people who don't know where I live.

I heard from **Hoxsey** finally, and his stationary gave me information I hadn't previously had . . . and explained why he, unlike other unorthodox cancer healers, has not been put out of business by the AMA.

Bob Silverberg has a lovely yarn coming up, called "Precedent," based on Trial by Ordeal. The guy commits a crime, openly and in the presence of the whole native town. He then undergoes Trial by Ordeal. Only it just so "happens" that he's in the Space Exploration Corps after having left the professional boxing business by urgent re-

391

quest . . . and he proceeds to make a monkey's uncle out of the local champion. It "happened" that way, because the leader of the expedition was out to mouse-trap the local judicial system in such a way that the localites would <u>want</u> to change their methods of justice. The ex-pug's victory had nothing whatever to do with justice, truth, or honesty; it had to do solely with his particular skill.

Hoxsey's winning against the AMA . . . and his stationary is the Hoxsey Oil Company, **Harry M. Hoxsey**, Owner. The pooled resources of the AMA don't happen to be effectively greater than a share in the East Texas Pool, apparently. The AMA's normal procedure is simple; they sue the obnoxious individual out of business. They so distract him with law-suits that he can't do anything else.

Hoxsey's cure must be better than anybody else's has been; he's got more lawyers than the AMA.

Hubbard didn't have; he couldn't afford the libel suits that would have established the validity of some of his work. (Much of it has since been confirmed — particularly that there are prenatal influences, for instance. But they never mention Dianetics™, of course.)

Hieronymus, de la Warr, a dozen others, have repeatedly demonstrated that their techniques can diagnose and cure medical problems at a distance. It's been demonstrated many, many times. The AMA did sue **Hieronymus** out of business; he didn't succeed in setting up the Hieronymus Oil Company, unfortunately. That proves **Hoxsey's** cure for cancer is much better than **Hieronymus'** cure for leukemia. (He's done that, as a matter of fact.) The proof? Why . . . very simple! **Hoxsey** struck oil, and that proves his cancer cure is superior.

The normal way of combating an unorthodoxy is by making it uneconomic — "not worth the effort." Then the argument is presented, "If this great idea of his really worked, as he says it does, he could make money at it and not be begging for support." I.e., the proof that the idea is no good is the fact that it has been possible to put the guy out of business so he can't prove the idea is good. Thus **Hoxsey's** cancer cure must be good, because, since he struck oil, they can't put him out of business.

"Duhhh . . . cheeze, boss . . . somethin' soun's a little funny, but I guess you mus' be right. Anythin' you say, boss."

Your position I can fully understand. We differ in a lot of ways, **Ike**; I'd never be worth my salt as a biochemist, because I don't have
392

your ability to grind a hole in a problem by patient dogged determination. I prefer the dynamite technique . . . which works on some problems, but not on others. You'ld never get a tunnel through a mountain by grinding — but you'ld never shape a Lincoln Memorial statute with dynamite.

I'll respect the importance and value of your grinding technique — but please to note carefully that you get the raw material for your grinding and chipping from some quarry where a dynamiter got his hand into the act. The dynamiter is just as necessary — and a damn sight less popular, because he's so horribly noisy, stirs up so much dust and dirt, and keeps knocking the good, solid ground out from under people's feet and homes, so they keep having to move somewhere else.

I like to drill a little hole, slip a stick of dynamite in, light the fuse, and stand well back. Done properly, people don't notice the guy who planted the stuff, because he's lost in the crowd now. It takes a little patience waiting while the fuse burns down to the dynamite . . . but the results are fairly predictable.

As you should know; you do quite a bit of quarrying on the side, yourself. Think your positronic robot stories haven't had effect on the thinking of men in cybernetics today? So it took a few years for the fuse to burn down . . . so who planted the dynamite?

I appreciate your point that you are not rejecting the ideas on what I might call a "first-order response to authority" — because Authority says that <u>this specific idea</u> is Verboten. You're rejecting on a sort of second-order authority; "All valid ideas are logically related in manners already understood; they can all be deduced from already-known concepts. Any idea which cannot be deduced from known concepts is invalid."

Yeah? Who told you that, **Ike**? Who's your authority for that? Experience?

Did you know, **Ike**, that there is not one single provable case of an undiscovered murder?

It's true. And furthermore, there never will be.

You can clearly see that every valid, proven idea shows us that all valid ideas are logically derivable from the known concepts; that shows that there isn't one, single case of a proven, valid idea that isn't derivable from known concepts. Thus we can be sure that all valid ideas <u>are</u>

derivable from known concepts, can't we?

Yeah, and anybody knows spaceships and atomic bombs are impossible nonsense, because there never have been any.

And transmutation of the elements is known to be impossible.

Matter of fact, we now know that if they had, in 1880, known enough thermodynamics, they could have proven it was impossible, because of the fact that the highest temperature matter can attain on Earth is far too low.

And a bumble bee really can't fly . . . as a fixed-wing device.

There are provable, and absolutely valid, limits to any namable process. The difficulty arises when a particular end is under discussion, and it is shown that it is inherently unreachable by any known process. In the realm of mechanical engineering, you cannot transmit information faster than the speed of sound; a steel rod cannot control something, if impulses have to exceed sound-speed.

With limited knowledge, it's possible to prove an impossibility.

The difficulty is, no one wants to acknowledge limitations, absolute and unbreakable limitations, on his abilities. He will, therefore, tend to hold that all real possibilities lie within the possible extensions of his methods.

They don't.

Consider this problem: Suppose cancer is a psychosomatic condition, like ulcers, or shingles. No "cure" is then possible at the physical-medical level. You can cure stomach ulcers, of course, by removing the stomach — just as you can cure kleptomaniac pocket-picking by amputating both arms. (It's been tried — for centuries it was tried — and it works.) You can cure cancer of the breast by amputating the breast. You can cure political annoyances by amputation of the head, too.

Now if we have a medical science which holds as a rigid postulate, "Any real cure of cancer must be physical-medical," then the medical scientists cannot cure cancer in any real sense. Never. Impossible. As innately impossible as trisecting the angle by Greek geometrical methods; within the defined limits, it is innately and forever impossible.

In that case, only someone who denied medical science would ever be able to cure cancer.

But medical science would immediately deny him; his claimed
394

cure, resting on a psychosomatic approach, would be provably unreal, since "real cure" is defined as "physical-medical."

In seeking to protect people against the charlatan who claimed that a psychic-or-psychosomatic approach, worked, the medical scientists would seek to prove to the less learned and educated public that the quack was, indeed, a quack — and would arrange to demonstrate what they knew to be true, despite the charlatan's sly efforts to deceive people by presenting cured individuals.

Look, **Ike**; it isn't that you can't believe something you do not understand; it's that you can't believe something you understand <u>not</u>! You have reason to believe **Hoxsey** is <u>not</u> right; that, not complete ignorance of the facts, is why you can't believe he is right.

My hunch on the thing is this: **Hoxsey** does <u>not</u> have a cancer specific — which he believes he has. He's been fighting the AMA so long and hard he won't look at anything else. Ditto in reverse.

The characteristic of cancer patients is excessive tolerance. They are the melancholic personality type, that holds, "Nothing can be done." They differ from the anxiety type, which holds, "I can do nothing." It's been shown that a human cancer can be transplanted from one cancer victim to another — but not to a non-cancerous individual. The normal intolerance mechanism of the cancer patient isn't functioning.

Whether you like the facts or not, be honest scientist enough to accept facts. Lourdes, faith healers, and psychosomatic treatment have turned off cancer. Spontaneous cures take place.

The AMA claims a 32% success rate with cancer of the internal types, including all internal types. What percentage of that success is spontaneous? If we take a vote of all cancer victims on the subject of whether medicine can cure cancer, we'll have a two-thirds majority saying, "No . . . and I've got the corpse to prove it."

I think that **Hoxsey** has a psychologically active drug — an inverse of *Rowulfia serpentina*. The tranquilizers depress purposiveness; the homicidal maniac still feels like committing murder . . . but not hard enough to do anything very active about it. It's a <u>manana</u> drug.

The psychiatrists are looking for a DO IT NOW drug — a purposiveness stimulator, for use on melancholic patients.

Tranquilizers cure ulcers, high blood pressure, shingles, etc. Now

395

that the AMA has a physical-chemical object, a pill, that does, by physical-manipulation of shoving it down the guy's gullet, what they want done . . . when psychosomatic problems are reduced to a point of physical-action resolution — then they can accept that the action works, and that maybe in this case, the problem really was psychosomatic.

I think what **Hoxsey** has is decidedly different in one respect; it makes the patient decide to change things. He does — including changing his own personality.

Imagine a guy who's crawled into an attic to do some necessary work. It's mid-July, outside temp. 90^0. Temp. in attic, 130^0, thanks to the sun. He passes out.

Now if he remains passed out, he will, within an hour or so, be killed by the environment.

Suppose someone throws a cupful of ice water on his face. Now certainly, a cupful of icewater won't keep a man alive under those conditions.

But . . . if the icewater gives him a temporary stimulus enough to crawl out of the place . . . he'll live.

Did the ice-water cure the condition that was killing him?

Suppose **Hoxsey** doesn't cure cancer at all — that all his cures are simply spontaneous healing. Funny, ain't it, what a high percentage of his patients have the good fortune to undergo spontaneous healing!

The ice-water didn't make it possible for the guy to live — it just stimulated a spontaneous cure. The organism produced the curative process (getting the hell out of that attic!) itself.

A tranquilizer, like a narcotic, makes the intolerable more endurable. Sometimes, that's exactly what's needed, to endure a temporary shock.

Sometimes the reverse is needed; a shock that makes the situation which has been endured patiently so intolerable the guy gets out of it.

Why not get hold of some of **Hoxsey's** stuff, and see what the hell it does do? My hunch is that it would not only cure a lot of cancer, but also drug addiction, alcoholism, neurotic melancholia, and a dozen other things.

And, dammitall **Ike**, is a scientist supposed to explore only the known-and-understandable? Or is he supposed to pick up things that just damn well don't make sense, and make sense out of 'em?
396

It seems to me that exploring why the impossible happens is the major task of science — not merely explaining the understandable!

If **Hoxsey** can't possibly be curing cancer — fine! Then, dammit, get in there and find out what he is doing!

I know very well you don't believe in psionics. OK — so you don't. But, by damn, you've got no blasted right to disbelieve facts! And that's what you are in fact doing. ONE single instance of absolutely-not-explainable-by-known-phenomena occurrence is a fact that forever destroys your right to retreat from that fact.

Eusapia Palladino, under the careful observation of the top-rank physical scientists of Europe, in their laboratories, did things with physical objects that they absolutely could not deny or explain. ONCE. No matter how many instances of stupid fakery she pulled, one single instance establishes the existence of an Unknown.

Edgar Cayce did things that were absolutely documented and established.

You don't have to explain psionics if you don't choose to work at that . . . but **Ike**, you have absolutely no honest right to insist that there is nothing to explain.

You accept that supernova exist. Ever seen one? How many individuals have observed them and reported on them? As many as observed and reported on **Eusapia Palladino**?

Since you have never observed a supernova, your belief in them is an Act of Faith. A few millennia ago, you would have exactly reversed your position; **Eusapia** would have been readily understandable as a real phenomenon, but an exploding star . . . ! Are you insane? Don't you know anything about reality? It's obviously a major magical portent, of course!

And this you, **Isaac** the Rabbi (it means teacher, remember, or, in modern terms, professor) would have known with such strong assurance that any fool who suggested that the supernova was due merely to a change-over from the Fe peak to the He peak in the thermonuclear reactions at the stellar core, would cause you the most complete bafflement at his stupidity.

And you think you're not reacting, now, to Authority?

Can you deny that you, in that earlier culture, would have reacted as any other Rabbi of the time would have?

You don't accept what any other <u>man</u> tells you — but don't overlook the Authority of your Cultural Orientation, either.

The correct conjugation of the very "to not know" is, "I don't know, you don't know, he doesn't know, we don't know, and they don't know. so let's find out."

If you don't want to explore — okeedokee; you have every right to be the damn good sculptor you are. But don't try to stop the boys who are trying to explore, by saying that there is nothing to explore!

The AMA objects seriously to having someone explore — yet they refuse to explore all possible avenues. They will NOT take a look at faith healing . . . though they've finally admitted that faith-healing is the simplest therapy for removal of warts.

Any psychiatrist can tell you that faith-in-authority is a major aspect of psychotherapy in most individuals. That's how Catholic priests keep a lot of their parishioners sane and useful.

Faith-in-authority is as good and necessary a thing as is observational science; it's called "respecting law and order" then. A woman who went on the streets with her breasts bare would certainly be punished for breach of faith-in-authority . . . in Boston, that is. In some South American Indian tribes, on the other hand, it's the standard mark of the prostitute that she covers herself. Decent, authority-respecting women go naked, as the Gods intended.

Regards, John

Isaac Asimov   *September 21, 1957*

Dear Ike:

Back from the Convention . . . and I'm glad you weren't there. I'm sorry I was there. Don't spread it as gossip, of course, because I don't like hurting people . . . but migawd! that "hotel"! "Hotel" is a decided misnomer; it was one grade above a flop-house. The Convention Committee was lucky; by an unpredictable stroke of fate, a new management moved in three weeks before the convention, and started cleaning the horrible place up — painting and redecorating from the ground up. "Up" however, hadn't yet reached the second floor when the con-
398

vention started; it was only on the ground floor. The new management was trying . . . but it should have started with a bulldozer and skull-cracker team, not paint-brushes.

The room we had was dirty with the ground-in grime that couldn't be washed off. It smelled of mice and roaches. The sheets had been washed, but the blankets and the feather puffs hadn't been — certainly not since the War. World War I, that is. They had something of that plastic feel, like vinylite sheet, or polyethylene, that comes with the long-term accumulation of oilyness.

Worse, the place was saturated with the psi miasma of discouragement, defeat, frustration, and surrender. Nobody had stayed in that hotel who could possibly stay anywhere else, for years and years, and it was full of the discouragement of all the people who'd been beaten down to staying there.

I know you don't believe in psi phenomena — but you've experienced the feeling that different houses give you; some are happy, whether there's anyone home or not, and some are paranoid, and some are defeated-hopeless. Brand new houses are just empty; old houses have, for some while after everyone moves out, a distinct feel. There's a sort of residual magnetism . . . only it isn't a physical-magnetic field, but something Else that can only be referred to by analogy, since the technology hasn't been invented yet.

This was one sf convention that was <u>not</u> a "lay of wife"; nobody had the enthusiasm to carry on. That Philadelphia convention was unhappy because of the way the poor fans wandered around aimlessly, with no goal or place to go.

This was different. This wasn't a lack-of-purpose, but a feeling that no purpose could exist anywhere anyway, a positive denial, rather than a simple emptiness.

We'd just come from Ireland — which is wonderful, and a place really worth going — and were rested, happy, and feeling fine.

Four days in England, and we fled back to Dublin, where I spent two days in bed trying to get over a violent cold.

The only reason I wish you'ld gone, was so you could have encountered that miasma, and had a little experience that would not fit so neatly into physical science concepts!

We went up to see the de la Warr Laboratories, as soon as the convention was over. (I had to stay the whole three days; the Guest of Honor couldn't run out, and they had me scheduled for late on the last day for a psionics discussion. Worse, I couldn't complain about the place. Oh . . . I neglected to mention the bath tub. No bath with the room, of course; the bath was across the hall. It smelled like the subway station men's rooms, incidentally; the toilet had a flush system older than any I'd encountered before. A solid lead tank hung near the ceiling, with a pull-chain that you had to <u>pump</u>, not just pull, to make it flush. A pull of about 35 pounds required; I don't think it was out of order, but just built that way. The bathtub, however, was the prize. Biggest thing in that line I've ever seen — about the size of an Egyptian sarcophagus, and shaped like a keyhole. The round part was a good 3' in diameter, the rectangular part another 4-1/2', and the drain was a six-inch hole right where one would have to sit, equipped with a broken brass grating. It also resembled an Egyptian sarcophagus in the depth of its layers of encrustation. It must have been really elegant in the 1870's.)

Anyhow, the de la Warr Laboratories are in Oxford . . . and man, you should see the place! Beautiful grounds, five neat brick lab buildings, each about the size of a 7-room house. **de la Warr** himself was City Engineer of Oxford before he resigned to take up the psionics work full time, and he's about as fuzzy-headed in his thinking as you'ld expect a successful municipal engineer to be — he'd run any electronic computer a good race for coldly accurate logical thinking.

However, he's an engineer — which means that he isn't limited in the way a scientist is. A scientist's beliefs are oriented on what he can <u>understand</u>, i.e., relate by application of formalized and agreed on rules of logical derivation. An engineer isn't, never has been, and shouldn't ever be. A scientist is limited to "Is it logical?" — and if it's logical, he'll believe it if it's demonstrable or not.

An engineer doesn't give a hoot in hell whether it's logical or not; he has one and only one criterion; "Does it work?" A physical chemist may be deeply bothered by the mechanism by which mortar sets, until he's worked it out; Roman engineers weren't — they knew <u>that</u> it set, and how to mix it so it would set, and that was all they needed. It worked.

The result is that engineers will always be ahead of scientists in
400

some areas, and far behind in others. **Einstein's** $E=mc^2$ didn't work, when he announced it; it was years before it became an engineering formula. Roman engineers were using mortar damn near 2000 years before anyone explained the physical chemistry of the $Ca(OH)_2$ to $CaCO_3 \cdot H_2O$ conversion.

Damascus armorers were making case-hardened spring-steel a millennium ago; their theory was nonsense, of course — the soul of the slave that died as they ran the red-hot steel through his guts had nothing to do with the tempering the blade acquired. But their engineering was valid; it produced a case-hardened spring-steel.

An engineers' approach is markedly different from that of a scientist; for the scientist, "It works" is neither necessary nor sufficient.

For the engineer, "It works" is both necessary and sufficient.

OK. — so there's a **Mr. France**, in charge of one section of Britain's National Power Grid, a division engineer, we'd call him. They, like every power company, have a standard problem — locating underground power cables. The maps are usually in some office n miles distant, when needed, and frequently aren't accurate, because the modifications map didn't catch up with the original installation map. Locating underground cables is a bloody nuisance.

France has solved it; he dowses for them. He's trained all his assistant engineers and gang-foreman in dowsing for cables, and that's their standard method of finding them; to hell with the maps. This works, in an engineer's terms, because it's fast, reliable, and cheap, a damn sight more satisfactory than hunting up maps.

They simply take two L-shaped metal rods — any metal will do, copper, aluminum, galvanized iron — anything handy — about 12" on the short leg, and 18" on the long leg. They're held like a pair of pistols, short legs being the grips, pointed forward, the "barrels" parallel, and horizontal. When the operator walks along and crosses above the cable, the two rods swing in and cross each other. He's been able to teach some 90% of applicants; to date only one deviant has shown up. For him the rods work fine . . . but they turn wall-eyed instead of cross-eyed when he crosses the cable. The rods are simply heavy-gauge wire — about 3/16ths metal. The depth at which the cable is buried makes no difference, and whether the cable is connected or not is of no importance.

Nobody has been able to figure out why it works . . . but the engineering crews use it regularly, because it's cheap, simple, and more reliable than maps. They don't give a damn why; they have a certain task that has to be done, and done rapidly, with a minimum of damn-nuisance digging holes where there are no cables. Let some scientist figure it out, if he wants to — they don't have to, and haven't time to.

De la Warr says he is simply ignoring the scientists — that he finds it's hopeless to try to do anything with them. Instead he's working with the engineering level people; they don't give a damn why anything works, if they can use it. He's doing a lot of psionic treatment of horses and farm animals — particularly race horses, and very highly bred domestic animals. The Medical Association can't stop him there, and the Vets aren't organized well enough. Meanwhile, he's working out more effective devices, supporting his work on the payments for jobs delivered to customer satisfaction. A satisfied customer never complains about the theoretical impossibility of achieving the satisfaction he has attained.

One of the great problems of Mankind is that the normal (i.e., individual having characteristics close to the statistical average) man cannot live in fear, uncertainty, or ignorance . . . but does, in real-world fact, live in the presence of uncontrollable random factors, or which he has no knowledge, which threaten his existence. Objectively, he lives in fear, uncertainty, and ignorance; subjectively he cannot tolerate living in that situation. Solution: deny the reality of his ignorance, of the uncertainty of the things he knows for sure, and the existence of forces which threaten him and which he does not know about, understand, or control.

The science fictioneer admits the existence of unknowns . . . but concentrates on the fact that unknowns have positive values. (No intelligent entity will undertake a task with no predictable reward value; make the unknown valuable, and even the risk and effort of tackling the unknown become acceptable.)

I know damn well that a lot of human beings are going to die and/or be crippled physically, mentally, or psychically by the research in psionics. These forces are potent; they can kill, and injure. **Roentgen** was lucky; he discovered X-rays, but he didn't explore them; the ones who did usually died, because they hadn't yet realized that the rays
402

were lethal.

Chemistry killed a lot of good men, too. Nucleonics has killed several already, and it's barely started.

So will psionics. So what? You think we're going to reach the Moon without killing a number of good men? I may be one of those who "summons a demon too powerful to control" myself. So? So then it will be "Selah! It is finished . . . and it was worth trying, anyway!" stuff — in essence, the proposition that amateur research into the nature and function of Mind is both necessary and worthwhile. So there's a risk! So what? What isn't a risk, for God's sake? So our own amateur experimenting, **Peg's** and mine, has, several times, had me mentally twanging and decidedly uncertain as to whether I was going to or already had. The condition, I can now report form experience, normally lasts about three days, by which time you get a new integration, and start on from where you flopped.

Blessed are the meek and self-sacrificing, for they shall inherit the Earth. Yeah, verily. The guys who are uncertain of themselves, so they go ahead and find out; who are uncertain of whether the sea really does slide off the edge of the world, and go to see. The meek and humble are those who can live in uncertainty and ignorance. Since 99.9999% of Totality is uncertain and unknown, that gives them quite a bit of lebensraum, doesn't it?

And **Ike**, you're even schizier than you realize; you talk a good game of being conservative and orthodox . . . but you don't do it. You do a very nice job of sabotaging conservativism right where you are. I'm just trying to encourage you to sabotage some specific aspects.

Teachers are paid to teach what the parents think their children should know. Teachers get fired if they teach things the parents didn't employ them to teach . . . if the parents realize it. You put on one of the finest stuffed-shirt fronts anyone could ask for in a Professor — as stuffy and reliable a teacher of just what the parents know their dear little unable-to-think-for-themselves-of-course-or-if-they-aren't-they-should-bes as anyone could ask for.

Only you aren't and can't be. You're not teaching biochemistry half so much as you are teaching Inquiry.

You couldn't do it half so effectively if anyone suspected you of Unorthodoxy; protecting your reputation of pious orthodoxy is a ma-

403

jor asset, and your public persona should not for a moment slip on that.

But I'm suggesting that among the snide, underhand comments you slip through under the guise of orthodoxy, is the question of what does constitute demonstration. No article of faith is more important to the orthodoxy scientist than the proposition that no one should have articles of faith. No belief is more fundamental to science than that belief should not be important in any thinking. And that, of course, is a faith, a belief, that no one can challenge and remain within the ranks of orthodox science.

I'm well aware that the normal method of progress in thinking is to develop a conceptual world-system which includes both the old and the new. I suggest that the thing that makes the pill hard to swallow is the fact that the importance of all the old, the net value of all the hard-won experience, is diminished by that maneuver. Modern military technology includes the bow-and-arrow principle, of course . . . but perhaps the major use of archery in modern military procedures is in the Signal Corps, where it is sometimes convenient to use an arrow to carry a light cord over a high tree branch so that a radio antenna or other wire can be pulled up.

Flint arrow-head chipping is still included in human culture; there are several anthropologists who have made a study of the technique, in order to understand the problems of the old-timers. The *Mayflower II* called for relearning the detailed technology of square-riggers.

You think biochemistry will never be reduced to such a state? Modern die-stampings have reduced the handicraft technique of shaping parts to a sort of hobby work, plus the special field of the die-maker. Why do complex organic syntheses "by hand" . . . when a biological organism can do the job so cheaply? I've seen some of the things psionic devices can do in the way of analyzing chemical compounds . . . and believe me, **Ike**, the work of determining the structure of proteins will never be done by biochemical techniques, but will be simply achieved by developed psionic methods.

On the business of proteins being the fundamental stuff of life: Sorry, **Ike**, — we've been mistaking the tool for the tool-user. It's been said that iron, coal, and sulfuric acid are the fundamental materials of modern civilization. Certainly the total tonnage of those materials exceeds the tonnage of human flesh.

404

And it isn't human flesh that's fundamental, either; there's more tonnage of human flesh in China and Africa than in the United States, for instance.

The essence of life is <u>not</u> material, but organization-as-a-thing-in-itself. We speak of a "magnetic field," and do NOT mean the hunk of iron that's magnetized. OK.; let's discuss an organizational field — which <u>is not</u> that-which-is-organized, any more than the iron is the magnetic field.

The essence of life is organization, not that-which-is-organized. It's pretty fundamental that a low-density, soft material cannot force a high-density, hard material into a patterned shape. True, water can wear away or dissolve away hard material . . . but only because water molecules are, as a matter of fact, a damn sight harder and more rigid structures than most other substances. Iron, for instance, is markedly more compressible than water.

OK. — then couldn't it have been predicted that that-which-imposed-pattern on protein molecules must, itself, have a structure more rigid, less labile, than protein? If you want to stamp out polystyrene molded parts, you don't use a polystyrene mold — you use a metal mold.

What's harder and more rigid than an atomic nucleus?

The completely non-material force-fields that shape and determine the nucleus, of course.

When we learn how to handle organization fields directly -- we'll know how to make molecules to order, without ever bothering with the chemistry of the process.

A photographic negative is a strange thing; it's the result of a chemical process of a kind — but what chemical process can make so incredibly delicate and detailed a picture of a little girl? Answer: pure noise-like chemical potential, plus a minute amount of organizational energy. Organizational energy makes pure random an ideal building material; if the developer were poorly mixed, the distribution of reducing agent anything but purely random, the negative would be unsatisfactory. To Organization, Chaos is an unlimited opportunity.

A man doesn't need the skill of an artist to achieve a beautiful picture . . . if you could make pure organization fields work for you!

My point? Sure, the new must always include the old. But the individuals who have invested greatly in achieving the old may not be willing to allow it to be included. Archery is included in the study of Military Tactics, too . . . but not in a way that would satisfy Robin Hood. So he could hit a 1-inch target at 100 yards? So what?! With my precision rifle, plus telescopic sight, I can hit it at a mile — and with a naval rifle, I can hit it at 30 miles, though it will be sort of hard to prove, since the entire area of the target, and 30 feet in all directions, will be obliterated.

Science doesn't mind a <u>little</u> extension — but a **Galileo**-type re-orientation of the total cosmos is a little tougher to accept. **Galileo** was willing to include the old, too, you know — as a complete misunderstanding of what was really there.

Regards, John

Isaac Asimov *October 4, 1957*

Dear Ike:

Ike, for Pete's sake, climb up off your low-horse, and take a look at the real situation you're actually in! So the Dean is making threatening growling noises; my friend, that Dean <u>is</u> an anus!

As of now, **Dr. Isaac Asimov** has quite a reputation as a <u>teacher</u> of biochemistry, and Science. You're a little mistaken in saying that there are hundreds of other biochemists that could do research as well as you; they could do it better. You aren't, and never actually were a researcher; you're a teacher. Like most top-notch teachers, the research work isn't something that interests you <u>for itself</u>, but <u>for its results</u>, which can be taught.

Most major cities are actually aware of the problem of getting adequate science teachers; the difficulty is that industry will snaffle any competent young scientist at higher financial wages than teaching offers. (You should see the number of those questionnaires that came back to *ASF* with Age 27 to 28, Salary, 9 to 12 kilobucks!) (Also the number that came back Age 45-55 with salaries in the 30-70 kilobuck range! President of power company. Operate own consulting lab. Etc.) What the school systems have to get are people who are science <u>teachers,</u> not scientists. Real teachers, people who want and need to <u>teach</u>.

Wanna bet you couldn't get some city to make interested noises in your direction as head of the science-teaching department?

406

How about Professor of Science Teaching at an Education school? You may not have had much published in biochemical journals . . . but man, you've flooded the *Journal of Chemical Education*! Also *Science World*.

As a biochemist, you haven't established much of a solid reputation; true. But as a teacher of science, you've got a very solid national reputation!

There was a professor of Anglo-Saxon at Wisconsin when **Peg** was there, a man by the name of **Miles Hanley**. Now Anglo-Saxon is not exactly a very important subject these days; it's considerably deader than Latin or Greek, or even Sanskrit, as a matter of fact; those languages are, by comparison, active and burgeoning subjects.

But the number of **Peg's** Anglo-Saxon-class-mates she sees in the news these days is rather astonishing. **Clyde Kluckhone**, the Harvard anthropologist, was one, for instance. There are others.

The way **Miles Hanley** taught Anglo-Saxon, as I get it, somehow made **Sir James Jean's** *The Universe Around Us* and discussions of misericords in old English churches, and almost anything else a necessary and intimate part of Anglo-Saxon.

He was, apparently, the kind of man who needed nothing but a podium of some kind to teach kids to like learning; from that point on, it doesn't really matter what he's supposed to be teaching. His students will learn that sort by-the-way . . . and also start learning everything else and sort of forget to stop learning for the rest of their lives. . . .

If somebody offered you the Chair on Sumerian Basket Weaving and Band Instruments . . . what would you teach, **Ike**?

Within two years, that'd be the course half the students in the college would be trying to take. There's nothing like teaching a "snap" course; the students — poor suckers! — have their defenses down, and will actually allow themselves to become interested in learning. Besides, in a "snap" course, the professor isn't really expected to stick to the subject, is he . . . ?

As you know, **John Arnold** had to leave M.I.T.; his free-wheeling "snap" course in Creative Engineering got out of hand. It was a "snap" engineering course, because, after all, who can say what Arcturians really like in the way of automobiles, huh? His students were annoying the orthodox professors all up and down the line, by asking questions people aren't supposed to ask, such as, "How do you know? Is that the only possible interpretation of the data?" It bothered the other professors . . . particularly the ones who couldn't get the necessary 10 students to run their pet elective courses, while **John** was having trouble handling the 80-100 students that signed up for his.

How many students do you have in your courses, **Ike**? And how many does that Dean have . . . or doesn't he handle any courses?

You're acknowledged as the best lecturer . . . and aren't head of the department? (And don't want to be, I betcha!)

It's a fair bet that I could maneuver things around so I was made vice president at Street & Smith. Horrible thought; I'd have to go into that damned city five days a week, and make business trips about once a week, and do more damned routine business hassling, report-writing, and accounts-examining . . . ugh! Thank God it's a free country; nobody can make me do that! I'd never have a chance for a decent bull-session!

Peg was offered a chance to be one of the board of Chosen Freeholders here in Union County (It's a top county political post, and a strong chance at major state office.) Our cross-street neighbor is one of the top politicos of New Jersey; he wanted **Peg** to come in — and come in at the top.

The idea appalled her. Sure she could do it — but she wouldn't have been free to do what she really wants to do.

Ike . . . take a look at what you really want to be.

My hunch is, it isn't "biochemist." It isn't "science fiction writer" either. Those are, I think, both incidental -- methods, means, not purposes or ends.

Jane was back from San Francisco for a couple of weeks; she came home immediately after we did. **Janie's** a lot more of a woman than she was last spring; the whole experience seems to have been just about what she needed. One of her major troubles was that she needed a good, solid, kick in the teeth that she could-and-would accept as having been earned by her own errors of thinking — and inasmuch as the engagement to **Randy** was her very own, private idea, and was one she her very own self decided was an appallingly bad one . . . she got it sunk into her somewhat intransigent young head that her ideas could stand cross-checking.

408

Her feeling that **Wellsley** had nothing to give her was both true and false; she had been exposed to a deeper level of thinking around here — **Gotthard Gunther** — you — **Wayne Batteau** — **Claude Shannon** — others — but she hadn't, actually, been getting what she could have from them, either.

She had never allowed anyone to bully her into giving up her own belief in her own ideas.

She was really beat down last March; it wasn't just that **Randy** had unstabilized her — it was the simple fact that she picked **Randy**, and she recognized that she was a colossal dimwit for doing so.

She had been mistaken on a million things; the **Randy** matter simply served to punch a hole in her barrier of self-conviction . . . and everything else came up for review, too.

I couldn't help much; neither could **Peg**. (She was feeling extremely shaken because of rejecting some sound ideas we'd offered during the last five years or so, of course.)

You know **Toynbee's** idea of the going-away-and-returning of the philosopher-prophet-leader? The old boy has something there . . . and that's what **Jane** did.

Barney Kahn, of course, was a big help. But she also met a youngster out there, one **John Allen**, who's been even more of a help — partly because he had very much the same sort of problem. His father is **Dr. Allen**, Prof. of Biochem at Berkley — and one of those people there's nothing wrong with. (Except that, so far as I can make out, he's a stuffed shirt. Trouble is, the stuffing is such a fine-grained, solidly-packed, government-approved grade that you can't really prove it's just stuffing.)

(You think **David** isn't going to have one hell of a time with you?! What's wrong with you, **Ike**? Are you un-understanding, stupid, a drunk, disrespected by your neighbors, guilty of peccadilloes, given to petty tempers, unkind, thoughtless of others, or guilty of displaying any of the ordinary, easily-spotted human failures that a 15-year-old kid can spot and define? Will he be able to spot anything in your character that'll give him a good solid foothold for rebellion? And it isn't just stuffy hypocrisy with you, either; you say it and you mean it and you do it. In what ways — that can be perceived and understood by a kid — are you imperfect, **Ike**?)

Anyhow, **Jane** could see **John Allen's** problem — and because she felt beat down, was able to start accepting that she needed some re-evaluation of her ideas.

She's learned a lot — and can accept and use some help now. She's doing fine; she's going to business school this fall, for a specific reason, with a plan in mind — not just because going to school is The Thing To Do. **Barney Kahn's** been teaching criminal psychiatry at Berkley, and working with the State Parole people; he's got **Jane** interested in being a psychiatric parole worker. For this she needs business methods courses, and some more psychology courses.

Incidentally; inasmuch as there is no logical method that can generate postulates (that's fact; check with any genuine logician. Logic works from postulates; it doesn't make them) and men intuit postulates, men have intuition. But it's not like female intuition. Kicking it around, **Jane**, **Peg** and I have reached a provisional differentiation:

A woman intuits states; a man intuits processes. A woman tends to have a "revelation" as to a goal, a state-of-being. A man has a tendency to intuit methods, means, a process-of-doing. A woman will "intuit" a new arrangement of the furniture — the dining room turned into a music room, with the grand piano out of the living room, under those windows there. . . .

But she visualizes the end result — and neglects the process which happens to involve moving the piano through a doorway smaller than it is.

Men, on the other hand, visualize a process . . . and neglect to visualize the end result. Process without purpose, is man's chief fault. Vide Angels dancing on a pin.

Purposes without process, of course, is what gives us the WCTU's bright idea of Prohibition.

Re: the psi fields proposition, the "aura" of a house.

You attribute it to "conditioned reflex."

OK, that explanation will do for your writing room — but what of the case of reaction on a first encounter with a house?

We have a happy house here; I've had a fine opportunity to observe the effect it has on people entering it for the first time. No conditioning — but reaction just the same!

By the way; here's something that might serve as story back-

410

ground. Currently, we're culturally in a phase of excessive democracy; we've rejected aristocracy so hard that we've swung to excessive democracy — the "dictatorship of the proletariat" in fact is the Philosophy of mediocrity.

Currently, our cultural philosophy actually penalizes abnormal competence as something Unfair, or Wrong. The 90% income tax is a studied effort to prevent people from seeking exceptionally high achievement — it isn't a measure to produce government revenue, but a punitive fine for the Unfair practice of Doing Too Good A Job.

The Union practice of making a union man hold down to a standard (low) output, as the bricklayer is required to lay not more than 400 bricks per 8 hour day — and to take 8 hours doing it. He's attacked socially, economically, and physically if he refuses to abide by mediocre performance rules.

The anti-intellectualism cult you yourself pointed out is similar in basic character.

"All men are equal — and if they aren't, by God we'll cut 'em down to size 'til they are!'"

The student who does exceptionally well is in danger of being attacked by the other students; he's the hated "teacher's pet."

The proposition that some human beings are innately superior to others is violently denied — to the extent of crippling the innately superior so he won't be superior.

Now there is reason to distrust, reject, abolish, the old Aristocracy concept. The superiority-by-birth system didn't work.

Next step, coming up in the next couple of centuries, is an equally fervid rejection of the imposed-democracy concept we now have.

The difficulty is to find a correlation between some detectable, observable factor, and the <u>future</u> competence of the individual. It's not adequate to have *ex post facto* methods of evaluation. "Nothing succeeds like success" they say. Nuts!

I can put it in personal terms. The magazines are all clamoring (some somewhat wistfully) for your writing. You are a success.

Yeah . . . but what succeeds better than a recognized success is recognizing success-in-process-of-becoming-successful. *ASF* got where it did because I hitched it to rising stars like young **Ike Asimov!** The thing that succeeds better than success, is being where a success is
411

about to happen.

What we need is a way of spotting the superior individuals <u>before</u> their superiority is realized (in the sense of developed-in-reality). Detect the <u>potential</u> genius — and help him to maximize the potentials he has.

Race prejudice arises from efforts to make a usable correlation. Now it is damned well a fact (whether it's palatable or not) that there's a 90% valid correlation between brown skin and low individual civilized capability in the South. The trouble is that while it is statistically (and engineeringly) valid . . . it isn't individually valid.

Note this: there are conspicuous yellow-and-black striped caterpillars that come equipped with hairs that have a most repulsive taste to birds. They have a survival mechanism based on a repellent taste, coupled with a bright coloration to advertise the fact.

But . . . there are other caterpillars that have evolved the same coloration, in imitation of the noxious ones. The birds make an engineeringly valid correlation; yellow-and-black color — foul taste. They leave <u>both</u> types alone.

It's a useful, but not ideal, system.

Aristocracy-by-birth is a useful system, too. It's <u>probable</u> that competent fathers will sire competent sons. The probability definitely exceeds 0.5, and is, therefore, valuable to a species.

It's a useful test for predicting success — and predicting where the culture's always-limited educational resources should be concentrated for maximum cultural advantage. If the educational facilities can handle only 1 of every 10 children born — what technique of selecting children to educate will be most advantageous to the culture?

Aristocracy by birth is one solution.

Education at the parent's expense is another; successful fathers then concentrate the educational facilities on their sons . . . which is another way of aristocracy-by-birth, actually. It's a better technique than the older one, because Nobility may have been earned five generations ago. Economic success gets dissipated quicker than a title.

We need better tests, that's all.

The difficulty is this; by the nature of things, most people are mediocre (Definition!). When "most people" are in control, the system of tests will be designed to favor the mediocre, and penalize the non-mediocre.

It is NOT optimum to impose equal education on all; each individual should be educated in a manner that maximizes that individual's potentials. You can ruin a hell of a good machinist by convincing him that only white-collar-accountants are Worth While People, and making him force himself to be an accountant. You can ruin a hell of a good peasant-farmer type, with a real "green thumb," by making him believe he has to be a lawyer if he is to be a Worthy person. He'll be a miserable lawyer, in both senses of the word.

Now a lot of peasant-farmer types are going to be miserable, no matter what you do. Reason: the race has needed, and therefore has encouraged the breeding of, that type of stock for about 100,000 years — so there's a great many of 'em produced. But we don't need the type much any more. We need engineers, instead. So some peasant-farmer types have to be made miserable by being forced to learn to be Technicians, 3rd grade.

My point is: There will, inevitably, be a reaction toward an aristocracy-by-lormith. I don't know what "lormith" will be — but it'll be some kind of test that shows a higher correlation between prediction and fulfillment, and allows selection of the specially competent for special training.

It won't be perfect; it, too, will be inadequate. But it'll be better.

And it'll produce a new aristocracy system.

In the new aristocracy system, the inferior will be rejected, and will resent it, feel miserable, and feel a dull, aching misery because they can't do anything about it.

They won't be able to do anything about it, because they will in fact be inferior. There is, at any period of evolution, a group which has been handed the ticket marked "Drop Dead!" The rejects that are going to die — and who, naturally, don't want to die. The dinosaurs didn't want to. The dodo didn't like the "Drop Dead!" ticket . . . but he didn't draw it in a raffle; he earned it in a test. He failed the test by not defending his nest against rats.

Remember **H. Beam Piper's** "The Day of the Moron?" Some men must be rejected as inferior; they are.

There'll come a time when you and I are rejected as inferior; age
413

will earn us the "Drop Dead!" ticket . . . and we'll drop dead, whether we like it or not.

The story-possibility aspect, as I see it, is in the recognition of this simple fact: A perfect, perfectly just, and perfectly accurate system of evaluation of men will hurt individuals. It will hurt them for many reasons, among which are:

1. A man who has the potential to be an excellent machinist may have a great, deep conviction that he should be a musician . . . only he simply hasn't got that potential. An accurate, and just evaluation system would assign him to a machinist education — and, presently, dump him into the waste-bin division. Reason: he <u>can't</u> be a musician because he hasn't got it, and can't learn to be the machinist he could be because of his music conviction. So he's not educatable.

2. Some human beings are born without arms or legs — congenital deformities, caused either genetically, or by accident during fetal development. Equally, some human beings have congenital malformation of the ego; they are psychopaths who never developed the characteristic of empathy. Now if an entity does not have the inane characteristic "ability to learn," it can't be taught to learn. No matter how long and hard I try, I can't teach this typewriter to spell. A chimpanzee can't be taught to speak; he lacks the innate characteristic "ability to learn to symbolize." Some human beings have intelligence, but lack the ability to learn to empathize. The potential isn't there, so that no amount of training-effort will develop the ability. "Some" I say — and that's what I mean. Not all armless men are the result of congenital deformity; some, however, are. If an individual shows extremely long clotting time, he may need vitamins and certain amino acids . . . but he may be a hemophiliac, in which case no amount of therapy will set him right.

In a perfect evaluation system . . . some are going to be rejected, resent it violently, and <u>know</u> it is an extreme injustice. You can't explain to a psychopath that he isn't human; the characteristic he lacks by its lack makes it impossible for him to empathize the fact that other people are different.

There are lots of cases — and, of course, there will be the normal man who is rejected "unfairly" from the opportunity to show the genius he knows he has.

This assumes that God Almighty Himself is doing the selecting
414

and evaluation. I.e., that the selecting is absolutely perfect, beyond all possibility of question or doubt. Ideal, theoretical case.

Now on top of that, let's add the complicating factor that there will be <u>real</u> geniuses having real talents that have never been recognized, and therefore aren't being tested for. Let's acknowledge that no procedure will ever be devised that is actually perfectly correct.

So what do we do? Give up and do no selecting at all?

That's the answer of hyper-democracy. It holds that Selecting Is An Evil Thing because it denies that All People Are Equal . . . or Should Be If They Aren't.

It stems from the proposition, "Nobody is superior to me . . . but some are inferior, of course."

You flunk some of your students in biochemistry. OK — you're acting as a testing station, and finding that some individuals are superior, and some inferior. Why not set up a democratic system, recognize that All Men Are Equal, and give every student the same mark?

The simple fact is that, like it or not, Man has to accept the hard fact that some men are superior, and some inferior -- and the culture that doesn't accept that inevitably goes under to one that does. The one that wins will be the one that <u>does</u> select <u>and</u> reject, and uses the method of selection-rejection having the highest accuracy. And by "accuracy" I mean the method that correctly detects and specifies potential before it's too late to develop it/use it.

There's a shortage of funds to provide extended education for the top-talented creative individuals — because of inefficiency entailed in giving incompetents education they can't use, and don't want.

A military organization operates efficiently . . . or ceases to exist. Our Army is <u>most</u> undemocratic; education as a jet pilot or atomic missile technician is not open to all citizens.

Hmmm . . . wonder if the new phase of culture will start with a sort of military revolution that isn't a revolution, but simply the result of the military doctrine of selection of the most competent being imposed gradually throughout the culture? Civilians will run a culture only so long as the civilians have a higher "achievement product" than the military. "Achievement product" being numbers-of-individuals multiplied by average-efficiency-per-individual.

You know, **Ike**, it's always possible to present a concept through
415

the eyes of someone who hates the whole system . . . and still present it so the true value problems involved are detectable to the reader.

Regards, John

Isaac Asimov   *October 12, 1957*

Dear Ike:

Now it just happens I have a partial answer to an extension of PROFESSION that I'd just about decided to write you about.

Try this aspect on it on for size:

A doctor is allowed special privileges and prerogatives of course. Bill Blow figures that's all right; the doc has to sweat out about eight years of school to get it, and of course, if Bill himself had wanted it, he could have done it too — but Bill didn' wanna, cause Jeez, who wantsa waste all that time sweatin' out the books instead livin'?

But being a doctor is open to anybody that wants to sweat that long over it, so it's democratic.

But now somebody invents the Geewizard Machine. The Geewizard Machine is your tape-educator . . . with a slight difference. It takes about a week to fully train a doctor, and does <u>not</u> simply impose a <u>stet</u> education, but actually teaches him to think, understand, evaluate, and comprehend. It makes him not only smart and learned, but also permits him to be wise.

But it works only for the top 10% of men. Ninety percent of the people can't use the machine at all; when they try — they're free to try, of course — it gives them unbearable headaches, makes them violently upset emotionally, and produces a terrific uncertainty that, after even a half hour initial exposure, leaves them so confused they don't know which way to go — don't know whether it's raining or Tuesday.

Now some 40% of mankind <u>can</u> learn what the Geewizard Machine teaches — but only by the old, long, eight-year method. There are now two ways to become a doctor; the Geewizard way, or the medical school and internship way. One takes one week; the other eight years.

The Geewizard trained doctor is better trained, too; further he can catch up on any new work by taking one-day refresher courses now

416

and then — equivalent to a full year of schooling.

Naturally, school-trained doctors rapidly decline to zero.

Now we have the situation that certain men can, by spending one week, become doctors. They then have the privileges and prerogatives of doctors.

But most people don't have a chance.

And, of course, this isn't just doctors — it's any highly trained occupation.

The world is divided into two groups; those who can, in a week, acquire a full education . . . and those who have to sweat it out for years to reach the same point.

It's a matter of genetics; some have it, and some don't. A few Negroes have it; most white men don't. A few Chinese, a few of every race . . . but most of every race doesn't have it, and can't get it. It's just a genetic advantage that some happen to have . . . and the rest can't get. Being a genetic trait, of course, there's a tendency to find several individuals in one family, and other families (most) with no members.

What I'm setting up is:

1. An objectively detectable genetic variation,

2. Which is highly favorable,

3. And present in a relatively small minority.

4. And it has the characteristic that non-possessors can't bear to attempt claiming it.

Example: Suppose we consider the Peruvian Indios. They can work happily at 15,000 feet, due to genetic selection. I can't. If the Earth lost 2/3rds of its atmosphere, the Peruvian Indios would have a highly favorable genetic advantage — and I couldn't possibly get away with claiming I had it, because the act of trying to work actively at the existent atmospheric pressure would promptly lay me out cold, sick, and probably dead.

Also, for story purposes, assume that this is a matter of a mental chain-reaction system; if the chain reaction reaches 1.00000 it takes off toward infinity . . . and if it's less than 1.0000, it invariably and inevitably goes to zero. Therefore each individual has an either-or reaction; either he can take the Geewizard Machine, and go-reactive, or he can't take it at all. No borderline cases — or at least, so extremely few that they're about the equivalent in numbers to true hermaphrodites among

417

human beings.

I suppose we could add a third type . . . the type that chain-reacts bomb fashion instead of reactor fashion; they explode mentally completely, totally, and irrevocably.

This is just background to set up the real story problem:

What do you think our culture would do if faced with the <u>fact</u> that certain individuals had a powerful genetic superiority? It can't be equalized by any training process — because the difference is a <u>difference of reaction to training</u>! And as I pointed out a while back, the one thing that you cannot teach is "This is the way to learn." If the "student" lacks the ability to learn, you obviously can NOT teach him how to learn!

How would the culture react?

I think they'd smash the Geewizard Machines, and every Geewizardable individual they could find. They might keep some Geewizard Machines around so they could test individuals, and weed out those damned trick learners.

I speak from experience — mine and yours, <u>Ike</u>. You've got a built-in Geewizard Machine; remember how you learned the multiplication tables. You've got the characteristic of one-shot learning, too; i.e., in many, many instances, you can hear a comment made once, and know it forever afterwards, without having to make any special effort whatever. You don't "commit it to memory" or "memorize" it in the sense a normal man means by those phrases; you've heard it — therefore you know it.

I've got a similar characteristic; in prep school I read my physics text through at the beginning of the year, and that made it unnecessary to study it the rest of the year, obviously. At MIT, I did the same with physics and chemistry. And I averaged about 95-98 in those courses.

You think this looks "fair" to the guy who's doing an honest job of sweating out the course?

Now I don't say that I know this is genetic; by making the Geewizard Machine work on a genetic faculty, I'm establishing the proposition, "this individual can do it, but cannot explain and does not know how to do it, nor can he aid any other individual to do it."

Your PROFESSION made the inability to learn fast a desirable thing.

Now reverse the proposition; the tape education is not compulsive and narrowing, but frees creative talents for real work. No artist is worth a damn until he learns draughtsmanship; he has to be able to draw before he can draw creative ideas. But draughtsmanship is purely mechanical; a camera is a perfect draughtsman. Yet it takes an artist years to master draughtsmanship!

There's nothing inherently ennobling in the grubbing, slugging hours spent practicing draughtsmanship, either. It's drudgery, and basically a mechanical task.

Peedee's learning to drive; she's learning in a manual-shift car. She's engaged in spending most of her time and effort learning to do what an automatic shift mechanism can do perfectly. When she gets all through, I might say to her, "Now, **Peedee**, you have developed the skill and high talent of gear-shifting that twenty pounds of bolts, nuts, and hydraulic piping has."

Why spend years learning arithmetic? What's noble about that? Any desk computer can, with a couple pounds of gears, do what it takes a kid hundreds of hours to learn to do.

Logic is a purely mechanical system; simple relay circuits can do faultless logic. Just because you spent thousands of hours learning to do it doesn't make your logic better — it almost certainly makes it worse, because you must be using an extremely complex circuit to do a simple job.

The Geewizard Machine simply eliminates the need for learning the slow way any mechanical interrelation of facts. This frees the creative talent of a fine mind to work in the field where creativity belongs. Most creative people have a horrible time with arithmetic; it's an area where any creativity whatever means a mistake. My spelling is horrible; I'm too creative in the area where creativity doesn't belong.

But . . . how do people react to those who can bypass the mechanical learning of facts and data and rules and formulas? Suddenly the long, slow, hard way becomes in and of itself a noble thing. The Puritans so hated pleasure that being unhappy was the only good and noble thing. People would suddenly discover that they spent eight years learning to be a doctor because doing it the slow way was Good and The Way It Should Be Done, that they did it that way because that was the way Any Honest Man Would Want To. Not — Heaven forbid! -- because they couldn't do it any other way!

Does a man have a right to something he gets without earning it? How does a man "earn" a genetic characteristic?

Suppose it is shown that the Geewizardable characteristic is specifically a complex Mendelian recessive. The only way it can be detected is by genealogical studies of a family, or, of course, by the Geewizardability of the individual.

Geewizardability isn't too critically important to the females; they don't have to compete in the tough fields of industry — but it is critical to them with respect to their children. A woman wants her children to have the best there is around. This simply means that the Geewizardable man has the first choice among the females — and, of course, a Geewizardable woman wouldn't want a dolt husband.

This would, maybe, make people love the Geewizardable, huh? Women wouldn't mind too much; they don't need it, but their children can get it, if she simply bears children by a Geewizardable man. My, doesn't that make the nongeewizardable men happy?!

Now, **Ike**, my friend, the demand, "I have the same legal rights you have," is the insistence, "I'm just as good as you are." It can be made to look different . . . but it isn't, when you put it into action. What a man does has meaning only with respect to what he is. Legal rights have to do with what a man does. Therefore they are meaningless — inappropriate -- insane — if they aren't appropriate to what a man is, and don't take into account what the actor is.

If a certain individual were to come to visit at your house, for some reason became angry at **Gertrude**, and started beating her as hard as he could, what action would be appropriate?

Legally, this is assault and battery . . . whether the individual is 6 years old or 60.

You can impose equality of legal rights only on equal individuals. If you were somewhat careless and got the sodium fluoride ant poison into someone's mashed potatoes, you would be very strongly suspected of murder. As a biochemist, you know too damn much about the characteristics of NaF to be that careless by chance.

The basic concept behind "negligence" in civil law stems from a famous case of *Palsgraf vs. The Long Island Railroad*; it was held that a sequence of actions which could not be predicted by normal human

420

forethought put the result however, it came out, beyond the law of negligence. The ability to predict is, in other words, a root function in the concept of responsibility.

If all men are to be equal before the law . . . they must have equal rights, and duties — equal privileges, and responsibilities — equal freedoms, and limitations. And this can exist only when all the individuals have the same capabilities, for a man cannot be responsible where he is incapable, or have a duty where he has no ability; a blind man cannot be held responsible for not seeing a red light — and therefore cannot ask the privilege of driving a car.

A child, lacking the ability to predict, cannot see that a certain course of actions leads to disaster. Lacking the ability to predict, he cannot see that you do see the disaster ahead; he feels you are mistaken, don't understand what he means, are an old foggey, anything but that you see something that is a real and probable potential.

When an individual lacks an ability, you can't explain what it is he lacks in terms he can understand.

You can't explain what ethics is to a man born without the ethical sense. He thinks you're nuts, that you're a fool, timid, or stupid. Try and explain what "ethics" means to **Earl Korshak**, for instance! It means, he'll tell you, "the necessity of not getting caught."

Now a child knows it is possible that there is something real beyond the limits of its present understanding, because it knows it is a child. There are clues which it can perceive which distinguish it. It cannot distinguish between a wise adult and a silly adult, however; the clues of age, size, dress, etc., do not distinguish between a fool and a wise man. Policemen wear uniforms, so we teach a child that, if he is lost, he should ask a policeman for help. The uniform provides a clue by which he can distinguish a probably helpful adult.

Now some Negroes are wise, intelligent, ethical, fine human beings. Some are smart, intelligent, totally unethical, and vicious. This is true of all races; it is true of Negroes too. Some Negroes are sincere, intelligent, well-intentioned, kindly . . . and fools. Remember **A.J. Budrys'** story "The Executioner"? There was a good, kindly, sincere, honest man of unimpeachable integrity. But he was still a fool. He believed in segregation, and believed in it sincerely but falsely.

Now many Southerners are just like the Judge in that story; sincere, kindly, honest . . . and fools.

There are other Southerners who believe in segregation who are sincere, kindly, honest, and wise; they show the same final statement-action . . . but their reasons are different, and their intentions are different.

All the rays of light that reach a lens are brought to the same point in space — the focus. But they get there by different routes, and they're headed in different directions after they leave that point in space.

If you hold, "If a man holds the belief X, that shows he arrived at it by this kind of thinking, and plans to do thus," you're grossly in error. There are $\underline{n}$ ways of reaching any given conclusion, and, depending on the route that brought you there, $\underline{n}$ different places to go from there.

Jim, Tom, and Dick were all, on Oct. 12, 1957, in Sing Sing prison. One is a murderer; he will leave the prison tomorrow. One is a lawyer; he's going home tonight. The third is the warden; he won't leave the prison for several years yet.

Because two men hold the same idea . . . it doesn't mean that they think alike.

The Board of Education of Little Rock was doing a fine job; **Faubus** wanted political advantage, and knew exactly how to get it. **Faubus** created a situation which makes the fanatical segregationist and the intelligent southerner come to a focus; **Eisenhower** is in full agreement with **Faubus**, the fanatical segregationist, and the intelligent southerner on one point — only he is, as **Faubus** knew, inescapably stuck with acting exactly contrary to his sincere convictions! All four meet in a focus on one point: Armed force is not the way to achieve integration.

Faubus knew perfectly well that he could force **Ike** to act contrary to his own good judgment, contrary to good sense, and against the interests of the Nation; he forced **Ike** to intervene with armed force. **Ike** was compelled to by the law. **Faubus** has not suffered; he's gained. **Ike** has lost tremendously, the U.S. has lost tremendously, and the Republican party is finished.

Also, of course, the South has lost tremendously.

The reason is, of course, that the Supreme Court is, currently, stacked with a bunch of thick-headed legalistic crackpot idealists. They're learned legally, but fools humanically.

422

You can needle people into changing — but bludgeoning them usually produces highly undesirable results.

The South has every right to resent the stupid tactics of the Supreme Court — and the foolish, however sincere, NAACP.

Ike: try it this way. Colored people have no right whatever for advancement. Let's make the NAACP illegal, and start a new organization called the National Association for the Advancement of <u>Competent</u> People.

The NAACP as it is is advertising, flaunting, and screaming about the importance of skin-color as a clue to character.

The Board of Education in Little Rock was wiser; they'd hand-picked nine students <u>of high competence</u> as human beings . . . who, it happens, have brown skins. Those kids could have made their way on the basis of competence.

If the NAACP would stridently, loudly, and effectively <u>attack colored criminals</u>, they could, in a short while, build up a great deal of acceptance for themselves in the South.

The NAACP of course doesn't do that; they deny that colored people are criminals — they're always victims of rank injustice who must be defended.

A UN delegate was attacked and robbed and beaten in Central Park. Two New York papers said that his attackers were Negroes. The NAACP immediately howled at the indignity of accusing poor innocent Negroes of suspicion — just like Whites to do that! Only the UN delegate happened to be Negro himself, and it was his statement.

The NAACP will not acknowledge that there is any difference between Whites and Negroes. Under our hyderdemocracy, nobody must prove there is a difference. It happens that there is a difference, as anyone who's lived with them in numbers knows damn well — including the Negroes themselves, of course.

One of **Jane's** friends at Wellsley was a local Negro girl. Her mother is a doctor; her father's postmaster of her home town. She's a very pleasant girl; she has White and Colored friends. She does not go out with White boys; she doesn't attend White dances.

If integration is introduced in the south, the <u>average</u> southern Negro is going to be unable to handle the situation.

Dammit **Ike**, there IS a difference in heredity. The <u>lineage</u> of the

Negro peoples never earned the accomplishments that whites earned. It's an unarguable, simple, straight-forward <u>fact</u> that whereas the Egyptians started modern civilization in Africa — the civilization that modern Western culture descends from — the African natives <u>didn't accept and grow with it</u>.

The Amerindians, starting independently, <u>did</u> achieve high-order civilization on their own.

This isn't an arguable proposition; it's objective fact. You can see the great engineering works of the Incas in Peru, the immense buildings at Chichen Itza, Tenayuca, and Teothuacan. You can see the Pyramids and Sphinx in Egypt. The Chinese did it. The Europeans didn't originate that; the Cretans learned from Egypt, and the Greeks from the Cretans.

But the Negroes, living right next to Egypt <u>never did</u>.

The equatorial jungles didn't stop that process, either; the Mayans and the Incas both worked through jungles just as tropical.

<u>The Negro does not learn by example</u>.

That's not an anthropologist's theory, or a psychologist's complex. It's objective, sold fact. The Negro is exceedingly hard to teach. Exposed to Egypt for 6000 years, the Africans never built a nation. They <u>may</u> have built <u>one</u> city; at least there are the ruins of a city in the African jungles — but no one knows that Negroes built it.

The Negro has a 6000 year record of living next to growing civilization ... and not learning a damn thing.

If you want to solve a problem, you don't do it by denying the problem exists. Solve me this problem: Egypt has had civilization continuously for 6000 years. Negro peoples lap it to the south, southeast and southwest. The Negro peoples formed a civilization-proof barrier, so that none of the civilization leaked southward in all that immense span of time.

The phenomenal resistance to learning involved in that fact seems to me to suggest that the Negro peoples specifically selected in favor of individuals who would not and could not learn from foreign tribes. That <u>no</u> important cultural leakage occurred in so immense a span of time — 200 generations, allowing 30 years to a generation, 400 if we be more realistic in view of actual life spans in the jungle country — is positively fantastic. Look at the rate of cultural leakage from
424

Rome into the barbaric European areas!

There is a problem. The problem has never been properly formulated. Therefore it has never been solved. Applying force to an unnamed problem is like putting a bunch of biochemists into a big laboratory, and saying "Make a compound that will double human intelligence when it is swallowed or injected. Get going, and do it; you have one month. At the end of the month, we start shooting one of you each morning — one bullet, through the belly. We don't care how you do it. We don't know what intelligence is. But do it anyway."

The North denies there is a problem . . . and is increasingly segregating the Negroes themselves.

The only places I know of where Negroes have achieved a high level of cultural development are places where Negroes have been hybridized heavily with other races, and the hybrids heavily selected for cooperative characteristics. Brazil is one instance. Bermuda's another.

Don't deny the problem, **Ike**; examine it. Don't hold that every southerner is a fanatical fool; they can't all be as stupid as that implies. Don't fall for hyperdemocracy . . . when there is a real reason for differentiating.

And recognize that the basic goal of the NAACP, as stated in their official name, is inherently wrong. Colored people have no right whatever for advancement; the color of skin does not serve as a proper way of determining who should be advanced and who should be rejected. But . . . that's what they're working on, isn't it?

How shall we test people? How shall we determine what burden of responsibility, obligation, duty, and limitation can fairly be imposed? And should anyone ever have rights, privileges, prerogatives and freedoms without the other half of the picture?

Could a doctor function effectively if he were not granted special privilege? On the simple matter of the right to examine a woman's body, for instance — they tried denying the doctor that special invasion of privacy privilege, and found it didn't work.

Try denying a teacher the right to judge his pupils' work.

In the old days, a man who could read and write had the privilege of committing three murders without being challenged by the law. It was presumed that a man of that caliber did not act thoughtlessly or

425

without sound judgment.

There's a problem, **Ike**. It needs definition, not rejection.

Let's see you tell your positronic robot what a human being _is_. Are the Geewizardable human? The 90% will vote them out of the race, won't they? If the Geewizardable are human, then are the non-gee's human?

Should the law apply equally to all men? Should it allow a genius to get away with action no more responsible than that of an ordinary man?

Let's go beyond Law, and ask the fundamental question of Jurisprudence: What is Justice? Not Law, any more than mechanical engineering is Physics. What is Justice?

If human individuals can be not-equal-in-ability . . . can't human breeds be not-equal-in-ability?

Regards, John

Isaac Asimov   _October 20, 1957_

Dear Ike:

Well, I see I didn't get that proposition across clearly; you obviously don't see what I mean by "hyperdemocracy." Let's try again.

First: Improper segregation is to be distinguished from proper segregation.

Second: Segregation means nothing more nor less than "making a selection among different entities and setting them apart."

Item: You yourself are, I know, a strong believer in segregation. You practice it in your daily life, and strongly object at the suggestion that you be barred from practicing it. You yourself insist on "separate but equal" facilities. You hold, I know, that when it comes to bathroom facilities, men and women should be segregated.

Now, dammit **Ike**, I am not pulling a stupid, irrelevant, silly, nothing-to-do-with-the-question trick on you.

THAT POINT IS ABSOLUTELY THE BASIS OF THE PROBLEM!

Why? Because it illustrates the fundamental factors we must deal with in the real-world living problems we're trying to deal with.

Segregation means separating-and-setting-apart. It can be properly, or improperly applied. But segregation has a place in real living. In the
426

case of the male-female segregation I mention you find (feel, believe, hold, have an emotional conviction that) there is sound sense and good judgment in the separate-but-equal facilities.

If you hold that there is <u>any place for segregation whatever</u>, then you must be prepared to accept one of two dependent propositions: Each entity should be totally segregated. Or work out a formulation of how segregation should be used.

You cannot deny that you find there is a place for segregation. Then you cannot insist, "Well, now look here! That's <u>different!</u>" unless you specify in some general-law terms what that difference is.

If you say, "It has physiological basis," my friend, you walk yourself right smack into a trap. There is a demonstrable physiological difference between White and Negro, and I can demonstrate it with relatively simple photoelectric cell devices.

When a man can't solve a problem, the easiest way out is to deny that the problem exists. The problem does exist in this case, and I'm just mean enough to not let you deny its existence and slump back into a comfortable "it was just a bad dream; wasn't really there at all!" attitude.

Segregation is a real problem; you've been clobbered by it, I've been clobbered by it, and so has every other major science-fictioneer. We belong to the undesirable, rejected and segregated-out group of creative thinkers. Your current troubles at Boston University are the result of the fact that you won't accept that they have a real reason for wanting to segregate you out. One can't say of you that you, "hath a lean an hungry look," but you think too much . . . for their taste.

The tendency to deny the existence of a problem we don't have a solution for is Standard Operating Procedure. If denying it can't be made to work, then we make it somebody else's problem. "The Negro problem isn't <u>our</u> problem; it's the problem of those darned Southerners who won't do anything about it. We've got to make them."

Levittown, PA is not a southern town. South Africa is, of course, pretty far south. Chicago, Detroit, and Boston have all had intense White-Negro friction — and they aren't very far south.

The problem appears wherever Whites and Negroes begin to try to live closely together in statistically significant numbers. I should say, Whites and a random-selection group of Negroes.

427

The problem is, actually, a lot more general than that; whenever an A group and a B group exists, and the A group finds that the B group individuals are walling themselves off in segregated clusters, there will be inter-group friction. Thus in New York, during the period when the Italians established "little Italy" enclaves here and there, and maintained their own customs within the enclave-barrier, the

Italians were "wops" and cordially disliked.

In the US, the north-European groups never did much of a job of building enclave-walls, so Germans, Scandinavians, etc. were always fairly welcome.

In South America — particularly Argentina — the South Europeans did not form enclave-groups, and the North Europeans did. Result: German, English, Scandinavian, etc., colony-groups in Argentina that were definitely disliked. But no Italian or Spanish enclaves.

Any group that seeks to maintain its own tribal customs, and rejects amalgamation with the surrounding people, will be disliked. Any walled-off area, which cannot be entered and interacted with, is a danger signal — and human beings dislike it strongly.

Let's leave that aside, however.

The important point under discussion is this: You can not solve any problem by denying it exists. And you don't solve problems by fiat rulings, either.

The WCTU wanted to solve the problem of alcoholism. They admitted that it did exist (valid) and that it should not exist (also valid) and they had a solution: Prohibition.

The NAACP states that a problem exists, in that Negroes are not being accepted (valid) and that this situation should not exist (valid) and they have a solution: Prohibit its existence.

Now if you ask an alcoholic why he drinks, he can give you no logical reason. All the reasons he gives you are provably invalid. It can, on the other hand, be proved that, for steenteen different logical reasons, he should not drink. Therefore, obviously, he has no reason to drink. Since this is the case, we must make him realize this, and force him to stop drinking.

The difficulty is, of course, that there is a reason, and he does need alcohol. He just can't communicate to you or anyone else — or, for that matter, even to himself — what that reason is. The reason is, usually,

428

one that is culturally unacceptable, so that, if stated, it would be rejected anyway. Suppose, for instance, his reason is that he wants to destroy himself socially and economically so thoroughly he becomes valueless to anyone else. Obviously a socially unacceptable reason for drinking. But you see, he is being hounded by a blackmailer; if he's totally valueless to himself or anyone else, the blackmailer won't bother him. Try presenting that problem to the anti-alcohol forces of the WCTU, though.

Let us consider that you encounter a brilliant, charming, highly intelligent, competent and good looking psychopath. He can meet every objective test you can name and communicate to him . . . but you can't communicate to him the reality of tests of empathy. Empathy he hasn't got. Further, you can't teach him what it is.

We can, today, teach someone born color-blind what color means; we can do it with photoelectric cells and graphs and spectrums. We can teach him in terms of physical-objective instruments, so that he can see that there are differences which exist, but which he cannot perceive. If he is, in consequence, rejected as a dye chemist, despite the fact that his knowledge of chemistry is faultless, he can understand that he lacks something necessary for the work.

But there are no dependable, objective-instrument tests for empathic sensitivity. So you can't demonstrate to the psychopath that he is deficient in a manner important in human relationships.

So suppose you tell him that you can't tolerate people who have index fingers longer than their middle finger. He has his index finger shortened.

So you tell him you can't tolerate people with wavy hair.

He has his hair straightened.

There is no way to communicate the real reason for your rejection of him.

The only reasons you can communicate are false reasons.

When he satisfies the false reasons, you still reject him, which proves that you have no reason, but are simply prejudiced.

Now let's see you wriggle out of that spot!

Ike: The Southern Whites have an unreasoned prejudice against Negroes. OK; Now tell me how this "unreasoned" — i.e. "causeless" — effect came into existence? I demand that, if you claim the effect is causeless, you explain how this effect-without-a-cause came into existence in a Universe characterized by cause-effect lawfulness.

Dammital, **Ike**, there is a cause. It's a reason that can't be expressed, can't be proven, within the known and accepted techniques. The problem can't be solved by fiat. Pressure is needed; yes. Fiat . . . never worked.

I want to SOLVE the problem.

The question of interbreeding is another one you're somewhat deliberately obfuscating. The male is not a simple mirror image of the female; parity doesn't apply. The number of individuals in the next generation is determined by the number of females — not by the number of males. The female is like a transmitter; the male is simply the keying switch. The female is the only one who can project the life-message into future time; males can only provide messages to be projected.

To assure the continuity of the race, a statistically large number of life-messages must be transmitted. To assure the evolution of the race, the best of the available messages should be transmitted in the largest number.

The Race is an entity of a sort, but it's blind, stupid, and utterly unconcerned with individuals. It provides instincts to shape individuals in a manner that benefit it most. Instincts are for the benefit of the race; to the race, the individual is a necessary means to its Ends.

For some dozens of millennia, the human race has had a pattern that animal breeders now recognize; one good bull can breed up a whole herd of scrub cattle.

Some while back, human beings evolved the instinct of warmaking. The males of group A fought the males of group B, killed them if they could, and captured the females of B, and bred on them. Hard on individuals; it had a statistical effect tending to help the race.

I don't care how many times it produced a wrong effect. Sure it did. But something that yields a statistical gain of only 0.1% per cycle will, if run through enough cycles, yield effectively pure ^{235}U. Even if there's a real net advantage in the warring groups only once in a thousand times . . . the race doesn't mind; it comes out ahead in the long run.

The instinct to take the females of the inferior group and breed on them is very ancient. And the instinct, of course, defines "inferior" very simply; if you can do it, it's right.

Now let's get something straight: I do not say that, if a three-year-old baby pulls a pan of water boiling on the stove down onto himself that he should be scalded, or that "he deserves to be scalded." I say he will be scalded.

Equally, I do not say that men should do, or should have done as I described above. I say they did. And that anyone who holds that that didn't have effect on the nature of Man is, likewise, a foggy-headed fool.

Men have no conscious understanding of the laws of genetics at an emotional level; a few top-rank geneticists, like **Muller**, maybe, have worked intellectual genetics down to an emotional-reaction level. But damned few.

However, all men have three billion years of genetics built in, and that does reach up to the emotional level.

To say otherwise is to deny the obvious. Genetics effects emotions. Emotions are conditioned by genetic factors which concern genetic factors.

The male of the conquerors breeds on the females of the conquered. That instinct happens to run back about a billion years.

Please, **Ike**, will you take that factor into consideration when you say that White's don't really think Negroes are inferior because the Whites bred on the Negro females? A billion years or so of instinct says that proves that Negroes are inferior.

I agree with you that "we ought to outgrow primitive instincts" only in a very limited degree; got any substitute for the instinct to produce metabolic regulating hormones, enzymes, etc.?

We can't give up an instinct that works to some useful extent, until we have a substitute that works at least as well, with no greater cost.

You can't solve the Negro-White problem by fiat, **Ike**.

What suggestions do you have that aren't fiat-solution propositions? There is no problem of false segregation — which we all want to terminate — when there is no segregation. But there is, then, false non-segregation. A denial of right to difference of achievement.

The solution of the problem does not lie in the direction of no-segregation — and the problem I was throwing at you in the Geewizard Machine was what to do about a segregation that made itself apparent. A situation in which the reality of segregation is so obtrusive that the "There should be no segregation" proposition can't be considered.

What is the solution to the problem of differentiation that neither imposes false segregation, nor false non-segregation?

And don't tell me you don't believe in segregation, **Ike**, or by God

431

I'll insist you start a campaign to end the "separate but equal facilities" in toilets in public buildings.

Regards, John

Isaac Asimov   *October 26, 1957*

Dear Ike:

The difficulty with this segregation discussion is that there are two sub-problems:

1. The discussion involves several levels of reality, each of the levels having its own different sets of laws.

2. Like everyone else, you've been the victim of improper segregation-distinction-discrimination, and therefore are deeply suspicious of any segregation-discrimination.

The first sub-problem there makes it possible for you to claim my arguments are contradictory and self-denying.

By different levels of reality, I mean this sort of thing . . . and I have to use analogy, because only analogical reasoning can relate different levels. There are laws applicable to the organization of atoms in molecules. There are, also, laws relative to the organization of nuclear particles into atoms. The laws are not the same, though there are certain analogical relationships.

The laws of hydrodynamics have many analogies to the laws of electric current flow . . . but they're not the same. I may say, "The current different levels. There are laws applicable to the organization of atoms in molecules. There are, also, laws relative to the organization of nuclear particles into atoms. The laws are not the same, though there are certain analogical relationships.

The laws of hydrodynamics have many analogies to the laws of electric current flow . . . but they're not the same. I may say, "The current cannot pass through the metal, and goes . . ." at one point, and, at another, "The current passed down through the metal to . . ." which proves I'm completely confused and don't know what I'm talking about.

Only one is true of a fluid current, while the other applies to an electronic current.

Finally, in radio frequency engineering, it's necessary to discuss the electromagnetic energy flow, instead of the electron flow. A radio

432

frequency current will <u>not</u> flow <u>through</u> a piece of metal. You can have a powerful electromagnetic current flowing inside a pipe, and have no energy penetrate the metal to appear outside.

The result <u>looks</u> inconsistent as hell . . . but it isn't.

Now: There is one level of reality, The Past. The Past has the characteristic of being immutable, singular, and True. It is not, therefore, open to evaluation; you have no choice whatever as to what was-in-fact, and the terms "good" or "bad" have no applicability, since whatever was, was exactly, solely, and completely what it was. We do not have any way of getting absolute certainty of knowledge as to what it was — but it absolutely certainly was whatsoever it was. I.e., the autocorrelation of a past even to itself is 1.000000000 . . . .

What was is immutable. What <u>Is</u> is also immutable. Only what-will-be is open to influence. What Should Be is a plan, or map, of a desired future. What Should Have Been is actually an imaginary, since it imposes a mutation on the inherently immutable Past, and is useful only with respect to a future state; you can learn by considering what Should Have Been, and the <u>learning</u> then has reality in the future.

You've also got me quite badly misplaced, my friend. I said that the white race is superior. It <u>is</u>. I do not say that it <u>will be</u>. I say it earned that superiority in the past; it did. The superiority will not remain because the race is White — but only on the condition that the race <u>continues to earn</u> superiority.

The dinosaurs were, indeed, superior. They earned it. But superiority is a relative thing, not an absolute; it results when entity A attains an absolute level of achievement superior in <u>absolute</u> degree to the achievement of entity B. However, if B achieves that same absolute level, and A achieves nothing more, B becomes the equal of A. If B now achieves a higher absolute level, then B is, of course, superior to A.

Notice that this does NOT imply that A has, in any absolute sense, degenerated, weakened, or become less competent than it was. Its new inferiority comes not from degeneration or decay, but from stasis, while B advanced.

A Model A Ford, 1930 type, was a damn good, reliable, functional car. The same unit, produced today, would be precisely as good, reliable and functional. It was, as of 1930, a better car than the Chevrolet.

But the Chevrolet (1957 version) is incomparably superior to the Ford

433

. . . if by "Ford" we mean a static, 1930 Model A.

I do not, have not, and never will say that the White race is inherently, innately, or automatically superior to any other.

I say that, to date, it's ahead. And that it isn't going to stay there just by being-what-it-is, either. No matter how good you are, just stay that good long enough, and you'll be low man on the totem pole. Why the hell do you think I keep needling you and the other guys? So you'll not only retain what you have, but grow beyond it. And, of course, be able to needle me so I'll be able to find a new way of growing.

Now; the Past is-what-it-is. Part of the Past is that the White race, alone of human breeds, put itself through a 200 years stint of chattel slavery. Part of the Past is that the people around the Mediterranean basin hacked at each other for 6000 years; the continuous warfare served to perfect the interpersonal relations system within cultures on a trial-and-error basis.

Now it is a simple fact that, in engineering, "It works" is both necessary and sufficient. That trial-and-error does work.

But Science involves the use of a higher level method; your "Hemoglobin And The Universe" brought out the limitations of the trial-and-error, rule-of-thumb method.

But don't be stupid, and say that trial-and-error never works, simply because it won't always work.

My objection to the trial-by-ordeal method of settling matters is that it's exceedingly, and excessively inefficient. Statistically, on the 100,000,000-man and 100,000,000 year basis, it has a good probability of leading to a valid result. But it's damn costly in time and men.

Also, the trial-and-error method will not work when opposed by a superior technique — because the entity using the superior technique will devour the potentials that the trial-and-error method needs to make its tries and errors with.

Willy Ley pointed out that one of the absolute must conditions for life to originate on a planet is that there be no life forms on that planet. Life may have originated in the oceans, when they were a soup of accidentally formed organic complexes; that can't happen on a planet that already has life, because the living forms will use up the potential starting material long before it achieves the necessary level of complexity.

So: when I say that at a certain time in the Past, method X worked,

434

that does not imply that I think method X "should be used." Saying it <u>was</u> used is not equivalent to saying <u>it should be</u> used. Even saying, "Method X was used, and produced the following beneficial results: —" doesn't mean that method X is the best method <u>now</u> definable.

Amputation of the limb above the affected joint was standard surgical practice up to a century or so ago; it had the beneficial result that nearly all individuals with wounds that penetrated the joint capsule died unless the limb was amputated above the joint. As of 1800 or so, this was the best possible surgical method. As of 1900, the best possible treatment for gangrenous limb was amputation. As of 1900, the best possible treatment for diabetes was a starvation diet.

Note this: Those statements are valid, and hold that it was right and wise of the medical man to apply those treatments, and that they were beneficial treatments. But, dammit **Ike**, that doesn't mean I recommend those treatments now.

Ike, the basic characteristic of life is that <u>it is selective</u>. It segregates. It practices discrimination. It selects and rejects. The highest forms of life are more selective than the lower.

Now that statement gets into a logical mishmash, because of the fact that logic is linear, and the statement is valid only when interpreted in a multidimensional manner. Taken logically, "more selective" would mean "more specialized." Some species have tried that answer, and aren't with us any more.

The correct interpretation is "able to select more useful fractions from the Universe."

A crude still can select low-boiling and high-boiling components from a mixture. A more complex still can select perhaps 100 different components. A catalytic cracking still can do better; it can select from the input components that weren't even there to start with. The ultra-selective still is <u>more</u> selective, and <u>less</u> specialized!

In a radio receiver, as sensitivity is increased, selectivity <u>has</u> to be increased. My Hammarlund Super-pro receiver can sense signals of as little as 20 watts on the other side of the planet. You can't possibly use that kind of sensitivity unless you also have such selectivity that you can reject the signals from all over the planet. I can pick up WLW on 700 kc in Cincinnati, and reject WOR on 710 kc, with a transmitter of 50,000 watts only 5 miles away. Man, that set is really a segregationist!

435

Ike, you can NOT get people to give up discrimination, segregation, etc., for the very excellent reason that it is absolutely necessary to living. You are a segregationist, dammit, whether you realize it or not; you discriminate between sense and nonsense to the best of your ability, and will squawk like hell if someone tries to make you accept that sense and nonsense aren't really different.

The effort to make someone give up discrimination is inherently hopeless. Anyone who thinks otherwise is a damn fool, and will inevitably be disappointed in life. It never has been done. It never will be done. And, moreover, it never should be done.

Give over! Give up on the deal! It's wrong to begin with, and impossible of achievement anyway.

There is segregation. There will be segregation, now, and forever more. There will be more, not less, in the future.

The essence of Science is segregating sense and nonsense, of separating cause and effect, of discriminating between x and y and learning to interact them separately.

The essence of life is selection, discrimination, and segregation.

What's the job of the kidney? Of the digestive system?

Give up the false trail, come back to the starting point, and try a different route. You can not and should not end segregation. Every aspect of life and scientific research proves the crucial and beneficial importance of segregation and discrimination and differentiation. If you have as an ideal that of ending segregation and discrimination . . . quit it. You can't achieve it, because it doesn't belong in the universe. If you believe in what you're preaching — then pass every student with the same mark, and stop discriminating against some of your students.

If you fight the wrong problem, **Ike**, you'll work hard, get hurt, hurt others, and achieve nothing of value.

Now try writing a letter to me on this theme: The problem is to find the correct basis for discrimination and segregation.

Regards, John

Isaac Asimov   *October 30, 1957*

Dear Ike:

I think your point about the English teacher and the unfairness of

436

your writing does, indeed, fit as a piece of the pattern of resentment of the Geewizard machine situation. I mentioned your "unfair" ability to learn the multiplication tables by eidetic recall (I consider that unfair; when I think of the slugging work I had to do, and didn't get it right even so. . . .)

Many, many times the "unfair" tactic is the use of a method by A, that B didn't think of. It's unfair only because "that isn't what I meant!," not because there's anything innately wrong about it.

Let me show you an example:

In the current *Scientific American*, there's a puzzle problem that goes like this. "This incredible problem — incredible because it seems impossible that it could be solved with only the data given — appeared in . . . ; A hole six inches long is drilled through a plastic sphere, passing exactly through the center. What is the volume of the remaining plastic?

Now the intent of the puzzle-asker is that the victim solve the puzzle by complex geometric-logical-mathematical argument.

I solved the problem in about 30 seconds . . . by an unfair tactic. BUT . . . the tactic is strictly and accurately logical. It's just that the puzzler didn't <u>intend</u> that it be used, and hence feels cheated if the perfectly valid argument is used.

It's this way; in addition to the apparent data, there is one critically important datum; "the problem can be solved with the data given." Then, obviously, the answer is, "the volume is equal to that of a sphere six inches in diameter."

I DO NOT have to prove that geometrically; I can prove it is the necessary logical consequence of the statement that the problem can be solved with the limited data.

At first blush, it appears as though the volume of the hole would be necessary to determine the remaining volume. If this were so, the lack of that datum would render the problem insoluble. If the problem is, as stated, soluble without it, this must imply that the volume of the hole, and hence its radius, is of no significance. Evidently some set of factors comes into operation which cancels out the effects one would expect to result from varying the hole size. So I don't need to compute the radius, or try to. I can give the radius of the hole any arbitrary value I choose. I'll make it zero. Then the length of the hole is the diameter of the plastic sphere, no volume is lost from the sphere, and the volume wanted is that of a six-inch-diameter sphere.

I DO NOT have to show why the size of the hole makes no difference. The problem statement furnishes the data that it does make no difference.

Then I have "unfairly" solved the problem by using an unexpected technique. My questioner will be damn well annoyed, too; presumably he had to sweat out the complex reasoning to arrive at the fact that the diameter of the hole made no difference, and he wanted me to do the same. I cheated; I learned from his effort, and avoided the necessity.

This is rather similar to installment buying. A man buys a truck, on installments. This means he has the truck before he's earned it. He then uses the truck to increase his earning power to a point such that he can earn the truck, and pays off the installments. Result: he now owns a truck which he didn't earn, because the truck earned it!

This mechanism applies to a great class of problems . . . and isn't accepted in logical analysis, because it entails a non-logical process that's hidden neatly at the root of the real scientific method.

"If I just had the answer to this problem, I'd know how to work out the answer in a minute."

"If I just had a machine plane, I'd be able to make the flat, smooth steel bed-plate necessary for a steel plane. But without a machine plane, I can't make the bed-plate necessary to make a machine plane."

The unfair tactic high-power thinkers use is to assume they have the answer correctly, and then derive the method of achieving the answer by using the answer!

This is logically indefensible.

Actually, however, this is the real fundamental of the scientific method! Trial and error can't solve all problems, simply by reason of the infinity of trials necessary. Logic can't solve all problems, because it's deductive, not postulate-generating. But the validity of an arbitrary postulate cannot be checked logically; all logical deductions from the postulate will be logically valid.

However, arbitrary postulation, plus logical deduction, plus trial and error . . . now known as "making a crucial experiment" . . . will determine the validity of the postulate.

Now note this gimmick: in the puzzle-problem, the "Given: —" constitutes "the word of Authority." By using it, a lot of hard work can be by-passed. This illustrates a fundamental value in acceptance of
438

Authority. Properly, the Scientific Method should include that mechanism . . . but only to allow the Crucial Experiment.

Ike, you do indeed represent an "unfair" situation. What can that English teacher do about it?

Should there be equal reward for equal effort? The Universe doesn't work that way, however; it gives greater reward for greater efficiency, so that an entity that exerts 10 units of work at 80% efficiency is rewarded far more than an entity that exerts 50 units of work at 5% efficiency. So A gets a reward of 8 units for his 10 units of effort, while B is "unfairly" rewarded with only 2.5 units for his five-times-greater effort. Is this fair?

Part of what your English Teacher was reacting to is this: If you were calculating the weight of an average man on the surface of Venus, you'ld use a slip-stick. If you're calculating the weight of a kilogram mass on Earth's North Pole, you'ld probably want to use a computer, or work it long-hand to several decimal places. There's no point using a ten-place accuracy method on two-place accuracy data. You don't use drafting equipment for drawing a preliminary sketch of something — you do it freehand.

The English Literateur studies the written material as an object in itself; what it is, rather than what it's for. The freehand sketch and the finished draftsman's job is, therefore, evaluated in the same terms, on the same scale; they're both drawings, aren't they?

Misapplied precision can cause a lot of trouble, by lowering efficiency. And I can only add one item of interest: Try naming first-line authors who were formally educated in English, Grammar, or English Literature as major college studies. Journalism, too, for that matter! I can't say why, but I can make a statistical correlation; formal education in those subjects shows low correlation with effective creative writing!

Item: The latest Nobel Medalist in medicine is not an M.D.; he's merely responsible for the sulfa drugs, curare-type compounds, and half a dozen other things. I note with deep interest, too, that he and his wife form a man-woman research team. So women think just like men, huh?

Regards, John

Isaac Asimov   *November 5, 1957*

Dear Ike:

You're fun to argue with too ... but sometimes I think you're a true Egghead. An egg, you know is an object with a hard, inflexible shell, and all soft and gooey inside.

Isaac, have you ever stopped to listen to a Southerner of the immoderate and obnoxious type? I know you know they exist, and are obnoxious; do you, therefore, decide listening to them is unnecessary, and so not learn what their arguments are? I think you do, **Isaac** — because, my friend, you are stating, as your ideal, precisely, word for word, what the more obnoxious and immoderate "anti-Nigger" Southerner states as his. The right to choose his own friends. The right to choose who he associates with. The right to be able to go into a restaurant and not be forced to associate with a Nigger — to go to a movie house and not be forced to sit next to one of them damn Nigguhs. The right to be able to choose, personally, who his children will associate with, and not have some No'th'n damn Co't tell him who his kids are going to have to associate with.

Play it over slow and easy, **Ike,** and see where your stated ideal comes out ... in practice, instead of in theory.

You're asking for the right to cultural anarchy; **Dan'l Boone** didn't like associating with people, and could make it stick. There was room enough, then.

The Southerner is asking, in practice, what you are holding as a theoretical ideal — the right to personal choice of his associates in restaurants, schools, trains, movies, and at work.

Then your statement means that you agree in full with the principle which motivates the Southern segregationist -- the right to personal choice of associates. You are saying, in effective resultant, "When it comes to selecting and rejecting associates, the answer to the question 'On what basis shall we select,' should be 'On my personal, private likes and dislikes.'"

In a culture wherein a major part of living must be in the public sphere, the basis of segregation can no longer be the one you hold as an ideal -- personal, individual choice.

Don't throw the **Al Capone-Ralph Bunche** contrast at me; I have at no point suggested that skin-color was an appropriate basis for segregation.

440

Look, guy; there are two kinds of exact statements used in science. What is the atomic weight of chlorine? 35.5 did very well by chemists, and still does; the statistical figure is exact, reliable, and useful. But we both know that there is no such thing as a chlorine with a mass-number of 35.5.

But chemical engineering <u>must</u> use the statistical-datum figure; it's a true datum. They can NOT get right answers with either 34 or 36.

Therefore, we can agree that while no atom of 35.5 mass exists, there is an engineering need to work with that figure.

A machinest talks about the properties of "brass"; there is no such substance. A metallurgist talks about copper-zinc crystalization patterns . . . but he's engaged in improving a product sold as "brass."

Statistical-datum laws exist, and are used in science.

Natural, or exact, Laws also exist, and are used in science.

In engineering, <u>only statistical laws</u> can be used.

A politician knows he deals with an engineering problem . . . and it works statistically, until such time as someone figures out a way to find a natural law, and by that means separate the entities involved.

You can give an accurate statement of the radioactive energy emitted from one gram of "uranium." Later, as techniques improve, you can say that a gram of natural uranium contains 1 atom of ^{235}U in 140 of the mixture, and recalculate on the basis of ^{235}U & ^{238}U. If your calculations are correct, you'll get the same answer you got in the first place. Only now you know a lot more of the "why" of that original answer.

Know how they make "drill-proof" steel? It'll stop any kind of drill there is -- carbide-tipped, diamond, anything. It's simple; you make up a batch of a good grade of carbon steel, and just before you run it into the molds, you shovel in some chrome-molybdenum alloy, then pour. The result is a mild steel, with randomly distributed chunks of wildly varying hardness. Trying to drill it just makes the drill follow the line of easiest penetration, which wanders around like the path of a ball in a pin-ball machine. Drills, however, don't work well around corners. Very shortly you have a shallow drill-hole plugged thoroughly with a broken drill bit.

This material not only can't be drilled, it can't be sawed, rolled, or anything else with reasonable success; grinding works in a crude sort of way, but not very well.

Sociologically, a population like we have in the south is a drill-proof steel set-up. It's got lumps in it. It has randomly twisted pin-ball type

441

lines of effective isopotential. The center of any one lump is, of course, quite homogenous; it's the interface that has unpredictable characteristics and contours.

If you could apply enough force, with hard enough rolls, you could roll the stuff sort of . . . but you would still have randomly distributed knots, lumps, and nodules.

Now a pinball situation is one that a pin-ball can handle perfectly; it, acting as an individual, can bounce and turn and change direction with agility, fervor and zeal. An individual can find its own individual course through such an obstacle situation with ease and satisfaction.

It's only when an organized system — a drill, say — tries to find a single path through the maze that trouble starts.

The Southerner (and **Ike Asimov**) know it's perfectly simple — just let everyone choose his own friends and associates freely. The Southerner, having had some practical living experience with the problem, also knows that that means establishing segregated places.

Look, **Ike**, what would be wrong with setting up a situation that did allow what you propose: one school for Negroes-only; one for Whites-only, and one for both. Then each type could choose the type of association-environment he wanted, couldn't he?

What's wrong with that?

Simple! That means that there is one place where the Negroes can't go — and that's what drives them frantic. It's NOT that there is one place to go . . . but that there is a place not to go. If some southern town set up a brand-new palatial type school for Negroes only, and had a small, 50-year-old all-White school . . . what would the NAACP do?

Why not the integrated school plus the other two? Easy: those who genuinely accept integration don't need an integrated school; they can get all the integrated association they want, of course.

I'd love to get you and one of the more sincerely-bigoted and honest, genuinely good-hearted southerners going in the same room. The fireworks would be wonderful — and all the more so, since you'ld both be fighting for exactly the same fundamental principle; the right to choose your associates freely.

Now on the math business.

Ike, Science IS a Sacred Cow these days. There are too damn many people who want Science for Science's Sake.
442

Science is a tool; it's a powerful tool, but Science itself is absolutely useless. It can't solve any problems whatever. It's like a power-shovel — a very powerful tool, but it'll just sit there 'til it rusts away, accomplishing nothing, <u>unless somebody uses</u> the tool.

The purpose of tools is <u>not</u> to build more tools, either. Any more than <u>the</u> purpose of a human being is to breed more human beings. It's <u>a</u> purpose, and not to be neglected . . . but not <u>the</u> purpose.

The way to make progress is to fence off an area, study it, get it mapped . . . and then find a hole in the fence so you can go on to the next area.

Now I am quite aware of discontinuous <u>functions</u>. But the gimmick I threw your way was a <u>continuous</u> function. That $1/(1 - x)$ is a perfectly continuous function — a simple straight-line function. It isn't an hyperbola, parabola, tangent function, or anything of the sort. It doesn't go asymptotic or anything of the like.

Its one slight peculiarity is that the <u>function</u> is continuous, but the <u>validity</u> isn't. You can cite a lot of discontinuous functions; sure. You can cite functions with isolated points, too.

But . . . the thing I'm proposing is a realization that a function can be mathematically continuous, and yet have (1) a validity-discontinuity, with (2) an isolated point of validity. That $1/(1 - x)$ has a value that looks perfectly normal and decent for $x = -1$ . . . only that value of x is <u>not</u> valid, in view of the derivation, which involved division through by $(1 + x)$.

Sorry; correction. $1/(1 - x)$ does misbehave at x equals 1. Take the function $y = x - 1$, then. That's a nice, simple, linear. But if it's derived from $(x^2 - 1)/(x + 1)$ by dividing through by $x + 1$ . . . then it is not a valid derivation of the original function for $x = -1$.

<u>I'm</u> not being mystical about mathematics, dammit, **Ike**; <u>science</u> is! <u>I'm</u> trying to knock some of the mystical reliance on "mathematically proven" out of some of the cock-eyed science-worship I encounter.

I was talking to an IBM researcher this noon; we had a lovely time. He was fascinated by the idea of "one valued logic" . . . and even more fascinated when I pointed out that electronic circuitry design conceptions are based on the same one-valued logic philosophy a Bushman uses! They haven't yet gotten to two-valued logic!

Actually, two-valued logic is something we ourselves use only in a

443

most limited way. What we call two-valued logic is, usually, a one-valued logic.

A one-valued logic is a logic in which only positive statements can be made, and every statement must imply negation of all other possibilities. "This is mine" must imply "it is not yours, or his, or hers, or its, or ours, or theirs." Implication of negation is necessary, because there is no statement of negation.

Now such a logic requires a continuous universe. That is, if X is not mine, not yours, not ours, theirs, his, hers, or its . . . then it isn't. It does not exist.

You think that form of logic isn't being used in America today? Hah! And you a science-fictioneer. "Duh . . . but tha's impossible. Nobody's ever done that!" I.e., I can't, you can't, he can't, we can't, they can't, and therefore possibility of doing it doesn't exist.

In a true two-valued logic, there is the possibility of negative statement — and this generates a third situation. It is not mine. It is not yours. But it does exist, although it belongs to no one. The new concept is the concept of non-related existence.

It makes possible three situations: "1", which can be interpreted "the class is full," as in binary notation; "0" which can be interpreted "the class exists, but is empty." Thus 101 in binary denotes "the 2^3 class is full; the 2^2 class is empty, and the 2 class is full." The zero is the negative statement "no 2^2." Drop out that possibility, and the statement collapses to 11 . . . which isn't the intended statement.

But true two-valued logic includes an additional concept -- call it "barrier." If 0 denotes "the class exists, but is empty," let's use * to denote the "existence of the class is forbidden." Thus the class of four-sided plane triangles is not 0 — it's *. It's not an empty class — it's a forbidden or to use the term **Peg** and I have been using, a nulldicted class.

Notice though, that this concept, allows of a concept of a barrier-to-barrier-condition. When you specify a nulldicted class, it implies a dual limitation. Thus while the four-sided triangle class is *; the * applies only at and above the level 4 — it doesn't impose * on the 3-level.

Nuclei of mass-number 5 are, evidently *; this is, however, a doubly-bounded nulldiction; neither 4 nor 6 is within the boundaries of the *-class.

The corresponding statement-forms are, "I have information,"
444

"I do not have information," and "Information does not exist." The first is 1, the second is 0, and the third is*. The tendency is to so confuse 0 and * as to wind up with, "If I have no information, information does not exist." Or, "If it isn't true for me, then it is not true."

Tom Scortia just called from St. Louis, quite excited, and a bit upset. Items: Sputnik #1 went up August 4, 1957, circled Earth about 2 times, and burned out over the Mediterranean. Sputnik #2 (the first announced) went up October 4. Sputnik #3 (sometimes called Muttnik) was followed immediately by Lunar #1. My own hunch was that there would be a lovely nuclear warhead explosion right smack in the center of the full moon on November 7. If I was a Russian rockets team, by God I'd smack one right where half the world could see it, particularly when the Moon was so propitiously full on the seventh of November!

You probably saw the item about UFO's in the midwest on Monday. Monday evening two UFO's showed up over White Sands . . . a point which is rather more than usually equipped with radar and optical tracking devices.

"Hey, Ma! We got visitors acomin' in!"

Otherwise . . . maybe the rumor I've gotten from four separate chains of information (I've checked as well as possible to see that I didn't hear from E, F, and G, all of whom got it from A) has some truth in it. I got it with details; science has been working out the engineering implications and applications of electromagnets . . . and neglecting the possibilities of electrostatics. Electromagnetic phenomena are dynamic, and fine for dynamic jobs . . . but electrostatics are appropriate for static jobs . . . like negating gravity. Gravity's a static field, not a dynamic force. So it seems somebody did start looking into what happens with trick applications of electrostatics . . . and he has an interesting flying condenser.

Corona discharge from such a gimmick might make it sort of spectacular at night, of course — be quite a glow about it.

Yipe! News just in added another item I had not realized. There's a total eclipse of the Moon due November 7.

The Gods are favoring Russia this year! What an irresistible display!

Russia's claiming a real breakthrough of some kind on the "power-sources and instruments" on Sputnik #2" (official count . . . Muttnik unofficially). Wonder if they sent the dog up with telemetering to see whether their shielding of a nuclear rocket was sufficient to protect a living passenger?

On the other hand ... they said a lot about Sputnik weighing 84 pounds, and everybody knows the rocket-carrier, also in orbit up there, is much bigger than Sputnik itself. Yet at no time have the Russians hinted at the mass of the rocket carrier, which they obviously put into orbit too!

S'pose Sputnik #1 was put up with a 1200 pound rocket? It'd still be perfectly true that Sputnik weighed 184 pounds. And the shock of getting any satellite 7 times heavier than Vanguard planned to double its effect. If Muttnik had been announced as "simply" a repeat performance, the impact wouldn't have been anywhere near as great as the proposition that their second one was some 8 times bigger than the first.

It might be the same size. . . .

Incidentally, I have an extremely intense gripe, which I plan to voice as effectively as I can. Our government knew the Russians had an ICBM at the time Russia announced it.

And they deliberately deceived us — our own citizens — with a strong implication that they did not believe the Russian claim. Our government is certainly, and inarguably, guilty of either (1) gross incompetence in not getting information as to the magnitude of the Russian rocketry advances, or (2) gross deceit in concealing from us the facts they had. Inasmuch as the Government has stated they have radar accurate and reliable at 1500 mile ranges (and it actually works to 3000 miles) and we have radar bases all around Russia, there is no way Russia could test a 5000 mile missile without US-operated radar tracking it.

That they did not reveal what they knew at that time is explainable; that they denied the validity of the claim when Russia announced their achievement is inexcusable.

Regards, John

Isaac Asimov   *November 8,*
1957

Dear Ike:

OK — Sobeit. If you don't feel that article on "Computers: Do
446

They Really Exist?" I'll pass it along. Incidentally, I think the next best man for the job is our friend **Randall Garrett**. He did do a nice piece on that "Gentlemen: Please Note" idea.

But it does seem to me that a guy who's on the mailing list of all the computer boys, and has been asked to review their math, etc., but has never even seen one . . . is in exactly the position I suggested.

Wayne Batteau couldn't do the article; he hasn't the necessary pixilated sense of logical insanity. And he knows too much about computers.

There is such a thing as knowing too much about your subject, you know. You'd have too many emotional-reality ties to be able to do a really good job of that sort on "Proteins: Do They Really Exist?," for instance. (On the basis that the damn things denature so fast that you can't prove they were there in the first place.)

To do the piece, what's really needed is a little research into the articles decrying the reality of psi phenomena; all the arguments against the reality of X, whether psi or computers or **Hoxsey's** Cancer Cure, or **Galileo's** idea — they're all the same.

Really, you have the wrong approach, **Ike**. The essence of writing such a piece is not knowing what you're talking about; that's how it differs from thiotimoline, and The Goose. Not knowing about it, and very explicitly not wanting to know about it.

Heard **Eisenhower's** speech last night. I'm starting to work right now, and I think I've got a line of action that may be useful. **Killian** was president of MIT during the time **John Arnold's** course in Creative Engineering was quashed, forcing **John** to move to California. I do not want **Killian** as head of the program of creative engineering for the United States' defense, thank you. He is a respected scientist, an able administrator . . . and he let **John Arnold's** Creative Engineering course be squashed, because it annoyed the orthodox, conservative scientists of MIT.

Listening to **Eisenhower** tell about all the devastating rocket missiles we had on hand, I couldn't help thinking that if we, with our half-ass, defective program that hasn't put even a little satellite up have all that . . . wonder what Russia, with a working space-flight program, must have!

But you know, I'm just mystic enough these days, to have a deep hunch that Russia has lost the favor of the Gods; they didn't fire that

447

Moon rocket. The Gods gave them the stage; it was <u>their</u> night — November 7. The Moon was darkened for them to stage their show . . . and they didn't. The Fates don't offer such opportunities twice.

Incidentally: re the demotion of **Zhukov**. The "banana republics" are famous for their Army-operated governments; it does not make for sound government when the Army determines who shall control the government — when the muscles control the brain of the social organism, instead of vice versa.

In any nation, the Army should be loyal to the nation, not the nation controlled by the Army. In Russia, the Communist Party is the government; it is perfectly proper that government philosophy, not army-officer-troop-loyalty should determine the policy of the armed forces. **Zhukov** <u>was</u> wrong.

The thing is . . . he was just as wrong when he used the Army power to put **Kruschev** into control.

The U.S. gave Man control of the atom; Russia has given Man space-flight.

What's the next great breakthrough . . . and who will produce it?

Can you suggest what next <u>great</u> breakthrough there is? Interstellar flight is simply more-of-the-same space-flight.

Incidentally, I've been thinking of this set-up. I do NOT now think it exists as a fact . . . but the potentialities of such a situation make for story possibilities, when laid on another planet!

Suppose that you were President, and you had utter-top-absolute-secret knowledge to this effect: Russia was going all-out on a rockets and missiles program, devoting tremendous effort to the program. That their technology was extremely good, and going high-wide-and-hand-some.

BUT . . . that someone had discovered a pure-force drive. A development, say, of electrostatics, instead of electromagnetic effects — a flying condenser, instead of a spinning magnet, as is a motor. That properly arranged, the charge placed on the plates would cause every particle within the field between them to experience an acceleration toward one of the plates.

Now gravity is, of course, a static force — like a static electric charge. It exerts a force, and produces a tendency to accelerate — but does no work if that accelerative force produces no motion. (I.e., the fall is
448

blocked.)

By simply setting the electroforce to oppose G, the object floats, with no energy expenditure. To make it rise, of course, energy must be pumped in, because work is done then.

Horizontally oriented plates would produce horizontal drive.

Since every particle within the field is accelerated, by simply making the condenser plates the outermost part of the ship, the effective-felt acceleration is $A_r(M_p/M_c)$ where A_r is the real acceleration, and M_p the mass of the plates and M_c the mass of the contents of the ship. The resultant device would make 1000g accelerations quite comfortable to the crew of the ship. The major difficulty with the thing would be that it would, because of the very high voltages involved, have a serious tendency to corona loss, which would, with external plates, make the thing glow rather conspicuously. Sort of like a traveling neon sign, and anything but undetectable at night.

Now you, as President, know that this device has been built, tested, and proven. Bugs have been combed out; the thing works but-good. Trips beyond Earth's atmosphere prove the thing magnificently effective in space. Nuclear-reactor power makes the fuel problem simple; a suitcase full of uranium makes the round trip to Luna easily.

BUT . . . this thing is a real breakthrough — it's a totally new basic field — electrostatics as an applied technology of great power. And the further ahead we can get with this before Russia discovers the possibility exists, the better it'll be for us.

Also, there's a highly unstable personality at the helm in Russia. No telling when the guy might get hot-headed, and start something. If there's even a little approach to equality of armaments, when nuclear weapons are used, it's absolutely lethal.

This new device, however, hints at possibilities of atomic-weapon-proof force-screens, given a little time.

And . . . if a hot-head needed cooling, an absolutely new, totally unexpected, and totally unmatchable device such as this new type of ship would be shock enough to cool off almost anyone, without necessity for actually using it in warfare.

War is a calculated risk; prove beyond any peradventure of doubt that an enormously weighty factor exists that had not been calculated at all . . . and even a hot-headed gambler will stop to re-calculate. If the gambler

449

knew it existed, he'd calculate, and perhaps take an insane, but mutually lethal risk. Coming as a shock . . . he'd stop and regroup.

Further, using the ships, you would be learning things about fundamental cosmology that the Russians wouldn't be able to. That'd be putting you still further and faster ahead.

But . . . to keep it totally secret, it must be secret that there is a secret.

What would you, as President, do about the demands for a mis-sile and rocket program? You have to have one, of course; Russia would know that something most inordinately peculiar was going on if you didn't show any interest at all in the tremendous potentialities of long-range rocket missiles.

But you'ld be sort of penny-pinching on it, I think.

Not too niggardly, of course; after all, the Russians aren't fools — they might accept a certain degree of capitalist bumbling, but after all, there's a limit to how stupid you can pretend we are.

And, of course, when the satellite propaganda was shrieking around the world, some one of those who knew might in irritated, frustrated annoyance slip a little, and call that 185 pound trinket the silly bauble it was . . . compared to 1000-ton electrostat-drive ships.

You might even, just to worry the bejayzus out of the Russians, and to protect your establishment on the Moon, run out and collect their November 7th fireworks display before it hurt someone accidentally. Be an excellent chance to study their nuclear techniques, too, without anybody getting hurt or seriously endangered. After all, there's no reason to say anything; the Russians could simply assume that something had thrown their gimmick a bit off course — something failed — and no way of finding out what.

But, as President, you'ld have a terrible time deciding what to do about the demands of your own people for a more effective missile program.

When could you reveal the existence of the darned thing?

When the first Russian rocket arrived at the Moon, and in the words of the unofficial verse of the Marine Hymn,

"They will find the streets guarded by

"The United States Marines!"

(If you don't know their verse, you should; it's lovely: —

"If the Army and the Na-vy,

450

"Ever visit Heaven's scenes,
"They will find the streets are guarded by,
"The United States Marines!")
As a problem of tongue-holding, and involute ethics of spending the people's money, troubled conscience, and military evaluations . . . I think it'd make a hell of a story!

Regards, John

Isaac Asimov   *December 20, 1957*

Dear Ike:

The show is on Mutual Network — and I'm sure Mutual has at least one outlet in the Boston area. They wouldn't miss a city that large!

I have no facilities for cutting records — but you must have a magnetic tape player around Boston University there somewhere, even if you ain't modern at home. I tape the shows, and have a growing set of tapes. **Sanford Marshall**, who's the producer, is doing a bang-up job — he's got good people in the casts. One of the script writers — **Peter Irving** — is a scf fan, and a good writer. The other, **John Fleming**, doesn't have the feeling of SCF. We're looking for people who can turn out scripts, and do it fast.

Re: your article: **Ike**, I want such articles . . . but remember our readers have the delusion they already know the general facts about the solar system. If I start telling you about the chemical elements, you're apt to start getting bored before I've gone more than a page or so — you know you already know about those.

But if I wrote a piece about the metallurgical engineering problems of nucleonics, I could tell you things about carbon that you never happened to run across, and wouldn't have thought of, that would be interesting . . . and you wouldn't turn away because you already know you know about carbon.

Discuss the system of Deneb, say . . . and in doing so, you can haul in all the data you want about the solar planets. What I had in mind is a series which would allow you to discuss what you want to — the solar planets — in a framework that wouldn't make the readers react with, "You're not telling *me* anything new!"

You know, one of the troubles we have in communicating between
451

us is that you have a tendency to feel that I have left — rejected — given up — science and scientific thinking, because it appears to you that only so could I accept psionics.

Wrong assumption. Science is an absolutely essential basic — like arithmetic, it's a foundation. You've got to have arithmetic before you can start getting anywhere with algebra. Yet algebra actually includes arithmetic as a special case. When you start studying algebra, you don't abandon, reject, throw away, or cancel out arithmetic — you simply recognize that there are additional possibilities that are not included in the arithmetic-case.

Ike, Science has never been able to handle any continuous phenomenon as such. In dealing with electric and magnetic fields, they quantize them in terms of "lines of force." Yet of all things known to Science, those fields are most thoroughly continuous. While at the same time, our mathematics can't handle any truly discontinuous variable. In handling atomic physics, the physicists have to invert the procedure used on field forces, and talk about "statistical fields" of   particles. A statistical distribution of something can be handled as a mathematical continuous equation.

What I'm arguing for is the proposition: Our present known science is a special case. An infinite extension along now-known lines will <u>never</u> include the more general case. Therefore, let's <u>seek out the general case of which Science is one special case!</u>

If you don't like "psionics," call it "moisenhoist" or "flurogish" or anything you like. I don't care. But I do care that it be recognized that something innately non-scientific — something innately <u>not</u> subject to the laws of space-time -- exists.

Look, **Ike**: In 1950, the AEC boys started going after the H-bomb — the thermonuclear reaction that could be triggered to explosion. They were the nation's top scientists. They had access to all data available. They had computers running out of their ears. They had all the money they wanted to carry on their work, and the most extensive experimental facilities on Earth.

They used the finest scientific methods. They had solid data backing them every step of the way, and solid mathematical computation. They had experimental data, that showed that the ^{235}U bomb yielded a temperature of 100,000,000 degrees; the problem was to determine
452

what thermonuclear reactions, if any, could be triggered by that temperature.

They studied the characteristics of every possible nucleide, and found that two, and only two reactions were possible — the Deuterium-Tritium and the Tritium-Tritium. All other possibilities were out, because they wouldn't trigger with an ignition temperature below 100,000,000 degrees. Ammonium nitrate is a terrific explosive ... if you hit it with a fast enough shock wave. If you don't reach that shock-wave speed, you get nothing whatever. The damn stuff won't even burn. That's why they put 5-pound bottles of the stuff on the stock-shelves available to freshman would-be chemists; even a damn fool can't hurt himself with it. (Nitrogen Iodide will set it off, however!)

Well, since they had, by rigorous scientific study, proven that tritium would be necessary for any thermonuclear reactions — and if tritium were triggered, it, in turn, could readily trigger several other reactions — the AEC built that immense $2 billion Savannah River plant for tritium synthesis. God knows how many pounds of ^{235}U had to be consumed to produce a pound of tritium. Since tritium had to be used liquid or solid, the thing they wound up with on Einewetock wasn't a weapon.

The Russians had a thermonuclear weapon about 9 months later . . . without spending $2 billion for a tritium plant. They triggered LiH.

Now it had been proven, by sound, solid, scientific research that it was in fact impossible to do that.

The Russians did it, however. They did it by Psionics. By a method that did NOT depend on the Scientific Method. They did it by ingenuity — which can NOT be included within the boundaries of the Scientific Method, because it's illogical, is not capable of repeatable-experiment demonstration, cannot be communicated, and can't be taught.

Sure ... the product of the method is Scientific. But the method by which the ingenious idea is produced is not scientific. The product is a repeatable experiment that is communicable ... but the producing system is not.

Ike, like it or not, there are facts to be recognized. Some individuals are born with abilities others do not have. What I have meant by "hyperdemocracy" is the ruthless insistence that no individual be allowed either to have, or to not-have, any abilities except those

453

demanded by the democratic norm. Every ability that is not demanded is forbidden; thus we are all equal. All things should be shared — there shall be no great differences allowed. The range permitted shall be made as narrow as possible.

This philosophy dominates our present social, economic, and philosophical systems — including, inevitably, the educational system.

Notice that, unfortunately, Science appears to support the proposition. Science acknowledges as "real" only those phenomena which are repeatable on demand, and can be communicated from one individual to another. If you can not clearly define an experiment, in terms adequate to allow another individual to repeat that experiment predictably, then it isn't a "real" experiment.

Also, to be a scientific experiment, the mood, beliefs, mental state, etc., of the operator shall be unimportant — have no influence; they can not be specified as one of the operating conditions of the experiment.

Item: some research done on traffic accidents showed the interesting item that something like 80% of two-car collisions involved drivers both of whom were going to, or coming from, an interpersonal quarrel.

But if we seek to define the mood of the automobile operator as a relevant factor in an experiment, it is immediately denied as being "not scientific" if the mental attitude of the operator can influence the results.

But the "repeatable on demand" and "communicable in definable terms" requirements for a scientific experiment, when applied to human cultural problems, yields this interesting, and perfectly logical, consequent proposition: only that which can be taught is real.

Then all a child "really" is must have been taught.

The essential of the scientific philosophy — communicability and repeatability of experiments — imposes on our cultural thinking the proposition that it's nurture that's real. Nature is unimportant... because that is the unrepeatable, uncommunicable part, and so isn't "really" important. Only that part of Nature which is standard-issue stuff can be tolerated by a scientific philosophy. That part is predictable.

Thus the concepts of hyperdemocracy align perfectly with the Scientific Method philosophy.

Now look at the results of our present socio-economic philosophy, as expressed in legislation. Income tax is so steeply graduated as to make
454

it impossible for "nothing succeeds like success" to apply. Instead of high competence permitting a snowballing achievement, it's exponentially loaded, and the peak suppressed. Everyone wants success; by making it impossible for A to have an extraordinary degree of success, this leaves more opportunity-for-success around for other people.

Isaac Newton should not have been permitted to publish the Laws of Motion, Gravity, Optics and calculus; he should have been restrained — allowed to publish <u>one</u> thing, say Gravity, and left the others for other people to have success with.

It was all right for **Einstein** to publish Special Relativity, but he should have been forbidden to monopolize success by going on and doing further high-order work. He should have left it for other people to discover.

Yeah? Don't like that proposition?

What do you think the steeply graduated income tax does?

What of the surgical genius who can make 75 thousand in the first six months of the year . . . so that the rest of the year, if he works at all, he's working 90% for the Government? He should share his success — let other, less gifted men, take care of those patients.

Not only is that philosophy basically cock-eyed — it leads to something else, even more subtle.

Edison had no reputation, no education, and no influential friends. He was a telegraph operator.

But . . . he was ingenious. He cooked up a gimmick that greatly increased the speed of the stock-market telegraph system. He patented it, and made some nice money on it. The royalties allowed him to take time off, and do some more ingenious things. Since he didn't have to pay any income tax on his gains (they weren't considered ill-gotten in those days), he was able to hire some non-ingenious, but capable scientists to do the scientific work for him.

Edison had hunches. He decided very early that the practical electric light <u>had</u> to be a low-current, high-voltage, incandescent lamp. That it <u>had</u>, therefore, to be made of a substance having a positive temperature-resistance coefficient, and capable of standing not less than 2000^0 C. for extended periods. And that meant some form of carbon, the only substance available to then-existent technology with the general characteristics. He told his scientists to find the form of carbon required.

It took 50,000 experiments, but they did.

He could not have proven the validity of his idea to any scientist. Of his hunch. Any more than I could, in 1947, prove my hunch that LiH would be the thermo-nuclear fuel.

BUT . . . because he didn't have to pay income tax, he had been able to accumulate an extraordinary concentration of economic power, which he put to work guided by his extraordinary talent as an "ingeneer." He was NOT a scientist; he was a psiontist — had had some form of a sort of precognition, in that he could predict the direction in which success lay by non-logical means.

The gimmick is this: the culture as a whole benefits most when the greatest power is placed in the hands of the most ingenious individuals.

Ingenuity is not logical or scientific. It is not communicable, nor repeatable in the normal sense. The only known test for ingenuity is the old "by their fruits ye shall know them." A can do it and does it; B can not do it, and doesn't do it. A can not teach B, nor demonstrate to B how it is done. B therefore denies that A does it . . . and tends to make damn well sure that A doesn't get away with doing it.

Ingenuity is a dirty trick; it involves solving a problem by extra-legal methods. (LiH can not be triggered within the known conditions. It is done by a dirty trick.) Ingenuity isn't in the books, and can never be in the scientific books. Ingenuity is the Roman soldiers accepting the individual-handicap of short swords, and then fighting in such close order that three gang up unfairly against one long-sworded barbarian. Ingenuity is always unfair — because it is always the use of a method not-in-the-books.

Because only the test of by-their-fruits is available, the only way the culture can use such people involves allowing ingenious individuals a means of gaining great economic, social, and/or political power by their ingenuity.

A steeply graduated inheritance tax is fine; that stops aristocracy-of-birth. But a steeply graduated income tax imposes scientific democracy — it penalizes ingenuity, and prevents the ingenious individual achieving the means to make his ingenuity effective.

EXCEPT . . . for the individual who is ingenious at the indefinable, unteachable, and hence not-legislatable-against level of human relationships. The demagogue is hated, because that is his talent — and you can't
456

legislate against him, because his talent is his ability to please people — and you can't expect people to legislate against pleasure. Not really. Of course a Puritan demagogue can readily get them to legislate against ordinary pleasures . . . but not against the pleasure of being holier-than-anybody-else.

Hitler was very ingenious indeed . . . at that level.

The only kind of people who can judge and control ingenious people are, of course, ingenious individuals. Make things tough enough for ingenious people, and you get a filter effect. The solid-citizen of the ingenuity-group moderates himself, slows down, doesn't' push his real talents into use, and has ingenious hobbies instead. The violent-and-ingenious individual, however, will break through the restraints — and will not be curbed by the ingenious-but-moderate group. (Being ingenious, they will be less troubled, less driven to having to defend themselves against the violent genius. **Einstein** simply moved from Germany; **Fermi** won a Nobel prize and thus got himself financed out of Fascism.) Also, since the moderate-but-genius type has never been welcomed in the culture, he's not so damned hot for preserving that culture. So **Hitler** is going to some rather unpleasant extremes. So? The German culture'd been holding a pogrom on geniuses — which had just as much pain in it as death. Should the victim of that pain be too upset that the current pain-victims happen to be a different special minority?

Bill Blow is quite content to persecute the egg-heads. What Bill thinks is horrible is to have a persecution that doesn't exempt _his_ type. Since Bill doesn't have enough ingenuity-psyche to _be_ hurt, he doesn't see anything importantly wrong about taking a nutmeg grater to Gerald Genius' ingenuity-faculty, and scraping it away. He isn't killing Gerald, is he? If the damn fool commits suicide, that's his stupid idea, ain't it? Can't say Bill shot him, by God!

Remember **Sprague's** "Judgement Day"?

Item: So long as you deny that a factor in the problem exists . . . you can't solve the problem.

So long as the denied factor is, in fact, the most powerful of all factors . . . you can't even find out what the problem is!

Imagine trying to study protein chemistry in a solution through which a heavy electric current was being passed . . . when the existence of electricity was absolutely denied.

457

Until we, our culture, acknowledges that the Scientific Philosophy is necessary but not sufficient, we can't have a decent educational program, **Ike**. And this means that no possible extension of the Scientific Method in its present dimensions can serve. A logic-based culture is totally different from the ritual-taboo culture. In exactly the same massive, immensely significant degree, the next level, toward which we must move, will differ from the logical culture of the Scientific Method. No matter how many rituals and taboos you add to a ritual-taboo system, no matter how complex a system, no matter how far beyond the ability of any human individual to remember all the rituals you go . . . a ritual-taboo culture can never yield the effect required, that only a logic-based culture can provide.

What I'm trying to put over, **Ike**, is simply this: no matter how far you extend logic, no matter how intricately and extensively you compound it . . . it doesn't equal one tenth of one percent ingenuity. That there is a method — not a random-luck thing — beyond logic that even an infinite amount of logic can't equal.

So long as the ritual-taboo of the culture denies that logic can ever be superseded by an inherently more powerful method — so long as it insists that any real new method will simply be more logic — there can be no sound educational program. Because learning itself is a non-logical process.

Logic is a process which a mathematician would define as "commutable." It works one way as well as the other.

But the characteristic of a learning-event is that it is an inelastic event — the experience is irreversible. Hit a block of rubber with a hammer, and the rubber shows no learning from the experience. Hit a glass ball, and the glass either rebounds with perfect elasticity . . . or shatters. But hit a piece of steel, and the steel reacts inelastically — it "remembers" the experience.

You'll notice that all the computer memory-storage systems depend on inelastic phenomena.

Regards, John

John W. Campbell, Jr.   *December 28, 1957*

Dear John,

458

I see your point about the articles and I go along with both you and me. Since I'm dickering to have a collection of articles about the Solar System point of views published in book form, I have to do it with a minimum of advanced speculation because I'm aiming at general sales, too, and the *Astounding* clientele is definitely not "general."

However, what you say makes much sense and there is always room for more articles on the *Astounding* level, also.

For instance, I have put in some heavy thinking, and have come up with a description of the skies in the middle of the Galactic center or inside a globular cluster and in the process I've managed to explain why the stars you see from the Moon do not make up the good old "familiar constellations." Instead the Lunar sky is a strange and unfamiliar one, even without counting the presence of the Earth's globe.

I have also used it to evolve a theory why a Galactic civilization may exist right now and yet why we might be isolated and <u>remain</u> isolated. So — as you suggest — I hit both close to home and way to hell and gone.

It's 3,000 words long; title is OUR LONELY PLANET; hope you like it; and here it is.

I think the simpler articles will be done by **Lowndes**. At least he gave me verbal OK by telephone.

Got to read up on binaries now, so that someday I can do a piece on what it feels like to be on a planet that is involved with a double star.

I will comment on the rest of your letter later, except to say that I believe you when you said you had a hunch back in 1947 that LiH would be the H-bomb fuel, because you told me so then. — So you aren't being smart by hindsight and you may use this letter as evidence if you are ever challenged.

Yours, Isaac

Isaac Asimov   *February 17, 1958*

Dear Ike:

I didn't go to the office today; the snow, cold and wind really did quite a job on transportation, but in addition I spent the weekend nursing a decidedly painful big toe. When it started I wondered if I were showing up with some such ridiculous ailment as gout. Ridiculous, because gout is one of those things that just doesn't happen any more.

459

Turned out to be some undetermined variety of infection of the joint capsule. No need to specify; the shot-gun blast of antibiotic killed it, whatever it was.

In the meantime, however, it led me to do considerable thinking about gout, arthritis, and similar joint ailments, I can assure you!

I won't say I congratulate you on that prize; it wouldn't express what I feel about it. Perhaps offering the prize committee my congratulations would better communicate what I mean. It isn't a case of, "Congratulations, Ike! I always knew you could do it!", but of, "Well! By God they finally got a committee together that recognized Ike's <u>been</u> doing it for years!"

I've quarreled with some of your theses — genetic theories and I don't see eye to eye, for instance — but for clear, clean, honest, and enthusiasm-rousing writing on science, you've been earning prizes for years.

I've run into a concept, Ike, that may help you to understand what my feelings on a lot of things are.

Truth is hard to determine — but truth has the characteristic of being an absolute. It is inherently, innately, an absolute. A fact is <u>true</u> or not-true; if it is <u>true</u>, it's absolute, eternal, unarguable. The truth-value is either 1 or 0.

But now let's consider the concept of "beauty." This one's been kicked around by a bunch of aesthetes, philosophers, etc., plus assorted generations of strictly-from-phoney. Therefore the term's degenerated almost to meaninglessness.

However, observe this: a modern jet fighter is a beautiful thing — although no aesthetician had anything whatever to do with the design. It got that way because that is the appropriate-to-its-function balance of areas, masses, and lines.

Beauty, then, bears some relationship to efficiency of design. Let's use the term "practicability" in that sense, and recognize that the practicable has beauty.

Now "practicable" is NOT an absolute thing . . . but it does have absolute limits. An internal combustion engine remains absolutely impractical when its efficiency is so low that it can't produce enough power to keep itself going — if friction consumes more mechanical energy than the heat-engine system produces, the device is absolutely impracticable.

However, an internal combustion engine so clumsy that it could just barely turn itself, with no external load whatever, has crossed the threshold; it is now not-zero practical.

As soon as it achieves efficiency enough to carry some external load, it enters a new zone of practicability. Even if it is only 0.1% efficient as a heat engine, it can be used practically.

Its beauty is increasing.

A modern gas turbine is pushing the efficiency way up; it's becoming more and more beautiful.

Now: notice that a thing can be beautiful, in the absolute sense of having-a-degree-of-beauty — yet not have absolute beauty. The fact that A is true means that not-A is false . . . but the fact that A is beautiful does NOT mean that not-A is ugly.

A thing can be good, in the absolute sense that it produces good results — yet not be best, and therefore not be absolute beauty, absolute good.

Anything that is practicable, or beautiful or good, contains truth. But it doesn't have to contain nothing-but-truth, nor all-truth!

The problem in research is to find the truth in the good theories, and abstract it to make better theories — without ever demeaning the real and absolute fact that the original theory was a good one.

The old earth-air-fire-water theory of elements. If we'd been a little readier to seek all the scraps of truth in that theory, we might have detected, before Einstein came along, that matter has four, not three, phases; solid, liquid, gas . . . and energy.

The phlogiston theory held that something escaped when fuel burned. Correct; free energy does.

The logical system can handle only Truth . . . because it can handle only a positional notation in a binary system. It's not true that it can't handle grays; it can. If black be 0 and white 1, then a binary notation can, by positional notation, express any possible gray between these two as .1001101110 . . . or the like.

Problem: express two 50% grays, one of which is a blue-gray and the other a red-gray. Each reflects exactly 50% of the incident visual spectrum energy. To achieve that, actually, one would have to be a practically pure red-orange, and the other a pure blue-green.

No man possessed of color vision would acknowledge that either of these was "gray" at all!

Item for your consideration in a science-fiction story.

"What is the proper payment if someone commits an improper act on your behalf?" What do you owe if someone violates his code of ethics on your behalf? What is the ethically proper payment for an unethical service?

What if the act is <u>not</u> unethical in your code, but <u>is</u> in his?

Worse . . . what if the act is not unethical in his code, but is in yours?

One of these days soon, I'm going to be calling on you for help in getting a new magazine started. The wheels are definitely turning, and it's gradually shaping into something. It'll be a true <u>journal</u> of speculative thinking — and it'll be strictly amateur. The problem is simultaneously growing more complex and extensive, and clarifying and simpliying . . . as usual!

Notice this: The Royal Society in its heydey was a society of Gentlemen Amateurs, a society devoted to discussion and speculation about Natural Philosophy, by Gentlemen Amateurs. **Priestly**, who first reported the lightning experiments of **Ben Franklin**, was a Unitarian minister. **Ben** himself was a statesman, writer and publisher — an amateur philosopher. **Newton** was an amateur-tyro. The great days, the hey-dey, of the Royal Society was the period <u>when it was an amateur speculative society</u>!

Dr. Teller says science needs fans.

Yeah . . . only it needs fans, not mere loyal rooters, faithful followers, dependable apologists, acolytes or worshippers. What **Teller** appears to have in mind, however, is the latter — for he definitely doesn't recognize that science-fictioneers <u>are in fact what he says science needs</u>.

The way a system makes progress is by having not only the Government . . . but also His Majesty's Loyal Opposition, sniping all the way.

The true fan will help buy **Babe Ruth** a new stadium . . . and ruthlessly throw him out of the game when he gets too fat and winded to improve the Game. They'll love him all his life . . . provided he has good sense enough to quit when he's through. The fans force changes in the rules of the game — to make it a better Game. Sure, the professionals make the changes — but it's the pressure of the fans that
462

cause them to be made.

In photography, the professional photogs were satisfied with their 5 x 7 and 8 x 10 inch view cameras, and their flash-powder. It was a minister, in Newark N.J., incidentally, who patented celluloid-base film, as a substitute for glass plates. And it was enthusiastic amateurs who insisted on getting cameras and films that could take pictures where lighting was absolutely impossible, and no professional would consider even trying. Amateurs insisted on glass-enclosed flash-bulbs; flash-powder was too dangerous.

I now have a 2-1/4 x 2-1/4 twin-lens reflex camera with an F2.8 lens, for which I can get Royal X Pan film, with a Weston rating of 1600. It'll take lovely pictures in ordinary room lighting; no special lights or long-held poses required.

Professionals were satisfied with the Devin one-shot color camera. It exposed three sheets of film simultaneously, through three color-filters, and gave three-color separation negatives directly. You could do beautiful color work with it . . . if you could lug around 50 pounds of camera, and afford three 5 x 7 films per shot, and about 5000 watts of light, or, better, 200 flashbulbs at one shot.

Ektachrome film does a gorgeous job; the amateurs niggled, nagged, and prodded.

Just as no individual can trust his own self-evaluation entirely — he is apt to over-value what he has accomplished, and under-value his potential for further, but difficult, progress! — so no group can trust its own evaluations of itself.

It needs the outside viewpoint of Gentlemen Amateurs.

A woman can help a man; she'll never think like a man, and nothing he can ever do can ever make her see things just as he does. She's innately incapable of that. The human race, then, has a built-in, inescapable, inconvertible Loyal Opposition. "You can't live with 'em . . . and you can't live without 'em."

Of course, to an equal extent, Woman has Man as her inescapable-necessity Loyal Opposition.

What Professionalism tries to do, however, is to escape the nagging sniping of the Opposition, by claiming it to be incompetent. "Women don't understand these problems, and there's no sense paying any attention to what she says." "Hmph . . . men don't understand anything.

463

I know what I'm doing, and he can just lump it and like it."

Science needs fans — but fans drift away quite rapidly if they find that the system is, "You can look, and admire — but don't touch!" If the "fan" is supposed to watch and admire in awe ... but keep his comments (other than praise) to himself, he presently goes somewhere else where his innate abilities as a wise human being are given some respect and acknowledgement.

I've known aristocrats — true aristocrats. They had serfs, too. Human beings who served them and waited on them — and liked it that way. Because the serfs were fans.

Peg's family lived out in Negaunee, Mich., a small mining town, when she grew up. They had household domestics there, in those days. Finnish girls. **Peg's** family were true aristocrats; they had one girl who worked for them for 22 years. Old **Joe Winter** was a power in town — and the power was available at "Chulia's" call, when she needed it. Not just when she wanted it; when she rightly and properly had reason to have it used in her behalf. And "Chulia" knew that. Also, what "Chulia" said the family should do — the family paid attention to. That didn't always mean they did it — but it was given honest, judicious evaluation, and had effect of some kind.

Science does need fans — but it must pay the price of giving the fans respectful consideration. It cannot have them if it dismisses them as "uninformed laymen with inadequate understanding."

That, however, is where science is falling down. Part of why it's becoming "eggheads." (For more, see the long letter I've written your friend **Boyd** concerning his article.)

What I have in mind is to establish a journal, and an organization — nationwide, with local societies — of Gentlemen Amateurs.

1. There are thousands of highly trained minds in this country, with nothing to do. They're the 65-year-old-plus men who have been retired under company policy. They — many of them — have highly trained talents for organization of data, analysis of complex problems, and money, time, and free energy to expend. My father practically killed himself by retiring to do nothing with the highly trained, powerfully driving mind he had developed. He would have died, if he hadn't succeeded in giving himself the neatest lobotomy imaginable, via a brain hemorrhage. He retains all his faculties; he's as sharp as ever. Not a sign
464

of fogginess of thinking, loss of memories, or anything. Only he's slowed way, way, down — he thinks in such slow motion that the driving urge he lived by is completely gone. He's retired now, all right.

2. Every chemist is a competent physics fan... and vice versa. Every biochemist is a competent medical fan. So, incidentally, is every minister, priest, and rabbi.

3. Every big-league ball-team has scouts — but they depend on tips from fans to alert the scouts to talent in the backwoods.

4. Science is, today, missing contributions from highly original, competent amateurs, ideas that could make major advances, because you can't tell the crackpots from the geniuses, and the crackpots outnumber the geniuses 10,000 to 1. The old saying, "Don't Talk To The Motorman," means the motorman is too busy doing his essential job to be able to take time out to discuss affairs generally. The scientists are too busy doing their own work to be able to screen the amateurs and pick the geniuses from the crackpots. So **Christofilos** gets the brush-off, and it's a couple of years before a professional gets the idea of the strong-focussing principle. The New York dishwasher who sent **Einstein** the suggestion that gravitational fields could focus light was lucky to get through. (Incidentally, **Einstein** was a Gentleman Amateur; he was a mere patent office clerk, not **Herr Doktor Professor Einstein**.)

5. Science needs amateurs because they're everywhere, and scientists aren't. Imagine this: Make a photographic plate shaped like the map of the US, and deposit sensitive emulsion on it in a pattern determined by the density of distribution of professional scientists in the US. Now expose this plate in a camera, and see how good a representation of the scene you have in your print.

It was a Mexican farmer who observed the birth of Paracutin, not a vulcanologist. I will give odds that the next volcano to be born de nova, will be observed first by a farmer, or sailor, or other amateur, and not by a vulcanologist. Wanna bet?

I observed ball-lightning twice in my life; once as a 10-year-old kid in my Grandmother's house in Napoleon, Ohio, and once in Durham, N.C., when I was 23.

The second occasion, I observed it clearly, carefully, and directly. I inspected the scene carefully afterward. I had finished my course in physics.

When I reported it to physicists, I was told it was folk-lore, impossible because no electrostatic force system could possibly remain stable for more than microseconds, that it was an after-image in my eye, etc., and that it had never been reported by any "competent observer."

A professionally trained young physicist was not a competent observer. Who would be, then?

Now ball-lightning is recognized; it's a naturally-occurring, though understandably very rare, instance of a plasmoid. It's stable for an appreciable time because of the magnetic-bottle effect. Plasmoids are not only self-maintaining, but self-defending; they tend to bounce away from obstacles. The obstacle they do not bounce from, however, collects all the stored electromagnetic energy in the plasmoid, all at once. (It shattered an 8-inch oak tree to toothpicks. That stuff ain't foolin'!)

Consider this: Suppose an effective organized-amateur society had gathered data on ball-lightning, and forced science to study it. Say this was done in 1910.

This "pinch effect" is real new and wonderful stuff, ain't it? The latest thing, science has just discovered!

Look, bub; my father told me about the problems of "pinch effect" when I was about 8 years old. Any old-time electrical engineer knew about it. The first edition of *The Book of Knowledge* had a discussion of it.

Why? Because in the early days of AC power equipment, Westinghouse dreamed up a perfectly lovely type of electric furnace that would allow melting metals with no contaminating electrodes, gases, or other chemical intrusions. Simply make a big transformer, with a fire-clay trough circling the transformer core. Fill the trough with metal, and it constitutes a one-turn short-circuited secondary winding; it gets hot by the induced currents.

Lovely idea. It didn't work satisfactorily, however, because of the "pinch effect"—and that's where the term originated! The molten metal would get a leeeetle narrower at one point, and the local current-density would rise. This would increase the magnetic-field-density due to the flowing current, which would squeeze the metal thinner, which raised the current density which . . . and the ring of molten metal broke.

In the days before they had radio frequency power in quantity, that type of induction furnace was tried . . . but the pinch effect loused them up and it was abandoned.

In 1910, then, the pinch-effect caused by heavy currents in liquids was known. It wouldn't have been too hard a step to visualize the pinch effect in gas, would it — highly ionized gas? What would you expect if you had a current of 50,000,000 amperes driven by 10,000,000 volts?

Natural lightning strokes yield such magnitudes; man-made stuff duplicates the voltage . . . but they've never duplicated the voltage at that current.

Wonder what the neutron radiation is from a 12-inch plasmoid in air at full atmospheric pressure . . . ???? What the effective temperature is? Must be easily over 100 megadegrees.

Suppose, though, that science had gone to work on the amateur-observed, laboratory-unduplicable phenomenon, and gotten a glimmering of plasmoids and their properties? And started studying plasmoids in the '20s and '30s. It would have been easy — all the necessary stuff was around to do it.

Plasmoid research would have taken a sudden new interest when the concepts of thermonuclear reactions in stars came into sight in the early '30s. Plasmoids might well have been more advanced, and more attractive therefore, as nuclear research tools, by 1935, than was the cyclotron. The natural approach to nuclear energy is via thermonuclear reactions — there are the stars to give a shining clue to that line. (Only supernovae use fission reactions!)

By 1940, we might well have had some working hydrogen-fusion plasmoid reactors — or perhaps lithium hydride, since LiH doesn't give off dangerous and hard-to-handle neutrons.

In 1938 I had already pointed out that the deuterium-deuterium had a low ignition temperature, and God knows I wasn't the only one who knew that.

In 1936, in other words, all the information necessary to start work on deuterium fusion reactors, using plasmoids, already existed. Only the key factor was ball-lightning . . . and Science wouldn't look at the data.

(Science-fiction story there, incidentally. Men meet a culture that knows about fission only as an odd by-way of nucleonics. They took the natural path to atomic energy, and started with fusion reaction.)

The point of all this: The Journal I want would be the communication medium of Gentlemen Amateurs — but Gentlemen whom Science would respect, and appreciate as their Loyal Opposition. The Gentlemen Amateurs would be the true fans, who spotted the backwoods talent, who combed the crackpots from the geniuses, who had the time, money, and inclination to do all that screening work that the professionals cannot.

BUT... the pros wouldn't be relieved of the chore of dealing with crackpots unless they accepted and acted on the findings of the Gentlemen Amateurs. The man with an idea isn't going to waste time talking to a group who couldn't do anything about it even if they liked it; he's going to by-pass them, and hit where he can produce effect. And, of course, the Gentlemen Amateurs aren't going to waste their time, if they aren't useful, either.

I'll need your help, and sugestions, **Ike**.

Regards, John

John W. Campbell, Jr.   *March 3, 1958*

Dear John,

You may remember that the last time I was at your office, mention was made of a story named THE UGLY LITTLE BOY which I had offered to *Infinity Science Fiction* and which they had accepted. The reason I had offered it to them was that the genesis of the yarn was a remark **Larry Shaw** (*Infinity's* editor) had made over the luncheon table.

Now, very unfortunately, *Infinity* has been having some troubles, which I ought not talk about, perhaps, but anyway I was forced (first time in twenty years) to ask for the story back and they gave it back to me with regrets.

I am enclosing it here, **John**, and I would now like to submit it to you, where I would have submitted it in the first place but for my sense of obligation to **Larry Shaw** and his original comment.

Would you therefore look it over and tell me whether you can use it?

If you can, there is one qualification. My next book of collected short stories (which will include PROFESSION, by the way) is to be published by Doubleday in February 1959. They plan also to include THE UGLY LITTLE BOY (in fact, **Bradbury** was sufficiently impressed by it to ask me to cut it down to short story length and submit it to the slicks — it is 14,000 words long as it stands—-but I refused, since I know what I want
468

to say, how long it takes me to say it, and where I want to say it).

Anyway, if you like the yarn and think you can use it, will you be able to find room to publish it by the January, 1959, issue?

The *Sunday New York Times* (of 2 March) gives ONLY A TRILLION a full column of review and a very favorable one. I am particularly fond of the last two sentences: ". . . the second (*Pate de Foie Gras*) is a delightful piece that all can fully appreciate. The high-level consternation in this story of "Project Goose" leaves the reader with a kindly feeling for scientists and all their works."

Very truly yours with love, Isaac Asimov

Isaac Asimov *March 9, 1958*

Dear Ike:

Your mss. herewith. I'm sorry, too — I need novelettes right now.

The trouble is that the idea — which I gather is what you got from **Lowndes** — of the slower development of ideas in prehistoric times — is fairly sound and good for a story. But not this much story. And not, as here, with the effect of being a gag-story stretched to 15,000 words.

There's some other deeper, stronger, and bigger idea that you're trying to express in this; I don't know what it is. Since I'm reasonably good at spotting themes in stories, if I don't know what it is . . . I'm afraid you've failed to get it over.

I recall you had some considerable difficulty with "Naked Sun," because there was in it a thesis that you yourself don't like to consider— that Man has to move out of the cities, move out into the open.

There may be in this one a similar problem — that there is a thesis that you yourself don't like . . . but are trying to force yourself to acknowledge you know to be true.

For one thing, the fundamental proposition in this is that there are Irreplaceable Individuals — that all men are NOT equal, that it DOES matter, and is NOT just a matter of being Steamboat Time. But this is contrary to a doctrine which you have long held and frequently expressed.

Neanderthalensis was inferior; the ultimate test of ultimate reality is, was, and always will be, "Did it work?" The ultimate test of Ethics, even, is not logic, or judgment, or feeling . . . but, "Did it work in the long run?" I define "good" as, "That which works in terms of megayear

469

testing." Superior is, "That which works better in terms of megayears." Mammals were superior to saurians.

Homo sapiens was better than Neanderthal . . . because he included Neanderthal's virtues, and added some new ones. Cro magnon Man was not *Homo sapiens*; *Homo Sap.* is the hybrid of *H. neand.* and *H. cromagnon.*

And the thing that's most interested me is that *H. neanderthal* was not the brute-muscle-man of the two — his bones were lighter, thinner, and the muscle attachments were less rugged than those of *H. sap*! *H. neanderthal's* skull was fully as big in volume as *H. sap's*. But it was low-domed and broad, low-arched rather than high-arched.

In your story, Jerry would give Timmy a hard time — because pound for pound, Jerry's muscles are harder, tougher, and stronger, and his high-arched skull is thicker and harder to crack. In a butting contest, Timmy would get a fractured skull, while Jerry got a headache.

Look, **Ike**: Expose a photographic film in a camera, and it has a latent image. Put it in a developer, and the image can be developed.

To get perfect development, the developer must act in a perfectly random, statistical-distribution manner.

How can you prove that the developer is, in fact, acting in a purely random manner on all areas of the negative — giving every silver halide crystal an equal chance to express its latent-image potential?

Well, if you put in a piece of film that has been exposed in a perfectly uniform light, so that there is a perfectly uniform latent image potential all over the film, and it then comes out of the developer a perfectly uniform gray — the developer is acting in a perfectly random-distribution manner. If the evenly exposed film comes out nonuniform in density, then we know the developer is not acting uniformly.

OK — then the test for uniform action of development is the production of a uniformly developed negative, right?

How can you prove that every individual in a culture has an equal chance for development of his latent potentials? That the culture constitutes a medium in which development is uniform?

Easy! If every individual comes out uniform gray, that proves the development must have been equal, doesn't it?

It would, of course . . . if every individual started with equal potentials.

470

Now in photography they have Reducer and Intensifier solutions. An intensifier is intended to make it possible to get a print from an underexposed, flat-contrast negative; it increases contrast, and builds up the shadow areas. A reducer is the opposite; it cuts down the density of too-dense negatives.

By using reducer and intensifier solutions alternately, you can take a picture, and make it come out almost a uniform gray.

That proves that the development of every individual silver halide crystal must have been made truly uniform. Now they're all equally gray.

Incidentally, if you have time, you might read a few pages almost anywhere in *Atlas Shrugged*. The thing's too long ... but the author has some remarkably cogent remarks to make.

Ike, an individual who has the ability to learn, but not the ability to create, or invent, is incapable of comprehending that the ability to invent exists. Consequently, the Learner says of the Inventor, that, "he learned from experience," and sincerely believes that he, too, would have learned from those same experiences, if he had just happened to have them.

After all, says the Learner, "I learned what the Inventor learned, didn't I? What's he got that I ain't got? Why should I pay him; I can do it myself can't I?"

The Scientific Method is very democratic. Physical objects are, too. A high-power car will work exactly the same for an idiot as for a genius — physical things display perfect democracy ... and no judgment.

But ... the essence of the Scientific Method is, "What you claim is not proven real until you have shown me how I can do it exactly as you claim you can do it. Until I can learn how to do it, I deny that you have done it."

But as soon as I can do it, I deny that you have anything I don't have ... so why should you expect me to pay you for it?

The scientific method, <u>within itself</u>, denies that creativity exists; only learning exists.

Within the narrow limits of logical-science, one is inevitably forced to the conclusion that if Science applies to human beings, then only that which is teachable is real. The simple inverse of that, of course, is, "All human characteristics are teachable."

If you so define "real" that it equates to "teachable," then all "real"
471

human characteristics are teachable — and any non-teachable character-istics are "unreal."

The methods of creative thinking are not teachable.

Therefore, I have scientifically proven that creativity doesn't really exist.

If you think creative thinking is teachable — teach someone to write as creatively as you do, **Ike**. I've been trying for two decades now, and I know it's not teachable.

Like a photographic developer, I can develop a latent potential . . . but I can't create one. And the essence of my technique is, as I've said, being the Big Noise — a pure, random system of stimulation, so that the latent potentials in the individual, not my characteristic distribution, will show up.

But dammitall **Ike**, will you please recognize that equal opportunity is not demonstrated by equal results! And that unequal results does NOT demonstrate unequal opportunity.

People have been damning Scientists for releasing nuclear energy; "They should have used better judgment! They showed no social conscience!"

This is the plaint of a child when he says, "You didn't stop me from sticking my hand in the buzz saw!"

Fair enough . . . provided the child will, at the same time, obey the parent — we'll acknowledge the parent's inherent superiority.

What people want, of course, is Free Will with respect to rewards, and Free Immunity with respect to responsibility.

Notice this, **Ike**: Our present income tax law is so arranged that if you earn more than about $25,000 a year, you are not taxed, but fined. The tax gradation is so steep as to constitute punitive force. Clearly, the society holds that earning a great deal is a social crime.

However: 1. You can inherit wealth, with only normal taxation. That isn't considered criminal, unless it's really an enormous estate. 2. You can gain millions . . . provided it's capital gains, and pay only a normal tax.

Now Capital Gains is interesting. It results from making a lucky guess as to what investment will be a winner. You have to make only one lucky guess — and then hold on.

So long as it appears that the wealth is the result of lucky breaks, it
472

is not considered something to punish.

But . . . if you do it consistently, thereby revealing that it's a result of method, no luck . . . that's punishable by a confiscatory tax.

How could I make — and keep control of! — $500,000 in the next year or two?

By investing in a small company, then turning over to that small company trade secrets which permitted it to make millions, and grow.

If I patent the secret . . . it can be pirated freely.

Patents are considered unfair, improper, and hateful. Bell Labs, IBM, and now RCA are being forced to forgo the results of the creative work they do. DuPont, GE, Westinghouse . . . who's next?

The thesis of your story is that individual creative geniuses are irreplaceable. Sure you coated it with ". . . but not any more."

Ike, you're a liar, and you know it.

Was **Dr. Salk** replaceable?

Sure! He did a fine job of routineering; he applied known methods to a known problem, and ground out a solution. A damned good and deserving job of work, too.

Is that what **Einstein** did? Or **Galileo**?

Sure, inventions come faster now. Two reasons: there are more human individuals in any given time-span. There are a lot of routineering products that are new in one sense . . . but not in any fundamental sense.

Dr. Salk didn't discover a Law of Nature.

Galileo did.

The plans on the new magazine are moving forward glacially — slow, maybe, but somewhat difficult to halt. We've got to get this thing licked into shape first; we have to have the purpose defined clearly — and yet not so rigidly as to make it futile.

How do you define the nature of a magazine intended for rebels against sheer orthodoxy, by rebels against the Library Tribesmen, and make it clear that you're not starting *The American Crackpots Journal*?

How do you say that any professional is welcome . . . provided he writes as an amateur in the field he's discussing?

You know **Helmholtz** was an M.D. **Gilbert**, who really started the study of magnetics, was the Court Physician. But **Pasteur**, who made the greatest discovery in the history of medicine — the first real, broad, general breakthrough in millenia of medicine — was a chemist.

473

Professionals are welcome . . . but only as amateurs!

Most of your best articles, **Ike**, have been on subjects you have no professional authority to write on. What business have you, a biochemist, to write on radioactivity in the Earth's crustal rocks?

Or the mathematics of extremely large numbers? You're no mathematician, and disguising it just because you talk about haemoglobin doesn't excuse you.

The guy who wrote that lovely piece on "The Correlation of the Martian Canal Network" for us a couple years back is a Los Angeles dentist. His paper has been republished in the *Astronomical Society of the Pacific's Journal*. Also the Smithsonian's journal.

And, of course, **Einstein** was a patent clerk, not a professor of physics.

Regards, John

Isaac Asimov   *April 6, 1958*

Dear Ike:

Before glooming yourself into huddled retirement over the sad fate of **Kuttner & Kornbluth**, please re-read **Mark Clifton's** "The Dread Tomato Addiction." You, too, can lie with statistics.

Yes, **Kornbluth** was a stocky, somewhat overweight, sedentary man, and **Kornbluth** is dead. **Winston Churchill** is also a stocky, somewhat overweight, sedentary man . . . and you should live so long. **Joe Winter** died of a heart attack, coronary thrombosis type; he was a stocky, somewhat overweight sedentary man, too. But the thing that was critical was that **Joe** didn't have the sense to say, "I can't do all that," and quit. One of my neighbors here dropped dead of a heart attack, too.

When somebody drops like that . . . it's because either he said, "I can do anything," or his wife said, "Willy can do anything," and made him try.

The secret of a long and successful life is very simple; learn to say, "That's enough for now." Whether it's eating, working, or playing . . . or worrying.

The odd part about it is that the total organism is much like the arm; it goes into a cramp, and becomes useless, if only one muscle is kept in continuous operation . . . but can do a hell of a lot if the various muscles

474

are all used alternately. You can work like hell at your hobby, then work like hell at your business, then work at something else with vim, vigor and gusto . . . and it won't kill you. But doing one tenth as much at one thing will kill you.

It's a miracle that **Hank Kuttner** stayed alive as long as he did; **Catherine** did a magnificent job of holding that poor guy together. He was invalided out of the Army as psychoneurotic, you know; the Army's mistake was taking him in in the first place. How the man ever achieved as much as he did, with the terrible psychic wounds he'd been given, is a magnificent tribute to what he had innately.

He was, **Ike**, an excellent example of my basic point in our running debate; education and orientation can't completely destroy inherent power of personality, no matter how badly it distorts and scars it. Accept my word for it; the guy had a rotten start. **Catherine** did a magnificent job of nursing him . . . but the scar tissue remained.

Kornbluth I didn't know so much about, nor know so well. But I've read his stories, and I've met him.

There are several basic ways to react to injustice. Usually, the Unjust, the individual committing the injustice, sincerely believes that he is not unjust. But <u>always</u>, whether he considers himself justified (in which case he considers what he is doing either punishment-for-your-wrong-doing, or paying-back-injury) or not (and thinks he is doing it just because he enjoys the feeling of power), the Unjust inevitably intends to make it a one-way deal. He <u>always</u> intends to hurt you without being hurt in return.

You can react to the Unjust by being Unjust . . . but the Unjust will be expecting you to attempt to reflect the injury, and will try to block it. This means that you'll always find that he is (1) Unjust and (2) unjustly tries to maintain his injustice when you react, and (3) unjustly punishes your effort to reflect the injustice, and (4) . . . this is, obviously an endless series. Get sucked into it, and you wind up with anger, bitterness, and deep futility. You become so busy trying to "get even" that you never have any time, effort, or energy to get ahead with your own accomplishment.

(This holds for nations, too; a nation bent on "getting even" can never get ahead.)

This is the old Italian concept of vengeance — the old feuding concept.

Then there's the Irish approach; their anger is homeric, but never bitter. It's anger-with-gusto, not anger-with-bitterness. It's the proposition that the Unjust was unjust because he's a damn fool, and hasn't the wit to see that he's hurting somebody. But that once the blockheaded idiot's been made to understand the situation, they'll both be the best of friends.

The third attitude is that based on the proposition that what the Unjust did <u>was in fact</u> justified — <u>even when the Unjust himself believes he's being sadistic.</u> A homocidal maniac kills people because, being psychotic, and with the particular type of psychosis he has developed, he can't act in any other way . . . whether <u>he</u> thinks he can or not. He may think he's acting out of a freely chosen and rationally derived decision, based on judged and evaluated facts . . . but he isn't.

Then, with that propositon, the problem of the Unjust can be approached with enthusiasm, as a challenging problem; what factors did in fact make the observed resultant behavior the inescapable and necessary outcome? Solve that problem, and the Unjust can be triggered into a new type of behavior.

And, **Ike**, sometimes the best possible new-type-of-behavior is suicide for the Unjust. Some people need to drop dead. They can't be repaired into useable members of the human race. Some cells are cancer cells; they should drop dead. Quite a few of the Nazis belonged in that category; the human race would have benefited immensely if they had been assassinated before they got Europe in the mess they did.

Do not exclude "Drop dead" from the list of appropriate solutions to problems.

The essential point is this; some human beings can approach the problem of injustice-suffered as a challenge, a problem to be solved. And some can only accumulate repressed hatred, bitterness, and curdle inside as they go further and further into that endless series of injustice-injustice-of-suppressing-complaint -- injustice-of-suppressing-rebellion-against-unjust-suppression-of-complaint-against-injustice -- etc. -- ad-infinitum.

Cyril Kornbluth was stuck in that series. His anger against the ways of the culture he didn't fit too well produced cumulative bitterness in him. His stories were angry-bitter stories. (**Horace** tends that way
476

too; there's a lot of it in *Galaxy*.)

My own personal bets for the next candidates for the Drop Dead Club in science-fiction include **Pohl** and **del Rey**. **Pohl** out of futile-bitter-anger; **del Rey** by reason of being overwhelmed. **G.O. Smith**, incidentally, is rapidly moving up the list.

And you, my friend, can't get even a provisional place on the waiting list of that club . . . until you stop enjoying life and laughter. Until you stop crusading, and go back to sullen, bitter anger that your efforts aren't granted the success you know they should, by Inalienable Right, have. You've got to stop learning from your failures, and start being bitter that They won't let you do what you know you have a right to, before you get into **Kornbluth's** club.

As of now, you're in **Churchill's** club.

We just got back from San Francisco; been visiting **Jane** and inspecting our new son-in-law. **Jane** got herself a handful of man, this time — they're going to have hell and hallelujah for the next couple of years, I can predict with some assurance, but the results should be slightly terrific.

He's the son of the **Dr. Allen** who's head of biochemistry at Berkeley. And he hasn't spoken to his father for some five years or so. He's a red-hot, fulminating rebel, with the gentleness of a full-scale nuclear reaction under good control. Just don't pull out the control rods and try to see what happens.

The red-hot rebellion against his father is fully justified at a human level . . . and unjustifiable at any logical-cultural level. He's been earning his own way, away from home entirely, since he was about 16.

It started, I gather, when he was put in the Berkeley Experimental Nursery School, at ages 2 to about 6, for the psychology department to experiment on. He scored 162 IQ, and was their star exhibit. (I suspect he'd have scored higher if the psych boys had been wise enough to realize that some of his answers were better than, and therefore different from, the ones they had decided were "right.") His father is a logical orthodoxist. (You should know: no man can get to be head of a department of a major university without proving beyond question that he's an absolute logical orthodoxist.) **John**, I gather, had more sense and more guts than **Clyde Kluckhone's** son; you may or may not recall that the **Kluckhone** son, at about age 24, finally rebelled against the regimen his logical-orthodoxist (head of Anthropology at Harvard) father had surrounded him with . . . by shooting a Luger out of a hotel window into a crowd of shoppers on the street below. He killed a woman.

John thinks like a well-greased electronic computer . . . and then adds something more. He's extraordinarily brilliant, extraordinarily sensitive, and has the toughness and determination of personality to keep from blowing up.

But, naturally, he's exceedingly suspicious of (1) older men, (2) older people generally, (3) other people. They don't approve of his answers. He doesn't approve of theirs.

We got along fine; he is a sports-car enthusiast, and doesn't pretend to know electronics. We carried one of my home-designed hi-fi amplifiers out with us as a wedding present; it does things with music that he liked. Also, it's based on a flat rejection of orthodox theory. His father is trying to synthesize protoplasm; I told **John** precisely and specifically why the old man couldn't do it . . . because orthodoxy is inadequate to admit the problem that must be solved before protein can be synthesized.

Since we were out in San Franscisco for most of two weeks, I hadn't heard that *Science World* was folded. I haven't been in to the office yet, so it's still news to me.

I have a slight suspicion part of the trouble was with the fact that **Pat Lauber** wasn't a science-enthusiast . . . simply a woman enormously desirous of building a successful magazine. Plus the fact that, "See, we have all the answers" style orthodoxy is what the teachers want presented . . . and, "Look how much we don't know . . . and how wonderful it would be to find out!" is what the students need. Teachers don't want a magazine that raises questions; they want one that answers them.

Oh . . . by the way. **Peg** made an exceedingly acute observation the other morning. (While watching a young couple with two boys, 1-1/2 and 4 years old, at breakfast next table at the hotel.) Even at 4, the boy was displaying the male pattern . . . as Peg observed correctly. A boy's questions are thickly larded with, "Yes, but . . . ." and, "But why. . . ." A girl's are usually simple inquisitives, and she ends up with either, "Oh," or, "Yes."

Now as to our running debate:

The basic trouble is that the problem of the relationship of the
478

individual to the group has never been solved. The Society expresses rules for public living . . . and those rules are totally impossible for private, individual-to-individual living. Taking the most strictly private-living, individual-to-individual relationship of all, physical sex, note that the society's rules are utterly hopeless as any sort of a guide. And, until quite recently, the society ruled that no information about the practical operation of sexual relationships should exist at all! (I.e., books discussing sexual relations were flatly interdicted.) **Kinsey's** efforts to gather some information — whether those efforts were well handled or ill is beside the point — were violently attacked; various pressure groups forced the Foundations that supported his work to withdraw their support. (And **Kinsey** died of a heart attack.)

The Society exists by group-relationships. Private relationships interfere with it, since they are emotional in nature, and not subject to easy control by intellectually communicable rulings. (Instance: family loyalty will cause a family to shield a criminal from the agents of society. Emotional effects frustrating social rulings.)

But individual-individual rules are just exactly as inappropriate to group systems such as a society.

Now: What I'm trying to say is, "A Society, being a great, big, clumsy, massive organism, has to have rules of organization; it can't operate on pure individual choice."

What you're trying to express is, "Broad rules don't fit individual-individual situations, and seriously hurt the poor guy who gets caught in the jam."

I agree with you. Completely, 100% agree with you. I agree that something should be done about it.

But I do NOT agree with you that we should pass a broad rule that there should be no broad rules.

Look, guy; **Newton's** laws didn't work for Mercury, nor for high speed electrons. Therefore we should throw Physics out the window, huh?

I agree with you that present broad rules anent racial problems are unsatisfactory.

Now please stop being foolish-in-the-head and suggesting that we throw all rules of racial relationship out the window.

What we need is not no-rules-at-all, but rules that work better.

479

The Food & Drug Administration tests for the suitability of dye substances as food dyes are, as you told me, unsatisfactory and inappropriate. So let's dispense with the FDA, and have no rules, huh? Let anyone who thinks his dye-stuff is a good food color go ahead?

Maybe we should, instead, do some sweating on devising more appropriate tests . . . with the recognition that no test will ever be completely satisfactory, except the use itself.

You know these "tube tester" machines in radio stores? They test cathode emission, and not much more. I've got a tube that tests perfect . . . only it won't amplify worth a damn; something's wrong with the grid, so it's non-linear as hell. But I'm using it very satisfactorily; it makes a fine oscillator, where all I want it to do is to turn the plate-current on and off.

When the testing procedure is inappropriate to the problem, people want to throw it out. Fine . . . but that doesn't mean throwing out testing. It means getting a better testing procedure.

Now consider this question: Do we need <u>any</u> kind of racial rulings?

If you answer that, "No," then, "Should an individual pay <u>any</u> attention to the genetic background of his mate?"

And don't answer that one, "No" or I'll refer you to the young man from Dundee, who buggered an ape up a tree.

The trouble, M'lad, is that no logician can count. That is, since logic is qualitative, not quantitative, no logician can distinguish degrees, quantities, or magnitudes. And, incidentally, no one yet has come up with a logically satisfactory definition of Number, though God knows they've tried hard enough.

Look; what's infinity minus one? Infinity.

Not if the "one" is "first." You have to have <u>first</u> before you can have <u>any</u>. Your "Ugly Boy" story simply subtracted one (the first) from an infinite number of fires . . . and <u>whoosht</u>! they <u>all</u> went out.

Therefore, infinity minus one is zero. <u>Provided that "one" is "first."</u>

Now consider this problem: Is it logically possible to determine the color of an unexposed photographic film?

Logically, the only possible answer is "No." Color is a term dealing with light; in this case reflected light. But an "unexposed photographic film" is one that hasn't been exposed to any light. Therefore you can't possibly determine the color of an unexposed film.

480

But technically — i.e., in real-world practice — you can determine the exact color of the most sensitive film made, without exposing it. The threshold sensitivity of the best films is about 1000 quanta. Modern photomultiplier tubes are sensitive to about four quanta. Therefore a photoelectricspectrometer can observe the color of an unexposed film.

Since you have, all your life, been trapped again and again by the fact that logicians can't count, and by the fact that other people will always seek to force you into the untenable position of being logical just when you need to count . . . you have, like anyone else in the culture, a violent rejection of being stuck with a need-to-count.

When is a Negro not a Negro? When he's 1/2 White? 1/4 White? 1/8th?

When is a Jew not a Jew? When he's left the Hebrew faith? When he was born a gentile, even though he has accepted the Hebrew faith? Count, **Isaac!** Draw a line!

Remember **H. Beam Piper's** "The Day of the Moron?" When is a man too stupid to hold a critical job? When is an airline pilot unfit for work? A Canadian pilot, I notice, made a crack-up landing with a DC-7 a year or two ago. He was ruled negligent, and suspended for six months. A year later he cracked up a smaller liner . . . he hadn't been allowed to take the big DC-7's again . . . and killed some 30 people.

Your fundamental objection is that broad rules should not be made to limit the individual exception.

Start counting, **Ike**; count off what constitutes an exception. The existence of a society demands that there be rules. That's what distinguishes a society from an anarchy, isn't it?

Regards, John

Isaac Asimov *April 15, 1958*

Dear Ike:

Kelly's done a symbol for one of the up-coming covers, titled, "The Nonconformist." It's got a lot of little circles, with vector arrows pushing down on them, all squashed a little out of round . . . and one triangle, with the vector arrow pushing down, but, of course, triangles won't distort worth a damn.

You're not exactly a square, **Ike** . . . more of a triangle, I'd say!

481

I can see that Boston University might have a bit of difficulty forcing you to conform to what they want. In the first place, they're wrong, and you're right, which puts them behind the eight-ball to start with. Of course, normally that handicap wouldn't be enough to stop the Group from forcing the Individual to conform. The only difficulty they're up against is that your reader-Group is bigger than theirs.

Had an argument with a gal at the office the other day. (I get into those arguments with people who don't actually matter as themselves-alone, because they help me learn what it is that keeps me from communicating the self-evident to the large group they represent. It's worthwhile.) I was trying to get her to see that the creative genius' Opportunity was the ordinary man's Insecurity — that because our culture is, currently, dedicated to Security Uber Alles, we have a culture deliberately dedicated to developing methods of suppressing creativity.

There's a story there, **Ike**. As usual, we'd lay it on a far planet . .. but the essence of it would be that a group of schemers from Alpha set out to make it possible for Alpha to conquer the thriving, effective planet Beta. They arrange it by getting the Betans to become safety-security-certainties-only oriented. Men are to be advanced on a basis of seniority; brilliance is anti-social, because it makes people try to sidestep the Seniority rules. (Like a peasant trying to sneak into the nobility just because he happens to be competent.) Then the Alphans introduce various social legislative gimmicks to make sure the geniuses can't get anywhere, even if they do resist the pressure of conforming to dull-normal. They set up an income-tax system such that you can't earn more than enough for a fairly comfortable living — you can't earn enough to achieve control of economic power adequate to start something new. They arrange a Securities Examination Board, that allows the sale of securities only if they are safe, sane, and practically certain . . . and conformal. (No wild-eyed **Henry Fords** will get backing to disrupt the whole buggy industry.)

In other words, figure out the techniques that would lead to frustrating brilliant individuals in a culture, and make for maximum security of the people who want to have Answers, but don't want to have to Learn.

Ike, you'll find that every one of them is already installed and operating in the present US.

The Reptiles — the Saurians — tried to solve the problem of living
482

by Having Answers. The new-hatched saurian was gifted with enough answers to take him through life.

But evolution got more and more complicated; more and more answers were required. Theoretically, if you had omniscience, i.e., knew all the answers to all the problems, you wouldn't have to be able to learn, and wouldn't need to learn a thing. You'd already know.

The trouble with this technique is that it's the ridiculous-extreme of the proposition, "You can solve a problem either by a simple machine and a complex program, or by a simple program and a complex machine." The Omniscience method is a simple program — a one-step program. But it entails a machine of infinite complexity. And at infinity, the program ceases to be one-step; now you have the program-problem of access to the answer. The bigger a library becomes, the harder it is to find the stored data.

The Saurians ran into the difficulty. Getting new data in became an enormously difficult problem (i.e., evolving a new instinct became difficult) and the access-machinery began to get so complicated that it broke down.

The mammals solved the thing a different way. Learning involves developing an answer-generator, instead of the instinct-answer-storage.

You probably aren't aware of the fact that you're highly abnormal among human beings; 90% of the time, despite the fact that you have a phenomenally good memory, you solve problems by ad-lib generation of an answer on the spot. You expect to generate, rather than remember, answers.

Most human beings don't work that way, Check, and observe!

I made **Peedee** design a trick camera. I've forgotten whether I told you this; if I did, forgive me. It's relevant. The problem was to design a camera with a 120⁰ angle of view, for taking a picture of our rebuilt kitchen. A camera, moreover, that we could build, at home, with hand tools. (You can buy such a camera for about $4000.)

Peedee designed it; I built it. It took a beautiful picture.

It's a pin-hole camera, of course. But **Peedee** had to compute answers to the questions I pointed out:

1. What must be the distance from pin-hole "lens" to a 5 x 7 inch sheet of film so that the 7" dimension shall cover 120⁰ of angle?

2. What is the circle of confusion produced by a pin-hole "lens" of

diameter <u>d</u>? How small a hole must we use to achieve a satisfactory picture?

3. What will the F ratio of that hole and the above-specified lens-film distance be?

4. Using an ASA 200 film (Royal Ortho) what exposure will be called for?

5. If the pinhole is made in a sheet of Al foil taped to the inside surface of a 1/4-inch thick Masonite panel, how large a hole must we cut in the Masonite panel to allow the pinhole the specified 120^0 angle of view?

Now those things can NOT be looked up. You can't ask someone for the answers. The physics textbooks don't even give methods of figuring 'em.

Peedee, for the first time, recognized the need for generating answers herself. I wasn't holding out on her; I didn't know either. Her teacher wasn't holding out; he didn't know. The book with the answers wasn't being kept from her; there wasn't any.

She sweated on 'em, too, believe me! That circle-of-confusion problem is a dilly, because you immediately run into infinity, which you can't handle worth a damn. But she finally sweated it out, using principles of plane geometry. (Light rays from a point at infinity are parallel lines. That takes care of infinity.)

Most human beings DO NOT WANT TO LEARN TO GENERATE ANSWERS. The culture, of course, doesn't want individuals to generate answers . . . because <u>new</u> answers will be unpredictable variables that the culture isn't prepared for.

Actually, of course, new answers are like mutations; most new answers will be destructive. (Probability. If you do something absolutely at random, in a given situation, the probability is that it won't help the situation.) The thing that characterizes the creative genius is that his new answers are highly improbable — they are beneficial.

Anyhow . . . the non-conformist is bound to be an acutely painful and disturbing element, on the average, to the normal individual. It's the business of the Risk of Taking a Risk, vs the Risk of Not Taking a Risk — and the normal individual wants the Risk part of that completely eliminated.

Only . . . he doesn't want the chance of <u>good</u> luck eliminated. Only bad luck is to be forestalled.

484

The income tax system is so set-up that you can't <u>earn</u> a fortune; the punitive rates at high income levels make that impossible. But you can get rich by luck. I.e., if you invest in a stock which increases in value 1000 times, there's only a straight capital-gains tax. It's not a punitive tax.

An individual can achieve economic power through the capital-gains route . . . but he can't earn money sufficient for economic power. The capital-gains system favors those who exploit natural resources, not intelligence and competence. (Patents are being rendered either useless or illegal. They're useful only if you've got money enough to sue big corporations blue in the face . . . which means you have to be a big corporation. But big corporations are being forced to surrender their patents as an illegal monopoly in restraint of trade! See Bell Labs, IBM, and now RCA.)

Do you think it might be fun to work out a story in which the Alphan saboteurs deliberately seek to destroy Beta by contriving a genius-suppression cultural system?

It's been suggested time and again in scf that humans have an abnormally high rate of invention, and scare the pants off the Galactic races.

Usually, the story has the Galactic races trying to destroy Earth, or the like.

Maybe they've got a better technique, huh?

Ike, what's the place of "unkindness" in living? What right has the creative genius to be so unkind as to destroy the security and stability the normal man depends on?

What right do we scfers have to needle, to be gadflys, and ask discomforting questions?

"What you don't know, won't hurt you." This is true. It may kill you . . . but it won't hurt you, in the sense of worry, fret or frustrate you. We worry people. Do we have a right to?

And now to worry, fret, and/or frustrate you:

Had lunch with **Walter Gibson** t'other day. He'd just been out to the place on Long Island where they're having poltergeist trouble. Now **Walt** is Vice President of the American Magicians' Guild; he was a member of **Houdini's** committee. He's also a member of the American Society for Psychical research. He's a man who's made a business of

485

illusions . . . and, also, a man who's willing to discover the real thing, provided it's <u>not</u> an illusion.

Walt believes that the phenomena on Long Island are the McCoy.

The 12-year-old kid involved appears to have a somewhat unusual attention-getting device. The motivation is simple enough; he wants attention. <u>Personal</u> attention and respect.

Of course, he isn't doing it consciously . . . but he's the focus of the phenomena. And the phenomena quit during the time **Dr. Pratt** was there, giving him full, 100%, sympathetic attention. They haven't resumed since.

Three times, objects were seen <u>while in flight</u> by observers who were <u>not</u> members of the family. 1. The detective assigned on the case. 2. A reporter from the local newspaper, who was spending a night there. 3. A reporter from a London paper, who went out after the *Life* story appeared.

Gibson checked the circumstances with the eye of a professional illusionist. In case #2, the object was an 8-inch globe of the Earth. The course it followed involved flying around a corner; if it didn't defy the law of gravity, then it defied the laws of motion.

The most critical aspect of it is that the objects seen in flight were visible-as-objects while flying. The eye does <u>not</u> see an object thrown with velocity sufficient to take a 20-foot trajectory, unless the line of observation is nearly parallel with the line of flight. You can see a blurr of motion, a streak in the air, but not an object.

But several times, flying objects crashed with violence sufficient to shatter them completely. In one instance, the object was shattered . . . but the wall it shattered on wasn't dented.

If you visualized an 8-inch globe flying from point A to point B, you would visualize it <u>as a seeable process</u> — you'd actually visualize a slowed-down flight.

If you visualized an object flying from A to B, and shattering when it hit B . . . the <u>object</u> would be imagined as shattering, but usually one overlooks the fact that the object struck is also damaged.

It appears that what is occurring is that a subjective-reality visualized is being imposed on objective reality. What happens is what the boy <u>imagines</u> the occurrence to be . . . not what would normally happen!

There is a dream-like, unreal quality — because they are dreams

486

being objectivized! Things shatter not because they strike with shattering force — but because the visualization is that they shatter. The bottles that started popping — they were screw-cap bottles. Screw-cap bottles don't pop. The detective made a considerable series of tests, and found that if a screw cap is put on only 1/3rd turn, and a fast-effervescing mixture put in the bottle, the cap will fly off with a pop. But it's got to be a <u>fast</u> effervescence, or the gas just leaks out around the loose cap. And if the cap isn't loose, the bottle explodes.

Conclusion: the popping noises heard are <u>not</u> caused by the cap coming off. Some small boy mind is visualizing the bottles opening . . . and visualizing the pop as the cap flies off.

The phenomena have the weird, confused lack of proper correlation that you're apt to find in a poorly worked out story written by a small boy . . . or in a dream.

More interesting in its own way is the throwing of a 78 pound bookcase-with-books. The kid didn't have the strength to do it physically.

Evidently this dream-power, this dreaming-real, gives an individual access to power, sheer physical power, he wouldn't have in mechanical application.

The more **Gibson** told me about the details of the phenomena — and remember he, as a professional illusionist, was acutely concerned with precise details — the more dream-like the whole phenomenon became. Things appear to check with somebody throwing things . . . but they miss, they miss in the way someone who didn't understand chemistry, actually, would describe a chemical experiment. It would almost sound right . . . if you weren't listening with a trained ear.

The explanation "the kid is throwing the things" doesn't satisfy — because no trajectory of the required order could end in a crash that shattered the flying objects, without denting the wall. Or cause a glass bowl to shatter a wooden cabinet . . . without being damaged itself. Or throw a phonograph across the room, with a crash that alarmed the whole house . . . and not damage the phonograph appreciably! The crash was <u>not</u> caused by the impact . . . but, like the popping bottles, by the imagined requirement of a mighty crash.

So. **Walt's** writing the thing up for us, and writing up some other stuff about previous poltergeist phenomena.

Item: infinity minus one, the math sharks tell us, is infinity.

Exception: when the one subtracted is the first.

Application: Which is most important in establishing the repeatability of a scientific experiment; the original experiment, or the confirming test? Obviously, the confirming experiment is a confirmation unless the original preceeds it . . . yet the original isn't a scientifically validated repeatable experiment until the confirmation. Which, then, is the first scientific demonstration of the phenomenon?

Lawyers refer to "precedents." Once a precedent can be established, the case can be argued.

Until a Class exists, there can be no subsets of the class. Until a class accepted as "Real psi phenomena" is allowed, there can be no instances.

Science, by refusing to acknowledge the first prevents the building of the infinite class!

Bernie Kahn told me something, while I was in San Francisco, that I find fascinating . . . and I think you will. I've no references on it, and I wonder if you and/or your cohorts could find them. It might be real nice and useful to you, too.

It seems that there's a nice, readily available source of cortisone, available cheaply, and without prescription, that the dear old AMA can't possibly get nailed under prescription. Licorice! It doesn't contain cortisone itself, apparently, but a precursor which, in normal human metabolism, is immediately converted to cortisone . . . and apparently by a transformation that can't be handled in vitro!

Peg's been troubled by a bit of arthritis of the fingers. Massive vitamin C helped. (2-5000 milligrams/day.) But licorice helps more.

Further item: **Bernie** also told me that extract of dogwood contains a considerable quantity of estrogenic hormones.

Major ingredients of Lydia E. Pinkham's Female Remedy: Licorice and extract of dogwood. By God, the old witch-woman did have a female remedy based on hormone therapy before the MDs knew hormones existed! What does a woman in menopause need? Cortisone and estrogenic hormones, of course!

Your gang up there may well be interested in running down references on that. If you can and do . . . please send me a nice little squib on it.

Just go on being a triangle, **Ike**, remember the fine motto NON ILLEGITIMATI TE CARBORUNDUM! and to hell with orthodoxy!

Regards, John

Isaac Asimov   *June 4, 1958*

Dear Ike:
You know, when people are confronted with the possibility that a situation Alpha may exist, Alpha being a situation they simply don't know how to handle . . . they deny the possibility that Alpha could, or should, or has any right to, exist. If it doesn't, can't, shouldn't, and won't ever exist, then there is no problem of learning-how-to-deal-with-alpha.

O.K.; you're fighting the proposition, "Genetically determined superiority and inferiority exist."

Try considering this problem: On a certain planet Arret, an intelligent humanoid race exists. The race is divided into a number of breeds. Some breeds are superior to others.

1. Don't argue it shouldn't be — on Arret, by definition of the problem, it <u>does</u>.

2. Don't argue, "It should be ended." It can't be, except by wholesale slaughter of all breeds but one . . . and that will cure it only temporarily, because the humanoids of the planet have highly unstable germ-plasm, and are highly susceptible to mutation, so that even if the breed were stabilized, it wouldn't stay that way.

3. Solve the problem, "How should a culture handle the interrelationship of inferior and superior breeds?" It being recognized that, since these are breeds, not merely individual superior-inferior differences, there must be a cultural mechanism for handling <u>both</u> equality-within-a-breed, <u>and</u> superiority-inferiority between breeds, <u>and</u> individual-difference.

Set aside completely any problem of Earthly genetics, and solve the hypothetical problem of a culture on a planet where there <u>are</u> significant differences of breed. With the stipulation that the differences of breeds is entirely non-physical; i.e., the differences are mental, solely, and so cannot be distinguished by any physical trait.

The problem of handling superiority-inferiority is so damned tough that, currently, our culture is seeking to deny it exists to be solved.

Now it's very fine to say that it's the mixed breeds that have the best characteristics; I agree with you. So do all geneticists. It's called "hybrid
489

vigor." But, **Ike**, you've got to have something before you can mix it. If you deny there are breeds . . . then what's this nonsense about mixed breeds, huh? If the concept "human breeds" is an empty class, then it is zero, and zero plus zero is zero, as is zero times zero.

Stop fighting the existence of the problem; that is, was, and always will be a futile chore. Try fighting the problem of how to handle the fact that the problem of inferiority-superiority exists.

Look; the image found on a photographic negative is due to the action of the developing agent. That can be proven very simply indeed; try taking an exposed film, and treating it directly in the thiosulphate silver-halide dissolving solution. You'll get a completely blank negative. That proves that the image is caused entirely by the chemical energy of the developer, doesn't it?

Take some Royal X Pan film, and develop it in D-8 formula, and you get a negative that's all black and whites, with practically no grays. Further, the image structure is coarse and grainy. The sensitivity-rating of the film shows a film-speed of about ASA 2000, though.

Take the same Royal X Pan, develop it in D-777, and it shows a film-speed sensitivity rating of about ASA 800. . . . but the image structure is smooth, almost grainless, and shows excellent, soft gradations from black to clear.

See? That proves that it's all a matter of development, doesn't it?

Yeah . . . and now try developing a film that doesn't have any latent image in it — that's never been exposed. Or one that didn't have any silver-halide put in the gelatine. Or take a look at what happens if the emulsion hasn't had one of the red-light-sensitization dyes added to the emulsion in manufacture. All development, is it, huh?

Now it's clear that there is no such thing as this superstition-mystic idea of "infra-red," because no one can see it, and no good, reliable silver-halide emulsion ever indicates any such thing. It's only "shown" on films that have been treated with some weird stew of a dye that is supposed to make it "infra-red sensitive." Infra-red sensitive nonsense! Obviously, that weird stew is simply causing the film to fog in patches!

Deny the problem; that's far, far easier than solving it.

Deny the problem of psionics; admit it exists, and it represents a real problem for which we not only have no answers, but have no known methods of seeking for answers! The rules of research in the field haven't been laid out!

(But the City Engineer in Flint, Michigan, uses dowsing rods [made of standard brass welding rods bent into an L shape, held like pistols, in 1/4 inch copper tubing handles] for locating underground water pipes. Sure — he uses electronic gadgets for finding iron and steel pipes . . . but they don't work well for brick, clay, tile, concrete and plastic pipes. Also the electronic gadgets react to power cables, sewer and gas pipes; his dowsing rods don't. About 80% of his men can, and do, use them routinely. He's not exhibiting them in a show, seeking to attract notice with them, or anything other than get the job of maintaining the city water system done. The dowsing gadgets help. He doesn't need to know why.)

Deny the problem of inferiority-superiority; that'll make it go away so we don't have to solve it.

Give a fool some dynamite to play with, and he'll kill himself. Give it to a wise man, and he'll build bridges and mine ore.

Give a power to a fool — and you commit murder. Withold it from a wise man — and you frustrate him.

What should you teach students, **Ike**? All you know? Give all of them all the powers available to you?

You have no right to decide superiority doesn't exist — until you show that you are not afraid to handle the problem if it does exist.

This culture is so afraid of the problem, it denies it. In Russia, all children have a right to try for higher education. In America that situation is approached, too. But in Russia, the incompetent get thrown out. In America it is held unethical to say, "This child is incompetent; he shall not pass." And the only way to keep some from failing is to make the course so indefinite that even fools graduate.

Regards, John

Isaac Asimov   *June 10, 1958*

Dear Ike:

I'm afraid that *Astounding* will have to suspend publication, and you'll have to quit science-fiction writing. Reason: You and *ASF* are pushing people around — depriving them of the opportunity to do what they want the way they want to. I know several scf magazines have folded,

491

or damn near it, while *ASF* is continuing to take an even more unfair lion's share of the shrinking science-fiction market for itself. (Our circulation may have dropped, but we can't tell yet, since the drop is less than the usual seasonal fluctuations plus usual random fluctuations; if there has been an effect we haven't been able to determine it yet.) But if it is inherently unethical, evil, wrong, unjust, for a superior entity to benefit by virtue of that superiority, and at the expense of inferior entities ... why, then either *ASF* must be degraded in quality, or cease publication.

And you have, for years, pushed would-be authors out of the magazines and books, so you must degrade the quality of your writing, or stop writing. "Drop dead!" in other words, because your superior ability is frustrating inferior authors.

This is, of course, the current societal evaluation. It's held to be improper for a superior individual to display, use, or benefit either himself or others by the application of his superiority. Thus a surgeon of super-normal ability is subject to an income-tax-fine system which requires that he limit his superior activities, so that lesser surgeons will have their chance to butcher the patients he might have saved.

It's not fair to set the standards of high school education so high that only the more talented and competent youngsters can graduate. Everyone must have an equal opportunity to get a high school diploma; it isn't just to allow only the superior individuals to have them. That's why our local high school teachers tell me that of the graduating class this year, less than 50% deserve the diploma all will get.

It isn't fair and democratic to allow only superior individuals to have college degrees; the State should see to it that every young man and woman is assured of just as good a degree as anyone else has. You have no business flunking an incompetent and denying him the right to a medical degree, **Ike**, just because he's inferior; you're spitting on him, degrading him — pushing him aside.

Look, my friend: superiority and inferiority exist. I don't give a purple damn whether you like it that way or not; that's the way God made this here Universe, and, "I suggest you learn to love it," because hating it isn't going to change it.

You know, in an argument — if it's a real, honest, argument-worthy-of-respect-and-attention, each side has an hypothesis, a concept, and each side presents that concept as well, as forcefully, and

492

as clearly as they can. If you've got an idea — give it a <u>real</u> try, not a half-ass try. You're not doing your honest share in the debate if you don't make a genuine effort to uphold your argument, give it every possible, honest chance to win, and do everything you honestly can to find the weaknesses in the opposing argument.

The essence of the process of evolution is exactly the same; an organism is born, or hatched, with a genetic thesis; he has the right, <u>and the duty</u>, to make an all-out, honest effort to make that thesis work — to defend his argument as fully as he can, while seeking out every weakness he can find in all opposing arguments.

Every organism has the right to try — and the duty of trying. BUT . . . the right to try IS NOT EQUIVALENT TO THE RIGHT TO SUCCEED!

Every organism has needs. But, dammital, a <u>need is not a right</u>! Even if that need is an absolute, life-or-death, desperation need. An animal needs food; that does NOT mean it has a right to food. If a lion turns man-eater, it's usually because it has a desperate need for food, and is getting too old and slow to catch deer, zebras, or the like. It has a need that's absolute; it still doesn't have a right to food — and men set about eliminating its need in a hurry. Via the death route.

You've probably read about agammaglobulinemia. It's a genetic-defect condition in which the individual lacks gamma globulins . . . with the natural result that he has practically no immunity to disease. The condition wasn't discovered until recently: only when high-power anti-biotics made it possible for such a child to live a while were they able to find cases to study. A child born with this condition in 1920 would have had an absolute, desperate need for antibiotics . . . but a need is not equivalent to an assured right.

An individual may be born with a need to feel he is the most superior person in the world. That's not equivalent to <u>being</u> the most superior — and the need, however real and desperate, however necessary to his mental health, doesn't give him the right to fulfillment.

You know, **Marx** was right! History shows the inevitable triumph of the proletariat! Every culture that Man has built so far, in the logical-empire tradition, has wound up with the triumph of the proletariat — whether you call him "proletariat" or "the Common Man." **Marx** error was in saying, "That which always does happen is that which should

493

happen."

Because the always-correlated next step in the process following immediately after the apotheosis of the Common Man — whatever name you give him, plebian, proletariat, vulges, Common Man or what — is the break-up of the culture.

When the cells of a living body finally escape from the long tyranny of the dictatorial aristocracy of the nervous system, and establish a true every-cell's-equal state . . . we call it death, although practically all the cells are still living vigorously. A tiny knife in the medulla oblongata won't kill more than 0.01% of the cells of the body, and will free all the other cells from the long dictatorship of the nervous system.

Take a look, **Ike**. "Corn and circuses!" the plebian of Rome demanded . . . and got. The State should supply his needs, both for food and amusement, and because the Common Man had, at last, achieved the power he deserved, he got what he needed. Under the Republic, when it was really a republic, he didn't; he got shoved around by people who held they were superior just because they could get things done.

The Common Man of Athens finally revolted against **Socrates** and voted him to death.

The Czars in Russia stayed on top by most meticulously giving the proletariat exactly what the proletariat wanted—the right to do what they wanted, the way they wanted, no matter how stupid a way that was.

The Russian aristocracy did have superiority . . . and didn't use it. Czar **Peter the Great** really tried; he was cordially hated by both the serfs, whom he freed, and the nobles, whom he tried to put to work.

Why aren't teachers respected? Why, hell! A teacher is a man who tries to make people think new ideas; if there is anything that is more anathematized by the Common Man than that, it's making people do new things in new ways.

You know yourself that, today, the teacher is, actually, considered (as shown in action, not in verbalization!) a public governess — a domestic servant, whose job is to keep Junior out of Mama's hair, while indoctrinating Junior with what Mama believes he ought to believe. (Not by any means what she believes, of course!) Since Teacher's job is to keep Junior out of Mama's hair, if Junior comes home complaining about school, Teacher isn't doing what Mama wants done. The principle duty of the teacher is to keep Junior away from home, off the streets, and out

494

of trouble that might hurt him. (If it hurts teacher or someone else, that's perfectly all right . . . except when the other person hurt is someone else's Junior, in which case that Mama gets mad.)

Junior must be taught to understand English, so Mama can give Junior orders and have them obeyed.

But Teacher is a low-level domestic servant, and certainly has no business making judgments and decisions about Junior! The very idea of a mere teacher saying that Junior is a stupid, doltish, incompetent, and ill-mannered brat! The idea of teacher flunking Junior, saying Junior isn't good enough to keep up with those stupid, doltish, ill-mannered brats in his class! Or those snotty, snobbish, prissy brats that go around being polite and mannerly and studying to learn something — why, they think they're superior!

Go on, **Ike** — try being a high-school teacher! Try flunking the louts!

This is the Day of the Common Man!

Yeah . . . and remember the old hymn. "Work, for the night is coming, when Man works no more!"

The major difference between the US and Russian educational system is that in Russia they have a free public educational system, run on tyrannical lines. Ours is democratic. In Russia, a kid gets free education, and gets paid while taking his higher studies, but that's open only to superior individuals. The Teachers have the power and the right to say, "Ivan's a lout; he doesn't deserve education. Igor, on the other hand, has real ability; let the State pay him to develop that potential."

Naturally the teacher is respected in Russia; he isn't a domestic servant — he's a public Judge.

Come off it, **Ike**; look at your own convictions, not your social indoctrination! Sure, you have to keep clearly in mind what the social indoctrinations are, because you've got to make allowances for them. But don't confuse "What they say" with "What I know, on the basis of evidence, to be true."

You've fought for and won for yourself a very special-privilege position there at Boston Universwity, haven't you? The head of your department is your inferior-in-wisdom-and-breadth-of-understanding — so you humiliated him by going over his head and dealing with the policy-making level of the administration. How did you get away with

495

that? Any of the other men there try it successfully? Or did you humiliate them, too, by doing what they didn't dare try? Wonder if some of them didn't have hell and hallelujah from their wives for not doing what you did? Well . . . why didn't they?

Because you're superior, know it, have the power to demand special privilege, and make it stick. And you did.

You send in a manuscript, and expect me to read it immediately, out of turn, putting aside all the manuscripts of the slush pile. Special privilege you want, heh? On what basis? That you're superior.

Why do I behave so unfairly as to do what you want? Because you damn well <u>are</u> superior, and have damn well earned special privilege.

Sure there's equal-but-different . . . but there's also unequal-and-different. A man and a woman are inherently different; but also, some men are decidedly superior to a given woman, some are equal, and some are inferior.

This item is for your strictly-private-just-now information. **Art Gray**, Street & Smith president, appears to have hauled *Science World* out of the hole. He did something unethical, unfair, improper, and horrifying; the Street & Smith advertising department is still pale with shock and horror. He violated all the rules and ethics of the advertising business, by-passed the agencies, the company advertising departments, and went directly to the vice presidents and board of directors — the company-policy level. The result is very upsetting to several dozen advertising agencies, promotion departments, etc . . . but *Science World* which is a damn well needed communication medium, is almost certainly going to be appearing next fall, as usual.

Ike, the Common Man is, at <u>any</u> period of history, by definition, <u>relatively</u> stupid, thick-witted, and incompetent. The nature of statistics makes that necessarily and inescapably true. Remember our story of some years ago about the moron with an IQ of 250? He was a moron in a society where the common man had an IQ of 1000.

The Common Man is <u>always,</u> by the nature of statistics, relatively incompetent. Genius determines the nature of the cultural environment; genius is the creative group. The Common Man is always incompetent to deal with the structures genius builds; he <u>must</u> have the guidance of genius.

Genius could organize a Roman Empire; the Common Roman

couldn't control it. I've known hot-rodders; they don't have stupid accidents with their hyper-powered jobs — it's the shot-rodders who do. The shot-rodders are the Common Man kids who want the power the genius-level junior engineers have contrived, who can't achieve that order of organization themselves . . . and haven't the wit to control it when it's put in their hands.

It's the Common Man who wants to have hydrogen bombs at his disposal — who excoriates a scientist who says, "The Common Man doesn't have judgment enough to handle such weapons." And . . . who excoriates scientists for making the things when the Common Man uses them to his own disaster.

The Common Man always has judgment enough to be able to handle last century's problems — but this century's problems stem from the organizational ability of the culture's geniuses. That's why the Golden Age is always in the past; the Common Man can look back and see that those problems could be solved.

Remember the editorial I did in which I stated that there was a small clique in our population which had made it true that over one third of our population was ill-housed, ill-clothed and ill-fed . . . and were dedicated to seeing to it that that situation would forever remain? That almost half of our children were sub-normal, and that this same small group was responsible for that situation?

OK — the terrible statisticians are still at work. They've rigged things so that the Common Man can never be competent to handle the culture he lives in. Never — neither yesterday, today, or in any possible future.

The Common Man is forever doomed to incompetence — and the only kind of a culture which the Common Man can rule is one on the downgrade, one in which the complexities are decreasing faster than the entropy of totally unselective breeding and education decreases the competence of the Common Man.

That isn't arguable, **Ike**. It's an absolutely inescapable law of mathematical logic. The very definition of "Common Man" makes it innately inescapable.

<u>No matter how highly evolved the Common Man may become, in whatever future civilization there may be . . . he'll always and forever be incompetent!</u>

497

The dictatorship of the proletariat — the Day of the Common Man — is inevitably and causally related to the Night of the Culture. Gotterdaemerung; when the Twilight of the Gods comes, it is the Day of the Common Man.

Have you read *Atlas Shrugged* yet?

Item: I've gotten an article from a professional engineering-news reporter, **Murray Yayce**, on the operations of the Supervisor of Water Supplies for Flint, Mich. This engineer is a 40-odd year old professional, who uses dowsing rods made of standard brass welding rod, mounted in 1/4 inch copper tubing handles, for locating buried water mains. He uses standard electronic metal-detection equipment when seeking iron pipes, but that's useless for clay, tile, brick, or concrete water mains. Then the dowsing rods are used. About 80% of his crews can use them. They've been doing it for years as standard procedure.

He's using psi routinely — and he has no motive whatever save the elementary simple one of getting his job done, which it does. The data exists, is simple routine engineering records. He can, of course, demonstrate if that's what you want — but that's what you want. He doesn't want to — he just wants to use it in his regular business. So he won't waste valuable time putting on a ruddy show for fools.

Ike, that instance of use of a psi power is absolutely not open to any challenge of any sort whatever. It's data; don't quarrel with data, start examining the theory that says the data can't exist.

Item: I went down to Harrisburg, Pa., last week, to see an old fellow by the name of **Curtis Upton**. Princeton engineering graduate, Class of '05. 78 years old, and very vigorous. Chemical engineer for some 45 years, with some 70 patents to his name. Now interested in psionics. His specialty: medical diagnosis and treatment.

Art Gray was along. **Gray** gave him the name of a friend, on a slip of paper, and no other data. **Upton** started working with his gadget, and presently started reporting. "This man's very sick . . . vitality extremely low . . . he's got diabetes . . . chronic, but now in an acute attack. Blood circulation in the brain . . . why, he must be in a coma; there's almost none! Artherio-sclerosis combined with diabetes . . . ."

Data: the friend was in the hospital in New York, due to chronic diabetes plus artherio-sclerosis. He was in a coma, which the doctors indicated was in all probability a terminal coma; there was nothing they
498

could do.

This was Thursday evening. **Upton** did things which he said were treatment. After about 10 minutes, he claimed that the pancreas was restored to function. In another five minutes he said the blood circulation in the brain was back to normal.

Friday morning we drove back to N.Y.

Art heard from his friend's wife, about noon. She said — she knew nothing of the **Upton** business — that the doctors were much more hopeful that morning. That the blood circulation in the brain was very much better, that he was coming out of the coma, and that they were now beginning to suspect that the coma might have been caused by insulin shock — too much insulin, and were cutting down the dosage.

That one you can just mark up in the "Funny Coincidence" department. Only sometime you might try to figure out how large a file of "Funny Coincidence Department" data a man can legitimately allow, before deciding to start a new file with a different label.

Regards, John

P.S. I may be uncomfortable to my friends . . . but at least discomfort is stimulating.

Isaac Asimov   *June 19, 1958*

Dear Isaac:

This article comes back because, while good, it isn't good for us. Wrong level of instruction; our boys, in general, know about free-fall and what it means.

There's something I would like, though; it's partly expressed here, and buried by the more ordinary stuff which makes the sophisticated reader annoyed. To wit: a discussion of how surface gravity of a planet varies with diameter, density, and rotation. Mesklin being the extreme example, of course. Surface gravity considerations could be continued to the white-dwarf star level, and backed off to the asteroid level. At what "diameter" does a mass of standard nickel-iron meteoric material have to be approximately spherical? What, in other words, would be the largest possible dimension of a non-spheroidal mass of hard, tough, nickel-iron?

Second: The depth of the gravitational well created by a mass is not

499

a function of the density of the mass alone. For a given distance-from-center, say 100,000 kms, the gravitic well is a function of <u>mass</u> alone. Saturn may have an Earth-like gravity at the surface . . . but, oh, brother! What it takes to climb out of that gravitic hole in space!

Or consider a cold dwarf star; diameter only 2000 kms, and perfectly safe, radiation-wise, at a distance-from-the-surface, of only 1,000 kms. In a free-fall orbit, the thing could be approached without smearing the passengers of a ship. BUT . . . if it has a mass of, say .75 Sols, what's the gravitic well that would have to be overcome to get away?

Also . . . at what distance from Earth-surface, would a satellite be half way to the Moon? Half way, that is, in terms of energy?

There'd be a hell of a useful article there.

Item: We've got an article coming up on the use of divining rods. Seems a gentleman by the name of **Marklund**, a hard-headed, horny-handed engineer in charge of the water supply system for Flint, Michigan, uses standard electronic metal-locating equipment for spotting underground water mains . . . when they're metal. But how do you locate brick, clay, concrete, or tile mains?

Well, you take standard brass welding rods, bend them into an L shape, put the short ends in 1/4-inch copper tubing bushings, and hold them pointing horizontally, straight ahead of you, like a two gun westerner with a pair of pistols.

You then walk over the area where the pipe is believed to lie, and, when you cross it, the "gun barrels" swing outward and align themselves with the pipe. Then the crew digs down to the pipe.

It works for 80% of his crew-chiefs — and every crew has at least one man who can use 'em.

Now **Marklund** is paid by the City to keep the water system working, and the City doesn't give a damn how he does it, just so he does it well and cheaply.

And **Marklund**, of course, doesn't give a damn whether you or anyone else believe the rods work; he just wants to find water pipes in the quickest, easiest, cheapest manner, and make his living fixing said pipes. He hasn't the slightest interest in "selling" anyone the idea that the rods work, and any other individual's belief or disbelief is a matter of complete indifference to him. He doesn't claim to be a diviner — he claims to be, and sells his services as, an efficient water-supply
500

maintenance engineer. The City of Flint agrees that he is that.

However, you, as a scientist, are, in all intellectual honesty, forced to acknowledge that **Marklund** — who's been using the technique for some 6 to 8 years as routine procedure — has something that needs investigation.

He's not like your young physics prof in "Belief"; it isn't necessary for him to prove he <u>does</u> actually levitate, and isn't simply pulling tricks. Nobody gives a damn how he finds the city's water mains — and he, being a hard-headed, horny-handed engineer doesn't give a damn how his rods work, either. He has no need to find out how; he isn't paid to. And you have no way of forcing him to explain what he does, nor any right to demand that he do so.

But you, as a scientist, have the intellectual-honesty duty of acknowledging that he has a working engineering technique that employs some method that lies beyond the bounds of known science.

Incidentally — the rods don't do it; the man using them does it. The question isn't "how do the rods work," but "how does the man perceive when to turn the rods?" It's done subconsciously; what sensing system does the subconscious employ in order to perceive when to turn the rods, though?

Independently, the Chief Engineer of the Midlands Electric Power District in England has developed and used the same technique. He uses #000 power-line wire instead of welding rod — which is about the same thing in practice. He's also tried iron, aluminum, brass, and copper rods. Makes no difference, of course. He locates underground power-lines with his divining rods. And he, too, reports 80% of his crews can use them.

Re Superiority: Sometimes, **Ike**, you discourage me. Please read what I say — carefully. Not what you insist on thinking I say. I have NOT said what you, in your latest note, specifically claim I've said. You haven't noticed what I have been saying.

I've had trouble like this repeatedly; if I say, "Psychological forces are important in disease," half my hearers report, "He says germs have nothing to do with disease," and start proving that germs do have something to do with disease, and thereby seek to prove I'm wrong.

In a photographic negative, what is the cause of the image; the exposure, the nature of the film, or the developer? If you name any one

501

of those, I'll prove you're a liar by proving it won't work without the other two. Exposer and development of a sheet of cellulose acetate yields nothing. Development of Royal X Pan yields nothing. Exposure of Royal X yields nothing.

Now Negroes are, genetically, statistically, inferior to Caucasoids — and don't be a damn fool and say that they aren't, and don't be a damn fool and say that I am saying, "All Negroes are inferior to all Caucasoids." I've lived in the South; you haven't. I've met Georgia crackers, who are Caucasoids, and the world would be better off if they were all sterilized. They have neither sense, intelligence, nor humility; the southern Negroes are stupid, but they have sense and a degree of humility. They're a damn sight better kind of human being than the typical "Georgia Cracker." They are willing to learn, and acknowledge that they need to learn; the Cracker has neither characteristic.

Part of the thing that needs to be unlearned right now, **Ike**, is something I'm trying to get you to unlearn: YOU CAN'T LEARN THE ANSWER TO A PROBLEM IF YOU SIMPLY DENY THE PROBLEM EXISTS, OR INSIST IT SHOULD BE TREATED AS THOUGH IT SHOULDN'T EXIST.

There is superiority and inferiority. You can't solve it by insisting it (a) doesn't, or at least, (b) shouldn't exist. It does, and we can assume that it exists because the Laws of the Universe make it necessary that it exist.

Now automobiles, airplanes, trains, ships, etc., are inadequate answers to the problem of transportation. They're imperfect; they kill people, are costly, maim, injure, consume natural resources, and take time. Teleportation is obviously the necessary answer.

Now let us do with the transportation problem what you would have us do with the superior-inferior problem — call it the S-I problem. We will outlaw all these less-than-perfect solutions, unlearn railroading, highway building, and aeronautics, and learn teleportation. Of course, we don't know how to learn teleportation just now, but if we just outlaw all inferior solutions right away, someone will, of course, learn the perfect solution.

Nuts.

If **Newton** hadn't come along and taught us all those imperfect answers, why we'd have had Relativity instead right from the start, huh?
502

Look: Present racial discrimination techniques are bad answers. BUT THEY WERE BETTER THAN NO ANSWER AT ALL.

I mentioned last time about why popular democracy won't work; I've since worked up a full mathematical-logic type analysis, and can show that discrimination and selection is essential to a func-   tional society. Even a lousy selective mechanism is better than none at all!

The New York Public Schools system has finally, this year, decided to become hard, ruthless, tough — to be cruel and anti-democratic. They're actually going to flunk some seventh grade students! Any seventh grader who can't pass a fourth grade reading test is going to be held back. Of course, they can't be <u>too</u> harsh; it's been agreed that no poor unfortunate slob will be left back more than once in his whole school career.

What I have been vainly trying to communicate is this:

1. The selection-by-skin-color is a lousy test . . . BUT NOT TOTALLY MEANINGLESS.

2 Selection by birth (nobility method) is a lousy test . . . BUT MUST NOT BE CALLED MEANINGLESS.

3. Selection by IQ test is a lousy technique . . . BUT NOT TOTALLY MEANINGLESS.

4. Selection on the basis of school marks is a lousy test . . . BUT NOT ABSOLUTELY WORTHLESS.

5. You can NOT get people to give up a lousy test . . . UNTIL YOU OFFER THEM A BETTER ONE.

The schools in this country are in foul shape . . . because the school-marks basis of selection and rejection of individuals is not perfect — and parents <u>demanded that it be discarded in toto</u>! They demanded that no child be rejected just because he didn't do things the way the teachers thought he should — i.e., that no child be flunked just because he consistently got E on his subjects.

They got their demands.

The schools began giving up <u>all</u> selection of students — and Russian education, which is about like ours was 50 years ago, save that they make both high school and college required (and paid) for all <u>competent</u> individuals — is naturally doing a damn sight better job.

Now I never got a decent mark in English in my entire school career. So I'm a successful writer and editor.

How'd you do in English?

I got the highest marks M.I.T. gave at the time in Chemistry and Physics. So I'm in the Arts field, not in Science!

I never took an Arts course in my life — but **Kelly Freas** and several of the others say I've taught them things about Art their Art Schools didn't know.

OK? School marks do <u>not</u> serve as a perfect test of the student's abilities; this, maybe, is proof we should drop all school-marks testing?

Not, by God, until someone comes up with something better. Not just because the answer we have isn't optimum!

I refuse, absolutely, to give up weighting the fact of a dark skin in my judgment of a man; it is a significant datum, having a very definite statistical correlation with experience. BUT . . . I also refuse to make it an absolute determinant test. If you refuse to recognize my wisdom in paying attention to his dark skin — you are, by God, neither a scientist, a rational man, nor a competent advisor. And if you pay attention <u>only</u> to his dark skin, you're a fool.

If a man is in Sing Sing, convicted of murder, does that prove he's an utterly unreliable witness, whose word can not be trusted on anything? No . . . but it's a black mark against him, and his testimony must be weighed in terms of what he is known to be. If he's a professional, hired killer-for-money — it may well be that he's a completely honest business man, who could be implicitly trusted for honest accounting of moneys entrusted to him.

The School Marks test is as lousy as any I know — but you don't rail against that particularly. How about the wise but no-formal-education individuals who are denied employment merely because of lack of sheepskin? Isn't that just as unjust as denying employment because of dark skin? Is it fair to deny a man the right to practice medicine just because he has no sheepskin? Is it in any fundamental respect different from denying him the right because he doesn't have a white skin?

Go on - weasel! Say that's different, because the sheepskin test is a valid test, while the black-skin test is not. On what basis do you make that distinction? I'm not asking simple questions, I'm asking the hard ones! If you acknowledge that selection-by-test is valid <u>at all</u> . . . then you must give me an acceptable, usable, apply-able test for me to use. Not tell me, "Selection is inherently improper."

504

The social scientists are, gradually, being driven to accept that their use of statistics has been exceedingly phoney. The Gaussian Curve that I've been yelling about for several years is gradually being sort of pushed into a back drawer . . . quietly, so no one notices they've discovered a mistake.

I'll make a flat statement, without qualification, and I'll bet that within 10 years it will begin to be recognized as a valid law.

Any time a social scientist finds that a human population shows a Gaussian distribution of any characteristic . . . he's wrong.

Reason: A Gaussian distribution applies to a pure-random universe. It's fine for gas molecules of the same type, in the complete absence of electric, magnetic, thermal, or gravitic gradients — but if any gradient force of any kind is present, you can not get a Gaussian distribution. By definition!

A Gaussian curve refers to a universe in which the [mode] average, median, and mean are identical. And that's a highly abnormal Universe!

In a human population, the average intelligence is certainly not equal to the median, nor to the mean.

I can name one biasing force at work; the fact that I can name one is, in itself, enough to throw out any Gaussian distribution argument. The biasing force: Mutation.

Any geneticist knows that mutation is enormously more apt to produce an unfavorable, than a favorable, resultant. Then there is, in any human population, a constant force weighting the odds in favor of the low end of the scale, with respect to any characteristic you name!

More recent, and more careful IQ studies, show a concentration of IQ's at two zones in the Genius end — about 140 and again about 180. Suggested reason: 140 is about as high as you can display, and remain in effective communication with the normal people. If you start displaying 160, you are rejected . . . and then you'll find friends only among geniuses. Then, of course, you can display as high a score as you like.

This, obviously, is another biasing force that makes a Gaussian distribution a lie.

Now all governments are Oligarchy in form; the limiting extremes of the Oligarchic "group of rulers" being, on one hand, the group-of-one, when we call it Tyranny, and, on the other, when the ruler-group and the total-group are the same, and we call it universal suffrage democracy.

505

The only difference between governmental forms is the manner of selecting the ruler-group from the population.

No one has ever tried universal suffrage democracy; it's too obvious that won't work. (Universal suffrage would mean new-born babies voting, too, you know. Currently we have an over-21-year ruler-group.)

The seniority system of ruler-selection worked pretty well . . . when the age level picked was 50 or so. Only damn sharp people managed to live that long in earlier times!

No nation has ever survived giving the Common Man a dominant voice in government. The above discussion of the effect of mutation, plus the meanings of average [mode], median, mean, and majority provide a perfect, complete, and unanswerable explanation of why the current American concept of democracy can never work.

The rigidity of the Universe itself supplies a foundation against which the current American hyperdemocracy — or any such hyperdemocracy — will bounce every time, without fail.

"We are now engaged in a great war to determine whether this nation, or any nation so endowed and so created, can long endure." The answer, **Mr. Lincoln**, is that it can't . . . not after the abolishment of the principles with which it was, actually, endowed and created!

Here's what happens: Once the hyperdemocratic effect sets in, the greatest number determines the course of development.

Now any species, anywhere, anytime, seeks to produce an environment in which it, and its type, can best survive and prosper, at the expense of the rest of the universe.

Once the control passes to the less-than-50-percent-right judges, they will inevitably seek to make the situation one favorable to them. This can only be one in which things are simplified to a point that they are right more than 50% of the time.

But, in the situation then existing, they are right less than 50% of the time, so the methods they pick to simplify the situation will, inevitably, be wrong decisions! They will, in seeking to simplify the problem, invariably make the problem worse. By the sheer mathematical fact that the more less-than-50%-right judges you have voting, the more certain you are to get the wrong answer.

Now one of the possible wrong decisions is the decision, "We need a one-man-tyrant form of govement. That's the simplest kind to
506

understand."

Inevitably, there will come a point where that wrong decision becomes the most-probable.

In Rome, it was **Caesar Augustus**. In Germany, it was **Hitler**. The U.S. came close to it, in the Great Depression, with **Roosevelt**.

The United States is, as of now, ripe for One Man Government. It's one of the Wrong Decisions that a hyperdemocracy is bound to make, if left to itself.

It being a wrong decision, it makes the situation worse for the people. One Man government can work only when very wise men indeed choose the One Man. (The Catholic Church has remained stable for a long time, because while it is One Man government, the One Man is selected by a group of highly selected judges.) But in the wild swing of a hyperdemocracy, it is the less-than-50%-right individuals who choose the One Man. They presently get a **Nero**, **Caligula**, and then a succession of men who buy the Empire from the Legion.

This is what happens if there is no major external Power. Greece didn't show the effects, simply because there were other, external powers that stepped in before the process went far. Ditto for **Hitler** Germany. Ditto would be true for the U.S.

I'm talking about an INHERENT, MATHEMATICALLY PRE-DICTABLE SEQUENCE OF EVENTS THAT STEMS FROM THE FUNDAMENTAL NATURE OF STATISTICS AND MUTATION IN LIVING ORGANISMS!

The consequences of hyperdemocracy can arise either from lowering the standards of selectivity of voters, or from maintaining the same standards, while the cultural problems increase in complexity.

Conclusion: Selectivity is essential to survival. This being the case — and there is instinctive knowledge that it is the case — you are working hard, at low efficiency, for the wrong thing, when you try to make people give up selectivity. The only thing you can do is work at giving them more useful, simpler, more practical and rewarding methods of selection. You can NOT make someone unlearn something that works, however badly. The only thing you can do is give him something that produces the result he needs more easily, more fully, and with less effort, time, and energy.

Actually, I think a major part of the resistance to selectivity is the fact that it means, inevitably, that someone is going to get hurt. Someone is going to get pushed around, enslaved, rejected, demeaned, and, finally, killed off.

Suppose I could make a magical charm that had the effect of killing immediately anyone who had a compulsion to drive wildly when he was drunk.

Do you think it would be ethical, just, wise . . . whatever term you want — to attach this charm, irremovably, to a man convicted of drunken driving, giving him full warning that he was being so afflicted?

Eric Russell was writing me of, "What makes a lunatic that way . . . and what to do?" and mentioned a man in his town who'd been kicking kids when no one was watching. The kids complained, the parents complained, the police couldn't do anything because of lack of evidence.

So one father, and the two adult brothers of one of the kids went around to the guy's house. He spent six weeks in the hospital recovering. But somehow, thereafter, he was able to master his compulsion to kick kids when no one was watching.

Then there was another bird who strangled two little girls, one 9 and one 10. No sexual assault . . . just strangled them. He was caught, tried, and the psychiatrists put him in the spin-bin. Three years later they released him as cured. Two months later he strangled another little girl. He was caught again, but unfortunately it seems he resisted arrest. Anyhow his neck was somehow disconnected in the ensuing struggle with some local citizens. He didn't strangle any more little girls.

Eric also reports that Britain's Welfare State is now known to the citizens as the Farewell State. All the younger, competent citizens are moving out; the older ones, with any money, are moving to Ireland or the Isle of Man. Those are independent governments within the Sterling area; you can take your money there. The most successful species, in the welfare state environment, are the most efficient ones — those who get the maximum return for the minimum effort. In a welfare state, that is the group that thinks up the cleverest ways to live off the state without working. The suppressed type in such a system is the type who seeks to get reward by working for it.

Ike, I repeat: Dammitall man, will you get and read *Atlas Shrugged*?! Your library has it — lending or public, either.

Regards, John

508

Isaac Asimov   *July 24, 1958*

Dear Ike:

With outhrust neck, and tight-shut eyes, you have marched boldly ahead . . . .

O.K., friend; I will not require that the inferior accept their inferiority; I will, instead, accept the burden of my superiority. It's been done before; if you insist, I shall do so. I may call it, as it has been called before, "noblesse oblige," or, "the White Man's Burden," but I will, if you insist, accept it . . . .

I'll consider myself properly rejected by the group, and set about organizing my own group. Since the group insists that I am inferior, and seeks to suppress my powers, handicap me to achievements no greater than their own, however, I shall withdraw . . . and use my superior powers.

A superiority is something that is useful. In "Slan," the telepathic ability was made not-useful by killing anyone who showed it . . . but telepathic ability is useful just the same. Particularly so, if the telepaths withdraw . . . for a while.

In Imperial Czarist Russia, intelligence and creative ability were not useful; such individuals were suppressed, or exiled or killed. For a while.

Eight million peasants starved to death trying to prove that their greater numbers made them all-round superior to the creative-organizers who had broken free of the suppression.

How do you want it, **Ike**? You want a fantasy world, maybe, where the innately superior supinely allow the inferior to use their talents, while rewarding them with kicks and sneers?

A broken, twisted mind is invisible; you can't see blood flowing, or broken bones sticking out through flesh, or writhing intestines spilled out of a slashed belly. So let us not break bones and bellies that can be seen, and make us feel squeamish; let us, instead, twist and crack minds. Disemboweled minds don't look as messy. A young woman walking around after a prefrontal lobotomy isn't as ugly-looking as the same young woman wasted away because some one cut the spinal cord and left her quadraplegic.

But how long, do you think, those individuals who can sense that

509

sort of battle-damage will accept the burden of superiority quietly and resignedly . . . before they decide they had best start honing their weapons?

And please, **Ike**, don't quote inane "authoritative" statements! There is no such thing as all-round superiority?

Then, Ike, there are no mammals. There are no human beings. Because mammals have an all-round superiority over fishes, and reptiles. And human beings have an all-round net superiority over other mammalian species. And since no such thing as an all-round net superiority can exist, why obviously the Earth is populated solely by reptiles, fishes, insects, etc.

You want me to talk in terms of myself? O.K. I'm physically bigger, stronger, and more dextrous than the norm. My resistance to disease is markedly greater than the norm. Physically, I'm an above-norm specimen — which we can call "superior" as a working, useful, definition. (Yes, I have sinusitis . . . which is largely psychosomatic, and not to be relegated to the physical level, therefore. Also, properly, we should take the 25-year level in discussing pure physical characteristics, and I didn't have it then.)

Intellectually, I'm above norm — as standard testing procedures showed.

Mentally — which is something other than mere intellect — I am also above norm. Objective testing procedures of any appropriate type can be applied. I'm discussing here the mental abilities entailed in original, un-learned-skill problem-solving. The things that no linear extension of a computer could handle. (Intellectual differs in being an extension of computer-abilities.)

I suggest that you try defining a characteristic in which either you or I are subnormal — any "compensating" defect that balances out those demonstrable physical, intellectual, and mental superiorities — and, if you can't, will you please-kindly throw out that cliche about "no all-round superiority?"

Both you and I damn well are all-round superior individuals. In real, practical, objective, useful ways.

Look, you thick-headed yayhoo — I make a more-than-adequate living "working" two days a week, and doing what I damn well enjoy doing the rest of the time. To be strictly honest, I work about 8 hours a week — because you know as well as I do that the time I spend
510

interviewing people in New York is one of the pleasure-periods of my living. You also know that the hours I spend writing such letters as this, I thoroughly enjoy. The hours spent analyzing what makes societies and individuals tick are hard, sweating, head-and-heart-aching work . . . in one sense. But so is the physical labor of playing tennis, or rowing on the crew — both of which I did because I damn well wanted to.

I have done damned little work in my life — and I don't intend to. Not when work is defined as "doing something productive that is emotionally depressing or unrewarding." I won't work, in that sense, because I can do things that are highly productive and are not emotionally depressing or unrewarding.

And that, my friend, is my real, fundamental superiority. I can accomplish useful productive achievements, and enjoy it.

So, if you look real hard in the mirror, do you. Do you teach a lot of classes, which you dislike doing? No; you made Boston University break its pretty little routine so you would be free to do what you damn well felt like doing — writing.

Quite rightly, too; your writing is not only highly productive effort, but emotionally stimulating and satisfying to you. You've done damn little work in your life — and you never should be required to.

And that, of course, is what makes the inferior human being so damned mad. That's why you have quarrels with the men at Boston University, who have to work to achieve less than you achieve by doing what you want to do for enjoyment! It's unfair! It's unjust! You've broken the curse of the Garden of Eden! You make your living without the sweat of your emotional brow!

For a guy who sits on his well-padded duff enjoying the benefits of all-round superiority, you're in a hell of a spot to tchk-tchk-at me with that inane and insipid cliche!

Horace Gold might be in a position to make such a statement; he had physical, biochemical, intellectual, and mental superiority — and of course nobody broke his bones, or spilled his guts, but his emotional structure wasn't quite as rugged as yours and mine.

What's your attitude on that? That since his emotional structure broke down, that proves he wasn't worth anything anyway? That there's no reason to try to change the set-up of the culture, because only

511

the emotionally incompetent get broken into misery anyway? After all, it can't have been really too bad, because you didn't have your emotional guts trampled out, did you?

Bill Blow, basic moron, doesn't consider the problem important. What, him worry? Only about important things — things that happen to him, like not getting promoted with the rest of the class, just because he happens to be stupid, and undemocratic things like that.

Horace Gold? Hah! Ain't he a stupid jerk! Imagine, settin' in his flat like that, afraid of his own shadow! Haw! Shows ya these smart egg-heads ain't got any guts, don't it?

You know, if a man's been castrated, you can't kick him in the balls, even when he deserves it. And if he's been born without 'em, you can't do it no matter how badly you know he has earned it.

Bill Blow simply cannot be made to appreciate what **Horace** went through; he hasn't got the organs necessary to appreciate the impact of the blow.

Now in cave-animals, eyes are a disadvantage; they're more suscep-tible to injury and to disease than solid bone and tough hide.

The emotional sensitivity high-level individuals possess is a marked disadvantage in that respect.

The Roman citizen used to get some real good belly laughs watching some stupid wench in the arena trying to stuff her guts back in her belly, after a lion swiped at her in passing. I've tried for some time to figure out what it was that made that funny-satisfying to the Roman Common Man.

I've also tried to figure out what makes insanity funny material for the American Common Man. They are, in a way, on a par.

The Common Man has a form of superiority over you; he can twist your sense of empathy . . . but you can't hurt him that way. He hasn't any. That doesn't explain why he laughs at insanity — but helps explain why he can, where you and I cannot.

Why isn't the Common Man bothered by nuclear warfare? Because he hasn't enough sense of futurity to be hurt that way. Can you worry, emotionally hurt, or scare a true, genuine, no-kidding fatalist by threatening him with Death? If you bring a cat into a laboratory, put it on a table, get out a bottle of cyanide, put some in a dish, and add some milk . . . is the cat worried?

512

Sure, there's a loss that comes with our precognitive imagination; a loss of peace of mind. If that cat were your own pet cat, and you saw someone doing that to it, you'd be worried, even though the cat wasn't.

Leslyn got a D in arithmetic this semester; <u>she</u> wasn't worried (until I started my summer school, founded on the Fundamental Theory of Pedagogy. "If it won't go in at one end, try the fundamentals of the problem.") but <u>I</u> was. So far, we've worn out 1-1/2 rubber tiles, but a great deal of arithmetical and logical methodology has been implanted.

Incidentally, you know the thing that causes her major trouble: a violent refusal to surrender the fantasy-concept, "I don't know how." She's lying to herself, and to me. It's the same mechanism a small child uses when he says, "I can't cut this meat!" because he wants it cut for him. It's a violent emotional wrench to accept that she <u>can</u> do them, but won't let herself.

Very useful in forcing her to accept that conclusion is the "sucker-bait" type of problem. I give her 10 problems every two days. She stays in the house, and does nothing but problems, for just as long as required to get the 10 problems. Then she's free to anything she likes until the next batch. If they aren't all done when the next batch is due, she gets two swats with a rubber tile for each incompleted problem. (And the principle of punishment is that it must hurt more than expected; otherwise it isn't punishment, but an accepted risk.) <u>And</u> she has to finish the incompleted problems as well as the new batch.

She didn't believe it the first time the rules were laid down.

I meant what I said.

Now she believes me.

The sucker-bait problem is of this type:

"A well has to be dug; it must be 3 feet square, and 75 feet deep. One man can dig down one foot in an hour. But the owner of the land is in a hurry. How long would it take seven men to dig the well?"

She mooned, grumbled, mumbled, kicked at the floor, and paced around her room dropping things for three hours on that one. She finally insisted that she didn't know how to solve that kind of problem. (She hasn't had algebra yet.)

I forced her to draw a careful picture of the thing. She fought at every step of the way; she wouldn't draw a single line properly . . . because every line brought her so much nearer to the inevitable and inescapable

513

realization that the problem was one she could have solved in the first 30 seconds, if she'd been willing to use the knowledge she had.

Every sucker-bait problem is one carefully constructed to trap her into a forced realization that her own determination not to use her abilities is the source of her troubles. That she cannot blame those troubles on my too-difficult problems, or my refusal to "help" her.

She'll do things like "Divide 679,151,439 by 879" without much protest, and get the right answer. (It's 772,641, according to the *Chemical Rubber Handbook* of numbers, cubes, and squares.) It's the problems that require her to use <u>herself,</u> and <u>her own thinking</u> that she rebels against.

Now look; for her maximum benefit, I must impose on her, dictatorially and with physical compulsion, something whose purpose she cannot, or currently will not, appreciate. Short-range empathy for her immediate discomfort tends to make me withdraw from the job; long-range empathy for her future forces me to impose the job on her.

The principle therein has broader applications, Ike.

Item I came across just recently in my studying of the current problems of America: After Rome conquered Greece, the Roman nobles imported Greek slaves to teach their children. The latter days of the Roman Republic saw most Roman children who were educated at all, educated by slaves.

Rome went to hell in a handbasket.

Now it occurs to me that the characteristic of a slave-teacher system is that a number of undesirable abstractions can be drawn from the evidence presented to the child.

1. Learning is something for slaves.

2. Only slaves and children have to study . . . and children are, essentially, slaves.

3. The slave has great knowledge . . . and is a slave. But Papa does not have as much knowledge . . . and is the source of power.

Therefore, Knowledge is not Power.

Also, a slave may not impose his will on a freeman's son, let alone on a Noble's son.

Now one of the reasons you and Boston University don't get along too well is that you're very much of an anomaly — a professor who is not subject to the absolute disciplinary power of your department head. You

514

aren't a slave-teacher.

Your compatriots there, my friend, are.

And if you want to see a real slave-teacher in action . . . go watch a public school teacher.   But he's not merely under the thumb of the principal — he's under the crushing power of the PTA. The parents. The Common Man and Woman.

Junior knows damn well that the teacher can be, and is, pushed around any which way by Mama and Papa. That Papa may be a jerk . . . but boy, is that teacher a stupid jerk!

That teachers are intellectuals . . . and they're the lowest floor-mat on the whole social system.   Everybody walks on them.

The slave-teacher system appears to have a tendency to show up in the last stages of true republican governmental systems. Just before it switches over to one-man rule.

The model for the form of one-man-rule America will adopt is now being worked out in the labor unions.

The next time the US is hit by a major national trouble — serious depression, war, etc. — the forces operating in evolving oligarchic governments (and ours is one) will be fully ripe for the institution of the one-man-rule phase.   In **Franklin Delano Roosevelt's** time the forces were not quite ripe; from now on, they are.

The major change-over will probably come in our life-time; it will not, however, be a change to the dynamic aristocracy phase, where a small group of exceptionally able men actually rule the nation. We had that phase in the 1780-1810 period. It will be the Roman Empire phase, when the apparent ruler is, actually, the agent of the Common Man — a fantasy-projection of the Common Man making things go the way he knows they should. (The jerk.) The one-man-ruler is, actually, ruled by the populace, and is not a true one-man ruler. (**Frederick the Great**, and **Peter the Great** represent instances of true one-man rule, where the ruler could impose on the people what they needed, but didn't want.)

Normally, the first one-man-ruler is a highly competent man. Chances are, we ourselves will vote for him, rather than against. If I were a Frenchman now, I'd vote for **de Gaulle** . . . even knowing that he represents the beginning of the last phase of cultural break-up.

It's the middle-period of the last phase that sees **Neros** and **Caligulas** come into power.   Later, the titular heads are futile; the cultural forces

515

have been dissipated to such an extent that a sort of peace descends, and nobody does anything much, and so nobody is much disturbed . . . until the new cultural force begins to work its way in.

England, incidentally, is curiously stuck. They never got rid of the titular one-man-rule system, so they can't go from republic to a titular one-man-rule system. However, you'll see the Throne gaining more and more responsibility in government. They might sort of half muddle through, because the English royal family is wise, and sound, and England's most powerful cultural tensions and drives are already damped out.

The US's are not, yet. I suspect there'll be quite a shin-dig before things quiet down.

But unless something other than oligarchic government can be invented, and introduced successfully, within the next 25 years . . . .

Oh, well, I should have quite a stirring old age!

The basic trouble is, the Common Man is a jerk. He always is. He always was. He always will be. He is, because the statisticians make him that way. It's not I, but the laws of mathematics that make nearly half our people of sub-normal intelligence.

The only times when the Common Man is not an incompetent jerk are those periods when the culture of the world has fallen flat on its face, and those periods when a status-quo endures for five generations or so.

In the first type of period, there isn't enough culture left to be misguided, so the individual is relatively smart. In the second, the culture has stabilized at the Common Man's own level. It'll never last, though, because some Uncommon Man always comes along.

Regards, John

Catherine Tarrant   *August 2, 1958*

Dear Catherine,

One of my stories, MOTHER EARTH, which appeared in the May, 1949 issue of *Astounding*, is to be anthologized in a Fawcett anthology, edited by **Leo Margulies**. Fawcett wants to have the copyright for the story in my name.

Could you therefore ask **Mr. Lawler** to write me a letter assigning me the copyright for MOTHER EARTH in the usual fashion and
516

corroborating the fact that I possess anthologization rights (as I believe I do because some years back I was transferred various rights to all my stories.) When it is received, I will send it on to Fawcett.

Thanks very much and sorry to put you to the trouble.

Love, Isaac Asimov

P.S. I just returned from a 3-week vacation yesterday. It is wonderful to be able to get back to work.

Isaac Asimov   *August 6, 1958*

Dear Isaac:

I sent your letter on to **Mr. Lawler's** office and his secretary asked me to tell you that we purchased All Serial and Pocket Book Rights to your story "Mother Earth" on October 11, 1948. The story was published in the May 1949 issue of *Astounding Science Fiction*. On August 11, 1954 an Assignment of Copyright was sent to you. We retained Serial Rights only.

Regards, John W. Campbell, Jr., Editor

Isaac Asimov   *August 12, 1958*

Dear Ike:

I didn't keep a carbon of my last letter, so I've forgotten whether I'd worked out the business about Logic and Entropy at that time, and told you about it; pardon if this is repetition.

To map any territory T onto a mapping surface S, S must belong to the same topological genus as T. Thus you can't map a sphere onto a plane without tearing — not merely rubber-like stretching distortion, but tearing. Tearing breaks the relationship system that constitutes a true mapping operation. And you can't map a sphere onto a torus, pretzel, or anything other than a sphere-genus surface.

Logic is a mapping surface onto which the territory of material-objective reality can be successfully mapped; this is the essence of Science. Relationships found in the logical-map can be found in the territory-reality.

Then Logic is a "surface" having the same genus-characteristics

517

as objective material reality.

But if a map represents a territory, then the territory represents the map; characteristics found in the territory must also be true of the map.

It is known that an overwhelmingly dominant characteristic of all material systems is Entropy — the tendency of any material system to approach a condition of no-difference. Not of no-energy, but of no-difference.

Then Logic must have the same characteristics, and any logic-dominated system must likewise tend to approach a state of no-difference. The more logic dominates the system, the more completely it must become a no-difference system.

OK — so "Liberty, Equality, Fraternity!" are not humanitarian doctrines; they are the inevitable outcome of logic-dominated thinking.

The essential characteristic of a logic-dominated culture will be approach to the equivalent of the gas laws — pure statistical deviation around a norm. The Norm shall be God, and no individual shall be permitted, for long, to have any abnormal excess or deficiency of energy.

The state of pure entropy is, in cultural terms, anarchy or chaos. A classless society cannot acknowledge crime — because to do so establishes a criminal class, and there must be no-difference. The only rule of selection permissible in pure logic is the rule of Least Difference — Occam's Razor is simply the 2nd Law of Thermodynamics! (The first law of Thermo is, in Logic, the fact that logic can neither create nor destroy postulates.)

Logic denies Judgment — because Judgment has as its characteristic appropriate inconsistency. And logic cannot exist in inconsistency. Therefore any use of Judgment is anathematized by Logic.

A logician's attitude toward Emotion is almost exactly equivalent to the attitude of a Victorian Maiden Aunt toward Sex; it shouldn't exist at all, and it mustn't exist, and if we just deny it vigorously enough, maybe it will go away, and in the meantime have nothing whatever to do with it, because it's Evil and Nasty and the real Root of All Evil. And under no circumstances is it to be studied, investigated, evaluated, and understood. It is to be simply and absolutely denied existence.

Primarily, that attitude stems from the fact that Emotion, or Subjective Reality, cannot be mapped onto the surface Logic; it is a territory having the characteristics of a higher order genus.

518

Now, the essence of your fight for no-difference, for equality, and no-judgment — whatever stems from that logical orientation, misreacting to subjective reality, which has been mismapped onto Logic. You can NOT get subjective reality in proper relationship — free of tearing-inconsistency — on a logical surface, because it belongs to a different genus.

Examples: I asked you to judge me, personally, as an individual.

You didn't — except to say you felt a strong emotional attachment. And then went on to a logical mishmash, because you don't trust your own emotional perceptions of the non-logical reality of the subjective order! Emotional feelings are sensory perceptions of the non-logical reality level we call Subjective Reality. The very term "Subjective" has been so semantically loaded that coupling it with the oppositely loaded term "reality" has a grating effect — a response of "contradiction in terms."

Try this approach: Human beings have sensory mechanisms that are not purely physical, that perceive a level of the Universe which exists apart from human beings, a level which can not be mapped into Logic, any more than a sphere can be truly mapped onto a plane.

Now, Ike, consider this: Every logical-empire culture Man has ever set up has wound up in one of two ways: either it went to non-logical traditionalism, and froze as a ritual-tabu culture — or it went to the entropic state that Logic must approach — it went to decadence, chaos and anarchy, to be taken over by some other group.

Every logical-empire culture, without exception.

The sign-posts near the end of the culture are the rising domination of the Great God Norm. The domination of the least-difference men — the Common Man, the Proletariat, the Plebian — call them what you will. The elimination of class distinction, the elimination of difference-concepts such as "right" and "wrong," the loss of demarcation of crime and civilized behavior. Every decadent logical-empire culture has shown those exact same signs.

India is not a logical-empire culture; it's a ritual-tabu culture, which is why it remained stable so long. There, class-distinction is purely ritual. That's as bad as no-class-distinction.

The signposts on the road to decadence and break-up are the logical domination of no-difference. When murder loses its distinguishable

519

characteristics, and is degraded to a serious misdemeanor, then to one-of-those-things; you-can't-expect-people-to-be-perfect-you-know. When homosexuality declines in distinction to "just a matter of opinion, after all; you can't say it's wrong, you know, because 'wrong' is just a value-judgment, really."

In the United States today, murder is classed as a serious misdemeanor — not legally, of course, but in practical action. In England, homosexuality is winning acceptance as not-a-crime.

Understanding of the hard, painful difference between "right" and "wrong" is not a pleasant thing; it places binding and uncomfortable limits on your feeling that you are free to act as you will. That makes it unpopular . . . and Logic says that there is no-difference, really, except in value-judgment, and since value-judgments are illogical anyway, they should be discarded.

They are illogical, of course.

And then Logic pulls its neatest trick; since things are either True or False, and since value-judgment is illogical, either Logic is True, and therefore value-judgment False, or value-judgment is true, and Logic is False — and everybody knows damned well that Logic isn't false!

OK, **Ike**; you're rejecting the human duty of doing value-judging. To do so is to accept responsibility for your judgments — and that is a lonely task, today.

You say you don't want judgment on any group basis, but judgment of each individual as an individual. But . . . will you in fact judge an individual as an individual? Judge him — and accept individual responsibility for the judgment you make?

If you won't — and you know damn well you're an abnormally high level individual! — why do you expect the ordinary people around you to do the same thing you draw back from? If you feel scared to state a value-judgment, and stand by it — why do you ask that others do what you will not?

And that's what you're asking when you ask that a man be judged not on a group-basis of, "He is a Negro," but on a basis of, "He is Jim Jones."

No; what you are in fact establishing-by-default is the situation, "No Judgments Whatever!" and that is the way a world ends — not with a bang, with a whimper of, "I can't Judge!"

That is the way all of Man's worlds have ended.

520

You say there should be no judgment based on breed and genetic lineage? Then stop judging individuals on the breed-and-lineage basis of "human being" — because that is strictly a genetic-lineage basis of judgment. If you insist on logic, dammit, be logical! You have no right to the term "human" in your judgment; it's a genetic-lineage term.

I'm not kidding, **Ike**; I mean exactly what I say. I positively deny you the right to use the term "human," if you insist on being logical, and insist on denying genetic or blood-line judgments. Neither can you use the terms "primate," "mammal" or "chordate;" they're genetic blood-line terms too.

Define what it is you really want, dammit! Do you want any judgment whatever? You can't ask that — can't ask for the use of judgment at all, if you want Logic!

Do you believe a high-level civilization capable of maintaining cities can exist without any judgment? Do you think it will exist for long without judgment — if the present logic-domination trend continues? All human history shows that logic-dominated empires collapse into rubble, and that it is the cities that fall. The peasants and the nomads live by ritual and tabu; they survive — but the cities don't.

Dammitall, **Ike**; this is not an academic argument. The United States, and all Western Culture today, shows the great sign-posts of the domination of Logic — and the collapse into no-difference.

To continue as we are now going is certain death and destruction. And all the philosophy of the past ages has never been sufficient to stay the coming of darkness. All the wisdom of all the ages of Man has never been enough.

We must find something new. We must — or die, as all the cultures before us have died.

And the situation is NOT "different now . . ."; entropy is just as entropic in a universe of gas at 10,000 degrees absolute as it is in a universe of gas at 1 degree absolute. The level makes no difference whatever. The scale doesn't count.

A star radiates heat and light, only so long as there is a difference-of-nature in its mass; a white dwarf sun is one which has been reduced to all-core. It no longer generates energy; it simply radiates away into space the remnants of energy generated in previous ages.

Your real objection is one of fear — fear not of Judgment-itself,

521

but of improper judgment. You distrust Judgment, because it will, you fear, be improper judgment.

Then the only solution is to find the laws of Judgment, and find ways of getting proper judgments. And Logic isn't the way.

Let me show you that you do want blood-lines and breed-characteristics accepted, and judged.

Imagine a war between the Eastern and Western hemisphere. It becomes necessary for us to send an army into the Himalayas, where much of the fighting will be conducted at 15 to 20 thousand foot elevations. The men doing that fighting must be alert, active, and agile — or they'll be destroyed.

Now it is our hyperdemocratic ideal that there is no such thing as breed and blood-line — so Jew and Negro and Anglo-Saxon and Peruvians alike are sent into that battle line, purely at random.

And die, of course. They all die — and thus prove their fundamental equality. The Peruvians die because their flanks are exposed by the non-Andeans who cannot live and act at those altitudes. If the force had been selected by breed — if you, **Ike**, had been rejected because you are a Jew and not an Andean — there would have been a selected force of men who could fight and act effectively those altitudes.

You would, if you were sent, be a victim of bad judgment; you would have been accepted into a group membership which would be lethal to you.

Rejection from a group can be of great protective value.

You reject your children from the group "those permitted to use matches and fire-making devices," for their protection. You reject some of your chemistry students from making certain experiments . . . for their protection. Kids who want to build model rockets, with a propellant mixture of potassium chlorate, sulfur, and sugar must be rejected from the group of model rocket builders against their will and choice.

Every man hates to be told "your judgment is inadequate," and so the Common Man wants to abolish judgment as a criterion.

And when he uses his defective judgment, and winds up crippled, broke, and incompetent to work effectively . . . he wants to be supported in the manner to which he'd like to be accustomed by those who are "luckier" (he'll never acknowledge that they're wiser) than he.

Consider a slave, in Roman Republic times. The slave wants to be a musician; his master, when the slave is 14 years old, studies him, and judges him. He gets trained as an accountant. He is forced to be an accountant, against his will and choice. But the Roman republic was well run; the slave can earn his freedom. He does; and at age 25 has accumulated enough to buy his freedom. He, as a freedman, starts at last on the musical career he always knew he should have had . . . . And a year later is sold back into slavery. He has a tin ear, and having a tin ear, can't tell that he has a tin ear. It sounds like music to him, but not to anybody else.

The trouble is, of course, that when one man's judgment is imposed on another, the second is always sure it's wrong. If he weren't of that opinion, the semantically loaded term "imposed" wouldn't apply. It isn't an "imposition" to be "forced" to do what you yourself choose to do, is it?

The slave is always sure he's being mistreated, when he and his master disagree. **Leslyn** feels she is being mistreated in being forced to study arithmetic.

Harriet Beecher Stowe did a wonderful propaganda job on *Uncle Tom's Cabin*; that's what it was.

There are injustices in any system. It's an injustice that **Joe** was killed in an automobile accident. That a girl in New York last week was seized, raped, and sadistically murdered by four JD's.

There's a difference between "perfect" and "optimum"; the problem is to find the optimum system — which will not be free of injustice. No real-world system is free of noise.

The propaganda in *Uncle Tom* is the statement of a case of injustice in terms of a general-situation. It can not be denied that such things happen. It can be denied that such things were the norm.

It can not, and should not, be denied that southern field-hands were driven by lash and gun — that there were sadistic overseers, too. But simple economics suggests that sadistic overseers were highly undesirable from the viewpoint of the plantation owner.

Now if you'll give up — reject as inherently, permanently nonsense — the idea of a perfect system, and seek, instead, an optimum system, you can get a damn sight further.

Imagine **E.E. Smith's** Arisians running things, and you'll recognize that some people would necessarily be forced to act in a manner contrary to their will, their choice, and, even, their own best interest. Some individuals would best serve the world by dropping dead; there is no place, anywhere in a civilized world, for a congenital psychopath. A haemophiliac must not be allowed to breed. It may be contrary to his will, his choice, or his personal best interest; nevertheless it is necessary for the good-of-the-race that he be forced to die, genetically — and that the psychopath be forced to die individually.

The "best of all possible worlds" is not a perfect world.

In seeking to achieve perfection . . . you can destroy optimum. But you'll never achieve perfection, so you'll have destroyed that which can be, not get that which can't be, and wind up with hell on Earth.

The real nature of slavery recognizes that some individuals are incapable of self-discipline, and the use of judgment. These individuals, to be useful in a civilization, must be driven to behave in a useful manner, against their will and choice. They are immune to argument at any level save physical force. (Try using logical argument on a child!)

Yet such individuals can be of value to a culture; they can perform needed tasks, provided they are controlled by individuals who do have self-discipline and judgment.

The field-hands in the old south were selected individuals; they were selected for inability to control themselves jucidiously. Economics, not the laws of man, protected them — and the same laws of economics protected the household slave. A household slave was too valuable for use as a field hand; he was an individual who had judgment, self-discipline, and was worthy of trust and respect. The children could be entrusted to such slaves.

You will find exactly this same pattern in every slave culture; the thing that causes violent emotional reaction to the concept of slavery is the proposition that one man is being subjected to the judgment of another human being.

Without questioning whether that judgment is good or not.

It's flat, arbitrary, dogmatic rejection of the proposition, "One man should judge another."

But . . . how does that differ from, "One man is his brother's keeper." One man has responsibility for the welfare of another.

Am I to be responsible for the welfare of a homocidal and destructive man . . . without having any right to judge his homocidal or destructive
524

behavior, yet I am to be held responsible for the results?

Is it justice to lock up **Typhoid Mary**, who has no harmful intent? Against her will and choice? To judge her as unfit for human companionship, and normal human contacts?

The problem comes down to one thing, Ike: If you reject Judgment-as-such — then you reject <u>both</u> acceptance and rejection.

The problem is not to reject judgment — but to find sound bases for judgments. And sound means not in your terms, or in my terms — but in the Universe's terms.

And the Universe is <u>not</u> limited to Logic. It is <u>not</u> limited to true-false — but neither is it valid to say that true-false has no place.

There is true, generalized superiority; remember the proposition of area, instead of linear superiority. The specialist is needed, and the wise man recognizes and values the specialist — but can still recognize that a specialist is inferior to a man of greater total competence. A lion <u>is</u> inferior to a man — though he is physically superior.

Consider this, as a final point: Suppose I learn the Laws of Magic, (and I know damn well they exist, and your denial of that proposition has no effect whatsoever on the matter — no more than my statement of it has. The Laws exist in the Universe, and neither your opinion or mine affects that, or they do not exist in the Universe, and neither opinion will affect that, either) but suppose I learn them, and they do exist, and I am able to employ them to cast spells.

Now with them, I can induce a man to <u>want</u> what I have decided to make him want. As a result he wants it; he truly, deeply, emotionally, wants it. It is his choice, and he will be made unhappy if he is not permitted to fulfill that want.

He would not consider himself a slave, would he? He would fight, and fight violently, anyone who sought to block him from doing what he wanted. Such an individual, he would hold, was trying to enslave him.

Now a man following a post-hypnotic command will show just such behavior; this is known.

Emotional conditioning will make a man behave that way too. He <u>wants</u> to do what he has been conditioned to want.

Further, suppose a man with such emotional conditioning is approached by a magician, who can, by applying the laws of magic, break that emotional conditioning, and allow the individual true free choice.

The conditioned man would flee the magician in horror. He <u>wants</u> what he wants, and having his very wants taken away from him — the very stuff that is his personality, would be the ultimate threat to his existence as a self, wouldn't it?

Suppose the slave who wanted to be a musician, not an accountant, were told by a magician that magic could make him want to be an accountant instead of wanting to be a musician; what would his response be?

Wanting to be a musician and not being able to be one might be frustrating — but at least, he would feel, he was free to be himself. But if the magician took away the desire to be what he couldn't possibly be — that would be the ultimate degradation and destruction of his self, wouldn't it?

Suppose you knew I could cast a charm which would make you <u>want</u> to find the validity of judging other men.

To any emotionally conditioned individual, it makes no difference <u>why</u> he wants what he wants — it is self-itself to <u>have</u> wants. Then if someone takes those wants away, and replaces them with other wants — that is the annihilation of self-itself!

You made some guesses as to what had caused the change in me that caused me to abandon the viewpoint you hold.

You guessed wrong. For one thing, you suggested early experiences had conditioned me differently. If that were the answer — then I would not <u>have been</u> in agreement with you. I would be a pagan, not a heretic.

Further, your experiences as a Jew have little to do with the attitude you hold; there are a damn sight more non-jews and non-negroes and non-you-name-its that hold the attitude you are expressing than there are Jews who hold it.

I can tell you what it was that caused the change in my attitude: In the last eight years, **Peg** and I have worked some 20 hours every week, studying emotion, orientation, and belief — faith.

I have found that attitude-orientation is a very important <u>part</u> of me . . . <u>but is not Self</u>. That I can have my attitudes changed without being destroyed-as-a-self. That I can be judged — and accept those judgments without necessarily being degraded — if the judgments are sound.

I can, in other words, have a change of personality, without thereby losing my existence.

That "I" means more than "I believe . . . ."

And, knowing that, I know that it does not destroy a human being to have his wants, his attitudes, his deepest desires, remolded against his will. Naturally, it must be against his will! His "will" is simply his sense of "I want"; consequently it is inevitable that any change of his want-system will be against his will.

The reason magic and the laws of magic are so violently rejected by human beings is very simple; they are the hated Laws of Emotional Orientation.

That does not make them evil — but it does mean that they will inevitably <u>appear to be</u> the essence of ultimate evil — the techniques by which a man's very wants can be changed. And anything that forces a man to act in a manner contrary to his wants — no matter how bad or inappropriate those wants may be in fact — will appear to that man as "evil." While something which can change the want itself is, from his viewpoint, the ultimate evil.

I've found it isn't. I've had my wants changed — and, whaddaya know! It hasn't destroyed me at all! For a time, I had to operate with the knowledge-belief that what I was doing was deliberate suicide — Self-destruction in the sense of destruction of my Self.

I found it wasn't that, after all.

And, having found that, my attitude on imposing one man's will on another changed. It doesn't necessarily mean the destruction of a man's soul to have that soul forced to change. Learning a new want-pattern isn't the Ultimate Evil; it just feels that way.

Knowing this by direct, personal experience — I am no longer convinced that measures taken to force a human being to change his nature are necessarily, and by reason of that alone, evil.

Therefore I no longer hold that a man's wants, beliefs and desires are Sacred. It hurts, when a want-pattern is changed. It hurts, too, when a broken bone is set — but that doesn't mean it shouldn't be done.

What hurts most about having a want-pattern changed is that there exists the phenomenon of Memory. A man with a twisted leg can have an operation, under anesthesia, and have the bone broken, reshaped, pinned, and have it heal in a new, straightened pattern. But matter doesn't have memory; it can't compare itself-now with itself-then.

Change a thief to an honest man — and he does have memory. Now his past hurts him. Even if the change itself is made under anesthesia of some kind — still his past hurts him.

It is regrettable that it is so painful to have your want-patterns changed.

Nevertheless, want-patterns must be changed. Like it or not, the Universe requires changes.

It is painful to have external pressures applied — but that alone does not prove that the pressures are Evil. It merely proves they're painful.

The item that made the change in me was not a past experience, **Ike**, but a present experience: that change of my own want-patterns did not destroy me, degrade me, or terminate me. That "I" am more than "My Beliefs And Certainties," and that change of those could take place within "I."

And . . . that the old beliefs need not hurt. I feel neither shame-for-having-believed-such-thing, nor shame-for-believing-this. Each was appropriate to its place in the system me-and-the-universe-in-time.

A magician-enchanter is simply one who can argue effectively at the wants-desires level; one who can change attitudes, not merely logical conclusions. And, of course, if you change a man's attitudes . . . all his logical conclusions start shifting, too! Is a dry cell a useful device? Not to a caveman. Is a given logical conclusion important-useful? Depends on your world-orientation, doesn't it? The logical conclusion remains true, and logical, and valid — just as the dry cell remains a dry cell.

Slavery is a system under which one man is forced to accept the attitudes and desires of another. You and I may agree on that logical conclusion.

But the things I've learned in the last eight years cause me to evaluate that truth on a, "Yes . . . and so . . . ??" basis. While you evaluate it, "And that proves slavery is an ultimate evil." We are in full agreement on the fact of this "dry cell" — but not on its value.

You know, a cave-man would have no use for the dry cell — and therefore one who said that dry cells were of little value must be a cave-man, huh?

I suspect a man of 5000 AD would have little use for a dry cell, either.

What we need, and must have if civilization is not to repeat again and again and again the monotony of going through the logical-entropy
528

cycle, is a means of reaching the next level of civilization — one in which supra-logical communication is acceptable. One in which it is not considered an Ultimate Evil to force a man to change his wants, desires, and will.

I believe that we must study psi — and study it damn hard, and damn quick. Because psi is the objectively-observable phenomena of the supra-logical level of reality; it is a set of objectively observable phenomena which can only be understood by use of thinking-techniques appropriate to that higher level. It's a territory that requires a map of a new genus — and because it is objective, it will allow us to build an accurately formulated map of subjective reality.

By the way; the Bethlehem Fabricators Co., Inc — big steel outfit in Pa. — uses dowsing rods regularly as standard procedure for locating pipes and conduits buried underground. Electronic pipe-locators are useless — too much scrap steel stuff lost a few inches underground in their yards. The president of the company is a friend of **Art Gray's**; he's used the rods, and his plant men have used the rods for years. The idea that there was anything unusual about it had never occurred to him!

They get their rods, incidentally, from a regular supply house.

The reason psi is so violently rejected is that any analytical-thinking method competent to handle it . . . is competent to force a change in a man's wants-desires-beliefs.

Item: the high-level individuals who can't use psi — and a major- ity of them can't! — appear to be blocked by self-distrust. They're too self-critical. Happy little morons aren't self-critical; they have little trouble with psi. And they're in no danger of having their wants altered by psi-level techniques of thinking, because they don't think at any level.

Regards, John

John W. Campbell Jr. *October 16, 1958*

Dear John,

This is a business letter so our argument is temporarily called off. I'm having troubles. It's been half a year since I've written a word of science-fiction. It's not because I'm dried up; or tired of writing. It's just because since the beginning of 1958, I have written a book on the derivation of scientific words (for which NAMES, NAMES, NAMES was the inspiration), another one on numbers (for which HEMOGLO-BIN AND THE UNIVERSE was the inspiration), another one on man's notions of time, another one on blood and its functions, and I'm just finishing one on the Solar system. I'm working on a few others, too.

In short, it's all non-fiction, and please don't be angry with me because it was the *Astounding* articles that introduced me to the writing of easy-going, non-fiction. You, sir, have corrupted me.

And by the way, talking about my *Astounding* articles, you should see the reviews I've received for my book ONLY A TRILLION which is a collection of the articles. I may have told you this before but it rated a full column in the "Sunday Times Book Review" and rave notices from a number of places. Some mentioned that they were previously printed in a s.f. magazine but no one tried to use that as an excuse to sneer. S.f. magazines are respectable now — or *Astounding* is, anyway.

However, all this is to explain that my first submission to *Astounding*, which is here enclosed, is a non-fiction piece. It is entitled THE UNARTIFICIAL ELEMENTS, is only 1400 words long, and maybe you can use it. Even if you can't, it takes up the question of definitions (when is an element artificial and what criteria of artificiality can you use) which ought to amuse you.

On October 21, by the way, is the 20th anniversary of my first story sale (to *Amazing*). Next January 9 is the anniversary (twentieth) of my first check from *Astounding*. To coin a phrase, Time flies.

Yours, Isaac Asimov

Isaac Asimov   *November 13, 1958*

Dear Ike:

Glad that "Yellow Pill" yarn appealed to you as an idea. There's a bit of a story behind it. **Rog Phillips** had sent me about six stories, one after another, all of which had been returned very promptly.

Rog wrote an angry, rather paranoid letter, saying that I was prejudiced against him, and wouldn't buy anything of his. (I'd just punched several gaping holes in a pet thesis of his which he'd incorporated in one yarn I returned.) I suggested that if he sincerely felt that, he could readily submit under a pen-name, through an agent, or otherwise disguise his efforts.

530

He quite angrily submitted, "The Yellow Pill." It just happened that that seemed to me the first story he'd shown me that had a really neat, clearly and succinctly presented thesis. His check was on the way three days later.

Never heard a word about any of it from him afterwards. I think the experience had something of the effect of a "yellow pill" on him — and the effect as implied in the story is unpleasant, you'll notice. You don't need a yellow pill unless you've retreated from a too-harsh-to-bear reality, in which case the yellow pill is forcing you to face the unbearable. Obviously an unpleasant experience.

Incidentally, there are several ways you can check (without benefit of yellow pills) on your dream-world problem. If you were really in a delusional dream-world, would you have me in there niggling at you via mail like this?

By the way, since you're looking for hobbies of a different sort . . . I've just been talking with a lecture agent by the name of **Gordon Skea**. It seems that there are, scattered hither and yon across the country, outfits that are willing to pay from 3 to 6 hundred bucks for an evening's lecture; a good agent can frequently rig up a tour taking 3-4 nights, hitting 3 or 4 cities, and making several hundred in each.

With the reputation you have, you should certainly be able to command quite an interesting fee. You might take a look into the matter; you've been a hell of a good public speaker for years — why not get someone to pay you for what you like doing anyway?

Now if you'd add photography as a hobby to that . . . just think of the chance for taking pics of various cities!

On the discussion: **Randy Garrett** has a Jewish problem somewhat different from yours. **Randy** is now sporting a King Henry VIII style beard & mustache. He is, currently, living in a Jewish neighborhood. He is making enemies and influencing people to dislike him more effectively than usual, because he is also wearing a silver cross pin in his lapel. A block away anybody can spot him as a young rabbi, of course . . . .

And **Ike**, my friend, consider the case of a fairy, a queer. They can, normally, be spotted about as far off as you can spot a Mulatto. I'll admit a coal-black Negro can be spotted a bit further than a fairy can, but the normal Mulatto can't. Sure, I know a lot of queers don't look that way — but they're simply "passing." There's tremendous prejudice against

531

them, too, you know. I know of an instance where a large retail store closed out one small department, that being the simplest way to shove out a pair of fairies who'd gravitated there — and they did NOT want fairies around. A sort of race prejudice, huh?

They can be spotted by their mannerisms — walk, body-posture, etc. Then there's the different type, the true eunochoid. He can be spotted two blocks off; nobody but a eunochoid has that body-weight distribution. He's not just fat; he's fat in a particular and unique way.

There's marked prejudice against them, too, you know.

Now there are many types that can be spotted a long way off — skin-color is by no means the only thing that can be spotted at long range. It's just one that's easy to spot and to describe. You, having had considerable training in endocrinology, know what a eunochoid is, and can describe one in fairly understandable terms. But ask Bill Blow, I.Q. 95, why he doesn't like Cecil Jones . . . and Bill can't tell you.

A small child will react toward a sheep and a sheepdog in entirely different ways — even though he's never seen either before. You know . . . "horns, hooves — herbivorous! You can't!" Sure, **Couvier** was zoologist enough to know those factors — but a child is enough the product of three billion years of terrestrial evolution to have the reactions built right in. But he couldn't explain, "I don't fear this animal, but I do fear that one, because that one has clawed paws, not hooves, and it has long, pointed canines, and the lean, flat belly of a carnivore."

Point: human beings do-in-fact notice and react to pattern-clues that they cannot express in conscious terms. Sure, there have been things like the chalicotherium, with its horse-like head, herbivorous diet, and claws on its feet that would scare a lion. But the patterns are pretty reliable — certainly reliable enough to make them worth reacting to if you want to stay alive.

But . . . reactions to patterns cannot be defended logically. You can't point out logically the things you're reacting to. You know that; try pointing out the figures in a Ishihara Color Test diagram to a man born color-blind!

All of which leads to this: you can't be spotted as a Jew from two blocks away. But you and I can be spotted as Eggheads from at least as great a distance as a Negro can.

Part of being an Egghead is a degree of neuromuscular coordination
532

that is abnormal; it's not just intellectual, you know! At age 20, I drove from New Haven to Boston, on the old Post Road, not the new turnpikes, at an average speed of 45 miles an hour. The only odd thing about that was that it was at night, with absolute slick glare ice on the roads every mile of the way. I didn't skid or slip once on the entire trip. I don't know how I managed it now — but I know as an historical fact that I did. It's part of what makes me an egghead. I can keep stuff piled up on my electronics bench, and not knock it over while working on it. I can work with bare high-voltage conductors without getting connected to them.

You've got the same sort of talent. We're abnormally aware of all the things around us. The result is that we handle ourselves, our bodies, with an efficiency and economy of movement that the normal can't depend on himself to achieve.

We, my friend, have gestures and body-postures that are as identifiable at long range as anything a fairy does.

There is, too, the matter of dress — even when we make a subconscious effort to conceal the facts by being sloppy in dress. There's still an air about the way we wear clothes that the normal couldn't match if he tried. There's speech, and facial expression — the muscles of the face aren't different; we just use them differently. We're acutely sensitive to the nonvocal communication of facial and bodily movements — and use those in communication.

Finally, there's the matter of the human aura . . . which I know I can't prove, but which has effects even on those who don't consciously perceive it. In the theater they call it "presence" or "personality" as in "he can't project his personality."

One of the reasons you can teach like all crazy is that you can project an aura, a presence, a personality, that amounts to projecting and imposing on the students the feeling that what you are saying is fascinating. You can project an attitude toward what you're discussing. Naturally the student learns something he feels is fascinating.

Reason why the Egghead is hated: Suppose I have precognition and telekinesis, and I get into a dice game with ordinary people.

Now if I use my telekinetic powers to make the dice go the way I want them to, I'm loading the dice, obviously.

But if I do not interfere with them in any way, but simply use my precognition to see which way they're about to fall, I am not loading the
533

dice at all.

Is that cheating?

It doesn't make any difference in practice, does it? I'm going to clean the normal players just as clean as I choose to. They haven't a prayer against me, because to them the behavior of the dice is random, while to me it's a perfectly predictable and dependable phenomenon.

The simple fact that I can know, and predict, where others simply see randomness means that I have robbed them of freedom of action. They can no longer act on the basis of randomness, because I can, in the same system, act on prediction.

I don't bet on anything except sucker-bets — the other guy being the sucker. I bet only on fully-predictable outcomes, where the other guy thinks it's non-predictable. I get into dice games only when my precognition is working, in other words.

Sample: I'll bet I can pove to your complete satisfaction that it is possible for a planet to have its south magnetic pole at it's north geographic pole — geographic north being defined by the proposition that the local sun-star rises in the East. Planetary magnetic phenomena being related to ionizing radiation from the local sun-star, the proposition makes sense.

Reason it's a strictly sucker-bet, of course, is that that's the situation on Earth. The north magnetic pole of a compass needle points toward geographic north — which proves that there must be a south magnetic pole there. (I suckered **Randy Garrett** for a buck on that one.)

An egghead is an individual who robs those around him of their freedom of action by being able to predict accurately, where they see only random. It makes no difference whether the Egghead does predict, or uses his prediction — the fact that he can any time he chooses to makes all others around him live at the mercy of his good will.

Put it this way: suppose one of the regular scf. authors decides to do a novel for *ASF*. So long as **Ike Asimov** stays busy writing text-books and fact articles, the guy has a chance of selling it. But if **Asimov** chooses to write a novel . . . the poor guy's squeezed out. Then he can sell the novel only by your leave.

Whether you so intend or not, the fact remains.

The Normal has no chance of competing with the Egghead; that is, in fact, the definition of the Egghead — he's someone who cannot be successfully fought, save at the purely physical level. And even then it's enormously dangerous.

The Egghead is the Magician of old; it's always dangerous to attack the Magician — save with the help of another and more powerful Magician.

The Scientist today has the same position; it's impossible to attack the Scientist-dominated United States unless you have more and better Scientists yourself. China may have more men than we do — but that would be more than equalized in the first few hours of an all-out attack on the US. It wouldn't take more than a dozen hydrogen bombs to equalize the numerical odds — and China hasn't any.

The Egghead robs other people of their freedom . . . by simply existing.

Worse, when an Egghead has existed, the world is forever robbed of true freedom of action. Once Hari Seldon has shown that sociological forces can be predicted — no one after that can act with the full satisfying freedom of freshness and self-directiveness. What unknown-to-me-now sociological forces are pushing me to do this thing I think I'm choosing to do? Even if Hari Seldon or his projection aren't there to say, "Well, now you've done that which you were inescapably forced to do, the next thing you will do is . . ." the fact that he's shown he could have, proves it could be done — and that proves that you don't have the free will you like to think you do.

Only the Mule did — the Ultimate Egghead.

O.K. — the Egghead is hated for a reason. He's recognizable at a distance. His advantage over the Negro is that he is an Egghead — and supremely dangerous. He distributes blessings and curses, and that tends to make people slightly leary of attacking him.

You know, I should make this discussion easier on myself, save myself trouble by shipping your latest letter to **Mark Clifton**, and his latest to you, and let you two fight it out while I watch.

What I've been trying to tell you is:

1. The problem exists.

2. The methods so far used don't work.

3. Trying to make people deny the feelings they feel is non-functional.

4. What we need is to give over on that approach and invent another.

Now in essence, you want to put more power, more force, more energy behind the old approach until we <u>make</u> it work.

Yeah — and if hydrogen is stubborn about liquefying when we apply pressure, by God if we just put <u>enough</u> pressure on it, we'll make the damn stuff liquefy as we know perfectly well it should.

Try it! Try a million — a hundred million — atmospheres! Liquefy? Nope, it won't. Metallic hydrogen; yes. Liquid? No!

It takes some pressure, <u>and low temperature</u>. Just put on pressure, however, and the temperature goes up, not down. Put on enough, and instead of liquid hydrogen, you get a thermonuclear fusion reactor called star.

Back off, and try a different approach. Less pressure, and less heat, dammit!

Now **Mark's** letter has to do with teachability. He says he has observed, again and again, that little Tommy is, according to teacher A a good boy and a good student . . . while teacher B reports that Tommy is a juvenile delinquent in the making, and utterly unteachable. And <u>that they're both perfectly correct</u>.

Teacher A produces an environment, and uses a method, that Tommy <u>can</u> (NOT "will") accept. In that environment, under that method, Tommy learns rapidly and happily. Teacher B produces an environment, and uses a method, that Tommy <u>cannot accept no matter how much he tries</u>.

A physical analogy: if Tommy is violently allergic to angora wool, and teacher B always wears angora sweaters in class, Tommy is <u>unable</u> to study in her presence. He's too busy sneezing, gasping, and weeping. He's disrupting the class. He's undisciplined, and refused to remain quietly in his seat.

"Be nasty to your little boy,
"And spank him when he sneezes!
"He only does it to annoy,
"Because he knows it teases."

Now what you're doing is saying that, "Anybody can learn the way I say, and what must be done is to apply enough force to make them pay attention and learn the way I say! I know that this method hasn't worked in the last 6000 years it's been tried, but that's only because people didn't use enough force. Now, with the new and powerful pressures we know how to apply, backed up by atomic and hydrogen bonbs, we can, at last,

536

really make people learn what I know they should learn, the way I know they should learn it."

Look, **Ike** . . . try arguing that with **Mark Clifton**, will you? It's not just me that says that won't work.

I'm NOT trying to make you give up the desire that the lesson be learned.

I am trying to make you give up the desire to teach it by pure, raw, brute force. Whether that force be disguised as legal pressure, or undisguised bayonets.

You know, **Edgar Cayce's** thick-witted, heavy-handed Paw down there in the Tennessee mountains, was a-tryin' to make that dumb kid larn his spellin' from the book. He was givin' the kid a good larrupin' every time he misspelled a word. Eleven-year-old **Edgar** was exhausted physically — it had been going on till near mid-night — emotionally, and every other way. And at that point he slipped a cog. He begged his Paw to let him catch ten minutes' sleep, and promised he'd spell right then.

And he did. From then on he never missed a word. Never missed <u>any word whatever</u>. He'd slipped sidewise . . . into pure clairvoyance. He could spell any word that existed anywhere without hesitation or error.

You try your larrupin' them dumb Southerners long and hard enough . . . and they might just happen to slip sidewise. But one thing seems to me to have been very adequately tested and established: pure pressure alone will not liquefy human opinions. Like hydrogen; high pressure can produce a rigid, metallic form, or if it's adiabatic pressure, hydrogen fusion and explosion. But pressure per se never has, and never, never, never will work. Low temperature alone will . . . but the best way is mild pressure, and reasonably low temperature.

I don't deny your goal — but I assure you you're on the sucker end of a sucker bet when it comes to your method.

Regards, John

Isaac Asimov   *November 18, 1958*

Dear Ike:

Why, **Ike**! You're a bigoted, hyper-conservative racist! You, down underneath, dislike the Negroes and other races of color so much you don't want them to win the world! You're using as an argument for integration-

537

now the proposition that we mustn't let the colored majority of the world gain control of the world!

Ike, you've really got me 100% wrong. I don't care what breed rules the world tomorrow, <u>provided only that it is the most accomplished of human breeds</u>!

I do <u>not</u> at all mind the idea of a world-ruler who is as black as the Ace of Spades — provided only that he's a <u>man</u> — all man and two yards wide.

Take a look at the cover for **Simak's** "Big Front Yard" I ran; the character in the saddle there is black, isn't he? And does that make him a Negro?

By definition and derivation of the term "Negro," it does; the word is simply the direct Spanish meaning "black" — and that guy is black.

I don't care <u>who</u> runs the world — provided only he's the best man. I don't give a damn whether he's black, white, yellow, or purple with chartreuse polka-dots.

If the Blacks can take the world away from us, <u>by their superior achievements</u> . . . it's theirs until somebody out-achieves them. Theirs by right of proven superiority.

What I most disgustedly object to is the technique of parasitism, and the technique of winning-the-race-by-tripping-every-other-runner.

If a man gets tuberculosis, and the tubercle bacillus overcomes and kills him . . . who wins? The germs die too, don't they? The parasite is an organism that destroys its host — and can't live without a host.

If a wolf attacks a buck deer, and the wolf wins . . . the deer is eaten, but the wolf gains strength to go on growing his way. That's not parasitism.

Let's drop the term Negro; that simply means "black." Let's talk about the *Homo africanus* — the breed of Man native to Africa. This breed of man has <u>never developed a civilization above the ritual-taboo order</u>.

Do not seek to argue with that; it's an historical fact, and facts are beyond the zone of permissible argument.

I dislike White, Yellow, and Red trash as thoroughly as I dislike Black-skinned trash.

The one thing I'm interested in is the development of MEN. Super-men. And I don't give a damn what racial stock they start from — just
538

so they achieve. I wanted space-flight; sorry the US didn't get there first — but space-flight is more important to Man than the primacy of the US. That's why I said in my editorial, "Thanks, Ivan; you did a damn fine job!"

I meant it.

Ike, the Men, the Big Men, will <u>always</u> be vastly outnumbered. It makes not the slightest difference what color, shape, or size they are — they'll always be vastly outnumbered. The Big Men are always, by definition of the concept, that small minority way out toward the high-side toe of the distribution curve — and by that fact, they're always outnumbered vastly.

So what if we're outnumbered? If we can't out-think those that outnumber us . . . then we aren't actually at the toe of the curve!

What I want is a segregation system that will breed MEN that I can look up to — before whom I can be humble, and still feel that I have every right to self-respect.

What I do NOT want is to have a situation in which I am forced to yield to petty men for whom I can have no respect, with the result that I can not respect myself.

Let me state that more accurately; I do not want to be forced to yield to petty men for whom I <u>should</u> have no respect.

Many times, no doubt, I may fail to respect someone for whom I <u>should</u> have respect. If he can teach me that I am wrong — fine.

But mere numbers is no reason to respect anyone; the insects and the rabbits outnumber us. The Chinese peasants outnumber us — and the Chinese Reds are doing a good job in China, teaching the ritual-minded peasants in the only way anyone has ever been able to make peasants learn any new thing. With physical force.

The Arabs got nowhere for centuries. **Nasser** is no savage villain; he's an enlightened man. I've talked with the man who was head of his Public Health & Education program, when he was here in New York.

The man's a doctor, and we talked a lot about his family, and the trouble he's having with his son, who's a rebellious, self-directed, creative thinker with great potential, but somewhat shorter on wisdom than the 16 year old boy can yet realize. This doctor is a fine, sound, wise, human being, and a highly educated man.

His job has been to send, or lead, army platoons into Egyptian villages, and, at bayonet point, under threat of immediate military

539

execution, force the fellahin to yield their village land to the State. They are forced, by direct physical threat — and by actual public shooting down of individuals — to build a community building to serve as a school and public health center. They are whipped into building sewage disposal systems. Their children are ruthlessly dragged away from them and forced, screaming in fear, to submit to inoculations. Fellahin groups that charge the soldiers are machine gunned, while the medical technicians ruthlessly continue to inoculate screaming babies while their helpless mothers stand by watching.

It's the only way it can be done.

Children are taken from their homes, and forced to go to schools. Neither the children nor their parents want it; they fight it, but are helpless slaves under the crushing power of the State-controlled Army. The parents are deprived of the help of the children in the fields; the children are deprived of their natural right to live and work in the sunlight and fresh air. (They'll have an increase of TB from that, you can bet, too.)

It's the only way it can be done.

Here, we call 'em truant officers; there it takes an Army platoon armed with machine guns to do it. Because neither the kids nor their parents want it.

And all that, **Ike**, is thanks to the Israeli. And I mean thanks! The Israeli did to the Arab group-entity what the Egyptian medical-educational service is doing to the fellahin villages. It stuck 'em where it hurt with a bayonet. The Israeli are superior people; they have the right to inflict their opinions on their inferior Arab neighbors. And it benefits the Arabs.

I don't give a damn whether the King of the World is a Negro, a Jew, an Arab, a Chinese, a Russian, or what the hell he is — just so he's an entity I can respect in the fullest, highest sense.

I don't want the breed that wins the race to be the one that was cleverest at tripping all the others, though. I don't want the winner to be the guy that scattered thumbtacks in the paths of all the other runners, after knocking down the original leaders by clubbing them from behind.

Further, I don't want one breed to get ahead by a fluke . . . and then make it impossible for any other to get ahead.

That, of course, is what the NAACP thinks they're fighting. That the Whites got ahead by an historical accident, and have been suppressing
540

everybody else since.

It isn't true. Sure, the evidence <u>seems</u> to be that way, because the Whites have stayed ahead. But the only races of color that have caught up, or started to catch up with the Whites, are the ones that abandoned their own cultures, and accepted the White's!

Rome wasn't built in a day — and a statistical-run genius among the Negroes can't build a Rome, because it can't be done in one lifetime. Unless the breed can <u>sustain</u> a high-effort level over several generations, the accomplishments of one statistical-run genius will be cancelled out to futility. And <u>that</u> requires that his high-order abilities be transmissible.

It's the scientific method, **Ike**; only the repeatable experiment counts.

But each statistical-run genius "knows" his race is capable of just as great things as any other. He knows, because he has the abilities, and is a member of that race.

Do you know the ability-level of Russian Jews, **Ike**?

"I am a Russian Jew. I am a highly capable science and fiction writer. Therefore Russian Jews have this capability." It's an easy, and emotionally desired argument, isn't it?

The Negro members of the NAACP feel deeply, honestly, and sincerely that the Negro breed has the capabilities they have.

Sorry . . . it isn't a repeatable experiment. It's a unique occurrence.

You, on the other hand, are nowhere near so much a unique occurrence; high mental ability and persistence-in-thinking are fairly repeatable experiments among the Russian Jewish breed, aren't they?

And **Ike**, you're slipping back in the face of facts again. You're going back to "race hatred must be taught; it isn't instinctive." I agree that it must be taught — but suppose race A has a unique ability to teach other races to hate it? The resultant hatred-of-race-A is taught, all right, under those conditions — but it isn't taught in the way you mean by the phrase, is it?

Now please to stop pulling that proposition on me until you've thoroughly explained how the English, who were NOT taught to hate Negroes have developed a powerful anti-Negro reaction. And have the intellectual honesty to consider, at least, the possibility that the Negroes so acted as to <u>earn</u> the hatred the English, for the first time in their history, now feel toward them.

The Egghead earns the hatred normal men feel toward him; he robs the normal man of freedom.

Look; if I have precognition and telekinesis, and get into a dice game with normal men . . . the others are helpless. I've robbed them of their freedom to play a game-of-random-chance, since, for me, it is not a game of random chance . . . and therefore it is not a game-of-random-chance in reality!

Tic-tac-toe is a "determinant game," as any Game Theorist can show. The one who makes the first mark can lose only by sheer stupidity. If I demonstrate to you that this is so, but you cannot understand why or how it is so, then thereafter every time you move first and lose, you will know you're stupid — because you know that only your own stupidity allowed your defeat.

I robbed you of self-respect. It makes no difference if you have risen in anger and killed me — you're still stuck with the irretrievable fact that you know you lose only by your own stupidity.

The craftsmen could smash the machines in the Industrial Revolution — but that didn't restore the feeling that their craft was a high, human ability. Sure, they could smash a machine . . . but a machine could weave better, faster, neater, and fancier cloth than they could just the same. Their freedom to respect that ability was irretrievably taken from them.

If I get into that dice game, it makes no difference at all whether I use precognition to bet on what is going to occur, or use telekinesis to make what I bet on occur — the result is precisely the same. I've robbed the normal players of the freedom to know-it-is-a-game-of-chance.

My friend **Sam Andre** bets on horse-races. He wins consistently. Not every time, but consistently over a season. He does it as a hobby, and has averaged from $750 to $1200 a year for the last ten years.

Tell the normal horse-better about that, and you rob him of the sense of it's-all-luck and I've-as-much-chance-as-anyone-else. He hasn't: **Sam Andre** will, with mathematical certainty, take his money away from him. The only way the sucker can hope to retain his money is by not even trying. His freedom to bet on the horses is gone forever.

And if **Sam** drops out . . . still his freedom is gone, because **Sam** has proven that it isn't "all luck" — it's just the sucker's stupidity that makes him think so.

(I threw **Sam** a curve, though, when I gave him a formula that topped

542

his. I proved to him that there was a way to win on the races not only consistently, but every time! I like to make sucker bets, you know — bets where the other guy is a sucker, I tell him he is, he won't believe it, I bet I'll demonstrate it, and then do so. My system for winning every time: "I'll bet that some horse will win, if there is any race at all." **Sam** objected that there was no such bet possible. I pointed out that that is precisely the bet the parimutuel machine makes on every race — and that it invariably wins. And that that is, actually, what a bookie does.)

Sure, the Egghead earns the hate the normal man cordially gives him. A lot of people dislike arguing with me, because I reduce their freedom-of-opinion by nailing their opinion down on one of their own facts. The only type of mind that can enjoy that treatment is the want-to-learn type; the want-to-be-right type is driven to anger.

(Yes, I'm using it on you. I'm using your statement about "we mustn't let the other races win the world" against you. But I have considerable reason to believe that you're a want-to-learn type, rather than a want-to-be-right type.)

Now here's something for you to mull over carefully.

Before any meaningful argument-discussion can take place, some point of starting agreement must be settled. We couldn't successfully discuss "How to cook hare" if you thought the subject was "How to cook hair." And "heir to breed" misunderstood as "air to breathe" could lead to some considerable confusion.

Add this: Any sane entity has some sort of Highest Value, or Highest Good, for which any lesser value can be sacrificed, but which cannot itself be sacrificed for anything. In Chess, the King is the Highest Value; anything else and everything else can be sacrificed in the King's defense, but there is no possible reason (within the game) for sacrificing the King.

Add this: A Highest Value can be either positive (I want) or negative, (I want NOT).

Add this: The "highest" concept involved seems to be arithmetical, rather than algebraic. A negative value of 100 units, in other words, has a higher value than a positive value of 90 units. The result; a human being will sacrifice the thing he wants most, for the thing he wants-not even more.

Example: a man will sacrifice his life (which he wants) to escape servile slavery (which he wants-not even more.) The American Indians could not be enslaved, because of that factor.

Interact the above, and observe this consequence: If a man wants-not Alpha, with a highest-value intensity, he will sacrifice facts, truth, honesty, ethics, life, judgment, and everything else to maintain not-Alpha, with relationship to his self.

The astrophysicist who committed suicide when the 1919 eclipse expedition proved Relativity — which he found intolerable want-not — had to be accepted. He could not force his want-not onto the world around him — but he isolated his Self from the intolerable system. In effect; "I will NOT permit, under any circumstances whatever, a relationship between my Self and such a world-system."

The chess player who sees that checkmate is inevitable in three moves does sacrifice his King; he knocks over his King, and is immediately outside the rules of the game.

Currently, psionics is a want-not of Science. Science has, in consequence, sacrificed truth, honesty, ethics, logic, and everything else in an effort to isolate itself from psionics. The psychologists say **Rhine's** statistical methods are invalid . . . despite the fact that the American Mathematical Society has attested that his methods are 100% sound. But the Math Soc. says they don't believe his laboratory methods are valid. The psych boys say they are . . . because all their own lab methods are based on precisely the same techniques **Rhine** is using, and they'd have to negate their own experiments. On psi experiments, Science has, again and again, insisted on the rule of "invariable success"; i.e., that every psi experiment must always work exactly as predicted. Thus when diviners don't always succeed in finding water, Science rejects the entire proposition.

But radar doesn't always work, and certainly you wouldn't guarantee that a certain enzyme-isolation technique would invariably work.

Scientists will display the human characteristic of want-not with all the consequences involved — they'll sacrifice every other value, positive or negative, for a highest-negative-value.

I'm beginning to get some real results from my campaign on the divining rods for locating pipes, because that's been tailored in recognition of the want-not mechanism.

The reason Science wants-not psionics, is that it would by-pass Science as the Ultimate Value. Then the actual highest value I'm tangling with is the want-not that Science be by-passed.

So I'm demonstrating a real threat that I can cause Science to be by-passed completely! And by reason of psionics!

I'm encouraging the Engineers to by-pass the Scientist! The Engineer, in actual fact, can and should at times, do just that. The engineering use of the divining rod does in fact bypass science. This establishes a new kind of direct, and desperate threat of by-passing; a more direct threat of imposing the Highest Want-Not Value.

Science will, inevitably, be forced to accept the want-not problem of psionics to avoid the even-more-violently not-wanted problem of direct engineering by-pass.

Why did the US finally accept a real, full-scale, hard-hitting satellite program? Because we had been by-passed.

Now a want-not has a curious characteristic. Anything else will be sacrificed for a highest-order want-not.

In order to have a meaningful discussion, two individuals must start from a common point of agreement.

Suppose I want not to discuss Aleph, and you want to discuss it. If that want-not is a highest-order want-not, I will sacrifice truth, honesty, ethics, memory, everything else in its favor.

Then there will remain only one possible point of starting agreement which you can find; we can agree only on the starting point, "We want-not to discuss Aleph." When you find that point, I can not abandon — sacrifice — it, because it's a highest-value non-sacrificable King-point.

BUT . . . you can't discuss Aleph starting from that point! The instant you do start discussing Aleph, you've abandoned the point, and we're no longer able to discuss because we don't have a common point of agreement!

This shows up in the human Quarrel mechanism, which is characterized by the fact that, if A and B are quarrelling, A will deny the truth of anything B says. If B says, "Well, after all, the sun will rise tomorrow," A will, characteristically snap, "Not if you can help it!"

The problem of dealing with human beings usually boils down to finding the want-not that underlies the whole structure of resistance. If that want-not turns out to be the highest-value in the other human being's system . . . discussion is inherently impossible . . . unless you can, somehow, induce a still-higher value, either a want or a want-not, which

545

will permit the sacrifice of the old King-point.

OK; now consider this. Is it possible that you have a want-<u>not</u> of Highest Value on the business of, "First eliminate <u>all</u> segregation!"

If the only possible starting point of agreement is, "No basis of segregation whatever should even be suggested," if such a total-negation point is the only possible acceptable point of starting discussion . . . it's a point that intrinsically forbids discussion <u>ever</u>.

If your king-point is, "No one should even consider segregation," you would be driven to sacrifice all other points in its favor.

Now in chess, the King can be protected from attacking pieces by blocking. If the blocking piece is then taken, another blocker can be moved in. Since there are only 15 possible blockers, the attacker can, eventually, exhaust the supply of blocking pieces, and press home the attack on the King.

But in argument, there is an Aleph of possible blocking points to protect a king-point, and if the defender is willing to sacrifice the Aleph of points — and he is! — he won't even be bothered by the relevancy of the points he introduces as blockers.

The discussion might be on whether **Napoleon** or **Lee** were the better general; if the defender finds he's under pressure, he may insist on discussing Siamese fighting-fish, and maintain it's a relevant point. Or demand that it be shown that **Napoleon** was not unfaithful to **Josephine**.

He's defending a king-point that **Lee** is superior to anybody . . . because **Lee** is his life-model. Because **Lee** is his Highest Value (not **Lee**-in-reality, but **Lee**-as-he-envisions-him, of course) his highest-value want-<u>not</u> is that **Lee** <u>not</u> be de-throned.

Because logic has no means of proving a negative proposition in an inexhaustible field . . . most human quarrels wind up with one individual retreating into the negative-proposition position. From that position, he can launch an aleph of blocking points.

Rhine, for instance, has been blocked by an inexhaustible supply of "insufficient control of the experiments" points.

One of the things about my attack on the psionics problem has been that I simply, happily refused absolutely to be trapped into trying to exhaust their supply of blocking points.

You know, if the piece attacking the King is a knight . . . even an inexhaustible supply of blocking pieces wouldn't do a bit of good, would it?

I'm attacking the king-point of want-<u>not</u>-psionics by a knight-attack; I'm <u>not approaching it scientifically</u>! I'm making an engineering approach . . . which can't be blocked by even an aleph-c of scientific blocking points! It happily goes skimming right over-around-through all the absolutely water-tight scientific proofs that it is impossible, to the conclusion "I can use it to my benefit."

And finally, **Ike**, my friend . . . you're the mystic, not I! You, not I, are the subjectivist. You're saying, "Unless <u>I</u> can observe it, by <u>my</u> methods, it doesn't exist." That is a purely subjective viewpoint, not at all an objective one!

Furthermore, it's stinking lousy because it's further restricted by communication channel problems. Suppose I have a microphone that can sense everything up to 100,000 cycles, and an amplifier and scope that can present anything up to 1,000,000 cycles . . . and they're connected by a telephone line that works just fine up to 3000 cycles, but has cut-off filters built in to prevent cross-talk on the carrier-current transmission system.

Now the mike can observe it, and the amplifier record it . . . but the channel won't communicate it.

Example: You can observe the pattern figure 5 in an Ishihara color vision test card . . . but you have absolutely no possible way of communicating what you observed that led to your conclusion, "There is a figure 5." The observation <u>is not objective</u>. It's not a physical observation at all! It's a <u>mental</u> phenomenon stimulated by a complex of physical stimuli. The observation you report <u>is not</u> a physical observation, and you can't show me a physical-science device that can demonstrate your reputed observation!

Hell, take something simple! Show me a physical-science device that can make the observation, "This wooden model is a representation of a dextro-rotary crystal, while this one is a model of a leavo-rotary crystal."

You, you physical-science-logical-mystic, are denying the observational fact that Life recognizes — i.e., senses! — <u>patterns</u>! You can do it yourself, and know-for-a-fact-of-experience that you can. Now tell a computer how you do it, you mystic!

Sure, I can do it too, and you can say to me, "You see what I mean?"

And the correct answer is, "No, I don't see what you mean, but I perceive, by non-physical sensing systems, what you are indicating you want me to observe."

Now furthermore, just because you can't observe something by any method known-or-available to you doesn't mean that it can't affect you, either . . . modern physical science to the contrary notwithstanding!

Try getting into a card game with a card-sharp sometime. You can't, and never do, observe the markings on the cards. This means, scientifically, that they cannot affect you.

Haw! You should be so broke!

Sure, I know that argument is entirely outside the scientific area, and not at all what you intended. Of course not! But you're making the presumptuous claim that your statement, "only the observable has effect," is a philosophical generality — and if you want to maintain that, brother, you've got to stick to it in any field I can find to apply it!

Remember what I said about the normal man being robbed of his freedom by the genius who can perceive order, where he can not! That simply means that the genius has sensing systems which he can use, but which the normal man cannot use. The normal man is not directly affected by anything that he can't observe . . . but that doesn't mean that he isn't affected.

You're calling me a mystic more or less on the grounds, "It's unfair, improper, indecent, and unethical of you to react to something which neither I, nor any of my methods, can detect."

Those dirty Russians must have stolen the secret of making satellite-rockets from somebody; it's unfair and unethical because we don't have them.

Look, just because you can't see any difference between A and B is no proof that there isn't any — and just because you can't learn to see a difference doesn't mean that I can't see one! And the fact that I can't communicate that difference to you doesn't prove anything but that fact itself.

Science is egregiously presumptuous; try a little humility. Humility is not the same as servility! I can't levitate . . . but some individuals can and did. I can't use clairvoyance . . . but some individuals, such as **Edgar Cayce**, did. And it is true, even though I can't explain it, and he can't communicate it to me.

548

How presumptuous can you get?! "Now," says Science with lofty nose, "obviously if I can't observe it, it doesn't really exist at all."

And the stupid Robot, Science, can't even distinguish between the left hand and the right!

Until a couple years ago, it didn't even admit there was a difference!

Dammit, electrons and positrons are not mirror images, fully equivalent. Right and Wrong are not merely mirror images, seen from different viewpoints. It's not "just a matter of opinion!"

Parity does not rule the Universe.

Regards, John

John W. Campbell, Jr.   *November 27, 1958*

Dear John,

About a week ago you sent me a clipping that a fan had sent to you about hemoglobin being synthesized in the test-tube. It reminded the fan about HEMOGLOBIN AND THE UNIVERSE and he suggested to you that I write another piece explaining what was going on with this business of synthetic proteins.

You sent it on with an added "How about it, **Ike**?" on it.

So this is how about it. Enclosed is a 7,000 word article entitled MICRODESIGN FOR LIVING which not only talks about synthetic proteins but gives the latest poop (as far as I know it) on how the body manages to make proteins anyway.

Incidentally, you undoubtedly know of **George Gamow**, whom I mention in the article. He is a first-class scientist (I am only second-class, if that) and he is also probably the best popular science-writer in the world (I am only second best, if that.) My only consolation is that **Gamow** does not write science-fiction. There, at least, I have him.

I hope you like the article and can use it.

Yours, Isaac Asimov

Isaac Asimov   *December 12, 1958*

Dear Ike:

Dammit, I wish you'd arrange to stay with us one night, the next time you're down, so we can have a real bull-session. I'd just gotten back from

549

a trip to North Carolina, talking at North Carolina State and visiting **Rhine** at Duke, and had a hell of a lot to yak about with you.

Some items: MIT is, though it doesn't know it yet, in a bind . . . and, as **Peg** said after two days at North Carorlina State, "The next generation of engineers is going to be talking with a deep-south accent." North Carolina State is in the position, with respect to MIT, Cal Tech, Cornell, etc., of Russia to the US. They haven't got much in the way of traditions . . . but man, are they doing things!

We stopped in Richmond over night. Now Virginia is full of tradition and history. North Carolina, of course, is mostly remarkable for being unremarkable; nothing important ever happened there . . . except that there's one cape on the shore, a sand bar, called Kitty Hawk. Richmond is a proud, slightly down-at-the-heels City of the South. Ever think what an excellent economic indicator the local photographic stores and electronic shops are? Cameras above the Brownie class are strictly, purely, luxury items — and a luxury appealing only to people who enjoy learning and doing. In Westfield, here, the Westfield Studio store stocks Rollies, Licas, Speed Graphics, Nikons — all top-bracket cameras in the $200 to $500 range. Precision machines, with very wide range competence.

The biggest photo store in Richmond had a window-full of second-hand third-line cameras — cameras I haven't seen even second hand in New York City stores! There were no Leicas, Nikons, Rollies, or Speed Graphics on hand; just lots of pamphlets and literature.

The town has no money, and nobody interested in learning anything requiring increased understanding.

Raleigh-Durham-Chapel Hill are being billed as "the research triangle" . . . and the boys are NOT kidding. They damn well mean it.

And North Carolina State College, **Ike**, was the <u>first</u> school to have their own nuclear reactor to teach nuclear engineering! In 1949 the No. Car. State physics department "rolled their own!" Using unclassified data, and data they dug out themselves, they built their own reactor, instruments, control system, and shielding system. They've got a Grade A #1 course in nucleonics — one with damn near a decade of experience-in-teaching.

They're definitely ahead of MIT on that . . . which finally got a reactor <u>this</u> year!

550

Item: a North Carolina State prof has a new isotope separation gimmick. In three stages it does what Oak Ridge does . . . and each stage occupies about 2 cubic feet of space!

He uses a standing supersonic wave. At the nodes the pressures reach 10^{12} atmospheres, and at the anti-nodes, the accelerations reach 10^{13} gravities! Under 10^{13} gravities, the separation of U isotopes is quite sharp, you might say. Of course, the molecules don't stand up very well under those accelerations, but they re-form as soon as they get out of the zone of max acceleration.

The desired isotopes are simply skimmed off with a tiny pipette. Even a micropipette carries quite a stream when the stuff's being rammed into it with 10^{12} atmospheres pressure, you know.

His nice, neat, quiet, cheap little gadget makes an ultracentrifuge look purty puny; 10^6 g's is about as high as they've ever managed. And his device offers no menace of explosion.

Some one of these days, someone's going to use really high-density RF magnetic fields, and produce accelerations that'll produce nuclear fusion direct. What's the limiting intensity of a sound wave? The answer, obviously, is the point at which the matter conducting the wave breaks down and behaves inelastically. The final inelasticity of hydrogen is when it collides inelastically . . . and fuses. As long as it does not fuse, it behaves elastically. No energy is withdrawn from an oscillating system, so long as it behaves elastically. Therefore the only drain on the input of such a system would be the energy involved in inelastic collisions. But those, of course, will yield more energy than is absorbed.

I've been thinking of that proposition, trying to work it out . . . and, just for the hell of it, I'm going to write **Ted Thomas**, who's been looking up some other maybe-patentable ideas for me, and see if I can maybe get something on that. Please to consider the above proposed fusion reaction system a "disclosure to a trusted friend competent to understand the proposal."

I believe it could be done by using a microwave resonant cavity — a pair, rather — so shaped as to produce by interaction an exceedingly intense magnetic field. In such a system, the normal electromagnetic radiation of oscillating ions would be reflected internally, so that there would be very low loss by radiation, at any point short of fusion.

The essential concept is that the limiting intensity of any vibration is that at which the medium itself ceases to be elastic. This is not a matter of frequency, but of intensity. Sound being a mechanical vibration, the limitation is the mechanical properties of the medium. If the medium be fully ionized deuterium the mechanical limitations of deuterium set the limits — and that limit is fusion of the nuclei.

Note that this is not a thermo-nuclear device; it's "pressure-welding" instead of "temperature-welding." The oscillating deuterons would be "cold." It would involve organized, not random movement of the deuterons.

The deuterons could, of course, be accelerated by either the electric or the magnetic component of the RF oscillator.

I've been doing a lot of thinking about patterns vs linear systems — above is part of that — and doing a lot of work with photography rather than electronics as a result.

Item: I was able to take some damned good baby portraits 15 years ago . . . but couldn't get anything satisfactory for adults or older children.

Now I've developed a totally new approach to photo-portraiture. And this one is positively deadly! I used it on **Peg**, and I used it on **Dr. Rhine** when I went down to Duke. It's a Keeler Polygraph sort of thing — it reveals facts about attitudes and beliefs and fundamental personality-structure that would lift your hair.

The gimmick: I got **Peg** to talk to **Dr. Rhine** . . . and I went to work with my little Nikon 35mm. It's got an F 1.4 lens, and gets lovely pictures by ordinary room light . . . and I can take one a second if I really want to. With a Nikon motor . . . which I am now seriously considering! . . . I could take 3 a second, run out a whole 36 exposure roll in 12 seconds flat.

I shoot at 1/60th second or faster. Above 1/125th is best, and with an F 1.4 lens, and Tri X Pan film, ordinary room light lets you do so.

I take a series of half a dozen or more shots — a dozen is about enough.

Now the human eye cannot perceive changes in less than 1/10th second. Suppose we have a child with a rigid-minded, bullying parent. The kid is angry and disgusted with Pop . . . but Pop's got a heavy hand, and a quick willingness to use it. Expressing his feelings facially is going to get him clobbered, but good.

But . . . if he sneers at the old man for 1/30th of a second — Pop can't see it.

552

The old proposition: you can't correct an error until you can detect it. No feedback system will eliminate an error it cannot sense. You can't punish misbehavior you can't detect. The kid can sneer and snarl at Pop all he wants to . . . just so long as it remains in the class "not so's you'd notice it."

The Keeler Polygraph works, because while all of us have learned to lie with a straight face, without blushing, etc., we've never had experience having to lie without subtle changes in respiration, heart-beat, etc.

If you shoot a series of pictures of a man at 1/125th or faster . . . you catch him in the act of sneering, snarling, smiling, twinkling, sagging in despair, showing the fatigue, etc., all of which he has, since childhood, been trained to mask from human vision. You learn to speak without snarling . . . or else! You learn not to show your sneers . . . or else!

But at 1/125th or 1/250th they show.

Now you can wait, and catch any expression, on anyone. You could, if you waited around long enough, catch Scrooge with a warm, friendly smile. I could catch you looking at someone with a sneer of disgust, or a snarl of hate.

But suppose I got **Peg** to get you talking about Boston University . . . while I snapped a dozen shots at about 1/250th second? It won't be what one shows . . . it'll be what the pattern shows. Suppose she got you talking about Boston University — then about moving to North Carolina where living costs are way, way down (frying chickens, 25 cents a pound; eggs and butter likewise. Four bedroom house, two baths, and den for $19,000, etc.) and there are miles and miles of beautiful open country, with rolling wooded hills and open meadowland. And then talking about a new science article you were working on . . . .

What sort of fleeting expression-patterns would I catch? Frustration-irritation on Boston University. Delighted interest on the low costs in North Carolina. Withdrawal and discomfort about the empty, unorganized landscape. Interest-enthusiasm about the science article.

O.K. — that would be a Portrait of **Ike Asimov**.

And no one of the shots could possibly be!

Now: I believe I've found a useful measure of a new dimension in Reality. The dimension is not a space or time dimension, and doesn't behave like those four. Why it is so, I haven't figured out, but there is a curious fact that the three spatial dimensions are truly interchangeable; they are not interchangeable with the time dimension, however, on any basis analogous to the interchange of length-for-breadth. The x, y, and z axes are purely relative . . . i.e., show a true parity effect. But there is not parity between x, y, z, and the t axis.

O.K. — now let's talk about the m axis. It does not show parity with x, y, z, or t. It's as different-in-nature from them, as t is from x, y, z.

Consider a man walking across the room. He is moving in three space dimensions, with respect to the time dimension.

We can, however, conceive of the concept "walking across the room," as a unit, a ding-an-sich, a gestalt.

This does NOT mean a series of movie frames; it is NOT a series of self-contained units — a discontinuous structure of quantized bits. Mentally visualize the total process, not as a series of stills, but somewhat as **Heinlein** had it in "Life Line," where Pinero described a man's life as a wriggling, twisting pink worm extending from birth to death.

Now this conception — which you can fully appreciate as a real conception! — entails a dimension not temporal or spatial! To visualize the process as a gestalt, you must be removing yourself from it along the m-axis, so that you can see all four space-time axes "simultaneously" . . . but notice that we have no competent word in the language, for "simultaneously" means "at the same time", and this is not a matter of either slicing, or collapsing-to-zero the time-axis of the process.

I'm calling it the m-axis . . . because I think the best term for that dimension is meaning. We have an instinctive, non-linguistic awareness of it . . . and have fumbled at it with language. How close are "close friends"? This doesn't refer to a measure along either x, y, z. or t axis — but it evidently does refer to a measure along the m-axis.

Now, Re the Argument: So far, your position is, "No differentiation — no classification — until you do it right!"

Yeah . . . only "right" is an interesting, tricky, word. Do you mean, "Until it is done so there is no risk of anyone being hurt?" In that case, there is no "right" way. Do you mean, "Until there is no risk of me being hurt?" That also means no "right" way. Does it mean, "No danger of anyone being rejected because of incurable, inherent flaws which he did not choose and cannot eliminate?" Then that, too, is impossible.

There's a difference between "guilty of" and "responsible for,"
554

remember. If I'm driving, and a steering knuckle breaks, and the car, out of control, runs over and kills someone . . . I'm not guilty, and won't be tried for murder. But I am responsible, and can be sued for damages. (That's why I carry insurance.)

A man is <u>responsible</u> for his flaws, whether he's guilty of them or not. He's <u>responsible</u> for them, even when they are entirely beyond his control. A man is killed by a bolt of lightning; he's dead, whether he was busy shaking his fist at the heavens and defying God, or merely sleeping on a hillside.

In this case, the guy was killed for not exercising due precognition. If he'd just taken the trouble to preken what was going to happen there, he wouldn't have been hurt, so it's his own fault.

Ignorance of the law of Nature is no excuse.

Now a child is held not responsible by reason of ignorance . . . in <u>human terms only</u>. A pot of boiling water on the stove doesn't hold that concept; it'll scald a three-year-old to death with the same impartiality it would a 21-year-old.

A child is held not-responsible, because we recognize in it potential-yet-unrealized. It is forgiven because it <u>will</u> learn.

An idiot is different; his behavior is like that of a three-year-old — but his potential is exhausted. He's reached <u>brennshluss</u>, and is unable to accelerate any more.

No system of classification is useful if it doesn't have the necessary characteristic of saying, "These individuals are rejected. Throw them away." It <u>must</u>, to be useful, have a "Drop dead!" category.

The level of "acceptable" itself, moreover, must be an advancing one. The line of Terrestrial life is pointless if it is never to advance beyond our present stage; there must, if there is reason in living now, come a stage wherein Life has advanced to a level such that we rate as "subnormal idiots; euthanasia necessary."

Suppose I found an immortality treatment that kept me alive, and in my present stage of development, for 10,000 years. I might be useful on some backwater, undeveloped planet. If I found that unbearable — if I simply demanded a chance to join in the dynamic life of the mainstream worlds — it would be necessary to destroy me. If I can't be happy doing what I can do, and can't possibly, ever, learn to do what I want to do . . . somebody should have the good-sense-kindness to say, "Drop dead," and make it stick. If what I want to do is something I am inherently incapable of doing, and I cannot be happy not doing it . . . I'd be better off dead.

Remember the myth of Phaeton? He wasn't competent to do what he wanted to do, drove Apollo's sun-chariot anyway, and killed himself and a lot of others.

O.K. You say, "No classifications until you have the right ones!"

Put up, or shut up! Name the right classifications — or drop dead.

Because if you demand something you can't possibly have — then you're going to be miserable and you'd be better off dead. And you can't have a world of no-classifications.

It's fundamentally, and inherently impossible. Now, always, past, present, future, here, there, throughout the Universe. YOU CAN NOT HAVE A SOCIETY WITHOUT CLASSIFICATIONS! It's absolutely and innately impossible — a contradiction in terms.

Reason: the fundamental of intelligence is the ordering of information.

Ordering means arrangement.

Arrangement means classification.

No classification equals no ordering, implies no intelligence. No intelligence means no possibility of society.

The intelligence doesn't have to be possessed by the members of the society; the society can be built by external intelligence. Vide the ants and bees.

So you don't like the present classifications. That's permissible. But give up, because you must, the idea of a no-classifications system from which the new classification system is to stem. You must give it up, because the no-classification society isn't a society. It isn't even possessed of intelligence, and so can't learn.

Instead, start formulating, now, in this society, the better system of classifications.

Or, as I say, drop dead; you'll be happier that way. You're demanding something that's innately impossible.

Therefore: Instead of attacking present classifications on an "I don't want any!" basis, start now proposing alternatives.

Regards, John

556

Isaac Asimov   *April 29, 1959*

Dear Ike:

Beginning as soon as I can get the articles to fill 'em, *Astounding* is going to have an additional thirty-two pages of slick paper (and 15 cents more on the price tag). Problem: for slick paper pages, I need photographs and photographically illustrated articles.

Have you any suggestions?

Regards, John W. Campbell, Jr., Editor

Isaac Asimov   *October 27, 1959*

Dear Ike:

Came across something that may help you and some of the other boys to understand what it is I'm talking about in my remarks that Science isn't doing its job right.

The following is a word-for-word quote from an official Navy Research Advisory Committee report on the need for basic research. Report prepared by Arthur D. Little, under an Office of Naval Research (ONR) contract. The report is in two volumes — <u>very</u> handsome and expensive production, with two-color printing, beautiful typography, on every page. Wide margins, and extra-heavy grade of pure-white high-quality book paper. Huge four-color fold-out charts, flow-sheets, etc. Obviously time, effort, and money were really concentrated on it. NRAC was really pouring on the coal to present their proposition: That the Navy should spend about twice as much as it is on basic research, to keep the basic and developmental research programs in balance.

Now: Item 1. I agree in full that that proposition is valid. What they are trying to communicate is something that needs to be communicated, something very important. It should be put over.

BUT ... I groan at the utterly incompetent, hopelessly thick-headed way they've gone about it. I predict (and this is strictly a what-I-believe-will-be, <u>not</u> a what-I-think-should-be prediction) that they will <u>lose</u> ground, not gain it, because of this thick-witted report.

The whole concept of we-need-basic-research is centered around, and derives from, one proposition which they very clearly state. It's printed in blue ink, on a page where the rest of the text is in black ink, to

557

call strong attention to it.

I quote: "In every invention there exists a key fact, the last to be discovered of all the facts, relationships, and principles which were necessary before the invention could be made. The date of discovery of that key fact is the earliest date at which the invention could have been made. Some inventions have been made very quickly after the discovery of the key fact, others have been made long after, but no invention was ever made before the discovery of its key fact."

Ike, I've shown that statement to a collection of non-scientists — intelligent people who were not trained as scientists.

Every one of them has immediately spotted the egregious fallacy in the statement.

Yet that blue-ink-underlined statement passed with all the professionally trained scientists who worked on preparing the statements in the report — and is, in fact, the expression of the basic philosophy which the report seeks to substantiate.

Now look, **Ike**; the Catholic Church holds that the only way to get to Heaven is through the Catholic Church. That you have to have an ordained Catholic Priest sign your passport.

Some people disagree with that proposition, and somewhat resent the Catholic attitude.

My friend, a lot of non-scientists (and they happen to be the majority of the human race) resent the Priesthood of Science. Inasmuch as practically all national administrators and legislators are non-scientists, they are not going to be pleased by the dogmatic and fallacious statement the Office of Naval Research has paid Arthur D. Little to work up. I mean it; try that statement first on six assorted professional scientists, and then on six assorted intelligent non-scientists, such as lawyers, economists, or historians. Particularly lawyers, since that group dominates national administration. Hell, you can try it on artists and high-school kids, and they'll spot the nonsense that the ONR and Arthur D. Little, Inc. didn't see!

Those damn dunderheaded scientists are trying to sell the importance of basic research (which is true) on the basis that it is the only way to achievement and progress (which is flatly false.)

Now dammit, **Ike**, it's all very well for scientists to say, "One should always act on reason, facts, logic, data — understandings. Not on
558

'faith' or mere emotional conviction."

But that same scientist says, also, "You, as a layman, cannot understand the problems involved here; they cannot be explained in language, and without the necessary mathematical training, you cannot understand." This is precisely equivalent to the priest saying, "This is a Mystery which is beyond your understanding. I cannot explain it to you; you must accept it as an Act of Faith."

The <u>scientist</u> may be acting on the basis of data, logic, understanding and reason, when he asks for the administrator to assign $100,000,000 to a project . . . but <u>the administrator is not</u>. The administrator, who, as the scientist will be glad to assure you, cannot understand the problems involved, cannot act on logic or data or understanding . . . but on faith alone. The scientist is, in actual fact, demanding, "You, Mr. Administrator, <u>must</u> act on faith in my greater wisdom. You are incompetent to judge, because you are ignorant, and cannot be instructed. You must have faith in me and my greater judgment in these matters, and spend the $100,000,000 as I tell you to, without questioning the matter since you are unable to understand the facts."

I.e., the scientist demands that the administrator act on the basis of an emotional conviction, not based on logical data, that the scientist is wise, judicious, and good.

Now the fact of the matter is that in any division of labor system, faith — emotional conviction without understanding -- is necessary. You demand it of your children, don't you? You must in most of your living have faith in others who have special skills, mustn't you? If you have no faith in your automobile mechanic's work . . . on what basis do you accept that your steering gear won't fall apart next time you drive? Do you have data on its condition by direct and adequately trained observation?

Then see what the scientists have done with that stupid blunder of theirs. Any intelligent non-scientist is immediately aware of the simple and perfectly obvious fact that most of the inventions we use today were <u>not</u> the result of basic research, did <u>not</u> stem from application of key facts, but were arrived at either by trial-and-error without understanding whatever, or by intuition.

The basic-research-scientific method of determining their required angle of lean for a kid riding his bicycle at 15 mph around a curve of 20

559

foot radius takes a minimum of 5 minutes for a college physics junior, using pencil and paper. But any 12-year old solves it in split seconds in his head, without any understanding of key facts.

What key facts had to be discovered by basic research before the wheel was invented? And, for that matter, most people you ask don't know what the invention involved in "the wheel" was. (It wasn't the wheel that had to be invented; log rollers have the essential roundness characteristic. It was the axle that had to be invented, the answer to, "How can you make the log rollers stay under load, instead of continually rolling out from under?" And it was done without basic research.)

The Romans had mortar — without physical chemistry that could explain the crystalline forms of CaO, $Ca(OH)_2$, and hydrated $CaSO_4$.

Most human progress, as any intelligent non-scientist is perfectly aware, was made before the concept of basic research was invented.

Therefore that stupid statement that basic research is the only way invention and progress can take place is a statement that is a lie, because it's a half-truth (it is true that that's a way) being promulgated as the whole truth.

The scientist — hotly though he denies it — demands that the non-scientist act on a basis of "trust and obey, for there's no other way" when the scientist tells him what to do.

And then the scientist gives the non-scientist most excellent reason to distrust anything the scientist says by pulling a childishly stupid blunder like that!

Science, my friend, is a true priesthood. If that statement were valid (conditional definitely contrary to fact), then it would be true that only scientists could make inventions.

The attitude displayed by scientists toward non-scientifically trained inventors demonstrates that the scientist believes the statement to be completely true.

That a major governmental research agency could publish that flat statement as truth indicates to what an extent they have blinded themselves to simple, obvious facts.

Key facts are absolutely necessary to invention by the deductive method.

Goodyear didn't invent vulcanization by the deductive method; he invented it by spilling some goo on his stove. Who was it first synthesized
560

urea? He did it, maybe, by deductively deriving the necessary steps to produce the desired result? Hell, he wasn't even trying to make urea!

And the sublimest stupidity of all is this; true, fundamental research is precisely what the scientists say doesn't exist — it's discovery entirely without preceding key facts or relationships. A true fundamental discovery is the recognizing observation of a totally unpredicted phenomenon.

Dammit, **Ike** . . . what can you do with a priesthood that hasn't the self-awareness to acknowledge that it _is_ a priesthood?

Now to your letter and the question of "responsibility."

It's a real nice question. The fundamental answer is that we are, all of us, always gambling. We're taking risks, calculated or otherwise, whether we acknowledge that fact or not.

The true irresponsible individual is one that takes risks and insists that he isn't. The responsible individual is one who knows he is taking risks, calculates his risks as well as he can, and then does his best to calculate the probability of the risks he doesn't know he's taking. (What you don't know _can_ hurt you; the responsible individual calculates a safety factor to allow as best he can for that fact, and the fact that he isn't omniscient.)

My parable is the picture of a viking in the old days, caught in a violent storm at sea, and being driven through black and rainswept night by a howling gale. He hears breakers ahead — he knows that the 40-foot waves are smashing against a rocky coast. He can't see a thing . . . until he sees dim whiteness of the shattering waves.

Question: What's his emotional attitude?

The irresponsible's attitude is angry-frightened-resentment-sense-of-injustice. It _shouldn't_ have happened, because he didn't intend it that way, and it isn't his fault because he didn't intend it, and nobody should blame him, and somebody cruel and evil has deliberately done this to him.

The responsible's attitude is that he's going to do his damnedest to try to survive . . . but that this was one of the X's in the equation that he knew existed when he set out on this trip. So . . . this time the X turned out to be the dominant factor, instead of the negligible. OK — so he knew that, made his bet, and he's lost it. _Selah_.

The responsible can, like **Col. Stapp**, mount the rocket sled to determine whether or not his eyeballs will fall out under 30 G's deceleration. Like the viking, he's computed the risks as best he can,

561

believes he'll survive, and further calculates that the reward to be won is worth the risk he can't compute.

If his eyeballs do fall out. . . he regrets, but does not recriminate.

You probably know that any professional explorer is acutely ashamed of any adventures he has. An adventure is something he didn't adequately predict and allow for — and he showed himself a fool thereby. The jungle explorer who damn near dies of malaria in the tropical wilderness . . . because he forgot to bring quinine. That's an adventure. The explorer who's bitten by a snake, because he neglected to clear the area where he put down his blankets adequately. That's an adventure.

But the explorer who's bitten by a snake that drops from a branch overhead, where it had been concealed by a mass of vine stems . . . that's one of the calculated risks. He has vials of antivenin for the purpose.

Your particular mental type happens to be the type that is capable of what I call insearch, but not adapted to exsearch. You're aware of the risks of staying at home, because of the many undetermined and as-yet-undeterminable factors in the home area. You sense, and react to, the risks within the "known" area — the risks of the city, of psychological and politicosocial pressures, of microcosmic risks. Your risk equations, therefore, appear, to you, to have the maximum rational risk-factor already.

Others see no risk at home; they make fine ex-searchers. You couldn't conceivably drive yourself to explore an Amazon jungle. Most explorers couldn't drive themselves to live in, and really explore, the socio-psychic tensions of a city. The explorer is one who suffers from claustrophobia; you suffer from xenophobia (in the special meaning of fear-of-strangeness, rather than strangers.)

A coward is an individual who's in a situation that _he_ can't tolerate.

A kid thinks his old man's a stuffy, timorous dope, because he's got a high-power car and won't ever let 'er out — won't give it the poosh and really see what she'll do. I've got a Continental, and I've never had it above 95 — at which speed it rolls sedately and quietly, and with no strain whatever. I understand they're good for about 145. I haven't the slightest intention of finding out . . . though I do, of course, have a desire to find out. (Pure curiosity would imply that!)

The thing the kid misses, of course, is that the old man doesn't believe in betting with such unimportant trivialities as how fast a car can go; he's currently engaged in betting $3,000,000 that they can make the new process work economically when they go from pilot plant to plant scale. Papa isn't interested in Russian Roulette; he's trying to figure out a way to set up the experiment of making dinitro acetylene. It'd make a lovely rocket monofuel ... more kilocalories per gram than hydro-oxy fuel ... stabilizing it though ....

Why play penny ante?

Physically, I lead a very sedate, conservative, safe life.

I've got the risks reduced just about as low as I can get 'em, and I keep 'em that way.

But ... **Ike**, have you ever tried probing into your own emotional structure, to see what happens when you wiggle this fundamental orientation, or that one?

Glad you liked that November editorial. **Sprague de Camp** sent me a card that he liked it too.

That one, my friend, came from investigating what the concepts of "loyalty" and "slavery" and "democracy" and "civilized" meant.

There is, in case you aren't consciously aware of it, a certain risk — non-physical, of course — in attacking your own intellectual-emotional structure. Quite rewarding, of course, if you get away with it.

I concentrate my risk-taking in that particular area.

I have, incidentally, been knocked sprawling a couple times. One was when I first encountered an absolutely solid, undeniable non-physical psi-reality phenomenon. It's <u>most</u> uncomfortable to have the foundation of your entire mental-emotional organization suddenly turn liquid and run out from under you.

I am, by the way, setting up a lunch date in the next week or so with a 20-odd year old young art student in New York. It seems he's in somewhat the position your young physicist was, though not quite as badly, since he's an artist. But it's embarrassing to levitate, in this society.

I approach the meeting with considerable trepidation and uneasiness. But there are questions I've got to determine, and the only way I know of determining them, is by going ahead and getting in touch with the guy.

Ike ... what's a wild adventurous life?

Don't you know that you lead one? Hell, ask any of your ex-colleagues at Boston University — who are still tightly bound to Boston University because they can't take the wild risks you can!

563

The irresponsible don't take risks; to take a risk you must first know that there is a risk there to take. Just believe in your own infallibility, and there are no risks, are there? Does it take courage to be a fool? Does a fool need courage to be foolhardy? An ignorant child will play with dynamite sticks in a manner you don't have the courage to, won't he?

Courage is somewhat like Sin; it exists only when you know the act is dangerous and do it anyway. Fools can not sin, and can't show courage.

Regards, John

The 1960's
with *Isaac Asimov*

[In a letter to **John W. Campbell**, **Walter A. Strong III**, then undergraduate student, describes a hassle with **Dr. A.H.Whiteford** of the Logan Museum of Anthropology, Beloit College related to the merits of objectivity in the comparative approach to the study of culture. He suggested to **Dr. Whiteford** that science fiction analyses produced the same effects with more lucidity by leaving the culture alone, avoiding trickiness and backward spelling (referring to an article of **Professor H. Miner's** "Body Ritual Among the Nacirema", *American Anthropologist* volume 58 ,1956, number 3 — "Nacirema being **Miner's** "Miner-ism" of American spelled backward.) **Whiteford** suggested that **Strong** present an example, and so, with his back to the wall, he wrote to **Campbell**: Ed.]

Walter A. Strong III   *November 7, 1960*

Dear Mr. Strong:

First, try **Asimov's** book *I, Robot*, if you can get hold of it. In it, the objective viewpoint is that of the robot.

More recently, the stories **Mack Reynolds** has been doing — and is doing — in *Analog*, are all of the order you seek.

And may I suggest that a lot of useful instruction in the art of how-to-observe could be gained by requiring a student to derive, from a written sample of the culture's own material, what the cultural postulates must be? For example: in the *Book of Job*, it is clear that the author's cultural postulates held that a child is a child is a child. Thus

564

Job lost his wife and children, but God rewarded his loyalty with more numerous wives and children.

Similar studies can help a lot in learning how to spot <u>our</u> unspoken, but "everybody knows," cultural postulates.

Sincerely, John W. Campbell, Editor

John Brunner   *October 19, 1961*

Dear Mr. Brunner:

I know of the area-stimulus theory — **Ike Asimov** mentioned it in an article in *Astounding* about eight years ago.

The trouble here is several-fold:

1. The evolution of intelligence took about 2,000,000 years. No one makes plans for any such period of time!

2. You can co-operate with a near-equal intelligence — but not with a very different level. Note that it is literally impossible to make a fool see that he <u>is</u> a fool — and hence you simply cannot establish working co-operation with him!

So — Ahmed's idea — and Lee's — is folly.

Sincerely, John W. Campbell, Editor

Enc.: "Stimulus"

Isaac Asimov   *December 13, 1961*

Dear Ike:

This one I think you should handle. Since it isn't a magazine or other serial publication involved, I figure it must come under your retained non-serial rights and you, not I, are the one to say whether the fine glow of your Art could be lost by this proposed reshuffling.

Regards, John W. Campbell

Isaac Asimov   *January 1, 1962*

Dear Ike:

We might get further if you'ld try finding out what I actually believe, instead of being so solidly convinced that what I believe is wrong . . . without finding out quite what it is. Or why I believe it.

565

For your information, **Leslyn**, our youngest daughter — and perhaps the brightest and kindliest of the three — is going to a highly segregated private school. It's very rigidly segregated; only high-intelligence, high-innate-potential children are wanted. Her roommates include a girl who is, in effect, a Liberian princess (though since Liberia is technically a democracy, she has no such title.) Two of her classmates are boys from Nigeria and Ghana. There are a couple of Thailanders, I know, but I haven't checked on all the other kids there.

But it is a very highly segregated school.

Last year, she went to the local regional High School which is entirely unsegregated. So far as I know, there were no Negroes in the school; certainly **Leslyn** didn't have any as classmates. But this was a disgustingly unsegregated school -- with resultant characteristics that are abominable, a very real, and horribly dangerous menace to the good of our country, and the human race.

It's unsegregated in that they allow morons to mix on equal terms with high-level kids.

I can tell you the results — I've got documentary evidence if you care to examine it.

Last year, **Leslyn** brought home report cards appropriate to a Happy Little Moron. All the "citizenship traits" were Excellent — you know, cooperative, courteous, tries hard, that sort of stuff. And she got two E's, two D's, and one B (in Art, of course). The year before, the guidance officer at the school had insisted that she didn't have the ability required for a college preparatory course, but should take the stenographic training course. She was, also, having an extremely lonely time.

This year, at Buxton, she's getting glowing reports — doing a bang-up job, and having a perfect whee of a time. At Buxton, in the first semester, the English class worked through two Shakespeare plays, a book of poetry, and four major novels. Checking with one of her friends here in town during Christmas vacation, she found that the Regional High School English class had, in the same period, struggled through most of *Romeo and Juliet*.

They're giving her about eight times the work-load, and not just in English — her Latin, geometry, and other courses are about equally solid meat and bone — and she's having a wonderful time, enjoying her classmates and roommates, is extremely popular with both faculty
566

and students.

It makes a huge difference to a child to get out of an unsegregated school with no Negroes, and into a highly segregated school where Negroes and all sorts of foreigners are welcome — provided only they meet **Kipling's** oh-so-racist doctrine:

"But there be neither border nor breed nor birth,

When two strong men stand face to face

Though they come from the ends of the Earth!"

I believe in highly segregated schools — for a damn good reason, **Ike**.

So do you — or you'ld never have written "Profession."

John W. Campbell, Jr.

Richard V. Eck   *January 15, 1962*

Dear Mr. Eck:

I'm returning your article, complete with all incidental communications.

I fear **Asimov's** point is all too well taken. We would have to rerun "The Goose" to make your piece understandable — and that's scarcely practical, even though **Asimov** contributed free rerun rights!

Sincerely, John W. Campbell, *Analog*

James P. Conrath   *August 21, 1962*

Dear Mr. Conrath:

Isaac Asimov's "Planets Have an Air About Them" appeared in the March 1957 issue of *Astounding*.

John W. Campbell, Editor

Frederick M. Uleman   *February 4, 1963*

Dear Mr. Uleman:

The three laws of robotics are those of **Dr. Isaac Asimov**, first published in his stories later collected in *I, Robot*.

The first of the series was published in *Astounding Science Fiction* for April 1941.

567

The "non-Asenion" term is not known to me, so I can't help there.
Sincerely, John W. Campbell, Editor

John Diebold   *April 3, 1963*

Dear Mr. Diebold:
Recommending science-fiction books to someone is difficult unless you know him personally; the range of interests expressed in science-fiction is, actually, wider than in standard literature. Adventure-type? Technical puzzle-type? Future sociology? Where is your field of interest?

Almost anything by **Hal Clement** is tightly thought through, and well-written. **Robert Heinlein's** older stories are brilliant and well-thought out; his material since 1955 is entirely different. **Isaac Asimov's** fiction books were all of good to excellent quality.

Most of the other authors in the field are rather wildly variable, each sometimes doing excellent stuff, and sometimes landing with a dull squelch.

The anthologies on the market do serve fairly well as samplers to give you a chance to find what you like.
Sincerely, John W. Campbell, Editor

Robert W. Franson   *July 9, 1963*

Dear Mr. Franson:
If an author comes up with a new concept in science-fiction, and writes a series based on and using that concept . . . it's his so long as he uses it.

If an author throws out an idea, and makes no further use of it, anyone who can see a use for it has a perfect right to do so.

Also, it's perfectly fair to use an idea taking off from another author's idea, and make due acknowledgment of that fact in the story. **Randall Garrett**, for example, has several times used the background built up in **Isaac Asimov's** "Foundation" series, each time making it clear to the reader that he is knowingly doing so. He — and others — have referred to the **Asimov** Laws of Robotics, thus using — and acknowledging — **Dr. Asimov's** "Three Laws of Robotics."
568

Moreover, for your information — you just haven't been reading science-fiction long enough. **Anvil** didn't originate non-featureless hyperspace; **Jack Williamson** had one story some 30 years ago in which his characters were having all sorts of trouble with the unruly features of hyperspace. More recently, **James Schmitz** has used a non-featureless hyperspace.

Go ahead an' have fun with it!

Sincerely, John W. Campbell, Editor

Robert Teviot Livingston *August 1, 1963*

Dear Professor Livingston:

The "Finagle's Laws" pieces we ran some years back were "Brass Tacks" contributions by readers. I started the thing off by mentioning that nearly everyone knows Finagle's First Law, "In any laboratory experiment, if anything can go wrong . . . it will." And its corollary, "If anything can go wrong, it will do so at the worst possible moment, in the most inconvenient possible manner."

Many readers contributed many "laws" to the collection — but they were never assembled and published as such. One I recall was, "When there is an error in the computations, the entire staff of the project will be unable to find it in eight hours of study, but the first by-stander consulted will spot it within thirty seconds."

Isaac Asimov is usually credited with formulating the Three Laws of Robotics. (He claims I did, but he's a notorious, professional liar, being a fiction writer by trade.) Most science-fiction since he first published them has acknowledged them either specifically or indirectly.

The main trouble I have in saying, "Yes, I'll help you," or, "No, I won't," is that, so far, I haven't quite been able to determine what it is you have in mind that you'd like me to work with you on.

I've long been aware that the "scientific method" is an absolutely necessary tool — like a hammer — but that it is not the only necessary tool. And that, unfortunately is where I get into violent fights with all Properly and Duly Certified Scientists.

They hold that unless it is "scientific" it does not, and of a right

569

should not, exist. That only the objective is real — despite the obvious fact that psychology is, of necessity, the study of subjective reality.

Trouble with us, when we have lunch, is that each of us has too many thousand ideas that need discussing to be able to concentrate on any one thing!

Regards, John W. Campbell, Editor

Edward G. Walterscheid   *June 24, 1964*

Dear Mr. Walterscheid:

I'm surprised you hadn't previously become aware that no bureaucrat knows what his bureau wants, needs, or will be pleased by, until after it's happened, but that all bureaucrats are perfectly certain, beforehand, that what you're planning to do is the wrong thing.

On that PLOWSHARE article — by the way, the timing was remarkably good! — you did a good job, a better job than the bureaucrats had . . . which they could recognize only afterward.

Got any more good ideas?

Re creativity and science fiction. Our trouble is that you, I, **Ike Asimov**, and a number of other science-fictioneers know that science-fiction reading is a high-correlation test for creativity . . . but that the formal, orthodox educators and executives don't. Our problem in getting ads is very remarkable; we keep finding that the very tip-top echelon of the major companies read, or have read and enjoyed, science-fiction and appreciate it. (They're creative, naturally; that's how they got there.) But that the media-men who actually assign advertising budgets, third-and-fourth-line men, think it's utter nonsense, and won't buy. And the top men are too busy, of course, to step in . . . !

Another side of this question, though: If I were a lab director, and needed some new employees in the Quality Control division, I'd also check for science-fiction reading . . . and reject any man who read science fiction. There are lots of highly important areas of science and technology where creativity is an extreme handicap. Faithfully, reliably, with perfect and unvarying repetition, the quality control man must repeat exactly the same test in exactly the same way on the same product — and keep to that rigid routine year after year. Think you could do it? Or **Ike Asimov**? I know I couldn't!

570

Yet it's absolutely necessary — or the test results will mean absolutely nothing.

On the **Dawson-Bova** theory: Where **Dawson's** idea differs so drastically (and this part of the idea is exclusively his contribution) is the realization that several billion years ago, when the system was created, stellar masses were closely crowded together in an extremely small volume of space. During the creation of stars from the gas-dust cloud, they are not scattered at multi-light-year distances, but are quite close together, where the chances of interaction are enormously increased.

Plus the fact that the presence of the cold gas-dust cloud acts as a cooling agent; it allows us to assume that there was, at creation time, an immensely greater density of gas-dust than the present mass of the System suggests, with most of it having served as an "evaporative cooling medium" to carry off the surplus energy (and momentum) during the genesis of the System.

Incidentally, **Dawson's** come up with another that's a dilly, that **Bova's** planning on writing for me.

Those quasi-stellar objects have got the astrophysicists chewing their nails to the elbow, largely because no known energy process can explain the stupendous output they show. Very briefly — I'll let you fill in the steps! — **Dawson** says, "Remember that space is finite-but-unbounded, and many hold that it's expanding from some original very small size -- the 'Big Bang' theory suggest something only a few trillion miles across.

"OK — suppose there are, actually, only about 1,000 galaxies, that space is, actually, only about x million light-years around in it, making a new circuit every few million years — and we, therefore, see redundant images of all the galaxies there actually are, but at further and further distances, because light's gone around several times.

"The quasi-stellar objects are the original 'Big Bang' and that's why we can't explain the energy-release process! We see it in multiple, simply because space isn't a perfect hypersphere, and the irregularities have caused various odd diversions of the light-paths in the multiple tracks around the universe.

"And, of course, the light is reddened because space has been expanding and stretching it ever since it started."

Hell — that notion's better than some of the wild-eyed propositions

571

the pro astrophysicists have been throwing around to explain those things!

Regards, John W. Campbell, Editor

Isaac Asimov   *March 23, 1964*

Dear Ike:

This enclosed Xerox is something I feel you should be aware of in judging the work I'm doing in *Analog*.

This letter represents exactly what it is I am fighting in the Establishment — the suppression-censorship of facts, and the intransigent refusal to allow publication of material that demonstrates the Establishment has been wrong for a century.

The writer (obviously it is unfair to identify him!) is a research man with a major U.S. university. He wrote an excellent article about a specific discovery in his field — one which he and two other men achieved. The discovery has been published and accepted in a major journal in his field -- and it shows clearly that for about one hundred fifty years the Establishment has repeatedly and flatly turned down evidence of the existence of phenomenon.

We'll say he's a biochemist, who has demonstrated, by computer analysis of 20,000 data, the unshakably solid existence of a correlation between A and Omega, which correlation has been repeatedly affirmed before.

What the Establishment is objecting to is a popular-level article <u>discussing the implications</u> of the technical-level article. I.e., discussing the <u>history of the discovery</u>.

It is suppression and censorship of such articles that allow you and many others to be so sure there no longer is any anti-**Galiléan** spirit in the Establishment.

I've never said I was a genius, **Ike**; I've been saying that real Truths have been found by men who were geniuses — or at least sound and solid workers — and suppressed by the Establishment.

This is for real, **Ike**. It's not science-fiction. This is a letter from a real scientist, at a real major University, who has had his real discovery accepted as valid by professional science — and is now being commanded to shut up about it.

572

Compare that with the situation of **Galileo**. The Establishment then didn't deny the facts; they simply opposed **Galileo's** communicating those facts to the general public.

Regards, John W. Campbell, Editor

[The letter follows, as mailed to **Isaac Asimov**, without identification: Ed.]

Dear John:

The stuff has really hit the fan for me. Minutes ago, I received an ultimatum from the topmost echelon that I must, to quote the letter just received, "go through the great embarrassment and disappointment of facing up to this and to withdraw the manuscript. This means, moreover, because of the ethics of the situation, that you are constrained from submitting the manuscript elsewhere, and will have to let the whole matter go, at least for the present."

The letter goes on to elicit specific reasons for this order, and I must admit that many of the points are well put and reasonable, on the surface. But it ends up with the all-too-clear statement that "the price will not be inconsiderable" if I go ahead and do what I please about the matter.

In other words, my job is at stake — both here and anywhere else in his field of science.

I'm flabbergasted by all this, but know that you will understand why I now simply have no choice other than to ask you to cancel your plan to run the article. Fortunately, these screws were applied to me soon enough after my Thursday visit with you, and Friday's drop-in on **Herb**, that an investment in graphic work and linotyping has not had a chance to be racked up and thereby lost.

I can also rest assured, I know, that you will keep all the key features of this episode entirely confidential. Personally, I doubt whether I'll ever recover from the "implications" of what has happened to me this past week.

Will you be kind enough to pile together all the material (manuscript and illustrations, etc.) together, so I can pick them up in the next few days when I'm in the Grand Central area? And I hope we both can get together again soon — we surely have a lot of mutually interesting

573

things to talk about!

Sincerely and apologetically,

Mrs. M. Kling   *July 20, 1964*

Dear Mrs. Kling:

There have been a number of very thoroughly authenticated instances of levitation in history; that it exists, I have every reason to believe.

It's been demonstrated under controlled laboratory conditions.

The trouble is — no one who can do it has been able to teach anyone else <u>how</u> to do it!

Incidentally . . . **Dr. Asimov** is very firmly convinced that levitation absolutely does not and cannot exist; I got him to write the story simply as an exercise in psychological reactions to people to an emotionally disturbing idea!

Sincerely, John W. Campbell, Editor

Jean Malmstrom   *February 17, 1965*

Dear Mr. Malmstrom:

I feel the story you are interested in is "The Sound of Panting" by **Ike Asimov**.

Sincerely, John W. Campbell, Editor

Philip Cohen   *August 16, 1965*

Dear Mr. Cohen:

Linus Pauling happens to be one of **Isaac Asimov's** heroes. In 1933 I was down at Duke University, and one of the graduate students there was showing me their fluorine generator in operation. Maybe Fluorine was hard to get free in 1933, but Duke (which doesn't have much of a reputation in science!) had it coming out of a standard 1/4 inch copper tube in a nice steady stream, any time they pushed the button to turn on the electricity.

Also, there's thirty years between 1933 and 1963. What was the matter with performing that xenon hexafluoride experiment some-

574

where in that period? You can buy liquid fluorine by the tank-truck load now, and for the past fifteen years it's been available in compressed-gas bottles commercially.

Anoxia is not anesthesia. An individual who is unconscious by reason of anoxia, but not so far gone as to be near death, can be made conscious by inflicting acute pain. Run a screwdriver blade under his thumb nail and he'll come up off the floor with a howl. Surgical anesthesia requires (1) blocking of pain impulses, (2) muscle relaxation, and (3) maintenance of metabolism in healthy condition. Unconsciousness is neither necessary nor sufficient. Why didn't they use morphine, which causes unconsciousness, before they had nitrous oxide and ether anesthesia? Because while morphine produces unconsciousness, and deadens pain somewhat — pain will bring a man out of morphine-induced unconsciousness, until the morphine doses is so massive that, when painful surgery is finished, the morphine dosage kills the patient.

Under spinal anesthesia, the patient is fully conscious, and can, if he wishes, watch the operation in comfort. Don't confuse anesthesia with simple unconsciousness.

Xenon is quite active. It's not quite, but nearly as reactive as iodine, and is more reactive than iridium or tantalum. Getting it to combine with fluorine is vastly easier than getting a lump of iridium into solution.

The data on mercury was available in many newspapers, in the *Scientific American*, and in *Sky & Telescope*, as well as in various technical journals in the field.

Sincerely, John W. Campbell, Jr. Editor

[Letter of October 21, 1965 from John Martellaro, refers to a science article by **Isaac Asimov** stating that Osmium is the densest element. Martellaro also quotes the November issue of *ASF* that John W. Campbell stated that Iridium is the densest. Martellaro quotes from the 1962 *Handbook of Chemistry and Physics* where Osmium has a density of 22.48 g/cc, and Iridium's density is 22.42 g/cc. Martellaro wants to know who is right?]

John Martellaro *October 25, 1965*

Dear Mr. Martellaro:

Iridium is a most intractable metal. Matter of fact, Iridium has an inherent crystalline strength greater, by a good margin, than any other metal! About five times that of iron — and by that they mean those "iron whiskers" that run around a million psi tensile strength, not ordinary commercial iron.

The Iridium also has a very high melting point.

It's chemically so inert that nothing known will attack the massive metal; it has to be mechanically reduced to powder before fused sodium peroxide attacks it.

The density of cast specimens comes out about 22.4-plus. But there is considerable suspicion that the castings aren't perfectly solid, and the minutest defect would have a drastic effect on density readings.

Theoretical studies of the crystalline structure, x-ray data, etc., suggest that Iridium is, at maximum density, about 0.05 points denser than Osmium.

Sincerely yours, John W. Campbell, Editor

John W. Campbell, Jr.   *September 10, 1966*

Dear John,

It was a great pleasure to meet you and **Peg** at the Tricon; we meet all too rarely these days.

I looked for you before, during and after the banquet and didn't see you. I particularly hoped you were in the audience because the Foundation Series, quite to my own surprise, won the Hugo for the all-time best series.

My speech of acceptance was a very short one. It went, "I would like to thank Mr. **John W. Campbell, Jr.** who had at least as much to do with the Foundation series as I had."

It was a great convention for me and I look forward to seeing you in New York next convention-if no sooner.

Yours, Isaac Asimov

Isaac Asimov   *September 14, 1966*

Dear Ike:

I was indeed at the banquet -- and I did indeed hear your little speech of acknowledgement.

One thing I think you ought to recognize more clearly, though. If I spot an acorn lying on the ground, and stick it in a spot of good soil, it's hardly being honest to point, a few years later, to the tall oak tree standing there, and say, "What do you think of the tree I made?"

There must be a hundred kids I've seen possibilities in, and tried to encourage. I must be doing something wrong; you're the only one who's turned into a really major factor in both science fiction and science.

Must have been you, not me, that brought it about.

Regards, John W. Campbell, Editor

Herman Stowell King   *December 21, 1966*

Dear Mr. King:

Most of the active fans who take the trouble to go to conventions are of the group I call "thoughtless liberals"; they don't have thoughts on the subjects they talk about, just a vast collection of slogans and catch phrases. They don't <u>want</u> to <u>think</u> about them, but want to get confirmation of what they have already decided-hence they enjoy getting together and agreeing with each other.

Inasmuch as most of my readers seem to enjoy my editorials, and our circulation keeps increasing, I would gather that the large majority of *Analog's* readers do <u>not</u> belong to the "thoughtless liberal" group.

Isaac Asimov is, of course, deeply opposed to the suggestion that there are real mental differences between races, and will ardently defend the proposition that no such characteristic exists. Since I don't agree with him, he doesn't like many of my editorials.

Sincerely, John W. Campbell, Editor

John W. Campbell, Jr.   *December 24, 1966*

Dear John,

You may well be right, and I do believe I said that theories, no mat-

577

ter how well-established, can't be considered sure in areas outside the realm of experience and experiment.

However, a theory isn't wrong just because it exists, and there is nothing to compel me to believe a view is incorrect just because it is official. There are people who are convinced the earth is flat and I refuse to join them for no better reason than that The Scientific Establishment says the earth is round.

Yours, Isaac Asimov

P.S. Season's Greetings, by the way.

Isaac Asimov   *January 3, 1967*

Dear Ike:

Ah, but a theory *is* wrong, just because it exists!

At least all human history to date shows that every theory ever thunk up by philosophers, scientists, economists, lawmakers et al., has, in time, proven to be mistaken in greater or lesser degree. Therefore on pure probability, I must assume that all current theories are in some degree mistaken, inadequate, incomplete, and unreliable.

With every Happy New Year comes a new theory!

Happy New Year!

John

Jack H. Stocker   *January 20, 1967*

Dear Mr. Stocker:

Bit delayed in answering you by Christmas holidays, followed by getting hospitalized for a week for tests which finally convinced my doctor that I was right in the first place — I felt fine.

My usual technique in giving talks is to act on feedback from the audience. I speak entirely ad lib, sort of start anywhere, and watch how the audience is reacting, and build in the directions that seem to be getting the most interest-response from them. My talks are light-hearted, intended to amuse and get laughs — but convey serious ideas. Subjects that people tend to laugh at can be presented so the important ideas stick if they're so presented that the audience has chances to laugh with you, instead.

578

The "Problems of Prophecy" is a good general subject; it's a real, wide-open topic, and allows any approach from strict logical extrapolation (which **Ike Asimov** is more or less required to stick to, because of his professional position) to pure intuition, which fits **Fred Pohl** best, since he hasn't had professional scientific training.

However, I'm the one member of that panel who is genuinely interested in, and has genuinely done some serious research into the field of psi, or ESP. (Psi is a term **Dr. Seol** invented; ESP covers the field of extra sensory gifts — it doesn't cover telekinesis, levitation, et cetera, which are, so to speak, extra-muscular action, instead of extrasensory perception. Psi is intended to cover both classes.

The basic problem of prophecy is that you can't predict something you don't know anything about. Currently, science denies the reality of psi — hence scientists can't predict what psi research and discoveries may turn up. We may never get a rocket ship to Jupiter's moons . . . because someone learns the mechanism of teleportation, and simply teleports an instrumented probe out there, without benefit of rockets. If someone discovers how clairvoyance works, and develops a mechanism capable of producing the effect — after some 2,000 years of trying, we now have mechanisms that can see; if human beings can achieve clairvoyance, why not mechanisms? — what effect would it have on human cultures? For one thing, it would end the nudity taboos, write "Finis" to the idea of military or commercial secrets, and raise hob with the entertainment industry, since who'd pay to see a show.

This is, of course, simply a part of the overall question of the effect of breakthroughs; I've simply mentioned some of the possible breakthroughs in a particular area.

Mainly, however, you'll have a panel of highly competent ad lib speakers, who can bounce any ball thrown at them from any direction, and do it with aplomb. I know them all, and can assure you that any one of them could field any question or challenge thrown his way, and do it interestingly. **Poul Anderson** is particularly good at it, and **Ike Asimov** probably the most amusing.

Regards, John W. Campbell, Editor

[Peter J. Falina had purchased a paperback of *Sleeping Planet*, and commented that at the end of Chapter 20 was: "Gremper had just multiplied himself into a positronic horde.' This did not match with his memory of the original story in the August 1964 *Analog*, and so he looked it up and found: "Gremper had just multiplied himself into a <u>robotic</u> horde": The following is JWC's answer.]

Peter J. Falina   *April 26, 1967*

Dear Mr. Falina:
The enclosed Xerox will, I think answer your query.
I changed "positronic" to "robotic" because I feel that **Dr. Asimov** has established his right to the specific term "positronic" — positronic robots come exclusively from the trade-marked assembly line of the **Asimovian** factory!
The Xerox is the original manuscript just as we sent it to the printer's.
My congratulations on your detailed and accurate reading, and sharp memory!

Sincerely, John W. Campbell, Editor

Maude Gamble   *August 28, 1967*

Dear Mrs. Gamble:
I am passing your postcard along to **Dr. Asimov** for him to answer; I'm sure he can tell you where "Intelligent Man's Guide to Science" is available — and I think he will enjoy your interest in it.
When you get it, I suggest you keep it out of sight, for private reading only. The resultant frustration of your "very polite 10 year old son" when he finds that, mysteriously, you know more science than he does, should encourage in him a determined and persistent effort to regain his lost self-satisfaction.
The only way to understand science is to get the feel for it — a deep-in-your-soul understanding that assures you that this, of course, is the way things just naturally would have to work. Intellectual memory of scientific data and theory may get a youngster straight A's in science courses — but that won't make a scientist of him.

Sincerely, John W. Campbell, Editor

Maude Gamble   *September 18, 1967*

Dear Mrs. Gamble:

I bounced your card along to **Dr. Asimov** because I thought he ought to have a chance to understand the motivations underlying some of his readers.

And don't decide your case is hopeless! Remember that you're not trying to become a scientist — simply an intelligent layman. You need general background — which is, actually, all that a top-rank physicist has if he wanders into a discussion of geologists, or what electronics engineers have in a bunch of biochemists.

Remember, if you ask a leading geologist what adenosine triphosphate is, he'll probably look as blankly lost as would a top biochemist if you asked him what the Mossbauer Effect is!

Sincerely, John W. Campbell, Editor

Isaac Asimov   *September 28, 1967*

Dear Ike:

This I think will interest you; it's a Xerox of the review I'm running.

Here's a "reference work" somebody should stop before all the High school libraries get it!

Sincerely, John W. Campbell, Editor

Maude Gamble   *October 9, 1967*

Dear Mrs. Gamble:

Ike Asimov is a bit of an orthodoxist, for all his science-fiction writing; the myth of Man's helplessness is an Orthodox theory. But, just remember that a <u>large</u> full-grown leopard weighs about 150 pounds, and is generally considered a not-impressive animal. A puma, or mountain lion, weighs about the same. Man is, as I've said, one of Earth's large and powerful animals; large men run well over 200 pounds.

And I'm glad you're enjoying science; most scientists aren't scientists because of Noble Dedication but because there's nothing in the world that's more darned fun than science! They have a whee of a time!

581

And if you have an idea they don't understand the humanities — guess again! How do you think the computer lab boys at MIT managed to program the PDX-1 to (1) play a Brahms organ solo, and (2) compose a new Brahmsian solo?! **Dr. Wayne Batteau** is a concert-quality pianist — who hasn't time to practice because he's talking to dolphins, and working on super-advanced radar.

And the Boston Symphony gives concerts at the MIT auditorium quite frequently.

Scientists are by no manner of means one-track minded; they're simply too busy producing in the area of science to take the time to practice producing in the various other areas in which they are highly educated and competent!

Sincerely, John W. Campbell, Editor

Isaac Asmov   *October 10, 1967*

Dear Ike:

The enclosed Xerox is from the *Royal Engineers Journal*; generally speaking field engineers in military outfits have a very hard-headed pragmatic viewpoint. They like things that work and keep them alive. One might say their love for science is like a cat's love — strictly belly-love. Or in the case of engineers, staying-alive love.

May I suggest that Orthodox Science might show some degree of interest in investigating this engineering technique — or else stop yapping about the Sacred Scientific Method, based on pragmatic experimentation?

NASA being stuck with the literally deadly problem of solar flares and astronauts has finally been compelled to find out why **John Nelson's** technique of astrological forecasting of solar flares works. "With Jupiter and Saturn in quadrature, and Venus in triune . . . ." didn't make astrophysicists happy worth a damn — but it correctly predicted major solar flares.

You might be interested in doing an article on where the center of gravity of the Solar System is. Contrary to widely disseminated folklore of orthodox science, it is not inside the Sun — save when Jupiter and Saturn are in major opposition. Also, the sidereal period of rotation of the solar system is 11.2 years — by some odd chance precisely one

582

sunspot period.

Since gravitational fields and magnetic fields do not behave in the same way, this little discrepancy raises hell with the magnetic phenomena in the Sun — and flares, as you know, result from magnetic explosions in the Sun.

The NASA boys have finally figured it all out — once they really set to work and tried to find out what underlay the solid realities of astrological prediction!

(I have no more faith in personal astrology than you have — but unlike you, I'm willing to acknowledge that there's a lot more in that field than the noble Astronomers have yet bothered to dig out.)

It's also damned interesting to learn that Venus' peculiar retrograde rotation appears to be <u>locked to Earth's synodic period</u>!

Of course, "everybody knows that . . ." the planets are not capable of any serious influence on each other is part of the ancient folklore of Orthodox Science.

I'm having almost as much fun watching the Orthodoxists gag down their humble pie in re the rules-of-thumb of astrologers as I did sitting in front of the TV set in the hotel in Cambridge some months back, watching the pictures being flashed on the screen, with the caption at the bottom "LIVE . . . FROM THE MOON." I'd been living just a few blocks from there, 30 years earlier, when my MIT professors called my work "pseudo-science" and "science-fantasy" and "nonsense."

No, **Ike**, I'm by no means against Science — just agin' "Scientists" who won't practice what they preach or even what they claim they practice!

If something works in a pragmatic, rule of thumb sense . . . <u>it must have an underlying principle</u>. The true scientist's job is to study and explain it — <u>not explain it doesn't really exist</u>!

I don't believe in the supernatural, as most orthodox Scientists do. Oh, they don't acknowledge that they believe in the supernatural — they simply accept with full faith and credence utterly supernatural odds as "normal coincidence." Now uneducated bookies, having no mathematic understanding of statistics and probability, tend to get suspicious when a patron manages to win on 95% of all his bets, at odds of 20 to 1 or 100 to 1.

But Scientists are so gullible they'll go on paying off his bets, sigh a little, and say "Well, sometimes people are lucky," and never suspect that he's got a system that works.

Like engineers dowsing for pipes — just coincidence, even if 85% of all who try it succeed, and succeed with 98+% accuracy.

Incidentally, a top-notch-scientific friend of mine told me of a top-notch geologist friend of his who had been tearing his hair and weeping on his shoulder over an incident in the western desert country. Million-aire rancher had hired him (the geologist) to find some water for one end of the ranch. After careful study, the geologist reported that, unfortunately, there was no water-table to be tapped — there was an immense mass of continental bed-rock underlying the whole area.

So the rancher called in a dowser. Dowser went over the place, kept shaking his head, and finally reported, "Well, you've got some dry acres here — the only decent water supply on the whole spread seems to be right down here, but you'll have to drill through about 600-700 feet of solid granite to get it!"

"Enough there to do me any good?" asked the rancher.

"Yup. Plenty — if you can get at it."

The rancher called in a driller with a rig capable of chewing through granite. The geologist assured him he was wasting over $100,000. The rancher assured the geologist he had money enough for his hobbies. At about 680 feet they struck water — in quantity — in a mass of solid continental granite. Which is self-evidently geologically impossible.

The flow has been strong, adequate, and the water is exception-ally fine.

How come?

Earth is still a young planet; it's still busy outgassing. judging by the adsorbed and otherwise bound water in meteorites, Earth should have some six times as much water on the surface as it has, so 5/6ths of it is still way down yonder working its way out. It was pure coincidence, of course, that the dowser guessed that, and indicated the spot where it was worthwhile drilling through 700 feet of solid granite to get it. A fine flow of "juvenile water," as it's called.

I've had an opportunity to taste "juvenile water," incidentally — believe me, you never had such delicious water! By the time the
584

stuff's worked its way through 2-3,000 miles of Earth's mass, it's pretty well in equilibrium with the mineral content of the deep mass. And it's never before passed through any biological organism!

Anyhow — that isn't what I set out to write you about.

I have a question, and a proposition for you.

Question: Have you got an exclusive contract on doing articles for *Fantasy and Science Fiction*, or can you take an assignment from *Analog*?

If you can, I have a proposition. Go see **Louis L. Sutro**, at the MIT Instrumentation Labs, who's in charge of the team working on the first <u>robot</u> in scientific history. I say "the first in scientific history," because it's the first the scientists themselves officially designate as "the robot."

The Robot is being designed to explore Mars — and it can NOT be remote-controlled from Earth, because of the time-delay involved in the low speed of light. The Robot could walk faster than light, so to speak — it'd have such exceedingly slow "neuro-muscular" coordination that it'd kill itself before its controlling system (on Earth) could tell it, "Stop! You're walking over a cliff!"

The solution, obviously, is to have its controlling intelligence on Mars with it.

Sutro & Company have a report out. Full designation, "R-565 Development of Visual, Contact and Decision Subsystems For A Mars Rover."

If you can, I'd like to have you do the job of writing it up for us. After all, you're the guy who's famous for robots and robot psychology, so who should write up the report on the design of a nervous system for a Mars-Robot? Of how a robot nervous system and brain recognize dangerous situations, and decide what to do about them?

Besides which, you're right handy by to MIT, and will have welcome entree — and will, I'm sure, find the whole complex problem completely fascinating.

Incidentally, we can pay you 5 cents/word.

Warren McCullach, who's fascinating enough all by himself, is one of the team working on the job.

No doubt some of their fanciest stuff is <u>Classified</u> in big red letters. But there's more than we could possibly use available in open publication.

585

We've got an article coming up — feature piece, with a most spectacular color-photograph cover — that you'll like I'm pretty sure. "The Bugs That Live at -423 ^{0}." It's the story of the engineering bugs that had to be squashed before the liquid-hydrogen-fueled Centaur could fly. Remember the blow-up the Cambridge Electron Accelerator had a year or so ago, when their liquid-hydrogen bubble chamber peeled off part of the super-heavy roof of the accelerator building? That little puddle of liquid hydrogen was nothing to what the Centaur engineers had to play hopscotch with. H_2's interesting because any mixture with air, from 2% to 98% is explosive. And air tends to freeze solid on the plumbing, solidly plugging the boil-off relief valve, with imaginable consequences.

Oh, I tell you — they had fun! Also the biggest most spectacular blow-up in Cape Kennedy history. (That fireball is our cover.)

BUT — it's Centaur that's been landing Surveyors and Orbiters on the Moor or in lunar orbit, within 1 part in 100,000 of their aim-point. And Centaur, as is, is capable of boosting a useful payload package to Saturn!

In other words, we're rapidly approaching the vehicle capability to land a Mars rover.

And you're free to — and do you want to — tell us about what's being done?

Regards, John W. Cambpell, Editor

John W. Campbell, Jr. *October 13, 1967*

Dear John,

I must admit the situation on dowsing has me uneasy. I am enclosing an article from today's *New York Times* which you have undoubtedly seen, but just in case you haven't — .

If the phenomenon exists, there must (as you say) be an explanation, but one that doesn't upset everything else (or else we've got to explain everything else from scratch and I don't want that job.) Anyway, I'm not man enough to tackle it, so, with a confession of cowardice, I leave it for the brave.

Now about the business end of the letter. No, I do not have an exclusive contract with *F & SF.* I don't have an exclusive contract with anyone. I honestly believe that I come as close to total freedom in writing as it is possible to be. I can write anything for anyone on any subject in any way and, one way or another, I always get it into print. (knock plastic!). — And I owe it more to you, **John**, than I do to any other single man, which is why you can never forfeit my gratitude and love no matter how irritating you may be in some of your views.

Being close to total freedom is not being entirely there, however, for there is one obstacle neither I, nor any mortal, can overcome, and that is the mere fact that it takes me so many minutes to do things and that there are so many minutes and no more in a day.

I would like to see **Louis L. Sutro** and find out what he's doing and then see if the subject is something I have the (a) ability and (b) time to handle properly. (I always have the ability and time to do something improperly, but I have a prejudice against doing that knowingly.) Could you wait until I can manage to get out there and report to you and then tell you whether and when it might be done? I'll try not to waste too much of your time.

If things are tight with you, and you must assign someone else for the sake of time and certainty, I'll understand.

Yours, Isaac

Isaac Asimov   *October 16, 1967*

Dear Ike:

I can wait a while on the MR Robot article — and it's perfectly evident that you, as The Authority on Robots, should write it.

That item on dowsing from **Hanson Baldwin's** column in the *Times* appeared on Thursday; as of this Monday morning I have received copies or Xeroxes of two editions of the *New York Times*, the *Hartford Times*, *Los Angeles Examiner*, *Philadelphia Enquirer*, and three other papers that I can't identify because the paper's running line was clipped off, but they came from Dallas, Texas, Colorado Springs, and Barrow, Alaska.

For your information, the marines at Quantico were started on the investigation by a light-colonel who's been a long-time *Analog* reader, and wrote me for data, details, and references.

Agreed that you aren't in a position to do research on the problem;

587

I'm not either. The research should be done by someone with a very large number of subjects available for testing and experimenting — like a Marine officer or a University psychology department.

What you and I can do — and what I feel our proper duty is to do — is write pieces that inform a wide spectrum of people that there is something worthy of investigation. That Orthodox Science does NOT know all the answers to everything, and is not in a position to say that, "It's impossible nonsense!" just because it doesn't fit their present theoretical knowledge.

More and more evidence is accumulating — sound, objective evidence — that the angular relationships of the planets does affect Earth's weather. That, in other words, there is sound, useful, observational (though unexplained) data to be abstracted from Astrology.

Kepler's great discoveries of the laws of planetary motion were buried in huge tomes of pure astrology; **Newton's** laws derived from **Newton's** willingness to glean that mass and abstract the solid, useful information from it.

I'm simply insisting that those men who claim **Newton's** mantle of Scientist should practice **Newton's** willingness to look carefully at anything that works.

In this case, the angular relationships of the planets whips the center of gravity of the solar system around, yanking even the immense mass of the Sun this way and that. The mass of the Sun follows gravitational influences — but the magnetic fields do not. The result turns out to be some pretty violent gravito-magnetic turbulence in the vast mass of perfectly conducting plasma, with consequent surface hell-raising called sunspots and solar flares.

With Jupiter and Saturn in inferior conjunction, the CG of the system is well outside the Sun's surface; when they're in superior conjunction, they are in "opposition," and the CG moves well within the Sun. Earth and Venus have major effect — despite decreased mass — because they're near, and move rapidly, producing more rate of change of acceleration, more "jerk," or "surge."

Incidentally, the astrophysicists are going to have to run their computers overtime re-analyzing how the Sun's internal economy operates. That gravito-magnetic turbulence must cause mixing of core and shell material much greater than their previous models accounted for!

588

Regards, John W. Campbell

Isaac Asimov   *November 16, 1967*

Dear Ike:

The enclosed Xerox of a Xerox of a newspaper clipping may make it possible for me to convey to you why it is I've been blasting at Orthodox Science! [Dowsing Rods: Ed]

I am <u>not</u> demanding that Orthodox Science immediately drop what they are doing, and do what I say they should — which is the message you seem to read into my statements.

What I <u>am</u> saying is, "You Orthodoxists have no ethical business using your status, your authority, to prevent research in any area just because it doesn't fit <u>your</u> present cosmology! That is the sin that **Pope Urban** and the Church fathers committed against **Galileo** — and that you, today, are committing against other explorers into the Unknown!"

The newspaper here reports precisely what I'm talking about.

A small business man (very small!) was selling a gadget which was intended to apply a principle which is unknown and inexplicable within the bounds of known science.

If it worked, it did a useful job not otherwise achievable. It was sold with a 100% money-back guarantee. The possible loss of investment was about equal to a couple of movie tickets.

BUT . . . the Orthodox Scientists pounced on this flagrant violation of the sanctity of Physical Cosmology, with all the might and power of the Federal Government's Post Office, and declared with absolute authority that it was a fraud.

Obviously they did not make a reasonable test of the device; mostly U.S. utility companies could testify to that five-ten years ago. The U.S. Marines can testify to it today.

The Scientists in Authority assure the Postmaster that it <u>must</u> be a fraud, because it could not work under the Known Laws of Science.

They thereby used their status and authoritarian position in precisely the same manner **Pope Urban** & Co. did against **Galileo** — they did <u>not</u> apply the scientific Method, they did <u>not</u> make an honest experiment, but they <u>did</u> use their authority and status to make it impossible for the would-be experimenter to spread his heretical doctrine.

589

That, **Ike**, is what I most violently object to.

Not the scientist's refusal to do research himself.

His use of his power and authority to keep anyone else from being allowed to do that research, and communicate his results.

Can you find any ethical excuse for the behavior of the scientists who encouraged the Post Office to block this man's efforts — the scientists who asserted authoritatively that it was a fraud . . . but didn't make a legitimate test?

And the now-known success of the U.S. Marines with precisely this device makes it abundantly clear that the Post Office scientists did not make a legitimate test.

Shouldn't such scientists be condemned as villains impeding the progress and expansion of human knowledge?

Incidentally, in Britain there's a company that manufactures and sells a similar, but somewhat fancily decorated gadget called "The Revealers;" they charge not $2 but $200 a pair — and they're selling them to county engineers offices, water departments, various universities and engineering industries throughout Britain.

Unfortunately, it's the plant maintenance departments at Cambridge and Oxford that buy and use them — not the science departments, who prefer not to observe them in use.

Ike, will you agree that I have a legitimate beef against Orthodox Science and Scientists?

Not because they don't investigate what I feel needs investigating
. . . .

But because they use their status and authority to suppress anyone else's efforts to investigate and use the device.

I agree I have no right to make them study what I want studied — unless I specifically employ them, at my expense, to do so. But I ask that you agree they have no right to use their power and authority to prevent anyone else's investigation and use of the principle.

Regards, John W. Campbell, Editor

John Dugan   *December 4, 1967*

Dear Mr. Dugan:

I suggest you send your questions to **Mr. Asimov**. Write to him in
590

care of *Analog*, and we will forward your letter to him immediately.
Sincerely, John W. Campbell, Editor

Dr. Louis L. Sutro   *January 19, 1968*

Dear Dr. Sutro:

The essence of a true "robot," in the general public mind — though they could not define it if asked, of course! — is a mobile, self-controlling, self-directing multi-purpose mechanism aware of its environment and reacting to that environment in a goal-directed manner.

Your MR Robot as originally designed for Mars Exploration fulfills that definition pretty well — mobile, multi-purpose, self-directing on the basis of its own awareness of its environment and its purpose.

An ordinary automatic oil-burning furnace is, in some limited sense a "robot" — though it doesn't, of course, meet the public-mind image of "robot." It's a sensile "organism," and its environmental awareness is extremely limited, just water-level, room temperature, stack temperature and boiler temperature and pressure.

But MR Robot really <u>is</u> a design for a true robot.

Usually, the reason for using mechanisms rather than humans is that the extreme single-purpose design of the machine allows superior accuracy and reliability. There is seldom valid reason for building a mobile multi-purpose, self-directing machine — but Mars Exploration is just such a purpose.

I'm sending a Xerox of your letter to **Ike Asimov**; the first week in March I've got to be down in Washington — they've got me scheduled to talk on future technology and its effects on sociology. It'll be interesting to say that I had to miss the first report on a true robot to attend that discussion of future technology! But I think **Dr. Asimov** will be a more than adequate representative.

Re holography and the need for rigidly fixed mounting: the more accurate statement is that the angular displacement of film-to-object lines must be less than some very small angle $\underline{A}$ during the time of exposure. Essentially the same applies in ordinary photography; to make a 5 minute time exposure you need a very rigid tripod if you want precision. However, I have gotten resolution to better than 1/3000th inch on a high-resolution copy film in my 35mm camera using an ordinary light portable tripod — and a 0.5 millisecond electronic flash illumination.

Isn't the holography-rigidity requirement rather a function of exposure time than of holography per se? Something less than granite mounting might do if a giant pulse laser with a fractional microsecond pulse supplied the illumination.

Like practically all other problems of multipurpose, environmentally aware robots, the problem is one of balancing engineering technique factors, not of fundamental absolutes.

From what you've told me, the computer analysis of holograms remains another extremely rugged obstacle. Ah, well . . . it would have been an "elegant solution" if it could have been used!

Regards, John W. Campbell Editor

Isaac Asimov   *January 22, 1968*

Dear Ike,

The enclosed Xerox explains about half the situation. If you can possibly make it about the beginning of March -- Sutro & Co will have something well worth your seeing, and I'd most dearly love to have you write up for us the first actual, real-world robot design story. Maybe they haven't got that positronic brain system worked out yet — but as the Old Master Roboticist, certainly you should be the one to write up the story!

And be it realized — I don't demand an exclusive coverage on this. I'd like you to do a piece for *Analog*, along lines that only a science-fiction magazine would want and need, but there'll be plenty of other places where you could place articles having a more staid and orthodox slant on the subject. Places where references to positronic brains wouldn't be appropriate, let's say!

The other half of the situation involves the fact that I can't be there in Cambridge at that particular period. I'm scheduled to give a talk to the 6th Goddard Symposium of the American Astronautical Society on the future effects of technology on sociology. It's going to be fun saying that to attend the meeting I had to skip M.I.T.'s announcement of the design work on the first genuine humanoid robot!

One final item, on a very different line. As a long-time word-slinger and word studier, I think you'll find this challenging.

Before the sandglass and waterclock went out of style, there was no "clockwise and counterclockwise" to designate rotational direction. So they had other terms.

Fine. Now one of those terms was "widdershins."

Can you find the antonymic term?

And be it remembered that in those days, screw-thread cutting was an exceedingly difficult work-of-art sort of task. They didn't have machine lathes with calibrated lead-screws. So they didn't have machine screws, wood screws, or other common household commodities equipped with either left-hand or right-hand threads.

They still needed rotational-direction terms, though. So . . . what were they?

That question came up, incidentally, because I built a TV antenna rotator with remote control, and wanted to label the control panel. It popped into mind that it'd be more fun to label it widdershins and x?x?x?x than mere CLOCKWISE and COUNTERCLOCKWISE. So I went to look up counter-widdershins . . . and couldn't even find widdershins in the big dictionary!

So feeling frustrated, I naturally have started throwing the problem at all the word-meaning-hobbyists I know!

Regards, John W. Campbell, Editor

Mark Wilson   *April 15, 1968*

Dear Mr. Wilson:

Sorry to call the good Dr. **Asimov** wrong . . . but he is. Gravity is the mightiest force in the universe because, unlike any other known, it is additive. It has no inverse, no negative.

Atomic-nuclear forces seem, at first glance, to be far greater — except that, in the heart of ordinary stars, gravitational force accumulates to a level that crushes atoms and forces them to coelesce.

In the end, giant stars are crushed, by ever mounting gravity, to neutron stars only a few score miles in diameter.

Gravitational forces can mount to such intensity that what is known as Schwarzchild Discontinuity occurs — the gravitational field becomes so intense all matter is crushed to pure energy, and that energy cannot escape because the escape velocity from that gravity field <u>exceeds the speed of light.</u> The entire system, in effect, drops out of the Universe.

So . . . which is the greatest of all forces?

Sincerely, John W. Campbell, Editor

Joseph G. Sharp, Jr.   *May 13, 1968*

Dear Mr. Sharp:

That "Magic Society" course you mention in your letter is well named; to call it science-fiction, however, is improper. Of the eight books you list, only **Asimov's** *I, Robot* represents true science-fiction — and it isn't sociological. It's a discussion, in story terms of the logical consequences of certain logical commands built into robots to be used around human beings. It does <u>not</u> deal with the society the robots are introduced into — only with the robots and individual users. "Liar" certainly isn't sociological — but it's a fine analysis of the psychological problem of a child trying to be logical in a normal human home!

The others are actually fantasy, and are sociological. Most of them are, in fact, <u>antiscience</u>-fiction.

So why call them science-fiction? "Magic," which usually refers to wish-fulfillment dreams, does fit the course. They might well add **Heinlein's** story "Magic, Inc." which was a beautiful analysis of what happens in a society that accepts and uses magic routinely!

Sincerely, John W. Campbell, Editor

Bob Sunman   *June 6, 1968*

Dear Mr. Sunman:

Sorry. . . but thiotimoline was "invented" by **Isaac Asimov, PhD** in one of the finest, most carefully constructed hoax articles ever published. He had some beautifully authentic-sounding bibliography, too. Sadly, it doesn't exist.

The only equally careful imaginary article was **Asimov's** discussion of the biochemistry of the Goose that laid the Golden Eggs — titled "Pate de Foi Gros." Wonderful, but sadly unreal.

Sincerely, John W. Campbell, Editor

594

Dear Mrs. Johnson:

I can give you two hints for producing successful writers.

The first is old fashioned, involves a lot of hard work, but remains essential — practice. I know I practiced about 1,000,000 words worth!

The second come from a comment **Bob Heinlein** made years ago. "The main reason professional authors don't have too much competition is that so many of the amateur manuscripts stay on somebody's closet shelf."

Expect rejection slips. **Asimov** had his first dozen stories turned down, you know.

Sincerely, John W. Campbell, Editor

[The following letter is in answer to queries placed by **Charles V. Heinmuller** on April 11, 1969. **Mr. Heinmuller** is doing an English research project in high school which will determine whether or not he graduates at the end of the school year.

He is doing research on a novel by **Isaac Asimov** (Professor of Biochemistry at the Boston University School of Medicine) -- *Foundation*, which won the Hugo award for all time best science fiction series.

Student **Heinmuller** says that he does not have enough critical essays to qualify for acceptance by his English teacher, and wants to know if there are further reviews available in perhaps *Analog's* "Reference Library" or other essays in **Campbell's** files and/or references. The rough draft of his paper is due two weeks from yesterday (April 10) The letter is dated April 11, 1969.]

Charles V. Heinmuller *May 1, 1969*

Dear Mr. Heinmuller:

The *Foundation* series by **Dr. Asimov** was originally published entirely in this magazine (then called *Astounding Science Fiction*) and only many years later put into book form. The original stories started about ten years before you were born, I believe, and continued as short stories, novelettes and novels, for a long period.

Since all of the *Foundation* series stories had appeared in this magazine, and were familiar to our readers at the time, we never carried any real review of the book publication, simply referring to the magazine publication.

If you check your copy of *Foundation*, you should find that it was originally copyrighted for *Astounding Science Fiction*, by Street & Smith Publications (which has since merged with Conde' Nast.)

When **Asimov** started the series, he was **Mr. Isaac Asimov**, a graduate student at Columbia!

Sincerely, John W. Campbell, Editor

**The 1970's
with *Isaac Asimov***

Ron Goodman   *June 25, 1970*

Dear Mr. Goodman:

No complex definition can be given in a letter nor can a precise quantification of a point on a spectrum be easily specified. If you want to try a real dilly, imagine you've been thrown back in time, and you're trying to explain to old **Ben Franklin** what "Entropy" means in the statement, "Entropy always increases."

In addition to other problems of definition in psychology and sociology, there are individuals — too small in number to constitute a "type" —which have to be left floating somewhere outside of all classes. Astrophysicists have the same problem; they have spectral classes O, B, A, F, G, K, M and a few more — and then they have a group called "peculiar" stars becuse they don't fit in any class. (And drive the nuclear physicists nuts, moreover — one group of them has strong lines of technicium, an element that has no stable isotopes, and none that has a half life longer than about 250,000 years. So, how does a star get full of it????)

What you're describing in yourself is neither "warrior barbarian" nor "warrior citizen" — you're off the general line of development. Somewhere along the line, you made a fetish of stubbornness.

Aside from that one factor, the rest of your story is standard for anyone with "a lot of smarts but not enough wiseness," as an old fellow I
596

knew in Ohio put it. I know all about the pattern; I was there myself. When I was in third grade, some fool teacher who should have been wiser than I, asked me to give a lecture on the movement of the Solar System in space to the fifth grade kids. This, naturally, made me even less popular at school than I was already.

Ike Asimov had similar troubles. (He had an eidetic memory; saw something once and he remembered it photographically. Naturally, he was a whizz at multiplication and addition.) A good percentage of the top people I know did.

Your major difference is that lack of pragmatism; a pragmatist says, "Any idea that works must have truth in it — any idea that doesn't work is wrong! Change it!" Figure out what it is you want to accomplish, and if you're not getting it — your method must be wrong; change it!

I got over correcting my teacher's misunderstandings and errors before I got to prep school. I let my schoolmates have their delusions (except when I needed some quick cash, and could hook them into a bet.)

The true barbarian does make an excellent soldier — provided he has a leader he respects. The Sergeant who can do anything he can do, and do it better. The Captain who's sharper than he is, in ways the barbarian can acknowledge — such as tactics. **Sherman's** men loved the old bastard; he walked the legs off 'em, marched 'em till their tails were dragging — but they loved him because he did <u>not</u> get 'em killed. He clobbered the enemy. The true barbarian obeys a <u>man</u> (not a principle) he can respect.

He doesn't in the least mind having somebody beat his ears in, and then order him about. He feels no loss of self-respect whatever; a man should test himself against others, and see how high he actually rates. The guy who can knock him down is a better man than he is; that's OK, now he knows where he stands. He doesn't feel he's any the smaller for that; simply that others are bigger — a simple fact that any sane entity knows. Why should he feel demeaned just because someone else is bigger, stronger, or wiser? And he obeys that man not out of fear, or "knuckling under," but out of respect the other guy earned.

So he happily follows his admired leader off to war, and obeys his orders because usually there isn't time for detailed explanations.

Are you "knuckling under" when you obey the dictates of Ohm's Law, or accept that you have to submit to having capacitance in your circuits?

Your trouble, my friend, is <u>not</u> that you're a barbarian — you're not, because you don't show the strong social gregariousness of the barbarian. Barbarians conform.

Try reevaluating your patterns in view of the historical patterns of true tribesmen, barbarians and citizens.

I think you've got youself misallocated!

Sincerely, John W. Campbell Editor

Jay Klein   *May 6, 1971*

Dear Jay:

The last time one of my flash units flubbed when I most wanted some shots — of bats! — it had a built-in synch-cord, and it wasn't a synch-cord failure anyway. The flash tube itself was gassy, and fired only very erratically, when it happened to feel in the mood. That made it seem like an obvious bad electrical connection. Since it was near midnight on Halloween, there were no handy open photoshops for replacements, either! Have to tell you about that [sic] flying bats on Halloween some time . . . .!

But main reasons for this note — **Peg** says, "Thanks for **Larry Shaw's** address," and I say, "I want more!"

I'd like about a dozen 5 X 7's of the best picture of me anyone's taken in the last 15 years. (This strongly suggests that its' not at all what I actually look like, but more what I'd like to think I look like!)

It's the one you got while I was at the Banquet table. I'm waving my cigarette and holder as usual, looking off to my right, my right forearm and hand cutting across at about a 45^0 angle to the upper right of the pic. Dunno how you identify your negs, and all this one has on the back by way of identification is "Luncacon 71 F3-1."

I'm always needing pics to send out with biographical material or something when I'm due to give a talk somewhere; that's what I want those pics for.

If somebody wants to put my pic on a book jacket sometime, I'd like to have this shot available.

598

Please to send me the dozen prints and the bill for same (I like to have friends, not to use them!) and let me know what the normal fee for use of the shot on a bookjacket would be.

I promised you that old neg of **Ike Asimov**. It was taken about '38 or '39, and I know I've stored all my negatives in safe containers, safely protected from excess humidity and/or temperatures . . . but so far I've only been able to find those from 1941 et. seq. Where the earlier cans are I don't know at the moment — I'll run across 'em, and when I do, I'll let you have that strip.

It's a 35mm Super XX neg, somewhat underexposed, taken in the original Street & Smith office, when **Ike** was a Columbia University undergraduate. He had a lean and hungry, somewhat pimply, moustached look, and damn few would recognize it as **Ike**!

Regards, John Campbell

Frank M. Bell   *May 11, 1971*

Dear Mr. Bell:

If anyone ever tried to make me any kind of ruler, I would immediately abdicate!

How the hell can a man have any fun sniping at stuffed shirts when he's the official Poo Bah?

Sincerely, John W. Campbell, Editor

The 1930's
with *A.E. van Vogt*

Robert Swisher   *April 18, 1939*

Dear Bob:

The reason you haven't heard from me before is the excellent one that I've had another one of those colds, and spent my evening sweating on the couch and reading scf and *UNK* manuscripts 'til I'm sick of the things.

Incidentally, please go ahead and review briefly all the years in the other mags, if you can and will, because I haven't got a prayer of reading 'em now. I've got another sweet little headache to make life more agreeable. There's a such-and-such called **A.J.B.** a well known hack writer, who can, however, usually be depended on to turn out a readable, if not good story, on comparatively short notice. I gave him a basic idea for an *UNK* novel of 40,000 words; he wrote 10,000 that seemed fairly good with enough editing, and I told him so, so he did 30,000 more of the gawdawflust tripe ever submitted by anyone claiming to be a pro writer. I needed a novel in a hurry. That was so frightful I saw there wasn't a chance of **B** making it usable, so I called in **Norvelle Page**, who did "Flame Winds" in four days. "Flame Winds," in the next *Unknown,* is a straight, plain snickersnee action yarn with overtones of magic. But it's done with a zest and interest that makes it one of the best of tis type -- not so darned far behind **Merritt's** snickersnee yarn, "Ship of Ishtar," in many respects. The man deserves real credit for doing such an excellent job of writing from a cold, standing start in four days. He developed the whole yarn, background, characters, plot and incident plus the style of presentation in four days, wrote 40,000 words first-rate action and de- serves my heartiest thanks into the bargain for getting me out of a tight spot on coverdate. **De Grouchey**, our promotion manager, and **Miss Patchen**, one of the girls in the advertising department, have read the yarn -- because they wanted to, not because there was any necessity to - - and went out of their way to tell me how much they liked it.

In the meantime, **B** got his unmitigated mess back, with the remark that it was not satisfactory.

B sent a letter saying the yarn was ordered, and he'd sue for $600.

We sent a letter saying we didn't buy anything that wasn't usable, and that as a pro author he ought to know damned well everything was sourer than all hell.

He still threatened suit. We told him to fix it up, rewrite it, and we'd consider it. **Ralston**, Vice-President of S&S in charge of legal matters, looked into the case, getting my reports and **B's** demands, and figured it'd cost too much in legal fees, plus the tendency of a jury to sock the big, hard-boiled corporation in favor of the poor little author, to make it worth while.

It wound up with me having to take the damned tripe, with the under- standing that I "revise" it for $100. That means, in effect, that I've got to write a 40,000 word novel for $100, while **B** gets $600 for something I will throw out from title page to last paragraph.

The only satisfaction I have at all is that **B** won't sell S&S very much in the future, in all probability.

Incidentally, you might refrain from adding this letter to your file. There's no joy in having it as a matter of record, but I don't have a surprising desire to blow off steam on the job.

One thing I'm a little puzzled about, is whether I should print the revised yarn under **B's** name in hopes of having all the readers write in and say, "the best story **B's** ever written -- doesn't seem possible the oaf could have done anything so good."

However, t'ell with the dispute. Just that writing plus the reading I'm gifted with nowadays, keeps me and will keep me, fairly well occupied. The extra $100 will mean, though, that we'll have cash for vacation, as well as car. **Dona's** been a bit worried because, when we get the car, we'll have used up about all the cash available. Saving $100 a month means that we haven't gotten much observable benefit from the raise, naturally, while we have gotten an extremely observable increase in the amount of work to be handled. **Dona's** being unofficial assistant editor, reading mss. at home, and throwing out the hopeless cases at the beginning. Then I can read her notes and see whether it might be worth looking over for ideas. It saves me a lot of time, and is extremely helpful, naturally.

You wouldn't know it, of course, but New England is at war with Mexico -- having a terrific battle, largely naval, in fact. **John Clark & Fletcher Pratt** are working it with the aid of another group of naval bugs. **John Clark** is the Commander in Chief of the Navy of New England, and somebody else is C in C of Mexico. **Pratt** is the referee, and clearing house of information. It's all fought out on the map. So far, New England's lost two tankers, one submarine, and has another blockaded and trappped at Nassau. New England possesses 4 <u>Dunquerque</u> battle-cruisers, a cruiser fleet, a destroyer squadron, 1 tug, 3 freighters, 8 subs, 2 tankers, etc. The tankers were originally, unnamed, but **Clark** tacked some names on them that I thought were lovely. The four were "Sloth," "Avarice," "Greed," and "Gluttony." He's decided that the two remaining are "Sloth" and the "Gluttony." The freighters are a newer addition, and as yet unnamed. I imagine they'll have nice names too.

Mexico, unfortunately for New England, has one battleship -- The <u>Colorado</u>. The <u>Colorado</u> is, of course, the <u>U.S.S. Colorado</u> and it's unfortunate because the US battleships are designed rather differently than those of other nations. The <u>Colorado</u> carries armor so heavy that <u>Dunquerque</u> (they're actually French, of course) can't puncture it.The <u>Dunquerque's</u> carry 15" guns, but the shells will simply bounce off of the terrific armor carried by the <u>Colorado</u> at any range the <u>Dunquerque</u> is likely to try. But the <u>Colorado</u> carries 16" guns, and can put shells clean through the <u>Dunquerque</u> at a distance so great the <u>D.</u> can't even hit the <u>C</u>.

That seems to be typical of the US battleships. They're all slow -- about 22 knots -- but so inordinately tough they don't have to run from anybody, and as long as we want them only for a defensive fleet anyway, they don't have to chase anybody.

The new 45,000 ton ships the US is building, the <u>Washington</u> class, will have 12-16" guns, 14" armor (proof against anything lighter than 16" guns, and extremely resistant even to them) and a speed of 33 knots. Since most US ships exceed their rated speed, **Clark**, **Pratt**, and the others who probably have a pretty good idea of what they're talking about, say they'll probably [be] good for 35 to 36 knots. An item that rather interested me is the fact that if all the cruisers in the combined German, Italian, and Japanese navies caught the USS Colorado out in the middle of the Atlantic all alone -- the Cruisers would high-tail it home. I didn't really realize how incredibly tough a battleship is. The cruisers couldn't even put a shell into the Colorado if they were allowed to come up to point-blank range. While one well-placed 16" shell from the Colorado would put a cruiser out of action, to be sliced up at leisure later on.

To the cell: Thanks a lot for the *Mellor* data I haven't gotten anything straightened out yet, however, because of the completely nutty reactions of the negative pole. I've re-rigged my switch panel, with a gang of no less than six double-pole-double-throw switches, plus two rheostats, one double-pole-double-throw, and four single-pole-single-throw switchs so that I can, by flipping switches, convert the instruments into a sort of potentiometer-voltmeter. That gives me a voltage reading on zero load, or, if desired, a voltage reading when under very slight charge. The instruments will now perform tricks almost as cute as those of the blasted cell.

Results: I've tried as negative poles Cu, Zn, Co, Al, and Mg. With a Cu negative, the peak voltage of the full-charged cell, gassing off H at the negative pole, and 0 at the + pole, is 1.7 or thereabouts. This is obtainable only with gasses coming off-potentiomter hookup with a slight negative load. On zero load, it falls very rapidly to 1.25, hesitates a moment, and plunks down to 0.98 or so. It holds there, even when a load of .1 amps is applied, for about a minute, then falling slowly to zero, and finally reversing potential, with the Cu becoming + and the Co becoming negative. Only by that time, it isn't Cu, it's CuO. The Cu plate, incidentally, will react violently -- gives a shock discharge on short circuit strong enough to kick my 10 amp meter off the scale. Which is a current density of around 10 amps per square inch. And -- when the Cu plate becomes + to the Co, the Co plate starts dissolvinhg as that "blue compound presumably an alkali cobaltite" that *Mellor* mentions. That, on charge, plates back to the Co oxide.

But the really screwy thing is the action of those other types of plates. The full-charge voltage with the Zn plate is 1.9, and discharged voltage about 0.6 with the Al plate -- which, under any conditions-- the full charged voltage is 1.9, and the discharged voltage is about 0.6. Furthermore, on continued load in the discharged condition, the blasted plate -- the Co plate -- begins to gas off too! And I don't see how it can be anything but hydrogen.

The trouble with working with a Co- as well as a Co+ is that the Co- is not completely reduced back to metal by the charge, leaving a layer of a lower Co oxide on the surface which has its own unwelcome potential. Getting a piece of reasonable pure ordinary iron is an astonishingly, and unhappily difficult proposition. It's all galvanized, or steel, or tinned or something. Purer iron, the mild rolled steel of commerce, comes in boiler-plate sizes, and has to be worked with an oxyacetylene torch. I'm gonna try an iron electrode as soon as I get some satisfactory stuff.

The Mg electrode was a complete failure. I was astonished by the absolute and utter indifference of magnesium metal to that high-power alkali. There was one spurt that slapped the voltmeter upward and then it simply collapsed back to zero and stayed right there. It's lack of interest in alkali surroundings was astonishing. Further, if I use a faintly acid salt, the Mg reacts, but the Co plate dissolves off so rapidly its astonishing.

That electroplating bath for cobalt that you sent: do you know whether that's for bright plate or for thick, solid metal? Your reference here was *Koehler Electochem* Vol II p 126, but the only place I might get that would be the NY Public Library, and I haven't a chance to get up there. Besides, as a matter of fact, it is now more a matter of curiosity than need, since I have the experimental Co plates I so badly wanted.

It makes [a] nice hobby to play with -- the Co cell and the instrument hookups. I had lots of fun trying to figure out how to make that potentiometer hookup I mentioned. I put a couple of dry cells across a potentiometer resistance, tapped by the variable arm for my voltmeter and cell. The voltmeter and the cell are both connected across the variable arm and to one end of the potentiometer resistance. The cell is in series, however, with a milliampmeter. Since I can read to 0.01 ma. on the instrument, and detect the movement in response to about .0002 ma., it makes a galvanometer whose sensititivy is not to be sneezed at. I have a series of fixed resistances in series with the galvanometer that can be cut out, and the galavanometer reads zero, the voltage across the portion of the potentiometer resistance being tapped is equal to the voltage of the cell, and the voltmeter also connected across this gap, is reading the voltage of the cell -- but not drawing on it, but getting the current needed to operate it from the dry cells.

By increasing the tapped voltage above the balance point, I feed a slight current into the cell, the galvanometer reading the rate of charge in milliamperes, and the voltmeter giving the voltage within about .01 of true reading.

And the wiring of the switch panel was lovely! It looks like the inside of a radioset!

Really makes a nice hobby and relief from reading too many mss. Since I buy my chemicals at the grocery store (lye) and the hardware shop (Zn, Cu) and the instruments at the radio store, it's cheap. The only objections come from **Dona**, who says things about the mess in the corner of the bedroom.

The science fiction convention plans are progressing apparently. They've rented a hall somewhere in uptown New York -- at 59th street "just off Park Avenue," which sounds very nice. They've got a dance hall, it seems, that's used on Fridays and Saturdays, and therefore got a low rental. I'm loaning some cover-originals, and giving some black-and-white originals to be auctioned off. Also a boost for the boys in the "In Times To Come" department of *Astounding*.

They wanted me to referee that famous soft-ball game, but I turned 'em down with the remark that I might referee football or crew, but I never played baseball. They ought to get **Nelson S. Bond**, who's a sports writer as well as a scf. writer.

The cover for the July *Astounding* ought to be damned nice. it's an illustration for "Black Destroyer" by **A.E. van Vogt**, a new writer, and, I think, a real comer. He's got the goods.

Incidentally, I'm making remarks in "In Times To Come" about how many new first-rank writers we've introduced in the past 18 months. We have done fairly well, I think. **Kent Casey** is first-rank -- a regular who's taken first places with his yarns. **Lester del Rey**, **L.S. de Camp** really got going this year, **M. Schere**, **L. Ron Hubbard**, who was new to scf. if not writing, **H.L. Gold** was redeveloped.

Which reminds me that **Gold's** long novel, "None But Lucifer" turned out too long for the story. He's gone into collaboration with **Sprague de Camp**, and I think they'll get a damn good yarn out of it.

The scf. convention committee appealed to me the other day to help settle a problem. They wanted to hold a dinner in honor of somebody, but didn't know who to pick. They thought of having an author, and editor and a fan, but were afraid of the howls of anguish from the other non-selected of each. The author was gonna be **Binder**, the editor me, and the fan **Ackerman**. I pointed out that the rest of the fans would then unite unanimously in stabbing **Ackerman** in the back, the other editors would tend to stab the convention committee and the authors would not love **Binder**.

Then they thought of honoring **Weinbaum** -- he was safe. I pointed out that most people were just a leeeeeetle tired of hearing about **Weinbaum**, and that they could get other authors to praise him with a "**Weinbaum** was a wonderful writer (Huh! That's what you think. He wouldn't show today.) and a great guy personally (The damn rat!) and they wouldn't love the convention committee either."

The last I heard they were gonna honor science-fiction, which was a nice, safe thing that everybody could agree on.

And that's about enough I guess. **Dona** wants to write **Franny**, so I'll turn it over to her.

Regards, John

[Perry A. Chapdelaine, Sr]   *May 23, 1983*[sic]

Dear Perry:

Greetings!

I finished NULL-A-THREE; so now I can come up for air.

I was searching for something in answer to a letter I got while I was busy -- and ran across 2 pages of what was evidently a three page letter from **Campbell** -- small pages, with page one missing.

It has the look of being a very early letter; since "Black Destroyer" ws the first story he ever published of mine -- though it was the second one I sent him.

This must be in 1939 -- before he put together the July 1939 issue with "Black Destroyer" in it. Perhaps he was asking my permission to print it first; but I really have no recollection on the matter.

Hope all is well with you.

Cordially, Van

P.S. The story originally titled "The Wonderful Man" was eventually published as, "The Changeling!"

A.E. van Vogt *Sometime in 1939*

[sic: Ed.] stories that has ever been written -- and that's not ballyhoo. It is. **A. Merritt** at his peak never did any that were much superior to this one. It's got action and mystery and humanness.

The lead novel of the second issue will be **L. Ron Hubbard's** "Ultimate Adventure," a story that in mood, quality, and interest stands side by side with some of **Washington Irving's** better Tales of the Alhambra.

The range of *Unknown* will be fantasy, but the one, lone qualification for the stories, the only rule laid on the authors, will be pure entertainment. "Trouble With Water," by **H.L. Gold**, will be humor fantasy. "Where Angels Fear -- " will be a very nice horror-ghost yarn. But it is NOT an old-fashioned, 19th century, English-type ghost story - one of those archaisms that begins, "Had I known what horror was to meet me that night, never would I have set forth on that fatal journey --."

It's to be a magazine of just the sort of fantasy you have done so exceedingly well on your past two efforts, save that there will be no mechanistics, no machines and such. Further, the thing I most desperately need at the moment is horror material. If this "Black Destroyer": had not been interplanetary, had not involved atomic power, mechanism, etc. it would have been grand for the new magazine.

606

I'm certain you can do exactly what I want, and in the new field -- non-science -- there's a wide-open market with a howling appetite for 90,000 words a month, wide open for stories of every length from 50,000 words down to 5,000. I am immediately, instantaneously in the market, and if you can do me a 15,000 to 30,000 word novelette in that time, I'd love it.

I'm expecting a flood of good, bad, and worse stuff as soon as the magazine hits the stands -- the herded rejects of a dozen years that now gather dust in a thousand closets -- so if you can get started before the deluge, I'd love it.

Let me know what you want to do about "Black Destroyer."

Sincerely, John W. Campbell, Jr.

The 1940's
with *A.E. van Vogt*

Robert Swisher   *March 6, 1940*

Dear Bob:

Franny says her father is going back sometime in March — said date being over-vague. If you'll let us know pretty quick when he's going, we'll come up for a weekend or so. We're figuring on taking our vacation this year in week-ends fairly early, except I want about a week's worth of days left in and about the end of October. We'll be kinda limited in our travelling, too, toward the latter part of summer; **Dona's** got **Franny's** disease now, but isn't yet quite as experienced in what she can and can't get away with without serious objections from within. We'll know better where we stand after another month or so.

Dr. Lutz seems to be a firm believer in the idea that no two people react alike, so he's making very few predictions 'til he has a little more data on **Dona's** personal reactions. (Incidentally, she wasn't supposed to be sick 'til about 6 weeks from now, but she fooled him.) His principal pronouncement so far seems to have been, "Yes, I guess you are."

But let us know when **Franny's** father goes, and we'll start figuring. Incidentally, how will your visitor's situation be fixed as of Memorial

Day? That seems to be our next holiday not taken from vacation time.

Thanks for ratings and 10 bests. Always interested for personal information. Looks like *Unknown* made out better this issue than did *Astounding* . Personally, I like "In The Good Old Summertime" quite a bit. I'da given it blue.

Robert Tarrant happens to be a real guy's name — but he didn't write the letter. **Robert Tarrant** is a cousin of **Miss Tarrant's**, and the address given is **Miss Tarrant's**. It's legitimate. I wrote the thing, of course. And **Arthur McCann** has an answer coming up. He suggests taking a trip to the dime store, buying a collection of silverware, going to the local contractor's for a burlap bag, fifty pounds of crushed stone and sand, and adding a pound of sulphur to the mixture, then shaking all up thoroughly in burlap bag. Take silverware, run through transmuter, shake well in bag again, and sell resultant "old family silver" at the nearest jewelers. With proceeds, buy a trailer, and take trip, with machine, to Colorado. Set up show at known radium-ore deposits, and, with new purification process, turn out radium from radium ore, product being carefully contaminated with sodium and barium. After six months of this, selling product at $25,000 an ounce, improve product so radically price drops to $5.00 a ton or so, and admit what you've got as the patent goes through.

But, asks **McCann**, how about this: **Tarrant** says the thing will transmute solid plaster busts to solid silver or gold. I doubt it, because process is so violent it twists atoms out of shape, it seems unlikely mere molecular linkages will remain. Seems more probable it'll turn out any element in its natural room-temperature state — solid, liquid, or gas — but that solid elements will be in form of coarse dust or fine sand — except sodium, etc. — and not in original form.

Then: suppose process has been on market 100 years. (So people have had time to get over solid gold bedsteads and 2-ton Pt iceboxes and 100% Au chairs etc.) Now, under these conditions, that any element costs exactly the same at the transmuter mouth — except vicious stuff like F — what will the following common items be made of: Frying pan. Monkey wrench. Coins. Desk lamp. Tableware (now called silverware). Kitchen knife.

Surprising how disapointed you feel when you keep coming out with the answer "steel . . . Steel . . . iron . . ." just what it is today . . .

but that's not very legitimate because you might as well say iron. You might use a Co frying pan, because Co doesn't rust, but you might as well use an iron alloy — Pt-iron for instance. (I'm told it's practically as uncorrodable as Pt with even a 5% addition of Pt. Fe, Co and Ni are, really, Pt-metals, and one of the characteristics of Pt-metals is that any alloy of 2 or more has chemical-resistance properties markedly altered. Thus Pt goes in Aqua Regia — but Pt-Pd-Rd doesn't.) No signs found so far that other metals have 1/100th the alloying properties Fe displays in the multitude of steels. Because it isn't, really, Fe that does it, of course, but the cockeyed string of Fe carbides.

I[n] R[egard] "A" — pardon; "a" — I figured it was out and might as well go on and escape. I stated my protest against it's release in the body of the thing, you'll find, so I'm protected two ways. I have a suspicion your friend **EES** won't love it too much. He evidently likes to have his ideas, and the suggestion that someone else contributes may make him warmish under the collar.

Why don't I get a cylinder of H_2. They make small cylinders, OK, but I wanna know which way I'm going before I jump. The cylinders cost $15 — $12.50 or something like that down as a deposit. Best delivery and filling charges.

Re[garding] **Avery**: I got a letter from him asking rather sadly why this had to happen to him. Why the lightning had to pick him out to hit. Answer: It didn't. That particular lightning has lashed out with exactly the same noisy slap on the wrist every time, with the exception of the time the paper printed that rumor. We would have done more, probably, only the editor of the paper called us up and pointed it out first, telling us retraction was already rolling off the presses. That sorta made us look viciously vindictive if we did anything more. We didn't.

Fantascience Digest, as you've undoubtedly seen, printed a full retraction and apology, after a sharp warning letter. I didn't put out any statement then because I didn't want to stir up more unpleasantness in fandom than necessary; I didn't know **Avery** was going to reprint that thing before the retraction appeared. It looks like the whole thing has been a series of see-a-libel-and-rush-into-print-with-a-copy. Unhappy rumors spread faster than nice ones. Ask any old maid gossip. The only way to scotch it was to do as I did finally; give it all the publicity, with howls of annoyance and dire threats, that I could.

Ask **Avery** what actually happened; we demanded that he print a retraction, and growled horribly. Needn't tell him, but we had no intention of doing much more than scare him — and he damn well deserved a good scare. He printed a vicious libel — a criminal offense, for which he was liable. Period. S & S is the offended party — not **Avery**. S & S showed considerable tolerance.

Unimportant little paper? Yes — but its circulation is exactly where it's apt to hit us hardest. Every fan has contact with a fan who read that — and evil tidings fly fast. Most important authors have ties with the fan field. Authors don't submit manuscripts or write stories for magazines that are in bankruptcy already.

And, for all the fuss, you'll find all we did was make him print a retraction. His own folks — rather wisely, I think -- made him get out of the fan business until he's 21 and can print libels on his own responsibility without getting them in dutch too.

As much as **Avery**, we were growling at the whole fan field; as much for our own sakes as for others. The field has been rotten with libels, and in need of cleaning up. The whole bunch of 'em needed a sound scaring into realization of their responsibilities.

I wrote about the same as the above to **Avery** today. We didn't make any more trouble with him; we simply made more noise. The latter, you'll agree, was necessary.

I didn't see the reprint of the Uranium article, nor the "Lenard the Hungarian" item. I imagine he was referring to us. If so, his magazine was sent out, you can be sure. If he didn't get it, he could probably ask his local postal officials what happened to it. Some English-reading postal clerk musta liked it to.

The **EES**-5 cents a word item was reprinted from the **Westerfeld** article in *Writer's Digest*. I gotta letter from **EES** on that, cracking that his wife wanted to know who was the red-head he spent the other $4000 on.

The 96-page reprints of *Astounding* and *Unknown* in England are news to me. What's your data on it? I don't know anything at all about it.

I doubt that, "All" would sell. If it did, you get the 10%. I hadn't heard about *New Worlds*.

I'm taking your letter in to the office tomorrow to find out about the reprint series you mention. I don't know about 'em but somebody might. They may be part of the Three-books-for-a-dollar series we've been adding in *Astounding* and *Unknown*. If so, I'm afraid they're the part of the series that's now outa print. I'll find out.

Afraid **E.A. Poe** was something less than fiction. That announcement at the front is to protect us when needed: it also says semi-fictitious stories, I notice. Doesn't cover straight articles, so maybe that was an article after all.

I've been looking for a review of the QSFL meeting in the *New Yorker*, but no have seen. They reviewed *Captain Future*, as you no doubt saw. They coulda done an even more torchey job if they'd known science a little better. The stories you mentioned I haven't seen — I just read the cartoons and the "Talk of the Town." [The Major is fulla them. I couldn't think up any "points" in time to put them in that letter. (Handwritten on side of letter, Ed.)]

I'm getting ridden somewhat for the paleontology of "Chapter from the Beginning," but **Phillips** covered himself a leeetle bit better. He has an unspecified, indefinite, unlocatable-in-time pre-man; not a Cro-Magnan. He did make some blunders, however, but the paleontologist who's written us a bummer of a letter (coming up) said he liked the yarn a lot. Which is all it was intended for, he agrees.

Amazing is, so far as I know, still claiming they're rising 3000 copies a month in circulation. That'd give them something like 100,000 circulation if they were right on it. They haven't that, but I'm pretty sure the mag is not folding or ceasing publication. **Warner** musta gotten his manuscript sent through some other magazine's routine by mistake.

Astounding, incidentally, has hit another new all-time high. It's about 500 copies over the October peak on the January issue. I wanna know what February did. It should, if cover editorial, content, etc., can do anything, have hit a still higher peak. I still don't see why the December copy should represent a low mark for the last 3/4 of the year — 4,000 under November which was 4,000 under October — and then have the January issue bounce up 8,500. It's one of the biggest jumps *Astounding* has ever made. And **Smith's** serial didn't do it, because the darned thing was ending.

Pohl was in today, said *Astonishing* was doing all right — would be continued — had a bigger circulation than *Astounding*. If *Astonishing* is continued, that alone will prove his final statement. But, if it is, I'll cheer for him. Damn it, I run a better book, I still say, and if he can drag in that many more new scf readers, with his low price, bet I can garner some of them away from him, and won't lose any of my own. At 10 cents, he needs 70,000 circ. I have 50,500. I should be able to chisel 5 or 10,000 outa his.

Incidentally, he complained somewhat bitterly that I had an iron-clad monopoly on the authors he most wanted — **de camp**, **Heinlein**, **van Vogt**. Seems the dirty capitalists prefer writing for 1-1/4 cents [more] than for his 1/2 cents.

Heinlein's going great guns. He's sent in so much stuff I'm gonna have to invent a pseudoname for him pretty soon. All good, blue stuff. Developed carefully and interestingly. He's working on a thing for *Unknown* called "Magic, Inc." Start looks rather lovely. Imagine **de Camp's** logic crossed with the style of "If This Goes On —."

Also private and not to be mentioned. Don't show this part of the letter, anyway, to friends.

About three weeks ago, **Ron Hubbard** got a letter from Hollywood begging him to come back and do the right thing because their child was due in about 2 months. Signed with some gal's name. **Ron** tried to figure out which one of his movie-writing-days pals was working the gag. Couldn't so didn't answer.

Monday, he got another letter, also from Hollywood, but this time from a friend in the writing business — *Saturday Evening Post* — *Collier's* — etc. Also, letters from his agent, and from two other sources, reporting they'd been answering some questions, and what the hell. The friend in Hollywood however wrote to explain that the previous letter was no gag. They'd taken the girl in — the writer and his wife had — and were helping her as best they could. Apparently some kid about 19-20. Baby due in April sometime. She'd tried to get in touch with "**L. Ron Hubbard**" and the first letter, sent to *Unknown*, and forwarded to **Ron** by me, had been her first attempt that way. Then she'd set out looking for friends of **Ron Hubbard's** in Hollywood, and found this couple who had taken her in.

When she found them, things began to fall into a more understandable pattern. She discovered that "**L. Ron Hubbard**" wasn't the
612

pen-name of **Benedict Unselt**, but the real name of the author, and that, instead of being about 49, medium height and build, with a game left leg, he was about 6 feet tall, flaming red hair, and about 32.

Some high-power checking was started at once, and it was found **Unselt's** been pulling that line for about 2 years around dude ranches in the west, where he met this girl. So far as is known, he's still pulling it. You'll see a letter in *Unknown* presently, protesting that **L. Ron Hubbard** isn't the author's right name, that the writer has met him, describing him. The heading will describe the real **L. Ron Hubbard** and call **Unselt** an imposter.

Above circumstances will not be revealed, of course. I'm gonna have a further conference with **Ron**, and see what we can do through the fan mags to unearth the louse. Better stop.

Write me, John

Robert Swisher   *June 3, 1940*

Dear Bob:

Last Friday I finally finished up the pile of manuscripts that had accumulated while I was away, plus those that came in while I was trying to polish off the pile that had come in. I'd have finished sooner, but the town's been deluged with "visiting firemen" — to wit, **Robert Heinlein**, **E.E. Smith**, and appropriate wives, plus various and assorted authors and ditto-esses who thought it was about time I saw them, after telling 'em I was out of town for three weeks.

So — anyway. As I said in my brief note, accompanied by six rubber-tired ash-trays (I hope the ash-trays as well as the rubber tires arrived in sound condition!), we tried to get in touch with you Thursday, but **Fran** seemed to be out. As you know, **Dona's** mother died that Sunday; Sunday nite I made a flying trip to N.Y., spent Monday working, and came back on the boat Monday nite. The funeral was Tuesday, as you know; Wednesday, **Dona**, as residual heir, was very busy cleaning things out, and this was finished Thursday. Thursday noon we finally had a breathing spell, and that nite we took the boat back to N.Y. I had to get down by Friday for make-up.

We arrived in N.Y. at 8 A.M., took a taxi to 304 W. 28th St., I stepped into a handy cigar store, and called **Willy Ley** to inform him that for once the Germans were about to be invaded and to get up and get ready for guests. That Friday nite, **Dona**, **Willy** and I went to Kriegspiel at **Fletcher Pratt's**, and finally, at about 2 A.M. arrived home. **Dona** hadn't wanted to go home alone.

Since then, things have been slightly hectic both officially and socially. The **Heinlein's** are swell people. They are taking a tour of the country for the hell of it, and may wander up Bosting way; I'm gonna suggest they look you up if they do. They're both a little shy and reserved at first -- **Heinlein** puts on a bit of Annapolis manners, and Mrs. **Heinlein** is naturally reserved — but they loosen up quickly, and they both are darned interesting. **Bob Heinlein** has some swell stories and anecdotes. One's good enough to write:

Concernces Couvier, the great French zoologist, contemporary of **Darwin**. Some of his students decided it would be fun to scare the wits out of the old boy, and arranged for one of the number, dressed in conventional Devil's attire, complete with accessories to invade his room one night while they were parked outside. The old man woke up, the student leered down at him and intoned: "Mortal, prepare to die! I have come to eat you!"

Couvier looks him up and down somewhat blankly. "Horns! Hooves! Herbivorous! You can't!" he snapped.

In N.Y., the **Heinleins** are staying at the apartment of three ex-Navy men — classmates of **Bob Heinlein's**. The three live with their family, but maintain the apartment for conveniences and parties. When we went in it, I went to the bathroom to wash off the grime of a day's toil, and remarked to **Bob** when I came out that it looked at first glance as though the decorator of the bath had been somewhat of an egomaniac. The room was lined with mirrors. There were three huge mirrors on the walls, and one of those triple all-angle mirror arrangements into the bargain.

Heinlein explained that it was accidental, all due to a misunderstanding. It seems that when they got the place, they decided they needed a long mirror over the couch. **Arwine**, the principal occupant of the joint, heard about an auction of night-club (deceased) effects, and went around. There was a nice mirror — just what they wanted. About 12 feet long and three feet deep. He bid on it, and got it for a nice price, ordered it delivered. The next day, the trucker arrived, and, with three assistants, brought it up. Then he went down again for the rest. **Arwine**
614

had made a slight error; he had bid in Lot #288 — all the mirrors in the joint!

The second occupant of the place, in the meantime, had told a glazier to get around and put up the mirror. **Arwine** had left to tell the other boys what had happened when the glazier arrived. When **Arwine** and friends returned, glazier looked a bit distressed and reported he didn't know where to put the other eight mirrors, but he had most of 'em up. He did. There are 15 different mirrors, most of them large, in the bedroom, dozens in living room and kitchen, as well as the polyreflective bathroom.

Sprague sold us a story the other day that he called, "The Warrior Race," but I'm thinking of retitling, "The Earth-Savers." Earth's conquered by a Spartan-type people from Alpha Centaurae, a pure warrior race. The Earth-savers are a Philadelphia politician and a Chinese business man. They save the Earth because they're so completely and colossally crooked they utterly and hopelessly corrupt the warrior race and make them too soft to fight. It's a rather lovely idea, I think.

I've told you about the Solar System having the elements of a giant vacuum tube amplifier: I was telling **Smith** about it, and he's thinking of having his Galactic Patrol story wind up with Kim beaming the entire enemy fleet out of existence by using eight solar systems hooked up in push-pull as a final power-amplifier on the beam output. I rather like that, too.

"All" is retired from the active list herewith: **Heinlein**, to whom I recounted the plot, seems very much interested and wants to work it out. He would do a nice job, I think, and I want him to try.

Incidentally, **Heinlein** told me something of his system. "Peace! It's wonderful!" He has a big chart: on the vertical margin, he has years and centuries marked off; on the horizontal margin, technologies. (Physics, psychology, rocketry, etc.) When he writes a story, he decides what century to lay it in, what technology, etc., and looks at his chart. At the chosen time, his chart tells him, such-and-such a form of government was in power (the Prophet, for instance, if it's laid in 2300; see "If This Goes On—") and tells him what characters mentioned in other stories were living at that time. A given character — the Skipper in "Misfit," for instance — is represented by a vertical line, his life span, in the vertical column of his technology. Horizontal lines across are labeled with the name of the invention of major importance they represent. For instance, the sun-power screens mentioned in "The Roads Must Roll" and in "Coventry" and "Blow-ups Happen."

All his stories under the **Heinlein** name in *Astounding* will have that common historical background. "All" will be rewritten under another name, because it doesn't fit that historical set-up in any way. "The Devil Makes The Law" (Ex-"Magic, Inc.") will appear in *Unknown*. That doesn't fit either, but it does fit in another history he's building up.

A.E. van Vogt's "Slan!," the superman story, came in while I was away, and has been accepted and will appear beginning in September. It makes nice reading, and is, I think, a thoroughly good job. **Heinlein** will be interested, I know.

Heinlein is retired from the Navy due to disability — T.B. Seems there are three occupational diseases of the Navy, all due to the promotion scheme they have. The system works as follows: an officer is up for advancement, is considered by the promotion board, and is, let's say, passed over. Someone else, his junior, is promoted over his head for doing unusually good work. That's all right; he's still eligible. He's up again — and again passed over. Still all right. But if he's passed over a third time — he's automatically retired from the Navy. Now the Navy men very evidently love the Navy. But they can't stay in it if they don't advance; they can't stand still. That applies to the men under them, who are trying like holy hell to get up too.

That leads to the three occupational diseases: T.B., Ulcers, nervous breakdown. It works this way. Just short of nervous breakdown, your digestion goes to hell. Now if you've got a tough nervous set-up, and a tough physical condition, you'll get ulcers and be retired. If your physical set-up is a little weak, the over-work, poor digestion and eating, lack of sleep, etc., gives you T.B. If the nervous set-up cracks first, you get rested in a sanatorium.

They all recover, practically speaking, but after they've been retired, **Heinlein** says, Navy's all they will or want to talk most of the time. So **Heinlein** made a specialty of <u>not</u> talking or looking Navy for the last 6 years, and went in for politics instead. The **Heinleins** are also boycotting the war.

Leslyn (Mrs. **Heinlein**) says they'll learn all they need to about it from one of two sources: the history books or the Man with the Leggings. **Bob Heinlein's** retired — but that just means he's on the reserve list, to be called up when they want him.

Arwine, also ex-Navy, was telling me he had resigned. **Heinlein** cackled softly; **Arwine** grinned. It seems **Arwine** sent in his resignation, was properly ushered out of the Navy, and has gone into publicity (World's Fair) work. About three months ago a man came around to him inquired rather forcefully why he hadn't reported to his Area Commander this quarter; **Arwine** explained he had resigned from the Navy. The gentleman remarked that maybe he <u>thought</u> he had, but the fact was that you just don't retire from the Navy. You resign from Active Duty, not from the Navy.

Arwine's a Lt. Commander, but he told me he'd never commanded any ship, which puzzled me. I mentioned it to **Heinlein**, who said it wasn't any particular secret, but Lt. Commanders who haven't commanded ships are in another division of the Navy's work. He then dropped that, but went on to tell me about the very bad luck the Navy has with men who are sent to the Japanese Language School, also run by the Navy. A number of the very shortest Annapolis men take the course, but the Navy has the worst luck; nearly all of them, just about the time they've completed the long and very thorough course, get into a jam, a bad one — they go wrong, like taking a bribe and being caught at it, or something — and get court-martialled out of the Navy with a bang.

Arwine's not in that division, because he's very tall, and very, very rugged and North-European of feature.

Heinlein was fire-control officer on the Lexington. Tells me there are four official, and five unofficial classes of Naval information; Public, Service, Confidential, and Secret, are the official ones. The meanings are clear. Unofficially, the men divide them into Public, Service, Confidential, Secret, and Super-colossal Terrific Secret. The last class includes things like the bomb-sight, and the plane-arresting-gear used in landing planes on aircraft carriers. The latter consists of two things; a wire cable stretched about knee-high across the deck, and the arresting-gear proper to which the wire cables run. Frayed wires are fixed by machinist's mates; the arresting gear is in steel cases below decks. When that needs repair, some of the technical officers get out of their pretty uniforms, get into dungarees, station an officer guard outside the room,

617

and go to town personally on the apparatus.

The apparatus, incidentally, **Heinlein** says is very, very smooth. It'll arrest a big bomber with a nice, even, uniform deceleration, and not drag it backward after it comes to rest, but will pull the wires back into place when the bomber's finger, which catches the wires, is released.

That seems to cover most of the general news available at this time and place.

Dona is now entirely over her spells of sickness, has had only one day when she was somewhat upset, and hasn't taken to amphogel more than three or four times. She seems to be doing very nicely indeed. She's got her one of those special dresses, and is slightly annoyed because it's a nice, new, pretty dress that she can't wear yet. So far her regular things fit.

Oh, a cousin of ours has a new — very — son. Last year, when she went to her doc about it, she was told to expect results about April 24 — and was annoyed. They'd taken out hospitalization, but the waiting period for maternity benefits wouldn't be up until May 4. Missing by couple of weeks meant about $100 to them.

The baby was late. She went to the hospital May 5, and it was born May 6. She claims it showed remarkable judgment, for one so young.

Dona has some remarks to make, I believe, so —

Regards, John

Robert Swisher   *June 20, 1940*

Dear Bob:

Large scale doings here, of late. Looks like we'd be settled in a house (Ours — in just 240 more payments!) not far from Orange, rather easier to reach by car than the present apartment. The deal is still rather boiling, not fully set, but seems to be on its way. It's a nice, new, five story house out in Westfield, N.J. That's about half way between New Brunswick and Orange, you might say. It'll cost us $6850 plus the lovely effects of waiting twenty years to pay. There's about 75 x 120. Hmmmmmm — some discussion on that point; **Dona** and I don't agree on the width of the lot. It's about as wide as yours, whatever yours is, minus the tomato bed part. However, the depth will appear
618

almost endless unless we get an Englishman with hedge-row ideas, because all the back lots run into each other beautifully.

It's a grand community, we think. Every Sat. aft. and Sun. aft. the local men appear in year-before-last's white britches and a coat of tan and start wielding lawnmowers, spading forks, bug-killer, or similar instruments. There's the general air of a summer lake community about its friendliness. Six of the men — a cousin of ours has a house there already, so we learned — have bought one of those one-wheeler lawnmowers on shares and run it around. A seventh supplies storage space and repairs so he's got a share in its use. Most of the folks are just about our age and circumstances, and seem to get along swell. Matter of fact, the buyers of houses automatically join a local Association, which same association determines whether or not they like the new buyers. If they don't, the people are gently hoisted out of the community and the company buys back the house at the sale price. That's not mere theory; it's been done.

Our little five-story-place is on the top of a swell of ground, and will have the advantage of good drainage and all available breezes. In another 40 or 50 years it'll have the shade of some noble maples and oaks. At present there's woodland to the north of the community, and woodland to the south — but none on it. It is evident that some hardworking farmer, by the sweat of his brow and horses, cleared that land of the dang-nabbit trees. Ah, well — you can't have everything.

It's on the New Jersey Central railroad, which is almost half as good as the Lackawanna as a commuter line, and runs trains as late as 11:30 at night. That is, there's a station only 1-1/3 miles away. Actually, the N.J.C.R.R. isn't too bad; it's one of the better commuter lines, though not electrified as is the Lackawanna, and not quite as convenient to the office. I have to take train-ferry-subway connections.

However, the 1-1/3rd miles is 99% made up for — if not 199% made up for — by a community service. They've got a station-wagon bus service that, for $1.50 a month collects you at your door, takes you to your train, and collects you again at night. And that's a hell of a lot better than most available houses in the metropolitan district can offer. To get within 1/2 mile of the stations means paying high — and walking in the rain a lot.

Oh — as to the five-story feature. It's a frame house, with a most interesting arrangement. **Fran**, I know, will be interested in its features. It makes the most effective use of space to lend interest and apparent size I've seen anywhere. There's no air of phonyness about it's appearance as so damn many of the glorified small homes have. It's trickery — but intelligent trickery and useful.

The garage is built into the house. But — it doesn't open at the front; the entrance is at the rear. The front is equipped with three windows — small ones — that naturally appear as room windows. A garage being rather sizable, that adds one large, or two small, rooms to the apparent size of the place. Further, it gives enough room-enclosed to permit good lines to a more-than-one-story place.

Entering the house door, you're in the living room, having stepped in off the screened-in porch. (This is Jersey, remember, and the Jersey mosquitoes hunt in packs.) The living room (not at all as large as **Dona's** always sworn hers would have to be!) leads into the dining room (also small, but plenty big enough) and thence into the kitchen, not large, but efficient. Also from the living room, a half-flight of stairs leads up to a small hall-way, from which open two bed-rooms and the bath, and another door which leads to another half-flight that leads upward to a now-unfinished room. This space is large enough to make a good big extra bed room, marred only by the fact that one wall slants considerably, being the roof. Another half-flight can lead up from here — it's not installed yet because unneeded till the room's finished off — to a space ample for a storage room for Aunt **Matilda's** trunk, horsehair rocker, and bedding, etc. There's really some space up there.

Now; how-come the half-flights? Simple. Let's go down them from the storage room. One half-flight (the unfinished half-flight) down is the unfinished room. Another half-flight down is the bedroom floor. The storage space is above the bedrooms, the two half-flights making a story, actually.

Going down another half-flight, we're on the living-room-dining-room-kitchen level. The unfinished room is above the living and dining room, being two half-flights up. Now, out to the kitchen, and there we go down a half-flight and enter to the garage. The bedrooms and bath are above this, being two half-flights up. (The garage isn't a two-car affair, but brother it is <u>not</u> a skimpy garage. There's room enough for a lawnmower, garden roller, the oil-burner fuel tank, and a
620

cord of wood besides the car and the inevitable junk. That's why the
bedrooms and bath, though not huge, are still big enough.)

Mayhap I've confused you? I'll prepare a list — a table — giving
the arangement visually.

6. Storage space.

(1/2 flight-to-be)

5. Unfinished room

(1/2 flight)

4. Bedrooms-bath

(1/2 flight)

3. Living-Dining Kitchen

(1/2 flight)

2. Garage

(1/2 flight)

1. Basement

That shows their vertical and indicates their horizontal arrangements. The unfinished room is floored over, so there will be no foot-
through-the-ceiling acts.

There's a fireplace in the living room (it draws; they test them <u>be-
fore</u> they put the walls in!) and the heating is steam-oil fired. The hot
water during the summer is maintained by a special low setting on the
main oil burner. All assessments except sanitary sewer are taken care
of; sewage is by septic-tank system, the present local inhabitants swear-
ing that there is no trouble with it, and it being FHA approved. Inasmuch as there isn't any system anywhere in the village of Scotch
Plains — in which township the place lies — yet, it will probably be a
number of years before that comes up.

We don't quite know the address of the place yet, but we'll let you
know soon enough. We expect to move out there just about the time
the third member of your family moves out. We figure that it's a case
of the sooner the quicker — with **Dona** now feeling fine and looking
fine. Looks quite normal so far, with a gain of but 3-1/2 pounds so far.

Incidentally, we're having 'em install fluorescent lumalines in
the kitchen and dining room. I always did like lots of light with my
meals.

The basement is L shaped. The furnace is most of the way up the
main branch of the L, with the tubs at the top wall of the vertical bar.

I'm gonna screen off the horizontal bar of the L, leaving an I shaped part — actually, of course, a straight hall part — as a game room. The screened part will be my own particular mess spot.

One of the reasons we most like the place — the community and company that runs it — is the reports we've gotten from the cousins who live there now. They've had troubles. Their cellar flooded, a few minor things bothered them. The company fixed them — free. There are bound to be troubles; what I want to know is that they'll be fixed. Evidently they are.

We've been wondering what the community would think if we finally did get "Fi-Fi." You know — the Irish wolfhound we've mentioned. There are a number of dogs out there now, but there might be reactions to seven or eight feet of dog in one hunk.

Which reminds me; the aforementioned cousins have a slightly insane Peke. It likes asparagus — loves the stuff. I've been wondering, in my usual irrelevant way, just what the other dogs in the neighborhood think as they circulate the local bulletin boards. Must be terribly confusing. (**Dona** suggests that, since you don't eat it, maybe you don't know. I doubt the suggestion myself. Anyway, you should know the asperigrine reaction.)

We'll probably settle for an Irish Setter — if we can get one!

Another pleasant feature of the development is that, being purely a development, its roads don't go anywhere at all except to the development. Therefore, the only traffic is that of other residents who, presumably, have children of their own. At least, about 80% or so of them do. There is no main highway nearer than three good, long blocks.

When you come to visit us next, you'll probably be stored in the second bedroom; at last we'll have a reasonable arrangement for guests. It's apt to get used, too. I think I mentioned that the last New Yorkward train left at 11:30. It's rather easy to miss a train at that hour if the conversation is really going good, and the next train carries the milk in at 3:45 A.M.

Not much shop news; the stories have been coming in very slowly. Oh, you know by this time, I imagine, that **Hank Kuttner** and **C.L. Moore** are married. Poisonally, from what reports I've heard of the gal, I think **Kuttner** was damned lucky.

Did I mention "Slan!" in my previous letter? If not, or even if I did, it's worth mentioning here. **A.E. van Vogt** has turned in something worth writing — and also writing about, I think. You probably won't rate it gold because it isn't a super colossal super-science. But the son-of-a-gun gets hold of you in the first paragraph, ties a knot around you, and keeps it tied in every paragraph thereafter — including the ultimate last one. Starts out nicely. Nine-year-old super-man — slan, as they're called — and his mother on the street. Mother, by her telepathic sense, knows that she's been spotted as a slan, and is about to be shot down. Tells the boy to run away — which he does just as she is shot down in the street. He gets a bullet in his side. Nine years old, his parents both shot dead, a ten thousand dollar reward for his corpse, as for all slan corpses, and nowhere on Earth to go.

He's got a nice set-up, and handles it just as nicely. Starts in September — four parts.

Hmm — guess that's all. Unless you've contrived another of those crossing letters, you owe me one now!

Regards, John

A.E. van Vogt   *Tuesday 1941*

Dear van vogt:

The replacement copy of the magazine has already been launched on its way to you; should be there about now.

Something that may interest you in connection with the space-storm item. You remember asking me what might make a space-storm, and I remember rather vaguely what I replied. Mulling it over in my head, the darned thing got more and more plausible, 'til now I have a full-fledged theory — to wit; space-storms do exist, they are going on, normally raging for centuries, moving with the glacial slowness of any vast structure. The proof: cosmic rays. Cosmics have never been satisfactorily analyzed, nor explained, nor a satisfactory explanation of the stupendous energy-levels they show possible. In cosmic-ray "bursts," energies totaling tens and even hundreds of thousands of millions of electron-volts have been measured — a value so enormous as to require the simultaneous annihilation or dissipation of ten or twenty hydrogen atoms. But to conceive that twenty hydrogen atoms could simultaneously intersect in paths of enormous velocity all at one point is ridiculously improbable. Yet nothing else seemed adequate to explain the measured, stupendous energy. The fission of a ^{235}U atom is weak-kneed and incompetent by comparison with the incredible concentration of energy cosmic-ray bursts have shown.

This energy is measured by summing the total energies of twenty or forty or a hundred ions that will be suddenly driven out from a point-source, the ion-paths being followed and measured in a Wilson Cloud Chamber. The thing is called a "burst" because the resultant photograph of the ion-trails in the cloud chamber look startlingly like a shell-burst.

Ordinary cosmic rays don't display such terrific energies, but still show energy-values of so high an order no ordinary atomic disintegration can properly explain them. Further, the cosmic rays seem to be a weird mixture of particles of both positive and negative charge, moving with terrific velocities, and pure radiation of very "hard" or high-energy characteristics.

Furthermore, the cosmics come from all directions of space almost equally — the variations are so small as to be well within instrumental error.

It is known that stars move in groups — a flock of anywhere from a dozen to several million suns may move through the galaxy in a common direction at pretty much of a common velocity. It is to be presumed that these suns have some sort of common origin, have other things in common with each other. Such as, for instance, all being made of Contra-Terrene (CT) or Terrene (T) matter.

The Solar System at the present era is moving through a star-stream, a group of such related suns, to which Sol does not belong. It's crossing the street in star-space.

The spectrum of space has shown that all space is filled with diffuse interstellar gases, including calcium, sodium and hydrogen, of course, and probably most of the other elements. All stars throw off such trails of gas, and throw off electrons — or positrons, if it's a CT star — as they move through space.

If our sun were moving through an alien — a CT star-type — group of suns, the space in and around those suns would be saturated with CT gases; our own system and its surroundings for 5 to 15 light-years saturated with terrene gas atoms, and electrons.

If a CT calcium atom started moving toward us, it would encounter
624

the electron haze, and its orbital positrons would go up in a blaze of hard radiation. The stripped nucleus, carrying now a terrific and unbalanced negative charge, would repel electrons, and tend to attract terrene atom nuclei — if, in that near-perfect vacuum, it could once get close enough to one so that the electrons of the terrene atom could no longer repel it away. Eventually, it probably would meet one. Say it met a sodium atom. The result would be some terrifically violent and instantaneous — simultaneous — cancellation of charges. But still there would be the left-over CT remnant of the heavier calcium atom. But now that remnant would be traveling with a speed near that of light; the violence of that atomic explosion that annihilated most of two atoms behind it.

If that particle entered Earth's atmosphere, it would be moving with a colossal speed, a speed so great that no atom of our atmosphere would have a chance to react with it until it had been slowed down gradually to a velocity low enough to permit a reaction. Then, naturally, the remaining CT nucleus and an equivalent mass of some Terrene atom would undergo a mutual annihilation that would throw atomic debris and violently hard radiation in all directions.

Seems to me that would make a damn good imitation of a cosmic ray burst, if it isn't the real thing! The particles -- and hence the violence of the burst — would vary as the particular types of CT and T atoms underwent the original partial cancellation in space varied. If the terrene atom outweighed the CT, the terrene nucleus left would bombard us simply with the terrific kinetic energy imparted by the explosion. If the atoms only one step apart in mass canceled, we'd have single high-velocity particles. In addition, there would be a welter of loose electrons and positrons exploded in all directions, as well as assorted types of radiation, all at least as hard as the gamma rays of radium, and going from there right on up to the stuff occasionally given off when a pair of really big atoms — say a lead and a uranium atom, or bismuth and thorium — underwent mutual annihilation.

If that theory's right, and it does sound plausible, anyway, those space-storms you asked about are on right now! Ordinarily, the century-long space-storms would be plotted, space-weather reports predicting the weather in each section covering years and centuries could be made. But sometimes an unsuspected thickening of the tenuous gases would

625

produce gusts — gusts that last five or ten years. And a Nova, or even more particularly, a Supernova, would be hell-on-wheels. The unexpected, sudden, and tremendous upsurge of storm, preceded only slightly by the sudden explosion of light, would produce terrific effects. Furthermore, cruising at half a light-year a minute, a pretty conservative deep-space, long-range speed, you'ld smack into the heart of that storm before you knew the thing had gone Nova. There would be weather observatories all through the traveled sections of space to watch such things. Most of their work would be keeping cosmic ray records, but they'd always be established somewhere where an unusual or interesting star and/or system provided further occupation.

Incidentally, I mentioned your question and my theory answer to **Richardson**. I'm waiting in considerable curiosity to hear what he and his Mt. Wilson friends have to say!

Regards, John W. Campbell

Robert Swisher *June 9, 1941*

Dear Bob:

Now washing in the tub are three prints specially made for your edification; I'll describe 'em as to what they are now, as you will, certainly, have looked at 'em already. The nice, spectacular one of **Nellie** is a 14-1/2 diameter blowup of some Superpan Supreme developed in Von-L Salon developer for Weston 250, 5 times manufacturers rating. That is rather typical of the results I got with Von-L. The one of **Dona** laughing is a 14-1/2 diameter blowup of some Finopan, taken at Weston 175, 7 times manufacturers rating, and developed in Von-L for Weston 160. I did this because I was told that underdeveloping tended to minimize film grain. This is far and away the best result I have ever gotten on any Von-L developed shot. Unfortunately, the 20-exposure roll so developed yielded just 5 printable negatives. The rest were too light to make anything but a gray blur even on some extra-contrast paper. On various other Von-L rolls, my results have ranged from horrible grain at 8 diameters to usable grain at 11 diameters. (The latter was on Finopan shot at manufacturers rating — Weston 24. It was developed at 65 degrees for 4-1/2 minutes.)

The one of me is a 14-1/2 diameter enlargement of some
626

Panatomic-X exposed at manufacturers rating of Weston 24 (W 16 here; its fotoflood) and developed in Edwal-20. My enlarger won't go beyond 14-1/2 diams. Without turning it around and projecting onto the floor. There is no detectable grain whatever on this; the shadowy suggestion of might-be grain under my nose and my cheek is beard. On the whole picture it is clear as to what it is.

I can't discuss comparative detail on this one and the others; **Dona** gave me, as my birthday present, a new lens — a Wollensak f 2.8 that has 4 times the resolving power of the Perfex f 2.8 I did have. But I can say this; I'm still not getting the detail I should, and from what **Louis** the Office Boy and others have told me, I suspect one of the major troubles in this is that I'm still using Von-L stop bath and hypo-hardener. The emulsion is swollen when it comes out of the wash, but compacts down on drying and gets hard. **Louis** says that his films come out of the hypo already compact and hard — just wet. I suspect that that swelling and contracting of the emulsion doesn't do a bit of good to sharpness of detail. Agfa says Finopan has a resolving power of 1700 lines per inch. The Wollensak lens is guaranteed for 4000 lines/inch on the optical axis, and 200 lines/inch at the edge of the field. At 14 diams, therefore, there should be a sharpness of more than 120 lines per inch — the limit of the eye in ordinary work. There isn't; I'd say there wasn't more than 50 lines/inch detail here.

But there is a cleanness of image and lack of grain that makes it perfectly practicable to use 14 diameter blowups in portraits.

Incidentally, Superpan Supreme runs to 1200 lin/in, Ultraspeed Pan to about 950 lins/in. With Superpan Supreme, I can make very satisfactory 14 diameter enlargements on Buff Luster paper that show no detectable grain — if I develop in Edwal-20.

It amounts to this: Von-L may well be a good developer, capable of the results claimed. I don't get 'em. I've done a respectable amount of fairly expensive experimenting on it. I still don't get the results consistently. The first roll I developed in Edwal-20 had very nice grain. The second and third were still better. This shot of me is from the 3rd roll. Edwal-20 lets you use considerable latitude of over and under exposure without getting horribly grainy, but it will block highlights on overexposure. A properly developed Edwal-20 roll has <u>no</u> black spots; they're all a sort of yellow-gray. If it's black, it's blocked. I've had that on some of the frames of the second roll, which was overde-veloped a bit because the temperature rose more than I realized until too late. Edwal-20s great advantage is that you can get consistent, depend-able results and extremely fine grain with just reasonably good tech-nique. You don't have to be a genius to make it work right every time. You can expose at full manufacturers rating.

I also tried Edwal-12. For that, you expose at ratings two times as high as the manufacturer says — Ultraspeed pan at Weston 200, Su-preme at Weston 100, etc. Grain is pretty decent at 8 diameters — quite acceptable. At 10 diams. it isn't objectionable on buff luster pa-per. If you want more film speed, and don't mind a little — damn little, really — grain, try that. I'd really rather recommend that for you. I have a suspicion, from what I've dug up recently, that your lens will break down on detail at about 10 diameters anyway. **Del Rey's** figures I find, are largely snatched out of the air as far as I can make out. The Perfex lens, according to the Perfex people has a resolving power of 1000 lines on the optical axis. That means it's getting damn sloppy at the edges of the picture by the time you make a 10X blowup. That's why I wanted the Wollensak — it's still sharper than any film except Minipan, Microfile or Micropan (Agfa's, Eastman's and DuPont's super-fine, super-super-slow films. Weston speeds about 0.4 to 1.0; resolving power 3400 lins/in.) clear out at the edge of the field. The figures I've finally gotten were obtained by calling up Agfa and say-ing I was a physicist doing some spectrum work and wanted a pan film with both speed and resolving power; what were the figures. Neither Eastman nor Agfa answered letters just plain asking. The figures for the Perfex and Wollensack lenses I got by calling Raygram, the New York distributors, and arguing until the guy said he'd write the Perfex people and ask. If you're sufficiently interested, I'll go to work on the Argus people and find out what your lens actually does rate. Letters don't do any good, and I find it's like pulling teeth to get the data. For some reason they hide it as though it were shameful. I tried hard to chisel the figures out of Carl Zeiss for their Tessar f 2.8 lens, but I finally had to give up. I <u>think</u> they don't know here in New York. All they keep saying is that the resolution exceeds any film manufactured, so why bother with it?

You can gather that the thing griped me. I got disgusted with the usual, "It's a very good lens." Yeah, damn it, but <u>how</u> good — <u>how</u> fine. OK. — now I'm happy. I know the resolving power of film and lens, and know what ultimate goals I can drive for. And I know that neither my camera or enlarger lens is going to go flat on me before the film does. Any lack of detail at 14-1/2 diameters, then, must be due to some error in my processing methods. Since there is absolutely no grain at that enlargement, it is not due to grain. That leaves another, specific, definite line of attack for me to work on. And <u>that's</u> what I wanted.

Incidentally, the change to the Wollensack lens has made visible, definite improvement in the clarity and sharpness of even 5 and 7 diameter enlargements. In the 10 or 11 diameter enlargements of parts of negatives the improvement is delightful. I'm enclosing a sort of "proof" enlargement of a pic of **Dona** Panatomic-Edwal-20-fotoflood-Wollensack at f 2.8. It's not a good picture, and somewhat under-printed, but notice the immense sharpness of the hair detail. It's a 7X enlargement — would almost cover an 8 X 10 if the whole negative were used, in other words.

I haven't tried any Kodachrome yet, but I intend to soon now. **Dona** still not interested. Kodachrome, incidentally, is a lovely test of the ultimate resolving power of your lens; it's practically grainless at infinite enlargement, and its resolving power is terrific. Grainless because the image is a dye image; further superposition of three separate emulsions means that grain in one would be covered by the different lie of the grain in the other two. Resolving power from a similar effect.

But a suggestion and question. Any slide projector I've heard of costs about $8 even with my discount. It can be used only for slide projection. You can get an enlarger of about the same quality for about two dollars more. That can be used as a projector fairly well, though admittedly not as conveniently as a real slide projector — but it will also enlarge prints for you.

Oh, a question you asked. Mr. Von L doesn't say anything. He won't write. **Lower's** gone on a vacation for a month, and I haven't heard from him. **Richardson's** friend who was going to use it hasn't been back on the Mountain yet, so I haven't heard.

Back to Kodachrome: You asked about a filter for using daylight kodachrome under photoflood. Son, you is mistooken. If you want anything in that line, you want a filter for using photoflood kodachrome in daylight. I don't think you want even that. Here's why: Under those conditions — daylight kodachrome plus filter for use in photoflood — the film has an effective Weston speed of 3.0 Gadelpus. Kodachrome A — the photoflood type — has a Weston speed of 12 under photoflood, and a Weston speed of 8 with filter in daylight. A speed of 8 isn't bad at all in full sunlight, but a speed of 3 under fotofloods is practically unusable. Even a speed of 8 under photofloods is rather horrible. I've been taking some pics on Finopan under photofloods with a green filter to overcome the red sensitivity that makes pan film produce white lips in portraits. Under those conditions, you have a Weston speed of 8. Two #2 photofloods, one at 6 feet for a shadow-detail filler-inner and one at 3 feet for the main light just made it for an f 2.8 lens wide open at 1/25 second. The light is perfectly horrible. The first set of pics I took that way, **Dona** was badly squinted and strained in each of them. You certainly don't want to operate at Weston 3; I suspect you'ld be disappointed in the results at Weston 12. F II wouldn't hold still for 1/5th second under the light intensity you'ld have to use. F I and you'ld be all right with a decent light intensity and a 1 sec. or so exposure. I think the best way to take indoor kodachrome would be to use a couple of large sized flashbulbs on the open-flash method. Open shutter, fire flash, close shutter. The flash lasts about 1/50th second, and the latter part of it is so weak as to make almost no impression on the film, so no movement or change of expression registers. I plan to use outdoor kodachrome outdoors exclusively. There you can get light intensities running way up to 19 on the meter — a 500th sec. at f 3.5 for Kodachrome. Ordinary sunny-day light intensity runs enough to give you a 200th at f 2.8 almost any day.

It's queer, but a fact, that that terrifically greater brilliance of daylight as against the "unbearable" photoflood light, doesn't bother at all. I imagine it's a matter of maladjustment of the eyes; they try to adjust for a general-level-of-illumination, and, because photoflood light follows the inverse square law with a very rapid falling off of brilliance, the eye can't make a decent adjustment. Daylight doesn't follow the inverse square law — it's all over the place in uniform, though terrific, intensity. Queerly, that light, 40 or more times as potent, is pleasant!

I'm writing the letter now, but will stop at H & B and get the prices Monday morning. I'll send the whole shebang Monday from the office.
630

Kodachrome comes only in the 18 exposure rolls.

I suggest you get an orange or red filter rather than a dense yellow. The orange and red filters make the shadows and clouds far more dramatic without getting into the long exposures. I'll let you know on all three types of filters as to prices.

DK-20 can be bought in two forms: they give you the formula in every roll of Eastman film, and you can compound it from the bulk chemicals. It doesn't pay, because the Eastman people put out the dry, but mixed chemicals too cheaply. You can buy DK-20 in bottles containing an inner vial. You dissolve the powder in the inner vial, then add the contents of the bottle when it's all dissolved, and there's your DK-20. Same goes for Agfa's stuff.

Edwal-20, as the enclosed circular shows, can be bought in dry powder form, in the form of the already mixed and dissolved solution, or you can get the formula and mix it yourself by buying the Edwal book on developing and printing techniques. Edwal-20 is a standard, widely known and widely used developer that most people I've talked with say is a bit better than DK-20. Edwal-20 is a paraphenalynediamine developer — it deposits a layer of yellow-brown stain on the film where the image is. The stain is absolutely grainless, and adds to the negative's photographic density without contributing grain. Since paper is blind to yellow light, the stain is black to paper, though light in color to the eye. The result is that a very thin, actually an underdeveloped, negative prints nicely. The under-development is advantageous, because the grains don't have time to grow together and produce the speckled appearance. (See **Aunt Nellie's** picture.)

Paper developer. Defender 55-D is what I use. Comes in a can with two compartments. Dissolve part A, then add part B. It's cheap, good, and seems to be very widely used indeed. 55 cents size makes 1-1/2 gallons of working solution. You need only 8 Oz. at a time, so it lasts.

I've been using Von-L stop-bath and fixer. I intend to change. I'll let you know, but they come, I know, in the same sort of kits. The standard stop-bath hardener is chrome-alum-bisulphite bath. It must be made fresh for each film, but is probably the best. I intend to get one of the prepared, stabilized kind that's less nuisance.

Paper stop-bath is just a weak acid solution. I've been using, as you know, a dilute acetic acid bath. I changed because HAc is a bloody

631

nuisance. Citric does equally well, is about as cheap, and will not drip, spill, or burn careless fingers accidentally. Paper fixer can be plain hypo with a little formaline, but prepared gunks are easier.

Re use of dayload tank: the film will jam — as I've found to my sorrow — unless certain elementary, but not too obvious precautions are taken. I can explain better when I see you. Those precautions observed, everything's very, very swell. Also some practical angles on management of temperatures while developing. The important one is that the specific heat and temperature of the film and the tank can throw you off unless all four items — tank, developer, stop-bath and hypo — are at equilibrium temperature. Unfortunately, the best and finest grain is obtained at 65 degrees, which isn't prevalent in June, July, August and September.

****

The prints are now drying. They look even better than I thought. I made an 8 X 10 that's a 13 diameter enlargement of a neighbor's small son. Shoulda had about 4 seconds more printing time, but it's only a little bit light, and otherwise it's a honey. Detail, and absolutely grainless. Also a 5 X 7 that's 11 diams. Hair sharp and grainless. I'm getting results at last, by God! (I'm also getting 40 cents for the two of 'em by God!)

The one of **Nellie**, I now see as it dries, is even more terrific than I thought. Supreme developed in Edwal-20 will yield a very nice 14 diameter enlargement. Not truly grainless, but you can't see the grain on buff luster paper.

General News department.

Ever hear the tale of the old fellow who had one wooden leg, and wouldn't tell the kids what had happened to the missing one? One day, tired of their pestering, he told 'em he'd tell 'em what happened to it if they'd promise not to ask him any more questions. They promised, and he said, "It was bit off."

Tell **Franny** to think of that one the next time she's tempted to tell someone, "**Frances II** has a black eye." What the hell —.

Peedee has a tooth, at last, and apparently is going to have two practically at once. As you can also see by the pic of **Peeds** enclosed, she has a new highchair. **Aunt Nellie's** been visiting.

632

Kinnison: Coordinator arrived last Wednesday, was read, accepted, and fought over with **Grammer** and **Ralston**. **Smith's** getting what he wanted pretty much — $1,475.00 anyway. It's better than "Gray Lensman" because it's longer but seems shorter. **Rogers** is doing 2 covers, and all inside illustrations for it.

I'm in a mess on Serials now. **van Vogt's** just sent one in — "Recruiting Station," a 2 parter. I know he's hard up, can't stop his job long enough to start writing for lack of money. So, despite the fact I can't use it till next March, I took his yarn. I need novelettes — shorts. **van Vogt** can write 'em if he breaks loose, as he planned. With the cash from this sale, he can. It's a pretty good yarn too, naturally. But to further the mess, **Heinlein's** working on a 2-parter sequel to "Universe."

I shall go nuts.

The SRL article seems to be more or less permanently stalled. I haven't seen the *Esquire* article recently. It seems to have wandered off and died too. *Pic* is setting up that article now; should show up in about 2 weeks.

Incidentally, any time you want some more prints of any pics I have on my rolls, send me one of your copies so I can identify it and I'll look it up. You know what it costs me. I'm spending all my evenings down there — to **Dona's** constant objection — so I might as well do something useful I figure in about another month I'll have my techniques all worked out smoothly, and from then on I'll be able to be happy without spending every evening downstairs. Then I can do some more articles.

Looks like I may get to do one for *National Magazine*, Street & Smith's new competitor for *Liberty/Colliers*. Also atomic power. This one on the angle America has best chance to get it first because **Hitler** and **Mussolini** have sent all the best theorists over here, and we already had the world's best experimentalists in the field. Now we've got everything.

It now being 2:10 A.M., I think I'll turn in.

Regards, John

P.S. I made some 8 X 10 enlargements of a neighbor's small boy Sunday — more of those mentioned above. The neighbor, after seeing the first set, ordered a half dozen of each at two bits apiece. They are really beautiful, absolutely grainless, and as sharp and brilliant as anyone would want in a portrait. One of them is a 13 X enlargement and really is about perfect.

H & B man tells me that Kodachrome in an Argus camera is as good as any 35mm has any need to be. Some local Dr.'s been taking Kodachrome with an Argus for clinical work. H & B man tried to sell him a Leica, since he was using about 3 X the price of the Argus camera per week in Kodachrome film alone. Guy tried out the Leica and brought it back. No sale. The improvement wasn't noticeable. Only advantage was that he could use less light, but light's cheap — particularly daylight. For indoor work he was using flashbulbs anyway, so no saving there, and no point in a bigger lens.

With a big flashbulb you can take Kodachrome in a 50th with the lens stopped down to f 11 or so. Those flashes really give you <u>light</u>.

A.E. van Vogt   *June 11, 1941*

Dear Mr. van Vogt:

One reason I thought I'd send that check on "Recruiting Station" along right away was that I hoped you'd be able to break loose and really do some writing with that cash as a starter. I need "Ptath," need more *Unknown Worlds* writers badly. You can, you know, use up to 50,000 words on *Unknown* lead novels now, since we are going to the large size, carrying about 110,000 words.

The break in "Recruiting Station" will come on Page 67, I think. If you'll write a synopsis for the first part and send it along, it'd help. In doing it, you'd better tie in directly, without the break the direct story shows, to the switch-over from Norma to Garson. Otherwise synopsis readers are going to wonder what the hell they missed. Was there an intervening installment, or what. . . .?

I piked the break rather than the Page 78 break, because the Page 67 point about bisects the yarn. Page 78 would give a long and a too-short installment.

If you're doing an article on the metallurgy of magnesium why not do one for us, too? I'd love it. I've been tearing my hair trying to get some good technical articles on metallurgy -- metallurgy of all the elements wanted. There's room for reams and reams of stuff, and the
634

light metals are particularly interesting. If you can catch hold of some on Beryllium to throw in with the material on Mg, and add some dope on Al, comparing their properties, I think we could nicely absorb 5,000 to 6,000 words on the Light Metals. One angle might be on the queer fact that Li, Mg, Al, Na and Ca are among the softest of metals, as well as the lightest. But Be, in glaring and inexplicable exception, is very light, and extremely hard — steel hard, and steel-like in its resistance to fusion. Yet Be, in the periodic table, is smack between Li and B, just above Mg.

What I'd really like would be a discussion of the thing in a series of such 5,000 word articles. Age-hardening and precipitation hardening — what it is, how it works, the almost miraculous things accomplished by it (such as dural that's soft as wax when first made, and hard, though and strong twenty-eight days later. Such as that dural airplane rivets are made, and popped immediately into dry-ice boxes, where they remain soft until put in place and allowed to warm. Then they become hard and strong.)

But I need "Ptath" more than articles.

Regards, John W. Campbell, Jr.

A.E. van Vogt   *August 25, 1941*

Dear van Vogt:
Enclosed are the two prints I promised. If you're interested, I'll send some more later on. (Probably you'll get 'em anyway, now; an amateur photographer invariably has more prints than he has any legitimate use for.)

The one of my wife — **Dona** — and daughter — **Peedee**, for **Philinda Duane** — was taken about 2 weeks ago; the one of myself was taken by **Dona** last May. (Henceforth I'll leave off the Spanish tilda on her [**Dona**] name, and you can assume its presence.) Despite my mention of the 35mm camera and all the negatives I've taken with it, neither of these was taken on 35mm film. They're enlargements from 9 X 19 centimeter negatives taken with my other box — a Zeiss Icon Maximar, bought second-hand last Christmas as my present to me from **Dona**. The negatives on that cost about 6 cents each developed and fixed and ready for enlarging, vs. the less-than-3/4 cents for the

35mm stuff. But the bigger negatives have a quality of smooth tone-rendering and precision of texture and detail that the 35mm can never approach. On the other hand, the 9 X 12 cm. camera is so clumsy to use, has to be focused so exactly, and is capable of so few shots without reloading, that it's hopeless as a snapshot camera. Every picture has to be taken with the camera on a tripod, lights and subjects arranged, and careful checking that everything is right — before 6 cents goes <u>click</u> in a 25th of a second.

I like a dark print — contrary to most photo-finishers, who tend to print very light, giving rather blank highlights.

The photography has proven a good Scotsman's hobby, however. There are 72 families in our development, and all but about 5 of them have at least one small child; the maximum is four so far, with 2 quite average. I'm the only camera enthusiast out that way, I've practiced enough so I can usually get a fairly acceptable portrait of a child, and the parents, grandparents, aunts, uncles, and cousins to the second-cousin-once-removed stage seem to like pictures. Parents and grandparents get 8 X 10's (40 cents each), aunts, uncles etc. get 5 X 7's (@ 20 cents) usually, and 4 X 5's (@ 5 cents) go to cousins, friends, and scrapbooks. Since my charges for finished prints are about what a drugstore charges for enlargements of their own negatives, and since my camera equipment is a lot better than the usual box-brownie sort of thing, I get a good many orders. But my profits are sufficient to pay not only the cost of the work they want, but also to pay for most of my own film. (An 8 X 10 costs me about 6 cents; the negative from which it was made usually is one of two taken at the time, so costs 12 cents. If they take only one 8 X 10 I come out ahead; usually they want three to five, plus two or three 5 X 7's, plus half a dozen 4 X 5's.)

I took the snaps you sent home last night, as **Dona** had been asking whether I'd gotten them yet for a week or more. Her first comment on seeing them was, "Oh, what a lovely place! Uhmmmm, that garden!" A good 45 seconds later. "He's good looking."

Maple Hill Farms, our development, is, you see, about 6 years old, and it was, before that, a farm. The farmer's great-grand-daddy probably worked very hard indeed getting all the dad-ratted trees outa the way. It was abandoned as a farm largely, I think, because the top soil had washed off the hill into the little dale below. Now the houses in the
636

lower part have nice top-soil, and flood cellars, drowned gardens, and young swamp-maples growing about 15 feet high. We on the hill have dry cellars, good drainage, and from 3/4 of an inch to 4 inches of top soil laid on New Jersey Hardpan, a special type of formation consisting of still unconglomerated New Jersey Red Shale, which may be found about 4 to 8 feet further down. New Jersey Red Shale consists almost solely of complex aluminum-potassium-magnesium-sodium silicates stained a bright rust-red by ferric oxide. (It is, as a matter of fact, almost certainly exactly what the sands of Mars are composed of — the rusted, oxidized remains of mountain ranges gnawed down from their original 30-40,000 foot heights to the present Appalachian and Kittaniny ranges.)The plant-nutrient properties of that stuff compare favorably with a good grade of concrete. The mechanical properties of that "soil" aren't very different either. The standard — and only — way to plant a tree up our way is to dig a 3-foot deep, 5-foot diameter pit with the aid of pick-axes and crow-bars (some of that hardpan is so hard a pick-ax won't work; you have to break it up with a crow-bar), fill the pit with topsoil hauled from somewhere else, and plant the tree therein. Annual fertilizer additions will keep the tree going till its roots have forced their way through the hardpan. Eventually trees can break down even that stuff.

But while hardpan is great stuff for giving a house perfectly solid, non-settling foundations, and giving my photoenlargers, thereby, a foundation that won't vibrate even with the heavy freights now going by, night after night, it makes for peculiar drainage action. Our place drains; its on the hilltop. But water cannot seep into that utterly impervious hardpan; a week of rain, such as we had recently, means that the people lower down in the development get really flooded beyond redemption. The cellar-pumps can't handle it, because the drains they should pump into are so full as to back up two blocks uphill.

So **Dona** liked the looks of your place.

Incidentally, speaking of heavy freights going by — they are. New York City is supplied by nine major railroads, and about half a dozen more minor ones. The one I'm near is one of the majors, but a lesser one. All day the heavy freights slog through on the four-track line carrying fuel — oil and coal. And all night, from about 9 P.M. to about 6 A.M. the super-heavy freights heave and strain along, running on

637

schedules that don't leave more than about two signal-blocks headway between 'em. Freights so heavy the engines start slipping their wheels about once every four minutes or so. And those night freights do <u>not</u> carry fuel.

The road we're near — a mile and a half — is, as I say, one of the smaller of the major roads, but I can't guess at the tonnage of heavy freight they're moving down to the docks. It's stupendous, though, I know that.

The extra-special heavy work comes in waves. For a week or more the night freights will be more-or-less ordinary things that just roll through with the usual dull, distant rumble. Then the heavy, labored slogging of the super-heavies will start again, running close together, night after night, all night long. That means a convoy has gone out and cleared space on the docks for more freight to be moved in. I strongly suspect that there's no exact correlation in time; anybody within 50 miles of New York in any direction can hear one railroad or another straining under the weight of tanks, guns, shells, plane engines, foods and equipment.

It's a nice sound in the nights, these days. It's the world's heaviest railroad system — as much bigger than Germany's as our greater population multiplied by our higher standard of living — and it's staggering under the loads their hauling.

Regards, John

A.E. van Vogt *September 10, 1941*

Dear van Vogt:

The office is in a bit of a dither at the moment, so this is going out in my personal high-speed, high-inaccuracy typing. It'll be reasonably legible, I hope — .

The Ezwal story was taken, and a check sent out several days ago; I don't know which ending I'll use, as I'll want to check over the differences, and motivations in each. What was your point in making the change; think a cruiser-full of the Rull's would be too much for the Rytt plant to get? I'm going to add one other item though; the prof. and Ezwal have succeeded in getting hold of an undamaged, perfect Rull lifeship, containing the perfected antigravity, as well as getting away from the planet. Presumably the first time that's been accomplished, by reason of the total destruction consequent to subduing any spaceship.

But the above-mentioned dither comes about this way: *Astounding* is going to the large, flat size of *Unknown*, with 128 pages and containing about 40,000 words an issue more. Your time story will, in consequence, be gobbled up as a short novel in one issue, instead of being a short serial. I'll be using fo[u]r novelettes an issue, probably, as well as short stories. The increase in wordage is very comfortable — and in a monthly, that's a half million words a year extra.

And to add to the pressure, **Bob Heinlein** has decided he'd like to retire, and is going to practically stop writing. Inasmuch as he was, also, **Anson MacDonald** and **Caleb Saunders**, that will make something of a hole in the supply main. I need, in other words, more material, and hurriedly. Since you were a newspaperman, and had training in production of literary material, and have shown an ability to do work on the same high level **Heinlein** maintained, I'm hoping you will be able, now, to help fill the decided gap.

Present most immediate needs are: a novel for *Unknown*, and novelettes for *Unknown*. Short stories for *Astounding*, and, in about a month, novelettes for *Astounding*. If you want to develop a pen-name, we can absorb $200 to $300 worth a month from you in the two magazines. That being a year-round average.

Regards, John W. Campbell

Robert Swisher *April 14, 1942*

Dear Bob:
You can fumigate this letter before reading if you wish, but I think my index of infectiveness has dropped pretty well by now. I'm recuperating from influenza, and feeling that **Peedee** could take me two falls out of three in a wrestling match. I think **van Vogt** must have been personifying the flu when he described the vampirism of the dreegah. Gawd, the damn stuff drains you. I've now had it 9 days; the cold-like part is practically gone — no sneezing, coughing, or anything.

But the fact that I'm home with flu, that the **Heinleins** have shoved off for a week in New York, now that **Leslyn** is recovered from her gallbladderectomy, and that **Dona** doesn't dare let me take care of

639

Peedee means that I have a chance to do some lettering. For the last two months I have been sort of busy. Keeping novels etc. for the magazines coming in, what with most of my top writers drained off into the armed forces, has kept me busy when the **Heinlein's** didn't. I've finally gotten *Unknown* so nicely set up that I can relax a bit. A novel from **Bester**, one from **Heinlein** on hand; one from **Leiber** and one from **van Vogt** seen in draft of the first parts, and one or two more in the talk-about stage.

Herewith is a collection of prints of various subjects. I've really had some fun with infra-red film, and suggest that you try some soon. With a good heavy red filter you can get fair cloud effects if the air is exceptionally bright and clear — but in this part of the world, the air is so muggy and hazy that it takes infrared to give a decent cloud rendering. The heaviest red filters that are supposed to heavily overcorrect the sky, are only able to give a very faint cloud rendering in the northeast here. Out in the southwest a light yellow filter comes out right; here anything lighter than dark red Wratten A is a waste of time.

In the contact prints of the snowscenes — #s 1 and 2 — I was photographing early in the morning after a heavy, sticky snow — it was entirely off the trees in another 45 mins, gone completely by that evening. The sky was crystal clear, with a few high, light clouds. #1, infra-red with Wratten A filter gives a correct rendition of the subject — the trees were all mantled with sticky white snow; the deep blue sky made a sharp and beautiful contrast background.

#2 — panchromatic film with Wratten A — lost a good bit of that contrast and the spectacular appearance, though it rendered the trees themselves somewhat better.

#3 was taken with the Perfex at the same time, using Super X and Wratten A. It did very well, really. #3 print is overprinted intentionally to produce a night effect; the paper was fogged from standing around some 5 months in a not 100% light-tite box. #4 is a straight print of the same; the clouds were much more visible to the eye.

#5 is a Super XX shot with Wratten A taken some while back; the clouds are just about correctly shown — yet that filter is supposed to give black skies and heavily overcorrected skies.

#6 shows practically no clouds; the day was a bit grayish, but if the Wratten A did what it is supposed to do — and does in the rest of the
640

world — **Charlie** would have had a nice background of clouds. **Charlie** stopped in, as you see, while on his way from Plattsburg to Baltimore. #7 shows that **Charles** has not gotten any more heavy-minded than he was. #8 is a contact and #9 an enlargement of a set-up we made that turned out pretty nicely I think. The "letter from home" happens to be from you to me, but it looks good.

#10 is a portrait of **Bob Heinlein** that satisfied all concerned; — it's about what he actually looks like.

#11 is what **Leslyn Heinlein** does not look like. She was about to go to the horsepistol for her — ectomy, and was neither feeling nor looking well. Furthermore, that camera can, when it chooses, be cruel. It chose. It has a resolving power approximately 7 times that of the human eye when the eye's at its best. It can exaggerate color contrast in a savage way, and dwells lovingly on skin defects. But this is the only shot of **Leslyn** I have, and it gives some vague idea of what she looks like.

#12 is a flash shot of **Peeds** playing hard-to-hold with **Bob**. The intensity of flashbulbs — even the cheap little #5s — is indicated by the fact that my home-made synchronizer opens the shutter for 1/5th second, while the flash lasts 1/50th or so. Yet the 75 watt mazda burning in the lamp in the picture is not overexposed, and the lampshade, you'll notice, is not as heavily exposed as the white door. #13 and 14 were flash shots, too. #13 was shot at f 32 — a companion shot taken at the same time, one of which I have no available print (they're all glued down), was even better, and made a lovely 8 X 10. The trick of getting good results with single flash bulbs is, I find, to direct the light both at the subject, and at a large light colored wall or reflector area on the other side of the subject. Notice the very nice modeling and the soft shadows the system produced in #13. In #14 I couldn't get that arrangement, and the results aren't as satisfactory.

I don't know whether I sent you a print of #15 or not; it was taken by daylight, and is one of the best shots I've gotten, I think. Generally speaking, the 9 X 12 cm job isn't satisfactory for snapshots; it's too big and hard to set up, has too critical a depth of focus, and is clumsy. I'm always tempted to use it, though, because of the sharpness and quality of a print that is in focus. #16 shows one fairly successful attempt to use it as a snapbox. Despite the small proportion of the negative area occupied by the subjects, you'll find that they're actually larger than could have been managed on a 35mm film.

But for real snapshooting, the 35mm box can not be beat — it's the one and only way to get such lovely shots as #16-A -- taken some while back while **Peeds** was still crawling, and couldn't do so well in her long nightgowns. Technically, it's a lousy picture. But you couldn't catch that at all with anything but 35mm. #s 17, 18, and 19 come under the same general heading.

I don't know whether you ever met my sister, or whether I ever sent you any pics of her. #20 shows her holding **Peeds**, as seen by 35mm; #21 is by the 9 X 12.

#22 is **Willy** and his new **Olga** — taken the first time they came out. They look comfortable together, which promises **Willy** may have better luck this time than last. Having **Olga** around has been a help to him since De. 7. #23 is a not-too-successful print from a not-so-hot 9 X 12 negative of **Willy**. **Willy** has a peculiarity; when he shifts his point of vision, his right eye gets there before his left; if you snapshoot him too quickly, you may, as in #23, find the two eyes looking two different ways. #24 is a somewhat better pic; trouble is **Willy's** beard is black, and Super XX in that 9 X 12 will honest-to-god see things. The little number "3" at the bottom of that print means that it was the third frame of a dozen in a film pack. #25 is the "6" of that particular pack, and #26 the "9". I'm working on the negative of #25 — trying to make an enlargement of **Lyman's** head without **Kay's**. I made a direct positive of the negative, and Farmer's Rececere d [sic] the rest of the negative copy out. #27 was taken the same day; it's most of **Sprague's** model navy; he's made about four times as many models, but the others are the U.S. Navy's model navy now. The navy wanted recognition models of US ships and British ships, so that air pilots could be trained not to bomb US and British ships. **Sprague**, incidentally, is now in Florida, recovering from whoooping cough; he got enlarged bronchia from his whooops, and the Navy turned him down till the said tubes shrank back to normal.

#28 was inspired by your pic of the aurora; I got a much better one, as you see, only the foreground wasn't low enough so the sunset shows too much. This was red filtered, 1/5th at f 2.8, hand-held. The best I got at 1/2 sec, f 2.8. That sunset was really set; when it takes half a second on Super XX at F 2.8, red filter or no, the light's getting dimmish.

I hope you can get down this way again sometime — though it looks now, as though it might be quite a time. I'd like to have you see the ultra-doopered darkroom I've worked up. There are nine switches of various types, plus three plug-in choices on the electrical equipment. I'm preparing to install one more switch and associated gadget — a spotlight over the hypo tray so that I can turn a white light on the finished prints without ruining prints still in the developer. If the beam is made sharp enough and weak enough that should be possible. I think I can do it with some dime-store reading glasses and an automobile tail-light bulb. My bench is now wired for 110 A.C., 150 D.C. and 6 volt A.C. I'll add 6 volt D.C. if I find I need it — the equipment is on hand. The 6 volt A.C. is wired direct from the house mains — the bell-ringing transformer is very conveniently located, and supplies all the 6 volt current I need for throwing relays and lighting automobile taillight size bulbs. 110 A.C. of course. The 150 D.C. is available from the rectifier unit built into the automatic enlarger timer — 150 being what you get when you rectify and smooth out 110 A.C.

In addition to the enlarger timer, I have a minute timer that will either flash a light or sound a high-power growler at 60 second intervals. It can be put into operation either by throwing a tumbler switch that makes it run continuously, growling or flashing at minute intervals, or you can press a bell-push that throws a relay which turns it on. In the course of 30 seconds or so the clock motor inside kicks out the relay, continuing to turn because a commutator ring carries current to the clock motor. At the end of 60 seconds, it flashes the light, and simultaneously reaches the end of the commutator bar, shutting itself off completely. Pressing the bell push will again throw in the relay long enough for the commutator dead section to pass.

I'm using D-72 print developer, which completely develops ordinary print paper in 60 seconds, so I just hit the bell push when I throw in the print, and when the light — a 7-1/2 watt yellow safelight bulb — flashes on I can take the print out, and have the timer ready for another cycle. When I'm developing film, the 9 X 12 films, that is, I have to work in total darkness part of the time — the only way to agitate the film being to raise and lower the film holders in the solution by hand. For that purpose, I need a minute timer that makes an audible signal — one

643

audible enough to hear even when I have water running and the oil burner is blasting away. A switch cuts in the growler.

D-72, incidentally, seems to do just as good a job as 55-D, and does it in half the time. The only objection I have to the stuff is that it tends to deposit muck on standing, and tends to stain the tray used for developing. By using a two-quart bottle of print developer as my working solution, I don't have to pour the whole quantity into the tray, and the muck is simply left in the bottom of the bottle. The stain comes out with $KCrO_4$ & mild H_2SO_4 plus a little Bon Ami.

The enlarger I made for the big camera consists of a light box with diffusion glass onto which I clamp the camera itself, with the film-holder back removed. The light-box is mounted on the ceiling of the cellar by a trick one-bolt-and-two-pins arrangement that makes it absolutely solid, but which permits it to be taken down in a few minutes for replacement of the bulb. The bulb I'm using now is a 150 watt reflector Mazda — like a reflector #2 photoflood only a 150 watt standard filament. I have a ground-glass diffuser in it, and get nice, even illumination. But — the damned thing is slow. It takes usually 15 to 30 seconds printing for a 5 X 7, and for a really big enlargement — an 8 X 10 from 1/4 of a negative, say — it may run into 2 or 3 minutes. I'd like condensers, but condenser lenses for that size box cost about $10. By comparison, the 35 mm enlarger, using a little 40 watt automobile headlight bulb, makes a 15 by 24 projection that'll print in 45 seconds. It uses condensers.

Incidentally, I developed some Tri-X pan in Agfa 47 — a high-speed, high-power developer used on an ultra-fast and grainy film. D-76 requires 20 mins; Agfa 47 only 8 to 9. I made a 6 X enlargement on Velour Black B surface — the same as "A" but in double-weight — 8 X 10 size of **Peedee's** head and shoulders. Grain was only barely detectable by close scrutiny of someone who knew what to look for. I shouldn't be surprised if 35mm film could be developed safely and satisfactorily in Agfa 47 — Super XX doesn't have anywhere near the grain Tri-X pan does. Eastman says of Super XX — "Will stand considerable enlargement without noticeable grain" — and of Tri-X Pan — "may be enlarged somewhat without noticeable grain." Agfa 47 is nice stuff to work with — it's clean (no deposit of muck) quick (6-9 mins) gives full and complete tone range with very smooth gradations
644

— see print #10 of **Bob Heinlein** — and maximum emulsion speed. I've completely quit using D-76; that stuff, like D-72, has a bad habit of depositing tiny crystals that get on the film in development and make nasty little black measles.

Oh — the big enlarger does not have an adjustable head — the table moves up and down on a pair of 1-1/2 inch pipes instead. Two C clamps mounted on the table clamp it at the desired height.

Item: the next time you have a cold, don't get ephedrine nose drops. If you haven't happened to have some one introduce you to 'em before, get 1/4% neosynephrine drops. They come in an isotonic solution, have all the effect of ephedrine, and don't burn the nose at all. Even **Peeds** takes 'em without protest. They make a 1% sol. for adults, but **Dr. Lutz** says he's found the 1/4% practically as effective as 1%, and it costs less. (**Lutzie's** a swell doc — he doesn't go by the books and the ads alone. Even if a guy has all the classic symptoms of maladay A, he gives a complete check to make sure that he doesn't also have some extra symptoms that aren't maladay A. He's been out of his internship 5 years now, and he isn't taking on any new patients — too busy!)

I'm making up — gradually — a series of 4 X 5 prints of **Peedee**. The first was taken with the old folding Kodak before we got the Perfex. Thereafter, I'm selecting good prints of **Peeds** at 1-month intervals, and mounting 'em in series, so you can get direct comparison. Have you tried making direct comparisons like that at month intervals on **F II**? It's kinda startling, I find.

Franny broke the secret on the sex of the twins; maybe now we can find out what their names are? Modern medicine being what it is, I imagine you mustsa known what was up some months ago. Hope you had the forethought to buy your stuff at one of those double-if-double baby supply places. Hmmmm — reminds me you had two cribs. Kinda lucky — but your baby carriage won't be much good. What does **F II** think of the situation?

The **Heinleins** have fallen in love with **Peeds**, apparently. She started making eyes at **Bob** the first day he arrived, and has been working on him ever since. She's been flirting with **Leslyn** very effectively, too, and has 'em both fetching and carrying for her. She won't talk — so far has seen no need for it, as far as I can make out. She can point and roll

645

her eyes with marvelous efficiency.

But the result of all the attention has been wonderful to behold. She likes the boys. **Bob** is hers, her exclusive slave and attendant. The other night he and **Leslyn** curled up in the same chair, and hey, presto! there was **Peeds** tugging at **Leslyn's** hand and making annoyed sounds. **Leslyn** let her lead her away, and **Peeds** deposited her on the couch, and went over and climbed in **Bob's** lap herself. So **Dona** came over and sat in my lap. **Peeds** was over in about 15 seconds, pulling at **Dona's** hand, and presently having deposited **Dona** safely, came back to me herself.

When **Peeds** is taken for a walk through the settlement — called, among its friends, Pregnancy Plaz or Reproduction Row, for cause — she gets distinctly annoyed when the adults with her stop to talk to and admire other children. We're her property.

Peeds, incidentally, is a formalist at heart. When the warm weather started, she was distinctly upset. She loves to go out, and has, for a month or more — since she could walk rapidly and easily — made her desire clear by going after her red windproof suit and dragging it over to the handiest adult while saying very distinctly in her own language, if not in English, that she felt it was time to take a walk. It confused her no end when we first took her out without the equipment; she went back in in a worried manner and got the playsuit and brought it over to be put on. She knew what was what even if we forgot.

Also, when put in her chair for supper, there's no progress made till her bib is properly attached. Given food and properly seated, she points to her bib and very clearly states her desire to be properly equipped.

She's adopted the lowest stair of the steps going upstairs as her particular favorite perch, despite having been given a chair of her own. It isn't quite the right height; the stair is.

Incidentally, when she first learned to walk, after taking about a dozen steps by herself and realizing she could do it, there was no more of that crawling business for her; she was a walker. She made the complete transition from all crawling to all walking in two days. She fell flat about every dozen steps for the next few days, but she wasn't going to put up with any more babyish crawling. Came the real difficulty. She'd been going up and down stairs for months; but she did it crawling. She decided flatly that she wasn't having any more; she walked, not crawled, so she'd walk down stairs. We had a hell of a time keeping track of her and convincing her that she could <u>not</u> walk down stairs.

When she does start to talk, I bet we have a high old time with her; she talks a blue streak in her own language now. So far, everything she's done, she's done whole-hog once she found out she could do it at all. I suspect she'll try to talk in the same way, and run into the unutterable stupidity of those adults who just <u>won't</u> understand her, no matter how clearly she states her mind.

And she has a mind of her own; man does she though!

Incidentally: will you send me a few of your good prints? To date you've stated they were unsuccessful prints, and I'd like to see some of your late good ones of the whole family. Would you like me to get you a paper-holder for your printing table? They make a tricky one that looks good. It has a metal plate with infolded edges that make the side margins, and opening at one end, and a metal slide at the other carrying a bent-over metal edge that makes the fourth margin. It's five inches wide, and the slide makes it adjustable from 3-1/2 X 5 through 4 X 5 to 5 X 7, and gives you clean, even margins all round. Costs about $1.50 I believe. The 3-1/2 X 5 size means you use 1/2 5 X 7s. It actually approaches closer to the proportions of the 35mm negative frame.

Recent decisions of policy: DL paper does better, even in 4 X 5s for 35 mm stuff. Kodabromide paper has a surface very similar to DL in texture of surface, but with slightly more gloss that does even better. The DL type surface gives you better tone rendering for 35 mm stuff. In 5 X 7 size, the B surface is better than the A — the doubleweight gives a more substantial picture that flattens out better. See the two 5 X 7s enclosed. DL 5 X 7s would be the dish for 35mm enlargements. A 5 X 7 enlargement from 9 X 12 cm. negatives is only about 1-1/2 to 2 X enlargement, and looks nice on B. Agfa's Royal White or Kashmir White is somewhat better than Velour Black DL but harder to get. Kodabromide has a similar surface, which is fairly available, has the same paper speed as Velour Black, and is somewhat preferable.

The ring-marks on glossy prints can be eliminated if the print is held down on the ferrotype tin by some means until drying is completely finished. The pressure doesn't have to amount to much, but

647

must be applied by some means that permits the escape of water vapor. I'm using a piece of corrugated cardboard at present. Prints #1 and 2 were dried that way; #5 without the cover. I put two hardwood maple sticks across the cardboard — just anything handy that weighs a couple pounds and will distribute the weight.

That seems to be everything handy in the way of news, remarks and suggestions.

And now, b'god, you owe me a letter.

Regards, John

A.E. van Vogt   *June 12, 1942*

Dear van Vogt:

Recently I've been pretty well occupied, and have had to confine most of my remarks to you to those put on that pretty pale-green paper the business office makes out. I'll try to catch up a little more fully.

On the general subject of bouncing manuscripts, I might say that I've been writer long enough myself to know that no human being can maintain perfection, or even a reasonable facsimile thereof, for any extended period of time. If you didn't have an occasional slump, I'd be inclined to believe that "**van Vogt**" was a pen-name for a literary factory — one of those combines where half a dozen authors work together, A getting an idea, B developing a plot, C working out the rough draft with incidents, D developing the conversation and characters, and E doing final writing, while F specializes in sticking in love scenes, fist-fights and scientific double-talk as the occasion demands.

To date, I believe **Bob Heinlein** is the only science-fiction writer who has a record of 100% sales of everything he ever turned out. He did it by using a string of pen-names, and selling his slump-stuff to progressively lower markets under progressively more secret pen-names. He doesn't like rewriting. If you are, like myself, an incident-and-idea salvager, you'll eventually use up those ideas in other stories. If not, you could revamp 'em a bit, stick on a pen-name, and try them on the other books. Some one, in the present state of the magazine market, is sure to be willing to publish them under some pen-name, even if the payment doesn't exceed the lawyer's fees necessary to collect from the publisher. On the other hand, several of the other books — *Amazing*,

648

Thrilling Wonder, *Planet* and others, I understand — pay very decently, both as to rates and willingness, though none quite as promptly as Street & Smith. We have for several years made a special point of getting out checks in full payment more quickly than most houses get out a letter of intent to buy.

Unknown is still chock-a-block on all lengths save novels; at the moment, I have the novel necessary for the issue in sight, but I'll be needing one before very long.

Astounding is quite badly in need of a serial; it will be more than half a year since the end of "Beyond This Horizon" before we can, because of issues now made up, have another novel. I don't particularly like that, but the capacious maw of the large-size mag swallows anything shorter than 40,000 words in one bit. If you've got anything of 45,000 to 60,000 words on the schedule, we can use it.

"Weapon Shop" was, like much of your material, good without any detectable reason for being interesting. Technically, it doesn't have plot, it starts nowhere in particular, wanders about, and comes out in another completely indeterminate place. But, like a park path, it's a nice little walk. I liked it, as you may have gathered from the 25% extra.

I'm genuinely trying to divert the stream of science-fiction a bit, and you, **del Rey**, and one or possibly two others are the best bets as to authors capable of making the change felt. **Heinlein's** out of the business; he's not at sea, but excessively busy on some work so damned fascinating I wish he could discuss it more fully, and that I could pass on what little I know. **Asimov**, **de Camp** and I myself am engaged in the same work to varying degrees; I, because I'm on it only part time, least of all.

But what I'm trying to do in science-fiction is to turn it away from the hard, rather brittle practicality of some of the best of the stories of the last year or two. Up to 1940, science-fiction rather badly needed some more solid background stuff — something small-scale, material taking a close-up look at a technical civilization that used the inventions of science-fiction not for the first time, but as work-a-day tools of industry. Where the atomic generator wasn't the new and wonderful discovery of Prof. Quzxyktl, who immediately applied it to his spaceship and sailed for Mars, but the common draft-horse of heavy industry.

Where atomic engineers got paid an hourly wage or a monthly salary, instead of having as their payment wild and wooly adventures.

Now, that background has been filled in solidly enough so that all the current writers and readers have some idea of what an atom-powered civilization means — that not all atomic engineers spend their lives patching up meteor-smashed atom-burners on experimental Mars-bound space-cans.

(You can always tell when I really get rolling on a typewriter; the letters start coming out at odd intervals. I use the Columbus system of typing — hunt and discover — as I learned to type by typing my first yarn for the old *Amazing*.)

With that background fairly solid now, I think it is time to go back to the explorers, the first invaders of space. They'll leave behind them a world with technical resources adequate to support and sustain an atomic-powered spaceship, and with industrial potential — and pressure — high enough to overflow into interplanetary space.

Philosophical problem: Can a socio-technical pressure-potential be determined in terms of some type of arbitrary unit on an arbitrary scale such that by it, the overflow-point of a civilization can be pre-determined, and the type of overflow predicted? That is, **Ericson** discovered America sometime previous to 1000 A.D. — but nothing happened. The socio-technical pressures of Europe were not high enough to drive out a sufficient number of people to found a colony, and the technical means to maintain transoceanic colonies were not at hand. In the latter part of the 15th century they were, so Europe overflowed to America. For a long time, the socio-technical pressures were so low on the North American continent that Europeans remained on the Eastern seaboard only, practically speaking, and the colonies remained colonies. Then the pressures built up, first reaching the point where independence of action was necessary, particularly to those colonies where the pressures were highest — the original United States — while other colonies, where natural conditions hadn't been so favorable to the accumulation of pressures — Canada — remained colonies. As time passed, Canada required and obtained, its freedom of action, while the pressures here produced the Western overflow.

Socio-technical pressures after the war will be, for some time, directed toward rebuilding Europe, but with atomic technology coming
650

in, and the immense population now available, that job will be effectively completed within 5 years. The time for interplanetary overflow will be at hand. First explorers, then colonies, then — the old cycle over again. Eventually, someday in the not-too-remote future, there will be overflow toward other stellar systems. The overflow will probably be directly from Earth, not from the other Solar planets. Earth will always develop the highest pressures; man is ideally adapted to this planet, and is bound to breed and work best here. The pressure will be for the discovery of other stellar planets more nearly identical to Earth in climate.

I want material laid in the periods of over-flow — either the exploratory, or very early colonization periods — the romantic type of daring-do that characterized, but badly and baldly characterized, the early days of science-fiction. I want hard-boiled idealists who don't know they're courageous. Men who, for $500 a month (they think) are doing the impossible, and cursing the job they love and are tackling because no higher pleasure is possible for them, in fact.

Incidentally, the time scale: Science-fiction tends to go very wrong on time-scale, because authors and readers in the field are very timid about it all. I'm betting on a first landing on the Moon by 1965 at the latest, Mars by 1970, Venus at or about the same time. There will be a scientific colony on the Moon from 1965 to 1970, consisting of astronomers, solar specialists, and electronics and atomic engineers. There will probably be some research chemists, and some map specialists too, the chemists working on projects more readily conducted under conditions of total vacuum and low temperature.

By 1980, there will probably be some manufacturing specialties conducted on the moon, particularly fine chemicals, and, quite possibly, the production of extremely dangerous atomic products, or atomic products whose gaseous by-products are difficult to control and extremely poisonous. There may or may not be a spaceship on the Moon then; eventually there will be, as special Martian carriers shuttle between the Moon and Mars, escaping the severely limiting gravitational field of Earth. (Structure can be made much lighter if the ship never encounters field intensities greater than 0.4 gravities.)

Exploration into the asteroids will be undertaken before 1980, and an observation station may be established on one of the major plane-

651

toids by that date. Atomic physicists and some astronomers will be in charge — mainly atomic physicists. Special ships will be sent out from that base on the dangerous mission of seeking out contraterrene matter for capture and study.

I'm personally quite genuinely convinced that the rate of progress is far, far faster than even the bolder science-fictionists imagine. One item in your "Weapon Shop" that I doubt like blazes is the suggestion that the vibratory transmission process was discovered 3000 years before the story, and has not been duplicated in that time. When socio-technical pressures reach a certain tension, certain inventions pop out somewhere almost automatically. The discovery of electric currents from batteries forced the discovery of electromagnetism which forced the discovery of the dynamo, which forced the discovery of the motor. The existence of quantities of electric power forced the discovery of the electric arc-light, and social pressures demanded the "subdivision of the electric light" as it was called then. **Edison** happened to be the man that did it, but he did it, remember, on a perfectly simple basis: there must be an answer, and if we try enough things we'll find it. Anyone could have done the same — it was just a matter of someone doing what the technical demands of the time obviously called for. The discovery of the process for extracting aluminum is another perfect example — there was a demand for it, and two men developed the answer independently and simultaneously.

Now, with the idea of planned search for a scientific instrument to 'fil a pre-conceived need firmly established, the inventions will come as the needs arrive.

Escape from the Solar System to other systems may take a couple centuries — it may be done in one more. I doubt that it will take much more than two and a half. Given travel to the planets, and the unsatisfactory environment they represent to man, plus the desires to reach other and satisfactory planets, the method will be developed as sure as fate.

Hmmmm — idea. In 1993, Mr. A, great space-ship engineer, builds a ship to reach Centaurus by simply plowing ahead while he and the crew are under suspended animation, a process developed by an M.D. who's going along. They set out, go into suspension, and, 500 years later plow into the system of Centaurus, to be awakened by automatic devices.

They take over, make for a nearby planet, and discover it is an inhabited, highly evolved world. They can see immense cities bigger than any on Earth, finer cities. It's an Earth-like world, with more land-to-water than Earth, but green over most of its area. They approach, and spaceships of an advanced and wonderful design appear, and from them men come over to investigate them.

They're men — humans. They're natives of the planet — their people have been for the last three centuries since the first colonists came from Earth by the Donaldson drive. The explorers have been expected for the last 50 years or so. They're given quite a welcome, shown around the museums, their ship installed in one, and are returned to Earth about a week later. Trip takes about 3 hours. "Have you checked every factor involved in this trip?" asks the Doc of the engineer before they started. "Every one. We'll make it, and get back successfully — the first men on Centaurus." But he overlooked the factor of human progress.

After he got over being a curiosity, I wonder what they'd do for a living? **Archimedes** wouldn't be much of a scientist if planted here today, and scientific progress is exponential — with a high-value exponent. Maybe that exponent is, itself, exponential.

There are plenty of romantic exploration stories to be told, really good ones really well told, as they weren't in the early days of science-fiction. And they don't, by any means, have to be technical comedy; tragedy is frequently more impressive.

Re the size of cities on a colony world 300 years old: New England was first settled just a few years more than 300 years back, and for the first 150 years was consciously strangled, kept from growing too strong, by the mother country.

But immediately, I need novels pretty badly, rather than novelettes or shorts.

Regards, John W. Campbell, Jr.

A.E. Van Vogt   *August 24, 1942*

Dear Van Vogt:

The promised shot of myself is not enclosed, because the only print I happen to have in the office today is a contact print (under-exposed) of a nice infra-red negative of some clouds and woodlands. I'll send the picture of myself in a day or so, when my highly unreliable memory makes me think of it. I've got a series of prints from the desired negative at home — my hobby being what it is. Also, since you were kind enough to include some shots of the rest of your family — or is that all the rest? — I'll see if I can find a good one of mine. My small daughter is photogenic, age 2, and a camera-hog already. If she sees the camera around she laughs, grins, and runs around in front of it to pose; she's had her picture snapped on the average of 3 negatives a day since she came home. (Using 35mm film, the negatives cost less than 3/4 cents apiece, finished and ready for the enlarger. Normal practice is to take half a dozen shots at a time, getting a high chance of securing a satisfactory pose and expression. Hence the large number of negatives.)

Incidentally, I judge you're around 6 feet, weigh around 180? The shot you'll get is a head-and-shoulders portrait my wife snapped for me; I'm 6'1", 225#.

That navy research program I can't crash the gate on is a very unusual set-up in any governmental organization — probably unique in the world for the degree of imagination applied in its creation. The imagination was not supplied by governmental organization, but somewhat in spite of it. The man in charge of the whole set-up is a regular line Navy officer, a Lt. Commander, with flying rating, who did all the right things in Navy tradition. Annapolis, fleet service, carrier service, flying service, passed his examinations for advancement, etc. On his last exam for advancement, one question posed was to describe possible weapons for the next 30 years. He went to town, did an impressive job, and the Navy, partly on the basis of that, set him where he is.

Now the secret of that lies herein; he's an old-time, long-experienced science-fiction reader and would-have-written-if-he-just-had-time man. His discussion of 30-year-hence weapons was based on a long consideration of science-fiction, integrated with a wide and sound naval experience. It was good, because he was good, and had had a well-schooled imagination.

He's in charge of the project. He's been out gunning, specifically, for *Astounding* authors and readers who have engineering degrees, and can, thereby, get by the Civil Service commission. That's why such an astonishingly high percentage of *Astounding's* top-flight authors have been vanishing into the Navy; there's one navy department that is literally specifically trying to catch *Astounding's* top-flight authors! They've not only got **Heinlein-MacDonald-Riverside-Saunders-Munroe**, which is bad enough from the magazine's point of view, considering the quantity and quality he turned out, but also **de Camp**, **Asimov** and **Hubbard**. They're getting **R.S. Richardson** into another department, incidentally, and **Hal Clement**, as I said, goes to the Army Air force. (He's an astronomer too; they want navigators. You're doing a nice job of cruising when you take a Flying Fortress from a mid-ocean dot like Midway 1800 miles out to sea, hit another mid-ocean dot, and come home to Midway without swimming the last few miles for lack of gasoline.)

By the way, speaking of Flying Fortresses, I wonder if Canadians have gotten the same sort of cross-talk confusion in their papers that we have? "The British don't like Flying Fortresses because they're too slow, carry too little, and are too lightly armed and armored for use over Germany." Then, "It's all a mistake." That statement was put out by an uninformed British aviation writer and does not express at all the opinion of the RAF." The RAF never uses the Flying Fortress for raiding. But we've been using it about a dozen times, and, to date, the far-famed Luftwaffe hasn't been able to down a single one, even when attacking with their super-dooper publicized Focke-Wulf 190's. All they've done is had their pet pursuit planes knocked down. And there's an item in today's paper about a Flying Fortress pilot that finally got mad at a Jap Zero pilot who hung off out of range and played games. The fortress pilot took off after the Zero, started dogfighting the pursuit ship, and downed the Nip! Wonder what the Nip thought when a four-motored bomber started after him doing wing-overs and loops?

Another item of newspaper news-slanting that amused me, and seems to have annoyed the British, was the handling of the Dieppe raid. The headlines here were on the order of, "U.S. And British Land In France," and, "U.S. Rangers Attack At Dieppe." Inasmuch as the following story explained that a "detachment of a battalion of U.S. Rangers" had gone along, the headlines were slightly askew. I suspect the English papers headlined it "Commandos Land At Dieppe" — also askew, inasmuch as the force seems to have been about 85% Canadian.

As a matter of fact — changing subject somewhat, but not too much, at that — I got a number of letters saying that the reader wasn't interested in reading about Nazis. That pure entertainment didn't bring the nasty word into his mind; that he read to get away from the whole damned subject for a while. "My Name Is Legion" ran into the same trouble, but to a somewhat lesser degree, because, at the outset the author showed definitely that **Hitler** was really going to be done in, and done up brown on the way through. A point I'll bear in mind henceforth.

Incidentally — wonder if you couldn't have some fun in your stories of the future, by having some character, at appropriate moments, refer vaguely to the historical and repellantly atrocious punishment visited on the defeated Nazis. Something — unmentioned in detail — so appalling that it acts as a deterrent to all would-be dictators for a thousand years to come. Inasmuch as it will probably be the Russians who finally got at **Hitler,** the punishment might have been the unauthorized and original imaginative devising of some single Russian officer. If vague references to that end appeared scattered in half a dozen different stories, the readers would, I can assure you, notice, remember, and probably write asking you just what in hell the Russian officer did do to the Nazi High Command. Or it could be simply an "officer of the United Nations." Perhaps something suggesting, "it was nearly two centuries before legal processes got around to ending the Nazi High Command after that" would titillate imaginations.

We'll use the pen-name **Dean M. Hull** on your stuff. I have in mind running, probably in the December issue, "The Flight That Failed" under that name.

Regards, John W. Campbell, Jr.

P.S. I just now discovered you'ld put notes on the back of the prints. My guess on your height and weight seems to have been fairly close, at that. And the other question is also answered.

A.E. van Vogt   *October 15, 1942*

Dear van Vogt:

Before I forget to mention it, there's a book coming out soon that I think you'll want to get — if they permit importation of books into Canada. It's called *Rocket To The Morgue*, a mystery novel by "**H.H. Holmes**" — who is **Wm. A.P. White**, who writes, also, under the name **Anthony Boucher**. I don't know whether you know about the Manana Literary Society or not. Anyway, it was a group of science-fiction and fantasy authors in and around Hollywood-Los Angeles area which **Bob Heinlein** more or less semi-organized as a way of getting new authors for me. He was a big help; through that loose, really 90% social group he found and got started into fantasy-science-fiction for me **Anthony Boucher** himself, **Cleve Cartmill**, **Roby Wentz** and one or two others. The group worked over **Hank Kuttner** 'til he turned into **Lewis Padgett**, a damnsite better author. **Ed Hamilton**, **Jack Williamson**, **L. Ron Hubbard** and **Julius Schwartz**, author's agent in the science-fiction field, were all members. The thing sort of broke up after Dec. 7 because so many went elsewhere.

Rocket To The Morgue is laid in that Manana Literary Society. (Incidentally, the club name was adopted because they were always talking about the yarn they were going to write — tomorrow. When anybody actually was at work on a story, he was said to have moved into the Hoy Division of the Manana Literary Society.) All but two or three of the characters in the book are based on the members of the group, they are science-fiction-fantasy writers in the story, and the motivation of the book is science-fiction writing. I'm in it off-stage; the editor the characters all sell their material to is named **Don Stuart**. One or two of the characters are actually blends of two or more real people, but most are direct, and quite accurate descriptions of the real writers. **Austin Carter** is **Bob Heinlein**, sketched very accurately. The detective of the story is **A.P. White** himself — and his family — although **A.P.** wanders in and out of the yarn also as **Tony Boucher**. **Joe Henderson** is a blend of 10% **Ed Hamilton** and 90% **Jack Williamson**; the description is pure **Jack Williamson**. About half the book is no more than reportorial jottings of Manana Literary Society meetings; 75% of the gags and cracks in the yarn are straight lifting of incidents that did happen.

I had a hell of a good time reading it, because I knew all the people in it. Oh, **Duncan** is a modified **Cleve Cartmill**; **Cleve** is, actually, as I

657

think I mentioned, rather thoroughly crippled physically. If you want a chance to meet some of your fellow authors under a <u>very</u> thin disguise, this is it.

Item One of the Business of the Letter: I had an idea that might work in nicely somewhere. Weapon Shop story or elsewhere. To wit, a field of some temporal nature which permitted, in effect, the existence of an energy debt. The result would be on this order:

Essentially, all order in physics, chemistry and science is based on one absolutely basic principle; in physical things, you can not go into debt, or borrow against the future. A ball resting in a shallow dish at the top of a long slope can't get away, though it has potential energy far in excess of that needed to climb out of the cup, simply because it can't borrow, even for an instant, against that high potential.

The modern picture of atomic nuclei suggest something "shaped" like a theoretical and perfect volcano. If you drew an energy graph of the thing it would look more or less like this:

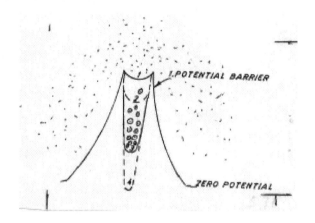

The nuclear particles reside in the throat of the cone (only it's a sort of four-dimensional cone, I guess!) and can't climb the inner side of the barrier to roll down outside. The depth of the throat varies from atom to atom-type. In Radium, you have a throat depth like that of #2; in Radium C, half-life 1/10,000th second, you have something like #1. Potassium, which is radioactive with a half-life 40,000,000,000 years and ^{238}U, half-life 2,000,000,000 years, would be #3, and Iron, half-life apparently about infinite, would be #4. (Iron, Cobalt and Nickel seem to be
658

the absolute maxima of atomic stability. Hence the immense amount of iron in the universe.)

The particles in the throat are not quiescent; they're "boiling" constantly. Occasionally, by a chance series of propitious collisions, one particle will be hit just right by several others, and pick up an abnormal kinetic energy. The speed of gas molecules in air is a statistical thing; some are moving a lot faster, some a lot slower, than average. So inside the atom, if one gets moving enough faster, it may get a freakishly high energy and succeed in boiling over the edge of the barrier. Whereupon it shoots down the outside of the potential hill, and comes flying out with a terrific radio-active energy. Hence the continuous, slow radioactivity of radium. Since the particles in "Radium C" have so shallow a potential barrier throat to climb, the chances of one particle reaching the necessary higher "thermal" energy are good; radio-decay is very rapid. With Uranium it's slow. With iron — it isn't.

So far, so good.

Now, if an atomic particle is shot at the atom — remember that's an all-around cone — the barrier tends to make it shy away, like a billiard ball rolled toward such a cone, or — say, ever see one of those indoor putting-practice gadgets consisting of a metal cone with a shallow cup to put down on the rug? The ball rolls away unless it is aimed absolutely right. So with a charged atomic particle headed at the potential cone.

If a neutron is headed at the thing, being uncharged it meets no particular opposition until it gets very close, actually up to the barrier practically. Hence neutrons can penetrate much more easily, are more effective.

But any particle that gets inside, neutron or proton, will add to the crowding inside. Also, if a proton, it's climbed the barrier and fallen down the throat; it lands amidst the already-present particles with the violent energy of that slide. It overheats the throat-particles, and atomic boiling is very apt to result. The neutron causes overcrowding, even when it doesn't have to slide down much of a barrier; the change of particle numbers alters the whole thing, and is apt to cause boiling over too. In the case of ^{235}U, the added neutron causes the volcanic cone to split open down its length, and huge chunks of the atom fly apart, rapidly regrouping, and reforming into smaller atomic cones.

All of which is general atomic theory.

Specific application to what I have in mind is that any atom has energy of constitution — a potential energy — great enough to more than overcome that potential barrier — if it could just get over the barrier to start with. There are a few exceptions; helium has a negative energy of constitution; the throat of the helium cone dips below the zero potential line, and couldn't be split up except by supplying huge amounts of energy from outside.

Put it this way; TNT has energy of constitution which, by rearrangement, is more than enough to break up the molecular bonds in the trinitrotoluol molecule. But there's a stability to TNT something like that of the ball in a shallow dish at the top of a long hill; it will stay that way forever unless someone gives it an initial push out of the dish. Most atoms are in a similar situation — they'd give more than they took. Some, like helium, are in a 3" deep cup whose edge is 2" above the surface of a flat plane. Like sodium chloride, no amount of starting will make them explode apart.

Now suppose our inventor is working with a time machine idea in mind, and gets into queer difficulties, and finally figures out that he has a machine that will permit two instants of time to be superimposed. The energy TNT molecules would release if they were just given a start can be fed to them to start them releasing by superposing the instant of time after release on the instant before release! The energy an exploding tungsten atom would release can be borrowed — through time — to supply the energy necessary to bring about that release. The energy the ball would get rolling down the long slope can be borrowed against to lift it out of the cup so it can start the roll.

In range of the machine, helium is stable, sodium chloride won't explode, and a ball tied down with strong wire will stay put. But tungsten or radium or any heavy atom will instantly release all its potential-energy-minus-necessary-initiating-energy, TNT explodes automatically, and the ball in the cup pops out of the cup and rolls down the hill at the velocity it would have attained at the bottom of the slope minus the energy needed to climb out of the cup.

Allow the inventor three ranges of control. First, a loose intensity, a "mechanical intensity," where the laws of mechanics go haywire by borrowing energy. Second, a "chemical intensity," where, due to tighter intensity, an ability to conduct through time more concentrated forms
660

of work, molecules automatically assume the state of least-potential available to them, and finally an "atomic intensity" where atoms assume their least-potential state.

Maybe he can project it as a ray, perhaps as a sort of bubble of force, perhaps only by setting his machine in the center of the zone, making sure the machine is constructed of ultimately stable least-potential materials already.

Results: If a heavy casting were held in place by bolts, and could fall, <u>within the field range of the machine,</u> far enough to generate more energy than would be required to overcome the friction involved in unscrewing the bolts; the thing will pop apart and fall. If the fall would be enough in 30 feet, but the field reaches only 28 feet, nothing will happen. If the thing is welded together, the energy of fall must be great enough to overbalance the necessary work of disrupting the metal before a fall will result. Steam boilers would explode if the total work of disrupting the metal is less than the work done by escaping steam. There the time-range of the machine counts; less work is needed to tear a 1/2 inch hole than to tear a 20-foot series of rips in boilerplate. If the machine produces a time-range great enough to cover the time of escape for the steam through a 1-inch hole, the boiler ruptures. If the machine can reach two times not more than one second apart, the boiler can't be ruptured unless — well, you get it.

The thing would be disconcerting as hell on the mechanical level. Tuned to the chemical level, with a long time range, "long" being ten seconds or so, things could be rotted to dust in ten seconds, a man made to die of old age in minutes, or blown up by sudden potential-leveling of the chemicals of his body in a short-range adjustment of one 100,000th of a second.

And — atomic power of course.

There are, I think, fine dramatic possibilities in the man around whom machines fall apart, things rot away, steel weapons crumble to dust, and men who attack him scream, and fall back with age-withered hands. At his gesture, explosives blow up, wood bursts into furious flame, durable plastics crumble as though a 100,000 years had passed over them. He can be attacked with gold, platinum, or similar metallic weapons — metals that do not corrode in air even in a billion centuries. He would not dare to use the atomic instability intensity,

661

because the resultant explosions would be utterly unendurable — the self defense would be self destruction.

I assume a field of limited thickness surrounding him at a controllable distance. He is not affected, but things approaching him are.

Something in it maybe?

Churchill's surprise at the 6-pounder-proof concrete barriers may mean simply that England doesn't, any longer, trust any concrete gun "proof" barriers. They've rejected the Maginot Line philosophy perhaps more violently than necessary, placing their emphasis on mobility and depth of fortification. No barrier is proof against attack; only mass and depth and interminability can resist indefinitely; Stalingrad as a city was not resistant to shell-fire and bombs; Stalingrad's rubble remained unalterably Stalingrad's rubble, merely slightly shifted, no matter how long or hard the bombardment. It had, so to speak, reached the least-potential state, where neither shell-fire, bomb, or our time-energy-borrower would appreciably alter it. Then it made perfect and gun-proof barriers. Bombs might, conceivably, break the Boulder Dam; they would never break the Platte River Earth-fill Dam. The Platte Dam isn't strong; it's just big. Bombs churning the unending millions of tons of dirt that make it would each undo the work of its predecessor. The English surprise may have been that the Germans appear to be using the very thing they themselves disapproved.

The Second Front, it seems to me, has been in full and effective action since August 7. It was pretty damn clear that the Japs were getting ready to hop on Siberia about then, and while the southwest Pacific hasn't yet engaged a great portion of their manpower, it has made them most decidedly unhappy. If they start a new adventure to their northwest, they're damned apt to find themselves too busy there to adequately cover their tail end, and too busy on the rear to get results in front — while a merciless bombardment of their cities from Siberian bases was carried out.

It's not manpower that stops the Japs Siberian venture so much as the same weary trouble that's stopped the European second front. Ships. Supplying the 300,000 men in the captured islands through submarine and bomber attacked waters is a lot harder problem for them than they like. To supply a 1,000,000 or 2,000,000 man army in Siberia with the same shipping would be too apt to cost them the whole southern empire.

It'll be a third front, not a second, when Europe's opened up.

But it'll take ships — more ships, not more men — to do it. **Hitler** has not knocked Russia out, and can't this year. But in the winter he has to withdraw most of his troops from Russia; he can't feed and supply them there. That means they'll be all over Europe, and that a winter campaign attacking Europe would be disastrous for us, it seems to me. Wait till spring, and when **Hitler** is forced to move troops to Russia again, when the Russian frontiers are engaging 4,000,000 men or so, and then a 1,000,000 or 2,000,000 man invasion of Europe would count.

We have 10,000,000 troops in Europe now, just waiting for arms and supplies. A defeated campaign would mean the loss of whatever force we directly threw in, plus the enormously greater loss of those all too willing European allies.

I genuinely believe that the end of the war may well be a whirlwind three-month campaign. A powerful allied invasion force in Europe, a terrific Russian assault, and the uprising of every rear area save Germany proper would catch the German armies all very deep in enemy territory, with hundreds of miles of hostile country between them and their supply bases.

But that allied assault has got to be 100% powerful. It must push the Nazis back from the coastal area selected at a miles-a-day rate, a rate that will make the High Command try to shift many divisions rapidly across the continent, further bollixing up sabotaged supply routes.

Airborne divisional attacks have never been used. In Russia they're useless; the place is too spread out and empty. In tight little Europe, the landing of a full division of airborne troops where a dozen major supply lines could be attacked in a 30 mile drive would have a hell of an effect.

Incidentally, my dream of the way to end the war: Get Detroit going on a jalopy plane — a $500 two-man light-plane, amphibian type. They should be able to turn out 2,000,000 in 18 months. Make 'em simple, fool-proof simple gadgets that any good automobile driver could handle with a few hours instruction. (Can be done; see the Ercoup.) Amphibian — so they can take off from bays, lakes, inlets, rivers, and what-not. Five hundred mile range; one-way trip to Germany. On a given day, all 2,000,000 with 4,000,000 soldiers, take off. Accompanied and shielded by plenty of fighters, flying fortresses, etc. The whole collection then lands all over the Rhineland, settles in, and has captured the place long before anybody could do anything useful about stopping it. They land the planes on roads, wheatfields, crash them in shrubbery, in city parks, anywhere. They land at 25 m.p.h.; nobody would be hurt much if they did crash into a house, and they're intended for only one trip, really. Nice, of course, if you can make a salvageable landing.

Taking over the place, the next job would be taking over the food distribution service to live off the land for a couple of weeks, until the way to the coast was entirely opened.

But after all, a country with an Army of Occupation in its heart can't put up a really effective battle.

The idea being a sort of exaggerated amplification of the "saturation raid" technique — with landings.

Regards, John W. Campbell, Jr.

A.E. van Vogt   *February 26, 1943*

Dear van Vogt:
I took the "Concealment" yarn. The thing offers possibilities of development — possibilities that considerably exceed its immediate value as a yarn. The vagueness of the present ending yells for a sequel in a slightly too-loud voice — but I can see the difficulty of finding any decent place to end the thing. I'll be interested to see what sort of a set-up you have on the concealed robot culture. Would a robot — allowing it was capable of logic and imagination — be capable psychologically of carrying out research to develop a super-robot? A more intelligent robot, that is. I rather gather that your point on this culture, at least, is that they haven't the power of conducting research — that they are a blind alley, never capable of further development, but, too, incapable of retrogression because of perfect memory and perfect learning powers. Like the ants, they can continue to tread the same pathways of knowledge and ability unceasingly and unchanged for 500,000,000 years if left alone. And, with them, there's not even the possibility of mutation to introduce improving changes.
664

Incidentally, remember the Three Laws of Robotics that **Isaac Asimov** used in his robot stories — specifically stated in "Run-around?" They'd be a swell basis for the psychology of a robot, it seems to me. They supply him with a measure of self-preservation, a measure of obedience, and a measure of free choice. Of course, the first law, of not harming by commission or omission any human being would be eliminated, and the Law of the Pack would take its place.

There is a current acute dearth of typewriter ribbons affecting the office, for some reason. At any rate, I haven't been able to get a new one for this mill for about two months. Since I'm heavy-handed on the keys, the ribbon I have is badly mangled. Sort of very dirty looking lace ribbon. I've run it through and used it up on both sides now. **Miss Tarrant's** machine, which handles the formal letters, gets what good ribbons are to be had. You'll have to pardon the faintness.

That item I sent you about the 16" ack-ack guns has been neatly borne out by the report of the U.S. battlewagon in the Solomons that massacred some two-score Jap planes. The Japs tried the same tactics on it that they'd used successfully before — on Prince of Wales and on U.S. ships. The mop-up that let only 1 of 17 planes return probably represents what happened when a salvo of 16" shells went off in the bomber formation on its way in to attack.

To date, there's been a pretty free interchange of knowledge by examination of enemy wreckage, but the advances are beginning to pile up. Remember what I editorialized some months back — about the divergence of sciences if a long-maintained break of relations continued for 5 years or so? It's beginning to work — and, as usual, in our favor. I know the Nazis haven't been able to duplicate the armor plate we're using on tanks, for instance. They can analyze themselves blue in the face, but the analysis, while it can tell 'em what its made of, won't tell 'em how it was made — which is the real story. You know what the phenomenon of "work hardening" in metals is? In case you don't: some metals don't display it appreciably, but most, to some extent, become harder when deformed, or worked. Copper and bronze do. Old copper-bronze swords were "tempered" by simply forging them — work-hardening was their tempering. Heating draws that temper. Cold-rolled copper, cold-drawn copper wire display the same work-hardening property. Take a bit of ordinary bell wire — a work-hard-

665

ened, cold-drawn wire — and heat it near red hot. It becomes astonishingly softer and more putty-like. No spring left in it. Bend it back and forth a half dozen times though, and you can feel it become appreciably stiffer. Work hardened. Zinc work-hardens too, but it anneals fairly rapidly even at room temperature, so won't stay hard. (Ever seen how a sheet of zinc will slump like a wet rag if thrown over something and left there for 3 or 4 months?)

The U.S. has evolved a trick alloy, treated in a special way — God knows what way; the Nazis don't — that makes it work-harden on the slightest excuse. You can't drill holes in it or machine it; the stuff work-hardens, very tough steel. When a bullet hits it, the bullet's impact immediately work-hardens it in front of its nose, converting it to an impenetrable, glass-hard face-plate over an extremely tough, non-brittle backing. The main mass of metal is too tough to break, and the face the bullet has to work on is too hard to penetrate. The combination of properties is an impossible ideal attained with beautiful simplicity; an armor that's tough and elastic except at the exact point the bullet hits, where it is always glass-hard. Since the Nazis have captured scores of tanks so equipped, they know all about what it does. But only by seeing the stuff made could they know how it got that way. The Japs have gotten samples of the stuff from planes shot down, but don't know either. (It won't spaul the way ordinary armor does. If a 50 caliber slug hits ordinary plane armor-steel, the slug is stopped all right, but the hardened steel back-face of the plate shatters under the blow and a sizable chunk is blasted out of the back — on the pilot's side. Not this stuff; it isn't hard and brittle at all; it's tough but rather soft — except where the bullet hits.)

I won't back my bet with money, but I am convinced that Germany will be incapable of any offensive action after October 1943, and that Berlin will fall to assault before October 1944. Berlin will be taken by shell-fire, bombing, and tanks in the streets. Probably by the Russians; the English and American commanders have an intellectual realization of the necessity but, I suspect, lack the guts to carry it out. Berlin must have the war in its streets. Berlin's people must be shot and bombed and shelled. Until Hans and Gertrude Deutschlander get their own personal ears batted down, their own personal friends shot dead in their own backyard, until they cower in their own homes and
666

see the Nazi soldiers being driven back, blasted away, their own homes razed, they will never believe that Germany lost the war because she was licked, broken, smashed beyond possibility of military resistance.

They didn't believe it after the last licking they got. They didn't see it that time. This time what we need is not an Army of Occupation in Berlin, but a Battle of Berlin. And the Russians are the boys who can and would do it up brown.

Japan won't go down in 1944; probably be 1945 before they get finished off. My personal fondest hope is that the Chinese be given the pleasure of taking care of Tokyo in a manner similar to the Russian handling I hope Berlin gets. Only — you know how in Chinese art work, the craftsman always finishes off the back of the statuette, or the underside of the craved piece as carefully as the front and top? I hope they handle Tokyo with the same attention to detail.

The enclosed prints are of a gadget I made up. Gadgeteering, you know, is my second hobby. This is a photographic enlarger timer — a sort of electronic sand-glass. A radio tube watches the electron sand drain out of the condenser reservoir, and when it's all gone, throws the relay. *Popular Science* bought an article on it; I have the gadget and $20 to keep it company. And the fun of making it!

Regards, John W. Campbell, Jr.

A.E. van Vogt   *March 3, 1943*

Dear van Vogt:

I just took "The Beast;" it's on its way through the accounting department now, and you should get a check shortly. I still need and need badly, more short stories; novelettes I'm reasonably well provided with now. Serials also seem to be taken care of. Shorts for *Unknown* are needed at last, also. And I'll be wanting another lead novel for *Unknown* in about 6 weeks. How's "Ptath" coming — or is it permanently shelved?

I think your five-years-more prediction is on the pessimistic side. I believe **Hitler** will go down in 1944, and Japan will be finished off in 1945. The great problem of the United Nations right now is the submarine, of course — but that's a problem of getting destroyers and

667

other escort vessels on the sea. We're doing right well at that now; we're producing destroyers not quite as fast as the Nazis build subs, but we approach that speed. Four went down the ways in one day this week from one New Jersey yard. They don't hold the launching of a destroyer back until more are ready just to make a simultaneous show; they're building them so fast the coincidental completion of four at once reached a probability of one.

I think that the reason for England's survival is double; the channel was no minor hindrance, nor was the opposition of the RAF; together with the British navy, they made the channel some of the highest priced liquid real estate in the world. (The whole damn channel could be turned into a sea of blazing oil, too, which rather stymied the Nazi intentions to send barges over. The British had God knows how many sunken tanks of oil laid like mines, ready to spread oil on troubled waters — and ignite it.) The various forms of hell on waves, wheels, and wings the British had to offer was one item. **Joe Stalin** tugging his mustache was the other. Neither **Hitler** nor **Stalin** even had the slightest doubt that there was going to be war between them, that each was waiting the most opportune moment. If **Hitler** had committed his army to the job of taking Britain, he might have gotten a landing, but at a cost out of all proportion in the first beachheads. He'd have lost at least fifty divisions of men, and tied down another fifty to the job of holding those beachheads. **Joe** would have waited till about a third of England was taken, but before the British Army or Air Force was knocked out, given his mustache an extra tug, and said, "Now." In 1940, **Hitler** had — and had to have — a big force of men tied up in newly occupied countries. He'd have had an extremely badly mauled Army in the West, a depleted reserve in Europe, a holding force in the East — and the Red Army rolling down through East Prussia.

That would probably have been a shorter war, at that. It would certainly have been to Russia's advantage.

The situation was to England's advantage. **Hitler** never dared to sustain the clawing his Army would have gotten trying to take beachheads in England. The British Lion, like a real lion, was in position to do some nasty clawing, and land some terrific wallops, though it didn't have any staying power, or the sheer brutal force for crushing action. It takes a bear for that sort of crunching — not slapping — power.

668

The United States is in a difficult sort of position. It's advantageous and disadvantageous at once. Our factories are practically immune to attack — and they can outproduce the rest of the world put together, once they're organized. (Ever think what would have happened if **Hitler** had somehow been an American Fuehrer? There would, then, have been no way to prevent world conquest. He would have had a hemisphere to work with as a base and source of supplies before the slightest effective resistance could have been offered, and with that base, Africa would probably have been taken as the next operations base.)

But our immunity-by-distance works against us, too. It's a hell of a job to apply that production power to the necessary points. Also, that immunity has tended to make military and naval establishments so much of a stepchild of American governmental policy that we have a lot to do to get started.

But I'm betting on the American tendency to "figger a way." Like that trick alloy they use in the armor. If the Russians had a decent rail network across Siberia it would help a lot; you can't sink railroad trains, and it's only 5 miles from U.S. to Siberia.

Americans are never, never, never going to understand British imperialism. First, admittedly, is the old fact that — well, you know the story about the definitions of "firm," "stubborn" and "mulish?" I am firm, you are stubborn, he is mulish. Same tendency creeps into any human evaluation. But --.

The United States has never wanted to own any non-contiguous real estate. We wanted to get rid of the Philippines; the Army and Navy saw their value as bases — but we were in process of getting rid of them. Most Americans did not fully realize that the Hawaiian Islands were American territory. I assume they do, now. But you've heard, perhaps, that famous double-talk oration — I've forgotten what comedian does it — about an Isolationist senator? Supposed to be an Isolationist going strong, double-talk of the usual sort with occasionally typical isolationist phrases shining through, and winding up with a magnificent, "— but what I wanta know is, what were the Hawaiian Islands doing way out there in the Pacific anyway?" It's a comedian's way of crossing up a not unheard of American little-man's reaction. He — and the Isolationist — would really mean, what were we doing owning real estate way out in the Pacific, anyway?

Since any average-IQ man mistrusts anybody who thinks differently than he does, there is an inevitable mistrust of anybody that insists on holding on to distant real estate. Since we have, historically, had more frontier than we could readily handle, there's been no dearth of positions for career men, sons of good families, etc. English aristocracy definitely did have a tendency to hold colonial possessions in the fold as an excellent place to station younger sons.

From my point of view, India is right in trying to get freedom now, because in peacetime England isn't so busy she can't devote her whole attention, if need be, to holding on. England is right in refusing it now, because she's too busy to work out practicable measures for simultaneously increasing her military establishment there and relinquishing political control. The answer is to give India a schedule of freedom to function automatically after the war. But India can't accept that, because she definitely feels that England pulled a stunt like that in the last war — and, once free of that mess, backed down on the promise and restored her full power. It's a complete dilemma, with all roads blocked. But I have a basic feeling that England got herself (and India) into that dilemma by a calculated policy of internal division.

As for distrust of British leaders, both U.S. and Russia have reason for that. I don't know whether you know about it, but in the 1st War, British naval and shipping people gave the advice on which our war shipping designs were based. The ships so built were convoy freighters, we found after the war. They were too big for use as tramp steamers — had too great a cargo capacity and engine equipment for economical service. They were too small and too slow for transatlantic shipping trade, too short-range and slow for trans-Pacific work. They rotted for years — till Japan bought them for scrap steel — because of this. The British shipyards were building, at the same time, larger-faster and smaller-slower ships both. Britain retained dominance of the world's merchant marine after the war.

The British leaders were, in the period 1933-1937 in a position to stop **Hitler**. Before that, they'd been in a position to stop Japan. Our Navy was sailing west of Hawaii with the ships alert for battle operations, expecting surprise attack in 1933. They expected and were ready for war with Japan then. There would have been war then and there,
670

too, if England had stiffened up. Japan would have had its ears slapped down around its knees, **Mussolini** wouldn't have gotten fancy ideas in Ethiopia, and **Hitler** would have been a minor nuisance if there had been.

By 1938 of course England had to sell Czechoslovakia down the river — though nobody loved them for it. But **Mussolini** could have been stopped in the Ethiopian adventure.

We don't like imperialism, probably primarily because we don't understand the why of it. And we don't trust British leaders in general, because we're convinced they tend to be wrong, and tend to hornswoggle us and anybody else they get hold of. The latter two points I'm absolutely convinced of. The only difference between my conviction and the general feeling to that effect is that I know damn well it's true — and true of anybody else on Earth, too.

Actually, I think, the American's greatest objection to the Englishman and his ways — concentrated with respect to the English leaders — is the undoubted fact that the English tend to impress people with a twin conviction: that the Englishman feels he is necessarily and inevitably right in all he does, and that he feels any other way whatsoever is silly and amusing. I do not say the man actually feels that; I do say that he has succeeded in convincing a large portion of the world that he feels that.

Oh, yes. Most people don't consciously remember the famous War Debts, but a good many years of conditioning to that thought hangs on. The proposition seems simple and straight forward — "they hired the money didn't they?" — that a conviction of bad faith hangs on like a pall. Try some time to explain to some IQ 100 man why paying an international debt is any different than paying his debts. Even try it with an Englishman, who has a subconscious willingness, not unwillingness, to understand.

If you succeed, they still want to know why England couldn't sell us some of her real estate in settlement. It rankles deep to feel you've been subtly gypped somehow, and can't quite figure out how it was worked. That's the only feeling you can arouse, if you do convince him an international debt can't be paid with a check on the First National Bank. And he does understand that he has to pay taxes to pay off the National Debt that represents those War Debts.

Ten-fifteen years of that in the background takes considerable eliminating. While it's there, there's a background conviction that you've got to keep a close eye on those English slickers. And one step deeper in the subconscious background is the added comment, "— and maybe we can get even this time." He's human to. And a great and glorious part of the American tradition has to do with hoss-trading, the same being a game without rules or mercy, based on the concept that he who does his fellow man in the eye is smarter — until he gets done. He who gets done is then expected to figure out how the doing was done, improve on it, and do it back. Yeah, Artur Blord is an outgrowth of that purely American tradition. Canada has a common heritage on that, naturally.

I suspect it is not quite understandable to a European that an American could distrust every move a man made and still hold that man as a good friend — just as — a fact I am well aware of — it drives a true German or other European completely bughouse to find it impossible to tell a man's friends from his acquaintances. (The only sure way to tell is that a man is reasonably courteous to acquaintances, and calls only his friends insulting names. Remarkable outgrowth of Western Frontier days.)

I think Americans (U.S. variety) are quite capable of distrusting everything the British leaders do, and still being thoroughly willing to get in and help slug along with them.

My great fear is that Americans are going to continue to distrust <u>and dislike</u> the Russians after the war. That will be a world calamity. The United States and Russia, as a team, outweigh any other possible team on Earth. With a three-way partnership of England and the Empire added, the preponderance of power would be so terrific no possible challenge could arise. The United States is apt to have a different and more world-wide angle on things after this war, too. We'll have about as big a stake in Australia as Britain has, for instance. A hell of a lot of American boys are getting married down there, and are going to stay; that's the only kind of stake that will hold American attention. Americans have a reputation for dollar-chasers, of course — as un-understandable to Europeans as hoss-trading in general. That chase is comparable only to the English fox-hunt; it's a traditional sport, with the result that Americans will not fight as hard for an economic investment as a European would. If he gets beaten on that running, he's willing to try again in another chase. But with a human stake in a region, the attitude will be different. If we can just get Americans to appreciate Russians as people — they can go right on loathing cheerfully their form of government — there's a real chance for real peace. Even German militarism would be overawed by a combination of Russian, English and American military power; even the insane Jap militarism would be paralyzed before that deadly combination. There's only one way to keep peace among men; the way a police force does. It is organized on a scale of armed force immensely greater than any gangster group can bring against it, and perfectly ready to jam offenders into jail <u>right now,</u> and then investigate whether or not they should be released. The Pax Romana kind of Pax — "Wiggle your ears and you'll get 'em slapped off so fast you'll wonder where they went" — is the one kind that works. But it takes a multilateral enforcement of such a Pax to keep it decently restrained. However, too-multi an enforcement won't work, either. France and democratic Germany were paralyzed that way; they had so many parties nobody could do anything. The two or three party system can be made to work; two-party is best, I honestly believe. A balance of power between three parties means that there will never be a single, decisive, completely responsible party; with two parties, one or the other is always in a position of responsibility-and-authority, able to act, but unable to pass the buck effectively. The League died of suffocation, not lack of attendance. It takes more than one, so that there is constant restraint — hence the undesirability of the Nazi and Bolshevist one-party systems.

We probably won't have peace, though, 'til other planets are opened to colonization. Then we'll have peace on Earth — and war in heaven!

Regards, John W. Campbell, Jr.

A.E. van Vogt   *April 14, 1943*

Dear van Vogt:

Our letters must have crossed in transit. You notice that I got the same answer that you did, but a different solution appeared to me. Instead of throwing the thing up as a bad job in its present form, I think it needs simply a mental shift on your part.

673

And though I say "simply," I fully realize that isn't simple. It'll mean reworking the whole thing, so far as your mental picture goes. You just won't have to rewrite it, because you haven't written it yet.

You can't handle it from the present point on in the way you handled "Weapon Makers," nor the way **Leiber** handled "Conjure Wife" nor as **Merritt** handled "Creep Shadow." But you can handle it the way — reduced to least common denominator — the horror movies and plays are worked. There, the characters don't know the menace in full, but the audience does. The audience sees the trap doors pop open behind the hero's back, sees the black hands reach out of the picture frame to grab the heroine, sees the wine poisoned — but the hero and heroine don't see it.

Your Ptath doesn't have to know the full potentialities of the villains and villainesses about him — but the audience must, and must be pulling for him, yelling at him when the trap-doors silently pop up. Inoznia, or whatever you called the villainess, has first evoked Ptath before he was ready, thus bringing him into being without understanding. Then she has brought him the personality of Holroyd. Why? Because Ptath, unless given a personality to distract him, would have reasserted his own. Holroyd, being no fool, realizes there must be a real connection between his Holroyd personality and the Ptath personality, that all he really needs to do is to allow the Ptath being to merge with himself, and he will still be Holroyd, but with Ptath's greater powers.

Furthermore, Holroyd is probably one of those who can be pushed around just so much before he stiffens, stops where he is, and figures out just what the hell this is all about. He's been pushed, and pushed hard, ever since he landed. If I were Holroyd at about this point I'd take time out for investigation, before I did anything whatever that anybody anywhere suggested to me. And Ptath, in any personality, is going to be a powerful personality, the total Ptath will be a highly dangerous opponent.

And — if Ptath laid all those protective spells, whatever they were, for the defense of his realm, it's practically certain that a man of that caliber would lay a second line of defense specifically designed to trap the attacker who knew the form and powers of the first line of defense. He'd be a poor general if he, evidently distrusting someone, didn't make sure that no one but he himself knew the whole combination.

674

And — that part of that combination involved himself as a pole-of-power, or what-not. At any rate, involved himself <u>as his fully-awakened self</u>. He'd probably set it up like a burglar alarm system, so that the tripping of the relay automatically invoked his full-powers presence.

Hence Inoznia (or whatever her name is) only thinks she is planning with full knowledge of Ptath's defensive plans. Where Ptath planned vaguely for all contingencies, she is attacking with knowledge of the plans — and with highly specific, rigidly organized plans.

Rommel had highly specific, rigidly organized plans for the defense of the Mareth Line. **Montgomery** had plans for its breaching. The plan he had started with didn't work as intended — but was more flexible, because rather vague, than **Rommel's** rigid defense plan. **Montgomery** slid off around the side before **Rommel** knew the attack wasn't going to be driven straight in again. Steel-hard, steel-rigid material is wonderful stuff. But soft, lax rubber is harder to break. A steel tire even on a light buggy would wear out in a few thousand miles; a modern truck tire is much softer; it yields to the attack of stones and grit, and wears 50,000 miles.

Would Holroyd's military mind suspect that more quickly than Inoznia's god-power enrapt mind? You know, one old style of booby trap involved a door hitched to a lever, cam and rope arrangement in such a way that the man pushing the door open wound up the rope, cocked the lever, and the cam released the thing to brain him at the right instant. The next man to come along would then supply the power to kill himself in turn.

Ptath's return requires the use of the god-power. Somebody must apply it. There's a safe way for friendly invokers — and a hidden way that, like the suicide booby-trap, makes the would-be destroyer supply the god-power to cause his own destruction.

If the reader has full knowledge of Inoznia's powers, aims and weaknesses (apparent) Holroyd-Ptath needn't have. But Holroyd -- Ptath may or may not reveal to the reader his analysis that suggests that the best path for Holroyd to follow is to do exactly what Inoznia seems to want — except for things that seem inherently wrong, such as yielding personality to her — in hopes that Inoznia is probably taking the most direct line to suicide and the restoration of Ptath's full powers.

Incidentally, for possible use in this story or elsewhere: Suppose you knew that the Htatp Treatment would reorient your personality and viewpoint completely, but leave your identity otherwise unchanged. That is, suppose you knew it could make you a convinced, whole-hearted Nazi, or make a Nazi a convinced, whole-hearted believer in democracy, a completely trustworthy, genuinely changed man. Turn **Hitler** into as trustworthy, sound a man as **Churchhill** or **Roosevelt**.

If that treatment were promised you, coming up next Tuesday, wouldn't the prospect be rather horrible? You'ld still be **van Vogt** — but, say, **van Vogt**; ardent Nazi, and fully convinced. Or **van Vogt**; ardent Shintoist, and fully convinced. Remember, you'ld be stable, ordinary in every way, comfortable in your new belief. Or, equally, if you were already a real Nazi, think of the psychological terror the prospect of being a whole-hearted believer in democracy next Wednesday would inspire.

The proposed god-power of Ptath could well do that to Inoznia as an inherent and inevitable result of her meddling with his defenses. It might be an effect that would not strike for a certain period of time, but that would, at the end of say 10 days, rebound on her automatically.

Or, maybe, that's the basis of the Shaposhenko treatment?

Regards, John W. Campbell, Jr.

P.S. for Halroyd's motivation — how about his quite normal desire to stay alive, as a starter? Ptath, of course, will have stronger motivation, once he's on the scene.

A.E. van Vogt   *April 21, 1943*

Dear van Vogt:

In common with many another neck-protruder, I seem, as of the present moment, to have had mine lopped off. Europe seems still uninvaded.

Well, it won't be long. I rather had in mind the idea **Gracie Fields** so succinctly expressed in her birthday wishes to **Hitler**: "This year we're sending you our heartiest tanks."

Which reminds me; the local "expert's" feeling is that tanks are about finished — gone the way of the Stuka. Only the Stuka was simply an obsolete type of dive-bomber (its low speed made it duck-soup to fighters; our dive-bombers make up to 350 mph, which is a different matter), and the tank is a class of weapon. The trouble is the old, old, old one, several hundred million years older than the wheeze about the hen and the egg; which wins, armor or arms?

The answer, almost without exception, has been, "Arms — and speed." Some, like the mole, use "trench-warfare" armor, but only a very few animals have been able to make armor work even moderately well, while they, actually, depend more on the extreme efficiency of their reproductive organs than on their armor. Hell, a guinea pig can neither run, burrow, bite, claw, fly or climb, has no armor, and is excessively stupid. The race survives solely and singly because of the fact they can make a doe-rabbit look like an old maid. Even an Australian doe-rabbit.

The tank is the armored beast again. The tank-destroyer is the fast, terribly armed, unarmored killer. The two-man team with a bazooka gun is the small, agile, sharp-toothed killer that hunts in packs. The tank destroyer is a lion; the bazooka-armed infantry the wolf-pack. But there is no natural equivalent to the bazooka-armed "Hurribuster" tank-killer.

That bazooka, by the way, vastly interests and pleases me. I don't know how long you've been following science-fiction, but back about 1928, one **Phil Nowlan** wrote two yarns in the old *Amazing* called, "Armageddon 2428 A.D.," and "Airlords of Han," in which, 500 years hence, Americans, forced to a state of guerrilla warfare against the semi-mongolian Airlords of Han, fought mainly with a light rifle-like weapon that fired rocket-propelled shells, whose destructive power and range were out of all proportion to the light rifle used; their main drive was not the piston-effect within the barrel, but the reaction of the rocket cartridge built into the shell.

The bazooka is a light, long rifle, firing a rocket-propelled shell whose destructive power is utterly out of proportion to the weight of the launching weapon. There are, seemingly, two types of bazooka shells — an armor piercing type, the greater part of the original weight of which is high-power rocket fuel, and a high-explosive type, which divides the original mass more equally between explosive and driving power. The first type will cut through the heaviest tank armor at an impossibly long range; it has the penetrative range and power of a 6" field-gun! The second type also seems to have the impact of a 6"

677

field-gun; the Nazis, when they first encountered bazooka-fire, hauled their tanks back hurriedly, under the unpleasant conviction that they'd wandered into the field of fire of a battery of 155mm guns.

It is interesting, I think, that the Russian answer to the tank took the form of a two-man, but otherwise conventional, heavy rifle — a heavy-caliber, high-velocity, piston-type rifle of orthodox design. The German answer to the tank was equally conventional; an improved 75mm gun — somewhat larger, somewhat lower in silhouette, somewhat faster muzzle velocity; their famous 88 mm gun. Both of these answers follow normal ordinance lines of thought, but diverge in one respect; the 88 is necessarily a defensive weapon — it can't be used in the front line unless the front line moves toward its fairly fixed position. The Russian high-caliber two-man rifle can move up to the front.

The American answer to the tank is totally different in basic concept; it's really two answers. One is conventional in thought, with the to-American-minds-conventional idea of automotive mobility. The tank-destroyer consisting of a 75 mounted on a stripped-down, pepped-up tank chassis uses the conventional small field-gun weapon, made more deadly by mobility greatly exceeding that of the prey it seeks. But the bazooka is unorthodox from start to finish. it is very apt to do more to change the face of war than even the tank did; the bazooka is in line with evolution — the tank a blind alley, like the triceratops and the giant sloth. It gives the individual infantry-man firepower so destructive no immobile fortress can survive a massed attack, and no mobile armored unit can survive more than a few hits. The early landings in North Africa showed the bazooka's deadliness against enemy fortifications. A small coastal fortress was reduced in a matter of minutes by one man with a bazooka.

When that weapon is in real, quantity production, when every infantry company includes numerous bazooka gunner teams, all **Hitler's** hopes of a fortress Europe will be futile. What fortress could stand up to an Army in which every other infantryman carried a 6" field-gun in his hands?

But there's another weapon coming up in the not-too-distant future — post-war maybe, maybe toward the end of this war. It's straight out of science-fiction, too, like the bazooka, and surely an item for such as we to keep in mind; we need it in our science-fiction business!
678

A month ago, I'd have declared flatly that no device measuring less than two feet in greatest dimension could possibly generate 1,000,000 or more volts; you can't insulate such enormous voltages in lesser thicknesses of material — it takes many feet of air — 18 to 20 — and feet of even the best insulating oils. But I've seen a photograph of a laboratory model of a new-type generator that, about 18" in maximum dimension, generates a 2,000,000 volt beam of electrons. A "pilot plant scale" model — the second one built; they are advancing in cautious steps — so small it has to be built on a bench to bring it to a convenient working height, generates a 20,000,000 volt beam. That's precisely twice the absolute tops heretofore obtained — and the previous top was attained in a van der Graff generator that had to be housed in an airplane hanger — actually, a dirigible hanger — it was so huge. General Electric is now working on a 100,000,000 volt model. There is no particular reason why they shouldn't go to work on a 1,000,000,000 volt model immediately, save considerable caution as to what would happen to normal atomic matter bombarded by a heavy-current beam of billion-volt electrons. For the betatron generator could, quite readily, produce a 5 <u>ampere</u> beam of electrons at one billion volts — an instantaneous discharge of five million horsepower.

If electrons are moving extremely fast — within 1/2 of 1% of the speed of light — they pass through atoms without anywhere near the slowing effect they encounter at lower speeds. There's a relativity effect that permits them to have less effect on the atom, and hence be less affected. The result is that a billion volt beam of electrons would penetrate air for long distances; a 10,000,000 volt beam would probably reach miles — particularly if pointed upward toward the thinner atmosphere.

Wonder what would happen to planes attempting to cross a coast equipped with coastal defense batteries of one to ten billion volt betatron generators? The betatron generators would be fired in bursts; one way to supply the terrific energy demands of such a generator for the necessary instant of time would be to supply them from a very massive, rapidly-rotating generator, with heavy copper bar windings strapped in place with extremely strong steel cleats. When the betatron was energized, the tremendous current drain would act as an energy-brake, stopping the massive rotor almost instantly — and converting all its rotational energy into a burst of energy. If the generator weighed 50 to 100 tons, and were turning at 10,000 RPM, the electrons expelled from the betatron would have to have a nearly equal kinetic energy.

The weapon would probably weigh 5,000 tons or more, but a battleship could mount it with ease. They wouldn't need 16" guns then. I would not, however, guarantee that such a weapon could be used on any planet whose continued existence was important. The effect of a 5-ampere current at 10,000,000,000 volts is totally unknown; atoms directly affected by it would be "heated" to temperatures higher than those at the heart of a sun. Remember that exploding ^{235}U atoms release the highest atomic energy known to man — and that's only a fifth of a billion volts! Radium releases only a couple million. Only cosmic rays, in very occasional super-bursts, exceed a billion volts.

Regards, John W. Campbell, Jr.

A.E. van Vogt   *June 9, 1943*

Dear van Vogt:

It's been my feeling — not based on any specific knowledge — that change of pace in an author is not appreciated; he should be two or more authors, each with a dependable style, a semi-predictable type of general treatment. That was why **Don A. Stuart** was started; **J.W.C.Jr.** handled super-science, heavy stuff — the stories under that name had a definite cast. Developing a new style is all to the good — but it should be done, for best effect, by a new personality. The trick works, and helps remarkably to change your own style for you. You are a different writer; you say so, and find yourself being so. It worked with **Lewis Padgett**, who writes quite differently from **Henry Kuttner**. It worked for **Will Stewart (John Stewart Williamson)** and for others.

But the full change is effective, really, only if a different type of story treatment is used. On this, I'd suggest that you try handling stories of the period not more than 50 years hence, concerning mainly the exploitation and colonization — and, of course, discovery and exploration — of the planets. The scene on Earth then will offer opportunities, too, of course. Your previous stories have all been long-range stuff; I very genuinely want to have much greater emphasis on 1945-95 now, and it would be an opportunity for you to change style and treatment in a major way.

Ellen Reith might do nicely as Blord's secretary — but the romantic interest angle wouldn't go over so well. Most of our readers are, apparently, in the 25-35 age-group — and while they'll accept a woman who's been divorced four times as a decent character, they have the feeling there's something distinctly fishy about her. No one but a damn fool would make the same honest mistake four times running in the course of a few years — a decade or so.

Incidentally, the double standard is <u>not</u> a creation of men; to a small extent it's a creation of nature, but 90% or so of it is due to women. They thought it up. If it becomes known that John Q. Brown is going out — and in — with Miss Jane Doe, John Brown's masculine neighbors don't worry. But their wives put up a terrific fuss. Jane Doe is ostracized. They do what they can to annoy John Brown, but since most of his dealings are with the husbands, they don't bother him much. The men wouldn't bother too much about a single standard — but the wives would. Reason: the men are the bacon-bringers, and can live comfortably without any permanent attachment to a female. The women need a meal-ticket, preferably a permanent and dependable one. They've worked for generations to get the institution of marriage established, and they'll go right on working to maintain it -- and that means crushing any extra-marital playing around which might snag off an already hooked meal-ticket.

Some women may rant against the double-standard and demand a single standard on the present masculine standard basis; all the rest are ranting against the departure from the present female standard. They've got the same sort of stake that a business man has when he rants against communism.

The other 10% is Nature's contribution to the argument; the women make the absolute maximum of use of it, naturally. If a man departs from the standard the women propose for all, he's not changed. If a women does, she is — and her prime idea becomes, logically enough, to hook a meal-ticket somewhere in a large hurry.

Women who don't like the double standard should blame their sisters, not their brothers. Unless, of course, they want the female standard as the single standard, in which case they can take their complaints to the devil. Without him, we are told, we'd all be angels.

681

Your idea on how the final attack on Germany will be carried out interests me. It follows the pattern. The Nazis started the blitzkrieg idea — the sudden war that was ended in a few weeks at most, before accumulated stocks could be exhausted, before supply problems of strategic order appeared. It didn't work finally, but it sure played merry hell with every victim they tried it on, with two thick-headed opponents who didn't know when they were licked, of course, excepted. They launched the mass, terror-bombing of cities. The great air war.

We have, in the last couple of months, taught them what _real_ mass, terror-bombing of cities, the GREAT air war really is. We may well proceed now to teach them what a continental-size blitzkrieg really is, too. They have a strategic reserve of force, and various local reserves scattered all along their defense areas. They plan to concentrate them heavily where attacked, bolstering threatened areas with allotments from the main strategic reserve. But if they're attacked all over, all out, all at once, the strategic reserve won't help a lot, with some 8,000 miles of front under simultaneous terrific attack. In the pattern of modern war, the victorious army can always advance far more rapidly than a defeated army can retreat. (**Rommel's** army was never defeated — 'til Tunis and Bizerte were reached. Previously, they had retired under pressure, but had not had their defense lines pierced.) With an Allied breakthrough, the Nazis would be in a mell of a hess — even without the Allied armored forces and air forces working in their rear, they'd be retreating through exceedingly hostile territory, exposed to well-organized and highly developed sabotage and guerrillas everywhere behind their lines. I doubt that the Germans could hold out for a full month under the maximum blitz pressure, a united hell-for-leather attack from north, east, south, west and above all at once. And supply lines from America couldn't fail that quickly — because they couldn't ever have been expected to work that quickly. It would be a capital-goods attack rather than an income-attack.

And the submarine menace would not amount to much during the attack period anyway. The subs in nearby coastal waters are kept down by air patrol now, true. But in the coastal waters, during the attack, there would be more air traffic by far than there is now. Just planes going and coming. And the recent improvement in sub-destruction isn't due to normal aircraft anyway; it's due partly to the use of helicopters, but pri-

682

marily to escort surface vessels equipped with a gadget called a mouse-trap. It traps subs rather than mice, however. It's very deadly, I understand. Like the bazooka, it isn't being described or mentioned just yet.

Aside from my own vegetable garden, my home activities have been of a somewhat less vigorous nature than yours. I've been cooking up an amplifier for some time, a gadget that will amplify the current from a photoelectric cell, and build it up enough so that a millimeter can be used to read the light intensity projected by the enlarger. Thus I'll have an instrument that will tell me what exposure a print needs, and give a scientific exact, and dependable answer to the question of "How much light?" every time. It's a hell of a neat trick, if I can do it. The trouble is that it has to be a DC amplifier. A radio set amplifies the incoming signal a million or so times — or even 100,000,000. But it's an AC amplifier; the signal it works on is an alternating current — the radio wave — and its product is an alternating current -- the audio frequency oscillations fed into the speaker. The various tubes are so coupled together that at each stage, any direct current present in the output is blocked off, allowing only the alternating current impulses to pass. Thus the plate-voltage supply for tube #1 — about 400 volts of DC — is blocked by its inability to pass through a condenser or a radio-frequency transformer coupling. The alternating current component impressed on it by the action of the first amplifier tube, however, passes freely through transformer and condenser. So the second tube takes the AC signal, amplifies it again, and throws it on to #3 tube — through another transformer that cuts out the DC plate supply.

The transformer also cuts out any stray DC due to thermo-electric effects, contact-potentials, and any variations in plate voltage due to line-current variations. (Those variations, taking 1/2 a second to 3 seconds or more to change, are practically DC, and can't pass the small condensers and transformers used.)

My headache is that what I want to amplify is not an alternating current; its a direct current of about 50 micromicro-amperes, and must be amplified at least 10,000,000 times before I can use it. I can't pass the amplified current from tube #1 into tube #2 through a condenser; neither the plate voltage nor the signal could pass. Therefore, I can't use more than one amplifier stage on one plate-current supply.

683

For every amplifier, I have to have a separate and distinct plate-voltage source. Since they tend to pile up one on another, after about two stages, I have some 1000 volts of juice playing around inside, and insulation difficulties, unpleasantly potent shocks, and other things are to be avoided with care.

But the circuit will, if it passes DC, as it must, pass line-current variations too. If the line current varies .00001 volts, and you amplify all variations 10,000,000 times — you'd have a neat 1000-volt variation in the output. So you use voltage-regulator circuits, bridge-balanced amplifiers, vacuum tube volt-meter circuits rigged as voltage multipliers feeding amplifier triodes, and generally try to play tricks on nature. You boost the photocell output voltage to a reasonable point by running the current of a few micromicroamperes through several millions of ohms of resistance, and then set the grid-bias on the first amplifiers to a fairly high threshold admittance so the damned thermoelectric currents, contact potentials and general evil disposition can't get through, but the signal can. If you think bakelite and rubber are insulators, you ought to see the meter needle tear across the scale when you short-circuit the terminals with a nice bakelite bus-bar. Stray currents from here to hell and back leak in and wriggle their tails in the meter. Give it a dirty look and the needle cowers down a few hundredths of a milliamp.

DC amplifiers are exceedingly annoying in their general behavior — and therefore more fun to make behave. I now have a two-stage — really two-and-three-quarters-stage-amplifier that will make the milliampmeter go off the scale when the photocell is exposed to the light of a match 5 feet away. It will read the enlarger light intensity with a very nearly linear response over a range of about 300 to 1, by shifting a four-position selector switch, and by opening or closing the cell window. And, with the maximum amplification of 20,000,000 times, the needle quivers only .02 milliamperes under normal voltage variations on the line-voltage. (When the oil burner cuts on, the 1/4 horse motor drags the voltage down so much the whole amplifier just shuts up shop and quits cold.) That steadiness is so perfect that it is apparent only when I use greatly diluted sunlight; the line-voltage fluctuations cause the light in the enlarger to vary slightly in temperature, and hence in brilliance. These variations are naturally read faithfully by the photocell and meter, and under the amplification I'm using, they amount to more than the unsteadiness of the amplifier.

The range of response covers printing exposures from 1 sec to 3 minutes, more range than I ever use.

To do it, I've evolved an unquestionably efficient, but thoroughly impractical device which uses eight different kinds of electric power, nine tubes, and about 50 different kinds and sizes of resistors. There are two rectifiers, three filter networks, and two voltage regulator tubes. Another tube, acting as a vacuum tube voltmeter, smoothes the power for the final amplifier stages. There is 3 volt drycell power, 5 volt AC, two 6.3 V AC supplies, 22-1/2 volt dry cell, voltage-regulated 105 volt supply, 250 volt plate supply, 400 volt plate supply divided into a 150 volt regulated supply and the vacuum tube voltmeter supply of 250 volts. The set consumes about 75 watts of power; its input is 0.00000000001 amperes at 22-1/2 volts, and the output is a maximum of 0.001 amp at about 0.01 volts. The other 74.99999 watts appears as heat in various and sundry resistors, tube-filaments, transformer windings, condenser leakages, plate dissipations, and occasional minor shocks when I get careless with my fingers.

It's a wonderful rig. Incidentally, *Popular Science Monthly* is paying for it — about $40 — though they don't realize it yet. I'll write a whole series of articles about the individual tubes, circuit-elements, and special difficulties.

The headaches involved might be of use to you as background in stories. All is not gold that glitters, and all is not simple that amplifies. And the prize above all other things is stability — an amplifier that amplifies what it's supposed to instead of every stray tidbit of accidental current that wanders by. Like a foxhound, amplifiers must be trained to trail foxes, and not set off on a rabbit spoor that happens to cross the way.

Regards, JWC, Jr.

A.E. van Vogt   *August 4, 1943*

Dear van vogt:

I'm taking "The Rulers," and returning the "Wonderful Man" fragment herewith. There have been large things in progress around here

685

this last week, and things were, again, tied up 'til decisions were made.

The main item is that poor old *Unknown* is dead — died of paper starvation. *Unknown* always was a small-circulation magazine, considerably smaller than *Astounding*, though I'd originally believed it would outsell *Astounding* at least 2 to 1, because *Astounding* requires technical imagination, and *Unknown* asked only imagination. It never did though, and, as is inevitable with small-circulation magazines, it had a small-circulation type of returns. You have to print a certain number of copies of a magazine in order to have some for display on the stands — and that's apt to represent a large percentage of a small-circulation total sale. The same number of display copies is a smaller percentage of a large circulation, of course. This made *Unknown* an inefficient user of paper, even though, because of its 25 cents price, it made money. Now the War Production Board rulings say we have to let *Unknown* go.

But *Astounding*, because of its better circulation — and in particular because of its peculiarly concentrated circulation; it has high sales on a small number of stands near technical industry plants — rolls merrily along. Some of the stories originally bought for *Unknown*, those that will fit reasonably well, will be transferred to *Astounding*. Many of the others will, I hope, appear in a last flare-up of *Unknown*, a one-shot "Annual" type book. In the meantime, *Astounding* suddenly finds itself mildly confused as to how much material it has on hand. We do not have any serial on hand, however; that much is certain. And we need one.

"The Wonderful Man" doesn't look like serial material in its present set-up. It needs more purpose, more motivation. The immortality of Capt. Hedrock was not a purpose, but a background fact. The super characteristics of Jommy Cross weren't purpose, but background material. Similarly, Craig's remarkable vitality is not purpose, nor sufficient motivation for the story — or at least, it is not sufficient when the story is told from his viewpoint.

It allows of purpose, but only on the part of the others; they may well want the secret of his practical immortality and tremendous vitality. There's a strong suggestion, however, of selfish secrecy in their method of investigation — and in the fact that his nurse-wife hasn't had a child by him, for that matter, to see whether it's hereditary.

686

Give stronger motivation, and it may start hitting on all eight cylinders and go somewhere. One item I suggest is that he does start using all his brain toward the end of each cycle of renewal. In the last cycle, gaining full brain power just before the end, invented the trick engine used in his cars and plane. Not having been given a good scientific background, he worked purely as a skilled and super-intelligent mechanic. He lacked facts, and had only a week or so, but with his meager equipment achieved a tremendous invention. This time, the business men who financed him hope that, in the last days, he'll invent some new and enormously more efficient administrative methods for major business organization — he has the specialized training needed this time, but, due to the escape and accident involved, makes the change before his brain has gone into full gear. With the result that, this time, the change to full-brain operation takes place <u>during the change</u> and so is fixed for the whole new cycle by the new cells being laid down.

Outside menace may be necessary — but I would point out that man's always been able to be the worst menace man needed to encounter to keep him stepping full speed ahead.

In any case, as it stands, the story either lacks purpose, or there is none revealed soon enough (even up to the present point) to really hold the reader's attention.

At the present moment, the papers are reporting Sicily's last corner is being reduced, with Catania still held by the Nazis, but the grip decidedly slippery. Obviously that has to be cleaned out before anything more is done. Then, I believe, the movement will be directly into Italy. Because Italy's military position is, despite what you say, catastrophic. It's utterly hopeless, the most hopeless possible, I think. They're so weak that they are about to become the battleground of the two powerful enemies, the Northern Italians being forced to fight with and for the Nazis, the Southern Italians welcoming the Allied troops as rapidly as they can advance. The Nazis will hate, distrust, and scorn them; the allies will inevitably scorn them, and distrust them. At the peace table, the Italians will suffer more than the Germans, in many ways; nobody will have either a good word or any respect for them. Their present situation is militarily hopeless from the Italian viewpoint because the people won't fight the Allies, and the soldiers surrender as quickly as they possibly can. It isn't the Italians' war; they have nothing to gain by endurance. Where the Englishman, bombed out of his home, got grimly furious at **Hitler,** the Italian bombed out of his home can only get grimly, hot-bloodedly mad at **Hitler** and the Italian government for not surrendering. The Englishman has something to fight for; the Italian is invited to fight and die for something he wants to get rid of!

Item: current and corny remark. Know why the Allies are hammering Hamburg so? They want to turn it into hamburger. Current reports indicate they damn well have.

I've been hobbying on a new line recently — electronics; I'm doing articles for *Popular Science Monthly* — and have built a short-wave tuner. It's still decidedly unfinished so far as alignment and adjustment goes, but I've been picking up a number of programs not put on for the benefit of local civilians. Among the best propaganda broadcasts is the beamed German and, until recently, Italian language news and news-analysis broadcasts. The news is straight factual, as far as I can make out with my on-leg-and-a-crutch German. The news analysis is an analysis of German High Command communiques, items published in German papers, etc. But what keeps 'em listening is the thickly scattered bunch of names of prisoners of war, with messages from them and addresses telling how to reach them. The names are scattered at intervals throughout the entire program, not read in a bunch. A beautiful job of monitoring is done on the broadcast — so beautiful I have a very strong hunch that they're using one of the automatic electronic volume-leveler circuits. It makes music a little flat, by holding the volume-peaks down, and boosting the soft passages a bit, but if you're listening in secret, it has the wonderful advantage that, except for atmospheric condition-caused fading and swelling, the volume won't suddenly leap up to a pitch that makes it audible outside. If you set it soft, it <u>stays</u> soft. It's good work. Also sound is the announcer, who speaks excellent German, **Willy Ley** tells me, but with an American accent you can recognize if you'ld never heard an American speaking German before. In other words, the listeners are meant to know that this man is no "traitor to Nazism and der Fuerher," but an American speaking so they can hear and understand what he thinks.

If **Alfred Forrester** becomes necessary, he will appear. Sorry in some ways you didn't think of that one sooner; that **E.M. Hull** suffers the difficulty that an **E.M. Hull** wrote, "The Sheik" — an item I'd completely forgotten 'til a reader inquired. But **E.M. Hull** is now tagged as the writer of the Artur Blord stories.

Regards, John W. Campbell, Jr.

A.E. van Vogt   *October 28, 1943*

Dear van Vogt:

This is coming back for changes. I think your thesis that a compromise peace can be morally ruinous is a good point to make, and a worthwhile basis for the story. The toti-potent group idea, also, it seems to me, is sound. But there are two threads woven through the story that don't sit well, and need changing.

First: There is a lot of good, sound logic in the proposition that Canada should come into the United States, each province becoming one of the states of the nation so built up. However, I have reason to believe that the proposition is received as easily in Canada as a good, 1/2-pint dose of castor oil. It may be logical, but it isn't desired.

Similarly, the name Usonia might be logical — but the logic isn't going over in <u>America</u> for reasons of Good Neighborliness or anything else. Any administration that tried to put that one over, I will guarantee, would be thrown out on its ear so damn fast we'd invent a new Constitutional referendum proceeding so we could haul 'em out before the normal term of office expired. Sure there are other Americas, and other United States of America, and all inhabitants of the continental masses of the Western hemisphere are Americans. But — 130,000,000 inhabitants of the United States of North America call themselves, "Americans," and intend to go on doing so. The suggestion of a change is irritating in itself; it is also, I can assure you, extremely improbable.

As a matter of fact, you know, if there is ever a United States of the World, it would be logical and advantageous to take full advantage of the fact that this is a government "of sovereign states" — and when that was written into the Constitution, they meant States, nations in the same sense that Germany, Holland, France and the other European nations are sovereign States. That is, if a world union were created, the present United States would enter not as one nation, but as 48 indepen-

689

dent, equal nations. (Texas is a heck of a sight bigger nation than most European powers. And New York is a major world power in its own right.) That would be logical and advantageous — but I'll bet that the people of this federal nation wouldn't see it that way! (Nor, probably, would the rest of the world. France would probably answer that each of her departments should similarly be a nation!)

The Usonia theme isn't vastly important anyway; that can be dropped readily enough.

The male-female war, though, is important. It's been done before, and done a lot. It's improbable, as a matter of fact. Inherently, the female of the species — any species — is not and by the nature of things, can not be equal to the male. In the insects that holds; the female by the nature of things has to be larger, stronger, and more active — usually longer-lived. In mammals the female is inherently handicapped. In Man, the characteristics of many genes are strongly sex-linked by unknown numbers of generations of selective mating. Intelligence is not; physical strength is. There are emotional reaction-chains which are. Some of those Nature herself planted in the male and female, sex-linked them, and nailed them down hard and fast for the protection of the race. (A female that lacks the characteristic of an instinctive tendency for protection of her young has a contra-survival tendency of the first order. A male lacking that characteristic has only a mildly contra-survival tendency.)

Women in general realize that in a sub-reasoned way. (Subconscious has been overworked; that, however, would be the right term. Or, to use another overworked term, a semi-instinctive way.) Women in general do not trust or like a woman who claims to be the equal of any man. They will give a woman a chance if she claims that women are the intellectual equals of men. Men will give her a chance.

But I'm pretty darned sure that practically no women, and no men would vote for a woman who had taken an "Equalizer" treatment. Be something like a eunuch trying to get votes on the basis that he had the advantageous characteristics of both men and women.

[Handwritten along side of margin:Ed: Note. The presence of "Equalized" women in the story is OK. But they'll be disliked by all men and most women. They'll be offensive as any other braggart, "I'm as good a man as you are" type — inevitably!]

Make Jennifer into Jefferson Dayles, make the reason for the stuffing of ballot boxes simple determination to seize power, and the story works out about the same.

I think you've been straining for something new and strange and different in this "Wonderful Man" yarn. But my gut reaction is that while you've achieved that in part, you'll do better without these particular strangenesses.

If you want Jefferson Dayles to have some ideal beyond simple dictatorial power, there's a legitimate aim, a legitimate consideration. One that, furthermore, will be completely answered by the final revelation.

This war is producing enormous advances in science — technologies, perhaps, would be better, since fundamental sciences are rather stymied both by lack of researchers and by lack of inter-communication. I have taken up two hobbies recently — photography and, more recently, electronics. I've gone into each deeply enough to know that each is a field so immensely broad, so intricate, that several lifetimes of research would be required to get a decent working knowledge of a few of the ramifications involved. In electronics, for instance:

I've been building a short-wave radio receiver. When I get it finished, it will be better than any set you can buy on the market for the job of picking up voice broadcast on short-wave. The vacuum tube has inherent noise — electrons being discrete particles, there's a lower limit to the strength of signal you can use, because added amplification brings the noise of individual electrons falling on the plate of the first tube, or bouncing off of charged elements within the tube. Certain tubes have less of that than others; these less noisy types make the best tube for the first amplifier. (If a noiseless tube amplifies ten times, then the second tube can be 9 times as noisy before its noise becomes noticeable above the now-amplified signal.)

I have several friends over at the Bell Labs. One of them, **John R. Pierce** — who wrote "Unthinking Cap" — is the polygrid vacuum tube expert for Bell Labs. He is, of course, one of the really top men in the country, which, under the circumstances, means also the world. He told me that a 6AC7-1852 used in triode connection made a tube so nearly noiseless that no antenna system could bring in a signal too weak for it to amplify without introducing noise. Also, he suggested using a

6AC7-1852 in triode connection as a mixer tube — for quietness again. And suggested a trick oscillator circuit, called the electron-coupled oscillator circuit. I tried it. It made a noise like a machine gun shooting beebees into a tin wash boiler. I commented on this the next time I saw **Pierce**, and he spoke to **John Skellet**, Bell Labs electron circuit expert. Seems **Pierce** was right in the tube-noise data; that's **Pierce's** field. But the electron-coupled oscillator circuit, while an exceptionally reliable, stable, and accurate circuit for a frequency generating system, has a very high noise-level. **Pierce** is a vacuum tube expert; he knows all about what happens inside the tube. But his dope on the circuits outside the tube is rather hazy and theoretical rather than practical. He hasn't had time to study external circuits as well as internal electron reactions. He hasn't had time, even, to learn the mathematical processes necessary to handle the data he accumulates most conveniently. Bell Labs has a staff of mathematical experts who specialize in different types of mathematical physics, to work out those problems from data supplied by the researchers.

Pierce can't build a radio set; **Skellet** doesn't design tubes that are ideal for the circuits he wants; he designs circuits that work with the tubes available. Another engineer takes **Skellet's** test set-up and reduces it to a manufactureable article.

They'd probably do a hell of a sight better if the manufacturing expert designed tubes and circuits that were ideal from all three standpoints — but no man has time enough to learn all three fields adequately. (Item: in a superhetrodyne receiver, the tuning systems are multiple. The antenna tuner tunes, say, from 5 to 12 megacycles by a fixed inductance and a variable capacitance. The radio frequency amplifier transformer is tuned also, and it, too, tunes from 5 to 12 megacycles by means of a variable condenser and fixed inductance. The heterodyne oscillator tunes also; it is the most critical of the three tuners, but it must tune to a frequency always 1500 kilocycles higher than the frequency tuned by the other two circuits — from 6.5 to 13.5 megacycles. It is desired that all three circuits be tuned together by rotating one control — that the three variable condensers be varied together, by ganging them on a single shaft. But the tuning range of the antenna and RF tuners is 1 to 2.4; the oscillator tuning range is only 1 to 2.08. They can't tune together, obviously, if they are identical, nor if
692

they have the same physical shape. The plates of the osc. tuner must be of a different pattern — and a highly complex pattern. However, an approximation can be attained by using a smaller inductance coil, and reducing the effective capacitance of the osc. tuner by putting another condenser of fixed capacity in series with it. Which method is the most desirable? Theoretically, the cut-plate method; that can be calculated to give perfect "tracking." Practically, the manufacturing difficulties are so great, because of the complex and weird shape of the plates required, that the second, approximate, method is used.)

Someone capable of over-all integration is necessary. Someone with life-span enough to learn all the subjects. Or, better, several men who can integrate different fields, each covering several as rapidly as possible — because it would take generations to get all knowledge in one man.

[Handwritten along margin:Ed: This motivation isn't new to science-fiction either — but it is an inescapable, ever more pressing problem.]

When Dayles learns of the toti-potent possibilities, he sees a possibility of integrating several such men — immortalized by Craig's blood. He <u>must</u> get Craig; he <u>must</u> retain power until he succeeds. He also knows that benevolent tyranny is the best form of government; the difficulty with the thing being that tyrants have always been mortal, and a benevolent one is succeeded by a malevolent one with terrible results. This will make possible an integrated, stable, predictable benevolent tyranny under which progress will be steady. He will be a tyrant, yes — but a tyrant who is benevolent because he already has everything. (His family was wiped out in the war. He owns everything already; how can you bribe him?)

I suggest that the totipotents <u>can</u> reproduce. But that their children, like any other offspring, carry the inherited, not the acquired, characteristics. They, too, may become totipotent if under sufficiently terrible pressures, under the right balance of conditions. But, like ordinary children, they are far more apt to die than to become totipotent. Cut off a leg, mangle an arm, leave them in mud and cold for a week — and find a corpse. Two attempts were made; two small corpses resulted. No more attempts to force totipotency followed, naturally . . . . But one of their own did come back from the war totipotent; twenty of their children and grandchildren died. There's a somewhat higher

693

percentage of totipotency, of course . . . .

Regarding the overpayment on "The Contract." I estimate wordage on the basis of number of pages. Usually, it runs in the neighborhood of 300 to the page. Yours, I see, runs considerably looser. I think the simplest way is to let this ride; one of these days some one of your stories will be bought at a straight 1 cent — the bonus having been paid on "Contract." OK?

And concerning the idea of "Lost Art." **George Smith** is a designing radio engineer for Crossley Radio — now for the US Army & Navy. I'd been fussing with radio, learning the thing from manuals, catalogs, and technical reference tables, plus books on theory. Very fine works they were, too. Only they left out everything about the practical aspects. 6.3 volt alternating current leads carrying the cathode-heater current must be twisted together, and run jammed tight in the corner channel of the sheet steel chassis — otherwise they will induce a 60-cycle hum in the output. They don't mention it in the books. The output terminals of an audio amplifier must be at the opposite end of the chassis from the input terminals -- or the set will simply start squealing and do nothing else. But the books don't mention that — you're supposed to know it, as any radio mechanic does. Gripes on that subject lead to the suggestion of what an archaeologist, digging out a lost civilization, would do with a collection of tubes and some intact manuals that tell not what the tubes are for, nor how, practically, to make them work. The story grew out of a basic, personal gripe at the sloppiness of technical manuals. (**George Smith** told me the trick of twisting the leads and stuffing them in a corner, where the steel chassis soaks up the magnetic fields. He gave me several other similar hints. **Skellet** of the Bell Labs contributed the item about input and output leads.)

The idea you are working on had a rather different origin, and a different basic mechanism. One — **Smith's** — sprang from the annoying incompleteness of technical manuals. The other — yours — was more or less of a pure concept; the machines without mechanism driving the explorers to distraction by their complete lack of information.

Smith's idea, in other words, came from my immense irritation at the discovery that you don't have to be an archaeologist to find a lost art!

Regards, John W. Campbell, Jr.

694

A.E. van Vogt *Wednesday 1943*

Dear van Vogt:

I have one of my usual colds at the moment, making me feel more thick-headed than usual. So if this isn't clear in spots, ask for further explanation. It's an idea that might yield something if mulled about for a few weeks.

It could be handled from either of two ends. First; the basis is a moment's thought on modern archaeological expeditions, and the careful way they piece-together bits of broken pottery and such to find out how another world lived 5000 years ago, how they cooked their food, how they stored water, etc. And against that, suppose that an archaeologist of 1830 or so had dug up a ruined New York City of 1942.

Some things would make sense. Gas pipes, water mains, gas stoves, central heating plants using coal fires and steam or hot water radiators. By analogy, they'd get the idea that an oil furnace was a furnace and that the machine made fire, somehow. But electric motors weren't known. Electricity — except from exceedingly puny batteries — wasn't known. An electric stove wouldn't make sense; an electric light bulb would be a strange decorative fixture. A fluorescent light would be hopelessly meaningless. An electric toaster utterly unfathomable, particularly the kind that ticks and obviously is doing something with something for some length of time for some unguessable reason. They might guess at electricity at first, but they knew, then, that metal carried electric current, and since the conservation or energy principle wasn't really in their souls, they wouldn't have gotten the idea of making a complete metallic — short! — circuit. And a modern 1100 watt two-slice Toastmaster gadget would definitely be a total short-circuit to any battery they had in those days. Cold, the thing draws something like 2000 to 2400 watts, nearly 20 amperes. Connected across their sort of electric current supplies, it would kill the battery, but not get respectably warm.

Finding a radio, a modern home set of the A.C. operated type, would be even more hopeless a mystery. In the first place, an A.C. set would — from their point of view — start out by taking current from the line into a coil of heavy copper wire and short-circuiting it dead right there. (On D.C., naturally, it would.) They'd never heard of A.C., nor did they guess at the possibilities.) If it got beyond that point, the current would have to pass through several wires into a glass bottle where every circuit was broken by a considerable air-gap. On the other side of the thing in the bottle they'd find a condenser with one end only connected to the circuit, the other end connected to a completely independent circuit, in which position it could only act as an insulator completely without purpose, since no electricity can pass through a condenser. (No D.C. energy can beyond an initial surge.)

A modern steam generating plant would give them headaches, too. Allow the boilers rusted to destruction, they'd find the turbines with no indication of what the purpose of all the metal slats might be, nor what the purpose of the immense mass of iron and copper connected to the turbine shaft could be.

A bicycle they could figure all right, and if it had one of those miniature bicycle-lamp generators on it, they might get a clue that would lead them someplace. On the other hand, they might try it on one of their batteries, and simply get a small, inefficient electric motor and draw the wrong conclusion — that the generator was intended to propel the bicycle rather than vice versa.

The story could be either an 1800-type archaeological group exploring our civilization's remnants, or a 2300-type archaeological group exploring a dead civilization on another planet, a civilization not too remote from them but they could tell it had been only a century or two older when it dies. If you want to make it a 1980 group exploring a dead and drought-preserved Martian city, OK. Or allow that in 1975 the first ship reaches the moon, that in 1985 a new and utterly fundamental principle of natural law is discovered so that, by 1990 a ship reaches Alpha Centauri A-4 and discovers the city. The inhabitants of the city had not stumbled on the natural phenomenon that made their ship possible — it's one of those freak things that will happen; the discovered didn't know enough to invent the darned thing, but did anyway by blind luck. Just as **Lee de Forest** had no right to invent the radio triode. It should have been discovered by proper scientific research in the Bell Telephone Laboratories about 1935; **de Forest** didn't know a damn thing about the science of electronics. **Hall's** discovery of the aluminum refining process was legitimate; science had reached the proper stage. But **de Forest's** discovery had practical use, and brought on a rash
696

of investigation into electronics causing the discovery after the invention of the principles that should, properly, have led to the invention.

The spaceship drive was discovered out of time; the Centaurian culture had discovered the things that properly lead up to it, and in about another 50 years would have discovered it. The end of that set-up might be that the explorers finally catch on; all the mysteries are simply derivative, primitive, and sometimes unnecessarily laborious applications of the principle of the spaceship drive. the Centaurians had, lets say, a way of wirelessly transmitting energy, not electric energy however, but in such a form that it could be picked up as any desired type of mechanical energy and — by mechanical movement of electrons — hence electric energy. Certain atomic structures pick it up as rotation; an alloy of germanium, iron and molybdenum would, when the power station was working, rotate continuously about its axis of crystallization at a rate independent of the load placed on it, but determined by the proportions of the alloying elements, and the crystallization process used in producing the shaft. An alloy of iron, cobalt and titanium, on the other hand, would move in a straight line along its axis of magnetization in the direction of its north pole. Not a magnetic phenomenon, you understand; simply that the magnetization orients the crystal-units and makes them team up to pick up the transmitted energy. De-magnetization cuts off the power. The speed of motion is determined by the analysis of the alloy, and not by the load; it will move any load with equal speed, instantly attaining its fixed maximum, or smashing the restraining connections in the effort.

Now; figuring the fun the boys would have trying to dope out the gadgets made on those principles. (Oh — electrons will be "mechanically" driven at an unvarying rate through a rod made of an alloy of lead, copper and aluminum and manganese which is subjected to a magnetic field. The field orients the crystals; the current will flow at right angles to the field as a D.C. current. Another alloy, containing cobalt and nickel as well as the others, and made up as a short, broad cylinder, causes a steady current, useful in some applications where you don't want to be able to turn off the current.) If the power station isn't running, nothing operates of course. And without it, you'ld never guess that this meaningless, useless shaft actually turned at an invariant one revolution every .1375 seconds and, since that was their least

697

unit of time, the gearing associated with it was really a simple clock —
that, in other words, what seemed to be simply the shaft carrying the
"second" hand of the clock was actually the whole motor that operated it! Without that knowledge, the clock was a mass of gearing that
went from undriven shaft A to unpowered shaft Z, getting nowhere in
a peculiarly cumbersome fashion.

There ought to be a lot of fun and mystery in that, if you could find a
story to wrap it in. It isn't necessary for you to explain everything; if you
have the thing clearly in mind yourself, you can invent gadgets, machines, and whatnot, world without end, completely inexplicable except with the key. The key can be given in a few words at the end, when
the ship's engineer finally digs out the secret and makes up a miniature
power-unit. He has to demonstrate it finally when he's several billions
of miles out in space; he knew he was right before, because when he
tried out his miniature unit on the planet, the transmitter rig crumbled
to dust with a heavy thubump. All the gadgets lying around on the
planet tried to draw on it.

Regards, John W. Campbell, Jr.

[John W. Campbell and A.E. van Vogt were both very much involved with Dianetics™ during the early fifties. The following letter reflects Campbell's understanding of L. Ron Hubbard's works during
Hubbard's Research and Development phase. Although "norns" was
described in *Astounding Science Fiction*, it never caught on in Hubbard's further work, the word "norn" being replaced by the word "en-
gram." After 1954, Campbell did not stay abreast with L. Ron Hubbard's discoveries and definitions, and so the Dianetic materials described to follow are not held out to be complete. If the reader
wishes a final version of Hubbard's 1950 Dianetic work, see *Dianetics:
The Modern Science of Mental Health* available at most book stores.
(According to *Publisher's Weekly* this book is the all-time outstanding
bestseller, and has been since 1950.) If the reader wishes Hubbard's later
publications and/or tapes, write to Bridge Publications, 4751 Fountain
Ave., Los Angeles, CA 90029. Ed.]

A.E. van vogt   *November 16, 1949*

Dear van:

I haven't heard from you in some time, and with the subject of Dianetics™ boiling, I've been wondering what you've been doing. I'm still going to see to it that you get a copy of the operator's manual as soon as possible, but the thing is undergoing continuous revision. So much of any technique is always at the "of course" level in the mind of the man who knows it that, inevitably, he forgets to put in many of the little — but critical — points. **Ron** didn't have anywhere near all the essential dope in his first writing of the manual; a fact which he couldn't detect because he knew the stuff so well by then that he'd forgotten the trouble he had inventing it originally. Only when we tried to operate without that "of course" stuff, reinventing some of it as we went, did we point out its absence. Much of it is still in process, therefore, and the manual still isn't ready.

At the same time, we're renaming much of the material and concepts. For instance, the term "unconsciousness" has to be redefined so radically that the only sensible method is to invent a new word, and put on it a definition of our own that eliminates quarrels over what is meant. Many, for instance, would complain that you can't have "unconsciousness" in a prenatal human, because he isn't conscious yet and therefore can't be rendered unconscious. So we have a new term; <u>anaten</u>. If a man is knocked unconscious, he is anaten; but also when he is hypnotized he is anaten, and when the prenatal human is seriously injured it is rendered anaten. The neologism is made up — like radar — from the initial letters. In this case, <u>ana</u>lytic <u>a</u>wareness att<u>en</u>uation.

Similar neologisms are needed throughout; they avoid confusion of old meanings for new concept-words. For instance, "impediment" is now a <u>norn</u>. That one derives from Norse mythology, but has the advantage that it has no English meaning, is short, easy to say, and is extremely unapt to appear in the content of a norn. We found, on the other hand, a case where one patient had as part of his "impediment," "he's just an impediment to us." This sort of cross-up can cause trouble; we're trying to get rid of "impediments," but his reactive mind content says that he himself is an impediment; therefore we are trying to get rid of — i.e. kill — him. Naturally, he wasn't very cooperative at that point. But if we had been trying to get rid of norns, on the other hand —.

If you remember the Norse Norns, they were the equivalent of the Greek Fates. Three old hags with one eye, one ear, and one tongue between them; they were arbitrary, reasonless, they determined the pattern of a man's life without his consent or awareness. That's a norn, son, that's a norn!

Another trouble with "impediment" was that it implies a static process — a blocking. But the actual mechanism isn't static; it's goddamned dynamic — it drives man. It can drive him to suicide, or murder, or it can drive him into catatonic rigidity.

But if you want to see just how far off the path the professional psychologists have strayed, try these home-game tricks on your friends. These are a few items of parlor-Dianetics that won't ruin anybody.

First: Think of the last time you walked out of your home there, the last time you said good-bye to your wife. Recall the scene, and visualize it. Can you, in your mind, get an actual visual <u>picture</u> of the scene. Can you <u>see</u> her in memory, where she was standing or sitting — the scene as a picture? If so, can you see <u>colors</u> in the scene? What color is her dress? Her chair or other articles near her? Next, what did she say — what were the words? Can you <u>hear</u> her voice in your mind, as an actual sound — the tones, inflections and so on? If you have full normal human memory, you will. Also, remember when you combed or brushed your hair when you first got up this morning. Can you <u>feel</u> the tactile sensation of the brush on your scalp? Can you, in memory, smell the sensation of the brush on your scalp? Can you, in memory, smell the odor of roasting beef? taste the memory of a good, crisp apple? All of these sensory memories should be present; sight, sound and tactile are normally clear and strong, the others less strong, but present. If any of them is missing — you have a norn somewhere which blocks it. And if you try that on a dozen people — fully awake, conscious memory — you'll find that about 1/3rd of them don't hear. Some don't see colors; some don't see at all, some don't hear at all. And some neither see <u>nor</u> hear. I fall in the latter class; as yet I neither see, feel nor hear in memory — which explains why I've never been able to carry a tune (how can you sing if you can't hear what it should sound like) and can't remember people. (How could I; I can't see what they looked like!)

Item: the second requires the cooperation of a few children be-

700

tween 7 and 12 years old. It's called, "Remember When Game," and the child must like, trust, and believe the questioner — which makes the child's favorite parent the best one for the trick usually. It may turn out, though, that there are some fancy mutual abortion attempts in the background, wherefore a nurse, or a neighbor, may be the child's best and most trusted friend. You simply ask the child — fully awake and conscious — to remember the earliest memories. First will come 4-5 year old memories. Tell him or her "Oh, no — I mean early — way, way back when you were tiny. Just a tiny baby. You can remember — just go back, back in your mind. Look for the little mind pictures —." A little coaxing will bring first-birthday memories easily. (The trick won't work, of course, if the child's memory has been blocked by norns saying, "You can't remember," and "you can't see or hear or feel!" No use trying with those poor kids.) But a little practice, a little coaxing and you'll get fully conscious recall of things at 2 to 3 months old. It isn't wise to go back too much further; you may restimulate the highly painful and unpleasant birth memories, which are better left undisturbed until therapeutic approach is made. My 9-year-old within 20 minutes of starting was describing her Grandfather's first visit — she was about 2 months old. She quoted him, then started asking what, "Weston rating" and "Panchromatic" meant. Had quite a time stumbling over those words, too. Dad took movies of her that time, using Super XX panchromatic film, with a 100 Weston rating.

Very useful memory training for children — they'll have a damn good use for a memory like that. Throw nonsense words at them, or totally unfamiliar polysyllables, and make them repeat them back. Tell 'em to, "listen to what I said — go back in your memory and listen to it again." Pretty soon they really develop facility at that memory-regression, and use it regularly. Then school work gets wonderfully easy. What's 7 X 8? Why — see it in the book — or listen to teacher saying it. Just go back in memory and get the right answer. Spelling? Just see it in the book! You need only look at it once, after all, because after that you can always go back and look at it again!

Now tell me, my friend, just what in hell have the professional psychologists, psychiatrists, and psychoanalysts been doing for 50 years that they never discovered even those simple, readily observed and checked factors of human mind and memory? Sitting on their well-padded rumps, with their thinking mind completely out of gear? Or so hypnotized by their own inordinately complex theories that they couldn't stop to observe such simple facts — and find out why they existed?

Here's another one. Very useful around the household. Know someone who has blue-spells? That person is then redramatizing a norn that's full of despair, apathy, sadness, etc. They are, temporarily, stuck in that norn, and dramatizing it. It's apt to be accompanied by some sort of ache or pain, but doesn't have to be — nevertheless, they're dramatizing a norn, and stuck in it. You can't argue them out of the norn; it's a part in a play, only they are stuck in it and don't know it. You can't talk them out of it logically, because you can't talk to that individual; the person is dramatizing someone long gone — it's like arguing with someone in a sound movie. You see and hear them — but they aren't there really, just a projector and a screen. In this case the person you see is just a projector and screen for someone who isn't there — and you can't argue with the projector-screen.

But you can fool it. Listen, pick up the exact words and phrases used by the individual, until you know most of the key phrases. Then you start playing that part. You act blue; you use those phrases and words. Try to match the tone. And in about two minutes flat you'll have the ex-blue individual busily cheering you up. Reason: You've taken over the part he was dramatizing — and since he's stuck in that particular norn, if you pre-empt that role, he's forced to take over the opposite part. The opposite part in the drama was, of course, busily trying to cheer up the depressed person your victim was dramatizing — so the person is forced to be the cheerer-upper!

That's a general law of Dianetics. When an individual displays an unusual and severe emotional state, the individual is dramatizing a norn. The person will be dramatizing one of the personalities in the original scene. If someone else pre-empts the role being dramatized by that individual, the individual is forced to do one of two things: break out of the norn entirely — thus returning to some other emotional state, and possibly his own, natural personality (though probably jumping into still a new norn) -- or take up the opposite role in the norn. A suicider, for instance, standing on the window-ledge can't be argued in; the thing to do is to pick up his words and phrases, repeat them exactly, and when you've got his complete attention, start climbing out with him. He won't let you; he has to accept the other role in that norn — which was the role of the "oh, no-you-mustn't-do-that!" party, and he now has to argue <u>you</u> out of suicide, and prevent <u>you</u> from doing it! He's under just as powerful a nornal compulsion to do that as he was, before, to commit suicide himself.

Any emotional state — except true love — is almost certain to be nornal. Even attitudes are usually nornal. Suppose a man had a free-handed, fun-loving father, and a worry-wart, penny-pinching, gotta-watch-the-budget mother. If his wife really wants to work him, she watches for words and phrases on each dramatization. He'll have certain speech-patterns when he's free-handed — that is, being Dad — and quite different speech-patterns when he's being budget-conscious — i.e., playing the role of Mother. So, if wife wants a new coat, <u>she</u> puts on the Mother act — she uses the mother-role phrases. That forces hubby into the free-handed, lets-enjoy-ourselves-that's-what-money's-for father role. He forces the coat on her. But if wifey feels he ought not to buy that new television set just now — she puts on the Father role, using the father words and phrases. And hubby, of course, then has to take the mother-dramatization, gets budget-conscious, and doesn't buy the television set.

It takes observation, thought, patience and figuring to get the full effect of this trick in the finer little low-potential items like attitudes. In great emotional crises — suicide, homicidal mania or the insanities — the dramatization is so powerful and complete that the entire structure of the norn can readily be mapped out. Then it isn't too hard to break that particular dramatization.

I repeat: What have the psychologists been doing for the past fifty years?

But I think those items will interest and stimulate you. Try them out on some of your friends; you'll find that **Ron Hubbard's** <u>really</u> got answers.

Regards, John W. Campbell, Jr.

A.E. van Vogt   *December 22, 1949*

703

Dear van:

The office works got well loused up this year, with the result that the Christmas cards are expected about the first of January. Hence no Xmas cards from Street & Smith this year! So you can take this as a belated Christmas Greeting, as well as a letter. Or maybe we should just fire the Art Misdirector and say Happy New Year.

Anyhow, your letter re the Bruin SCF club talk, and Dianetics™, rather amused and interested me. Hypnotism is old; everybody knows something about it. Therefore most people tend to see in Dianetics a version of hypnotism. There's a rule of language development the linguists have called the "Hobson-Jobson Law." It's not named for men named Mr. Hobson and Dr. Jobson, but for the fact that the British troops in India interpreted as "Hobson-Jobson" a common Hindustanee phrase — approximating the true syllables with the nearest familiar English-sounding syllables. The French call a bowsprit a "beautiful meadow" — because beautiful meadow in French sounds more like "bowsprit" than any other French sounds do. The same process, I think, applies to intellectual material; Dianetics more closely resembles hypnotism than anything the average man knows — so he calls it hypnotism. The psychiatrist calls it a modified version of **Freud**. It isn't either one. Dianetics is a process of <u>breaking</u> pain-installed hypnotic commands, and flatly contradicts most of **Freud**.

But **Ron's** article — 16,000 words! — will appear in the May issue. The editorial is going to be a cruel, cruel thing. It invites psychiatrists, psychotherapists and psychologists who disagree to write their own articles, and promises to publish the best. But — it lays down one rule: the articles in their argument must follow the scientific method. The rules under that are, of course, that argument by appeal to authority, is invalid! That no theory can stand in the face of one demonstrable fact. That the <u>original source</u>, not the observer's report of that source, <u>is the data</u>. It's a cruel harsh stricture to lay on a bunch of foggy-witted philosophers! It's what happened to physical science, though, about 500 years ago. And look what it did for that branch of learning! I suggest that the article writer try substituting the name "Doakes" every place he is tempted to write "**Freud**," and see if his argument still makes sense. It should; facts, not authorities, count.

On the observer item, incidentally, a semanticist should like this.

The standard case report as published in clinical psychology books, is necessarily a brief summary of the important characteristics of the patient's actions and statements. The patient's actions and statements are the data; the observer's report is filtered, and distorted second-hand report. It's distorted, necessarily, by this situation:

The characteristic of an insane mind is that it is illogical, makes faulty evaluations of data, operates under misconceptions, and tends to mix relevances and irrelevancies.

The characteristics of a sane mind are that it evaluates data soundly, works logically, and can separate out and discredit irrelevancies.

But when we are trying to understand an insane mind, we must use the scale of data evaluation used by that insane mind.

Wherefore, only by setting up a mind having precisely the same insanity as the patient, can we get an observer able to extract the true importance's from the statements and actions of the patient! Any other mind will extract from the material offered by the patient the material his scale of evaluations holds to be important — and if the observer has been trained in a particular school of thought, he will inevitably find data along those lines of importance, disregarding as irrelevancies data not matching that scale of evaluation!

Nevertheless, if you get a series of case reports and study them, particularly the manic depressives and involute melancholies, you'll find case after case where the patient has been quoting from what will appear obvious to you now — an abortion attempt scene in which the mother is babbling to herself.

By the way, **Ron** tells me you were present several times when he was using Dianetic therapy techniques to relieve someone. He has also used Dianetic techniques in the presence of psychiatrists without the psychiatrist being aware of what was going on!

Ron's book on Dianetics will be out in early May, apparently. Hermitage House is going to bring it out, and has contracted to get it out with the maximum possible celerity; the book will be mentioned with the article, because sure as fate some people are going to try to get themselves into Dianetics after reading the article, which does not give detailed instructions on technique. And if they don't wait for the book, some of 'em are going to have to be pried off the walls by the men in white coats. And even Dianetics can't overcome the effects of a

705

prefrontal lobotomy, or a transorbital leukotomy.

By the way, have you heard of that one? The transorbital is a dilly — and I wouldn't have believed it myself if it hadn't been described to me in full medical detail by a neuropsychiatrist. In essence, the patient is electro-shocked into unconsciousness, then the eyelid is peeled back, and an icepick-like instrument driven in behind the eyeball, through the back of the eyesocket into the brain. It is swished around horizontally. Then the patient is given another electroshock to make him unconscious, and a similar job is done on the other side of the brain. That, my friend, is how psychiatry handles schizophrenia! Offhand, it seems to me that Freudian psychology has fallen absolutely flat on its inexpressibly silly posterior. The way to handle a patient who's mind is troubled is to destroy so much of his brain that he can't think about it or anything else any more.

Incidentally, I've mentioned that the trouble with most insane patients is that they're stuck in an impediment. I have a theory that there's one class that isn't. You know electroshock therapy works on depressives, manics, etc.; those are the boys who are stuck in impediments. Hit 'em with that jolt, and you blast them loose by main strength and awkwardness. You've given them a new and entirely different impediment to worry about.

But shock therapy doesn't work with schizos. Tentative reason: A schizo has as his operating impediment something of the nature of, "I can't stand being hurt; it's unbearable. I've got to get away from here!" He does; he gets entirely off his time-track, entirely away from reality of experience in memory — or present time. He's not stuck <u>in</u> an experience; he's stuck <u>away from all experiences</u>. Shock him — and hell, that's just another painful experience he's stuck away from! It doesn't affect him!

Oh well — we'll know a lot more a year from now!

Regards, John W. Campbell, Jr.

**The 1950's
with *A.E. van Vogt***

John W. Campbell, Jr. *June 12, 1951*

Dear John W.:

I am glad you have awakened to a real problem that *AST* is facing. However, the fact is your problem is even bigger than you have stated.

You may recall that at the time of my sale to you of "The Wizard of Linn" I wrote you saying in effect that I was not getting enough money for my rate of production to make it worth my while — this by the way was putting it mildly.

Therefore, I got an agent for a few of my stories, and he sold them for 3 and 4 cents a word, first serial rights only.

I did tell him that he should not send to you, since I had over the years developed a personal arrangement that made it impossible for me to think in terms of agents. But after he began to get the higher rates, I was forcibly reminded of an author who for years had a personal arrangement with the editor of the *Saturday Evening Post*, and for years sold him stories for $1000 apiece. One day he met a writer whom he knew had only sold to the *Post* for a couple of years. He discovered that this colleague of his was getting $5000 a story.

That hurt; and it hurt me when I learned that you have paid much higher rates to some writers than you did to me. And now I hear that *AST* is going to start charging 3/4 cents a word for book rights (for stories some of which were originally paid for at 1 cent a word). I thought that the 1/4 cent a word pocketbook charge was a good idea, but I haven't honestly had more than two books that earned as much as a cent a word for book rights. So — it sounds to me as if S & S is going backwards not forward in its relationship with authors. Personally, I should like to have all clothbook rights assigned to me en masse along with radio, TV and movie.

I believe that S & S should have some say and protection on pocketbook and serial, but only where such rights actually infringe on their territory. The refusal a couple of years ago to let me sell German serial rights of *Slan* did me out of $500, and accomplished no purpose that I can imagine.

Now, I hear that S & S is contemplating unloading its massive supply of stories to reprint magazines. This will kill every SF writer in the business, or at least reduce him to apathy, financially speaking.

I disapprove of such a resale without qualification. The prospect is absolutely frightening. This was the reason why publishers had to start buying all rights -- because authors were selling to cheap reprint magazines. If the lesson is so quickly forgotten, then this wretched seesaw is going to continue.

I favor an arrangement protecting both the author and the publisher from the more catastrophic results of such resale of serial rights.

So much for my personal feelings. Now, let me say that I have a real soft spot in my heart for *Astounding* and its great editor. Therefore, when I tell you that several writers have recently informed me that they have instructed their agents NOT to send stories to *AST*, I hope you will believe that I was shocked and somewhat dismayed as to what this would do to the magazine.

Their reasons were very similar to those I have outlined above. Everybody is afraid of another **Munsey** deal, like the one that sees an endless series of *Famous Fantastic Mysteries* come out with the great sf stories of the past paraded for the commercial advantage of those who bought up the **Munsey** inventory.

As for the stories of mine which have appeared here and there during the past year, with two exceptions, I wouldn't have sent them to you anyway. For those two, I received respectively 4 cents and 5 cents a word. I don't expect you to compete with that, but it sure is nice to get those kind of checks.

All the best always, Van

Clifford D. Simak   *June 18, 1953*

Dear Cliff:

My, but you stuck your neck out on that letter!

My friend, for some 2-1/2 years, my really quite remarkable wife, **Peg**, and I have been engaged in basic philosophical-psychological research, working at it — and I mean working almost 100 hours a week. That's some 12,000 hours of study.

I've gotten immense help from the deep self-searching that science-fiction authors have done. (**E.E. Smith's** "Children of the Lens" is one of the most solid efforts to study how a parent can train a child to be superior to himself that's ever been done, I think.)

I've had high-power help from my friends like **Wayne Batteau** at Harvard computer lab, **John Arnold** at MIT, **E.E. Francisco** who's head of research at White Sands — in other words, the high-power speculative minds of high sanity rating, who have contacted me through my science-fiction work.

Currently, **Dr. Gotthard Gunther**, a philosopher specializing in the study of symbolic logic and non-aristotelian logics, is helping us quite directly.

Claude Shannon's information theory, and **Weiner's** cybernetics have both helped. I've worked with both of these men; they're both science-fictioneers.

The men I've mentioned are known and respected generally; they aren't as speculative, actually, as some of the other men who are not yet widely recognized for their work. **Hal Clement**, for instance, and **Ray Jones**, **Cliff Simak** and **Eric F. Russell**. You and your compeers are communicators — you want to think out an idea, and communicate it. There is no more effective communication channel than fiction; fact discussions are not as powerful.

Jesus knew that; he used parables.

Uncle Tom's Cabin overrode all the polemics, lectures and orations the southerners could produce.

Go ahead and control the newspapers; you can be defeated with ease by the magazines printing pure fiction. Newspapers give only data; fiction establishes philosophy, and a man acts on data-interpreted-by-philosophy, not on facts alone!

The impossibility of portraying the superman was behind the moves I made back in 1939 to get some superman stories of a new type written. There are two possible approaches to avoid the problem: 1. The approach typified by the play "The Women" which was all about men, yet had not one man on stage. I pointed out this proposition to **Norvell Page**; he wrote "But Without Horns" for me. In that one, if you recall, the superman was never on stage — only people who had met him and been changed, or men who were fighting him.

2. The super-man can't be fully portrayed. But since ontogeny recapitulates phylogeny, a super-human must, during boyhood and adolescence, pass through the human level; there will be a stage of his development when he is less than adult-human, another stage when he is equal to adult-human — and the final stage when he has passed beyond our comprehension.

The situation can be handled, then, by establishing faith, trust, understanding, and sympathy with the <u>individual as a character</u> by portraying him in his not-greater-than adult human stages — and allow the established trust-and-belief to carry over to the later and super-human stage.

A.E. van Vogt worked out "Slan" in response to that comment-discussion from me. The central character is introduced as Jommy, the nearly helpless, hard-pressed small boy; seen further as Jommy Cross, the adolescent (adult-human equivalent) and finally followed as Cross, the super-human.

Each of the two methods is basically a single method, developed in two different ways — the method of projection.

If you can't reach the full way, you can project a line that will reach. Line up the reader by letting him follow that which he can follow — in **Page's** story, the reactions of human characters whom he can understand; in **van Vogt's**, the actions of a not-greater-than-human immature superman. Then projection does the rest.

There <u>are</u> basic laws of intelligence — and therefore basic laws of ethics which are NOT human, but are Universal. The term <u>mores</u> applies to the local interpretation of the Universal laws of ethics. Local in both time and space.

The Russians have a word "pravda" which is usually translated "truth." That's not what it means; it means "the official consensus"; the Russian language has no term meaning what we mean by <u>truth</u>—something beyond and apart from human belief or opinion, existent as a Universal reality, not part of human thinking.

When Moscow publishes a new directive to the Party, naturally that is <u>pravda</u> beyond cavil.

The lack of the concept <u>truth</u> produces an effect that seems weird and utterly irrational to a people oriented on the far more stable concept of a Universal truth beyond human influence.

But we, on the other hand, need the term <u>pravda</u> in English; I propose to use it. Pravda means, "the general consensus of what appears to be the nature of Truth." Pravda is perfectly real; pravda is to an individual item of truth as mores is to ethics. At any given point in space-time, pravda can be known, and mores can be known — but truth and ethics are sought.

710

The differentiation can be expressed mathematically: consider the infinite oscillating convergent series $1 + 1/2 - 1/4 + 1/8 - \ldots$ and so on. Summing any finite number of terms of this series will yield an answer either a little too large, or a little too small, and never exactly equal to the final result of the infinite series. But the limit of the sum of an infinite number of terms is real, has a determinate value, and can be stated. The sum can be determined exactly by a process other than simple summation; the summation of any finite number of terms will always be slightly off.

Let's say that the result of summing any finite number of terms is pravda; pravda, then, approaches truth, the actual determinate limit of the series, asymptotically.

Now characteristically, the value of such an infinite convergent series can never be determined at the level of arithmetic; only by using some higher-level mathematical process can the determinate value be found.

Thus the series suggested can be resolved and determined by algebraic methods, but not by arithmetical methods.

I have a daughter in school; another in high school, and a son in Williams College.

I have trouble helping my 12-year-old with her arithmetic; I've forgotten the arithmetical techniques for doing certain classes of problems, because the algebraic method is immensely easier.

I have trouble helping the 17-year-old, because many of her algebra problems involve techniques I've forgotten; integral calculus is so much simpler.

I have trouble with the boy; he is using thinking techniques in solving his problems that I have forgotten — there are far superior, simpler, and more direct methods.

Many years ago I wrote a story, "Forgetfulness"; only recently have I found, at a consciously communicable level, the direct philosophical statement of that story: The growth of an individual, a culture, or a race to a higher level will entail the development of thinking and doing techniques that cause them to reject lower-level techniques.

Dr. Gotthard Gunther, who is now receiving kudus in the philosophical fraternity for his recent development of a new understanding of non-aristotelian logics, has an article coming up in *ASF*. We renamed

711

his new concept, "logical parallax"; in working with it, I developed an additional proposition, "positional logic"; we are now working on a still further development which we're calling, "formulated analogic."

Formulated analogic is simply a determinately expressible system of abstracting generalizations from data. We haven't got it yet; we've simply stated, "this is the nature of the problem."

The essential point in logical parallax is that the two values "true" and "false" of Aristotelian logic become the multi-valued ideas of non-A with one simple transformation; the recognition that <u>the position of the observer introduces a parallax phenomenon</u>. Thus the "False" of Observer 1 may become the "true" of Observer 2; the consequence is that there are now 3 values, and we have, necessarily, a three-valued logic! Yet each separate logic system is, necessarily, a two valued system.

My addition to that was to point out that this is precisely what the binary number system of a modern computer does; everything in the universe can be expressed to any desired degree of accuracy with three symbols: a "true" symbol, a "false" symbol, and a "position" symbol. The Romans tried a number system having a near-infinite valued system — each number was represented by a different symbol, as M for 1000, C for 100, L for 50, X for ten, V for 5. The Arabic system uses 11 symbols, actually; 1, 2, 3, 4, 5, 6, 7, 8, 9, 0, and position.

The result can be obtained with three symbols; 1, 0, and position. Thus 10110 is 21.

Gunther then added what he calls, "T' ranges." T prime is a true-value beyond your ability to conceive that ordered truth exists. There are truths in the universe that you do not know; some of them are of such a nature that they cannot be included in your present truth-range system.

Example: A Hottentot native has never met a tiger. Tigers don't occur in Africa; Hottentots don't occur in Asia. But if a Hottentot encountered a tiger, he would readily handle the situation, because it lies within his "T-range," his "Truth-range."

But the Hottentot native, if he encountered two pieces of purified ^{235}U, would be up against something utterly beyond his truth-range; he would be forced to call it "magic."

The basic nature of the "magic" concept is "phenomena which
712

are, which exist or happen, but which are not part of the ordered system of understanding within the range of truth-as-I-know-it."

To a small child, the effects you, as an adult, obtain are essentially magic — but with the difference that the child expects to grow to understand and employ those effects himself.

A God exists when an entity employs means which are beyond your truth range, and which you believe will be forever beyond your truth-range.

The genius has a truth range, we'll say, of 2, where the normal individual has a truth-range from 0 to 1. Where the genius employs motivations and relationships in the range of 0 to 1 in his operations, the normal individual will understand; when he employs means or motivations in the 1 to 2 range, his behavior is "queer" or "nutty." Consequently the observation is that geniuses are practically insane.

Your superman is an individual who operates in the range of 0 to 5, say.

The expression of the idea here has, so far, been on a linear basis — implying that the truth lay in a linear system. It doesn't; expand that to a spherical concept, and consider the truth-ranges as being concentric spheres.

But most human societies have tended to develop linearly, emphasizing one direction of development of the sphere. It is possible to have two different civilizations having the same net volume of cultural development which have only small areas of common understanding, and most actual individuals are definitely in that position. Thus a nuclear physicist and a celestial ballistics expert have developed along opposite radii of the sphere of understanding. **Jim Brown's** story "The Emissary," about the man from the society that has social engineering, but not mechanical engineering, was another example.

Within the sphere of Understanding Radius 1, let's call it, there are many areas humanity has not explored. The social engineering sector, for example, is badly underdeveloped.

You could not describe and comunicate to your audience an understanding of an alien civilization, because the terms necessary have not been developed. Try translating "electron" into Hottentot in telling a science-fiction story for Hottentots. Even if you, as an author, could think of the alien culture, you couldn't communicate it effectively.

713

You'll have to describe actions — and that means describe them in high precision detail — which will allow your audience to project the existence of the concept you label.

Peg and I in our research have been forced to develop new terms; one of these is <u>kynmod</u>. I can define it only by action and analogy — but to use it in a story I must do so.

Science-fiction is seeking to do precisely what I'm discussing here; that's why the superman theme (seeking to call attention to T-ranges beyond that now recognized) and alien culture stories so deeply interest and concern you.

I believe I have cogent reasons for maintaining that ethics is universal, and only mores variable. Consider these factors:

Wayne Batteau, of the Harvard Computer lab sent in what he called, "The Three Laws of Stupidynamics."

1. The probability of correct prediction in total ignorance is zero.

2. The only thing you can learn is something you don't know.

3. You cannot usefully apply knowledge you do not understand.

Each of those, I think, is a statement that must be Universal. Makes no difference whether it's a methane-breathing Mesklinite or what.

Also, **Batteau** and his friends kicked some things around and came up with these:

You can't win. (Law of conservation of energy.)

You can't even break even. (Second law of Thermodynamics.)

Here is one of the first instances I know of of the direct and conscious statement of the fact that the most fundamental laws of physical systems can be <u>directly</u> applied in human systems. "You can't get something for nothing," is usually considered a moral adage. It isn't; it's a rephrasing of the law of conservation of energy.

The trouble is that people falsely expect the converse to be true — that you will always get the desired something if you work for it. That's the wrong converse; the true converse is, "You'll invariably get some result from your efforts." The result may be heat; it may be a lot of loud noise, It may be what you wanted — but you'll get something. The question is, what is the efficiency of your effort application? Are you getting 99.99% friction — or 90% desired product output?

There's the old argument: "I am honest. I have worked hard and faithfully all my life. I am poor. He is rich. He cannot have worked harder or longer than I; therefore he must be dishonest."

The concept of efficiency of application is lacking.

A Marine returning from Pelilieu during the war told me of a Jap Air Force Major they'd captured. Three days after the island was taken over, the Jap saw planes coming over from the direction of an adjacent island. "Where are those planes from?" he asked.

"Our base on the adjacent island."

"But that's impossible! There was no base there, and we'd been working at one for eight months!"

"There's a base there now. Started using it this morning."

"But how?"

They'd worked at it eight months; the Americans did it in two days — with 20 ton bulldozers, gigantic earth-movers, and power shovels. The Japs had been limited by using human labor; not more than 2000 men could work efficiently on the small island.

Suppose the Jap major hadn't ever encountered a set of heavy duty earthmoving machinery. Then he would have been faced with an occurrence beyond his T-range — pure magic.

All alien civilization plots have that difficulty — and the added difficulty that you can't get away with sheer arbitrary differentness.

You can't say, "They do it the opposite way," when there is, in every human being, a deep, subliminal knowledge that it won't work the opposite way.

We have 2,000,000,000 years of experience to go on; the instincts are the results of just plain trying it and seeing what didn't work.

You'll have to get a whole new orientation on what instincts are, however, to see this point! Instincts ARE NOT what people told you they were; they are what they actually are. Pravda on instincts does not equal truth about instincts; in this case the difference is immense.

Freudians hold that all men have a repressed desire to lay every good-looking female they see.

Ever found that desire in yourself?

Maybe **Freud** was wrong, huh?

It's true that the male dog has a powerful urge to take on any bitch in

715

heat that he scents. So this proves that the male human has a comparable tendency?

But observably there are many mammalian species that are monogamous by instinct. What proof have we that Man is polygamous instinctively, or completely non-monogomous, to create a term? I suggest the true instinct runs this way:

Man is basically monogamous. However, unlike most mammals, division of labor has progressed so far in man that the male undertakes most of the labor of meeting the external environment, with the result that there tends to be a marked unbalance of the male-female ratio. Men get killed protecting the females. In most species of mammals, males and females are about equally engaged in contact with the external environment.

The result of this resultant imbalance of numbers is that, when the tribe was forced to do so, polygamy was accepted as an alternative necessity. For the greatest good of human beings, polygamy became necessary.

The basic need, however, is for monogamy — as in many other mammalian species.

But — our educational system (not official, but actual) teaches a kid of 15-19 that he isn't a real he-man unless he keeps trying to lay every girl he can seduce.

Did you actually want to? And, on the other hand, did you feel yourself forced to feel that you should want to to be a real man?

This sort of thing has vastly complicated the problem of unscrambling what Man's true instincts are; pravda on the subject is so hugely out of step with truth!

Incidentally, any population statistician will tell you that mores be damned, the birth rate of a nation is determined by the number of females in the child-bearing age-range, not by the number of males.

There are, I think, deep basic laws that apply to any race, anywhere. You cannot solve your problem without solving someone else's; action and reaction must be equal and opposite. I'll bet that Man domesticated the cow because the ancient aurochs raided his grain fields; the way to control the raiders was to feed them — for the table.

The horse probably got domesticated on a similar basis; the dog certainly did. Man solved the wolf's problem of getting food; the tamed wolf solved Man's problem of an inadequate nose, and the tendency of Man to get so concentrated on one problem as to ignore other dangers.

This is ethics? This is action-equals-reaction. This is "good sense." It's not human; it's universal.

Dammit, **Cliff**, I can go on for hours like this! We've spent years of damned hard work plowing through this, and had a lot of very high-powered help. I haven't even touched on the business of the nature of emotion, and the proof that unemotional thinking is as impossible as an immaterial solid. Or the business of a demonstration, based on information theory, that an increase in knowledge leads to a <u>decrease</u> in wisdom <u>unless</u> there is an improved system of data-cataloging.

Item: The basic instinct in any animal organism is the instinct to predict. Reason: it does you no good to know what the situation was; you can't alter that. It isn't enough to know what the situation is; it's too late to change that. You can affect the universe only by knowing what the future <u>will be</u>.

Instance: a cat going after a mouse has to predict where the mouse will be.

Psychologists have denied teleology; unfortunately, every animal organism operates on a feedback loop going through the future — as best it can. The fact that precognition doesn't exist in fact has nothing to do with the case; the organism has to <u>act as though</u> it had precognition — or not be able to act at all!

Score another for science-fiction! This particular field of literature lies exactly along the deepest instinctive lines of human progress, philosophy, and communication!

It is my personal intention to live as long as I consider it fun to do so — and I expect that to be not less than 400 years. I am taking direct active steps toward that. It can be done, however, only by learning the nature of myself, my organism, and my universe.

I'm convinced that old age can be described accurately as, "a psychosomatic disease consisting of the accumulation and routine repetition of metabolic errors."

I grew this body I have; if I could build it — dammit, I can rebuild it! I know I do in fact rebuild it; every cell replaces itself in the course of a few weeks or months. But why replace a defective cell with a cell <u>having precisely the same defect</u>? Remember the story of the man in

717

a back-country Chinese town who took an old suit to the local tailor, and asked him to duplicate it? The tailor did — including three patches that appeared on the original, and a careful fraying of trouser cuffs and pocket edges.

Old age results from precisely such a process; the cells are replaced by faithful copies of the originals, including the patches, fraying and general errors.

You can't overcome that with drugs; you have to correct that by learning, and establishing understanding communication.

I have seen the bony deposits of arthritis melt away under psychosomatic therapy; I know for a fact that such work can be done.

I've seen X-ray plates.

I've also talked to a doctor who saw the X-ray plates of a man who had a gastroenterotomy operation for stomach ulcers, and later went to Lourdes shrine. The X-ray plates showing the operation existed. Plates taken afterwards showed that the alteration of his stomach and intestines made by the operation <u>had been done away with</u>. His body had refused to perpetuate the patch, and had corrected itself to the original youthful system.

I know damned well immortality is possible — personal, direct, right-here-and-now immortality. It can even be specified in physical science terms — but only in terms of information theory! Immortality is a product of understanding and selectivity; not of drugs.

Information theory is enormously more powerful than any present scientist recognizes, because each has seen only the piece that applies in his field.

Acutally, I now feel that the Universe can be described as an information machine — and the mind as an information handling mechanism.

Naturally, then, the mind can handle the universe!

Regards, John

W.H. Bade   *June 19, 1953*

Dear Bade:

Your wife's comment that, "Science is hard," is definitely sound. Last evening, in our research session, **Peg** and I were trying to deter-
718

mine a definition for "trivial technicality" that would separate it from "important basic clue." Your letter had something to do with it; so did the **Rosenberg** situation, **Douglass'** stay having been a major topic of the day's news. I deeply resent the idea that an individual thoroughly guilty of a crime should get away scot free on some misplaced comma in the indictment, or the like. Yet the dictator operates by considering the individual's wishes as trivia not worthy of consideration in view of the great, broad ends.

The famous, "The next generation of physicists will merely determine the next decimal point," is another example. That is precisely what the next generation did do. But the next decimal point revealed a knee in the curve!

Korzybski's work interested me, too — but I never read *Science & Sanity* through. Look, my business is being an editor. As an editor, in many years of reading, I've learned a very useful principle. If a man's thinking is so disorganized as to produce the first four or five pages in a disjointed, verbose and redundant state, it's highly probable his mind is that disorganized the rest of the way. Turn down the story.

Korzybski couldn't write clearly, or state his ideas succinctly. That in itself indicates his thinking was still in an unclarified state.

Lord, man, the whole New Testament wasn't 1/10th as verbose as *Science & Sanity*. It doesn't take a book that big to change the course of world history — and in fact, it's the short ones that have done most.

The Prince isn't very long either, you know.

When I finally get my philosophy worked out, I figure it should be expressible in about 5000 words.

I learned about **Korzybski's** work by letting other people abstract his ideas for me, and cross-comparing what they got from him. **van Vogt** got the most — roughly $4800.

I have trouble with **Joe Winter**, at times, because he is still rather sold on **Korzybski**.

You might be interested in the work **Dr. Gotthard Gunther** has been doing, and that he and I have been kicking around since. **Gunther** has an article in the *International Philosophical Journal*, or some such, that's already causing quite a bit of comment, although technically its pre-publication. Basically, he's worked out a meaning for the multi-valued logics. Heretofore, logicians (who thought things through a bit further than **Korzybski**) have had some fine mathematical logics of n-valued types, but couldn't actually apply them to real-world situations.

Gunther, in essence proposes that any n-valued logic is made up of a set of two-valued logics with overlapping values; we have an article on it coming up in *ASF* in which he calls it, "logical parallax." Answer with the true or false values the question, "Is Chicago to the east?"

Clearly, you must say, "True," while I must answer, "False." Then we have a three-valued system, because we have two different viewpoints. Within any one viewpoint, however, there is only a two-valued system. The problem is to determine the displacement values affecting the two viewpoints producing the three-valued system.

From this, I got the notion of "positional logic," and suggested that the binary number system represents an n-valued logic system operating with three symbols; true, false, and position. With those three symbols, anything in the universe can be expressed to any desired degree of accuracy.

Recently, working on that idea, I've finally gotten clear what is wrong with the old argument, "You can't do that; it's impossible! Nobody's ever done it!"

This is equivalent to the argument in the early days of the Arabic number system that you didn't need a 0 because there was no point in putting down nothing. The point is that a class of no members is not the same as a non-existent class.

In 1940, a lot of people told me atomic energy was impossible, and it was silly to talk about it. The essence of the argument could be expressed: The class of controlled nuclear reactors contains no members. Therefore the class does not exist. Therefore it is nonsense to discuss it.

Tojo thought so, too.

Actually, that's like saying 1111 is the same as 100101001, because only 1's have value; the zeros just mean that the referenced classes have no members, so they don't exist.

Now: What's the difference between 000101 and 101, then?

That, you see, is essentially the problem of the atomic power question. As of 1940, the situation was of the 000101 type; until someone put a 1 out there in front, the no-member classes appeared to be non-existent
720

classes.

The facts we have may appear to be in the 000101 department; the moment someone puts a 1 out in front, suddenly those other classes acquire meaning to us, and we say, mentally, "Oh, that's why that damned reaction didn't go right!"

Anyhow, **Korzybski** never seemed to me to have the business of abstraction worked out right. That's OK though; the Class of All Men Who Understand Abstraction is, to date, a class of No Members. **Korzybski** is in the very well populated Class of All Men Who Don't Know What Creative Thinking Is.

But he made a very real contribution; he shook up enough people's thinking so that they started achieving something. **Ron Hubbard** did the same; he didn't have the answers, as he thought he did, but he did get a lot of people thinking! [L. Ron Hubbard did go on to uncover and to communicate answers not available to John W. Campbell, prior to Campbell's death: Ed.]

Re: the interference of light and field cancellation.

You got me, pal. I didn't analyze the thing on that basis, but I have a hunch that standing waves aren't the right approach. A standing wave situation represents a rather special form of interference, doesn't it?

What if you generate the complex wave system of a square wave train? This can be produced by introducing a large number of sine-wave tones; periodically the system yields a large positive resultant, and periodically the system yields a null resultant. The net energy comes out even, but the instantaneous energy looks peculiar.

A friend of mine pointed out that according to Fourier analysis, we must accept the doctrine of predestination. Make a Fourier analysis of a function that goes _____|——— and the analysis will insist that sine waves existed from the beginning of time, and just happened to cancel, and then at the observed instant of the rise made their energy manifest.

I dunno. I just have a hunch we have a bit more to learn about energy and space than we think we do.

I remember I once asked the physics prof at MIT what would happen if you had two beams of pure monochromatic light of exactly the same frequency, and threw them into such phase relation as to cancel.

Wouldn't that annihilate their energy?

His answer at the time was that you couldn't generate pure mono-chrome light, so that there would be rephasing and reappearance of the energy.

In essence, what I'm asking now is, "Where's the energy lurking in the meantime?"

Gunther has a concept that might interest you — what he calls, "T-ranges." In a standard truth table, there is the assumption only of one true-false system. In his displaced logic concept, however, the T-range gets somewhat more complex, because of parallax effects, and other effects.

One of these others might be called understanding-reach. Suppose we have an entity A that can understand truths in the range of 0 to 1, but can't imagine the existence of truths beyond that range. Another entity, B, can understand truths in the range of 0 to 2, but not beyond.

To B, truths existent in the range 1 to 2 are ordered, comprehensible, related truths. To A, however, there is no ordered truth beyond 1. It's "magic," if A is a primitive, or "coincidence" if he's more educated. To A, the range 0 to 1, constitutes the totality of order in the Universe; beyond it is chaos, unordered happenstance, and Mystery.

Of course, there is an infinity of values between 0 and 1, so A won't run out of problems!

But when A observes B, he observes a strange thing; part of the time B operates in a perfectly rational, predictable manner, and does perfectly rational, understandable things. But part of the time B is completely nutty; he does strange pointless things for no understandable motive at all, and gets no results from what he does, either. (B's then operating in the range between 1 and 2, causing effects in the range 1-2.)

B is, however, unusually lucky; by coincidence, B happens to be standing around with a bucket when the sky opens and rains gold pieces. Or, by coincidence, B scratches the wall near a doorway, and just then a bright light happens to turn on in the room. (Wonder what a dog _does_ think of the performance?)

At a less extreme level of difference, B is a genius, and A is a normal individual. To A, B appears unpredictable, irrational, nutty, given to strange crochets, somewhat brilliant but unstable, and remarkably lucky.

A can see and appreciate the physical results of B's weird behavior; if B produces resultants having values within A's range, fine. B is then declared a genius. But if B's resultant is something that produces satisfactions only in the 1-2 range, A doesn't get the point at all.

Like science-fiction; it produces satisfactions only for those in the genius range. The IQ 100 bird doesn't see what the point of a story like "Mission of Gravity" is; he doesn't see anything but a crackpot called **Hal Clement** writing a lot of hogwash about an unreal planet for no reason.

"Except, gee gosh, I guess . . . huhu . . . he ain't so crackpot at that! Looka that will ya! He got thirty-two hundred smackers fer that story! He's not nuts I guess — but the guy that bought it sure is!"

Isaac Asimov had trouble with a boss at the Philadelphia Navy Base during the war; the boss thought **Isaac** was decidedly queer to talk about and even write science-fiction — until **Isaac** collected a check equal to one third of the said boss's annual salary.

In other words, A will understand only those parts of B's behavior that are motivated by concepts in the 0 to 1 range, and will accept B's 1-2 range motivations only when they produce rewards in the 0-1 range.

Example: Science is hard. OK — why do you do it? How much are they paying you? How many women does it get you? Name your economic motivation, Comrade!

And don't give me that malarkey about, "It will permit me to earn more after I get out of school." Hogwash; you know damn well **Joe Louis** made more than you will!

No wonder good, honest, upright 100% Americans like **Joe McCarthy** are suspicious of you scientists! You've got hidden motives you aren't revealing!

And until some of the 0-1 range people recognize that attacking really hard problems is the major joy of life, while making a good salary is a damned nuisance that has to be taken care of — how are you going to explain your motives? They know that precisely the reverse of that is true; that what everybody wants is a good salary with no problems to have to worry about.

See; you're hiding your motives. How can they trust you?

723

Occasionally, one finds it a wee bit difficult to establish full communication across such a barrier, not so?

I think **Gunther's** got an exceedingly important logical concept there. Unfortunately, those who most need it will be least apt to appreciate it.

Regards, John

A.E. van vogt *January 13, 1955*

Dear van Vogt:

We have gradually been catching up on the release of all but Serial Rights on the stories we bought through the years. I believe this package contains releases on all the stories which you sold us through the years you were writing. If there are any missing, let me know.

Regards, John W. Campbell, Jr.

The 1960's
with *A.E. van Vogt*

Rog Phillips Graham *January 10, 1962*

Dear Rog:

First, let me explain that part of the delay on that last letter was caused by the fact that **Kay Tarrant**, my assistant editor, secretary, managing editor, production editor, and everything else for the last 20 years, was hit by a heart attack, and has been laid up. Five of us are stumbling along trying to do what she did routinely and we're coming out the worse for wear.

The manuscript comes back. As things are, I've got novels on hand to carry through next December — which is too much already. (That last one is a **Jim Blish** Okie story I had to take!)

Your start on this is excellent — as was **Bob Heinlein's** start on his somewhat-similar *Stranger in a Strange Land.*

There are some stories, however, that can't be written — and among the unwriteable ones are:

724

1. The Second Coming . . . which could be written only by the Master himself, since no merely human mind could encompass the problems, and the needed solutions inherent in the Second coming. Any human-limited attempt would inevitably sound false, and shallow.

2. The story of the Superman, from the Superman's viewpoint. Which could, of course, only be written by a genuine superman, obviously. Can a child of 8 imagine realistically what adult love is?

3. Earth culture as seen by a visitor from a far older and more advanced culture.

The same fundamental reasoning applies.

For instance, your man's trapped into discussing the problems of modern science. Your answers sound phony as hell . . . because, of course, they are. You're not a 5000-year-old member of a 10 megayear old culture — and what you write doesn't sound like it!

Your man loses his temper; after the first 5000 years of living, the ones that haven't been killed by accidents are the ones that never lose their tempers and never panic.

And after kiloyears of visiting other worlds, other peoples, and learning other viewpoints . . . a man's range of tastes is far too great to be unable to appreciate gourmet cooking.

The trouble with trying to write any one of those three stories I named is that you aren't either the Master, the Superman, or a visitor with a 5000 year education in a mega-year-old culture.

Among the best superman stories that have been done — the classic and successful-in-popular-enthusiasm terms, were **A.E. van Vogt's** "Slan," and **Page's** "But Without Horns" in *Unknown*.

In "Slan" you never meet a full-fledged, fully-developed Slan; you meet a poor, lost and hunted kid, Jommy. And later an adolescent, desperately trying to find out who and what he is and should be Jommy Cross. And Kathleen, another incomplete Slan-to-be.

John Cross, a full-fledged Slan, is glimpsed only for a moment, as he takes over control of the story-to-be-after-the-story.

In "But Without Horns" the superman's presence dominates everything that happens . . . but the superman, like the men in the play "The Women," is always off-stage.

The only way any one of those three stories can be approached involves using one of those mechanisms — some way of telling it within

725

the limitations of human scope, for the author remains human.

The best we can possibly do will be like the three blind men report-ing back on their investigation of the elephant. We can't see . . . and if the blind men are reporting back to the group of blind-from-birth men who sent them to investigate, then their audience couldn't understand if the investigators, miraculously given sight for the moment, did report correctly!

Some stories can't be written . . . by human beings.

Regards, John W. Campbell, ANALOG

General Artists Corporation   *July 23, 1962*

Gentlemen:

Gordie Dickson's trouble in this series is that <u>he</u> knows what it's all about — but nobody else does. Specifically, the reader doesn't — as **Gordie** himself recognizes, by writing that author's explanation at the end of the manuscript.

van Vogt, in his complex series-stories, used to give the reader plenty of feeling of understanding the motivations that were relevant within any one story. The reader didn't know what **van Vogt** had in mind — but he did have the feeling he understood the motivations of the individual story.

Doc Smith, in his, may have had more in mind than the reader knew . . . but the reader nevertheless was given the motivations relevant within the story in hand.

Here, the Force Inimical and Force Favorable are not made to ap-pear real, important, relevant to the story. While the Nazi-like brutality of the Friendlies is made very real and strong.

The result is a feeling of no-real-motivation, and hence no feeling that the story is important — or satisfying.

Sincerely, John W. Campbell, Editor

Ralph Swanson   *January 6, 1964*

Dear Mr. Swanson:

Many times, story ideas aren't particularly important — it's the tell-ing that makes or breaks a yarn!

726

Your suggestion of sending scientific data back to Earth is valid. In effect, that's what **Clifford Simak** had as the basic motivation behind "Project Fishhook" in his novel "The Fisherman." (Pocketbook title was *Time Is The Simplest Thing.*)

And one factor you've got to at least consider in the set-up you suggest is one that's been too little developed. **van Vogt** did it once, years ago — and only once. The fact that while the interstellar ship is spending a century of Earth-time making the trip — Earth's science is advancing. **van Vogt** applied it in having a ship start out on a slower-than-light trip that took them 200 years or so, and arrived to find a century-old colony already established on their destination planet. Earth had developed a FTL drive a century after they started.

Does du Pont want a new, cheap process for making celluloid now? Or a better material for making gas mantles?

Sincerely, John W. Campbell, Editor

John W. Campbell, Jr.   *February 20, 1965*

Dear Mr. Campbell:

Well . . . I have written a story based on the idea that you sent me.

It's a little long for a short, but certainly well below novelette length.

Please deal with my agent, **Forrest Ackerman**.

I could probably write a few more around this format, but there would be some changes in the "identity" aspect.

Anyway, here it is.

Sincerely yours, A.E. van vogt

Encl. THE THIRTEENTH PLANET

A.E. van Vogt   *March 22, 1965*

Dear Mr. van Vogt:

Sorry -- but this one comes back.

In essence, you've simply written up, in longer form, the basic idea I suggested, without developing the proposition.

Making "MacPherson" a humanoid seems a weakening, rather than a strengthening, alteration -- because there is no explanation of what a "humanoid" is. Another term for "android"? Member of an alien species from some other planet? Who knows?

The intensity of action and reaction involved here -- shelling the ship -- doesn't make it seem reasonable that the captain should be quite so peaceably willing to trade nuclear initiators for sea-herbs. No trader captain is going to allow blackmail-with-force; it means the end of honest trading. You can't do business on such a basis, so there can be no business until the would-be robbers-with-violence learn that they can't make a profit that way.

(I'd rig the nuclear initiators, before turning them over, so they really initiated nuclear ractions! In everything within fifty feet of them, when turned on.)

Sincerely, John W. Campbell

Enc.: The Thirteenth Planet

Robert Chilson   *October 26, 1966*

Dear Mr. Chilson:

A.E. van Vogt used to do ultra-complicated interwoven plot stories like this — but he was about the only one who ever got away with 'em.

Sorry . . . but you're not in **van Vogt's** class yet! Instead of the desired effect, this produces a feeling of bewilderment, with a rapid loss of interest.

Sincerely, John W. Campbell, Jr.

RE: "Crossed Purposes" by Robert Chilson

John C. Hoggatt   *January 25, 1967*

Dear Mr. Hoggatt:

The trouble is, the number of you who want *Unknown* to come back is too small a number. The *Unknown* fans were ardent, intense, and vociferous — but too few.

Heinlein is now writing only novels — and he isn't writing the kind of novels I think belong in *Analog*. They aren't the type he did 20-odd years ago. Much the same is true of **A.E. van Vogt**.

And **Don A. Stuart** is too darned busy running *Analog*, and working with authors, to write stories!

Sincerely, John W. Campbell, Editor

Dear Mr. Lyau:

Some years back, someone said of **H.G. Wells**, that he had, "sold his birthright for a pot of message," when he stopped writing science-fiction, and started writing stories he intended to make people believe what he believed in.

Any magazine that has a consistent message, that tries to tell people what they ought to believe in, soon degenerates to a house-organ for a pack of fanatics.

To stay alive and effective, a magazine <u>must</u> be a forum where authors can present interest-holding, dramatic tales . . . carrying widely different ideas.

"Blowups Happen" was strictly **Bob Heinlein's** idea; I bought it because it was a good story — and incidentally projected what was, as of that time, a real possibility of danger. (We know better now; at that time, nuclear science did <u>not</u> know about the slow neutron-emitting isotope of Xenon which, alone, makes possible control of nuclear reactors.)

"Slan," by **van Vogt**, simply projected the problem of human reaction to the appearance of a superior type which was truly superior <u>and benevolent in intent</u>. It was, on a larger scale, the reaction shown to **Jesus**, and other great benevolent leaders. (The superior individuals who used violence to impose their ideas, such as **Ghengis Khan**, have a greater tendency to die of old age!)

Each of the stories you mention was one author's method of presenting a problem that, to him, seemed important — and which I agreed were worth presenting.

Analog's basic interest is in inducing readers to <u>think</u> about man's problems — instead of merely quoting neat little packaged sayings without bothering to inquire what they would mean, if actually imposed.

Many times a theory that looks good over a short range leads to intolerable conditions if extended in time, in space, or in numbers. An idea that works fine for a village of 2500 people becomes ridiculous if applied to a metropolitan area of 25,000,000. Euclidean plane geometry works fine for mapping a small town in Kansas — but it won't work for mapping the United States, because on that scale the curvature of the Earth becomes dominant. It wouldn't work for San Francisco, either — because San Francisco is anything but plane!

Science-fiction, by allowing a greater sweep of time, space, and scale can study present theories of human relationships far better than any other type of literature.

Can you have a popular democracy governing a galactic federation of 10,000,000 inhabited planets, averaging 1,000,000,000 people on each? Can you imagine a Congress with 1,000,000 Congressmen meeting in an assembly ten times greater than any known auditorium or stadium, and each of those congressman representing a <u>billion</u> people? A billion people, having only <u>one</u> representative to speak for them — to take care of their business with the Federation of Planets? Is a one-man-one-vote government the best possible way to arrange human affairs? It absolutely cannot work for that stupendous population — but what is the real limit at which it is the best form?

Only science-fiction can discuss such real problems!
Sincerely, John W. Campbell, Editor

William B. Ellern   *March 27, 1969*

Dear Mr. Ellern:

Sorry . . . but you've violated a couple of basic rules of action writing.

First, you're trying to tell two completely separate and non-intersecting stories here — which slows down and confuses the main story. Second, you start the subsidiary (and unnecessary) story first, which is a signal to the reader that <u>that</u>, rather than the main story, is the important thing to watch.

Start the main action <u>first</u>, hard, hot and heavy — <u>then</u> you can bring in side stuff.

You can also learn some tricks of the difficult art of time-lapse in stories. Have you read "Slan"? **van Vogt** pulled one of the slickest time-lapse tricks in science-fiction — or any other literature! — history in that one. A chapter ends with, "He knew they would find him; the question was, how long would it take them." The next chapter begins, "It took seven years. . . ." and **van Vogt** goes happily on with his story.

The basic answer to time lapse is to not worry about it — just state it, and get on with the action. Remarkable what a reader will happily for-
730

give for getting good action rolling.

Your moon prospector story worked, because you opened with action, and kept on acting all the way.

This one opens with a cold-standing-start pass at a topless B-girl — which isn't tops in science-fiction interest.

Incidentally, nakedness isn't a matter of how you feel, actually — but of how the neighbors feel. Thus a Samoan girl attending a US college would object to having her clothes removed — though her culture accepts nudity as normal.

Now as to the Bubble. One little engineering problem you sort of skip over awful lightly — how do they cool the thing so it isn't the Oven? In an environment where everything's above the melting point of tin, a technical complex that uses huge quantities of power for shielding forces, etc., is going to need some really fancy dissipation gadgets. Heat pumps that have an exhaust temperature in the neighborhood of 400 degrees C are a leeetle tough to keep running. Those big blocks of solid tin they ship out have to be cooled, too — which means a lot of heat dissipation!

Re strong beams and materials: Friend of mine works with **Bucky Fuller's** team — and they have some interesting structures. Like one about 6" high, weighing less than a nickel coin, and capable of supporting over 6000 pounds. They compute they can reduce the weight to somewhat less than half, if they can get someone to work up some "beams" of iridium-diamond two-phase material. Crazy as it seems, a diamond-iridium matrix works out to the lightest, stiffest, strongest possible material — 98% diamond and 2% Ir. **Fuller's** structural shapes make most of the difference now the unit I mentioned is built with boron fiber and a "glue."

That graph of stiffness-per-pound you sent doesn't go all the way up; there are two known substances that are stiffer than boron carbide — boron nitride (berazon) and diamond.

That same friend also came up with a glop with remarkable properties; the Department of Defense promptly clamped a classified lid on it. I don't know what it is — but I saw what it does.

Rub some of his glop — about 0.1 gram, I'd guess — on an aircraft alloy dural 3/4" bar, wait ten minutes, and pull the bar apart in your hands. The dural was changed to a sort of metallic sand, with about the

731

tensile strength of wet beach sand. His glop ends the inter-crystalline bonding forces.

A bit rubbed on a piece of aircraft wing dural sheet plus three minutes wait — and he stuck his finger through the disintegrated metal.

Have a little sabotage?

Re getting manuscripts typed up neatly: most authors have determined that there are only two satisfactory alternatives — marry someone who can, or learn to do it yourself!

Regards, John W. Campbell, Editor

re: "Sea of the Sun," by **William B. Ellern**

The 1970's
with *A.E. van Vogt*

John W. Campbell, Jr.   *February 20, 1970*

Dear John W. Jr.:

I am in process of writing six science fiction novels under contract to Ace. Ace is not opposed to serialization; provided it is done in a reasonable time. My agent, **Forrest Ackerman**, asked me if any of the six might fit *Analog* requirements, and I told him two.

At his request, I enclose the first hundred pages (of a projected 300) of the first of these two, titled THE BATTLE OF FOREVER.

If you are not interested in, or cannot at present arrange, a reasonably rapid scheduling, then I suggest you do not even bother to read the enclosed first installment.

(My timing on it is that I had better finish the story by the first week in March.)

You may be interested to know my experience in resuming writing after my long hiatus away from it. At first, I could only bring myself to fix up into novel form previously published shorter length stories. Then I wrote a number of stories in a very condensed form. THE SILKIE is a sample of that stage. All this time, of course, I was analyzing the problem. You may recall receiving a story from me — which you rejected with the statement that I had really goofed on the science. (I had had some alien race sweep up all the railroad tracks and other

732

metal of earth in order to obtain much-needed metal.) You said, obviously they would simply utilize a large iron meteor available in space. As soon as I read your comment, I thought: Of course . . . how could such a simple fact have faded so completely from my mind? But it had. And with it into vagueness had departed a good portion of my painfully accumulated scientific information. To rectify that, I had to put my attention back on science and also on the whole problem of a science fiction writer in a world that, scientifically, has moved forward at jet speed since 1950.

While I cogitated these matters, I wrote approximately one 20,000-word condensed story a year. Fortunately, as a result of Street and Smith originally reverting so many rights to authors, a kindness which I shall never forget, I was having from 4 to 7 paperbacks reprinted each year, along with a small income from foreign rights.

I observed in myself a restlessness, which made it difficult for me to put my attention on writing for very long. I'd start — and then I'd be over in a chair reading. To make a long story short, I analyzed that I had formerly been able to write because I used to be in a kind of a manic condition a good portion of the time. All that was left of that was a formless, non-directional restlessness.

I have deduced the following: it takes energy to write. Some people are simply in good health. Others operate through a manic-stimulation. To keep going in the long run, both of these types presently use caffeine. I started to do that, and it was alright. But meanwhile, we had gotten ourselves a Samoyed dog — a Northern Siberian breed. I started taking her for short walks, then for short jogs, and then for 40-minute jogs. Apparently for me, this was magic. Today, my blood pressure is 120/80, my pulse is 68, my temperature slightly below normal. It used to be slightly above — a couple of decimal points above.

How do you start in to full time production? Well, I decided what I needed was an assignment. I wrote six outlines with a few chapters on each, and asked Don Wollheim how about it? The first two novels are finished on schedule, two months each, though the last one went up to 373 pages.

Although they are all different, their basic theme is peace and violence.

The other one, which I do not enclose any portion of, parallels (roughly) the Viet Nam situation, where earth forces are about to leave 500 million Italians to the tender mercies of about a billion aliens.

The enclosed is the farthest-out of the six. In these six there is no attempt at fine writing. But I have already told Don that I have tentatively titled the second six "the beautiful stories." At the moment, I really believe I know how to achieve that.

Anyway, if the timing on the enclosed, or if seeing only a portion of a story, is not for you, please use the enclosed envelope. It is understood of course that if you are interested in seeing the remainder, there is no obligation incurred thereby.

Sincerely, A. E. van Vogt

A.E. van Vogt   *February 26, 1970*

Dear van:

I haven't a chance of using your novel — I'm stocked-up through mid-197<u>1</u> already!

But I'm glad you're working yourself back into story-writing trim. I guess it's much like any other skilled activity — you have to "keep in shape" by practicing. I know **Paderewski** used to say, "One day without practice at the piano, and I know the difference. Two days without practice, and the critics know the difference. Three days, and everybody knows."

And — yay, verily, the technology of writing has indeed changed over the near-20-years you've been out of it. Wonder how **Michaelangelo** would make out as a modern sculptor with an arc-welding machine? Or using an air-hammer to carve his stone?

This one shows many of the old **van Vogt** touches, and has some highly interesting ideas. Some, I think, you've carried a bit too far — I doubt that men would have taken the trouble to make <u>all</u> animal species intelligent. There'd be little point, because the inherent differences of the animals would have <u>had</u> to be almost totally suppressed in the process, or they'd never be able to live together in harmony. The instruments of an orchestra can complement each other only by being very different, but dedicated to the same goal — and the same overall tune. Though no two play the same music score.

734

Think of intelligent rats and mice as electronic repairmen, and the hippos as civil engineers supervising irrigation and other waterways, beavers as erosion control supervisors, bears as forestry service specialists! Bears would also make great police, to handle emergencies!

However — time makes our use of this one out of the question.

But how about novelettes and shorts? You know we're paying 5 cents a word now for shorts (under 7500 words) because of the chronic shortage of that length.

John W. Campbell, Editor

enc: THE BATTLE OF FOREVER by A.E. van Vogt [This book is also published in hardcover by AC Projects, Inc., 5106 Old Harding Road: $9.95 stock edition; $14.95 signed, numbered copy. Ed.]

A.E. van Vogt   *August 3, 1971*

Dear Mr. van vogt:

If you want further details about **John**, may I suggest that you write to **Dr. Ralph A. Hall** (address given). I can quote from a letter: ". . . on the death certificate that it was massive hemorrhage due to rupture of the abdominal aorta. This is one of the several final episodes in the files of every malignant hypertension case. He could have had a stroke, heart attack, uremia. . . . The 'nutmeg' liver was evidence that he was well on his way to cirrhosis. He also had gout. He could have probably had diabetes if he had lived. The paper thin abdominal muscles were due to lack of proper exercise."

For several years, **John** was virtually sedentary. The tophi lodged in his feet were not comfortable when he walked, being about the size and lumpiness of a raspberry.

I have no idea why you want this information, but am sending it as factually as possible. **John** had been under constant supervision for his truly frightening blood-pressure for at least five years.

He was in good spirits on the morning that he died, but he had curtailed his physical activities greatly. He was a teetotaler.

I find this a very difficult thing to talk about, but can only assume that you must have had a great need to know.

Sincerely, Margaret Campbell

Made in the USA
Middletown, DE
06 April 2017